Informatik aktuell

Herausgeber: W. Brauer
im Auftrag der Gesellschaft für Informatik (GI)

B. Walke   O. Spaniol (Hrsg.)

Messung, Modellierung und Bewertung von Rechen- und Kommunikationssystemen

7. ITG/GI-Fachtagung
Aachen, 21.-23. September 1993

Springer-Verlag
Berlin Heidelberg New York
London Paris Tokyo
Hong Kong Barcelona
Budapest

Herausgeber

B. Walke
RWTH Aachen, Lehrstuhl für Kommunikationsnetze
Kopernikusstr. 16, 52074 Aachen

O. Spaniol
RWTH Aachen, Lehrstuhl für Informatik IV
Ahornstr. 55, 52074 Aachen

Rheinisch-Westfälische Technische Hochschule Aachen

CR Subject Classification (1993): C.4

ISBN-13:978-3-540-57201-5   e-ISBN-13:978-3-642-78495-8
DOI: 10.1007/978-3-642-78495-8

Satz: Reproduktionsfertige Vorlage vom Autor/Herausgeber

33/3140-543210 – Gedruckt auf säurefreiem Papier

Vorwort

"Messung, Modellierung und Bewertung von Rechen- und Kommunikationssystemen" ist die 7. Veranstaltung der gleichnamigen Fachgruppe.
Die Tagung verfolgt die Ziele, Interessierten und Fachleuten aus dem deutschsprachigen Raum einen Rahmen zu schaffen, Erfahrungen und neue Ideen auszutauschen, entwickelte Werkzeuge vorzustellen und über Methoden und Lösungskonzepte für die Leistungsbewertung von Rechen- und Kommunikationssystemen zu diskutieren.
Gegründet wurde die Fachgruppe 1978 anläßlich eines GI-Workshops 1977 über Modelle von Rechensystemen in Bonn. Organisiert ist sie als gemeinsame Fachgruppe des GI-Fachbereichs 3 (Technische Informatik und Architektur von Rechensystemen) und des ITG Fachbereichs 4 (Technische Informatik), um

-       die Kräfte für das genannte Fachgebiet zusammenzulegen,
-       Fachleute möglichst unmittelbar die Arbeit bei den Gesellschaften auf diesem Fachgebiet gestalten zu lassen,
-       eine Partnergruppe für die internationale Zusammenarbeit zu haben.

Die Mitgliedschaft ist kostenlos und kann durch einfache Erklärung erfolgen.

Folgende Fachtagungen wurden bisher durchgeführt:

1981: Jülich (Mertens)	1983: Stuttgart (Kühn)
1985: Dortmund (Beilner)	1987: Erlangen (Herzog)
1989: Braunschweig (Stiege)	1991: Neubiberg (Lehmann)

Diese 7. Tagung wird zusammen mit der ITG-Fachgruppe 1.2.1 Verkehrstheorie durchgeführt und bezieht erstmals quantitative Aspekte der Leistungsbewertung von Kommunikationssystemen ein. In Form von Vorträgen, Kurzberichten, einem Werkzeugpraktikum und Werkzeugausstellungen werden neue Konzepte, Lösungsverfahren und Erfahrungen bei der Messung, Modellierung und Bewertung von Rechen- und Kommunikationssystemen vorgestellt.

Aus den über 70 eingereichten Beiträgen konnte ein anspruchsvolles Programm zusammengestellt werden, welches sich an Forscher, Entwickler und Anwender aus Industrie und Wissenschaft richtet. Durch die Einführung paralleler Sitzungen besteht die Möglichkeit einer individuellen Auswahl. Neu ist auch das Hands-on-Tools-Praktikum, das im Rahmen der Tagung die Möglichkeit gibt, praktische Erfahrungen im Umgang mit einem von drei Werkzeugen zur analytischen bzw. simulativen Leistungsanalyse zu sammeln.
Für die vier Hauptvorträge konnten international bekannte Persönlichkeiten gewonnen werden. G. Balbo, Universität Turin, leitet die Tagung mit einem Vortrag über die Leistungsbewertung von nebenläufigen Programmen ein. Der zweite Hauptvortrag von J. Wong, University of Waterloo/Canada, gibt einen Einblick in die Modellierung und Leistungsbewertung von ATM-Netzen. In den beiden abschließenden Hauptvorträgen behandeln K.S. Trivedi, Duke University, USA, Techniken und Werkzeuge für die Zuverlässigkeits- und Leistungsanalyse und A. Zeyn, Siemens-Nixdorf Informationssysteme, den Entwurf neuer Rechnersysteme.

Der Tagungsband enthält vier eingeladene und 24 referierte Beiträge. Daneben erscheint ein Band für Tagungsteilnehmer und andere Interessierte mit 20 Kurzberichten (Berichte aus laufenden Arbeiten) und der Kurzvorstellung von 14 Werkzeugen zur analytischen, simulativen und meßtechnischen Leistungsbewertung von Rechen- und Kommunikationssystemen. Dieser Band ist auch nach der Tagung erhältlich.

Vor der Tagung findet ein eintägiges Tutorium über Grundlagen, Methoden und die Anwendung der Leistungsbewertung von Systemen statt, zu dem ebenfalls ein getrennter Band mit Unterlagen verfügbar ist.

Danken möchte ich allen, die beim Zustandekommen der Tagung und des Tagungsbandes beigetragen haben, insbesondere

- dem Programmausschuß,
- den Autoren und Vortragenden,
- den Rezensenten der eingereichten Beiträge,
- den Sitzungsleitern,
- allen unten aufgeführten Förderern der Tagung,
- der RWTH Aachen für die kostenlose Überlassung der Hörsäle,
- dem Lehrstuhl Informatik IV (Prof. Spaniol) für die Organisation des tagungsbegleitenden Programms,
- meinen Mitarbeitern Frau Dr. C. Görg und C. Wietfeld für die Übernahme und sorgfältige Durchführung der zahllosen Vorgänge, die im Hintergrund ablaufen, ohne die eine solche Tagung aber nicht möglich ist.

Die Tagung hat folgende Gliederung (abgedruckt sind in diesem Band nur die Beiträge der Sitzungen 1, 2A, 3A, 4A, 5A, 6A, 7A):

Dienstag, 21. September 1993	
9.00	Eröffnung und Begrüßung
9.30	Hauptvortrag
10.45	1: Parallelverarbeitung
13.30	2A: Methoden 2B: Hands-on-Tools
15.30	3A: Wartemodelle 3B: Hands-on-Tools
Mittwoch, 22. September 1993	
9.00	Hauptvortrag
10.15	4A: ATM-Netze 4B/C: Werkzeuge I + II
13.30	5A: Komm.-Netze 5B: Rechnerarch. (KB)
15.30	6A: Komm.-Protokolle 6B: Methoden (KB)
Donnerstag, 23. September 1993	
9.00	Hauptvorträge
10.45	7A: Monitore 7B: Kommunikation (KB)

In der Hoffnung, daß die Einführung von Parallelsitzungen und das Angebot des Werkzeug-
praktikums auf positive Resonanz stößt, wünsche ich der Tagung einen guten Verlauf!

Aachen, 25. Juni 1993   Bernhard Walke

Inhaltsverzeichnis

Kommunikationsnetze

Analyse von Kommunikationsprotokollen

Monitore

Performance Evaluation and Concurrent Programming

Gianfranco Balbo *

Dipartimento di Informatica
Università di Torino, Italy. corso Svizzera 185, 10149 Torino, Italy
e-mail: balbo@di.unito.it

Abstract. Concurrent programs are developed to meet the demands of
high performance computing of many new scientific and real time applications. concurrent programming is however still difficult because of
the lack of tools that help in developing and debugging new efficient implementations. Concurrency, communication, synchronization, and non-
determinism make the manual assessment of the correctness and of the
efficiency of concurrent programs extremely difficult. Models of concurrent programs must thus be used since the early stages of their development to support their debugging and tuning. In this paper we discuss
the role that Performance Evaluation techniques may play within this
environment using as an example a methodology that has been recently
proposed for the automatic construction of GSPN models of concurrent
applications. In particular, it will be shown that a GSPN model of an
application can be directly derived from its code and that its evaluation
provides the parameters that are needed for obtaining the optimal allocation of the components of the application on the computational units
of a parallel architecture.

1 Introduction

The main obstacle to the diffusion of parallel computers is the cost and the complexity of their software development due mainly to to the low predictability of
their performance, and to the lack of tools that help in designing and debugging
new implementations.

Concurrency, communication, synchronization and nondeterminism make the
manual assessment of the correctness and of the efficiency of concurrent programs based on common sense arguments absolutely unreliable. Indeed, sets of
"unforeseeable" events may instead happen very frequently due to the different
speeds of individual concurrent processes. Moreover, currently available parallel
architectures are such that resource allocation has an important effect on the
performance of an application which becomes unpredictable when it is ported

* This work has been supported in part by Ministero dell'Universita' e della Ricerca
Scientifica e Tecnologica - 40% Project - and by the Italian National Research
Council - Progetto Finalizzato Sistemi Informatici e Calcolo Parallelo, Grant N.
91.00879.PF69.

from one architecture to another. The study of the characteristics of an application both from the point of view of correctness and performance, must thus be done since the earliest stages of the software life cycle [13]: formal models of concurrent programs need to be developed since the beginning of their design and tools must be available that work on real application models whose level of abstraction may differ depending on the goals of the analyses.

Different representations allow to characterize the behaviour of a program with different levels of detail [16, 14]. It is however important that these representations be compatible so that abstract models can be augmented with more detailed descriptions of specific components to allow a modular and efficient analysis of large programs. The choice of the modelling formalism that is used throughout the software life cycle must easily integrate within the programming environment and must allow the characterization of both the static and dynamic behaviour of the program by means of analytic as well as simulation techniques.

Concurrent programs are developed to obtain high-performance computing and is thus a major aspect of their implementations that of allocating their components on the computational units of parallel architectures in order to maximize their efficiency. Real parallel architectures are however characterized by a limited number of processors and by a limited degree of connectivity (not every computational unit can directly communicate with any other) that constraint their capabilities. Intuition suggests that processes that are concurrently active should be allocated on different nodes of a parallel computer in order to exploit parallelism. Communication among processes can however modify this picture. Indeed, processes allocated on the same processor communicate through common memory in a very fast manner. Communications among processes allocated on different processors, on the other hand, take place through relatively slow links. It follows that when mapping a concurrent program on a parallel architecture, several counteracting effects must be taken into accounts. These considerations are usually formalized as an optimization problem, called the *mapping pronlem*, whose objective function accounts for the communication and processing costs. The form of the objective function depends on the structure of the concurrent program and the coefficients depend on the amount of data exchanged among processes, on their mutual distance, and on the amount of local processing performed by each processor [10].

Because of the computational complexity of this problem, different approaches to the mapping problem can be found in the literature. One direction of research proposes the restriction of the generality of programming languages by providing the programmer with a limited number of predefined high level constructs that he must use to express the parallelism of his application. The individual optimization of these primitives allows the development of efficient applications. The other proposal conceives the automatic translation of a concurrent program into a formal model that can be used during a tuning phase of the application to obtain a performance efficient implementation.

In this paper we first briefly discuss both methods, and then we focus our attention on the second one that has been used to implement a programming environment for a concurrent language called DISC [9] that extends C with message passing primitives following the CSP [8] paradigm. In particular, we will show the role that Generalized Stochastic Petri Net (GSPN) [1] models can play to support the validation of concurrent programs and to characterize their behaviour for obtaining the parameters that are needed to solve the mapping problem.

The balance of the paper is the following. Section 2 presents the methodologies that can be used to solve the mapping problem. Section 3 discusses the possibility of using static analysis techniques for characterizing the behaviour of concurrent programs. Section 4 describes the transformation steps that must be undertaken to produce GSPN models of concurrent programs. Section 5 briefly discussed the possibility of representing the same program with different levels of abstractions. Section 6 indicates how the model of a concurrent program can be used to improve the performance of its parallel implementation. Finally, Section 7 concludes the paper.

2 Concurrent Programs and Parallel Architectures

The need of predicting the performance of concurrent applications requires that a complete characterization of the behaviour of a program is known before its execution. This very ambitious goal can be partially achieved only for programs whose behaviour is only weakly dependent on input data. Indeed, good performance for data dependent programs must rely on runtime methods (e.g., dynamic load balancing) that monitor their execution and perform a restructuring of their allocation when they observe an unbalanced use of system resources. Focusing our attention on concurrent programs that possess an *internal structure*, we can observe that a careful characterization of the computation may yield important advantages when the program is repeatedly executed.

Most of today's concurrent programming environments provide the user with monitoring and profiling tools that allow the analysis of the performance of a concurrent application, but that are of little use for predicting (let alone, assessing the optimality of) the performance of a concurrent program. In this situation, all what is possible to do is some *performance debugging* in which, based on the observation of the actual use of resources, new allocation schemes can be tried with the hope of improving the performance of the program.

A more scientific methodology for the solution of this problem is that of using models that can be studied before actually completing the development of the application. These models must be produced automatically, and two different approaches can be followed for this purpose.

The first methodology is based on concurrent programming by means of high level constructs called *skeleton functions* [6] in which a concurrent program is obtained by instantiating pre-packaged basic algorithms that capture the most common forms of parallelism. These forms include the *PIPE*, *FARM*, and *DC* (Divide and Conquer) basic parallel primitives with which many concurrent applications can be expressed. A performance model is associated with each skeleton/architecture pair and is parameterized in order to identify the most suitable allocation of processes that cooperate within this basic scheme. Given the allocation structure, an estimate of the time required to execute the skeleton is computed using a formula that corresponds to the solution of the model for a set of parameters deriving from the characteristics of the specific instance (e.g., number of processes cooperating within a PIPE). Most of these formulas correspond to worst case analyses. The composition of the results obtained for each individual skeleton provides an estimate for the execution time of the program. The effectiveness of this approach relies on the accuracy and on the robustness of the models developed to estimate the cost of allocating the skeleton on specific architectures. With this approach, the allocation problem is solved once for each skeleton during a preliminary and extensive study of the environment and the optimality of the allocation performed for each individual concurrent program is insured by the compositionality of the skeleton both in terms of functional capabilities and of performance predictions. Obviously this last step represents the critical aspect of the whole methodology and is thus the subject of extensive research [6, 12].

The second approach deals with this same problem from an opposite point of view. When a concurrent program is compiled, the parallel structure of the program is identified and an overall model is automatically produced. A programming environment that implements a methodology of this type is, in principle, more general but complex models may derive from this translation. Moreover, this generality is paid also in terms of solution time since no preliminary results can be exploited to compute the performance estimates provided by the model. Because of the complexity of these models, simulation is often used as the solution technique for the computation of the estimates.

This second method is, in principle, simpler to implement and some experience on its application is now being accumulates. For this reason the following sections will be devoted to a deeper discussion of this approach with the help of a simple example that will be used to clarify some of the issues of the methodology.

3 Static Analysis of Concurrent Programs

The static analysis of an application consists in characterizing a program with a formal model that is subsequently studied to infer its properties. This model is used first to analyze the correctness of the program and subsequently to assess its efficiency. Since during static analysis nothing is known about the run-time behaviour of the program (for example its input data), no assumption is made on which of the possible execution paths is actually followed by the program. Static analysis may thus account for many behaviours that would never occur in real executions. Focusing on validation aspects, three types of anomalies may be detected by static analysis in a distributed/parallel environment [14]: unconditional faults, conditional faults, and nonfaults. Unconditional faults correspond to errors that will definitely occur during program executions. Conditional faults represent instead errors whose occurrence either depends on non deterministic choices or on specific sets of input data. Nonfaults, finally, are errors which are reported by the static analyzer although they will never occur during program executions: nonfaults are detected when the correct behaviours of programs are ensured by control variables that are ignored during static analysis.

Once a concurrent program is considered correct it must also run fast. It is thus of paramount importance to be able to estimate the performance of the adopted solution. Again in the case of a static approach, this optimization must relay on the formal model of the program and must disregard any information on input data. A probabilistic interpretation of the formal model can be convenient to concisely account for the many possible executions of a program using probability distributions.

This discussion outlines the importance of having a formal model of a concurrent program that can be easily employed to study both validation and performance evaluation aspects of program behaviours. GSPN represent one of the formalisms that satisfy this requirement for their capability of supporting both validation and performance evaluation of real systems using basically the same model [11, 3]. Moreover, GSPN are also particularly well suited for the study considered in this paper because of the possibility that they offer of representing both the characteristics of the architecture (the hardware) and the peculiarities of the program (the software) of parallel computers [2].

4 Modelling CSP-like programs

Concurrent programs that conform to a CSP style are organized as sets of procedures that include statements equivalent to the **SEQ, ALT, PAR, if, while, repeat, for, ?** and **!** of CSP. The two operators **?** and **!** are used to indicate inputs and outputs; communications are of the rendez-vous style. Communication among processes is assumed to happen through declared common channels. This is the facility provided by Occam and it represents a generalization of the basic mechanism of CSP.

Depending on the objective of the analysis different models of the same program can however be constructed which exhibit different levels of details In particular, it is clear that, if we want to study deadlocks, all process synchronizations must be carefully described; similarly, if the objective of our study is the analysis of the communications among processes, all the possible rendez-vous must be taken into consideration. In what follows we shall describe two different possible choices of the level of abstraction used to represent our programs.

4.1 Modelling process schemes

A first choice is that of building a GSPN model that includes control flow, process activation and communication statements only [16, 14, 7]. In particular we model every single communication statement as well as each **PAR, SEQ, ALT, if, while, repeat,** and **for** statement that includes in its body a communication. All the sequences that do not include any of these instructions are represented

6

```
        Main                          P1
        while true                    while true
            ALT                           ⟨ P1 computes pckt[1..k] ⟩
                Chan₁ ? x :                   Chan₁ ! k
                    for i=x-1 downto 0        for i=k-1 downto 0
                        P₁Sp? pckt               P₁Sp? pckt[i]
                        ⟨ Print pckt ⟩        endfor
                    endfor                endwhile
                Chan₂ ? x :
                    for i= x-1 downto 0
                        P₂Sp? pckt        P2
                        ⟨ Print pckt ⟩    while true
                    endfor                    ⟨ P2 computes pckt[1..n] ⟩
        endwhile                              Chan₂ ! n
                                              for i=n-1 downto 1
                                                  P₂Sp? pckt[i]
                                              endfor
                                          endwhile
```

Fig. 2. A spooler system code

(whose associated delay is an estimate of their execution time).

The third translation step consists of replacing all transitions which represent named processes with their net representations. The substitution can be easily performed by superimposing the input (output) place of the process equivalent subnet with the input (output) place of the transition that represents the named process. This translation is performed by proceeding in depth-first mode, until all the names have been replaced.

The fourth translation step consists of implementing the rendez-vous. Pairs of communication transitions that belong to different processes and that represent their (mutual) communication are fused to concretely represent the synchronization deriving from the rendez-vous protocol. In the language we are studying a rendez-vous is caused by any pair of input/output (communication) statements sharing (naming) the same channel. When several input (?) and output (!) statements on the same channel exist in the code of the concurrent program, then many rendez-vous are possible. Without making any assumption on the program behaviour, we can only say that each input statement on channel x can represent a rendez-vous with any output statement on the same channel. We therefore need to superpose each transition which represents an input from x with *all* transitions which represent an output on x.

Figure 3 presents the results of the translation of the program of Fig. 2. The center portion of the net represents the *Spooler* process, while the left and right portions represent processes P_1 and P_2 respectively. Observe how the **for** has been translated: since the static analysis doesn't include any variable, the exit from the **for** is probabilistically controlled. The *Spooler* code consists of a **while true**, an **ALT** and two **for**s, one on each branch of the **ALT**. The **ALT**, which is represented in the translation table as a free choice subnet, after the inclusion in the complete model of communication becomes a non free choice conflict among communications on the two channels $Chan_1$ and $Chan_2$. The **while true** is represented here simply as a feedback to the beginning of the process code.

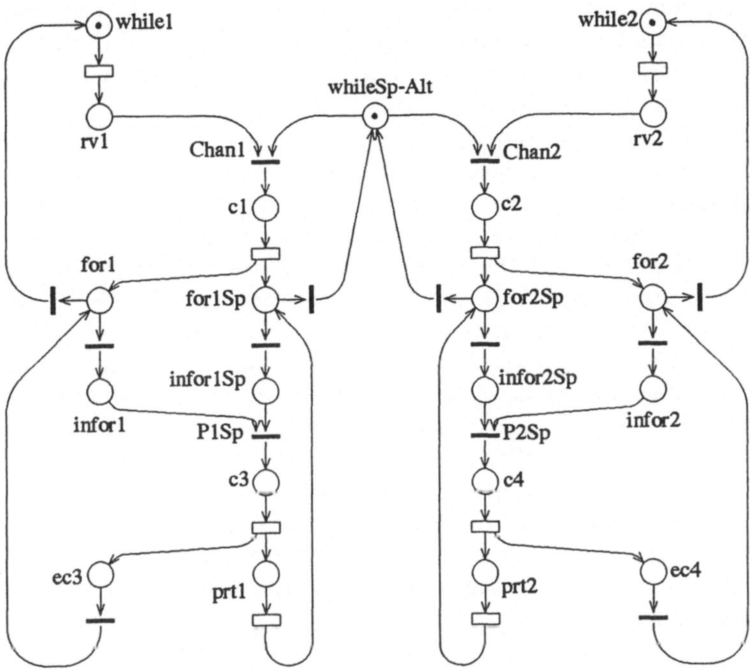

Fig. 3. The GSPN model of the "Printer-Spooler" example

5   Concurrent Program Representations

The GSPN model of a concurrent program discussed in the preceding section contains all the information that is needed to statically characterize its behaviour. Its solution (numerical evaluation of the associated continuous time Markov chain or simulation) provides indications on its efficiency under the hypothesis of the availability of infinite resources: all the activities that can be performed in parallel are actually carried on simultaneously and without interference, and all the communications take place at nominal speed.

Unfortunately, this optimistic situation is seldom found in real implementations where the physical limitations of commonly available parallel architectures introduce interference during the execution of the different components of the concurrent program. Whenever the structure of a concurrent program does not naturally fit the organization of a parallel computer, the problem of allocating processes to computational units becomes difficult to solve, since two contradictory objectives need to be reached: keeping the communication low and distributing the computation over the architecture. To solve this problem, a more abstract representation of a concurrent program is needed in which processing loads and communication traffic are accounted for in a compact manner. This information can be extracted from the GSPN model exploiting structural results as well as quantitative evaluations that yield the parameters of the concurrent program *communication graph.*

Communication graphs [15] correspond to a different view of concurrency in which concurrent applications are decomposed in modules that cooperate throughout the whole execution of the program. Cooperation is carried on by means of message exchange, and synchronization is introduced because of the synchronous property of the message passing mechanism (rendez-vous). Communication graph represents the interaction among processes in terms of the amount of exchanged information. Using their formal definition [4], communication graphs can be naturally built for any class of concurrent programs written using a message passing language. The model can be used for quantitative studies of the behaviour of a concurrent program by assigning weight factors to both the nodes and the arcs. Weights are associated with the nodes to represent the resource consumptions implied by the corresponding processes. Estimates of the amount of data exchanged among processes annotate the arcs in the model. Figure 4 represents the communication graph for our simple "printer-spooler". It differs from the scheme of Fig. 1 because of the annotations for the nodes and for the arcs that represent computation times (W_i) and amount of exchanged data (C_{ij}). Communication graphs of this type have two disadvantages. First, they flatten into a static representation the many communication patterns that may take place among program components during the whole execution. Second, they yield allocation methods that have exponential complexity and that thus suffer from the presence of useless communication graph nodes.

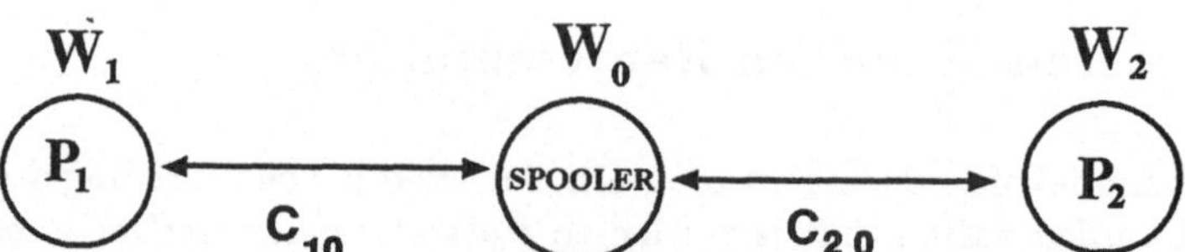

Fig. 4. Communication graph for the "printer-spooler" application

By introducing the concept of *phase* that represents a temporal interval during which an interaction pattern among processes takes place, many *phase communication graphs* can be identified for a single application that are usually individually smaller than the communication graph referring to the whole computation. The importance of having the computation of a program divided into

in the GSPN as timed transitions whose associated delays depend on the length of their executions.

Using this level of abstraction, concurrent programs are translated into GSPN models according to a procedure that is discussed in detail in [4].

Fig. 1. A "printer-spooler" system

In this paper we illustrate this translation process with the help of a simple example represented by a "printer-spooler" system that accepts the print requests of two user programs P_1 and P_2. A scheme of the structure of the *Spooler* and of the user programs P_1 and P_2 is depicted in Fig. 1, where $Chan_1$ and P_1Sp ($Chan_2$ and P_2Sp) are the channels used for communication between the *Spooler* and process P_1 (P_2).

The corresponding Occam-like code is presented in Fig. 2. Process P_1 (P_2) executes a loop of computation and requests to print the results. If process P_1 (P_2) wants to send a sequence of packets to be printed to the *Spooler*, it first sends a message on channel $Chan_1$ ($Chan_2$) containing a request to transmit k (n) packets and then enters a loop where at each iteration one of the k (n) packets is sent on channel P_1Sp (P_2Sp). The *Spooler* process executes a loop (the external one) looking for print requests coming from the two programs. When it receives a request for $k(n)$ packets from $Chan_1$ ($Chan_2$) it enters a reception loop of $k(n)$ messages from P_1Sp (P_2Sp).

The first translation step consists of generating the net representing the control structure. This task requires an abstraction phase that eliminates all the parts that are irrelevant with respect to control. This consists of coalescing into single macrostatements all those sequences of statements that do not include any communication or any **PAR** with named processes. This step can be easily obtained as by-product of the compiler of the language. The code presented in Fig. 2 is already in a form where only control structures that include PAR and communications have been kept. All other operations are summarized within angle brackets.

The second translation step consists of producing a first GSPN structure from the process scheme. Each process is considered separately and a corresponding net is constructed using the following general rules: named processes are represented in the net with single transitions (i.e., they are not yet substituted with their translations), communication statements are represented as immediate transitions (thus disregarding any type of synchronization connected with the rendez-vous), and macrostatements are substituted by timed transitions phases is the possibility of studying its behaviour phase by phase. In particular if a program spends most of its execution time in a given phase, then it can make sense to allocate the program following the indications provided by that phase only. This has the advantage of a reduced computational cost (even when the problem is solved with heuristic methods). Obviously the result obtained with this approach is suboptimal, but chances are that this solution be still valid and that the cost for its computation be considerably reduced.

GSPN models of concurrent programs can be used to compute the parameters of both communication and phase communication graphs. Details on how to obtain this more abstract models from the GSPN representation of the programs can be found in [5].

6 Concurrent Program Performance Tuning

The allocation of a concurrent program on a real parallel architecture always produces a loss of efficiency due to the physical limits of parallel computers. Indeed, if several processes are allocated on the same node, chances are that these processes will actually interfere. Of course, the allocation algorithm uses the information coming from the static analysis to keep minimal such possibility. An evaluation of the entity of such a loss can still be done using the GSPN model of the program augmented with a representation of the resources (processing units and communication links) shared by the different components. These shared resources can be easily represented by places initially marked with as many tokens as there are resources. The acquisitions of such resources are implemented with immediate transitions.

The solution of the augmented model in terms of throughputs and mean response times provides the performance indices that can be used to evaluate the efficiency of the final implementation and that can be used as the basis for deciding whether a reorganization of the program is needed. Indeed, the availability of a formal model of a concurrent program allows to proceed with a fine tuning of the application that may involve several iteration steps.

When the concurrent program is compiled for the first time, the workloads of the individual processes are estimated using simple statement counts. This information is used as a parameterization of the GSPN model that produces a (set of) communication graph(s) based on these initial guesses. When possible, the evaluation of the GSPN model is performed with analytic methods, but often simulation is needed. On the other hand, simulation can also be used for debugging purposes, since the animation of the GSPN model contributes to precisely understanding the exact behaviour of the program. When the mapping of the concurrent program is decided, its execution can be measured using the monitoring tools available within the programming environment and better estimates of the per-process computation times can be obtained. If the performance of the concurrent application needs to be improved, the modelling, evaluation, and mapping cycle can be repeated leading to a possible restructuring of the application itself. In the case of the DISC programming environment considered for our example, this iterative procedure is illustrated by Fig. 5

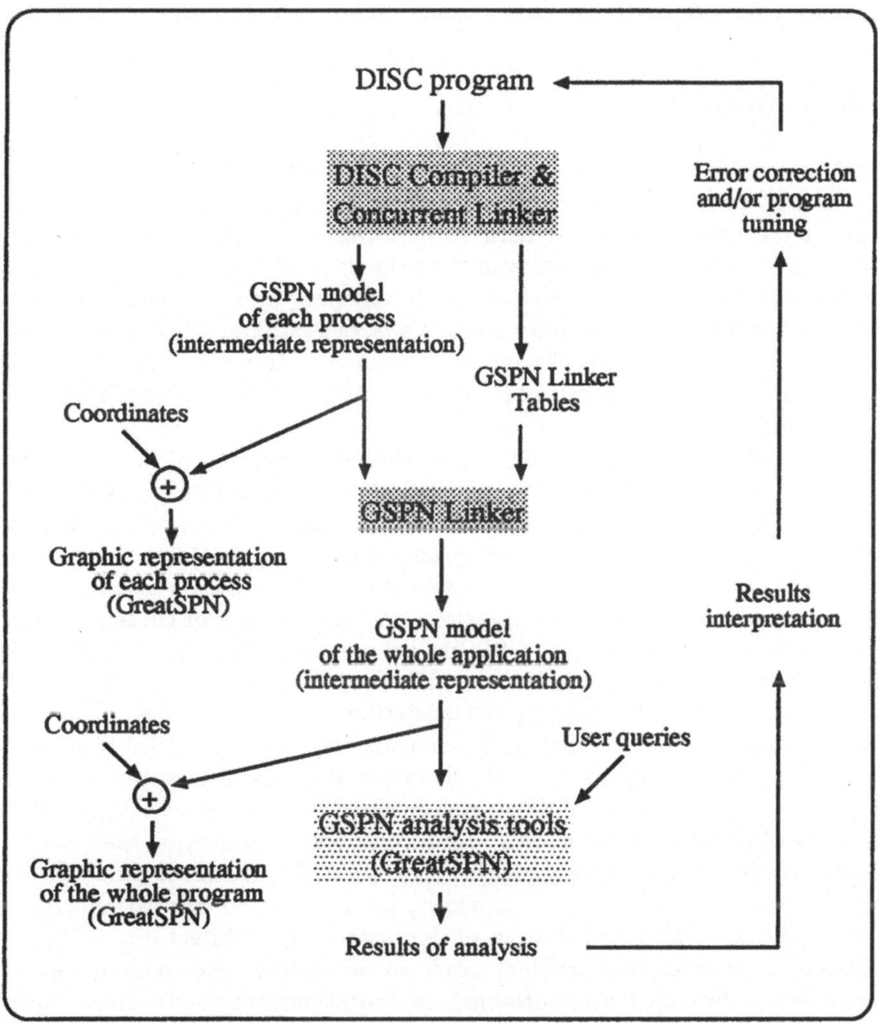

Fig. 5. Tuning of DISC concurrent applications

A concurrent programming environment of the type implemented for DISC allows also other uses of the formal model underlying the application. Testing a complete concurrent application is difficult because of the complexity of its behaviour. It is thus conceivable proceeding with an incremental approach and thus with the debugging of each individual component as soon as it is completed. To make testing reliable, we must account for the dynamics of the "scenarios" within which the components are meant to operate. In this case the availability of an overall model allows a simulation that drives the execution of the individual components when they are available, and that behaves according to standard principles when the components are specified, but not yet implemented.

7 Conclusions

In this paper we have discussed the role of formal models in the study of the behaviour of concurrent programs. Concurrent programs developed by means of skeleton functions yield predictable performance under the assumption of having a complete characterization of the behaviour of these basic blocks. GSPN models capturing the control-flow of concurrent programs can be automatically generated and used as the basis for a static analysis that identifies the qualitative properties of the programs. The models obtained in this way are very detailed and a control of their complexity can be performed by a proper use of abstraction mechanisms.

The use of GSPN as the formalism for the representation of the structure of concurrent programs satisfies the requirement of constructing models that are well suited for both validation and efficiency evaluation. This provides the basis for the development of concurrent program design tools that help the programmer reasoning about his concurrent application both in terms of adherence of the development to problem specifications and of efficiency of chosen solutions. When the models deriving from CSP-like programs are too big, it may become impossible to compute their solutions with theoretical/analytical tools. GSPN models are however suitable for their translation in event driven simulation programs that can be used for their animation and for statistical estimation of the results. Moreover, seeing the dynamic evolution of the parallel computation represents an extremely powerful debugging method for concurrent programs. The possibility of measuring the efficiency of a concurrent application that has been validated by the programmer allows to identify which part of the parallelization effort is actually beneficial, thus providing information on how to allocate the different processes on the processors of the underlying architecture.

Several aspects of this problem needs to be further investigated; more research needs to be done for an automatic computation of the performance indices that are relevant for the evaluation of concurrent programs. finally, prototype implementation of these methodologies are needed in order to prove the validity of the approach and to obtain insights on the supports that are required for an effective development of concurrent programs.

Acknowledgements

The author wishes to thank C. Anglano, S. Donatelli, G. Franceschinis, A. Mazzeo, N. Mazzocca, M. Ribaudo, and S. Russo who participated in the original development of the DISC programming environment mentioned in this paper.

References

1. M. Ajmone Marsan, G. Balbo, and G. Conte. A class of generalized stochastic Petri nets for the performance analysis of multiprocessor systems. *ACM Transactions on Computer Systems*, 2(1), May 1984.
2. M. Ajmone Marsan, G. Balbo, and G. Conte. *Performance Models of Multiprocessor Systems*. MIT Press, Cambridge, USA, 1986.
3. G. Balbo, G. Chiola, S.C. Bruell, and P. Chen. An example of modelling and evaluation of a concurrent program using coloured stochastic Petri nets: Lamport's fast mutual exclusion algorithm. *IEEE Transactions on Parallel and Distributed Systems*, 3(1), January 1992.
4. G. Balbo, S. Donatelli, and G. Franceschinis. Understanding parallel programs behaviour through Petri net models. *J. of Parallel and Distributed Computing*, 15(3), 1992.
5. G. Balbo, S. Donatelli, G. Franceschinis, A. Mazzeo, A. Mazzocca, and M. Ribaudo. On concurrent programs characterization. To appear on Performance Evaluation, 1993.
6. J. Darlington, A.J. Field, P.G. Harrison, P.H.J. Kelly, D.W.N. Sharp, and Q. Wu. Parallel programming using skeleton functions. In *Proc. PARLE '93, Parallel Architectures and Language Europe*, number 694 in LNCS. Springer Verlag, 1993.
7. A. Ferscha. Modelling mappings of parallel computations onto parallel architectures with prm-net model. In *Proc. IFIP-WG 10.3 Working Conference on Decentralized Systems*, Lyon, December 1989.
8. C.A.R. Hoare. Communicating sequential process. *Comm. of ACM*, Aug 1978.
9. G. Iannello, A. Mazzeo, C. Savy, and G. Ventre. Parallel software development in disc programming enviroment. *Future Generation Computer Systems*, 5(4), 1990.
10. O. Kramer and H. Muhlenbein. Mapping strategies in message-based multiprocessors system. *Parallel Computing*, 9, 1989.
11. T. Murata, B. Shenker, and S. Shatz. Detection of Ada static deadlocks using Petri nets invariants. *IEEE Transactions on Software Engineering*, 15(3):314–326, March 1989.
12. S. Pelagatti. *A Methodology for the Development and the Support of Massively Parallel Programs*. PhD thesis, Informatics Department, University of Pisa, Pisa, Italy, March 1993. Technical Report TD/93.
13. C.V. Ramamoorty and W.T. Tsai A. Prakash. Software engineering: Problems and perspectives. *IEEE Transactions on Computer*, October 1984.
14. S. Shatz and J. Wang. *Tutorial on Distributed Software Engeneering*. IEEE-CS Press, 1989.
15. J.K. Aggarwal Soo-Young Lee. A mapping strategy for parallel processing. *IEEE Transactions on Computers*, C 36(4), Apr 1987.
16. R. Taylor. A general purpose algorithm for analyzing concurrent programs. *Comm. of ACM*, 26, May 1983.

Performance Modeling of ATM-Based Networks

J.W. Wong

Department of Computer Science
University of Waterloo
Waterloo, Ontario N2L 3G1
Canada

Abstract. Asynchronous Transfer Mode (ATM) has been chosen as the multiplexing technique for Broadband Integrated Services Digital Networks. Under ATM, all information types (voice, data, image and video) are represented in terms of standardized units called cells. The acceptance of the ATM cell by the computer and communications industry as standard unit of information exchange will have a significant impact on the future development of communications infrastructure and end-user equipment. In this paper, we consider the performance modeling and evaluation of ATM-based networks. The performance issues at the ATM Layer and the ATM Adaptation Layer (AAL) are discussed. These include traffic characterization, multiplexing and switching, quality of service classes, call acceptance, congestion control, and AAL performance. Performance results on multiplexing and switching, and LAN interconnection using an ATM switch, are presented.

1   Introduction

Asynchronous Transfer Mode (ATM) has been chosen as the multiplexing technique for Broadband Integrated Services Digital Networks [1]. Under ATM, bandwidth is allocated on demand using 53-byte data units called cells. ATM supports a wide range of services, including voice, data, image and video, and provides a flexible means to multiplex these traffic types on the same physical network.

The acceptance of the ATM cell by the computer and communications industry as a standard unit of information exchange will have a significant impact on the future development of communications infrastructure and terminal equipment. In general, an ATM-based network is configured with a number of switches interconnected by trunks in a meshed topology. Standardized transmission speeds are 150 and 600 Mb/s.

Advancements in technology have resulted in the development of high-speed ATM switches at relatively low cost. ATM switching technology, although initially designed for the wide area environment, is also well-suited for local area networking, e.g., as a local-area network (LAN) or a backbone for LAN interconnection.

In this paper, we consider the performance modeling and evaluation of ATM networks. Our focus is on the ATM Layer and the ATM Adaptation Layer

(AAL). An overview of the functions of these two layers are provided in Section 2. The corresponding performance issues are discussed in Section 3. These include traffic characterization, multiplexing and switching, quality of service classes, call acceptance, congestion control, and AAL performance. In Section 4, recent performance results on multiplexing and switching, and LAN interconnection using an ATM switch, are presented. Finally, Section 5 contains some concluding remarks.

2 Protocol Structure of ATM Networks

Communication in an ATM network is based on a set of layered protocols [2]. These layers are depicted in Figure 1.

Higher Layers
ATM Adaptation Layer
ATM Layer
Physical Layer

Fig. 1. Protocol Structure for an ATM Network

2.1 ATM Layer

The ATM layer provides for the transport of ATM cells between AAL entities. Such transport occurs over pre-established connections. Cells belong to a given connection are routed along the same path (or ordered set of trunks); they will therefore arrive in sequence at the destination. The addressing mechanism in an ATM cell allows the possibility of routing several connections along the same path. At the ATM layer, each connection has a set of negotiated Quality of Service (QoS) parameters such as cell loss rate, cell delay, cell delay variation, and throughput.

2.2 ATM Adaptation Layer

The ATM Adaptation Layer (AAL) enhances the service provided by the ATM layer to support the functions required by AAL service users. It supports multiple protocols to fit the users' needs. Specifically, Type 1 provides a constant bit rate service and is intended for services that have specific delay, jitter and timing requirements e.g. video and circuit emulation. Type 2 supports a variable bit rate service that has timing requirements, and is intended for services such as packet video. Types 3/4 and 5 are designed to support data transfer services.

Between the two, Type 5 is more efficient in the sense that the payload field is larger, but message multiplexing along the same connection is not provided.

In addition to the above, packet segmentation (into cells) and reassembly are functions of the AAL.

3 Performance Issues

From the viewpoint of performance modeling, the characteristics of an ATM network are similar to those of a packet-switched network. Much research has been done on the performance of packet-switched networks; the initial work was published almost 30 years ago [3]. Topics investigated include delay-throughput analysis, routing, flow and congestion control, switch buffer management, and virtual circuit modeling [4], [5]. These investigations are based on networks with much lower transmission speeds (e.g., 56 Kb/s), and larger packet sizes. The results may therefore not be applicable to ATM networks, especially in the areas of traffic characterization, switch architecture, and traffic management which includes call acceptance and congestion control.

3.1 Traffic Characterization

Modeling of ATM networks is often done at a level of detail where cells are explicitly represented. Accurate modeling of the cell arrival process is therefore an important issue. An ATM network may carry several types of traffic with widely different characteristics (e.g., mean rate and burstiness). Models suggested include the Markov Modulated Poisson Process [6] and Semi-Markov process [7]. Exact analysis of queueing models with these arrival processes is often restricted to the single server case. While some of the queueing problems are analytically challenging, the need to understand end-to-end performance should not be ignored. Simulation seems to be a more viable approach when one is dealing with end-to-end performance.

Further work is needed to understand the traffic characteristics seen by the ATM layer. It is now possible to set up an experimental facility using off-the-shelf components. Traffic measurements on an ATM network supporting distributed applications would provide valuable insight into the impact of user applications, operating system software, and AAL on the characteristics of a traffic source.

3.2 Multiplexing and Switching

ATM multiplexers and switches are often treated separately in performance studies. The merit of such an approach is that one can investigate in detail a key component of an ATM network, under different traffic sources and user scenarios. The results are often valuable to the design of multiplexers and switches, e.g., output buffering is considered superior to input buffering with respect to throughput performance [8]. Again, there is a need to understand the end-to-end performance where a network model is required. We have investigated the effect of multiplexing and switching on the characteristics of a traffic stream [9]. Some of our findings are summarized in Section 4 below.

A likely application of ATM switching technology is local area networking or backbone for LAN interconnection [10]. Organizations engaged in distributed computing are expected to see a substantial increase in LAN traffic in the future. Shared-media LANs (e.g., Ethernet and FDDI), together with devices such as bridges and routers for their interconnection, may not be effective in meeting the increasing demand. ATM switching technology is an attractive alternative because it offers higher aggregate bandwidth. For LAN interconnection, the traffic sources are characterized by the departure of packets from a LAN, and the pattern of inter-LAN traffic. Results on end-to-end performance will provide valuable guidelines to local ATM network design and capacity planning.

A performance comparison of alternative configurations for LAN interconnection using an ATM switch has recently been completed [11]. A summary of the results is included in Section 4 below.

3.3 Call Acceptance

A key objective in the design of an ATM network is to achieve high resource utilization while meeting the users' QoS requirements (e.g., cell loss rate, cell delay, delay variation, and throughput). The QoS is negotiated between the user and the network when a call connection is established. Network resources such as trunk bandwidth and switch buffers should be managed such that the negotiated QoS is met. A central question is under what condition should a new call be accepted, keeping in mind that the traffic generated by the new call may affect the QoS of the existing calls.

To facilitate resource management, a user is required to specify the source traffic characteristics at call establishment. The current approach is to define an appropriate set of traffic descriptors. Ideally, these descriptors should be simple enough that the users can develop an intuitive understanding of the specification, and flexible enough that inaccurate specifications do not have serious negative effects [12]. Suggested traffic descriptors include mean cell rate, peak cell rate, burstiness, and mean burst length [13]. At call establishment, the user specifies the values of the traffic descriptors. The network then estimates the resource requirements of the call, using the specified values, the network state, and the QoS of the new and existing calls. A popular approach is to estimate the "effective bandwidth" requirement, and the call is accepted if this requirement can be met without degrading the QoS of the other calls [14]. There is a need to understand the accuracy of the effective bandwidth estimate, and a good measure is the frequency that an accepted call leads to QoS degradation.

3.4 Congestion Control

At call acceptance, the specified traffic descriptors constitute a "bandwidth contract" between the user and the network. It is possible that a user may violate the bandwidth contract, either temporarily due to the bursty nature of the traffic source, or more long term because of inaccurate specification of the traffic descriptors. Such scenarios may have a negative impact on the QoS of the other calls. A congestion control mechanism could be used to enforce the bandwidth contracts. Congestion control has been extensively studied for traditional packet-switched networks; most proposed schemes are reactive rather than preventive, e.g., the window mechanism. It is generally recognized that reactive control may not be effective for ATM because of the high transmission speeds and small cell size. Information needed for congestion control decisions may not be received in time, especially in the wide area environment. Congestion control schemes suggested for ATM networks are therefore preventive in nature; the most commonly proposed schemes are variants of the leaky-bucket mechanism [15].

Leaky bucket is an admission control mechanism which either drops or tags cells that violate the bandwidth contract. Dropped cells are rejected from entering the network, and any recovery is performed at a higher layer protocol. In the ATM cell, the cell header has a Cell Loss Priority (CLP) bit which can be used to indicate cells that are tagged. Tagged cells may be given low priority as far as switch buffer allocation is concerned. For example, an untagged cell may displace a tagged cell if the buffer is full, resulting in the tagged cell being lost. This last point raises the issue of buffer sizing and management at the switch in order to meet the QoS of the calls. Most schemes proposed for traditional packet-switched networks are applicable, although simplicity is an important consideration because of the high-speed operation of ATM switches.

Much research has been done on the performance of variants of the leaky bucket mechanism. More work is required to understand the interaction among call acceptance, traffic descriptors, bandwidth enforcement, and switch buffer management. Performance results taking these factors into consideration can provide valuable insight into the design and operation of ATM networks.

3.5 AAL Performance

As mentioned previously, several AAL types have been defined (Types 1 and 2 for services such as video and circuit emulation, and types 3/4 and 5 for data services) and an important function provided by AAL is segmentation and reassembly. AAL Types 3/4 and 5 support both message mode and streaming mode services, each mode may offer an assured peer-to-peer operation where lost or corrupted cells are corrected by retransmission, or a non-assured operation where retransmissions are not performed. The performance of AAL implementation is of interest because an inefficient implementation may result in a reduced bandwidth seen by AAL service users. Another performance issue is the impact of AAL on the traffic characteristics seen at the ATM layer.

It was also mentioned previously that ATM switching technology is attractive for local area networking. An important requirement, however, is the support of connectionless LAN traffic on a connection-oriented ATM network. Two approaches have been suggested [16]. In the indirect approach, end users establish permanent or temporary connections, onto which packets are forwarded. The direct approach requires the availability of connectionless servers which perform a mapping of packets onto established connections (permanent or temporary) at every switching node, based on the destination information. A study of the architectural and performance issues of connectionless services on an ATM network can be found in [17].

AAL Types 3/4 and 5 are designed for data service. With appropriate buffering, they may be able to support constant bit rate service also. It is of interest to investigate the effectiveness of AAL Types 3/4 and 5 in supporting a constant bit rate service, as compared to AAL Types 1 and 2.

4 Performance Results

In this section, we present recent results on multiplexing and switching, and LAN interconnection using an ATM switch.

4.1 Multiplexing and Switching

In [9], the model shown in Figure 2 was used to investigate the end-to-end performance of an ATM network. Each user node Ui is assumed to be fed by 8 traffic sources, corresponding to 8 calls already accepted by the network. Cells from these calls are multiplexed (in FCFS order) onto an access link (to a switch). The switches are internally non-blocking, and assumed to have unlimited output buffers. The Dj's are destination nodes and the paths are selected such that a balanced traffic scenario is obtained. All links in the network have a capacity of 150 Mb/s. Time is measured in slots, where a slot is defined to be the time required to transmit a 53-byte ATM cell at 150 Mb/s.

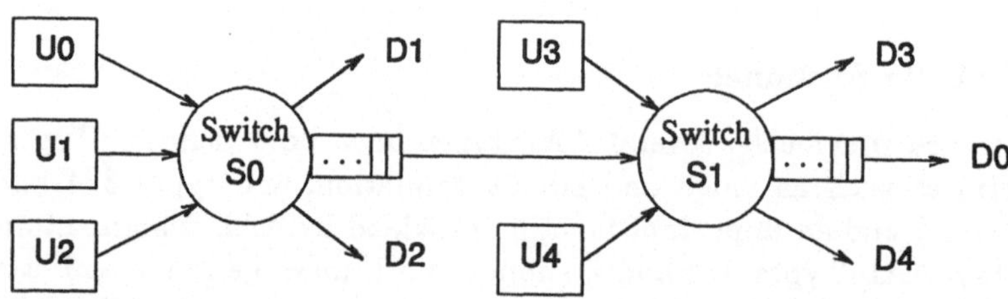

Fig. 2. Network Configuration

Two traffic source models are considered: MMPP and IPP (Interrupted Poisson Process which is a special case of MMPP). The parameters for these models are selected such that they have the same mean cell rate, peak cell rate, and mean burst duration. Simulation results for the mean queue lengths for different link utilization ρ are shown in Table 1. We observe that the queue length at switch S0 is smaller than that at the user node, indicating that multiplexing has a smoothing effect on the traffic stream. There is no observed difference between the queue lengths at S0 and S1, and hence no evidence that traffic was being smoothed by the switching process. However, further experimentation with finite switch buffers reveals that some smoothing does occur (see [9] for details).

A more important observation is that the two traffic sources exhibit substantially different queue lengths (or switch buffer requirements), even though they have the same mean cell rate, peak cell rate, and mean burst duration. These parameters are therefore not sufficient to characterize the resource requirement of a call. In Table 2, the squared coefficient of variation of cell interarrival times (denoted by CV^2) of the traffic sources are shown. We observe that IPP has a substantially higher CV^2 than MMPP. This is consistent with the earlier observation of a larger queue length. CV^2 is therefore a useful parameter for characterizing resource requirement.

Table 1. Mean Queue Length Results (95% Confidence Interval)

	IPP	MMPP
$\rho = .40$ User S0 S1	0.3140 ± 0.0031 0.2242 ± 0.0062 0.2337 ± 0.0112	0.1715 ± 0.0010 0.1228 ± 0.0015 0.1218 ± 0.0016
$\rho = .60$ User S0 S1	7.3277 ± 0.1477 6.1219 ± 0.5859 6.2280 ± 0.5199	1.5145 ± 0.0537 1.2540 ± 0.0513 1.2607 ± 0.0743
$\rho = .80$ User S0 S1	96.2755 ± 2.0820 76.3588 ± 4.7241 74.7214 ± 2.2881	29.0742 ± 0.9314 23.8471 ± 1.1850 22.8972 ± 1.5426

Table 2. Squared Coefficient of Variation of Cell Interarrival Times

		IPP	MMPP
$\rho = .40$	User Node	48.90	1.582
	Switching Node	48.87	1.577
$\rho = .60$	User Node	72.89	1.584
	Switching Node	72.08	1.565
$\rho = .80$	User Node	96.80	1.587
	Switching Node	90.62	1.526

4.2   LAN Interconnection Using an ATM Switch

In [11], a network model consisting of LANs and host computers interconnected by an ATM switch was developed. The switch is internally non-blocking, and assumed to have unlimited output buffers. Multiplexer/demultiplexers may be used to combine/separate streams of traffic from and to a group of LANs or hosts. Interface modules, situated between each LAN or host and the ATM portion of the network, perform segmentation and reassembly of packets. The indirect approach to interconnection is assumed where permanent connections are established between each source-destination pair.

Link speeds are assumed to be 45 Mb/s, and the time unit is given by the time required to transmit a 53-byte slot at 45 Mb/s. The LANs (Ethernets) are modeled explicitly while the hosts are modeled as packet sources. The packet arrival process to each Ethernet station is assumed to be Poisson. On the other hand, packet arrivals from a host to its interface module is assumed to follow an IPP.

Three configurations to interconnect two hosts and eight Ethernets are evaluated. These configurations are depicted in Figure 3 to 5, where the number of switch ports used are 2, 4, and 10 respectively. Note that multiplexers are used in Configurations 1 and 2. Ethernet-Ethernet, Host-Ethernet, and Ethernet-Host packets are assumed to be 64 or 1500 bytes, with equal probability. Host-Host packets have a similar distribution, but the sizes are 64 and 2400 bytes respectively. The destination of a packet is characterized as follows.

> Ethernet packet: 50% to same Ethernet
> 10% to hosts (equally likely)
> 40% to some other Ethernet (equally likely)
> Host packet: 20% to the other host
> 80% to Ethernet (equally likely)

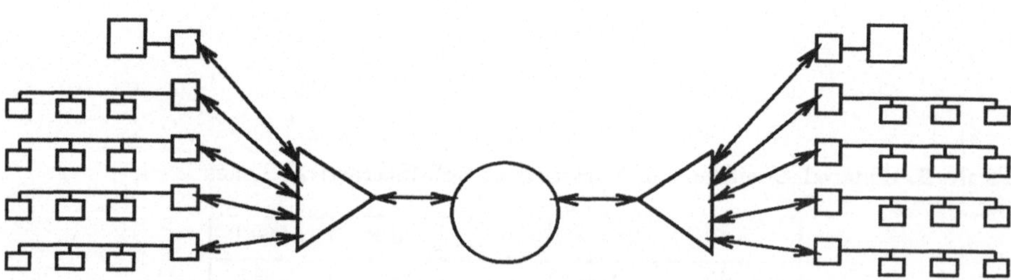

Fig. 3. Configuration 1

Table 3 shows the mean delays and delay variances of Ethernet packets when the mean bit rate of each host is 27 Mb/s (the link speed for host connection is 45 Mb/s). The offered load from Ethernet stations is assumed to be 30%; traffic

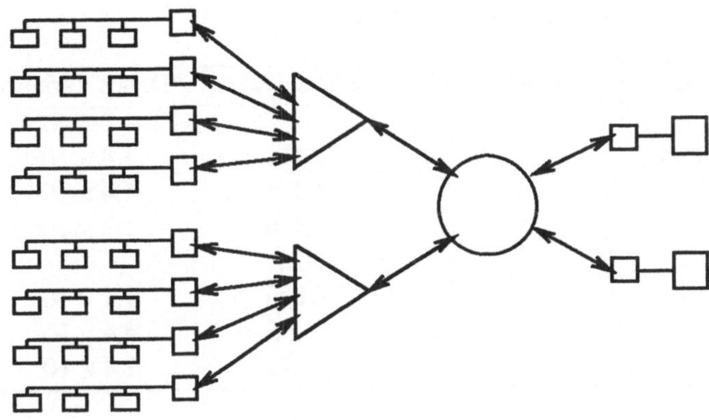

Fig. 4. Configuration 2

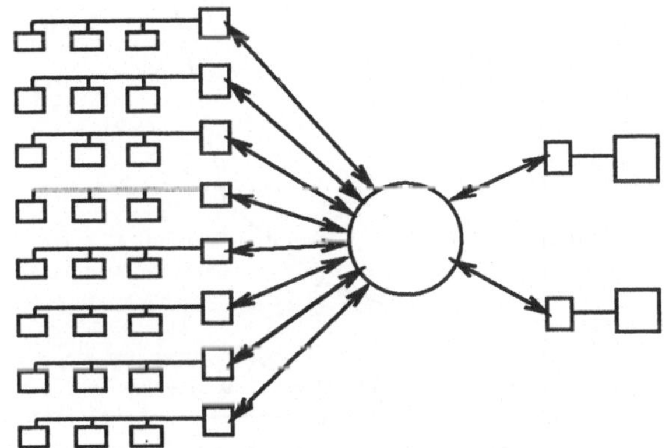

Fig. 5. Configuration 3

from interface module would add to this load. We observe that both station-to-station and interface-to-interface delays drop significantly as we remove the traffic-intensive hosts from the multiplexers and provide them with direct links to the ATM switch (Configurations 2 and 3). The delay variance within the ATM portion of the network is also improved.

The interface-to-interface delay of Ethernet packets for various levels of host traffic is plotted in Figure 6. We observe that by providing a direct link for each host to the switch, the delay is much less sensitive to load. The delay performance of Configurations 2 and 3 is quite similar, indicating that there is no significant performance advantage in providing a separate link for each Ethernet.

5   Concluding Remarks

In this paper, we have provided a discussion of the performance issues of ATM networks, and presented some results on network performance. It is expected

Table 3. Delay Statistics for Ethernet Packets

Delay Type	Configuration	Mean Delay	Delay Variance
Station	1	411	1.4×10^5
	2	333	1.4×10^5
	3	326	1.3×10^5
Interface	1	116	1.1×10^4
	2	35	4.4×10^2
	3	28	2.4×10^2

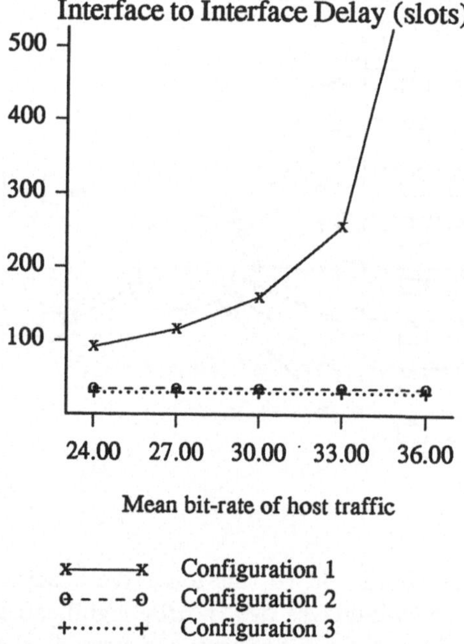

Fig. 6. Ethernet Packet Delay for Various Loads

that more work will be done in the future to gain further understanding of the performance characteristics of call acceptance, congestion control, AAL performance, etc. As to performance evaluation techniques, one would likely find that exact analysis is only possible for a component of the network, e.g., an ATM multiplexer or switch. To obtain performance results for a network model, one often has to resort to simulation. Another possibility is to do performance measurements using an experimental network. ATM network equipment is quite affordable now, and it is quite feasible to set up a local ATM network, and measure its behavior under various application scenarios.

Acknowledgement

The author would like to thank V.J. Friesen for her comments on an earlier draft of this paper. The results in Section 4 are taken from papers co-authored by her.

This research was supported by a grant from the Canadian Institute for Telecommunications Research under the NCE program of the Government of Canada.

References

1. CCITT Recommendation I.121: Broadband Aspects of ISDN. December 1990.
2. Asynchronous Transfer Mode: Bandwidth of the Future. Telco Systems, Norwood, MA, 1992.
3. Kleinrock, L.: Communication Nets: Stochastic Message Flow and Delay. McGraw-Hill, New York, 1964.
4. Wong, J.W. and Lam, S.S.: Queueing Network Models of Packet-Switching Networks, Part I: Open Networks. Performance Evaluation 2 (1), May 1982, 9-21.
5. Lam, S.S. and Wong, J.W.: Queueing Network Models of Packet-Switching Networks, Part II: Networks with Population Size Constraints. Performance Evaluation 2 (3), Oct. 1982, 161-180.
6. Heffes, H. and Lucantoni, D.M.: A Markov Modulated Characterization of Packetized Voice and Data Traffic and Related Statistical Multiplexer Performance. IEEE Journal on Selected Areas in Communications 4 (6), September 1986, 856-868.
7. Rodriguez-Dagnino, R. and Leon-Garcia, L.: Broadband Traffic Characterization. Canadian Conference on Electrical and Computer Engineering, Toronto, September 1992.
8. Karol, M.J., Hluchyj, M.G. and Morgan, S.P.: Input versus Output Queueing on a Space-Division Packet Switch. IEEE Transactions on Communications COM-35 (12), 1347-1356.
9. Friesen, V.J. and Wong, J.W.: The Effect of Multiplexing, Switching and other Factors on the Performance of Broadband Networks. Proc. IEEE INFOCOM '93, San Francisco, March 1993, 1194-1203.
10. Herman, J. and Serjak, C.: ATM Switches and Hubs Lead the Way to a New Era of Switched Internetworks. Data Communications, March 1993, 69-84.
11. Friesen, V.J., Hassanein, H.S., Wong, J.W. and Mark, J.W.: A Performance Study of LAN Interconnection Using an ATM Switch. To appear in Proc. International Conference on Computer Communications and Networks, San Diego, June 1993.
12. Turner, J.S.: Managing Bandwidth in ATM Networks with Bursty Traffic. IEEE Networks 6 (5), September 1992, 50-58.
13. CCITT Recommendation I.371: Traffic Control and Congestion Control in B-ISDN. June, 1992.
14. Guerin, R., Ahmadi, H. and Naghshineh, M.: Equivalent Capacity and its Application to Bandwidth Allocation in High-Speed Networks. IEEE JSAC 9 (7), 1991, 968-981.
15. Turner, J.: New directions in Communications (or Which Way to the Information Age). IEEE Communications Magazine 24 (10), 1986, 8-15.
16. CCITT Recommendation I.327: Broadband ISDN Functional Architecture. June 1992.

17. Box, D.F., Hong, D.P and Suda, T.: Architecture and Design of Connectionless Data Service for a Public ATM Network. Proc. IEEE INFOCOM '93, San Francisco, March 1993, 722-731.

Reliability and Performability Techniques and Tools: A Survey

Kishor S. Trivedi[1]* and Manish Malhotra[2]

[1] Dept. of Electrical Engineering, Box 90291,
Duke University, Durham, NC 27708-0291, USA
[2] AT&T Bell Laboratories, Holmdel, NJ 07733

Abstract. Reliability and performability modeling techniques and tools have been an area of lot of research activity in the last ten years. We present a survey of different techniques and tools that can be used for reliability and performability analysis. A unified mathematical framework for reliability and performability models in terms of Markov reward models is presented. Among modeling techniques, we describe reward-based hybrid hierarchical modeling, combinatorial multistate models, queues with server breakdowns, completion time approach, and iterative modeling. Software packages METFAC, NUMAS, SHARPE, SPNP, and Ultra-SAN are considered in detail while DyQNtool, PENELOPE, PENPET, and SAVE are briefly discussed.

1 Introduction

Fault-tolerant systems provide continuity of service despite component failures. However, the performance delivered by the system may degrade. A very simple example is that of a mirrored disk system. The system operates as long as at least one disk is operational. If both the disks are operational, then the reads are serviced from the disk with minimum seek time. Thus the system delivers higher read performance when both the disks are functioning than when one of the disks has failed. Performability analysis aims to capture this interaction between the failure-repair behavior and the performance delivered by the system.

Significant advances have been made in performability modeling and analysis since Beaudry [7] defined combined measures of performance and reliability and Meyer [71, 72] proposed a general framework for performability analysis. Several new algorithms have been proposed for calculating performability measures and a number of tools have been designed for performability analysis. In this paper, we present (in Section 2) a unified framework for performability and reliability analysis using Markov reward models. We survey (in Section 3) a number of different techniques which have been used for performability analysis. We illustrate how some of these techniques may be used for reliability analysis. We

* This work was supported in part by the National Science Foundation under Grant CCR-9108114 and by the Naval Surface Warfare Center under grant N60921-92-C-0161.

also survey (in Section 4) a number of software tools that have been developed for performability and reliability analysis. In Section 5, we discuss some of the computational problems that arise in performability analysis.

2 Reliability and Performability Measures

In this section, we present a unified framework for reliability and performability models in terms of Markov reward models. We shall see that performability analysis framework can be naturally adapted to reliability analysis framework by suitable assignment of reward rates. A comprehensive account of Markov reward models for performability analysis appears in [102]. Several references on solution methods for the measures defined below can be found in [21, 30, 47, 89, 102].

2.1 Definitions

Let $\{\Theta(t), t \geq 0\}$ be a continuous-time finite-state homogeneous Markov chain (CTMC) with state space Ψ. A constant reward rate r_i is associated with each state i of the Markov chain. With the reward rate specifications, the CTMC can be termed as *Markov reward model* (MRM). If the MRM spends τ_i time units in state i, then $r_i \tau_i$ is the reward accumulated. It is also possible to associate reward rates with the transitions of the CTMC. For more basic information on MRMs, refer to [51].

Let $\mathbf{Q}$ be the generator matrix and $\mathbf{P}(t)$ be the state probability vector of the MRM. Here $P_i(t)$ denotes the probability of the MRM being in state i at time t. The transient behavior of this MRM is given by the Kolmogorov differential equation:

$$\frac{d\mathbf{P}(t)}{dt} = \mathbf{P}(t)\mathbf{Q} \ , \tag{1}$$

given the initial state probability vector $\mathbf{P}(0)$. The steady-state probability vector π assuming that it exists and is unique is obtained by setting the l.h.s. in Equation 1 to zero vector:

$$\pi\mathbf{Q} = 0 \ , \tag{2}$$

subject to the condition $\sum_{i \in \Psi} \pi_i = 1$. Here π_i is the steady-state probability of the MRM being in state i. Let us now define a cumulative state probability vector of the MRM as $\mathbf{L}(t) = \int_0^t \mathbf{P}(x)dx$. $L_i(t)$ denotes the expected total time spent by the MRM in state i during the interval $[0, t)$. Integrating Equation 1, we get:

$$\frac{d\mathbf{L}(t)}{dt} = \mathbf{L}(t)\mathbf{Q} + \mathbf{P}(0) \ . \tag{3}$$

For MRMs with absorbing states, the state space Ψ can be partitioned into two: Ψ_A (absorbing states) and Ψ_T (transient states). Corresponding to the non-absorbing states, the submatrix $\mathbf{Q}_T$ of $\mathbf{Q}$ can be defined. The mean time spent by the MRM in state i is given by $\tau_i = \int_0^\infty P_i(x)dx$, which can be computed by integrating Equation 1 from 0 to ∞:

$$\tau\mathbf{Q}_T + \mathbf{P}_T(0) = 0 \ . \tag{4}$$

The mean time to absorption in such a Markov chain is given by:

$$MTTA = \sum_{i \in \Psi_T} \tau_i \quad . \tag{5}$$

2.2 Performability Measures

Let $\Upsilon(t) = r_{\Theta(t)}$ be the instantaneous reward rate of the MRM. The accumulated reward over a period of time $[0, t)$ is given by:

$$\Phi(t) = \int_0^t \Upsilon(x)dx = \int_0^t r_{\Theta(x)}dx \quad . \tag{6}$$

The expected instantaneous reward rate at time t of the MRM is:

$$E[\Upsilon(t)] = \sum_{i \in \Psi} r_i P_i(t) \quad . \tag{7}$$

The expected reward rate in steady-state of the MRM is:

$$E[\Upsilon_{ss}] = \sum_{i \in \Psi} r_i \pi_i \quad . \tag{8}$$

The expected accumulated reward in the interval $[0, t)$ of the MRM is:

$$E[\Phi(t)] = \sum_{i \in \Psi} r_i L_i(t) \quad . \tag{9}$$

The expected time-averaged reward in the interval $[0, t)$ is given by $\sum_i r_i L_i(t)/t$. For an MRM with absorbing states, expected accumulated reward until absorption is:

$$E[\Phi(\infty)] = \sum_{i \in \Psi_T} r_i \tau_i \quad . \tag{10}$$

The distribution of $\Upsilon(t)$ is computed as:

$$P[\Upsilon(t) \leq \psi] = \sum_{r_i \leq \psi, i \in \Psi} P_i(t) \quad . \tag{11}$$

The distribution of accumulated reward until absorption and distribution of accumulated reward over a finite period of time can also be computed.

Let the time to accumulate a given reward r be denoted by $\Gamma(r)$. Then the distribution of $\Gamma(r)$ is known once the distribution of accumulated reward is known [58]:

$$P[\Gamma(r) \leq t] = 1 - P[\Phi(t) < r] \quad . \tag{12}$$

For example, the distribution of time to complete a job that requires r units of processing time on a system which is modeled by an MRM can be computed in this manner.

2.3 Dependability Measures

In a dependability model, a reward rate of 1 is assigned to all the system operational states and reward rate 0 is assigned to all the system failure states. The *instantaneous availability* of the system is then $E[\Upsilon(t)]$ and *steady-state availability* is $E[\Upsilon_{ss}]$. The *cumulative operational time* of the system in time interval $[0,t)$ is $E[\Phi(t)]$. *Interval availability* is the proportion of time a system is operational in a given interval of time and it is given by $E[\Phi(t)]/t$. Measures related to time to first system failure are also of interest. To compute these measures, all the failure states are made absorbing (outgoing arcs from these states are removed). *Reliability* is then given by $E[\Upsilon(t)]$. The lifetime (analogous to cumulative operational time) [30] of the system in interval $[0,t)$ is $E[\Phi(t)]$ and *mean time to system failure* (MTTF) is $E[\Phi(\infty)]$. The *repairability* of the system is computed by making all the operational states absorbing and reversing the reward rates (i.e., making reward rate 1 to 0 and vice-versa) and computing $E[\Upsilon(t)]$.

3 Approaches to Reliability and Performability Analysis

MRM framework is not the only one available for performability analysis but it is the most commonly used one. We now discuss several different approaches that have been shown to be useful for performability analysis.

3.1 Markov Reward Models (MRMs)

MRM framework naturally leads to a separation of the performance and reliability models of the system. Performance model is solved to obtain reward rates which are assigned to the reliability model (also known as *structural model* [73]). However, this separation introduces an approximation in that reward rates assigned to any state of the reliability model are typically constant values (i.e., time-independent). Thus, it is assumed that for the sojourn in a state of the reliability model, the system provides a steady-state performance. The accuracy of this approximation depends upon the difference in the rates at which the events in the performance and the dependability model occur. Smaller the difference, the less accurate the results. It is for this reason that this approach is said to be based on a time-scale decomposition. In [102], we gave an example where this approach yields inaccurate results.

For the case, when reward rates take only two values, 0 and 1 (as in reliability models), de Souza e Silva and Gail [28] computed the distribution of interval availability using uniformization. Rubino and Sericola [90] obtained distribution of interval availability for semi-Markov models under some conditions. Goyal and Tantawi [45] and Reibman et al [89] evaluated interval availability by solving a partial differential equation (PDE).

For acyclic nonrecoverable MRMs (which arise in case of nonrepairable systems), the distribution of accumulated reward has been obtained [25, 44, 46, 72]. Nonrecoverable MRMs are characterized by a reward rate assignment in which reward rate of a future state is less than that of the present state. Donatiello and Iyer [34] used Laplace transforms to obtain closed form solution for this distribution for acyclic MRMs without imposing nonrecoverability condition.

For general MRMs, Kulkarni et al [58] and Smith et al [98] evaluated double Laplace transform of this distribution and developed a method of numerical inversion. Iyer et al [54] developed an algorithm for the computation of all the moments of accumulated reward. The $(k + 1)$st conditional moment of accumulated reward is expressed in terms of previous k conditional moments. Ammar et al [4] computed this distribution using Laguerre transforms. de Souza and Gail [29] compute this distribution using uniformization technique. This method has computational complexity that is exponential in the number of different reward rates assigned to system states. Donatiello and Grassi [33] have proposed another uniformization-based method that computes this distribution but its computational complexity is polynomial in terms of number of states and reward rates. They allow Coxian distribution for failure and repair times. Several authors have used the PDE approach to computing the distribution of accumulated reward [89, 85].

The MRM approach has been extended to allow the underlying reliability model to be semi-Markovian [22, 54, 59]. Pattipati and Shah [86] extended the work of Iyer et al [54] by allowing for nonhomogeneous Markov models. Furchtgott and Meyer [38] proposed a method that can be used for acyclic nonrecoverable semi-Markov models. However, the computational complexity is exponential in number of states of the model. Pattipati et al [85] allow a non-homogeneous Markov model with time-dependent reward rates.

The MRM approach is not directly applicable if parameters of the reliability model depend on parameters of the performance model (e.g., workload dependent failure rate of a server) and vice-versa.

3.2 Integrated Performability Model

Unlike the previous approach, the performance and reliability models are combined in this technique to yield a single monolithic performability model. Such an overall model of system behavior can potentially yield more accurate results than the time-scale decomposition model considered earlier. However, this approach typically results in a very large and stiff model (assuming state-space models such as Markov chains). Intuitively, largeness occurs because of a cross-product of states of the performance and reliability models. Stiffness occurs because the events associated with a performance model (arrival and service rates in a queue) occur typically at a much faster rate than the events associated with a reliability model (failure rates). Thus the tradeoff in performability analysis is that of solving a large, stiff model that yields accurate results versus solving two smaller, less stiff models that yield an approximate solution. We should note, however, that numerical difficulties arising from largeness and stiffness may very well negate this gain.

3.3 Queues with Server Breakdown

These can be considered as integrated performability models, but the research in this area is so extensive that we treat it separately. This problem has been studied for a much longer time. Some of the earlier references date as far back as 1958 [105]. *Priority queuing systems* with different customer types and *queuing systems with vacations* are two approaches that can be used to model queues with server failures and repair. A two-priority queuing system consists of two types of customers: regular jobs that arrive at a queue for service and breakdown jobs. Breakdown jobs have a higher pre-emptive priority than regular jobs. Arrival of a breakdown job implies server failure and pre-emption of any regular job currently being serviced. After server failure, the server undergoes repair (i.e., serves the breakdown job). Once the repair is finished, the server resumes servicing regular jobs if any. Alternatively, one could consider the repair period of a server as server vacation period. In this case, the model becomes a queuing model with vacations. The standard performance measures (such as mean queue length, waiting time distributions etc.) obtained by analyzing these queues are then the desired performability measures.

These queuing model types also lend themselves to model maintenance procedures in systems [35]. Regular maintenance is crucial for high reliability. In a priority queuing system, different maintenance strategies can be modeled by assigning appropriate priority (relative to the priority assigned to regular and breakdown jobs) to maintenance jobs. Similarly, the maintenance may be considered server vacation. Assuming that maintenance jobs have lower priority than regular jobs, maintenance begins when the queue becomes empty. If there is only one vacation period, then the model is known as *single vacation model*. If there is more than one vacation period (i.e., the server schedules another maintenance period if after completing a maintenance period, it finds the queue to be still empty), then it is known as *multiple vacation model*.

For a survey on single server queuing systems with vacations and evaluation techniques for steady-state measures, see Doshi [35, 36]. Several generalizations and extensions to these queuing models have been studied. Baccelli and Trivedi [5] analyzed an M/G/2 standby redundant system. Mitrani and Avi-Itzhak [75] analyzed multiserver queue using *generating functions* approach assuming that processors fail and are repaired independently. Neuts and Lucantoni [82] analyzed a similar model where servers may queue for repair and job arrival rate may depend upon the number of operational servers using *matrix-geometric* approach. They showed that congestion in queue length due to server failure causes the effect of failures to be felt long after the repair is completed. Recently, Chakka and Mitrani [17] solved an M/M/N queue with server breakdown and repair using *spectral expansion approach*. They generalize by allowing multiple simultaneous repair and failures which could depend upon the arrival and departure of jobs. Arrival and departures may occur in batches of fixed or random (bounded) size. Sztrik and Gál [100] proposed a recursive computational technique to evaluate a multi-terminal system with a CPU. Geist et al [40] proposed perception-based measures that capture both the mean and variability of response time in a multiserver queue with failures. King and Mitrani [57] presented an empirical study of a multiserver system with failures.

Kulkarni and Choi [60] analyzed steady-state behavior of a single server retrial queue (where customers conduct retrials until they find the server to be free) with server failures and repairs using Markov regenerative processes. Altiok [3] analyzed steady-state behavior of a single server queuing model with failures where service and repair times are allowed to be mixtures of generalized Erlang distributions. Mixtures of generalized Erlang distributions can approximate any general distribution. Van Dijk [32] computed simple bounds of steady-state congestion and throughput for multiserver systems with failures. The operational and failed periods can be generally distributed. These bounds depend only upon the mean of operational and failed periods. All these approaches focus on the steady-state behavior.

3.4 Queuing Networks (QNs) in Performability Modeling

Schoen [96] considers BCMP [6] QNs in which failure rate depends upon the workload. Müller-Clostermann has [78] analyzed a class of degradable QNs (similar to BCMP QNs) where each server may operate at several levels of (degraded) performance. He obtained approximate product-form solutions for steady-state probability distributions by exploiting the nearly-complete decomposability of these QNs. Haverkort and Niemegeers [48] proposed *dynamic queuing networks* (DyQNs) which combine parameterized QNs and generalized stochastic Petri nets (GSPNs). A behavioral decomposition approach is employed where the QN models the performance but some of its parameters are obtained from the GSPN which models the reliability. Szczerbicka [99] combined QNs and GSPNs for performability analysis but solved these models using decomposition and aggregation.

SHARPE facilitates specification and solution of hierarchical models where submodels can belong to a large class of model types including product form queuing networks, GSPNs, Markov reward models, fault-trees, reliability block diagrams, etc. For performability applications of SHARPE, see [63, 52].

3.5 Iterative Modeling Approach

If the parameters of the reliability model and the performance model are interdependent, then an iterative solution approach may be applied. Gelenbe et al [42] consider a distributed system in which nodes recover from failures based on a checkpointing strategy. The workload of a failed node is routed to some operational node thus affecting the performance of that node(s) which in turn influences the total recovery time of a node through checkpointing strategy. Such models may be solved using an iterative solution approach. In principle, the reliability and performance models are separated. However, instead of solving both these models in isolation, an iteration scheme (e.g., fixed-point iteration scheme) is devised which obtains the solution in a combined manner. In general, iterative schemes yield approximate solutions. Convergence of the iterative schemes and uniqueness of the solution remain an area of active research.

3.6 Completion Time Approach

The completion time problem assumes a task oriented view as opposed to accumulated reward approach which assumes a system oriented view of performability [10]. In the MRM approach, the unstated assumption was that no loss of reward occurs when a state transition occurs (i.e., accumulated reward until any time instant is preserved). This is known as *preemptive resume policy*. In queuing systems with server failures, accumulated reward may be lost upon server failure [39]. This is classified as *preemptive repeat* policy. Castillo and Siewiroek [16] and Kulkarni et al [58] obtained the task completion time distribution for a Markovian server. Kulkarni et al [59] extended this to semi-Markovian server. Bobbio and Trivedi [13] computed completion time distribution when work requirement is PH distributed using phase-type expansions. Bobbio and Roberti [11] computed distribution of minimal completion time for parallel tasks executing on a semi-Markovian system. Duda [37] and Kulkarni et al [60] allow for checkpointing. Using completion time as a basis, further queueing analysis has been carried out in order to compute the mean [84, 60] and the distribution of response time [18].

3.7 Multi-state Combinatorial Models

This approach is similar to the MRM approach in that reliability and performance model are separated and that performance measures are associated as reward rates with system states in the reliability model. However, unlike MRM approach, the reliability model in this case is a combinatorial model such as a block diagram or a fault-tree. Veeraraghavan and Trivedi [103] show how multi-state combinatorial models can be used for performability analysis. Unlike traditional combinatorial models where a system (or a component) can be in only two states (failed or operational), these models allow for multiple system (and component) states so that degradable system behavior can be modeled.

4 Tools for Performability and Reliability Analysis

In this section, we focus on software packages that allow both the performability and reliability analysis. Nearly all the tools that can be used for performability analysis can also be used for reliability analysis, although these may not be the most efficient tools for reliability analysis. For a survey on software tools for reliability analysis, we refer the reader to [41, 55, 68, 76]. For earlier surveys on performability modeling tools, see [48, 50]. The software tools that we consider are: METFAC, NUMAS, PENPET, SHARPE, SPNP, and UltraSAN.

The degradation modes of the system are obtained by taking a cross-product of degradation modes of all servers. To overcome largeness problem, the states with the same system degradation mode are merged into a single macro state. This aggregation is based on the observation that transitions within a macro state take place at a much faster rate than the transitions between macro states (since these transitions imply system upgrade/degrade which is rarer). The macro states define an aggregated matrix which is solved for steady-state measures. The performance model (which is a Markov submodel) associated with the states within each macro state is solved. These results are passed as parameters to aggregated model. Thus an approximate overall model solution is obtained by iterative and aggregation methods. Steady-state probability vectors are obtained by iterative aggregation, Gauss-Seidel iterations, or Gaussian elimination.

NUMAS can perform steady-state analysis of very large Markovian models. However, no support is provided for transient analysis. Thus many of the reliability measures and cumulative performability measures cannot be computed. Dependencies between failures of servers cannot be modeled.

4.3 SHARPE

SHARPE (Symbolic Hierarchical Automated Reliability/Performance Evaluator) was originally developed in 1986 by Sahner and Trivedi [92]. It has been significantly updated in 1991 [93]. It is written in C and runs on UNIX and VMS. The main feature of SHARPE is that hybrid and hierarchical models can be easily constructed. The overall system model may consist of several submodels of possibly different types. The model types allowed are fault-trees, reliability block diagrams, reliability graphs, Markov chains, acyclic semi-Markov chains, single and multi-chain product form queuing networks, GSPNs, and series-parallel task graphs. For example, the reliability of a system can be modeled by a reliability block diagram where reliability of each block is computed by solving a Markov chain. If a single Markov model for such a system was constructed, then it could have a state space of exponential size. Hierarchical modeling alleviates the problems of model largeness and stiffness to a large extent.

The model can be input either in interactive mode or by means of batch files. Submodels may be specified in the syntax of appropriate model types. These submodels may then be used in defining higher level models. Hierarchy is established by passing parameters from lower level models to higher level models as specified by the user. Each model is specified by the user manually which could be a drawback if for instance a large Markov chain is to be specified. SHARPE allows exponential polynomial ($\sum_j a_j t^{k_j} e^{b_j t}$) distributions to be attached to components (tasks, states). Thus failure distribution associated with basic components in case of combinatorial models (fault-trees, block diagrams, and reliability graphs) or sojourn-time distribution associated with state transitions in a (semi)-Markov chain could be an exponential polynomial.

The combinatorial models (fault-trees, block diagrams, and reliability graphs) are used for reliability and availability analysis. With each component (or link)

4.1 METFAC

This tool has been been developed at Polytechnical University of Catalunya by Carrasco and Figueras [15]. It is written in Fortran 77 and runs on VAX/VMS systems. The model is input by means of production rules which provide a higher level behavioral description of the system. These rules describe an event, the rate at which the event can occur and its response. For example, an event could be the occurrence of a fault and its response could be repair, performance degradation, or system failure. The production rule description of the system model is automatically converted to a CTMC. However, the reward rates (if any) must be manually specified for every state. This is a drawback for models with large state-spaces.

Transient and steady-state measures can be obtained. A cumulative performability measure known as *serviceability* can be obtained. It is defined as the probability of completing a certain amount of work before first system failure. Among a variety of other measures that can be computed are: reliability, availability (instantaneous or steady-state), maintainability, life-cycle reliability, life-cycle maintainability, mean up time, mean time to failure, mean time between failures, and mean time to operation after a system failure. Cost-related measures can also be computed. However, not all performability measures can be computed.

Steady-state solution is obtained by LU decomposition exploiting sparse storage. For transient solution, a multiple order, multi-step Gear, implicit method for integrating a system of ordinary differential equations (ODEs) is employed. This method is efficient and stable for stiff models. If the state-space is large, then a technique called *state dissolution* is used in which states with small probabilities are dissolved into parent states whose transition rates are modified suitably.

4.2 NUMAS

NUMAS (NUmerical Methods for the Analysis of computer Systems) has been developed by Müller-Clostermann at the University of Dortmund [77]. It is implemented in Simula 67 for Siemens BS2000 systems. Besides the performance analysis, it supports performability analysis via degradable queuing networks. In these networks, each server may operate at different (degraded) levels of performance. The failure and repair of each server takes place independently of other servers. However, the failure rate may be load-dependent and the repair rate may depend upon the number of operational servers.

The model for NUMAS can be input via two different interfaces: an interactive NUMAS interface or the HIT modeling tool developed by Beilner et al [8]. Both the interfaces allow specification of degradable queuing networks. The output measures are reported back in terms of input model (and not in terms of the Markov chain used for solution). These specifications are automatically translated into a (large) Markov chain. Typically, this Markov chain is very large since every state is defined by the number of customers at every server and the degradation mode of each server.

a failure-time distribution may be specified as an exponential polynomial (symbolic in t). SHARPE computes distribution function (symbolic in t), mean, and variance of time to failure of the system. User may opt for numeric solution in which case a numeric value of the distribution function at a given time t is computed. If failure probability or availability (instantaneous or steady-state) is specified for each component, then system failure probability or system availability is output. Specialized solution algorithms are used for different model types.

(semi)-Markov chains may be used for both reliability and performability analysis. Semi-Markov chains must be acyclic or irreducible. The sojourn-time distribution in case of a semi-Markov chain could an exponential polynomial. Reward rates may be associated with states of a (semi)-Markov chain and reward based performability measures can be computed. These reward rates may be specified either as a numeric value or as the output of a performance submodel specified by a queuing network, series-parallel task graph, (semi)-Markov chain, or a GSPN. In this case, the performance model is first solved to obtain a numeric value for the reward rate. For irreducible chains, SHARPE computes expected steady-state reward rate. For chains with an absorbing state, SHARPE computes distribution of accumulated reward until absorption, expected instantaneous reward rate, and expected accumulated reward until a given time t.

For irreducible Markov chains, SOR or Gauss-Seidel is used for steady-state solution. For transient analysis, uniformization with steady-state detection [81] is used. Symbolic solution of state probabilities is obtained using Laplace transform and partial fraction expansion approach [87]. For fault-trees and reliability graphs, a disjoint sum of products algorithm is used [104]. For task graphs, the algorithm used is discussed in [91].

4.4 SPNP

SPNP (Stochastic Petri Net Package) has been developed by Ciardo et al [23] at Duke University. It is written in C and runs on a variety of operating systems including UNIX, AIX, OS/2, and VMS. The model type used for input is a *stochastic reward net* (SRN). SRNs incorporate several structural extensions to GSPNs [2] such as marking dependencies (marking dependent arc cardinalities, enabling functions, etc.) and allow reward rates to be associated with each marking. The reward function can be marking dependent as well. SRNs are specified using CSPL (C based SPN Language) which is an extension of C with additional constructs for describing the SPN models. Whereas CSPL exploits the full power of C and makes the SRN specification very flexible, it also makes it imperative that the user knows C. There is no interactive interface, but a graphical interface exists. The user can either specify the SRN graphically or type in the CSPL file.

SRN specifications are automatically converted into an MRM which is then solved to compute a variety of transient, steady-state, cumulative, and sensitivity measures [21]. Standard measures such as average number of tokens in a place, average throughput of a timed transition, probability (transient or steady-state) that a place is not empty, and probability that a timed transition is enabled can be computed. These basic measures are combined or interpreted (according to the user) to yield various reliability, performance, and performability measures. For example, suppose that a token in place p implies that the system has failed. Then the probability of a token in place p at time t is the unreliability of the system. For a given reward function, expected value of the function, expected accumulated reward over a finite time interval, and time-averaged expected value can be computed. For SRNs with absorbing markings, mean time to absorption and expected accumulated reward until absorption can be computed.

For transient analysis, a highly accurate and efficient version of uniformization is employed. This incorporates steady-state detection of the underlying discrete-time Markov chain and computation of Poisson probabilities using Fox and Glynn's method [65]. For steady-state solution, Gauss-Seidel or near-optimal SOR method [21] is used. Sensitivity analysis may also be carried out by computing the derivatives of some of the output measures w.r.t. model parameters. Hierarchical models can be constructed by parameter passing from lower level models (subnets) to higher level models (subnets). Iterative solution approach [20, 24] based on fixed-point iteration can be employed by parameter passing via a shell file. State truncation is also easy to incorporate [56, 80].

4.5 TANGRAM

TANGRAM has been developed by Berson et al [9] at University of California at Los Angeles. It is written in object oriented Prolog and C and runs on SUN 3 systems. It provides an object-oriented environment for model specification. Submodels are defined in terms of instances of objects and interactions between the objects. Each object has an internal state which may change either due to an event occurring within the object or due to a message received from some other object. A library of object types is provided. The user may also define application specific object types and combine those with object types from the library. Hierarchical modeling is possible. Dependencies among objects is modeled by message transmissions among them. For example, consider the scenario when failure of a component makes several other components dormant. This is modeled by simply transmitting a message after the component failure to other dependent components which change their internal state to dormant mode. This generality and flexibility make TANGRAM a powerful modeling tool.

The overall model is specified as a collection of objects and interactions among them. A graphical interface is provided that is used to define icons for object types. Reward rates may be associated with internal states of the objects. A Markov reward model is automatically generated from the specifications of various object types. However, the transition rate matrix is incrementally built and only the reachable states are looked at. For steady-state analysis, power method is used. For transient analysis, uniformization is used. Reward based measures are computed as weighted sums of state probabilities and reward rates. It is not clear if cumulative performability measures can be computed.

Output measures are obtained by a querying mechanism. Queries regarding internal states of objects and rewards may be defined. Conceptually, SHARPE and TANGRAM both allow hierarchical modeling. A basic difference between the two approaches is that TANGRAM converts all the object types into a single, possibly large and stiff, Markov model for analysis whereas SHARPE uses specialized solution algorithms for different model types and does not generate a single large model.

4.6 UltraSAN

UltraSAN has been developed by Sanders et al [26] at the University of Arizona. It is written using C and X window interface library and runs on UNIX on DEC, SUN, and AT&T workstations. It is a successor of METASAN, a tool previously developed at University of Michigan and the Industrial Technology Institute [94]. Reliability, performance, and performability analysis based on stochastic activity networks (SANs) [74] can be performed using UltraSAN. Extensive support is provided for performability analysis. SANs are extensions of GSPNs [2] with primitives such as places, activities (same as transitions), input gates, and output gates. The input and output gates are used to model enabling and completion of an activity respectively. Both impulse-based and rate-based rewards are allowed. Impulse-based rewards are associated with the completion of an activity and rate-based rewards are associated with markings.

The SAN is input graphically under the X window environment. The entire model description is done in three parts. Structure file is used to define the structure of the SAN (places, activities, etc.). Experiment file is used to define the desired output measures and solution method. These files are independent of each other and therefore different experiments may be specified for the same SAN. Finally, a specification for combining various submodels in a hierarchical manner may also be provided. In the experiment file, two types of performability variables may be specified: activity variables and reward variables. Activity variables are specified for an activity and estimate the time between two completions of the activity. Reward variables include the rate-based and impulse-based rewards. Instantaneous values of these variables at a given time, accumulated value over a time interval, and time-averaged accumulated values over an interval may be computed.

For solution, a SAN is converted into a state-level representation (via markings) called Stochastic Activity System (SAS). If this is Markovian in nature, then a Markov model is generated. Steady-state solution is obtained by LU decomposition or an iterative method like SOR. Transient solution is obtained by uniformization. Largeness of state-space is overcome by constructing a reduced base model [95]. This model retains only the necessary information for a desired output measure. Reward based performability measures are computed using behavioral decomposition (i.e., performance model is solved to obtain reward rates for reliability model). For non-Markovian and analytically intractable models, simulation (transient and steady-state) is provided. However, behavioral decomposition is not employed for performability analysis via simulation. Instead, a single performability model is simulated. The timing distributions in the SANs are allowed to be general. UltraSAN is one of the few performability modeling tools that allows simulation. Hence several models which cannot be analytically solved can nevertheless be solved.

4.7 Other Tools

There are several other tools also available for performability analysis. Due to space limitations, we mention these only briefly.

DyQNtool (Dynamic Queuing Network tool) has been developed by Haverkort et al [49] at University of Twente. A GSPN models the reliability while performance measures are computed as product-form solution of a dynamic queuing network. As in MRM approach, a Markov reward model is generated for performability analysis. However, the parameters of the dynamic queuing network may depend upon the states of the reliability model.

PENELOPE has been developed by Munkert and de Meer [79]. It is unique in that it allows for performability evaluation and optimization. It uses MRMs which are extended by allowing for impulse rewards and reconfiguration edges [31]. The reconfiguration edges imply the notion of decision making, i.e., whether or not to reconfigure a system in a given state. This tool computes an optimal strategy of the system by optimizing some performability measure. Both transient and steady-state optimization is allowed.

PENPET (PEtri Net based Performability Evaluation Tool) has been developed by Lepold et al [61]. It is designed for performability evaluation of fault-tolerant multiprocessor systems based on MRM approach. GSPNs are used as the model type. Reward rates for different system states in a reliability model (a GSPN) are obtained as performance measures by solving GSPNs.

SAVE (System AVailability Estimator) has been developed by Goyal et al [43] jointly at IBM and Duke University. It employs MRM approach for performability analysis. There is no support within SAVE to compute reward rates. These must be supplied by the user. Transient, steady-state, and cumulative measures of MRMs can be computed. Simulation using importance sampling is also an option.

5 Computational Problems, Extensions, and Current Trends

From the discussions above, several bottlenecks in performability and reliability analysis become clear. We discuss some of the major issues:

5.1 Largeness

Largeness of state-space is a major problem for Markovian models. To overcome this problem, we may resort to either largeness-tolerance or largeness-avoidance schemes. In the former approach, a large overall model is automatically generated starting with a more concise description [50]. The model is solved using sparse storage techniques and sparsity preserving efficient numerical methods. In the latter approach, the model size is reduced during model generation and therefore a large model is not generated. State truncation methods [80], hierarchical model solution [67], and hybrid models that judiciously combine different model types [53] are examples of largeness avoidance.

5.2 Stiffness

Stiffness of the model is another problem that plagues its solution. It arises mainly due to large difference in failure and repair rates or failure and job arrival rates. The MRM approach reduces stiffness by separating the performance and reliability models but the stiffness within reliability model remains. Stiffness may be avoided by using aggregation [14, 13] that yields approximate solution. To tolerate stiffness, special stable stiff solvers may be used [69, 64, 88].

5.3 Non-Markovian Models

In Section 3.3, we mention several studies that focus on performability analysis of queues with server failures in which different distributions (job inter-arrival, service time, failure time, repair time, etc.) are allowed to be non-exponential. However, there does not seem to be much software support for these approaches. Most of the software packages support performability analysis via MRM approach.

For analyzing non-Markovian models, there are three different approaches:

– *Discrete-event simulation* of the non-Markovian model. The reader can easily obtain the vast literature on this subject.
– *Phase-type expansion* of the non-exponential distributions. There have been several efforts to analyze non-Markovian reliability models using phase type expansion [97]. For other references, see [52, 66, 101]. For performability analysis of non-Markovian models, there have been a few efforts in the past. Bobbio [10] has proposed how SPNs with generally distributed firing times can be used to generate stochastic reward models for performability analysis. He notes that the algorithms proposed in [27, 70] to solve the class of SPNs with PH distributed transition firing times can be used to solve completion time distribution problem when work requirement is a PH random variable [12]. Cumani [27] has implemented ESP package that allows analysis of timed Petri nets with PH distributed firing times using phase-type expansions. Distribution of completion time can be obtained. Further numerical examples of computing performability measures using ESP are in [83]. We have implemented a front-end package to SHARPE called GSHARPE [66], which permits analysis of a class of non-Markovian reward models (where after a change of state in the reliability model, the system cannot keep track of the past and any task being executed on the system must be restarted – the preemptive repeat different policy). The non-Markovian (reward) model is converted to a Markov (reward) model using phase approximations which is then solved by SHARPE. All the other features of SHARPE

are supported and performability analysis as supported by SHARPE can be carried out.

– *Analytic numeric solution* of the non-Markovian model. Recently there have been significant new developments in this area. Ajmone Marsan and Chiola [1] analyzed stochastic Petri nets with deterministic and exponentially distributed firing times which have come to be known as DSPNs (deterministic and stochastic Petri nets). Lindemann [62] has designed a software package called DSPNexpress that allows steady-state analysis of DSPNs under certain restrictive conditions. Choi et al [19] have proposed a more general class of timed Petri nets known as Markov regenerative stochastic Petri nets (MR-SPNs). These are analyzed by Markov regenerative processes under certain restrictive conditions. Both the transient and steady-state solutions can be obtained numerically. Although none of these studies discuss reward based measures, reward rates may be associated with markings of the net and reward-based performability measures can be computed. Presently, there is no software package that supports performability or reliability analysis using these classes of timed Petri nets.

References

1. M. Ajmone-Marsan and G. Chiola. On Petri nets with deterministic and exponentially distributed firing times. In *Lecture Notes in Computer Science*, volume 266, pages 132–145. Springer-Verlag, 1987.
2. M. Ajmone-Marsan, G. Conte, and G. Balbo. A class of Generalized Stochastic Petri Nets for the performance evaluation of multiprocessor systems. *ACM Transactions on Computer Systems*, 2(2):93–122, 1984.
3. T. Altiok. Queuing modeling of a single processor with failures. *Performance Evaluation*, 9:93–102, 1989.
4. H. Ammar, S.M.R. Islam, and S. Deng. Performability analysis of parallel and distributed algorithms. In *Proc. of 3rd Intl. Workshop on Petri Nets and Performance Models*, pages 221–227. IEEE Computer Society Press, Silver Spring, MD, June 1989.
5. F. Baccelli and K.S. Trivedi. Analysis of an M/G/2 standby redundant system. In A. Agrawala and S.K. Tripathi, editors, *PERFORMANCE '83*, pages 457–476. North-Holland, 1983.
6. F. Baskett, K.M. Chandy, R.R. Muntz, and F.G. Palacios. Open, closed, and mixed networks of queues with different classes of customers. *Journal of the ACM*, 22(2):248–260, 1975.
7. M. Beaudry. Performance related reliability for computer systems. *IEEE Transactions on Computers*, C-27:540–547, June 1978.
8. H. Beilner, J. Maeter, and N. Weissenberg. Towards a performance modeling environment: News of HIT. In R. Puigjaner and D. Potier, editors, *Modeling Techniques and Tools for Computer Performance Evaluation*, pages 57–75. Plenum Press, 1989.
9. S. Berson, E. de Souza e Silva, and R.R. Muntz. A methodology for the specification and generation of markov models. In W.J. Stewart, editor, *Numerical Solution of Markov Chains*, pages 11–36. Marcel Dekker, 1991.

10. A. Bobbio. Petri nets generating Markov reward models for performance/reliability analysis of degradable systems. In R. Puigjaner and D. Potier, editors, *Modeling Techniques and Tools for Computer Performance Evaluation*. Plenum Press, 1989.

11. A. Bobbio and L. Roberti. Distribution of the minimal completion time of parallel tasks in multi-reward semi-markov models. *Performance Evaluation*, 14:239–256, 1992.

12. A. Bobbio and K. Trivedi. Computation of the distribution of the completion time when the work requirement is a PH random variable. *Stochastic Models*, 6:133–149, 1990.

13. A. Bobbio and K. Trivedi. Computing cumulative measures of stiff Markov chains using aggregation. *IEEE Transactions on Computers*, 39(10):1291–1297, October 1990.

14. A. Bobbio and K.S. Trivedi. An aggregation technique for the transient analysis of stiff Markov chains. *IEEE Transactions on Computers*, C-35(9):803–814, Sept 1986.

15. J.A. Carrasco and J. Figueras. METFAC: Design and implementation of a software tool for modeling and evaluation of complex fault-tolerant computing systems. In *Proc. of IEEE 16th Fault-Tolerant Computing Symposium*, pages 424–429, July 1986.

16. X. Castillo and D. P. Siewiorek. A performance reliability model for computing systems. In *Proceedings of the 10th International Symposium on Fault-Tolerant Computing*, pages 187–192, June 1980.

17. R. Chakka and I. Mitrani. A numerical solution method for multiprocessor systems with general breakdowns and repairs. In R. Pooley and J. Hillston, editors, *Computer Performance Evaluation*, pages 289–299. September 1992.

18. P. Chimento. *System performance in a failure-prone environment*. PhD thesis, Department of Computer Science, Duke University, Durham, NC, 1988.

19. H. Choi, V. G. Kulkarni, and K. S. Trivedi. Markov Regenerative Stochastic Petri Nets. In *16th IFIP W.G. 7.3 Int'l Sym. on Computer Performance Modelling, Measurement and Evaluation (Performance'93)*, Rome, Italy, Sep. 1993, To appear.

20. H. Choi and K. S. Trivedi. Approximate performance models of polling systems using stochastic Petri nets. In *Proc. of IEEE Infocom 92*, pages 2306–2314, Florence Italy, May 1992.

21. G. Ciardo, A. Blakemore, P. F. Chimento, J. K. Muppala, and K. S. Trivedi. Automated generation and analysis of Markov reward models using Stochastic Reward Nets. In C. Meyer and R. J. Plemmons, editors, *Linear Algebra, Markov Chains, and Queueing Models, IMA Volumes in Mathematics and its Applications*, volume 48. Springer-Verlag, Heidelberg, Germany, 1992.

22. G. Ciardo, R. Marie, B. Sericola, and K. S. Trivedi. Performability analysis using semi-Markov reward processes. *IEEE Transactions on Computers*, C-39(10):1251–1264, Oct. 1990.

23. G. Ciardo, J.K. Muppala, and K.S. Trivedi. SPNP: Stochastic Petri Net Package. In *Proc. Intl. Workshop on Petri Nets and Performance Models*, pages 142–150. IEEE Computer Society Press, Kyoto, Japan, Dec. 1989.

24. G. Ciardo and K.S. Trivedi. A decomposition approach for stochastic reward net models. *To appear in Performance Evaluation.*

25. B. Ciciani and V. Grassi. Performability evaluation of fault-tolerant satellite systems. *IEEE Transactions on Communications*, 35(4):403–409, 1987.

26. J.A. Couvillion, R. Freire, R. Johnson, W.D.Obal II, M.A. Qureshi, M. Rai, W.H. Sanders, and J.E. Trivedi. Performability modeling with UltraSAN. *IEEE software*, 8:69–80, Sept. 1991.

27. A. Cumani. ESP – A package for the evaluation of stochastic Petri nets with phase-type distributed transition times. In *Proc. of International Workshop on Timed Petri Nets*, pages 144–151, Torino, Italy, July 1985.

28. E. de Souza e Silva and H. R. Gail. Calculating cumulative operational time distributions of repairable computer systems. *IEEE Transactions on Computers*, C-35(4):322–332, Apr. 1986.

29. E. de Souza e Silva and H. R. Gail. Calculating availability and performability measures of repairable computer systems using randomization. *J. ACM.*, 36(1):171–193, Jan. 1989.

30. E. de Souza e Silva and H. R. Gail. Performability analysis of computer systems: from model specification to solution. *Performance Evaluation*, 14:157–196, 1992.

31. H. DeMeer. Transiente leistungsbewertung und optimierung rekonfiguierbarer fehlertoleranter rechensysteme. *Arbeitsberichte des IMMDder Universität Erlangen-Nüremberg*, 25(10), October 1992.

32. N.M. Van Dijk. Simple bounds for queueing systems with breakdowns. *Performance Evaluation*, 8(2):117–128, 1988.

33. L. Donatiello and V. Grassi. On evaluating the cumulative performance distribution of fault-tolerant computer systems. *IEEE Transactions on Computers*, 40(11):1301–1307, 1991.

34. L. Donatiello and B. R. Iyer. Analysis of a composite performance reliability measure for fault-tolerant systems. *Journal for the Association of Computing Machinery*, 34(1):179–199, January 1987.

35. B.T. Doshi. Queuing systems with vacations. *Queuing Systems*, 1:29–66, 1986.

36. B.T. Doshi. Generalizations of the stochastic decomposition results for single server queues with vacations. *Stochastic Models*, 6(2):307–333, 1990.

37. A. Duda. The effects of checkpointing on program execution time. *Information Processing Letters*, 16:221–229, 1983.

38. D. G. Furchtgott and J. F. Meyer. A performability solution method for degradable nonrepairable systems. *IEEE Transactions on Computers*, C-33(6):550–554, June 1984.

39. D.P. Gaver. A waiting line with interrupted service, including priorities. *J. R. Statist. Soc.*, B24:73–90, 1962.

40. R. Geist, M. K. Smotherman, K. S. Trivedi, and J. B. Dugan. The reliability of life-critical systems. *Acta Informatica*, 23:621–642, 1986.

41. R. Geist and K.S. Trivedi. Reliability estimation of fault-tolerant systems : Tools and techniques. *IEEE Computer*, 23:52–61, July 1990.

42. E. Gelenbe, D. Finkel, and S.K. Tripathi. Availability of a distributed computer system with failures. *Acta Informatica*, 23:643–655, 1986.

43. A. Goyal, W.C. Carter, E. de Souza e Silva, S.S, Lavenberg, and K.S. Trivedi. The system availability estimator. In *Proc. of IEEE 16th Fault-Tolerant Computing Symposium*, pages 84–89, July 1986.

44. A. Goyal and A. N. Tantawi. Evaluation of performability for degradable computer systems. *IEEE Transactions on Computers*, 36(6):738–744, June 1987.

45. A. Goyal and A.N. Tantawi. A measure of guaranteed availability and its numerical evaluation. *IEEE Transactions on Computers*, 37(1):25–32, 1988.

46. V. Grassi, L. Donatiello, and G. Iazeolla. Performability evaluation of multicomponent fault-tolerant systems. *IEEE Transactions on Reliability*, 37(2):216–222, 1988.

47. B.R. Haverkort. *Performability Modeling Tools, Evaluation Techniques, and Applications*. PhD thesis, University of Twente, Netherlands, 1990.

48. B.R. Haverkort and I.G. Niemegeers. A survey of performability modeling tools. *Q-Passport*, 7:1–12, October 1989.

49. B.R. Haverkort, I.G. Niemegeers, and P.V. van Zanten. DyQNtool – a performability modeling tool based on the dynamic queuing queueing network concept. In G. Balbo and G. Serrazi, editors, *Computer Performance Evaluation, Modelling Techniques and Tools*, pages 181–195. Elsevier, 1992.

50. B.R. Haverkort and K.S. Trivedi. Specification and generation of markov reward models. To appear.

51. R. A. Howard. *Dynamic Probabilistic Systems, Vol.II: Semi-Markov and Decision Processes*. John Wiley & Sons, New York, 1971.

52. M. C. Hsueh, R. K. Iyer, and K. S. Trivedi. Performability modeling based on real data: A case study. *IEEE Transactions on Computers*, C-37(4):478–484, April 1988.

53. O. C. Ibe, R. C. Howe, and K. S. Trivedi. Approximate availability analysis of VAXcluster systems. *IEEE Transactions on Reliability*, R-38(1):146–152, Apr. 1989.

54. B. R. Iyer, L. Donatiello, and P. Heidelberger. Analysis of performability for stochastic models of fault-tolerant systems. *IEEE Transactions on Computers*, C-35(10):902–907, October 1986.

55. A.M. Johnson and M. Malek. Survey of software tools for evaluating reliability, availability and serviceability. *ACM Computing Surveys*, 20(4):227–260, December 1988.

56. H. Kantz and K.S. Trivedi. Reliability modeling of MARS system : A case study in the use of different tools and techniques. In *International Workshop on Petri Nets and Performance Models*, Melbourne, Australia, 1991.

57. P.J.B. King and I. Mitrani. Multiserver systems subject to breakdowns: An empirical study. *IEEE Transactions on Computers*, C-32(10):96–98, 1983.

58. V. Kulkarni, V.F. Nicola, R.M. Smith, and K.S. Trivedi. Numerical evaluation of performability measures and job completion time in repairable fault-tolerant systems. In *Proc. 16th Intl. Symp. on Fault Tolerant Computing*, Vienna, Austria, July 1986. IEEE.

59. V. G. Kulkarni, V. F. Nicola, and K. S. Trivedi. The completion time of a job on multimode systems. *Advances in Applied Probability*, 19:932–954, 1987.

60. V. G. Kulkarni, V. F. Nicola, and K. S. Trivedi. Effects of checkpointing and queueing on program performance. *Stochastic Models*, 6(4):615–648, 1990.

61. R. Lepold. Penpet: A new approach to performability modeling using stochastic petri nets. In B.R. Haverkort, I.G. Niemegeers, and N.M. van Dijk, editors, *Proc. of the First Intl. Workshop on Performability Modelling of Computer and Communication Systems*, pages 3–17. 1992.

62. C. Lindemann, M. Malhotra, and K.S. Trivedi. Numerical methods for reliability evaluation of closed fault-tolerant systems. Technical Report DUKE-CCSR-92-017, Center for Computer Systems Research, Duke University, 1992.

63. N. Lopez-Benitez and K.S. Trivedi. Multiprocessor performability analysis. *IEEE Transactions on Reliability*, Dec. 1993. To appear.

64. M. Malhotra. A computationally efficient technique for transient analysis of repairable Markovian systems. To appear in *Performance Evlauation* subject to revision, 1993.

65. M. Malhotra, J. K. Muppala, and K. S. Trivedi. Stiffness-tolerant methods for transient analysis of stiff Markov chains. Technical Report DUKE-CCSR-92-003, Center for Computer Systems Research, Duke University, 1992.

66. M. Malhotra and A.L. Reibman. Selecting and implementing phase approximations for semi-Markov models. To appear in *Stochastic Models*, 1993.

67. M. Malhotra and K. S. Trivedi. Reliability analysis of redundant arrays of inexpensive disks. *Journal of Parallel and Distributed Computing*, 17:146–151, Jan. 1993.

68. M. Malhotra, K. S. Trivedi, C. Y. Wang, and M. Veeraraghavan. Reliability modeling with computer-based tools. In H.T. Nagle and R. Schneider, editors, *Quality and Reliability in Computer-Based Medical Products*. TAB/IEEE Press, 1993. To appear.

69. M. Malhotra and K.S. Trivedi. Higher-order methods for transient analysis of stiff Markov chains. In *Third international conference on Performance of Distributed Systems and Integrated Communication Networks*, Kyoto, Japan, 1991.

70. M. Ajmone Marsan, G. Balbo, A. Bobbio, G. Conte, and A. Cumani. On Petri nets with stochastic timing. In *Proceedings of the International Workshop on Timed Petri Nets*, pages 80–87, Torino Italy, July 1985.

71. J. Meyer. On evaluating the performability of degradable computer systems. *IEEE Transactions on Computers*, C-29:720–731, Aug 1980.

72. J. F. Meyer. Closed-form solutions of performability. *IEEE Transactions on Computers*, C-31(7):648–657, July 1982.

73. J.F. Meyer. Performability: a retrospective and some pointers to the future. *Performance Evaluation*, 14:139–156, 1992.

74. J.F. Meyer, A. Movaghar, and W.H. Sanders. Stochastic activity networks: Structure, behavior, and application. In *International Workshop on Petri Nets and Performance Models*, pages 106–115, Torino, Italy, July 1985.

75. I. Mitrani and B. Avi-Itzhak. A many-server queue with service interruptions. *Operations Research*, 16(3):628–638, 1968.

76. M. Mulazzani and K. S. Trivedi. Dependability prediction : Comparison of tools and techniques. In *IFAC SAFECOMP Proc.*, Toulose, France, 1986.

77. B. Müller-Clostermann. NUMAS, a tool for numerical analysis of computer systems. In D. Potier, editor, *Modeling Techniques and Tools for Performance Analysis*, pages 141–154. North-Holland, Amsterdam, 1985.

78. B. Müller-Clostermann. An approximate product form for a class of degradable queuing networks. *Performance Evaluation*, pages 165–171, 1988.

79. F. Munkert and H. de Meer. XPenelope user guide. Technical report, June 1993.

80. J.K. Muppala, A.S. Sathaye, R.C. Howe, and K.S. Trivedi. Dependability modeling of a heterogenous VAXcluster system using stochastic reward nets. In D. Averesky, editor, *Hardware and Software Fault Tolerance in Parallel Computing Systems*. Ellis Horwood Ltd., 1992.

81. J.K. Muppala and K.S. Trivedi. Numerical transient analysis of finite markovian queueing systems. In U.N. Bhat and I.V. Basawa, editors, *Queueing and Related Models*, pages 262–284. Oxford University Press, 1992.

82. M.F. Neuts and D.M. Lucantoni. A Markovian queue with N servers subject to breakdowns and repairs. *Management Science*, 25(9):849–861, 1979.

83. V. F. Nicola, A. Bobbio, and K. S. Trivedi. A unified performance reliability analysis of a system with a cumulative down time constraint. *Microelectronics and Reliability*, 32:49–65, 1992.

84. V. F. Nicola, V. G. Kulkarni, and K. S. Trivedi. Queueing analysis of fault-tolerant computer systems. *IEEE Transactions on Software Engineering*, 13(3):363–375, March 1987.

85. K.R. Pattipati, Y. Li, and H.A.P. Blom. A unified framework for the performability evaluation of fault-tolerant computer systems. *IEEE Transactions on Computers*, 42(3):312–325, 1993.

86. K.R. Pattipati and S.A. Shah. On the computational aspects of performability models of fault-tolerant computer systems. *IEEE Transactions on Computers*, 39(7):832–836, July 1990.

87. A.V. Ramesh and K.S. Trivedi. Semi-numerical transient analysis of markov models. Submitted for publication, 1993.

88. A. Reibman and K.S. Trivedi. Numerical transient analysis of Markov models. *Computers and Operations Research*, 15(1):19–36, 1988.

89. A. Reibman, K.S. Trivedi, and R. Smith. Markov and Markov reward model transient analysis : An overview of numerical approaches. *European Journal of Operations Research*, 40(2):257–267, 1989.

90. G. Rubino and B. Sericola. Interval availability analysis using operational periods. *Performance Evaluation*, 14:257–272, 1992.

91. R.A. Sahner and K.S. Trivedi. Performance and reliability analysis using directed acyclic graphs. *IEEE Transactions on Software Engineering*, 14(10):1105–1114, Oct. 1987.

92. R.A. Sahner and K.S. Trivedi. Reliability modeling using SHARPE. *IEEE Transactions on Reliability*, R-36(2):186–193, June 1987.

93. R.A. Sahner and K.S. Trivedi. A software tool for learning about stochastic models. *IEEE Transactions on Education*, 36(1):56–61, Feb. 1993.

94. W.H. Sanders and J.F. Meyer. METASAN: A performability evaluation tool based on stochastic activity networks. In *Proc. ACM-IEEE Computer Soc. Fall Joint Computer Conf.*, pages 807–816, Los Alamitos, Calif., July 1986.

95. W.H. Sanders and J.F. Meyer. Reduced base model construction methods for stochastic activity networks. *IEEE Selected Areas of Communications*, pages 25–36, Jan. 1991.

96. O. Schoen. On a class of integrated performance/reliability models based on queuing networks. In *Proc. FTCS 16*, pages 90–95, 1986.

97. C. Singh, R. Billinton, and S. Lee. The method of stages for non-Markovian models. *IEEE Transactions on Reliability*, R-26(1):135–137, June 1977.

98. R.M. Smith, K.S. Trivedi, and A.V. Ramesh. Performability analysis: measures, an algorithm, and a case study. *IEEE Transactions on Computers*, 37(4):406–417, April 1988.

99. H. Szczerbicka. A combined queuing network and stochastic Petri net approach for evaluating the performability of fault-tolerant computer systems. *Performance Evaluation*, 14:217–226, 1992.

100. J. Sztrik and T. Gál. A recursive solution of a queuing model for a multi-terminal system subject to breakdowns. *Performance Evaluation*, 11:1–7, 1990.

101. K.S. Trivedi. *Probability and Statistics with Reliability, Queuing, and Computer Science Applications*. Prentice-Hall, Englewood-Cliffs, NJ, 1982.

102. K.S. Trivedi, J.K. Muppala, S.P. Woolet, and B.R. Haverkort. Composite performance and dependability analysis. *Performance Evaluation*, 14:197–215, 1992.

103. M. Veeraraghavan and K.S. Trivedi. Composite performance and reliability analysis using combinatorial multistate models. To appear in *IEEE Transactions on Computers*.

104. M. Veeraraghavan and K.S. Trivedi. An improved algorithm for symbolic reliability analysis. *IEEE Transactions on Reliability*, R-40(3):347–358, August 1991.

105. H.C. White and L.S. Christie. Queuing with preemptive priorities or breakdown. *Operations Research*, 6:79–95, 1958.

Leistungsmodellierung und quantitative Analyse der Einflüsse neuer Mainframe-Architekturen auf Betriebssysteme

Autor: Dr. A. Zeyn SNI BS2000

Kurzfassung*

In diesem Beitrag wird unter einer Mainframe-Instanz ein System verstanden, das in einem Netzverbund die Rolle eines zentralen Datenservers, eines Administrationszentrums und/oder eines Hochleistungs-OLTP-Servers spielt. Daraus ergeben sich Anforderungen an die heutige und zukünftige Leistungsfähigkeit von Mainframe-Systemen. Die Weiterentwicklung dieser Systeme unterliegt jedoch noch weit gravierenderen Einflüssen.

Zum einen erzwingen die enormen Leistungszunahmen der CMOS-Technolgie und der von der Open Systems-Welt ausgehende Druck auf die Systempreise eine Abkehr von der klassischen Mainframe-Architektur, des Tightly Coupled Multiprocessor, häufig realisiert in teurer ECL-Technologie. Zum anderen zeigt der permanente Leistungsmehrbedarf im Top Range der Mainframe-Systeme bereits jetzt das Ende der Leistungsfähigkeit der heutigen Mainframe-Architekturen auf, so daß auch hier Neukonzeptionen zwingend sind. Die neuen Wege, die zur Lösung beschritten werden,

- gehen von Tightly Coupled Multiprocessors (TCMP) aus, bei denen jedoch einige Grundprinzipien abgeschwächt werden, um zu höheren MP-Graden zu kommen,

- führen über Hybride TCMPs, die Standard- und RISC-Architekturen vereinen bei wahlweise skalierbarer Leistung

- zu eng vernetzten Rechnerverbänden mit Single System Image.

Um eine bestmögliche Unterstützung dieser neuen Mainframe-Architekturen durch die Betriebssysteme zu erreichen, kommt jetzt die Modellierung ins Spiel, mit deren Hilfe, geeignete Mechanismen evaluiert und ausgewählt werden, um sie dann auf Basis von Lasttraces einer quantitativen Analyse im Hinblick auf das Mainframe-Rollenverhalten zu unterwerfen. Es wird aufgelistet, welche Mechanismen zum Beispiel bereits mit welchen Ergebnissen zur Realisierung für das SNI-Betriebssystem BS2000 ausgewählt wurden. Ein Schwerpunkt liegt dabei auch auf der Einführung HW-adaptiver Basismechanismen, die in besonderem Maße spezifische Architektur-Konzeptionen der HW zur Kenntnis nehmen und die Ablaufsteuerung entsprechend ausrichten. Erläutert wird diese Vorgehensweise beispielhaft am Affinitäts-Dispatching der Ablauftasks. Den Abschluß bildet eine kurze Darstellung, wie Leistungsmodellierung und quantitative Analyse unverzichtbar in den Entwicklungsprozeß der SNI Mainframe-Betriebssystems BS2000 eingebunden sind.

---

*Der vollständige Beitrag lag bei Drucklegung noch nicht vor.

Performance Evaluation of Parallel Programs — Modeling and Monitoring with the Tool PEPP

Franz Hartleb, Andreas Quick
Universität Erlangen–Nürnberg, IMMD VII
Martensstr. 3, D–91058 Erlangen
email:quick@informatik.uni-erlangen.de   Tel.: 09131/858339

Abstract

There are many possibilities how to parallelize an algorithm and how to map a program onto a parallel or distributed system. Performance models help to predict which implementation and which mapping are the best for a given algorithm and for a given computer configuration. Stochastic graph modeling is an appropriate method, since the execution order of tasks, their runtime distribution, and branching probabilities are represented. In this paper the modeling capabilities and the analysis techniques implemented in our tool PEPP are presented.

In order to obtain relevant modeling results, measured and not only estimated model parameters are needed. They can be obtained through monitoring existing programs. A method to carry out monitoring efficiently is model-driven monitoring: model tasks are mapped onto their corresponding program activities which allows systematic and automatic program instrumentation. Model parameters can easily be calculated since the set of events is the same in modeling and monitoring. A model without timing information can be enhanced to a performance model with realistic parameters.

1. Introduction

In order to minimize the time for solving big problems, given problems are divided into subproblems which are then solved in parallel with $p > 1$ processors. During the search for optimal parallel solutions the execution times of different algorithms and implementation strategies have to be evaluated. Since the implementation of different versions is too costly — or even impossible if the desired hardware is not available —, predicting the runtime with a model is an appropriate method.

As the runtime of a user program normally depends on the input values and on the mostly unknown duration of library and system functions, it is not easy to predict, even on a monoprocessor system. In parallel systems where processes communicate with each other and share resources, there are additional factors that have an influence on the runtime, e.g. race conditions, mutual waiting of processes, or access conflicts on interconnection networks.

Graph models have been used extensively in order to model and to analyze the behavior of parallel programs [17, 21]. Experiences showed that realistic models often consist of hundreds of nodes. If large models are not series-parallelly structured, exact evaluation methods fail because of excessive computation times. Two ways how to overcome this problem are approximate methods and methods to obtain lower and upper bounds of the mean runtime.

Performance prediction yields more relevant and accurate results if not only estimated values but measured values are used. Runtime distributions and branching probabilities can be obtained by monitoring an already existing program. Additionally, the analysis based on numerical functions instead of parametric functions has two essential advantages. First it is much more efficient, and second modeling the tasks' runtime is not restricted to a particular type of distribution functions such as exponential or phase type. Therefore event-driven monitoring is necessary to support modeling!

In order to calculate the model parameters efficiently, we developed a new method, called model-driven monitoring. The model determines the places at which the program to be monitored should be instrumented. This kind of instrumentation guarantees identical sets of events in modeling and monitoring and is the basis for model-driven monitoring. The model is used for automatic program instrumentation, debugging, monitor configuration und event trace analysis. This method determines the right events for monitoring and provides results immediately after the measurement is finished.

For model creation, model evaluation, and model-driven monitoring the tool PEPP (*Performance Evaluation of Parallel Programs*) [2] was developed. In section 2 we define the stochastic graph model, the node types, and the runtime distributions used in PEPP. The analysis techniques developed and implemented in PEPP (series-parallel reduction applied to the numerical representation of the tasks's runtime, a new approximation method, and powerful bounding methods for the mean runtime) are described in section 3. The accuracy of the new evaluation techniques is shown in section 4. In section 5, the use of PEPP for model-driven monitoring is described.

2. Stochastic Graph Models

A parallel program is modeled by an acyclic, directed, stochastic graph $G = (V, E, \underline{T})$ which consists of a set of nodes V, a set of directed edges $E \subset V \times V$ (arcs), and a vector of random variables $\underline{T}$. Each task t_i of the parallel program is modeled by one node v_i and the corresponding random variable T_i which describes the runtime behavior of task t_i. The tasks' runtimes are assumed to be independent random variables. The dependency between tasks is modeled by arcs. An arc from node v_i to node v_j means that task t_j can start execution only if the execution of task t_i is finished. In the following section, we also use the set of predecessor nodes $p(v_i)$ and the set of successor nodes $s(v_i)$ of node v_i. If $p(v_i) = \emptyset$, then v_i is called a start node. v_i is called an end node, if $s(v_i) = \emptyset$. The level $l(v_i)$ of node v_i is defined as the longest path from a start node to node v_i:

$$l(v_i) = \begin{cases} 0 & \text{if } p(v_i) = \emptyset \\ \max_{v_j \in p(v_i)} l(v_j) + 1 & \text{else} \end{cases} \tag{1}$$

2.1. Node Types in PEPP

Obviously, there is a gap between programs which are not acyclic since they contain loops and acyclic graph models. In order to bridge over this gap and to make modeling and model evaluation more efficient in PEPP, we define four node types:

- An *elementary node* represents one task t_i of the parallel program with service time distribution $F_i(t)$.
- The execution of n identical tasks on n processors in parallel is modeled by a *parallel node*. All the n tasks are assumed to have the same runtime distribution $F_i(t)$.
- Iterations and loops are modeled by *cyclic nodes* or *hierarchical loop nodes*.
  A cyclic node is characterized by the runtime distribution of the body of the iteration or loop and the probabilities p_k which are the probabilities that the body is executed again after the k-th iteration. The body of a hierarchical loop node may be described by any PEPP graph. Both node types allow us to model cycles and iterations and the graph remains acyclic.
- A *hierarchical node* contains an arbitrary graph model consisting of elementary, parallel, cyclic, and hierarchical nodes. Any graph model can be included in a higher order graph by this node type.

2.2. Runtime Distributions

For the tasks' runtime distribution $F(t)$ many parametric distributions and numerical distributions can be used in PEPP. The runtime distribution may be

- deterministic $F(t) = \begin{cases} 0 & \text{if } t < d \\ 1 & \text{else} \end{cases}$

- exponential $F(t) = 1 - e^{-\lambda t}$

- Branching Erlang $F(t) = 1 - \sum_{n=1}^{N} p_n e^{-\lambda_n t} \sum_{j=0}^{k_n-1} \frac{(\lambda_n t)^j}{j!}$

- one deterministic and one exponential phase $F(t) = \begin{cases} 1 - e^{-\lambda(t-d)} & \text{if } t \geq d \\ 0 & \text{else} \end{cases}$

- numerically given

The deterministic, the exponential, and the Branching Erlang distribution are well known and often used in performance models. In many cases the approximation of the real runtime behavior with deterministic or exponential distributions is not appropriate and the approximation with Branching Erlang distributions often leads to a very high number of phases which makes the model intractable. In order to avoid the problems of inappropriateness and intractability we developed two approaches for describing measured runtime distributions.

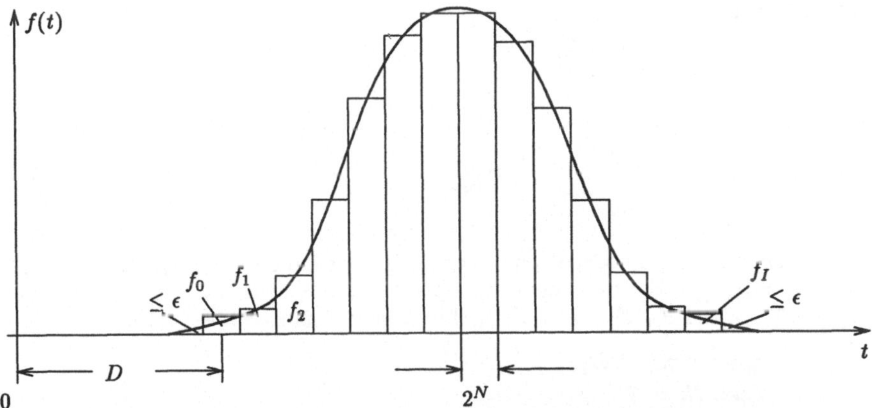

Figure 1: Continuous density function and the corresponding numerical function

Approximating the runtime with one deterministically and one exponentially distributed phase (de-approximation) allows us to adapt the first and the second moment of the runtime and we get only two phases for one node.

In the second approach we describe any parametric or measured distribution function by its numerical representation (fig. 1). A numerical density function f of an arbitrary density function $f(t)$ is defined as a tupel $f = (D, N, f_0, f_1, \ldots, f_I)$ [11] with displacement D, order N, and

$$f_0 = \int_0^{D+2^{N-1}} f(t)\,dt; \qquad f_i = \int_{D+(2i-1)2^{N-1}}^{D+(2i+1)2^{N-1}} f(t)\,dt; \qquad f_I = \int_{D+(2I-1)2^{N-1}}^{\infty} f(t)\,dt \qquad (2)$$

The width of the discrete steps is defined by the order N. To make the order of different densities adaptable, we always choose $D \bmod 2^N = 0$. This is important for model analysis. The numerical density is called ϵ–exact, if

$$\int_0^{D-2^{N-1}} f(t)\,dt \leq \epsilon \qquad \wedge \qquad \int_{D+(2I+1)2^{N-1}}^{\infty} f(t)\,dt \leq \epsilon \qquad (3)$$

This definition keeps the number of intervals small by neglecting the left and right tail of the density function. In our implementation in PEPP ϵ is 10^{-6}.

3. Model Analysis

3.1. Series-parallel Reduction

The analysis method depends heavily on the structure of a given graph. In order to classify the models in *series-parallel* and *non-series-parallel* graphs we define two reduction operators:

- *serial reduction*: This operator can be applied on two nodes v_i and v_j, if $s(v_i) = \{v_j\}$ and $p(v_j) = \{v_i\}$. By the serial reduction operator the two nodes v_i and v_j are replaced in the graph model by one node v_{sr} with $p(v_{sr}) = p(v_i)$, $s(v_{sr}) = s(v_j)$, and

$$
F_{sr}(t) = \int_0^t F_i(\tau) f_j(t - \tau) d\tau \qquad \text{(convolution)} \tag{4}
$$

  If the tasks' runtime distributions are given by numerical descriptions f_i and f_j, f_{sr} is obtained from

$$
\begin{aligned}
D_{sr} &= D_i + D_j \\
N_{sr} &= N_i = N_j \\
I_{sr} &= I_i + I_j \qquad\qquad \text{(num. convolution)} \\
f_k^{sr} &= \sum_{l=\max(0,k-I_i)}^{\min(I_i,k)} f_l^i f_{k-l}^j
\end{aligned} \tag{5}
$$

- *parallel reduction*: Two nodes v_i and v_j can be reduced to one node v_{pr}, if $p(v_i) = p(v_j)$ and $s(v_i) = s(v_j)$. The two nodes are replaced by one node v_{pr} with $p(v_{pr}) = p(v_i)$, $s(v_{pr}) = s(v_i)$, and $F_{pr}(t) = F_i(t)F_j(t)$. In the numerical case, the product is built by

$$
\begin{aligned}
D_{pr} &= \max(D_i, D_j) \\
N_{pr} &= N_i = N_j \\
I_{pr} &= \max(I_i - d_i, I_j - d_j) \quad \text{with } d_i = \frac{D_j - D_i}{2^{N_i}}; d_j = \frac{D_i - D_j}{2^{N_j}}; \\
f_k^{pr} &= f_{k+d_i}^i \left(\frac{1}{2} f_{k+d_j}^j + \sum_{l=0}^{k-1+d_j} f_l^j \right) + f_{k+d_j}^j \left(\frac{1}{2} f_{k+d_i}^i + \sum_{l=0}^{k-1+d_i} f_l^i \right)
\end{aligned} \tag{6}
$$

A graph G is called a series-parallel graph if G can be reduced to one node by the operators serial reduction and parallel reduction. All other graphs are called non-series-parallel graphs. Obviously, if we have a series-parallel graph, we are able to obtain the runtime distribution of the modeled parallel program by reducing the graph to one node v_{sp}. The random variable T_{sp} corresponding to v_{sp} describes the runtime behavior, and the mean runtime as well as higher moments can be obtained. This technique was used in [16, 18, 17] and [7] to analyze series-parallel graphs where the tasks' runtime distributions are modeled by exponential polynomials. However, applying this method the number of parameters grows so fast that it can be used only for small graphs. We cope with this problem by transforming the parametric functions to numerical functions and applying the reduction operators to the numerical functions [11, 15]. This allows us to evaluate series-parallel graphs of nearly arbitrary size.

If a program can be modeled only by a non-series-parallel graph, PEPP offers two evaluation methods, an approximate state space analysis and bounding methods.

3.2. Approximate Transient State Space Analysis

The exact analysis of non-series-parallel graphs is very costly, even for small graphs. In [12] a method is introduced to compute the runtime distribution of non-series-parallel structured graphs in which the tasks' runtimes are described by polynomial functions. If the tasks' runtime distributions are given by General Erlang functions, we can use the well known transient state space method. As the number of states grows exponentially with the number of Erlang phases, this method is not applicable in general. An approximate method for analyzing regularly structured non-series-parallel graphs is described in [7].

We propose to reduce the number of states by approximating the runtime distribution of each task with one deterministically and one exponentially distributed phase. The parameters of the deterministically distributed phase d and of the exponentially distributed phase λ are obtained from the expected runtime E and the runtime variance V. In order to adapt the first and the second moment we get:

$$\lambda = \frac{1}{\sqrt{V}} \quad \text{and} \quad d = E - \sqrt{V} \quad \left(\text{if } E \geq \sqrt{V}\right) \tag{7}$$

If $\sqrt{V} > E$, we approximate the task's runtime with a two phase hyperexponential distribution. The mean runtime of a graph consisting of deterministically and exponentially distributed phases can be obtained with the approximate state space method [20]. The analysis is done in three steps:

1. The runtime distribution of each node is approximated, depending on the mean and the variance of the node, by one deterministically and one exponentially distributed phase or by a two-phase hyperexponential distribution.
2. Serial reduction by adding the expected runtime and the runtime variance of serially connected nodes.
3. The remaining non-series-parallel graph, consisting of deterministically and/or exponentially distributed phases is analyzed by an approximate state space method (for details see [8]).

This method is much faster than the exact transient state space analysis. However, analyzing large models, this method may also fail due to the number of states in the state space.

3.3. Bounds for the Mean Runtime

If all these methods fail because of computational costs, we apply methods for obtaining bounds of the expected runtime [9]. There are several published bounding methods. Devroye [5] uses only the first moment and the variance of the tasks' runtime in order to obtain bounds for the mean runtime of the whole program. Lower and upper bounds are also obtained by Yazici-Pekergin and Vincent [22] where the nodes' runtimes are assumed to be independent and identically distributed of type NBUE. The mean service time of the critical path is used as a lower bound. This does not yield good results for high parallelism because only the first moments of the runtime distributions and no parallelism are considered. The upper bound is obtained by replacing the tasks' runtime distribution functions by exponential distribution functions with the same first moment and building the product of the distributions of all paths from a start node to an end node. Again only the first moments are considered and therefore the bounds are poor in general.

Our efforts were oriented towards getting better lower and upper bounds for the mean runtime of parallel programs by using the whole information contained in the tasks' runtime distribution. The three methods implemented in PEPP are based on the same principle. To get an upper bound of the mean runtime we add nodes or arcs to a given non-series-parallel graph in order to make it series-parallel reducible. The mean runtime of the remaining graph is an upper bound. Removing nodes or arcs from the original graph leads to a lower bound of the mean runtime. If a given graph already has a series-parallel structure, the bounding methods always lead to exact results. A detailed description of the different methods and a comparison is given in [13].

Bounding the Mean Runtime through Adding/Removing Arcs

The first bounding method is based on the fact that modifying a graph by adding/removing arcs leads to a graph with a higher/lower mean completion time [11].

Our goal is to get the series-parallel reducibility by applying a number of such modifications on a given non-series-parallel graph. Obviously, the exclusive adding of arcs leads to an upper bound and by analogy the exclusive removing to a lower bound of the mean runtime.

Generally there are many possibilities to reach the series-parallel reducibility of a graph by adding or removing arcs. Consequently, there is more than one upper and lower bound. The main question now is, how can we obtain the tightest bounds, i.e. the smallest upper bound and the largest lower bound for the mean run time. To decide which bounds are the best for a given graph we have to compute all the bounds. Obviously, this method is too inefficient, therefore we solve the problem in a different way: we developed a heuristic algorithm for inserting/removing arcs which enables us to get very tight bounds for the mean runtime in an efficient way.

The algorithm for the upper bound will be briefly discussed: a number of arcs is added to our graph until it is series-parallel reducible. The quality of the bounds depends on the number of arcs added, i.e. the less the number of new arcs, the better the resulting upper bound. The algorithm for the upper bound mainly consists of two steps [13]:

1. Series-parallel reduction of the graph until no more reduction is possible.

2. Search for a pair of nodes which allows us a parallel reduction through adding new arcs. The following conditions must be fulfilled:

   - It is not allowed to add arcs between nodes on the same level.
   - The number of new added arcs which lead to the next series-parallel reduction must be minimal.
   - If this condition is satisfied by more than one pair of nodes we demand that the number of nodes of the resulting graph must be minimal.

These steps are repeated until we have one node left. The resulting mean value of this node's runtime distribution is our upper bound.

The algorithm for the computation of the lower bound is similar to the algorithm described above. Instead of adding arcs we remove arcs. Removing an arc may lead either to a serial reduction or to a parallel reduction. In most cases it is impossible to decide which modification is better. Therefore, we decided to provide two different algorithms for the lower bound. The first one makes only modifications that lead to a serial reduction and the second one only removes arcs which allow a parallel reduction. If there is more than one arc which leads to a serial reduction, we assign the sum of the mean runtime of the start node and the end node as a label to each arc and remove the arc with the smallest label. The maximum of the two different lower bounds is our result for the lower bound. This solution costs two times more computation time than the algorithm for the upper bound, but we obtain a very good lower bound.

The Method of Shogan

The following method was developed by A.W. Shogan for the evaluation of PERT networks. The main difference between PERT networks and stochastic graph models defined in section 2 is that the tasks are represented by arcs instead of nodes. It is not difficult to transform our model into a PERT network, but here we will explain how we can use this method directly for our graph models.

First, we will introduce an additional notation. Let f_1 and f_2 be two densities and F_1 and F_2 the corresponding distribution functions. Then, we define

$$f_1 \leq f_2 \quad :\leftrightarrow \quad (\forall t \geq 0)(F_1(t) \geq F_2(t)) \, .$$

The same inequality between the corresponding first moments follows from the above definition of the relation '$\leq$' [11]. Now, we will describe the method of Shogan. The proof of the correctness of this method is given in [19].

Let $G = (V, E, \underline{T})$ with $V = \{v_1, \ldots, v_n\}$ and $E \subset V \times V$ be a stochastic graph, F_{T_i} the distribution function of each node, and f_{T_i} the corresponding density. Then, we can recursively compute the lower bound $g^<$ and the upper bound $g^>$ for the whole distribution density g as follows [11, 19]:

$$g^< = \text{shogan}\left\{ g_j^< \mid s(v_j) = \emptyset \right\}$$

$$g_i^< = \begin{cases} f_i & \text{if } p(v_i) = \emptyset \\ \text{conv}\left(\text{shogan}\left\{ g_j^< \mid v_j \in p(v_i) \right\}, f_i\right) & \text{else} \end{cases} \tag{8}$$

$$g^> = \max\left\{ g_j^> \mid s(v_j) = \emptyset \right\}$$

$$g_i^> = \begin{cases} f_i & \text{if } p(v_i) = \emptyset \\ \text{conv}\left(\max\left\{ g_j^> \mid v_j \in p(v_i) \right\}, f_i\right) & \text{else} \end{cases} \tag{9}$$

where

$$\min(F, G)(t) = \begin{cases} F(t) & \text{if } F(t) < G(t) \\ G(t) & \text{else} \end{cases}$$

$$\text{shogan}(f, g)(t) = \frac{d}{dt} \min(F, G)(t)$$

$$\text{conv}(f, g)(t) = \int_0^t f(t - x)g(x)dx \tag{10}$$

$$\max(f, g)(t) = f(t)G(t) + F(t)g(t)$$

$$\max(f_1, f_2, \ldots f_n) = \max(f_1, \max(f_2, \ldots, \max(f_{n-1}, f_n)))$$

$$\text{shogan}(f_1, f_2, \ldots f_n) = \text{shogan}(f_1, \text{shogan}(f_2, \ldots, \text{shogan}(f_{n-1}, f_n)))$$

The first moments of the densities $g^>, g^<$ now build upper and lower bounds of the mean runtime.

Obviously, these bounds are easier to compute, i.e. with lower computational effort than with the first method. Unfortunately, Shogan's lower bound is not as good as the bound obtained by removing arcs. The upper bound of Shogan, however, deserves special consideration. It is noteworthy that in some cases Shogan's upper bound is better than the least upper bound obtained by adding arcs. According to our experience the upper bound obtained by adding arcs is better than Shogan's upper bound in most cases.

The Upper Bound of Dodin

This method was also developed for the evaluation of PERT networks [6]. The main idea behind this method is to modify the PERT network through duplicating some arcs until it is series-parallel reducible. Applying this method to stochastic graph models means that nodes are duplicated. The method is based on the fact that duplicating nodes always leads to an upper bound of the mean runtime.

At the first view this looks like the upper bound of Shogan, where the max operator can be considered as the duplication of nodes, too. However, there are two big differences between these methods. The first difference lies in the duplication process. Computing Shogan's upper bound, we observed that during the duplication of a node we duplicated all predecessor nodes, too. The duplication process of Dodin, however, doesn't have this disadvantage.

Another difference is the non-determinism of Dodin's method. There are many ways to bring a non-series-parallel graph into a reducible form. For a close look on the duplication process we need the definition of nodes which can be duplicated.

Definition: The node v can be duplicated by adding v', if either

    a. $|p(v)| \leq 1 \wedge |s(v)| \geq 2$ (case 1),   or   2. $|s(v)| \leq 1 \wedge |p(v)| \geq 2$ (case 2)

The duplication of a node v can be processed as follows:

    case 1: For the duplication of node v choose one of the successor nodes v_i of v, and add an arcs from the predecessor arc of node v to node v' and arc (v', v_i). Then, remove arc (v, v_i).

    case 2: Choose one predecessor v_i of v, and by analogy add the arc (v_i, v') add an arc from v' to the successor node of node v. Then, remove arc (v_i, v).

Finally a few words about our implementation of this method. We compute the upper bound of Dodin as follows: 1. Series-parallel reduction. 2. Identify and duplicate all nodes which can be duplicated and integrate the new nodes by adding two new arcs into the graph and removing one arc. Repeat both steps until only one node remains.

The Analysis of Hierarchical Graphs

Both, graph construction and graph analysis can be done hierarchically. Choosing a hierarchical evaluation method means that the subgraphs of level $i - 1$ are analyzed and the distribution functions or the mean runtimes are inserted into the graph of level i. Applying the approximate state space method each subgraph is replaced by one deterministically distributed phase and we obtain a lower bound for the mean runtime. With the series-parallel-reduction method each subgraph is replaced by a lower or an upper bound inserting the best bounds which are obtained by the different methods. Therefore, we use the advantages of the different methods to get the best bounds for the mean runtime.

4. Numerical Results

In this section we show the quality of the de-approximation and of the bounding methods dependent on the distribution functions of the task runtimes.

4.1. The Accuracy of the de-approximation

Many simulations with the Petri net tool GreatSPN [1] were done to compare the approximated runtimes with simulation results. The differences between both results lie between 0 and 5 % of the greater result in all investigated examples.

It is readily seen that the introduced method in section 3.2 is exact, if a model consists of only deterministically or only exponentially distributed task runtimes. The graph in fig. 2 shows a model of a parallel program for multigrid solutions of a partial differential equation on a shared memory multiprocessor [10]. These graphs are regularly structured and can be described by the height n and the width m. The data dependencies constrain that a task on level i must wait until its own

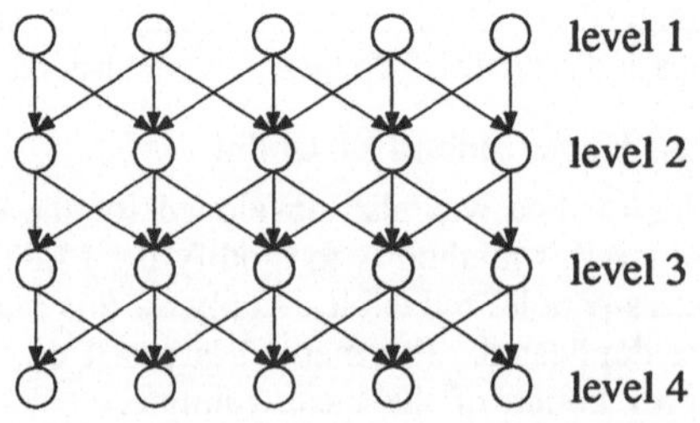

Figure 2: Model for a 4×5 neighbor synchronization

predecessor and the predecessor of its left and right neighbor have finished the computation on level $i-1$ (neighbor synchronization). We compare approximated results with exact values and simulation results for the model in fig. 2. As a workload we assume identically distributed runtimes for all tasks. The accuracy of the proposed approximation is tested by workload distributions of type Erlang. In order to be able to compare results, λ and k have been chosen in order to get the first moment constant and the variance different.

| task runtime | exact | | de-approxi- | simulation result |
(workload)	# states	value	mation	
$E_1(0.2)$	260	40.80	40.80	40.64 ± 0.25
$E_2(0.4)$	6052	34.72	34.70	34.35 ± 0.44
$E_5(1)$	too high com-		29.24	29.26 ± 0.39
$E_{10}(2)$	putation costs		26.47	26.67 ± 0.51

Table 1: Comparison of exact, approximated, and simulation results

The column with *de-approximation* contains the computed runtime for approximated models. The $E_k(\lambda)$ distributed task runtimes are approximated by one deterministically and one exponentially distributed phase. We get exact results only in the case, the task runtimes are modeled by $E_1(\lambda)$ or $E_2(\lambda)$ distributed random variables. In the case of $E_5(\lambda)$ and $E_{10}(\lambda)$ distributed task runtimes the computation costs of a markovian analysis are too high (number of states in the state space). We can compare the approximation results with simulation results to get information about the quality of the approximation method. The task runtimes in the simulation models are also approximated by one deterministically and one exponentially distributed phase. Table 1 shows that the approximated runtimes lie in the 0.99 confidence interval of the simulation results.

4.2. Comparing the Bounding Methods

Evaluating neighbor structures we observed that the quality of the computed bounds depends on the size of the given structure and the task runtime distributions. In order to demonstrate these dependencies we will first consider neighbor $(8 \times m)$-structures with $m \in \{4, 6, 8, 10, 12\}$. All task runtimes are identically $E_{10}(2)$ distributed, where $E_{10}(2)$ denotes the Erlang-10 distribution with rate $\lambda = 2$ s^{-1}.

The results are shown in fig. 3. The extensions .u and .l stand for upper bounds and lower bounds, respectively Klein is the abbreviation of Kleinöder. We observe that Shogan's lower bound is always less than the lower bound obtained by removing arcs. Unfortunately, for $m > 6$ the upper bound obtained by adding arcs is not as good as the other two upper bounds. Adding arcs to a neighbor-structured graph leads only to a series-parallel graph if each node is connected with every node of the previous and the next level. Accordingly, for the series-parallel reducibility of a neighbor-$(n \times m)$-structure it is necessary to add $(n-1)(m^2 - 3m + 2)$ new arcs.

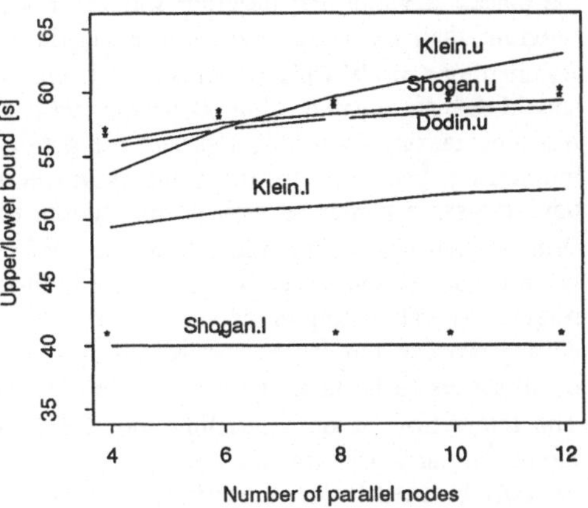

Figure 3: Bounds for the mean runtime

With Dodin's method, however, it is possible to reach the series-parallel reducibility through $(n - 1)(2m - 2)$ new nodes.

Hence follows that for $m > 4$ we have to add more arcs than nodes needed for the series-parallel reducibility. Nevertheless, we observe that for $n = 8$ and $m = 4$, Klein.u is less than Dodin.u, although for both methods 42 new arcs respectively nodes are necessary. The reason for this is that the duplication of one node leads, according to our experience, to a higher mean runtime of the whole graph than adding one single arc.

m	de-approximation			bounding methods								
				Klein				Shogan				Dodin
				lower		upper		lower		upper		upper
	result	#states	$T_c[s]$	result	$T_c[s]$	result	$T_c[s]$	result	$T_c[s]$	result	$T_c[s]$	result	$T_c[s]$
4	51.1	4252	15	49.4	2	53.6	1	40.0	1	56.2	1	54.8	1
5	52.4	62329	1430	49.2	3	55.6	1	40.0	1	57.0	2	55.8	1
6				50.6	3	57.2	2	40.0	1	57.6	2	56.3	2
8				51.1	5	59.7	6	40.0	2	58.3	3	57.2	2
10				52.0	9	61.5	10	40.0	2	58.9	3	57.8	3
12				52.3	14	63.0	18	40.0	2	59.3	4	58.2	3

Table 2: Comparison of the computation costs

Table 2 contains the computation costs T_c for obtaining results with the de-approximation and the different bounding methods. Exact results are not available for models of this dimension. We see that the de-approximation can be used only for $m < 6$ due to the state space explosion with increasing m. The best lower and upper bound is typed in bold style. Using the bounding methods, the computation costs are small and grow only polynomially with m.

5. Model-driven Monitoring with PEPP

Monitoring existing programs helps to calculate parameters which can be used as an input for models making them more realistic Both methods, modeling and event-driven monitoring, abstract the dynamic behavior of a program to a sequence of events. Since the aim of monitoring in this context is to calculate model parameters, eg. runtime distributions of program activities and branching probabilities, it is tempting to use the model for determining the places at which the program should be instrumented, i.e. to define which places in the program shall be recognized as an event during monitoring.

By creating a model (this model is called *monitoring model*) we also define where the program should be instrumented: all model events will be transformed to program events (model-driven instrumentation). With this approach we get exactly the same sets of events in modeling and monitoring. For automatically mapping model tasks onto program activities model tasks must have the same names as their corresponding parts in the program.

With model-driven instrumentation, the user is not overloaded with traced data which are not relevant for the current considerations. Instead, tracing is restricted only to data which is relevant for calculating model parameters. Beside, instrumentation is no longer an error-prone editing process, but can be carried out by an instrumentation tool, since a formal description of all places to be instrumented can be derived from the model.

The integration of our modeling tool PEPP into the ZM4/SIMPLE tool environment for monitoring and performance evaluation [3] is shown in fig. 4. It can be seen that PEPP can not only be used for creating (function `Creation`) and evaluating stochastic graph models with one of the methods explained in section 3 (function `Model Evaluation`) but also for supporting monitoring: PEPP creates files for automatic program instrumentation with

AICOS, for executing a measurement with the distributed hardware monitor ZM4, and for supporting trace analysis with the SIMPLE tool environment. In fig. 4, the six rectangles in the box **PEPP** represent the main functions of PEPP. The following four functions are necessary for monitoring and calculating model parameters:

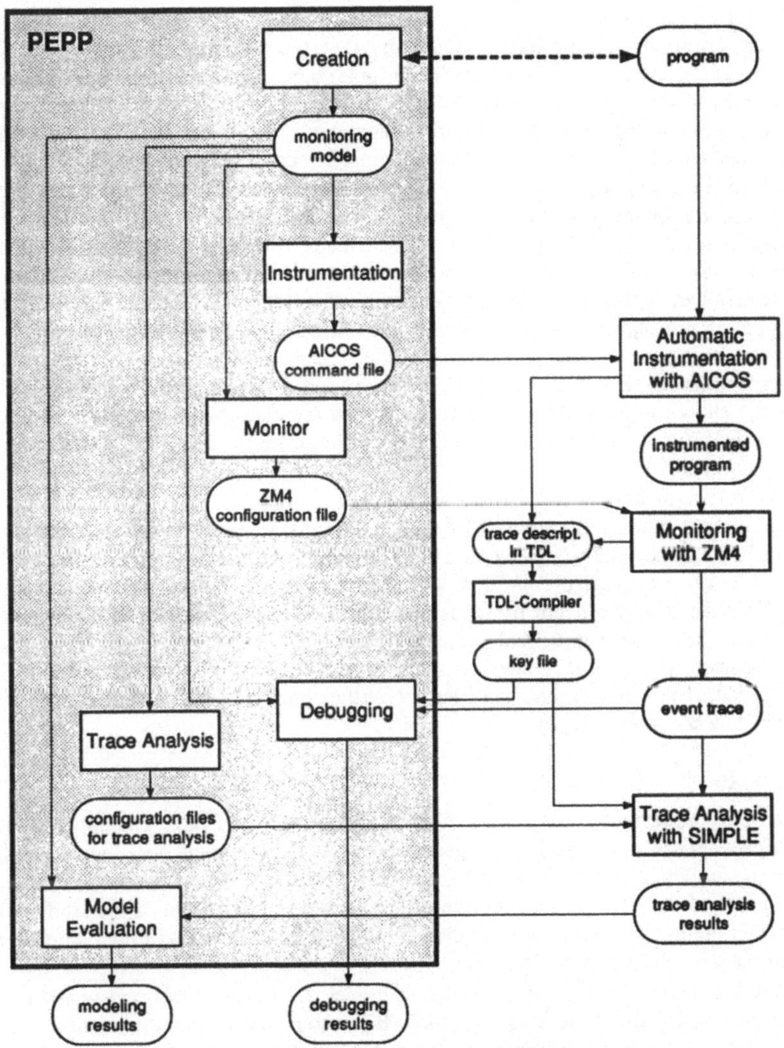

Figure 4: Model-driven monitoring with PEPP

- Function Instrumentation

  For automatic instrumentation an instrumentation description is created. This description contains information where the program should be instrumented and which statement should be inserted. For each event the statement to be inserted can differ. The event token for identifying the monitored event will be generated by the instrumentation tool. Since trace analysis should be carried out in a problem-oriented manner, knowledge of the event semantics during instrumentation can be used to automatically create an event trace description for trace access [14].

- Function `Monitor`
  In some cases not all processors of a parallel system have to be monitored. If the processors to be monitored are selected in the graph model with PEPP, this information can be used to automatically create a configuration file for the distributed hardware monitor system ZM4. Such a file helps adapting the monitor to the object system and executing measurements.
- Function `Debugging`
  Typically, programs are not derived automatically from a model or a formal specification. Therefore it cannot be guaranteed that the program behavior represented by the event trace corresponds to the expected behavior in the monitoring-model, which makes debugging necessary. Applying model-driven instrumentation, debugging can be regarded as a consistency check between the monitored program behavior and the monitoring-model (model-driven debugging). The monitoring model created for instrumentation serves as a reference for debugging the monitored program behavior. If there is no error in the program, a monitored event trace is a trace which can also be obtained by walking through the model. Such a trace is the input for further trace analysis and for calculating model parameters. Debugging a parallel program with respect to a model eases the understanding of erroneous program behavior. It is not only shown *what* is wrong in the program, but also *why* the error occurred. This is possible, since the dependencies between parallel processes are represented in the model. With our tool PEPP the results of the consistency check are shown graphically and textually. Errors are classified and related to the source code of the program and to the event trace. Furthermore, in PEPP the validation process can be animated [4].
- Function `Trace Analysis`
  For calculating runtime distributions for all model tasks from a measured trace a configuration file for the analysis tools `trcstat` of the trace analysis environment SIMPLE [14] can easily be created. While these files are available before the measurements are carried out the resulting event traces can be evaluated immediately after the measurement is finished. Beside this statistical evaluation, based on the program behavior represented in the monitoring model it is often known which aspects of the dynamic behavior should be analyzed. Therefore description files for further trace analysis (Gantt charts, etc.) can also be created automatically.

6. Conclusions

This paper gives a survey of analysis techniques implemented in PEPP. The approximate state space analysis allows us to obtain very accurate results for the mean runtime of graphs with a non-series-parallel structure. The series-parallel reduction based on numerical distribution functions leads to the runtime distribution of the modeled program in a very efficient way. Applying this method to non-series-parallel graphs, we get lower and upper bounds for the mean runtime and the runtime variance.

For realistic modeling it is necessary to derive model parameters from real-world problems, i.e. by monitoring existing programs. Our tool PEPP can be used for automatically creating an instrumentation description, a monitor configuration description, for debugging purposes and to create configuration files for trace analysis. With this method the (functional) monitoring model can easily be enhanced to a performance model, since monitoring can be carried out efficiently and results can be calculated immediately after monitoring is finished.

References

[1] G. Chiola. *GreatSPN Users' Manual*, 1987.

[2] P. Dauphin, F. Hartleb, M. Kienow, V. Mertsiotakis, and A. Quick. PEPP: Performance Evaluation of Parallel Programs — User's Guide – Version 3.1. Technical Report 5/92, Universität Erlangen–Nürnberg, IMMD VII, April 1992.

[3]   P. Dauphin, R. Hofmann, R. Klar, B. Mohr, A. Quick, M. Siegle, and F. Sötz. ZM4/SIMPLE: a General Approach to Performance–Measurement and –Evaluation of Distributed Systems. In T.L. Casavant and M. Singhal, editors, *Readings in Distributed Computing Systems*. IEEE Computer Society Press, 1992.

[4]   P. Dauphin, M. Kienow, and A. Quick. Model-driven Validation of Parallel Programs Based on Event Traces. In *Proceedings of the "Working Conference on Programming Environments for Parallel Computing"*, *Edinburgh 6–8 April*, 1992.

[5]   L.P. Devroye. Inequalities for the Completion Times of Stochastic PERT Networks. *Math. Oper. Res.*, 4:441–447, 1980.

[6]   B. Dodin. Bounding the Project Completion Time Distributions in PERT Networks. *Operations Research*, 33(4):862–881, 1985.

[7]   G. Fleischmann. *Performance Evaluation of Parallel Programs for MIMD-Architectures: Modeling and Analyses (in German)*. Dissertation, Universität Erlangen–Nürnberg, 1990.

[8]   F. Hartleb. Stochastic Graph Models for Performance Evaluation of Parallel Programs and the Evaluation Tool *PEPP*. Technical Report 3/93, Universität Erlangen-Nürnberg, IMMD VII, 1993.

[9]   F. Hartleb and V. Mertsiotakis. Bounds for the Mean Runtime of Parallel Programs. In R. Pooley and J. Hillston, editors, *Sixth International Conference on Modelling Techniques and Tools for Computer Performance Evaluation*, pages 197–210, Edinburgh, 1992.

[10] R. Hofmann, R. Klar, N. Luttenberger, B. Mohr, and G. Werner. An Approach to Monitoring and Modeling of Multiprocessor and Multicomputer Systems. In T. Hasegawa et al., editors, *Int. Seminar on Performance of Distributed and Parallel Systems*, pages 91–110, Kyoto, 7–9 Dec. 1988.

[11] W. Kleinöder. *Stochastic Analysis of Parallel Programs for Hierarchical Multiprocessor Systems (in German)*. Dissertation, Universität Erlangen–Nürnberg, 1982.

[12] J.J. Martin. Distribution of the Time through a Directed, Acyclic Network. *Operations Research*, 13(1):46–66, 1965.

[13] V. Mertsiotakis. Extension of the Graph Analysis Tool SPASS and Integration into the X-Window Environment of PEPP (in German). Internal study, Universität Erlangen–Nürnberg, 1991.

[14] B. Mohr. SIMPLE: a Performance Evaluation Tool Environment for Parallel and Distributed Systems. In A. Bode, editor, *Distributed Memory Computing, 2nd European Conference*, *EDMCC2*, pages 80–89, Munich, Germany, April 1991. Springer, Berlin, LNCS 487.

[15] H. Pingel. Stochastic Analysis of seriesparallel programs (in German). Internal study, Universität Erlangen–Nürnberg, 1988.

[16] R. Sahner. *A Hybrid, Combinatorial Method of Solving Performance and Reliability Models*. PhD thesis, Dép. Comput. Sci., Duke Univ., 1986.

[17] R. Sahner and K. Trivedi. Performance Analysis and Reliability Analysis Using Directed Acyclic Graphs. *IEEE Transactions on Software Engineering*, SE-13(10), October 1987.

[18] R. Sahner and K.S. Trivedi. SPADE: A Tool for Performance and Reliability Evaluation. In N. Abu El Ata, editor, *Modelling Techniques and Tools for Performance Analysis '85*, pages 147–163. Elsevier Science Publishers B.V. (North Holland), 1986.

[19] A.W. Shogan. Bounding Distributions for a Stochastic PERT Network. *Networks*, 7:359–381, 1977.

[20] F. Sötz. A Method for Performance Prediction of Parallel Programs. In H. Burkhart, editor, *CONPAR 90–VAPP IV, Joint International Conference on Vector and Parallel Processing. Proceedings*, pages 98–107, Zürich, September 1990. Springer–Verlag, Berlin, LNCS 457.

[21] F. Sötz and G. Werner. Load Modeling with Stochastic Graphs for Improving Parallel Programs on Multiprocessors (in German). In *11. ITG/GI–Fachtagung Architektur von Rechensystemen*, München, 1990.

[22] N. Yazici-Pekergin and J.-M. Vincent. Stochastic Bounds on Execution Times of Parallel Programs. *IEEE Transactions on Software Engineering*, 17(10):1005–1012, October 1991.

Performance Prediction of Parallel Programs

H. Wabnig, G. Kotsis, G. Haring
University of Vienna
Institute of Applied Computer Science and Information Systems
Lenaugasse 2/8, A-1080 Vienna, Austria
Tel: +43 1 408 63 66 10, Fax: +43 1 408 04 50

e-mail: wabnig@ani.univie.ac.at, gabi@ani.univie.ac.at, haring@ani.univie.ac.at

Abstract

The CAPSE (Computer Aided Parallel Software Engineering) environment is
proposed to support a development process, launching the performance engineering activities that accompany the whole software development lifecycle. In this
paper a first subset of tools is described, which illustrates the basic ideas for performance prediction in early stages of development. The toolset consists of an
automatic performance model generator, a special purpose simulator to generate
performance results and the well known visualization tool ParaGraph. The tool
implementation, the concepts to integrate existing tools (e.g ParaGraph) and the
tool restrictions are described. Timed Petri nets are used as the underlying performance model. The models for workload description, for the specification of the
hardware and for the mapping of the workload to the topology are shown. In order
to demonstrate the usage of the performance prediction toolset, a case study of
a parallel LU-decomposition algorithm on a hypothetical parallel computer system
with a hypercube communication network is elaborated by experimenting with a set
of different matrix sizes, mappings and hardware parameters. Achievable speedup,
efficiency, efficacy and the total execution times are compared.

1 Introduction

Having in mind the traditional (sequential) software development process where performance issues are insufficiently considered [Fox 89], one is now convinced that performance
analysis is a critical factor in the upcoming parallel software development methodology.
Today, the major challenges are to support the process of developing parallel software
by effective (automated) performance tools during the whole software development cycle,
i.e. performance engineering approaches in the early design phases of parallel software,
accompanying this process until the completion of the parallel application. Performance
engineering activities [Smit 89] range from performance prediction in early development

stages, modelling (analytical modelling and simulation) in the detailed design and coding phase, to finally monitoring and measurements in the testing and correction phase.

There are no general rules guiding the designer of a parallel program or algorithm from the problem specification to the final program. The possibilities range from parallelizing a sequential program, finding a new parallel solution or transforming the structure of the problem to one for which a parallel solution is known. Assuming that this process – whatever way the designer decided to choose – has lead to an algorithmic idea which he is now willing to implement, the following steps are to be taken towards an efficient application in the performance sense: For expressing the rough idea of a parallel program the designer at first should not have to use traditional programming languages and immediately start with an implementation, as this is usually time consuming and error prone. A high level graphical specification method is used to support automatic performance prediction, simultaneously gaining from its graphical expressiveness and hence preventing the designer from getting lost in implementation details. After arriving at an implementation skeleton in the specification phase, the designer is now interested whether the predicted performance is justifying to make a working program out of the high level specification. If the performance figures are acceptable, the designer can now turn to assign components of his program to devices of the target architecture. Finally, if a running parallel program has been achieved, performance studies using monitoring techniques can be fruitful in detecting system bottlenecks and aid in 'fine-tuning' the application. Further toolsupport in this phase is required for visualizing the running system on the basis of computation and communication events.

The CAPSE (Computer Aided Parallel Software Engineering) environment [Fers 91, Fers 92] is a toolset to support this performance oriented parallel program development covering the whole software lifecycle.

2 The Performance Prediction Toolset

2.1 The Methodology

The performance prediction toolset is one element within the CAPSE environment. The general methodology for the toolset bases on three layers:

The first layer, which is called specification layer, contains information about the workload of the parallel algorithm, hardware characteristics and mapping information. These three inputs can be varied to a high degree independently of each other[1] which makes it possible to easily experiment with various different hardware configurations and mappings of workload elements to the hardware. For scalable workload descriptions it is also possible to investigate several different problem sizes without additional efforts for specification adaption.

The second layer is the transformation layer. The transformation layer takes the

---

[1] Of course, for example, the mapping has to be done with at least the knowledge of the number of processors specified in the topology.

information defined in the specification layer to generate performance models appropriate for the third layer.

The third layer is a set of methods for performance analysis and prediction.

Various characteristics of parallel programs and objectives of the investigation make it necessary to use different methods for performance analysis. The methods can be based on various performance models (e.g. Petri nets, queueing networks). With the concept of the three layers it should be possible to verify performance results or select appropriate solution methods, which, for example, optimize accuracy vs. effort, without having to change the specification. Furthermore existing tools can be integrated into the toolset by generating appropriate input-files for the tools.

2.2   The Current Implementation

The current implementation of the performance prediction toolset includes only one solution method which is a timed Petri net simulator. In contrast to other tools for simulating Petri nets (e.g. GreatSPN [Chio 91] or Design CPN [Soft 91]) this simulator can only be applied for a very restrictive class of timed Petri nets and therefore several optimizations have been made in order to minimize the simulation time. The simulator recognizes events during the simulation that are relevant for the performance of the workload under investigation and optionally generates a tracefile in PICL syntax (Portable Instrumented Communication Library [Geis 90]). PICL is a portable communication library, which has certain features to collect event and statistic trace information. ParaGraph [Heat 91] is a widely known visualization tool, which has a multitude of different graphical displays giving insight into the execution of parallel programs. ParaGraph reads PICL tracefiles. In our case ParaGraph is integrated into the toolset by generating appropriate tracefiles during the simulation. Unfortunately ParaGraph does not support multiple processes running on one processor in parallel (with time-slices), preventing an interpretation of some ParaGraph diagrams, but preserving many useful diagrams.

Currently all specification elements (i.e. program, resource, mapping) are defined in textual form. A language syntax has been developed to do this in an easy and convenient way. Nevertheless for the specification of bigger workloads this is a time consuming and error prone task. We solved this problem by using another tool, supporting the definition of scalable descriptions, by means of a special language.

2.2.1   The Program Model

The program model is represented by a directed acyclic graph where the nodes represent the tasks to be executed (called computation node or CN for short) and the arcs represent communication or precedence relations. A CN starts execution if all precedence relations are statisfied and all communication dependencies are resolved.

Each node of the task graph executes in three phases: First receive data from all input CNs, then execute the task body and the last phase is to send data to all output CNs. Communication with other CNs is only possible at the beginning and at the end of the node execution. All the data necessary for the execution of phase 2 are read in during phase 1 and all the results needed by other CNs are communicated during phase 3.

To each CN in the task graph a computational demand is assigned. This computational demand can be zero, if the node does not represent computations, i.e. it is used to represent structural properties of the model. The computational load of a CN is characterized by instructions and floating point instructions. For each CN an estimate of the absolute number of instructions and floating point operations has to be given. For each arc in the task graph the communication demand has to be characterized by the amount of data (in bytes) which must be transferred across the arc.

2.2.2 The Resource Model

The considered model of the parallel hardware distinguishes between processing elements and communication links. Communication links are unidirectional and define the possibility to transfer data from one processor to another. The resource model assumes the possibility, that there is more than one process executed on a single processor in parallel. If more than one process is running on a single processor, time-slices are assigned to the processes. The resource model also assumes a routing mechanism for transparent message exchange among processors. I.e., if there exists a path from one processor to another processor, messages can be sent along that path. The routing paths are generated by an algorithm, selecting one shortest path with nondeterministic selection if there are more than one shortest paths. There exists no load balancing mechanism to dynamically select alternative paths.

Each message, that has to be sent to another processor is cut into small packets which are transferred to the destination processor where the message is reassembled (packet switching). Modelling communication in this way results in transfer delays if there is need for more than one message being routed over the same link at the same time. None of the messages is completely blocked but has to share the resource with others (the granularity is the basic packet size). Because all the packets are propagated in a pipelining fashion, the overall communication speed is not much influenced by the number of routing steps needed to implement distant communication.

The processing element is characterized in terms of computational speed. The model distinguishes between instructions and floating point operations per second. The communication links are characterized in terms of setup time and transfer rate. The setup time specifies a certain amount of time, required to physically establish the communication path. The transfer rate determines the speed at which data can be transferred over a certain link. All the parameters mentioned above can be individually set for any processing element and communication link in the topology.

2.2.3 The Mapping Model

The mapping information defines the assignment of task graph nodes to physical processors. All the arcs in the workload model which do not represent communication over

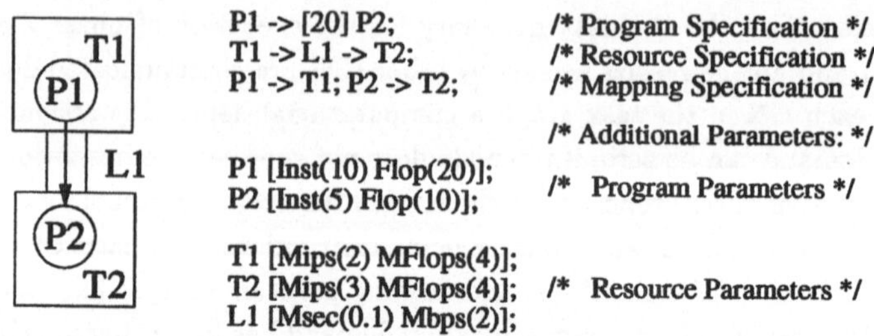


```
P1 -> [20] P2;                          /* Program Specification */
T1 -> L1 -> T2;                         /* Resource Specification */
P1 -> T1; P2 -> T2;                     /* Mapping Specification */

                                        /* Additional Parameters: */
P1 [Inst(10) Flop(20)];
P2 [Inst(5) Flop(10)];                  /*  Program Parameters */

T1 [Mips(2) MFlops(4)];
T2 [Mips(3) MFlops(4)];                 /*  Resource Parameters */
L1 [Msec(0.1) Mbps(2)];
```

Fig. 1.: Example for textual specifications.

links because the sender and receiver are mapped onto the same processor, are treated like precedence relations. They do not require any communication resources and hence their execution time is zero.

Figure 1 shows an example how a textual input for the program, resource and mapping information looks like. The small example specifies two processes which have to be executed sequentially on a topology consisting of two processors which are connected by the communication link "L1". Process "P1" is mapped to processor "T1" and process "P2" to processor "T2". Process "P1" requires ten instructions plus twenty floating point operations, "P2" five instructions plus ten floating point operations. Twenty bytes have to be communicated between the two processes. The speed of processor "T1" is two million instructions and four million floating point operations per second; "T2" can execute three million instructions and four million floating point operations per second. The communication facility has a startup time of one hundred microseconds and a transfer rate of two million bits per second.

2.2.4   The Petri Net Performance Model

Timed Petri nets [Mura 89] are used to analyse the specifications. Resource tokens represent hardware resources. Deterministic timed transitions represent computation or communication efforts. If a computation or communication needs a resource, it has to compete for the resource token. This behaviour is used to implement time-slices for multiple processes, active on a single processor. A common time basis for all timed deterministic transitions representing potentially parallel tasks has to be defined and the actual execution time is modelled by the appropriate number of firings of the timed transition. If multiple tasks are enabled at the same instance of time, each task executes a basic unit of time in turn. An appropriate granularity has to be selected to maximize accuracy and efficiency. The bigger the time basis is, the bigger can be the error for either the calculated execution time compared to the execution time specified in the performance model (which has to be a multiple of the basis time), or the time-slice behaviour to the real behaviour. On the other hand the smaller the time basis gets, the more transition firings are needed to simulate the Petri net. Therefore a tractable tradeoff has to be found. The tool supports two different approaches to solve this problem: The definition of a maximum time basis (because the time basis is limited, also the possible error is limited) and the definition of the minimum number of transition firings for the smallest task execution time in a set of potentially parallel tasks. Due to the conception of resource tokens, the execution time of a directed acyclic task graph is not deterministic.

The packet switching mechanism of the communication network is modelled in the following way: At the beginning of the communication an appropriate number of tokens is generated to represent the amount of data to be transferred, by dividing the number of bytes by the basic packet size, which has to be the same in the whole network. These tokens are propagated to the destination processor whereby every token has to compete for the link resource token at every routing step.

2.2.5 Results

The special simulator generates two different kinds of results: The first kind is a tracefile in PICL syntax. Depending on the specified simulation options, information about the simulation are collected at different levels of accuracy. Among other, the following information can be collected in the tracefile: The begin and end time of computation (with trace messages denoting which particular CN was executed), the begin and end time of communications (with trace messages denoting the sending and receiving CNs), information about the amount of data which was be transferred, identity of the sending and receiving processor, etc. ParaGraph uses this information to visualize the execution of the specified workload on the user defined hardware.[2]

The second performance result is a text file, generated by the simulator. It contains information about each processor in the topology (utilization, number of messages and bytes sent and received) and the total execution time for all communications, for all computations and the parallel program. Additionally the speedup is computed by dividing the sum of all computations by the total execution time of the parallel specification. If multiple simulation runs are performed, average values are computed.

3 Gaussian Elimination on Hypercubes

3.1 Problem Specification

The LU-decomposition algorithm [Quin 87, Lord 83] is taken as an example to demonstrate how performance prediction is done with the toolset. The starting point for the

---

[2]As mentioned before not all displays are meaningful because ParaGraph was not designed for multiple processes running in parallel on a single processing node. Some minor changes in the source code of ParaGraph had to be made to avoid error messages caused by this problem. In addition user displays have been included to support the visualization of the activity of multiple processes on one processor; e.g. showing the number of active tasks per processor.

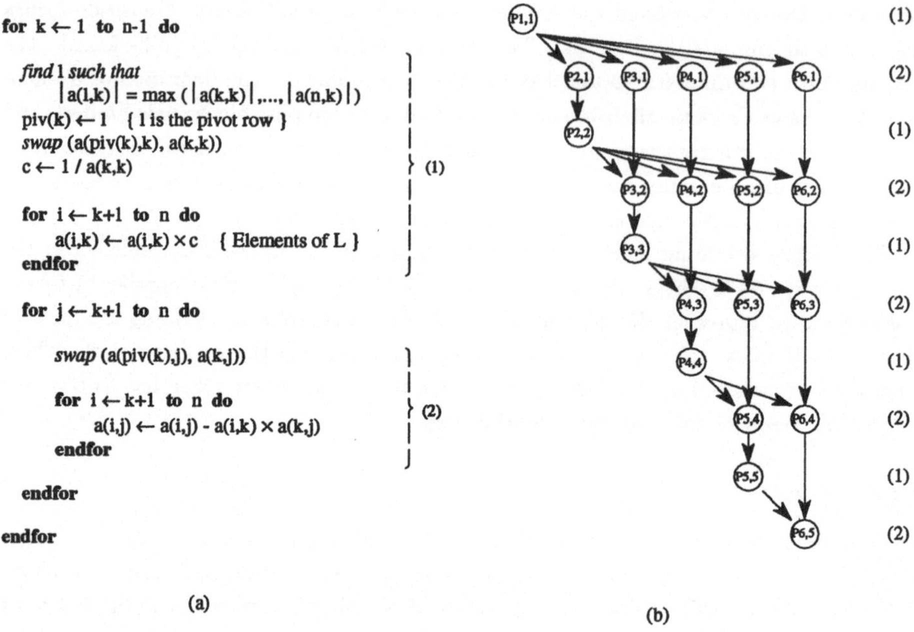

Fig. 2.: The sequential LU-decomposition algorithm described in pseudo-code (a) and as a DAG for a 6×6-matrix (b).

development of a parallel program for LU-decomposition is the parallel algorithmic idea. Figure 2 (a) shows the sequential algorithm for performing the LU-decomposition. There can be identified two main parts in the algorithm. The first part determines the pivot row and computes the first column of the matrix (1). The second part computes all the remaining columns of the matrix by using the elements in the first column and combining them with the elements in the other columns (2). The data dependency graph in figure 2 (b) shows that the computations of the remaining columns in the matrix are independent of each other. This leads to the parallel algorithmic idea: The for-loop which computes the columns[3] in the sequential algorithm is parallelized. The shape of the algorithmic skeleton is then the dependency graph interpreted as a task graph.

Input Specification and Parametrization of Program and Resource Description
The workload structure is generated by extending the algorithmic skeleton of the LU-decomposition for a given matrix size.

Looking at the LU-decomposition we can find linear growth in computational demands for both part (1) and part (2). This linear growth has to be translated into the actual number of instructions and floating point operations. Using a scalable specification these values can be generated automatically. Only two values for each workload parameter

---

[3]I.e. parts (2).

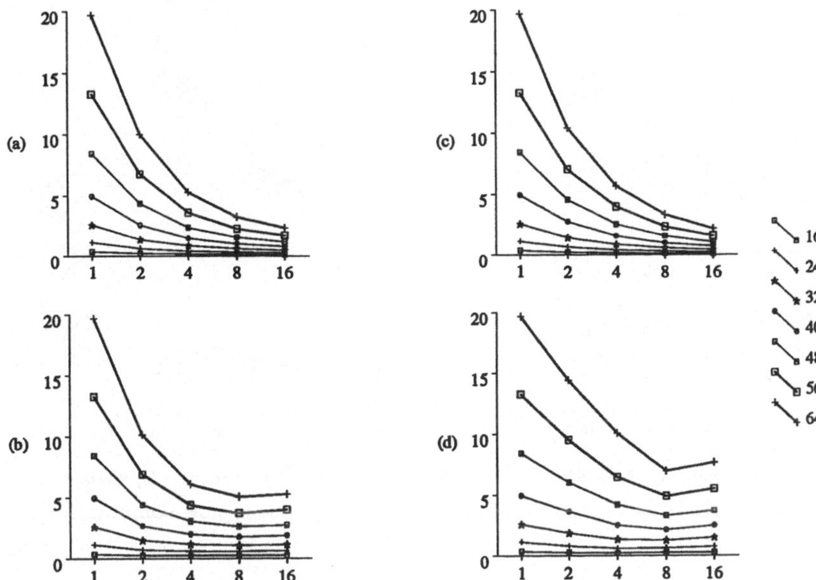

Fig. 3.: Total execution time (in milliseconds) for (a) mapping 2, fast communication, (b) mapping 2, slow communication, (c) mapping 1, fast communication, and (d) mapping 1, slow communication.

are necessary to specify the corresponding linear function. The amount of necessary communication is determined by the size of the matrix in each step of the computation and can also be generated automatically when using a scalable specification.

The basic hardware topology is a hypercube. We used hypercube topologies of dimension 1 to 4 (i.e. 2 to 16 processing elements).

For the investigations about the LU-decomposition algorithm we use hypothetical hardware parameters. We specified a very fast communication network with startup time 0.6 microseconds and transfer rate 2 gigabit per second and one which is more realistic (startup time 1 microsecond, transfer rate 100 megabit per second).

Mapping   Each node in the task graph workload description has to be mapped onto the actual hardware topology.

Two alternative mappings are considered: In the first mapping (called mapping 1 furtheron) the longest sequential computational path (tasks $P1, 1$, $P2, 1, \ldots, P5, 5$, $P6, 6$) is mapped onto a single processor, and all the other elements are assigned to the remaining processing elements in such a way that the maximum parallelism in each iteration is exploited. The second mapping strategy (mapping 2) tries to minimize communication efforts by assigning the tasks columnwise to the processing elements (i.e. distributing the matrix to the processing elements columnwise).

If the number of processors is smaller than the degree of parallelism, modulo operations

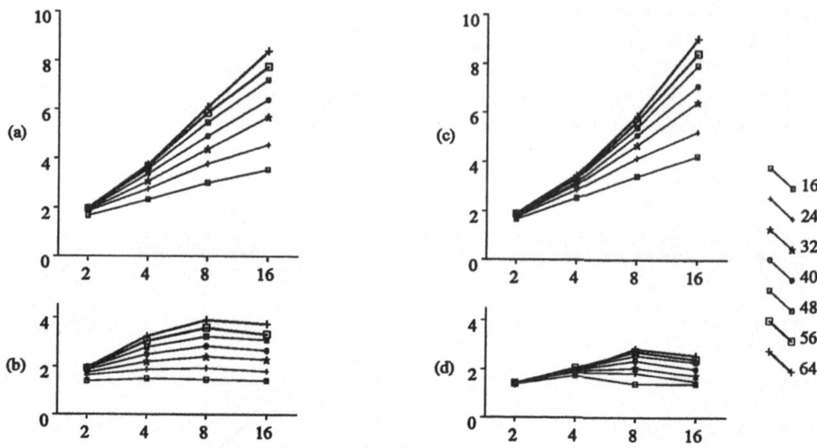

Fig. 4.: Speedup for (a) mapping 2, fast communication, (b) mapping 2, slow communication, (c) mapping 1, fast communication, and (d) mapping 1, slow communication.

are performed to assign them to existing nodes. This might lead to a load balancing among the processors.

Optimization of the Workload Specification   The modulo mapping strategy places multiple nodes of the task graph onto a single processor. The LU-decomposition demands that part (1) has to distribute the first column of the matrix to all parts (2). Therefore if more than one part (2) is mapped to a processor the first column is sent multiple times although the information is always the same. Of course a real implementation would not perform this redundant communication operations. But in the workload model there is no possibility to specify such circumstances and adjust the performance model automatically. Therefore we slightly change the workload specification and add dummy nodes to the task graph, which do not consume any computation time. Each arc from a part (1) to a part (2) is changed to an arc from part (1) to the dummy node for the processor on which part (2) is executed and a second arc from the dummy node to part (2). The arc parameters are not changed. In order to do that, the scalable workload specifications for the LU-decomposition had to be adapted to generate the additional dummy nodes and arcs.

3.2   Analysis and Interpretation of the Simulated Behaviour

Our objective is to find the optimum number of processing elements and the optimum mapping for a given matrix size and given hardware parameters (computation and communication speed). To do this we generated the following information for all combinations of program, resource and mapping possibilities: Total execution time, speed up (defined as the ratio of the execution time on a single processing element and the execution time on p processing elements), efficiency (defined as speedup divided by the number of processing

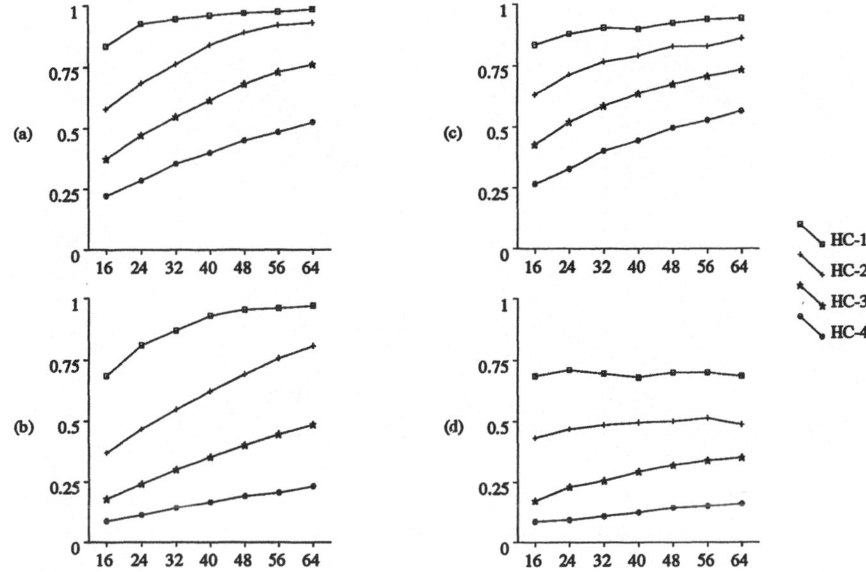

Fig. 5.: Efficiency for (a) mapping 2, fast communication, (b) mapping 2, slow communication, (c) mapping 1, fast communication, and (d) mapping 1, slow communication.

elements, thus indicating the average utilization of the processing elements) and efficacy (defined as the product of speedup and efficiency; the maximum indicates the optimal number of processors).

The diagrams in figures 3, 4, 5, and 6 depict these measures for matrices of size 16×16 to 64×64 comparing mapping 1 (longest path mapping, right diagrams) and mapping 2 (columnwise mapping, left diagrams) and the two different communication speeds (fast in the first rows and slow in the second rows). Either the number of processing elements (in the execution time, speedup, and efficacy diagrams) or the matrix size (in the efficiency diagram) is shown on the horizontal axis.

The execution time diagrams show that for the slow communication network mapping 2 (low communication) is better than mapping 1 (high communication). Eight processors provide the minimal execution time in both mappings. In the fast communication network mapping 1 is slightly better than mapping 2. Sixteen processors offer the fastest execution times in both mappings. The observations about mapping are valid for all matrix sizes.

In the speedup diagrams the above statements are visualized more clearly. Comparing mapping 1 with mapping 2 in the speedup diagram, one can see, that for the fast network mapping 1 gives higher values, and for the slow network mapping 2 is better. But the difference between mapping 1 and mapping 2 in the fast network is not as big as in the slow network. To choose the right mapping is an important factor, if the communication network is slow, while for fast communication networks the mapping is almost neglectible

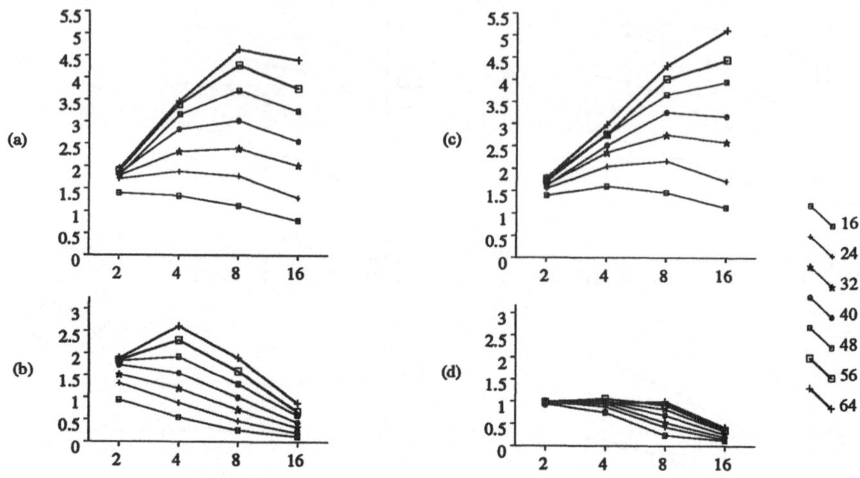

Fig. 6.: Efficacy (a) mapping 2, fast communication, (b) mapping 2, slow communication, (c) mapping 1, fast communication, and (d) mapping 1, slow communication.

for matrix sizes in the range discussed here.

The correlation between the matrix size and the efficient use of processors is shown in diagram 5. For the sixteen node hypercube and all studied matrix sizes, the efficiency never reached 25% in case of the slow network and 55% in case of the fast network. Two processors is the best choice with respect to efficiency for all networks and investigated matrix sizes, but the large amount of communication in mapping 1 limits efficiency to approximately 70% for the slow network and approximately 90% for the fast network, whereas in mapping 2 efficiency approaches to nearly 100% for large matrix sizes and two processors.

The optimum number of processors is matrix size dependent. For the fast network sixteen processor elements are the optimum if the matrix size is sufficiently large ($\geq$ 48 × 48). For smaller matrix sizes the optimum decreases to four processors. If the communication network is slow, then even for the biggest matrix size the use of only four processor elements is optimum. Again, mapping 2 is preferable over mapping 1 if the communication network is slow.

Figure 7 shows two selected PICL displays for a matrix of size 20 × 20 on a hypercube of dimension two (four processors). The task gantt chart displays the load of the different processors over the execution time. Task changes are represented by change of shading. Very frequent task changes indicate that there are multiple processes executing in parallel (i.e. the time-slices are displayed). White space between shaded areas reflects processor idle times. Idle times on a node are situations where all processes on that node are waiting for input data or have already been executed. The spacetime diagram shows the begin and end time and the source and destination processors of communications.

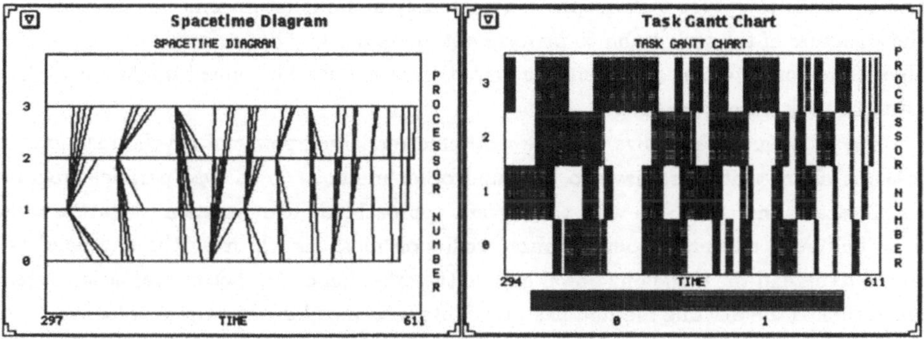

Fig. 7.: Some of the displays provided by the ParaGraph visualization tool.

As mentioned before there are other displays for critical path analysis, statistics, animation of the communication, communication traffic, etc.

4 Conclusions and Future Work

There are limitations with the existing system. The tractable problem sizes are rather small. For models with more than about 10000 task graph nodes it is not possible to generate the performance model, because the number of Petri net elements which have to be generated, is too big. The memory requirement exceeds available resources of average workstations. But even if the performance model can be generated, it is not said that it then can be simulated in reasonable time. The simulation of the packet switching communication network generates huge amounts of tokens for relatively small messages. For example, if the basic packet size is 10 bytes and a message of 10000 bytes must be transferred along a routing path with three hops, 1000 tokens would be generated and 1000*3 transitions have to be fired to simulate the data communication. This is the same for multiple processes mapped onto a single processor. The execution time of the process must be split in a number of smaller execution times to allow other processes access to the CPU resource and simulate time-slicing behaviour. Consider for example a set of 101 processes with one having a very small execution time (1 microsecond) and the others with very long execution time (1 second). Every 1-second-process has to be adjusted at least to the minimum execution time in the set of potentially parallel processes. Therefore the simulation would at least demand 100*1000000 transition firings to simulate the 101 nodes in the task graph. If the achievable firing rates[4] are considered, the execution of these 101 nodes would take at least 20000 seconds (about 5,5 hours). All these things have to be kept in mind when the modelling of the algorithm is done. We are trying to

---

[4]Firing rates are in the range of 100 to 5000 transition firings per second depending on the size and structure of the task graph. But as a rule of thumb, simulation speed decreases with growing size of the Petri net.

find methods to reduce task graphs automatically and exploit information contained in the structure of the task graph to perform optimizations for the performance model. But algorithms for detecting situations where optimization can be applied might themselves often be very time consuming.

The problems cited above and the restricted modelling power of acyclic task graphs make it clear, that there have to be found other methods to analyse parallel program specifications, not tractable with the current approach. So one direction for future work is to find such alternative performance prediction methods which on the one hand are suited to extend the modelling power and on the other hand offer better evaluation speed. Nevertheless the existing method has proved its relevance for a class of problems.

Other directions for future work are the design and implementation of a graphical user interface supporting scalable hierarchical specifications and the investigation whether task graphs can be extended to include loops and conditional branches without loosing the property of being performance predictable with the current solution method.

References

[Chio 91] G. Chiola. "GreatSPN1.5 Software Architecture". In: *Proc. of the 5th Int. Conf. on Modelling Techniques and Tools for Computer Performance Evaluation. Torino, Italy, Feb 13-15, 1991' (to appear)*, pp. 117 –132, 1991.

[Fers 91] A. Ferscha and G. Haring. "On Performance Oriented Environments for the Development of Parallel Programs". *Kybernetika a Informatika, Proceedings of the 15th Symposium on Cybernetics and Informatics '91, April 3-5 1991, Smolenice Castle, ČSFR*, Vol. 4, No. 1/2, 1991.

[Fers 92] A. Ferscha. "A Petri Net Approach for Performance Oriented Parallel Program Design". *Journal of Parallel and Distributed Computing*, No. 15, pp. 188–206, 1992.

[Fox 89] G. Fox. "Performance Engineering as a Part of the Development Life Cycle for Large-Scale Software Systems". In: *Proc. of the 11th Int. Conf. on Software Engineering, Pittsburgh*, pp. 85–94, IEEE Computer Society Press, 1989.

[Geis 90] G. A. Geist, M. T. Heath, B. W. Peyton, and P. H. Worley. "PICL: A Portable Instrumented Communication Library". Tech. Rep. ORNL/TM-11130, Oak Ridge National Laboratory, July 1990.

[Heat 91] M. T. Heath and J. A. Etheridge. "Visualizing Performance of Parallel Programs". Tech. Rep. ORNL/TM-11813, Oak Ridge National Laboratory, May 1991.

[Lord 83] R. E. Lord, J. S. Kowalik, and S. P. Kumar. "Solving linear algebraic equations on an MIMD computer". *Journal of the ACM*, Vol. 30, No. 1, pp. 103–117, January 1983.

[Mura 89] T. Murata. "Petri Nets: Properties, Analysis and Applications". *Proceedings of the IEEE*, Vol. 77, No. 4, pp. 541–580, Apr. 1989.

[Quin 87] M. J. Quinn. *Designing Efficient Algorithms for Parallel Computers*. McGraw-Hill International Publishers, New York, 1987.

[Smit 89] C. U. Smith. *Performance Engineering of Software Systems*. Addison Wesley, 1989.

[Soft 91] M. Software. "Design/CPN. A Tool Package Supporting the Use of Colored Petri Nets". Tech. Rep., Meta Software Corporation, Cambridge, MA, USA, 1991.

Modellierungs- und Bewertungskonzepte für ODP-Architekturen

B. Meyer, C. Popien

RWTH Aachen
Lehrstuhl für Informtik IV
Ahornstr. 55, D-52056 Aachen

Telefon: +49 241 8021440
Fax: +49 241 8021429
e-mail: bernd@informatik.rwth-aachen.de

Kurzfassung

Open Distributed Processing (ODP) verfolgt das Ziel, der wachsenden Komplexität verteilter Systeme gerecht zu werden. Kernstück ist der ODP-Trader, ein Objekt, das eine dynamische Schnittstellenbindung realisiert. In Abhängigkeit der Struktur eines verteilten Unternehmens und entsprechend der internen Abarbeitung werden mögliche Architekturen in vier S/A-Modellen klassifiziert.
Gegenstand dieses Artikels ist es, ein Verfahren zur Leistungsbewertung paralleler Warteschlangennetze abzuleiten, das allen ODP-Anforderungen gerecht wird. Dazu wird ein von Duda/Czachorski vorgeschlagener Ansatz von ineinander verschachtelten Fork/Join-Netzen paralleler Stationen mit unterschiedlichen Bedienraten betrachtet. Atomare Netze werden auf geschlossene Produktformnetze zurückgeführt und die Modellierung um die Einführung einer Synchronisation von Tasks erweitert. Das resultierende Verfahren ist eine geeignete Methode zur vollständigen Bewertung aller S/A-Modelle.

1. Einführung

Bedingt durch die steigende Vernetzung heterogener Rechnersysteme reicht die durch OSI modellierbare Offenheit der Kommunikation nicht mehr aus. Um den neuen Anforderungen gerecht zu werden, ist von ISO und CCITT das Basic Reference Model of Open Distributed Processing (BRM ODP) entwickelt worden. Parallel zu dieser Entwicklung haben Konsortien von Computerherstellern produktorientierte Projekte gestartet. Zu nennen ist das Distributed Computing Environment (DCE) [Sch 92] der Open Software Foundation (OSF), welches eine Umgebung für die Entwicklung verteilter Anwendungen bereitstellt, und die Object Management Group (OMG), die ins Leben gerufen wurde, um objekt-orientierte Technologien zu unterstützen. Die Architektur für einen Objekt Request Broker (ORB) [Gei 92] ist Gegenstand der Entwicklungen, um die Funktionalität eines ODP-Traders zu realisieren.

Das BRM ODP [ODP P1-4] stellt grundlegende Modellierungskonzepte bereit, die es ermöglichen, die Komplexität verteilter Systeme zu reduzieren. Um eine größere Abstraktion zu erreichen, werden im BRM ODP fünf Viewpoints (Enterprise, Information, Computational, Engineering und Technology Viewpoint) unterschieden. Sie sind Voraussetzung für das Design Trajectory verteilter Systeme [Po 92]. Eine zentrale Position in allen ODP-Architekturen nimmt der ODP-Trader ein. Er hat die Aufgabe, eine dynamische Schnittstellenbindung zwischen Objekten zur Laufzeit zu realisieren [ODP Tr]. Arbeiten mehrere solche Trader zusammen, so spricht man von einer Trading Federation [PoMe 93]. Basierend auf diversen Architekturen gibt es eine Vielzahl von Modellen zur Federation Realisierung.

In Abhängigkeit der Organisationsstruktur eines verteilten Unternehmens und entsprechend der internen Abarbeitung einzelner Traderanfragen werden mögliche Architekturen in vier Struktur-/Ablaufmodellen klassifiziert. Diese Modelle sind Gegenstand des nachfolgenden Abschnitts. Erfahrungsberichte ähnlicher Problemstellungen raten uns im jetzigen Bearbeitungsstadium von simulativen Untersuchungen ab. Deshalb werden zunächst analytische Studien bevorzugt. Das 3. Kapitel untersucht Ansätze zur Leistungsbewertung der einzelnen Modelle. Während die beiden sequentiellen Ablaufmodelle mit herkömmlichen analytischen Verfahren bewertet werden können, genügen die untersuchten Ansätze den Anforderungen an die parallelen Warteschlangennetze nicht mehr. Aus diesem Grund leitet das 4. Kapitel aus einem Ansatz von Duda und Czachorski zur Modellierung ineinander verschachtelter Fork/Join-Netze paralleler Stationen mit unterschiedlichen Bedienraten eine Methode ab, welche eine Synchronisation von Tasks mit einbezieht. Der fünfte Abschnitt diskutiert abschließend die Möglichkeiten dieses Verfahrens und faßt weitere Ideen sowie offene Probleme zusammen.

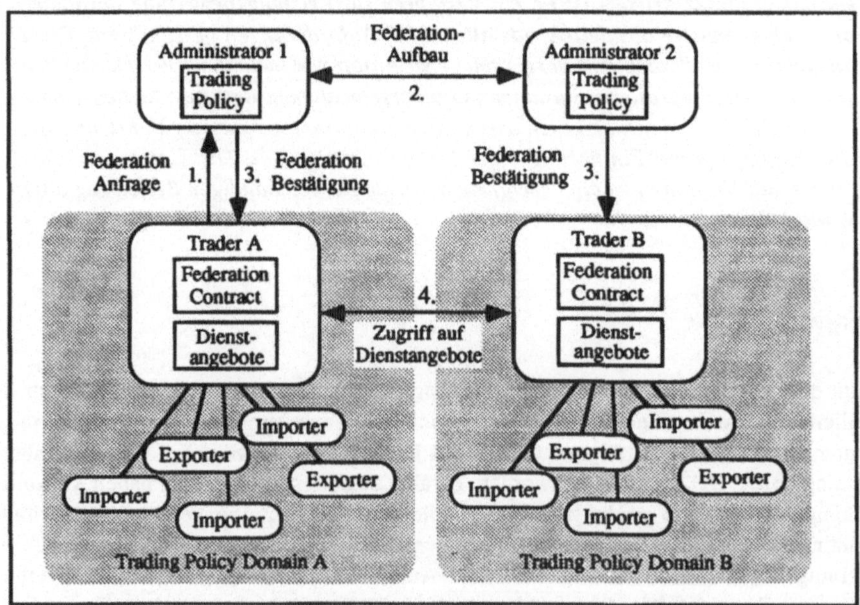

Abb. 1: Architektur einer Federation aus zwei Tradern

2. Modell einer ODP Trading Federation

In einem offenen, verteilten System besitzt der ODP-Trader die Aufgabe, dynamische Bindungen von Schnittstellen zwischen Objekten zu vermitteln. Für einen Benutzer stellt der Trader Operationen zum Anbieten, Zurückziehen und Ersetzen eines Dienstes zur Verfügung. Unabhängig davon kann nach bestimmten Kriterien eine gegebene Anzahl geeigneter Dienste gesucht werden.

Ein Objekt, das einem Trader Dienste anbietet, besitzt in ODP die Rolle eines Exporters. Objekte, die von solchen Dienstangeboten Gebrauch machen, heißen Importer. Zur Benutzung eines Dienstes erstellt der Importer eine Kommunikationsverbindung zum Exporter. Ein Trader und alle mit ihm verbundenen Importer und Exporter bilden einen Trading-Policy-Domain (TPD), siehe Abbildung 1. Mehrere TPDs können zu einer Trading Federation zusammengefaßt werden. Dabei wird jedem TPD ein Administrator zugeordnet. Dieser kann auf Anfrage eines Traders A einen Federation Contract mit dem Administrator des Traders B aushandeln. Kommt es zu einem Abschluß, erhalten die beiden Trader den Vertrag als Bestätigung der Zusammenarbeit. Dann kann der Trader A auf die im Vertrag festgehaltenen Dienstangebote des Traders B zugreifen. Für jeden Trader besitzt ein Administrator eine Trading Policy, die Grundlage für Entscheidungen betreffend der Zugehörigkeit zu einer Federation ist.

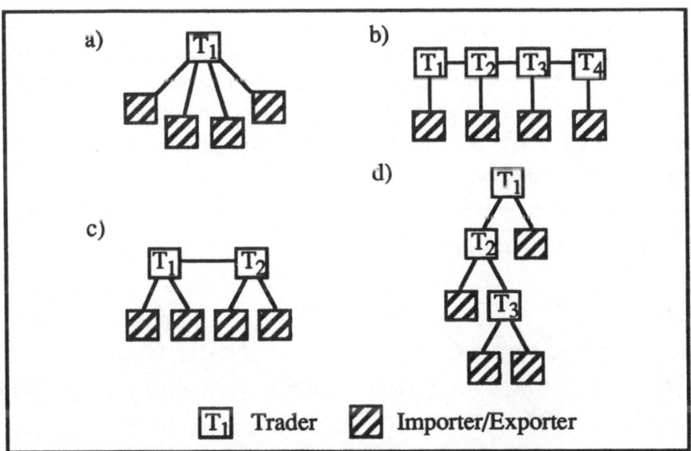

Abb. 2: Verschiedene ODP Trader-Modelle

Zu dieser Architektur gibt es verschiedene Strukturen, wie eine Federation von Tradern realisiert werden kann. Prinzipiell gibt es die Möglichkeit, einen Trader zentral oder verteilt zu realisieren. Extreme Modelle sind zum einen der zentrale Trader in Abbildung 2a, der alle Importer und Exporter bedient; zum anderen erreicht man eine maximale Dezentralisierung, wenn jedem Objekt ein eigener Trader zugeordnet ist, siehe Abbildung 2b. Im allgemeinen werden Kombinationen gebildet, siehe z.B. Abbildung 2c. Ein besondere Stellung nimmt die hierarchische Struktur ein, vgl. Abbildung 2d. Oft wird das Spektrum aller denkbaren Modelle durch organisatorische Zwänge eingeschränkt. Dies äußert sich darin, daß ein zentraler Trader, beispielsweise aus Sicherheitsgründen, nicht allen verbundenen Objekten zugänglich ist. Neben der Möglichkeit, zwischen zentraler und dezentraler Struktur zu unterscheiden, können Implementierungen verschiedene Arten der Ablaufsteuerung realisieren. Hierbei ist eine

Einteilung in parallele und sequentielle Verarbeitung möglich. Aus der Kombination der Strukturierungsarten mit den Möglichkeiten für die Ablaufsteuerung ergeben sich vier grundsätzlich verschiedene Struktur-/Ablaufmodelle (S/A-Modelle) innerhalb von ODP Trader-Federationen, die atomare Module für komplexere ODP-Architekturen darstellen. Die S/A-Modelle sind in Abbildung 3 dargestellt.

S/A-Modelle der Klasse 1 stellen alle Strukturen dar, die Anfragen an einen zentralen, sequentiell arbeitenden Trader richten. Bei Tradern des Modells 2 sind Dienstangebote in zwei Gruppen eingeteilt, und es kann parallel nach einem geeigneten Eintrag gesucht werden. Im Gegensatz zu diesen Modellen, welche sich durch nur einen zentralen Trader im Gesamtsystem auszeichnen, sind die Unterverzeichnisse der verbleibenden S/A-Modelle dezentral auf alle Trader in der Federation verteilt. Durchsucht man diese sequentiell, so erhält man S/A-Modelle der Klasse 3. Alternativ dazu kann man Trader einer Federation parallel nach einem Dienst suchen lassen. Dies wird durch Struktur-/Ablaufmodelle der Klasse 4 dargestellt. Zwar wird in [Kl 84] festgestellt, daß bei gleicher Rechnerkapazität ein zentrales System immer günstiger ist als ein verteiltes System, jedoch kann gleiche Rechnerkapazität nicht immer vorausgesetzt werden. Außerdem läßt sich nicht in jedem Fall eine zentrale Lösung realisieren.

3. Ansätze zur Leistungsbewertung von S/A-Modellen

Es soll davon ausgegangen werden, daß S/A-Modelle der Klasse 1 mit herkömmlichen Methoden zur Bewertung von Warteschlangennetzen analysiert werden können. Für Modelle der Klasse 2 kann diese allgemeingültige Aussage nicht gemacht werden, da Standardverfahren keine parallelen Auftragsströme behandeln. Auf die Untersuchung solcher S/A-Modelle wird deshalb im folgenden eingegangen.

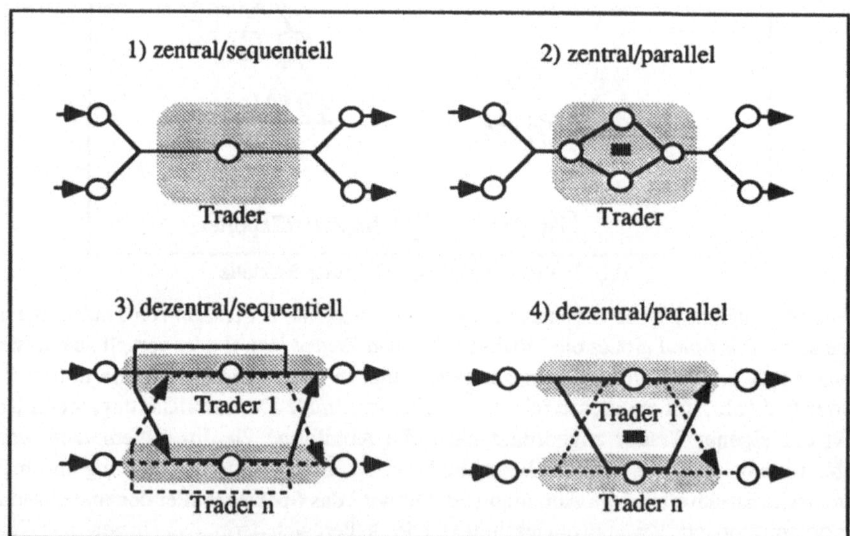

Abb. 3: Die vier Struktur-/Ablaufmodelle

Die Möglichkeiten zur Bewertung von sequentiell arbeitenden Modellen der Klasse 3 sind die gleichen wie die der Klasse 1. Deshalb soll im weiteren auf diese weniger eingegangen werden. Weitaus größer sind die Probleme bei Klasse 4-Modellen, da hier neben der Parallelität und Synchronisation verschiedener Aufträge auch verschiedene Klassen von Aufträgen benötigt werden. Dies folgt aus der Tatsache, daß Aufträge, welche die gesamte Federation betreffen, von allen Tradern bearbeitet werden müssen.

Alle Ansätzen, die hier behandelt werden, haben gemeinsam, daß der Ablauf eines Programms in mehrere, möglicherweise parallel ausgeführte, atomare Tasks unterteilt ist. Die zeitliche Folge der Tasks wird mittels einer partiellen Ordnungsrelation beschrieben. Daraus entsteht der Task-Präzendenzgraph (TPG), siehe Abbildung 4.

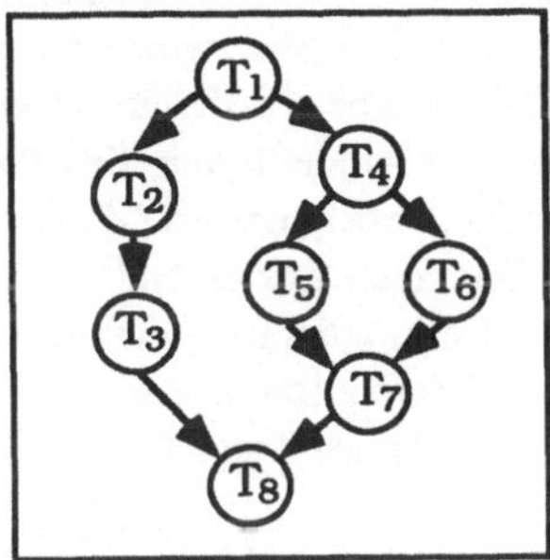

Abb. 4: Ein aus 8 Tasks bestehender Task-Präzedenzgraph

Im folgenden sollen verschiedene Ansätze auf Eignung zur Modellierung und Bewertung von S/A-Modellen der Klassen 2 und 4 untersucht werden.

Der Ansatz von Thomasian und Bay

Ziel dieses Ansatzes [ThBa 86] ist es, die mittlere Ausführungszeit eines einzelnen Programms zu bestimmen. Dabei wird das System in einen Programm- und einen Rechnernetzteil gegliedert, welche getrennt voneinander analysiert werden. Der Progammteil wird durch einen gerichteten, zyklusfreien TPG beschrieben. Zusätzlich können den Kanten des Graphen Gewichte zugeordnet werden, wodurch eine ausreichende Mächtigkeit bezüglich der untersuchten Programmstrukturen gegeben ist. Da Zyklen im TPG durch einen zusammengesetzten Task approximiert werden, ist der Ansatz zur Modellierung von Parallelität prinzipiell geeignet. Einfache Strukturen von Modellen der Klassen 2 und 4 lassen sich mit Hilfe des Ansatzes von Thomasian und Bay bewerten.

Mit diesem Ansatz ist es auch möglich, weitere Eigenschaften von Tasks, wie Geräteanforderung, Umfang der zu anderen Tasks übermittelten Daten und mögliche Rechnerknoten für die Ausführung zu spezifizieren. Der Rechnernetzteil wird durch ein herkömmliches Warteschlangennetz beschrieben. Kernstück des Ansatzes ist der Algorithmus für einen Scheduler. Er berechnet mit Hilfe des TPG und der Beschreibung der Systemeigenschaften die gesuchten Leistungsparameter. Gleiche Bedeutung kommt der Synchronisation der Tasks zu, d.h. der Scheduler legt fest, welche Tasks im nächsten Schritt aktiviert werden. Aus dem TPG erzeugt man eine Markoff-Kette, wobei die aktuell aktivierten Tasks den Zustand bestimmen. Diese Markoff-Kette ist wiederum zyklusfrei und kann deshalb iterativ erzeugt werden. Ausgehend von einem Initialzustand werden zunächst alle Folgezustände betrachtet, die durch einen Taskwechsel erreicht werden können. Analog wird dies für alle Folgezustände durchgeführt.

Für das Verfahren ist allerdings eine gewisse Einfachheit der Struktur des Markoff-Prozesses vorausgesetzt, und es basiert auf der Tatsache, daß nur ein einfacher Programmdurchlauf analysiert wird. Eine weitere Einschränkung besteht darin, daß dieses Verfahren die Zerlegung des TPG in kleinere Teilgraphen nicht unterstützt. Dadurch kann es sehr schnell zu einem immensen Rechenaufwand kommen, wodurch dieser Ansatz weder für komplexere Modelle der Klasse 2, noch für solche der Klasse 4 geeignet ist.

Der Ansatz von Kapelnikov

In Analogie zu dem ersten Ansatz unterscheidet Kapelnikov ([Ka 87], [KME 87]) bei der Modellierung und Bewertung verteilter Systeme zwischen einem Hardware-Modell, genannt Physical Domain Model (PhDM), und einem Software-Modell, dem sogenannten Program Domain Model (PrDM). Während zur Modellierung des PhDMs Netze mit gewöhnlichen Warteschlangenknoten genutzt werden, besteht das PrDM aus einem TPG, der im Gegensatz zu dem Ansatz von Thomasian und Bay auch Zyklen enthalten darf. Er wird der Computation Control Graph (CCG) genannt und ermöglicht es, mehrere Arten der Parallelisierung und Synchronisation von Tasks zu spezifizieren. Daraus folgt wiederum eine prinzipielle Eignung zur Bewertung von S/A-Modellen der Klassen 2 und 4.

Bestimmt wird bei diesem Ansatz die mittlere Laufzeit eines Programms in einem Rechensystem, das gleichzeitig kein anderes Programm bearbeitet. Zunächst muß das zugrundeliegende Rechnernetz analysiert werden. Dabei besteht das Ziel darin, den Durchsatz aller Rechnerknoten für verschiedene Systemzustände zu bestimmen. Ausgehend vom CCG wird ein Markoff-Prozeß konstruiert, der die wesentlichen Zustände bei der Programmausführung beinhaltet. Die Zustandsübergangsraten werden mit Hilfe der Durchsatzwerte aus dem physikalischen Modell bestimmt. Nun muß dieser Markoff-Prozeß gelöst werden und dann kann die durchschnittliche Programmausführungszeit bestimmt werden. Da die Lösung des Markoff-Prozesses aufwendig sein kann, schlägt Kapelnikov vor, den CCG solange hierarchisch zu unterteilen, bis der zugehörige Markoff-Prozeß effizient zu lösen ist. Mittels von ihm entwickelter Heuristiken ist es sukzessive möglich, den CCG wieder zusammenzusetzen. Insbesondere werden Zyklen im Graph ersetzt, so daß er zyklenfrei wird. Dadurch vereinfacht sich die Lösung des Markoff-Prozesses analog zum vorherigen Ansatz. Jedoch gelten diese Vereinfachungen nur für Modelle mit zentraler Task-Synchronisation, d.h. für Modelle der Klasse 2. Für die Dezentralität der Klasse 4-Modelle wird keine Vereinfachung vorgenommen, so daß eine Eignung für diese Modelle weniger gegeben ist.

Der Ansatz von Duda und Czachorski

Bei diesem Ansatz ([DuCz 87], [Bo 89]) geht man von einem Fork/Join-Netz (FJN) mit n parallelen M/G/1-Stationen mit unterschiedlichen Bedienraten aus. Es ist auch möglich, mehrere FJNe ineinander zu verschachteln. Dadurch ist dieser Ansatz in der Lage, Systeme zu analysieren, die durch einen gerichteten, zyklusfreien TPG beschrieben werden können. Eine solche Modellgrundlage ist sowohl für S/A-Modelle der Klasse 2 als auch Modelle der Klasse 4 für die Bewertung notwendig. Ein FJN, das nicht weiter verschachtelt ist, wird durch eine M/M/1-Station mit zustandsabhängiger Bedienrate ersetzt, siehe Abb. 5. Ersetzt man das FJN durch ein geschlossenes Produktformnetz, so kann man aus dessen Lösung den lastabhängigen

Ersatzknoten bestimmen. Im Gegensatz zu den bisherigen Ansätzen, die nur die einfache Ausführung eines Programms bestimmen, wird hier mit einer poissonverteilten Ankunftsrate für Programmaufträge gerechnet. Dieser Sachverhalt weckt ein besonderes Interesse.

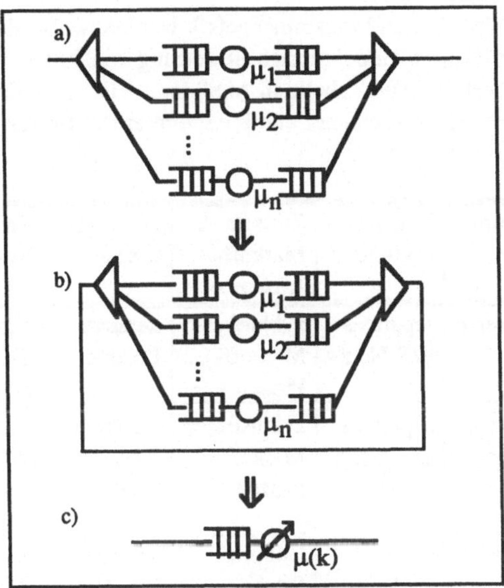

Abb. 5: Vorgehen nach Duda/Czachorski

Der Ansatz von Duda/Czachorski ist sehr gut geeignet, die in S/A-Modellen der Klasse 2 bestehenden Anforderungen zu modellieren. Dabei ergeben sich keine Einschränkungen. Auf der anderen Seite bedingt die fehlende Task-Synchronisation gewisse Restriktionen für Modelle der Klasse 4. Eine Eignung für einfache Modelle dieser Klasse ist unabstreitbar, jedoch nicht uneingeschränkt für komplexere Modelle einsetzbar.

Der Ansatz von Balsamo und Donatiello

Ausgangspunkt für diesen Ansatz [BaDo 90] ist ein FJN, das aus M/G/1-Knoten mit unterschiedlichen Bedienraten besteht. Im Gegensatz zu dem Ansatz von Duda und Czachorski beachtet er jedoch keine weiteren Unternetzte. Aus dem FJN entwickelt man eine Markoff-Kette, wobei ein Systemzustand durch die Länge der Warteschlangen der parallelen Bedienstationen bestimmt ist. Daraus folgt, daß dieser Ansatz in der Lage ist, Parallelität zu handhaben. Da er außerdem theoretisch sehr interessant ist, soll auch dieser Ansatz auf Anwendbarkeit hinsichtlich der Klasse 2- und Klasse 4-Modelle untersucht werden.

Die Zustandsübergangsmatrix hat keine Gestalt eines Quasi-Geburts-Sterbe-Prozesses (QGS-Prozesses). Erst durch eine geeignete Reduzierung des Zustandsraums erreicht diese Martix die Gestalt eines QGS-Prozesses. Aufgrund dieser Eigenschaft kann zur Lösung des Warteschangenmodells die matrix-geometrische Methode, siehe [Ki 90], eingesetzt werden. Effizient ist dieses Lösungsverfahren jedoch nur für M/M/1-Knoten, und es hat auch dann noch kubischen Aufwand bezüglich der Anzahl der Zustände. Daraus resultiert für die von uns untersuchten Anwendungsgebiete keine akzeptable Einsetzbarkeit des Modells. Für einfache

Modelle der Klasse 2 könnte das Verfahren noch verwendet werden, erhöht sich jedoch die Anzahl der parallelen Stationen, so stößt man schnell an die Grenzen der Leistungsfähigkeit.

Vergleich der Verfahren

Diese Analysen sollen abschließend zusammengefaßt werden, wobei die Eignung für die Modelle der Klassen 2 und 4 durch eine 5-stufige Bewertung von +++ = "problemlose Eignung" bis - = "nicht geeignet" erfolgt. Der Tabelle in Abbildung 5 ist zu entnehmen, welcher Ansatz sich durch welche Merkmale auszeichnet und inwiefern er die Bewertung der Klasse 2- und Klasse 4-Modelle unterstützt.

Ansatz	Programm-struktur	Netzdar-stellung	Struktur des Markoff-Ansatzes	Lösungs-ansatz	Task-Synchro-nisation	Ein-satz Kl. 2	Ein-satz Kl. 4
Thomasian/ Bay	zyklusfreier TPG	separates WS-Netz	zyklusfreier Markoff-Prozeß	iterative Lösung	explizit durch Scheduler	+	+
Kapelnikov	erweiterter, zyklischer TPG	separates, erweitertes WS-Netze	zyklusfreier Markoff-Prozeß	hierarchi-sche Zerlegung	explizit WS-Netz im Netz-modell	++	+/-
Duda/ Czachorski	zyklusfreier TPG	dazu analoges WS-Netz	Geburts-Sterbe-Prozeß	analoges WS-Netz, hierarchi-sche Zerlegung	implizit in Zustands-übergän-gen	+++	+(+)
Balsamo/ Donatiello	elementares Fork/Join-Netz	dazu analoges WS-Netz	Quasi-Geburts-Sterbe-Prozeß	matrix-geometri-sche Methode	implizit in Join-WS	+	-

Bedeutung:	+ ... nur für einfachere Modelle geeignet
+++ ... uneingeschränkt geeignet	+/- ... weniger geeignet
++ ... für komplexere Modelle geeignet	- ... nicht geeignet

Abb. 6: Gegenüberstellung der vier Ansätze

Es läßt sich feststellen, daß keiner dieser Ansätze in der Lage ist, allen Anforderungen zu genügen. Modelle der Klasse 2 können prinzipiell von jedem Ansatz bewertet werden, jedoch ist dies aufgrund des erhöhten Rechenaufwands nur für exponentiell verteilte Bedienraten durchführbar.

4. Ein Verfahren zur Analyse von Klasse-4-Modellen

Bei den vier vorgestellten Ansätzen ist die Analyse von Klasse-4-Modellen nur sehr bedingt möglich (siehe Abbildung 6). Als Ansatz für eine geeignete Modellierung wird auf das Verfahren von Duda und Czachorski zurückgegriffen. Einerseits können Modelle, die auf einem zyklusfreien TPG beruhen, bewertet werden; andererseits ist dieser Ansatz aufgrund der Zurückführung auf Produktformnetze gut erweiterbar. Im Gegensatz dazu sind die anderen Verfahren weniger als Ausgangspunkt für weitere Betrachtungen geeignet. Das Verfahren von Kapelnikov bietet für Klasse-4-Modelle eine Approximation, bei der jedoch nur Schranken für die Programmausführungszeit bestimmt werden können. Es ist sehr fraglich, ob die somit erzielten Resultate aussagekräftig genug sind. Bei Thomasian und Bay fehlt die Möglickeit, den TPG zu zerlegen, um mit komplexeren Task-Systemen fertig zu werden. Daher ist dieser Ansatz kaum für diese Modelle zu verwenden. Gleiches läßt sich über den Ansatz von Balsamo und Donatiello sagen.

Die durchgeführte Analyse der wichtigsten Verfahren zur Analyse von parallelen Abläufen mit Methoden der Leistungsbewertung von Warteschlangennetzen hat ergeben, daß keines der bestehenden Verfahren die Anforderungen der Modelle der Klasse 4 befriedigend erfüllen konnte. Folgende Punkte beschreiben die wichtigsten Schwachstellen dieser Verfahren:

- es müssen Teilanfragen einbezogen werden, d.h. Anfragen, die auf beliebig viele Trader in einer Federation zugreifen,
- es müssen die durch das Aufkommen von Anfragen an alle Trader in einer Federation entstehende Lastabhängigkeiten berücksichtigt werden und
- unterschiedliche Bedienraten der Trader müssen modellierbar sein.

Manche Verfahren haben nicht alle diese Schwachstellen, zumindest eine, wobei der letze Schwachpunkt bei keinem der Verfahren der einizige ist.

Zunächst soll das Problem der Berücksichtigung von Anfragen an Teilmengen der Federation behandelt werden. Genauer betrachtet, besteht das Problem in der Sychronisation der Teilergebnisse, welche von den betreffenden Tradern der Federation zurückkommen. Eine Anfrage kann erst dann beantwortet werden, wenn alle Teilergebnisse vorhanden sind. Jedoch genügt es nicht, die minimale Bedienrate zu betrachten, da diese die größte Bearbeitungsdauer in einer parallelen Abarbeitung bedingt. Dieser Spezialfall gilt nur unter der Annahme leerer Warteschlangen.

Teilanfragen berücksichtigen
Sei n die Anzahl der Trader in einer Federation und k die Anzahl der Trader, die von einer Anfrage beansprucht werden. Dann gibt es $\binom{n}{k}$ Auswahlmöglichkeiten. Eine Summierung über alle Trader der Federation ergibt $\sum_{k=1}^{n} \binom{n}{k} = 2^n - 1$ möglichen Auftragskombinationen. Unter Berücksichtigung der Tatsache, daß Anfragen, die nur an einen Trader gestellt werden, nicht synchronisiert werden müssen, verringert sich die Anzahl auf $\sum_{k=1}^{n} \binom{n}{k} = 2^n - n - 1$.

Eine Möglichkeit der Reduzierung dieser Komplexität besteht darin, alle Anfragen, die mehr als eine bestimmte Anzahl s, beispielsweise s=n/2, aller Trader in Anspruch nehmen, so zu bewerten, als ob sie n Trader benötigen würden. Durch diese Approximation läßt sich eine obere Schranke für die mittlere Antwortzeit errechnen. Bewertet man diese Anfragen nicht als komplette Federation-Anfrage, sonderen als s-Trader-Anfragen, so ergibt sich analog eine untere Schranke für die mittlere Antwortzeit. Dieses Vorgehen ist jedoch nur sinnvoll, wenn die k-Trader-Anfragen für s<k<n selten auftreten. In diesem Fall wird der Abstand zwischen oberer und unterer Schranke sehr groß und die Aussagekraft der Ergebnisse sinkt.

Ein zweiter Ansatz teilt die Bedienraten μ_i in Mengen M_k, wobei alle μ_i sich in dieser Menge befinden, die von μ_k maximal um den Wert ε von μ_k unterscheiden.

$$M_k(\varepsilon) = \left\{\mu_i \mid i \in \{1,\ldots,n\} \text{ und } |\mu_k - \mu_i| \leq \varepsilon\right\}$$

Diese Klassifizierung ist im allgemeinen nicht eindeutig, da eine Bedienrate μ_i zu zwei unterschiedlichen Mengen gehören kann. Um das Ziel der Anzahlreduktion der Kombinationen zu erreichen, ist es jedoch notwendig, daß die Mengen M_k disjunkt sind. Sinnvollerweise sollte eine Bedienrate zu derjenigen Menge gehören, von deren Zentrum sie weniger weit entfernt ist. Durch die Wahl des Wertes ε kann das Verfahren adaptiv an die Variation der Bedienraten angepaßt werden. Sind die Schwankungen gering, so muß auch ε klein ausfallen, damit nicht nur eine Klasse entsteht. Andererseits kann die Anzahl der Klassen durch ε so bestimmt werden, daß ein gegebener Rechenaufwand erreicht wird.

Lastabhängigkeiten zwischen Tradern berücksichtigen
Der zweite Schwachpunkt des Duda-Czachorski-Verfahrens ist, daß Klasse-4-Modelle aufgrund der Abhängigkeit der Trader untereinander nicht analysiert werden können. Das im folgenden entwickelte Verfahren beruht auf der Idee, Klasse-4-Modelle auf FJNe zurückzuführen.

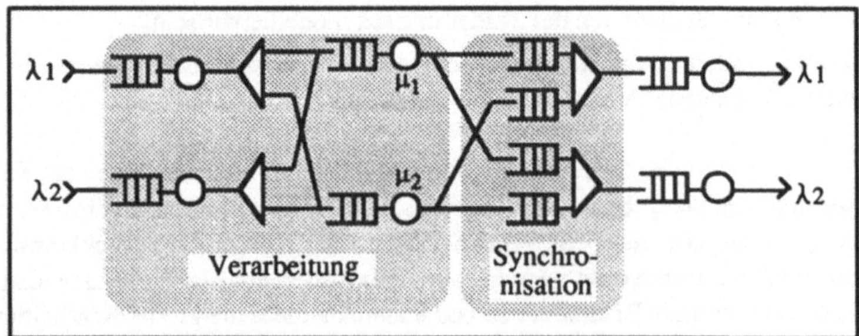

Abb. 7: Einteilung eines Klasse-4-Modells

Zunächst wird ein Klasse-4-Modell in zwei Teile gegliedert, siehe Abbildung 7 für n=2 Trader. Der Verarbeitungsteil beinhaltet alle Stationen bis einschließlich der parallel arbeitenden Stationen i mit Bedienrate μ_i, welche Trader-Anfragen auswerten, während die Join-Warteschlangen und die Join-Stationen den Synchronisationsteil bilden.

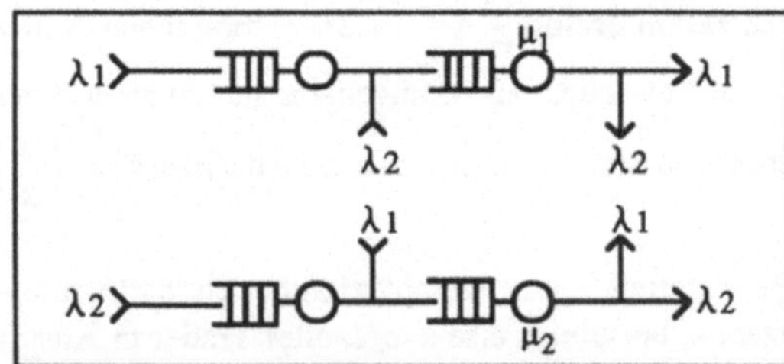

Abb. 8: Trennen des Klasse-4-Modells in zwei FJNe

Im folgenden wird nur der Verarbeitungsteil betrachtet. Diese getrennte Analyse ist nur deshalb möglich, da keine Rückflüsse im Klasse-4-Modell auftreten. Erster Schritt ist das Trennen der

Übergänge zwischen den Tradern, siehe Abbildung 8 für n=2 Trader. Die Ankunfts- beziehungsweise Abgangsraten λ_j errechnen sich aus dem Produkt von p_{ji} und der Ankunftsrate λ_j der Aufträge des Traders T_j. Hierbei stellt p_{ji} die Wahrscheinlichkeit dar, daß k-Trader-Anfragen an Trader T_j auch den Trader T_i betreffen. Auf die Fork-Station kann verzichtet werden, da jeder Trader isoliert betrachtet wird. Damit das System einen stabilen Zustand erreicht, muß folgende Bedingung erfüllt werden:

$$\mu_i = \sum_{j=1}^{n} \lambda_j \text{ mit } \lambda_i = p_{ji} * \lambda_i.$$

Da es sich bei der Bedienstationen i um M/M/1-Stationen handelt, kann die mittlere Antwortzeit $\bar{t}_i$ mittels der Formel

$$\bar{t}_i = \frac{\frac{1}{\mu_i}}{1 - \sigma} \text{ mit } \sigma = \frac{\sum_{j=1}^{n} \lambda_j}{\mu_i}$$

berechnet werden. Nun soll die neue Bedienrate μ_i der Station i berechnet werden, die jedoch nur noch λ_i als Ankunftsrate besitzt.

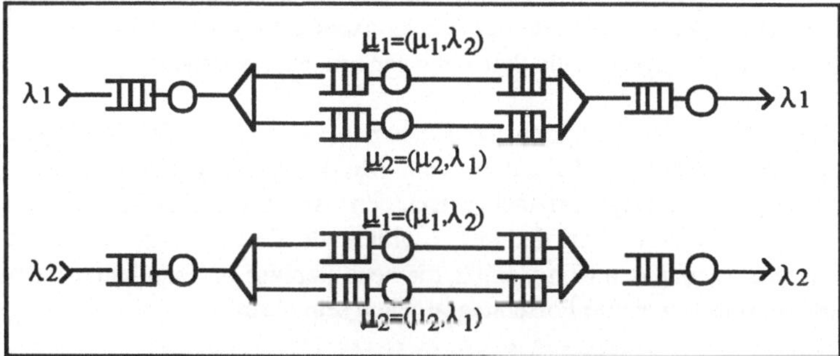

Abb. 9: Die beiden resultierenden FJNe

Mit Hilfe der eben berechneten mittleren Antwortzeit $\bar{t}_i$, der Ankunftsrate λ_i kann μ_i wie folgt berechnet werden:

$$\mu_i = \mu_i - \sum_{j \neq i} \lambda_j.$$

Mit Hilfe der neuen Bedienraten können nun n FJNe konstruiert werden, welche jeweils das Verhalten eines Traders beschreiben, siehe Abbilung 9 für n=2. Die Leistungsparamter der n FJNe können nachfolgend mit dem Algorithmus von Duda und Czachorski bestimmt werden.

5. Zusammenfassung und Ausblick

Im Rahmen von ODP entwickelte Architekturen verteilter Systeme besitzen ausschließlich den ODP-Trader als Kernstück. Die mittlere Anwortzeit soll mit einer Analyse von Warte-schlangennetzen bestimmt werden. Da klassische Verfahren hierfür nicht geeignet sind, wurden vier Ansätze untersucht, die diesem Ziel dienen. Der Ansatz von Duda und Czachorski wird als der günstige ausgewählt.

Zusammenfassend soll auf zwei Ergebnisse dieses Artikels noch einmal verwiesen werden: Zum einen wurde ein systematischer Vergleich existierender Ansätze nach von uns gewählten Kriterien durchgeführt, der eine Eignung der untersuchten Ansätze für den Kontext ODP ergab; zum anderen wurde die Erweiterung eines Ansatzes von Duda und Czachorski in drei verschiedenen Anforderungen vorgenommen.

Diese Erweiterung beseitigt Schwachstellen, in denen der Ansatz unseren Anforderungen nicht genügt. Im wesentlichen betrifft dies die Berücksichtigung von Anfragen, die sich nur auf einen Teil der Federation beziehen, die Einbeziehung des Aufkommens von Anfragen verschiedener Trader und das Betrachten unterschiedlicher Bedienraten. Diese unterschiedlichen Bedienraten ergeben sich daraus, daß sie umgekehrt proportional zum Umfang eines Trader-Directories sind. Durch die Organisationsstruktur des verteilten Systems bedingt, sind in der Realität stets Directories mit unterschiedlichem Umfang vorhanden.

Mit den durchgeführten Betrachtungen ist eine Basis zur Modellierung von ODP-Strukturen entstanden, die innerhalb des Open Distributed Processing von grundlegender Bedeutung für den praktischen Entwurf einer Systemarchitektur ist, wie sie beispielsweise in [HePo 93] und [PoHa 93] betrachtet wird. Aus Sicht der Leistungsbewertung ist die Möglichkeit gegeben, frühzeitig quantitative Analysen in die Betrachtungen mit einzubeziehen.

Die hier für ODP-Trader-Architekturen entwickelten vier Grundmodelle sollten auch für andere Architekturen im Kontext von ODP nutzbar sein. Mit der vorliegenden Arbeit sind zahlreiche Ideen für künftige Forschungsvorhaben entstanden. Allein der Ansatz zur Einteilung von Tradern in gewisse Typen und die dadurch resultierende Verringerung der zu betrachtenden Fälle führt zu einer reduzierten Komplexität, die neue Impulse für Parallelitätsuntersuchungen gibt und Ausgangspunkt weiterer Forschungsarbeiten sein wird.

Die geführten Betrachtungen sind Grundlage für Simulationsansätze. Dabei sollte zunächst von einer festen Anzahl von Tradern ausgegangen werden, wobei die Bedienraten der Trader und die Auftrittswahrscheinlichkeit der Auftragstypen variiert werden sollen. Einzelne Modifikationen der zugrundeliegenden Ansätze sind denkbar, so daß eine Bewertung der Ansätze an sich mit zum Ergebnis der Simulation gehören könnte.

Literatur

[BaDo 90]   Balsamo, S.; Donatiello, L.: Approximate Performance Analysis of Parallel Processing Systems. In: Proceedings of IFIP WG10.3 Working Conference on Decentralized Systems, Lyon 1989, North Holland 1990, 325-36

[Bo 89]   Bolch, G.: Leistungsbewertung von Rechensystemen. Teubner 1989

[DuCz 87]   Duda, A.; Czachorski, T.: Performance Evaluation of Fork and Join Synchronization Primitives. In: Acta Informatica 24 (1987), 525-53

[Du 87]   Duda, A.: Approximate Performance Analysis of Parallel Systems. In: Proceedings of 2nd International Workshop on Mathematics and Computer Performance and Reliabilty, North Holland 1987, 189-202

[Gei 92]   Geihs, K.: Object Request Broker. In: Praxis der Informationsverarbeitung und Kommunikation (PIK), 15 (1992) 4

[HePo 93] Hermanns, O.; Popien, C.: Modelling Heterogeneous CIM-Interfaces with ODP. Special Issue of Journal of Information Science and Technology on Applications of Open Distributed Systems, New York, July 1993

[Ka 87] Kapelnikov, A.: Analytic Modeling Methododlogy for Evaluating Performance of Distributed, Multiple-Computer Systems. UCLA, PhD Dissertation CSD-870061, November 1987

[Ki 90] King, P.: Computer and Communication System Performance Modelling. Prentice Hall, 1990

[Kl 84] Kleinrock, L.: On the Theory of Distributed Processing. In: Proceedings of the 22th Annual Allerton Conference on Communication, Control and Computers, University of Illinois, Monticello 1984, 60-70

[KME 87] Kapelnikov, A.; Muntz, R.; Ercegovac, M.: A Modeling Methodology for the Analysis of Concurrent Systems and Computations. UCLA, Technical Report CSD-870038, July 1987

[ODP P1] ISO/IEC JTC1/SC21 N7053: Basic Reference Model of Open Distributed Processing - Part 1: Overview and User Model, Jul. 1992

[ODP P2] ISO/IEC JTC1/SC21 N7524: CD Basic Reference Model of Open Distributed Processing - Part 2: Prescriptive Model, Nov. 1992

[ODP P3] ISO/IEC JTC1/SC21 N7525: CD Basic Reference Model of Open Distributed Processing - Part 3: Descriptive Model, Nov. 1992

[ODP P4] ISO/IEC JTC1/SC21 N7056: Working Draft for Basic Reference Model of Open Distributed Processing - Part 4: Architectural Semantics, Aug. 1992

[ODP Tr] ISO/IEC JTC1/SC21 N7047: Working Document on Topic 9.1 - ODP Trader, Jun. 1992

[Po 92] Popien, C.: System Design Trajectory based on Open Distributed Processing. In: Proceedings of International Zurich Seminar on Digital Communication. IEEE Catalogue No. 92TH0439-0, 315-31, Zürich, 1992

[PoHa 93] Popien, C.; Hager, R.: The ODP Trader Functionality Applied to the Integrated Road Transport Environment. Angenommen bei: IEEE Conference Globecom'93, Houston, Texas, Nov. 1993

[PoMe 93] Popien, C.; Meyer, B.: Federating ODP Traders: An X.500 Approach. In: Proceedings of IEEE International Conference on Communication (ICC'93), Conference Record 1/3, 313-7, Genf, 1993.

[Sch 92] Schill, A.: OSF/DCE. In: Informatik Spektrum, 15 (1992) 6

[ThBa 86] Thomasian, A.; Bay, P.: Analytic Queueing Network Models for Parallel Processing of Task Systems. In: IEEE Transactions on Computers, 35 (1986) 12, 1045-54

Bounds for Blocking and Deadlock
in Transaction Systems with Two-Phase Locking

Gerhard Haßlinger
Technische Hochschule Darmstadt
Institut für Theoretische Informatik
Frankfurter Str. 69A, 6100 Darmstadt

Abstract: The influence of data contention on the performance of database systems is increasing with the level of concurrency required for parallel processing. Besides simulation studies and measuring of a system, analytical models can help to estimate the effect of parameters and to optimize them in a multi-user environment. A transaction system using the strict two-phase locking protocol is considered, based on the assumption of independent renewal processes for the sequences of requests and transactions of each user. Simple upper bounds of the probabilities of blocking and deadlock situations are derived, including fixed or variable multiprogramming level, several transaction types with arbitrary distribution of size and arbitrary distribution of access to the data granules.

Keywords: Concurrency Control, Blocking, Deadlock, Database Thrashing, Renewal Processes

1. Introduction

A widely used mechanism of concurrency control and recovery for transactions in a database system relies on the strict two-phase locking protocol. In this scheme, transactions dynamically require locks for each accessed data granule and release them at the termination, thus providing serializability and the opportunity of isolated resets.

In contrary to static locking strategies, where all data required for a transaction is locked and thus must be known at the start, transactions with conflicting requests may run simultaneously. The number of active transactions in a dynamic locking scheme is reduced due to the effect of blocking, which causes a transaction to wait for the termination of another. In addition to temporary blocking, deadlocks arise corresponding to a cycle in the wait-for graph of blocked transactions. Deadlocks are observed to be rare in many cases [2, 4, 11], but also applications with critical deadlock rates are reported [12]. In any case, provision against deadlocks is necessary to guarantee permanent availability of the system.

We mention some methods of deadlock handling, that also avoid lifelock situations, which may arise by permanent cyclic resets of conflicting transactions [21, 22], and which are as intolerable as deadlocks:

- *deadlock detection* followed by the reset of the shortest transaction;
- *wound-wait:* if a request of transaction T_A is rejected by a lock, then the transaction that holds the lock is reset, if it is the younger one or else T_A waits in a blocked state;
- *wait-die:* if a request of transaction T_A is rejected by a lock, then T_A is blocked, if T_A is older than the transaction holding the lock or else T_A is reset.

Instead of *younger, shorter* any time invariant ordering relationship can be used among transactions to prevent lifelock. Studies of deadlock handling in systems with high data contention [3, 7] have shown that deadlock detection, which can be implemented at low cost [14], and the conflict rule wait-die outperform other alternatives.

Data contention may become a bottleneck of the performance in recently appearing requirements with increasing multiprogramming level, large transaction sizes or a high rate of conflict among individual requests e.g. in case of hot spot data. Database thrashing can be observed in extreme situations, when the mean number of active users decreases with a further increase of the multiprogramming level [10, 13, 18, 19, 20, 21]. Therefore methods have been suggested to avoid thrashing by dynamical control of the multiprogramming level [13], or control mechanism using analytical estimations [15], as well as alternative techniques e.g. virtual execution proposed in [10].

Besides many simulation studies concerning the performance of concurrency control in database systems, analytical approaches have been developed in the past decade [4, 7, 11, 16, 19, 20, 21].
Based on the concept of independent renewal processes for transactions and their requests, bounds can be derived for the blocking and deadlock rates, that clearly reflect the influence of the main parameters. The results of our approach, which are partly reported in [7], include variable transaction size, extending other models restricted to constant [11, 19] or geometrically distributed [4] size of transactions. Similar results are obtained in [20, 21] using approximations instead of the straightforward worst case analysis described in the sequel. As a further generalization, transactions of multiple classes are admissable with heterogeneous characteristics of their arrival processes and their access pattern on the data granules.

The analytical results are based on information about the mean transaction size and its distribution, the distribution of the requests among the data granules and their correlations for distinct transaction types of multi-class users. Accurate predictions of blocking and deadlock rates are possible at low data contention, while an increasing overestimation is observed in the near of the thrashing region. The results are pessimistic due to the worst case analysis and they indicate, whether the effects of thrashing or deadlocks on the performance are essential or neglegible.

The prepositions of the considered database model are stated in section 2, from which simplified bounds of blocking and deadlock rates are derived (section 3) and extended in several ways (section 4). The effect of indirect blocking is included in the more detailed analysis of section 5, followed by some comparisons of the results with simulation studies (section 6) and a conclusion.

2. Renewal Process Modelling of Transactions

In this section, assumptions about transactions and data requests are specified, which make an analysis of the blocking and deadlock rate feasible within a multi-user database employing a strict two-phase locking scheme.

(1) There are N users, who simultaneously share the database.

(2) The activity of each user is subdivided into transactions, each of which covers a sequence of coherent data requests. Transactions are assumed to follow each other immediately.
The random variable L denotes the number of requests of a transaction with an arbitrary distribution $p_L(i) = Pr\{L = i\}$ and the mean and higher moments

$E(L^k) = \sum_i i^k p_L(i)$. Each interrequest time S of consecutive requests of a user is described as a continuous time random variable with finite moments $E(S^k)$. The duration of a transaction is a sum of L interrequest times.

(3) The starting points of transactions and the instances of requests are furtheron viewed as independent renewal processes for each user, i.e.
   - successive interrequest times (S) are independent and identically distributed;
   - the sizes (L) of transactions are also i.i.d.;
   - activities of distinct users are assumed to be independent.

(4) Each request refers to a data granule, corresponding to a data item or a collection of items of the database. The conflict handling is based on a locking protocol, such that each request is connected with a lock on the referred data granule. A lock is held until the termination of the transaction. If another transaction requests a locked granule, then it is blocked and the user has to wait until the lock is released. The degree of multiprogramming is reduced below N, when users are inactive due to blocking.

(5) Let $\mathcal{M} = \{D_1, \cdots, D_M\}$ be the set of data granules. Then q_i denotes the probability that a request requires a granule D_i. The references to data items are again assumed to be independent even within the same transaction.

The interrequest time S may correspond to the access time to data from disk, cache or main memory or to the thinking time of interactive users. Extensions of the model are concerned with heterogeneous users (section 4.2) and with delays being inserted between the termination of a transaction and the start of the next, which may include completion and initialization procedures (section 4.3).

2.1 Conflict Rate of Independent Requests

From the supposition of fixed and independent probabilities of access to each data granule, we can conclude, that the probability of two distinct requests requiring the same granule is given by $q = \sum_k q_k^2$. This includes non-uniform references to data, e.g. hot-spot-data effects.

The *b-c-access* on a database of size M considered in [19] can be handled as a special case, where a request refers to a fraction of $c\,M$ granules with probability b and to the rest with probability $1 - b$ with a uniform access within each fraction, yielding

$$q = b^2 \frac{1}{c\,M} + (1-b)^2 \frac{1}{(1-c)\,M} = \frac{1}{M}\left(1 + \frac{(b-c)^2}{c\,(1-c)}\right) \qquad (0 < b, c < 1).$$

A uniform access over the entire database yields $q = 1/M$. In that case the probability of a conflict among independent requests is minimal within a database of M granules, since $\sum_{k=1}^{M} q_k = 1 \Rightarrow \sum_{k=1}^{M} q_k^2 \geq 1/M$. Therefore an almost uniform access should be intended as a design goal of the lock granularity.

2.2 Shared and Exclusive Locks

Another aspect with main influence on the conflict rate of competitive requests is the distinction between read- and write-locks. While several read-locks to a granule may be granted, the write-locks conflict with both read- and other write-locks.

If we assume the requests to be independently subdivided into read- and write-requests and if α denotes the fraction of read-requests, then the conflict rate is reduced by a factor $1 - \alpha^2$, since two requests to the same granule are permitted with probability α^2, when both want to read. The same result is obtained in [4,19] from more detailed database models. Different kinds of locks can be included in the *conflict rate* μ of requests, which is defined by

$$\mu = (1 - \alpha^2)\, q = (1 - \alpha^2) \sum_k q_k^2. \tag{2.1}$$

An interpretation is given in [19], viewing non-uniform *b-c*-access as a decrease and shared locks as an increase of the database size. Note, that the assumption of independence for the requests is not suitable, if e.g. the fraction of read-requests is higher at the beginning of a transaction than towards its end.

3. Blocking and Deadlocks among Two Competitive Users

This section is restricted to two users A and B working in parallel on the database, where deadlock situations initiated by a transaction T_A of user A in connection with transaction T_B of user B are considered. To initiate a deadlock, a transaction at first blocks a simultaneously running transaction and lateron requests a data item locked by the blocked transaction, thus causing a mutual blocking situation.

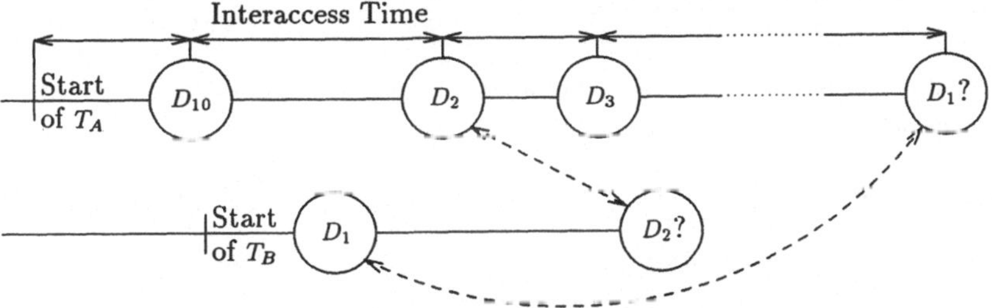

Fig. 3.1: Deadlock due to mutual Blocking

The following derivations of an upper bound of the probability p_D of a transaction causing a deadlock do not take into account reverse situations with user B as initiator, which may occur at the same frequency.

Let $p_C(i,j)$ denote the probability of user B being blocked between the i-th and j-th request of transaction T_A $(0 \le i < j)$, provided that B has been active at the instant of the i-th request of T_A.

Then $p_C(i, i+1)$ is determined by the number I of requests of user B within the i-th interaccess time of T_A, whose probability distribution is denoted by $p_I(j) = Pr\{I = j\}$, and by the probability of a request of user B conflicting with a previous request of transaction T_A. Since there are no more than i distinct data granules locked by T_A at that moment, the latter probability does not exceed $i\,\mu$. We can conclude:

$$1 - p_C(i,i+1) \ge \sum_j p_I(j)(1 - i\mu)^j \ge \sum_j p_I(j)(1 - j\,i\,\mu) = 1 - \sum_j p_I(j)\,j\,i\,\mu \quad \Rightarrow$$

$$p_C(i,i+1) \le i\,\mu \sum_j j\,p_I(j) = i\,\mu\,E(I) \quad (\forall x \in \mathbb{R}_0^+, j \in \mathbb{N}_0 : (1-x)^j \ge 1 - x\,j). \tag{3.1}$$

Furtheron, $E(I) = 1$ follows for independent users with the same mean interrequest times. Simple upper bounds are then obtained for the probabilities of user B being blocked by T_A until the i-th request of T_A ($p_C(0,i)$) or in the total course of T_A (p_C):

$$p_C(0,i) \le \sum_{j=0}^{i-1} p_C(j,j+1) \le \sum_{j=0}^{i-1} j\,\mu = \mu\,i\,(i-1)/2;$$

$$p_C = \sum_i p_L(i)\,p_C(0,i) \le \mu\left(E(L^2) - E(L)\right)/2. \tag{3.2}$$

When another transaction T_B is blocked by T_A, subsequent requests of T_A may cause a deadlock. Then the frequency of deadlock situations mainly depends on the number of locks held by T_B, which does not exceed the number R of requests of T_B prior to blocking.

If T_B comprises k data accesses and if the transactions of users A and B are assumed to be independent renewal processes, then the number R is uniformly distributed in $\{0, \cdots, k-1\}$ with mean $(k-1)/2$. Considering an arbitrary distribution for the size of T_B, we obtain $k\,p_L(k)/\sum_k k\,p_L(k)$ as the probability, that a blocked transaction T_B has size k [9]. The mean number $E(R)$ of requests of a transaction before entering a blocked state is given by

$$E(R) = \frac{\sum_k k\,p_L(k)E(R\,|\,L=k)}{\sum_k k\,p_L(k)} = \frac{\sum_k (k-1)\,k\,p_L(k)}{2\sum_k k\,p_L(k)} = \frac{E(L^2) - E(L)}{2\,E(L)}. \tag{3.3}$$

Now we can bound the probability $p_D(i)$ of a transaction evoking a deadlock by its i-th request as follows:

$$p_D(i) \le p_C(0,i)\sum_j Pr\{R=j\}\,j\,\mu = \mu\,p_C(0,i)\,E(R) = \frac{\mu^2\left(E(L^2) - E(L)\right)i\,(i-1)}{4\,E(L)} \tag{3.4}$$

Finally we are able to give an upper bound of the probability p_D, that a transaction causes a deadlock by any of its requests:

$$p_D \le \sum_j p_L(j)\sum_{i=1}^{j} p_D(i) \le \sum_j p_L(j)\sum_{i=1}^{j} \frac{\mu^2\left(E(L^2) - E(L)\right)i\,(i-1)}{4\,E(L)}$$

$$p_D \le \frac{\mu^2\left(E(L^2) - E(L)\right)}{4\,E(L)}\sum_j p_L(j)\frac{j^3 - j}{3} = \frac{\mu^2\left(E(L^2) - E(L)\right)\left(E(L^3) - E(L)\right)}{12\,E(L)} \tag{3.5}$$

Note, that the result depends on the first three moments of the size L of the transactions, but not on the distribution of the interrequest times S.

3.1 Two Users of Different Types

The results can be extended in an obvious way, when the statistics of the transaction size and the behaviour of requests differ for each user, provided that the assumption of independent renewal sequences is still valid for the starts of transactions and for their requests.

Random variables L and S are assigned with indices A and B refering to the users. The mean number of requests of user B within an interrequest interval of user A now is given by $E(I) = E(S_A)/E(S_B)$. We can conclude:

$$p_C(0,i) \le \mu \frac{E(S_A)}{E(S_B)} \frac{i\,(i-1)}{2};$$

$$p_C \le \mu \frac{E(S_A)}{E(S_B)} \frac{\left(E(L_A^2) - E(L_A)\right)}{2};$$

$$p_D(i) \le p_C(0,i) \frac{E(L_B^2) - E(L_B)}{2E(L_B)};$$

$$p_D \le \mu^2 \frac{E(S_A)}{E(S_B)} \frac{\left(E(L_B^2) - E(L_B)\right)}{12\,E(L_B)} \left(E(L_A^3) - E(L_A)\right).$$

$$(3.6)$$

4. Deadlock Cycles of Length 2 in a Multi-User Environment

When N users are simultaneously requiring access to the database, deadlock situations are possible with $i = 2, \cdots, N$ users involved, each of them waiting for a locked granule and himself blocking another user in reverse. An extension of the upper bounds (3.5) is straightforward, when only deadlocks between two users are considered. The analysis of section 5 also includes arbitrary length cycles.

Simulation and empirical observations indicate [11], that deadlock cycles are almost always of length 2, when at the same time deadlocks are rare. This result is also confirmed by the model, since a deadlock cycle of length i is set up by i conflicting pairs of requests. In that case the corresponding probability includes μ^i as a factor, which makes cycles of length $i > 2$ rare at a low conflict rate μ.

Assuming independent renewal processes for transactions and requests of distinct users with i.i.d. size of transactions and i.i.d. interaccess times, we again have $E(I) = 1$ for the mean number of requests of a user within the interaccess time of another, even if both users may be temporary blocked by other users.

Then we obtain bounds of the mean number $\overline{n}$ of transactions, which are directly blocked within the course of a single transaction, and of the probability p_{D_2} of a transaction causing a deadlock with one of the remaining $N - 1$ users being involved:

$$\overline{n} = p_C\,(N-1) \le \mu\,(N-1)\,(E(L^2) - E(L))/2;$$

$$p_{D_2} \le \mu^2\,(N-1)\,\frac{(E(L^2) - E(L))\,(E(L^3) - E(L))}{12\,E(L)}.$$

$$(4.1)$$

Similar formulae are derived by approximations in [21].

4.1 Influence of the Distribution of Transaction Size

The result (4.1) can be compared to other known results in case of a constant or geometrically distributed number of data accesses within each transaction.
For a constant transaction size, we obtain from $E(L^i) = E(L)^i$:

$$p_{D_2}^{const.} \le \mu^2\,(N-1)\,E(L)\,(E(L) - 1)\,(E(L)^2 - 1))/12.$$

Approximation formulae for that case are given in [11] and [19] with uniform access to M data granules $(\mu = 1/M)$. Both are similar to the upper bound of p_{D_2}, but for large

$E(L)$ they even exceed the bound by a factor 3 and 4/3 respectively:

$$p_{D_2}^{const.} \approx \frac{(N-1)\,E(L)^4}{4\,M^2} \quad \text{and} \quad p_{D_2}^{const.} \approx \frac{N\,E(L)^2\,(E(L)-1)\,(E(L)^2-1)}{9\,M^2\,(E(L)+\frac{1}{2})}.$$

Considering a geometrically distributed transaction size $p_L(i) = (1-p)\,p^i$ $(0 < p < 1)$, the higher moments and the upper bound are given by:

$$E(L^2) = 2\,E(L)^2 + E(L); \quad E(L^3) = 6\,E(L)^3 + 6\,E(L)^2 + E(L) \quad \Rightarrow$$
$$p_{D_2}^{geom.} \le \mu^2\,(N-1)\,E(L)^3\,(E(L)+1).$$

Again the result is similar to an approximation [4]: $p_{D_2}^{geom.} \approx (1/M)^2\,(N-1)\,E(L)^4$.

Comparing both cases, an essential influence of the distribution of the transaction size on the deadlock probability is apparent. The upper bounds of constant and geometrical distribution differ by a factor > 12 with the same mean $E(L)$.

4.2 Heterogeneous Users

Considering heterogeneous users, we denote by L_i, S_i random variables belonging to user i, furtheron the mean number $\overline{n}_i$ of transactions being blocked by user i in the course of one of his transactions, and the probability $p_{D_2,i}$ of a transaction of user i causing a deadlock. Let $\mu_{ij}(= \mu_{ji})$ define the conflict rate of a pair of requests of user i and j respectively $(1 \le i,j \le N)$. Then an extension of $\langle 4.1 \rangle$ can be given for user i causing blocking situations and deadlock cycles of length 2:

$$\overline{n}_i \le \sum_{\substack{j=1 \\ j \ne i}}^{N} \frac{\mu_{ij}}{2}\,\frac{E(S_i)}{E(S_j)}\,\left(E(L_i^2) - E(L_i)\right)$$

$$p_{D_2,i} \le \sum_{\substack{j=1 \\ j \ne i}}^{N} \frac{\mu_{ij}^2}{12}\,\frac{E(S_i)}{E(S_j)}\,\frac{\left(E(L_j^2) - E(L_j)\right)}{E(L_j)}\,\left(E(L_i^3) - E(L_i)\right). \tag{4.2}$$

The results can be applied to a mixture of several types of users sharing the database system, when at least partial information is available about the decisive parameters of their interaction. For those users, who demand read-locks only or who work on distinct subsets of granules, the conflict rate is $\mu_{ij} = 0$, while a high rate of conflict is expected among users, who share a small subset of data granules. If $q_{k,i}$ denotes the probability, that a request of user i refers to granule k and α_i denotes the fraction of read requests of user i, then we obtain:

$$\mu_{ij} = (1 - \alpha_i)(1 - \alpha_j)\sum_k q_{k,i}\,q_{k,j}. \tag{4.3}$$

Finally, we are able to bound the overall rates γ_C and γ_{D_2}, at which blocking and deadlock situations are expected to occur per unit of time:

$$\gamma_C \le \sum_{i=1}^{N} \overline{n}_i \Big/ \left(E(L_i)\,E(S_i)\right); \qquad \gamma_{D_2} \le \sum_{i=1}^{N} p_{D_2,i} \Big/ \left(E(L_i)\,E(S_i)\right). \tag{4.4}$$

Considering some special alternative of conflict rule or deadlock handling with information available about the duration of blocking situations and the losses of transaction resets, we may continue the analysis to estimate the overall performance reduction.

4.3 Users with Vacations

As a further extension of the model, we drop the assumption that each user produces an uninterrupted sequence of transactions. Instead we assume a vacation being inserted after each transaction with i.i.d. duration S^* with mean $E(S^*)$, preserving the renewal nature of the sequences of transactions of each user.

A vacation may include actions necessary to terminate a transaction and to initiate another. The degree of multiprogramming is reduced due to vacations in the range from 0 to N with mean κN, where

$$\kappa = E(L) E(S)/\big(E(L) E(S) + E(S^*)\big) \tag{4.5}$$

denotes the fraction of time a user is busy running transactions.
The mean number of requests $E(I)$ of a user within an interaccess time of another user is then reduced by the factor κ and the bounds (4.1) of blocking and deadlock probabilities are reduced by the same factor, according to their linear relationship with regard to the number of competitive users.

5. Indirect Blocking and Database Thrashing

The bound of p_{D_2} (see (4.1)) includes mutual blocking between no more than two users, although at a less degree, deadlock cycles of length $i > 2$ arise with increasing data contention. Indirect blocking must be taken into account to examine database thrashing at high data contention.
In order to model database thrashing, we consider blocking situations in the course of a transaction T_A, assuming homogeneous users without vacations. In the sequel, $\mathcal{B}_{T_A}$ denotes the set of users, who are inactive until the termination of T_A because of direct or indirect blocking. $E(|\mathcal{B}|)$ denotes the mean size of $\mathcal{B}_{T_A}$ at an arbitrary access time of T_A.
Since the set of transactions can be partitioned at any time into subsets, each containing an active transaction accompanied by all transactions, which are directly or indirectly blocked by it, we obtain

$$\overline{N}_{act} \left(1 + E(|\mathcal{B}|)\right) \geq N, \tag{5.1}$$

where $\overline{N}_{act}$ denotes the mean number of active transactions. We use the fact, that the mean size $E(|\mathcal{B}|)$ observed at the end of an arbitrary interaccess interval serves as an upper bound of the mean size of $\mathcal{B}_{T_A}$ at an arbitrary point in time.
The fraction $\overline{N}_{act}/N$ is a measure of the performance reduction due to data contention. When $\overline{N}_{act}$ decreases with an upgrading multiprogramming level N, database thrashing is indicated.

Let $\overline{n}(i)$ denote the mean size of the set $\mathcal{B}_{T_A}$ at the instant of the i-th access of T_A and let $p_B(i)$ denote the probability of a transaction joining the set $\mathcal{B}_{T_A}$ in the course of the interaccess time following the i-th access of T_A. The mean number of locks held by T_A and the members of $\mathcal{B}_{T_A}$ is upper bounded by $i + \overline{n}(i + 1) E(R)$ within the considered interaccess time, where the mean number $E(R)$ of locks held by a blocked transaction is again given by (3.3).

Note, that the probability of another transaction joining the set $\mathcal{B}_{T_A}$ does not depend on whether this transaction is blocked or active, since an active transaction joins the set $\mathcal{B}_{T_A}$ together with all transactions, that are blocked by it. We can conclude:

$$p_B(i) \le \left(i + \overline{n}(i+1)\, E(R)\right) \mu\, E(I);$$
$$\overline{n}(i+1) \le \overline{n}(i) + (N-1)\, p_B(i); \qquad (\overline{n}(0) = 0). \tag{5.2}$$

Since the mean interaccess time of each transaction is prolonged by a factor $N/\overline{N}_{act}$, we obtain $E(I) = N/\overline{N}_{act}$ as the mean number of requests of an active transaction within an interrequest time of T_A, which may include blocked periods. Then an iterative scheme is obtained for $\overline{n}(i)$:

$$\overline{n}(i+1) \le \overline{n}(i) + \rho\left(i/E(R) + \overline{n}(i+1)\right) \quad \text{with } \rho \stackrel{\text{def}}{=} E(R)\,\mu\,(N-1)\,N/\overline{N}_{act} \quad \Rightarrow$$
$$\overline{n}(i+1) \le \frac{1}{1-\rho}\,\overline{n}(i) + \frac{\rho}{(1-\rho)\,E(R)}\,i \qquad \text{if } \rho < 1. \tag{5.3}$$

The iterative relationship can be converted to a direct bound of $\overline{n}(i)$:

$$\overline{n}(i) \le \frac{1-\rho}{E(R)\,\rho}\left((1-\rho)^{-i} - 1\right) - \frac{i}{E(R)}. \tag{5.4}$$

Figure 5.1 demonstrates the increase in the mean size $\overline{n}(i)$ of the set $\mathcal{B}_{T_A}$ of users, who are directly or indirectly blocked by transaction T_A in its course, considering an example of constant transaction size ($L = 16, N = 70, \mu = 8.06 \cdot 10^{-5}$) near the database thrashing region.

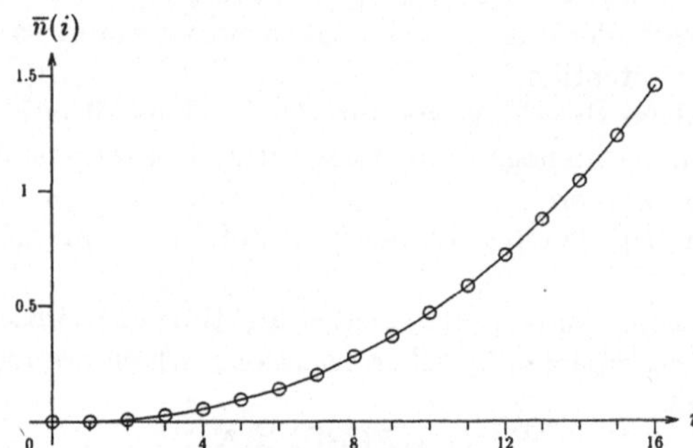

Fig. 5.1: Increase of blocking in the course of a transaction

That leads to a bound of the mean size $\overline{n}_A$ of the set $\mathcal{B}_{T_A}$ at the termination of T_A, considering the probability distribution $p_L(i)$ of the number of requests of T_A with generating function $G_L(z) = \sum_i p_L(i)\, z^i$:

$$\overline{n}_A = \sum_i p_L(i)\,\overline{n}(i) \le \frac{1-\rho}{E(R)\,\rho}\left(G_L(\frac{1}{1-\rho}) - 1\right) - \frac{E(L)}{E(R)} \tag{5.5}$$

Now we can also estimate the mean $E(|\mathcal{B}|)$ at the instant of an arbitrary access of transaction T_A, which also serves as an upper bound of the mean size of $\mathcal{B}_{T_A}$ at an arbitrary point of time:

$$E(|\mathcal{B}|) \leq \frac{\sum_i p_L(i) \sum_{j=1}^{i} \overline{n}(j)}{\sum_i p_L(i) i} = \frac{1}{E(L) E(R)} \sum_i p_L(i) \sum_{j=1}^{i} \frac{1-\rho}{\rho} \left((1-\rho)^j - 1 \right) - j$$

$$E(|\mathcal{B}|) \leq \frac{1}{E(L) E(R)} \sum_i p_L(i) \left(\frac{1-\rho}{\rho^2} \left((\frac{1}{1-\rho})^i - 1 \right) - \frac{i}{\rho} - \frac{i(i-1)}{2} \right)$$

$$E(|\mathcal{B}|) \leq \frac{1}{E(R)} \left(\frac{1-\rho}{E(L)\rho^2} \left(G_L(\frac{1}{1-\rho}) - 1 \right) - \frac{1}{\rho} \right) - 1. \tag{5.6}$$

Combining the results $\langle 5.1 \rangle$, $\langle 5.6 \rangle$ and the definition of ρ (see $\langle 5.3 \rangle$), we can conclude:

$$1 + E(|\mathcal{B}|) \geq \frac{N}{\overline{N}_{act}} = \frac{\rho}{(N-1)\mu E(R)} \quad \Rightarrow$$

$$\rho^2 \leq (N-1)\mu \left(\frac{1-\rho}{E(L)\rho} \left(G_L(\frac{1}{1-\rho}) - 1 \right) - 1 \right) \stackrel{\text{def}}{=} f(\rho). \tag{5.7}$$

Then an upper bound $\rho_{max} \geq \rho$ can be found, if

$$\exists \, \rho_{max} \in (0,1): \; \rho_{max}^2 = f(\rho_{max}) \quad \text{and} \quad \forall x \in (0,\rho_{max}): \; x^2 < f(x). \tag{5.8}$$

The upper bound of ρ in turn leads to a lower bound

$$\overline{N}_{act} \geq E(R)\mu(N-1)N/\rho_{max} \tag{5.9}$$

of the mean number of non-blocked users by definition of ρ. Finally, we obtain an upper bound of the probability p_D, that a transaction completes a deadlock cycle:

$$p_D \leq \sum_i p_L(i) \sum_{j-1}^{i} \overline{n}(j) E(R) \mu \leq \mu \sum_i p_L(i) \sum_{j=1}^{i} \frac{1-\rho}{\rho} \left((\frac{1}{1-\rho})^j - 1 \right) - j \tag{5.10}$$

$$\leq \mu \left(\frac{1}{\rho^2} \left(G_L(\frac{1}{1-\rho}) - 1 \right) - \frac{1}{2} E(L^2) + \left(\frac{1}{2} - \frac{1}{\rho} \right) E(L) \right).$$

The bounds $\langle 5.5 \rangle$ and $\langle 5.10 \rangle$ can be simplified, when ρ is replaced by ρ_{max} satisfying the condition $\rho_{max}^2 = f(\rho_{max})$:

$$\overline{n}_A \leq \frac{2 E(L)^2}{E(L^2) - E(L)} \frac{\rho_{max}^2}{(N-1)\mu} \quad \text{and}$$

$$p_D \leq \frac{E(L)\rho_{max}}{N-1} - \frac{(E(L^2) - E(L))\mu}{2}. \tag{5.11}$$

In both examples of geometrically distributed and constant transaction size, an upper bound ρ_{max} can be determined. In the former case $G_L(z) = (1-p)/(1-pz)$ holds with $E(L) = p/(1-p)$, yielding

$$\rho_{max} = \frac{1 - \sqrt{1 - 4(N-1)\mu E(L)(E(L)+1)}}{2(E(L)+1)}. \tag{5.12}$$

If the transaction size is constant, $G_L(z) = z^k$ holds with $E(L) = k$. Then ρ_{max} is the smallest positive solution to

$$\frac{k \rho_{max}^3}{(N-1)\mu} = (1 - \rho_{max})^{1-k} - 1 + (1-k)\rho_{max}. \tag{5.13}$$

6. Validation

Comparing the upper bounds of blocking and deadlock rates with simulation studies, the bounds are observed to be asymptotically tight at low data contention [7]. Direct simulation with very small deadlock rates can be extremly time consuming due to the rareness of measured events.

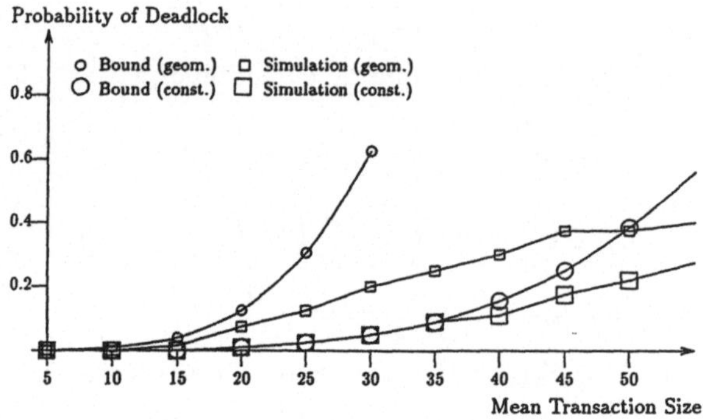

Fig. 6.1: Deadlock Rate

In figure 6.1, the fast growth of the deadlock rate with increasing transaction size is illustrated. The bound (4.1) of p_{D_2} is compared with simulation results in the case of constant or geometrically distributed transaction size. The simulations were carried out on a file server system at a low degree of multiprogramming ($N \leq 10$), but with complex transactions.

Analysis and simulation results are in good agreement, unless the bound of p_{D_2} exceeds 0.05. In the latter case, blocking and deadlocks lead to a non neglegible reduction of the performance, while the bound overestimates that effect at the same time.

The simulation performs deadlock detection followed by the reset of the shortest transaction involved, which is ignored in the analysis. An examination of the strategies wound-wait and wait-die, which avoid deadlocks by selective blocking and resets of transactions, must take into account the modified blocking behaviour.

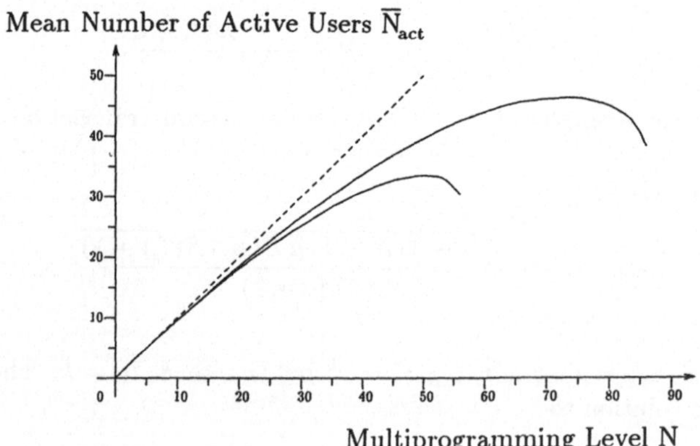

Fig. 6.2: Database Thrashing

Furtheron the bounds of the thrashing effect derived in section 5 are contrastet to simulations of a system at a high multiprogramming level. We refer to results presented in [10], where standard two-phase locking is compared to a virtual execution approach of concurrency control. Simulation studies of an example of standard two-phase locking with b-c-access ($b = 0.25$; $c = 1/32$) on $M = 32000$ data items ($\Rightarrow$ $\mu \approx 8.06 \cdot 10^{-5}$, see section 2.1) and transactions of fixed size $L = 16$ are reported to be subjected to thrashing at a multiprogramming level in the range $60 \leq N \leq 70$.
Figure 6.2 shows the bound of the mean number of active users $\overline{N}_{act}$ depending on the multiprogramming level N for a fixed transaction size $L = 16$ (upper curve) and for geometrically distributed size with $E(L) = 7$ (lower curve). The prediction of the thrashing area is in accordance with simulation, whereas $\overline{N}_{act}$ is underestimated in $\langle 5.9 \rangle$. If N exceeds a limit beyond the thrashing region, the bound is no longer applicable, since no solution $\rho_{max} \in (0,1)$ can be found satisfying $\langle 5.8 \rangle$. In the example of fixed size transactions, the limit is $N = 86$ and in the case of geometrically distributed size $N = 56$. A similar cusp catastrophe effect is reported in [20], following a different analysis. It is apparent, that this effect is partly due to the inaccuracy of the analysis, but it also corresponds to an increased instability of the database performance.

Conclusion

Based on the assumption of independent renewal processes for the transactions in a database with standard two-phase locking, simple upper bounds are derived for the probability of blocking and deadlock. When only direct blocking is considered, the result $\langle 4.1 \rangle$ confirms, that the probability of deadlock depends on the first three moments of the distribution of the transaction size and increases approximately
- linear with the multiprogramming level N,
- quadratic with the rate of conflict μ and
- by $E(L)^4$ with the mean transaction size $E(L)$, if the type of the distribution $p_L(i)$ remains unchanged e.g. constant or geometrical.

Making use of straightforward generalizations, heterogeneous users with distinct access pattern and arrival processes are included.
If indirect blocking situations are also taken into account, bounds are developed depending on the complete generating function of the distribution of the transaction size. A lower bound is given for the fraction $\overline{N}_{act}/N$ of active transactions as the performance measure of main interest.

Comparing the worst case analysis to simulation, good agreement is observed for low data contention, whereas an increasing overestimation of the performance losses versus underestimation of the reduced degree of parallelism occures near the thrashing region of the system. The results allow a useful estimation of the thrashing point, although they are not applicable, if the multiprogramming level exceeds a limit close beyond.

References

[1] Agrawal D., El Abbadi A. and Jeffers R.: An approach to eliminate transaction blocking in locking protocols, *Proceedings of the 11th International ACM Conference on Principles of Database Systems*, pp. 223-235, 1992

[2] Agrawal R., Carey M. and Livny M.: Concurrency control performance models: alternatives and implications, *ACM Trans. on Database Systems 12*, pp. 609-654, 1987

[3] Agrawal R., Carey M. and McVoy L.: The performance of alternative strategies for dealing with deadlocks in database management systems, *IEEE Trans. on Software Engineering SE-13*, pp. 1348-1363, 1987

[4] Becker A.: Leistungseinbußen in einem DB-System mit Zwei-Phasen Sperrprotokoll, *Informatik Fachbericht IFB 110 zur MMB-Tagung*, Springer, pp. 217-232, 1985

[5] Bernstein P., Hadzilacos V. and Goodman N.: *Concurrency Control and Recovery in Database Systems*, Addison-Wesley, 1987

[6] Bohn V., Härder T. and Rahm E.: Extended Memory Support for High Performance Transaction Systems, *Proc. of the MMB-Conference, Informatik Fachbericht IFB 286,* , Springer, pp. 92-108, 1991

[7] Breitenbach C., Hasslinger G. and Herold P.: Deadlocks in einem verteilten System mit zentraler Datenhaltung: Vergleich von Auflösungsstrategien und Abschätzung der Deadlockrate, *Informatik Fachbericht IFB 267 zur Tagung Kommunikation in verteilten Systemen*, Springer, pp. 320-334, 1991

[8] Dan A., Towsley F. and Kohler W.: Modeling the effects of data and resource contention on the performance of optimistic concurrency control protocols, *Proceedings of the 5th International IEEE Conference on Data Engineering*, pp. 418-425, 1988

[9] Feller W.: *An introduction to probability theory and its applications*, John Wiley, 1957

[10] Franaszek P., Robinson J. and Thomasian A.: Access invariance and its use in high contention environments, *Proceedings of the 7th International IEEE Conference on Data Engineering*, pp. 47-55, 1990

[11] Gray J., Homan P., Obermarck R. and Korth H.: A straw man analysis of the probability of waiting and deadlock in a database system, *Technical Report RJ 3066*, IBM Research Lab., San Jose, California, 1981

[12] Hartzman C.: The delay due to dynamic two-phase locking, *IEEE Trans. on Software Engineering SE-15*, pp. 72-82, 1989

[13] Heiss U. and Wagner R.: Adaptive load control in transaction processing systems, *Proceedings of the 17th International Conference on Very Large Data Bases*, pp. 47-54, 1991

[14] Jiang B.: Deadlock detection is really cheap, *ACM Sigmod Record 17*, pp. 2-13, 1988

[15] Moenkeberg A. and Weikum G.: Conflict-driven load control for the avoidance of data-contention thrashing, *Proceedings of the 8th International IEEE Conference on Data Engineering*, pp. 632-639, 1991

[16] Ryu I. and Thomasian A.: Analysis of database performance with dynamic locking, *Journal of the ACM, Vol. 37*, pp. 491-523, 1990

[17] Shum A. and Spirakis P.: Performance analysis of concurrency control methods in database systems, *Performance '81*, F. Kylstra Ed., Elsevier North-Holland pp. 1-18, 1981

[18] Tay Y.: Issues in modeling locking performance, *Stochastic Analysis of Computer and Communication Systems*, H. Takagi Ed., Elsevier North-Holland pp. 631-655, 1990

[19] Tay Y., Goodman N. and Suri R.: Locking performance in centralized databases, *ACM Trans. on Database Systems 10*, pp. 415-462, 1985

[20] Thomasian A.: Performance limits of two-phase locking, *Proceedings of the 7th International IEEE Conference on Data Engineering*, pp. 426-435, 1991

[21] Thomasian A. and Ryu I.: Performance analysis of two-phase locking, *IEEE Trans. on Software Engineering SE-17*, pp. 386-402, 1991

[22] Weikum G.: *Transaktionen in Datenbanken*, Addison-Wesley, 1988

[23] Wang P. and Li O.: A unified concurrency control algorithm for distributed database systems, *Proceedings of the 5th International IEEE Conference on Data Engineering*, pp. 410-417, 1988

Estimating Parameters of Cox Distributions

Manfred Kramer[*]

Abstract: An algorithm for the least square approximation of an empirical distribution function by a Coxian distribution function is developed. We derive a representation of the Cox distribution function in terms of divided differences of the exponential. The parameters of the distribution are subject to simple ordering constraints. We propose a variant of gradient minimization to solve the nonlinear programming problem and illustrate the method by a numerical example.

Keywords: Parameter estimation, Cox distribution, Least square approximation, Divided differences, Constrained minimization

0. Introduction

This paper deals with the approximation of empirical distributions by Cox distributions. These distributions have a rational Laplace transform.

Many analytic or numerical solution methods for queueing networks, especially for networks covered by the BCMP theorem, exploit this property [2, p.74]. In stochastic simulation it is also often more appropriate to use the compact representation provided by a continuous Cox distribution than to work with discrete histograms.

Several approaches to estimate parameters of the Coxian distribution are reported in the literature. There are methods to estimate moments and distributions under the additional restriction of uniform phase completion rates [3]. An elaborate procedure based on mixtures of Erlangian distributions, reducible to Coxian distributions after optimization, was presented in [10].

It was pointed out that by allowing distinct or repeated delay parameters accurate approximations with fewer stages can be expected than with homogeneous Coxian distributions [6]. Although outlined as a research problem, no direct estimation

---

[*] Current address: Dr. M. Kramer, AEG Electrocom, Konstanz, Germany

method without restrictions on the parameters involved seems to be known up to date.

Similar difficulties are reported from attempts to approximate by mixtures of exponential distributions. The extreme sensitivity of exponential sums in fitting data has been noticed in [11]. Divided differences as a remedy of these computational difficulties have been proposed in [5].

Our approach starts with a general representation of the Coxian complementary distribution function in terms of divided differences of the exponential function. In Appendix A the most important relationships concerning divided differences are listed for ease of reference.

The quality of the approximation is measured by the mean squared difference between the empirical and the approximating distribution. The first few moments are taken into account by adding a penalty term. Closed form expressions of the total error and of its first order partial derivatives with respect to the unknown parameters are derived.

The mean squared residual can be represented as a positive definite quadratic form. All parameters are subject to simple ordering constraints.

Minimization subject to such constraints is possible by an algorithm which is only a slight modification of the steepest descent method for unconstrained minimization [1]. We illustrate the method by a numerical example.

1. The Cox Distribution

The class of Çox distributions is dense in the set of probability distributions on $\mathbb{R}_+$ with rational Laplace transforms [2, Theorem 6.2]. We derive first a closed form expression for the complementary distribution function .

Let us consider the pure birth process $\{Z(t),\ t>0\}$ with transition epochs X_k, $k = 1, 2, \ldots$, starting at $X_0 = 0$ in state 1. Let $\nu_k > 0$ be the transition intensitiy in state k. The state probabilities $F_k(t;\nu) = P\{Z(t) = k\}$ satisfy the following first-order differential equations

$$\frac{\partial}{\partial t} F_k(t;\nu) = -\nu_k F_k(t;\nu) + \nu_{k-1} F_{k-1}(t;\nu), \quad t > 0, \quad k = 1, 2, .,.. \tag{1.1}$$

subject to the initial condition $F_k(0;\nu) = \delta_{k,1}$.

Let us generally write $F(t;x) = \exp(-xt)$ and apply the divided difference operator $\Delta_x[\nu_1,\ldots,\nu_k]$ on both sides of the functional equation

$$\frac{\partial}{\partial t} F(t;x) = -x F(t;x). \tag{1.2}$$

(see Appendix A for the definition of the operator). Using identity (A.6) in rewriting the right hand side it is not difficult to check that the solution of system (1.1) admits the following representation

$$F_k(t;\nu) = \Delta_x[\nu_1,\ldots,\nu_k] F(t;x) \quad, \quad t > 0, \tag{1.3}$$

Divided differences of the exponential are easily computed even for confluent arguments, since derivatives of any order are available.

Obviously, the functions $F_k(t;\nu)$ are linearly independent. Let $\nu = (\nu_1,\ldots,\nu_K)$ be the vector composed of the first K transition intensities. Let us also introduce the K-vector $F(t;\nu)$ with components $F_k(l;\nu)$ according to the notation of Appendix A.

Assume the process is stopped after M transitions, but in any case after K transitions. The stopping time X_M is then distributed by a Coxian distribution. This definition is obviously equivalent to the original defintion formulated in terms of branching probalilities and Laplace transforms [2].

The events $\{Z(t)=k\}$ and $\{X_{k-1} \le t < X_k\}$ are equivalent. Let α_k be the probability $P\{M \ge k\}$ and define the K-vector $\alpha = (\alpha_1,\ldots,\alpha_K)$. Thus writing $F(t;\alpha,\nu)$ for the complementary distribution function, or in other words, for the survival function $P\{X_M > t\}$, we have by the law of total probability

$$F(t;\alpha,\nu) = \alpha^T F(t;\nu). \tag{1.4}$$

Thus the survival, and equivalently, the distribution function is completely determined by the pair of K-vectors (α,ν). Without loss of generality the components of ν can be ordered by decreasing magnitude according to $\nu_1 \ge \ldots \ge \nu_K$. This property of the Cox distribution was first proved in [5], it is essential for its identifiability.

The m-th moment, $f_m(\alpha,\nu)$, of the random variable X_M is given by

$$f_m(\alpha,\nu) = \int_0^\infty m\, t^{m-1} F(t;\alpha,\nu)\, dt, \quad m = 1,2,\ldots, \tag{1.5}$$

according to a general relation between the survival function of a nonnegative random variable and its moments. (See [9, p. 27]). Substituting (1.4) we may write

$$f_m(\alpha, \nu) = \alpha^T f_m(\nu) . \tag{1.6}$$

where the vector $f_m(\nu)$ contains the divided differences of the associated scalar function

$$f_m(x) = \int_0^\infty m t^{m-1} F(t;x) dt . \tag{1.7}$$

Expressing the exponential function $F(t;x)$ by its derivative, as in equation (1.2), and evaluating the intergral by parts yields the following recursive relation

$$f_m(x) = \frac{m}{x} f_{m-1}(x) , \quad m = 1, 2, \ldots , \tag{1.8}$$

with $f_0(x) = 1$. The obvious explicit representation resulting from this recurrence is not particularly useful in numerical calculations.

2. The Mean Squared Residual

Assume that we are given a ordered sample $T_1 < \ldots < T_N$ of measured realizations of the random variable T, whose distribution is to be estimated. An empirical survival function can be derived from that sample, namely

$$G(t) = \frac{1}{N} \sum_{n=1}^{N} \chi[T_n > t] , \tag{2.1}$$

where $\chi[\cdot]$ denotes the indicator function. The m-th empirical moment is given by

$$g_m = \frac{1}{N} \sum_{n=1}^{N} T_n^m . \tag{2.2}$$

The Laplace–Stieltjes transform $\gamma(x) = E \exp(-x T)$ of the distribution of T can be rewritten as

$$\gamma(x) = \frac{1}{N} \sum_{n=1}^{N} F(T_n;x) , \tag{2.3}$$

where $F(t;x) = \exp(-xt)$, as defined above.

We shall use two basic scalar functions in the sequel. The first one is the Laplace integral of the survival function and is related to the the Laplace–Stieltjes transform $\gamma(x)$, see [12, Theorem 2.3a], by

$$\varphi(x) = \int_0^\infty F(t,x)G(t)dt = \frac{1}{x}(1 - \gamma(x)) . \tag{2.4}$$

The second one is the Laplace integral of the exponential survival function, in our notation

$$\varphi(x,y) = \int_0^\infty F(t,x)F(t,y)dt = \frac{1}{x+y} . \tag{2.5}$$

We would like to approximate the observed survival function by a corresponding Coxian survival function. The distance between both survival functions is assessed by the mean squared residual, that is, by the integrated square of the residual error function.

This error measure is analytically convenient, and in most cases appropriate too. It can be augmented by a penalty term in order to match the first M moments. So we arrive at the following objective function to be minimzed.

$$\rho(\alpha, \nu) = \frac{1}{2} \int_0^\infty \{G(t) - F(t;\alpha,\nu)\}^2 dt + \frac{1}{2} \sum_{m=1}^{M} \lambda_m \{g_m - f_m(\alpha,\nu)\}^2 . \tag{2.6}$$

One can show that the required moments finally are matched for an increasing sequence of penalty coefficients, that is, for $\lambda_m \to \infty$.

After substituting (1.4) and (1.6), the augmented mean squared residual can be rewritten as

$$\rho(\alpha,\nu) = const - \alpha^T \Phi(\nu) + \frac{1}{2} \alpha^T \Phi(\nu,\nu)\alpha , \tag{2.7}$$

where we have used the vector-matrix notation for divided differences introduced in Appendix A, adopting the notation

$$\Phi(x) = \varphi(x) + \sum_{m=1}^{M} \lambda_m g_m f_m(x) \; , \tag{2.8}$$

and

$$\Phi(x,y) = \varphi(x,y) + \sum_{m=1}^{M} \lambda_m f_m(x) f_m(y) \; . \tag{2.9}$$

The left hand side of equation (2.7) is our objective function, represented by a quadratic form in α with coefficients depending on ν. The first term of the matrix $\Phi(\nu,\nu)$ is a Gramian matrix of independent functions. It is therefore positive definite, a favorable property, which is not spoiled by adding some positive semidefinite matrices.

Let us introduce the Laplace transform of the residual, that is, of the deviation between observed and approximating survival function

$$\delta(x;\alpha,\nu) = \Phi(x) - \alpha^{T} \Phi(x,\nu) \; . \tag{2.10}$$

From this scalar function all partial derivatives of the objective function needed for the minimization process can be derived by forming divided differences.

For the partial derivative of $\rho(\alpha,\nu)$ with respect to the variable α_j the following relationship can be shown

$$-\frac{\partial}{\partial \alpha_j} \rho(\alpha,\nu) = \delta_j(\nu;\alpha,\nu) \; . \tag{2.11}$$

The right hand side is the j-th component of the vector $\delta(\nu;\alpha,\nu)$ obtained by taking divided differences of the scalar function $\delta(x;\alpha,\nu)$ for the specific argument vector ν..

Let us apply the differentiation rule (A.7)–(A.8) in the same way on the objective function $\rho(\alpha,\nu)$. After some algebra we find that the negative partial derivative with respect to ν_j can be written in compact form as

$$-\frac{\partial}{\partial \nu_j} \rho(\alpha,\nu) = \frac{1}{\nu_j} \{ \alpha^{T} \delta(\nu;\alpha,\nu) - \alpha_{(j)}^{T} \delta(\nu_{(j)},\alpha,\nu) \} \; , \tag{2.12}$$

where the vectors $\alpha_{(j)} = (\alpha_1,\ldots,\alpha_j^2,\ldots,\alpha_k)$ and $\nu_{(j)} = (\nu_1,\ldots,\nu_j^2,\ldots,\nu_k)$ are derived from α and ν by repeating the j-th component.

In the next section we show how to evaluate these quantities numerically by linear recurrences.

3. Recursive Computation of Divided Differences

The vectors $\varphi(\mu)$, $f_m(\mu)$, and the matrix $\varphi(\mu,\nu)$ result by taking divided differences of the associated scalar functions $\varphi(x)$, $f_m(x)$ and $\varphi(x,y)$. The argument vector μ is arbitrary in this section.

First we start remarking that divided differences of the primary function $\gamma(x)$, which is directly related to the sample, can be computed especially for confluent arguments, since derivatives of the exponential function of any order are available in analytic form.

The accuracy of these calculations may be sometimes doubtful, especially if several arguments nearly coincide. A way to avoid divided differences altogether is to compute the component $\gamma_j(\mu)$ directly by averaging the terms $F_j(T_n;\mu)$, which are nothing else than the solutions of the system (1.1) of ordinary differential equations at fixed time points T_n.

Let us apply the decomposition formula (A.6) on $x\,\varphi(x)$ to obtain the following recurrence for the components of $\varphi(\mu)$,

$$\mu_j\varphi_j(\mu) = \mu_{j-1}\varphi_{j-1}(\mu) + \delta_{j,1} - \gamma_j(\mu) \ , \tag{3.1}$$

where quantities with nonpositive indices are understood to be zero.

The same procedure applied to $x\,f_m(x)$ given by (1.8) yields the following recurrence for the components of $f_m(\mu)$

$$\mu_j f_{m,j}(\mu) = \mu_{j-1}f_{m,j-1}(\mu) + m\,f_{m-1,j}(\mu) \ . \tag{3.2}$$

Finally, the divided differences of $\varphi(x,y)$ follow in the same way by applying corresponding divided difference operators on $(x+y)\varphi(x,y)$. So we obtain the following linear recurrences

$$(\mu_i + \nu_j)\varphi_{i,j}(\mu,\nu) = \delta_{i,1}\delta_{j,1} + \mu_{i-1}\varphi_{i-1}(\mu,\nu) + \nu_{j-1}\varphi_{j-1}(\mu,\nu) \ , \tag{3.3}$$

for the components of $\varphi(\mu, \nu)$.

With the components of $\varphi(\mu)$, $\varphi(\mu, \nu)$ and $f_m(\alpha, \nu)$ we are able to compute the corresponding components of $\Phi(\mu)$ and $\Phi(\mu, \nu)$ by (2.8) – (2.9). The vector $\delta(\mu; \alpha, \nu)$ follows from (2.10) in the same way.

Upon inserting ν and $\nu_{(j)}$ in the above recurrences in place of μ, we get the objective function $\rho(\alpha, \nu)$ with all its derivatives straightforwardly from (2.11)–(2.12).

4. The Minimization

Our final goal is to find a pair of vectors α and ν that minimize the nonlinear objective function $\rho(\alpha, \nu)$ subject to the constraints $\alpha_k \geq \alpha_{k+1}$ and $\nu_k \geq \nu_{k+1}$, $k = 0, \ldots, K+1$, where $\alpha_0 = 1$, $\alpha_{K+1} = 0$. In order to stabilize the minimization process we impose additional side constraints in form of upper and lower bounds ν_0 and ν_{K+1}.

Since all derivatives of the objective function are available, the steepest descent method in its variant outlined in Appendix B is applicable. The separability of the objective function suggests to minimize first the quadratic form as a function of α, as long as possible, and then to improve the parameter vector ν in turn, and so on.

Gradient-based minimization procedures find only local minima and require a good initial guess of the parameter vectors. A coordinate relaxation method based on replacing one by one vector component by a random convex combination of its neighbouring components meets all constraints and proves quite satisfactory.

5. Numerical Example

The elapsed times of 90 interactive user connections to an IBM370 time sharing computer system as reported in [4] were adjusted to a scale ranging from 0 to 50 and used as the sample data in our example. The quality of obtained survival curves conveys some impression about the capability of the algorithm.

An initial parametrization was found by a random search method. Only the first two moments were considered. Convergence of the gradient method towards the minimum was apparently slow, depending heavily on the choice of the starting point.

The linearly interpolated empirical and an approximating survival function of order $K = 10$ are shown in Fig. 1.

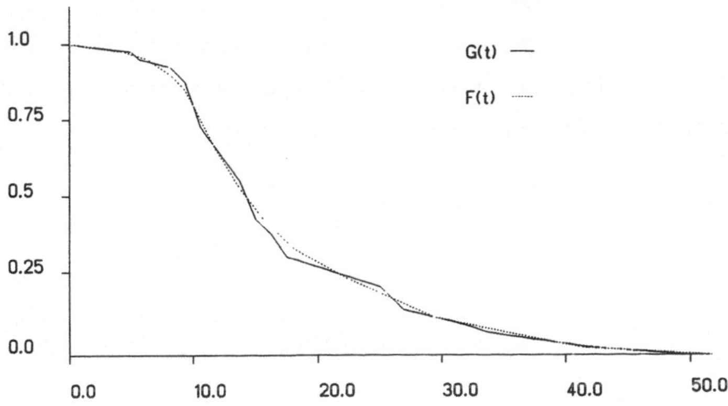

Fig. 1. Survival function of interactive user connection times

The sample moments are given by $g_1 = 20.61$ and $g_2 = 607.08$. The moments of the Cox distribution are $f_1. = 20.12$ and $f_2 = 550.69$. The parameter vectors are shown in Table 1 below.

k	1	2	3	4	5	6	7	8	9	10
α_k	1.0000	1.0000	1.0000	1.0000	1.0000	1.0000	1.0000	1.0000	0.6137	0.5403
ν_k	1.2277	0.9405	0.8269	0.7593	0.6844	0.6192	0.5252	0.3830	0.3079	0.0882

Tab .1. Parameters of the best approximation

A second run with a Cox distribution of degree $K = 20$ improved the mean squared error slightly to 19.8427 and the first two moments to $f_1 = 20.58$ and $f_2 = 627.84$ respectively.

The numerical stability of the divided difference calculations was sufficient for distributions of degree up to 10, beyond that value a system of differential equations was solved. The algorithm was implemented in the C++ language on a personal computer.

6. Concluding Remarks

The numerical example clearly demonstrates the feasibility of the proposed approach for estimating the parameters of Cox distributions. The algorithm outlined in Appendix B is just a cheap but efficient instance of a plethora of possible minimization algorithms and intended to demonstrate the basic approach, more sophisticated algorithms may exhibit improved accuracy and performance.

References

[1] T.S. ARTHANARI, Y. DODGE, *Mathematical Programming in Statistics*, J. Wiley, New York–Toronto. 1981

[2] S. ASMUSSEN, *Applied Probability and Queues* , J. Wiley, New York–Toronto, 1987

[3] W. BUX, U. HERZOG, *The Phase Concept: Approximation of Measured Data and Performance Analysis*, Computer Performance , K.M. Chandy and M. Reiser (Eds.), 1977, 23–38

[4] E. J. DUDEWICZ, Z.A. KARIAN, *Modern Design and Analysis of Discrete–Event Simulations* , IEEE Computer Society Press, Washington , 1985

[5] J.W. EVANS, W.B. GRAGG, R.J. LEVEQUE, On Least Squares Exponential Sum Approximation with Positive Coefficients, *Math. Comp.* (**34**) , 1980, 203–211

[6] V.B. IVERSEN, B.F. NIELSEN, *Some Properties of Coxian Distributions with Applications* , in: N. Abu El Ata (ed.), Modelling Techniques and Tools for Performance Analysis '85, North– Holland, Amsterdam 1987, 61–66

[7] D. KINCAID, W. CHENEY , *Numerical Analysis* , Brooks/Cole Publishing Company, Pacific Grove, California 1991

[8] A.M. OSTROWSKI, *Solutions of Equations in Euclidean and Banach Spaces*, Academic Press, New York – London 1973

[9] S. M. ROSS, *Stochastic Processes*, J. Wiley, New York – Toronto 1983

[10] L. SCHMICKLER, *Approximation von empirischen Verteilungsfunktionen mit Erlangmischverteilungen und Coxverteilungen*, in: U.Herzog, M.Paterok (Hrsg.), Messung, Modellierung und Bewertung von Rechensystemen, Springer 1987, 118–133

[11] J. M. VARAH, On Fitting Exponentials by Nonlinear Least Squares, *SIAM J. Sci. Stat. Comp.* (**6**) 1985, 30–44

[12] D. V. WIDDER, *The Laplace Transform*, Princeton University Press 1946

Appendix A: Divided Differences

In this Appendix we present a modification of the concept of divided differences adapted to the context of Coxian distributions.

Let $v_1 \geq \ldots \geq v_k > 0$ and let $f(x)$ be an at least k times continuously differentiable function. The divided differences of $f(x)$ are recursively defined by

$$\nabla_x [v_i, \ldots, v_j] f(x) = \frac{\nabla_x [v_{i+1}, \ldots, v_j] f(x) - \nabla_x [v_i, \ldots, v_{j-1}] f(x)}{v_j - v_i} \quad , v_j > v_i , \quad (A.1)$$

and by

$$\nabla_x [v_i, \ldots, v_j] f(x) = \frac{1}{(j-i)!} f^{(j-i)}(v_i) , \quad v_i = v_j \quad (A.2)$$

All divided differences $\nabla_x [v_1, \ldots, v_k] f(x)$ for $k > 1$ can be generated by repeated application of these recursive formulae, [6, Theorem 5].

The divided difference is a symmetric function of its arguments [6, p.301]. Divided differences of continuous functions are continuous. By Leibniz´s formula for divided differences of products [6, p.304] the following rule can readily be shown

$$\nabla_x [v_1, \ldots, v_k] x f(x) = v_k \nabla_x [v_1, \ldots, v_k] f(x) + \nabla_x [v_1, \ldots, v_{k-1}] f(x) . \quad (A.3)$$

Forming the partial derivative of a divided difference with respect to a variable v_j is easy, one has only to repeat this argument once to obtain the derivative. Thus, if all arguments are distinct, we have

$$\frac{\partial}{\partial v_j} \nabla_x [v_1, \ldots, v_k] f(x) = \nabla_x [v_1, \ldots, v_j^2, \ldots, v_k] f(x) , \quad (A.4)$$

for $j \leq k$, and 0 otherwise [6, p. 315]. There are efficient algorithms to compute divided differences.

Divided differences appear in our text exclusively in specific aggregates, which we continue to call divided differences without causing confusion, since we introduce a special operator symbol for them. Let us define the following aggregate

$$\Delta_x[v_1,\ldots,v_k]\,f(x) = \prod_{i=1}^{k-1}(-v_i)\,\nabla_x[v_1,\ldots,v_k]\,f(x)\;, \tag{A.5}$$

which is a symmetric function of its first $k-1$ arguments only.

The following results are merely restatements of known results for ordinary divided differences in terms of this new operator. Rewriting (A.3) yields the following decomposition rule which is essential for our approach

$$\Delta_x[v_1,\ldots,v_k]xf(x) = v_k\,\Delta_x[v_1,\ldots,v_k]f(x) - v_{k-1}\,\Delta_x[v_1,\ldots,v_{k-1}]\,f(x)\;. \tag{A.6}$$

Forming the partial derivative of the modified divided difference with respect to one of its argument variables v_j is also easy. If all arguments are distinct, we have

$$\frac{\partial}{\partial v_j}\Delta_x[v_1,\ldots,v_j]f(x) = -\frac{1}{v_j}\Delta_x[v_1,\ldots,v_j^2]f(x)\;, \tag{A.7}$$

for $j = k$,

$$\frac{\partial}{\partial v_j}\Delta_x[v_1,\ldots,v_k]f(x) = \frac{1}{v_j}\{\Delta_x[v_1,\ldots,v_k]f(x) - \Delta_x[v_1,\ldots,v_j^2,\ldots,v_k]f(x)\}\;, \tag{A.8}$$

for $k > j$, and 0 otherwise.

To avoid a clumsy notation we denote divided differences of the functions $f(x)$ and $f(x,y)$ with respect to vectors $\mathbf{\mu} = (\mu_1,\ldots,\mu_I)$ and $\mathbf{v} = (v_1,\ldots,v_J)$ as follows

$$f_i(\mathbf{\mu}) = \Delta_x[\mu_1,\ldots,\mu_i]\,f(x)\;,\quad i = 1,\ldots,I, \tag{A.9}$$

and

$$f_{i,j}(\mathbf{\mu},\mathbf{v}) = \Delta_x[\mu_1,\ldots,\mu_i]\,\Delta_y[v_1,\ldots,v_j]\,f(x,y)\;,\quad i=1,\ldots,I,\; j=1,\ldots,J\;. \tag{A.10}$$

Successive divided differences are collected in the vector $f(\mu)$ with i-th element $f_i(\mu)$, and the matrix $f(\mu,\nu)$ with i,j-th element $f_{i,j}(\mu,\nu)$. This notation is used throughout the text.

Appendix B: Minimization subject to Simple Ordering Constraints

Let $\rho(x)$ be a continuous and differentiable function of K variables. The components of a solution vector $x = (x_i)$ are subject to ordering constraints of the form $x_i \geq x_j$ for $i < j$, $i, j = 0, \dots, K+1$.

$$\text{minimize } \rho(x) \text{ subject to } x_i \geq x_j \text{ for } i < j, \, i, j = 0,\dots,K+1 \tag{B.1}$$

The upper and lower bound x_0 and x_{K+1} impose additional side constraints. We show that these simple constraints can be incorporated into the classical method of the steepest descent.

First we note that constraints satisfied as equalities induce a subdivision $\mathfrak{J}$ of the index range $[0, K+1]$ into contiguous intervals. Let x_i be the common value of all components x_i with indices i from an interval $\mathfrak{i}$. Thus a condensed vector $x = (x_\mathfrak{i})$ which retains only components with different values indexed by intervals $\mathfrak{i}$ can be identified with the original vector. It will be clear from the context, which representation is intended.

The negative derivative of the objective function with respect to the new variable $x_\mathfrak{i}$ is then

$$\delta_\mathfrak{i}(x) = -\sum_{i \in \mathfrak{i}} \frac{\partial \rho(x)}{\partial x_i} \, , \quad \mathfrak{i} \in \mathfrak{J} \tag{B.2}$$

Suppose $\delta_\mathfrak{i}(x) \geq \delta_\mathfrak{j}(x)$ for all adjacent intervals $\mathfrak{i} < \mathfrak{j}$ in $\mathfrak{J}$ with $x_\mathfrak{i} = x_\mathfrak{j}$. Otherwise any pair of adjacent intervals $\mathfrak{i}$ and $\mathfrak{j}$ violating this condition must be merged into a single interval. On the other hand, an interval should be split into two, whenever possible, in order to refine the feasible subdivision $\mathfrak{J}$.

Obviously, points on the ray determined by the negative gradient have coordinates

$$y_\mathfrak{i} = x_\mathfrak{i} + \lambda \, \delta_\mathfrak{i}(x) \, , \quad \lambda > 0 \, , \tag{B.3}$$

and these coordinates will be again ordered if the step length λ is limited by

$$\lambda \leq \min \left\{ \frac{x_i - x_j}{\delta_i(x) - \delta_j(x)} \;\middle|\; \delta_i(x) < \delta_j(x), \, i < j \in \mathfrak{J} \right\} \, , \tag{B.4}$$

where i and $j \in \mathfrak{J}$ are adjacent intervals. Clearly, since $x_i > x_j$, this upper bound is strictly positive, if $\mathfrak{J}$ is a feasible subdivision.

A new point $y = (y_i)$ is only acceptable, if $\rho(y) < \rho(x)$. Otherwise the objective function must be recomputed for an halved step length λ until this condition is satisfied.

A necessary condition for a minimum is that all derivatives $\delta_i(x)$, $i \in \mathfrak{J}$, vanish for an admissible subdivision $\mathfrak{J}$, and that this subdivision cannot further be refined. This is the stop criterion for the minimization process.

A Heuristic Approach for the Aggregation of Markovian Submodels

Peter Buchholz *

Informatik IV, Universität Dortmund, D-44221 Dortmund

Abstract. Decomposition and aggregation is a very important technique for the approximative analysis of large scale hierarchical models. In particular a decomposition on model level rather than on the underlying Markov chain allows to reduce the solution effort for a complex model significantly. We introduce here an extended approach for the aggregation of Markovian submodels including different types of entities. Aggregate construction is based on numerical pre-analysis of absorbing Markov chains. The resulting aggregates can be interpreted as queueing network stations with Coxian service time distributions, special subnets of coloured GSPNs or as specific station types in process interaction models. The aggregation approach has been automized and integrated in a tool environment. The resulting aggregation errors are most times much smaller than errors resulting from standard flow equivalent aggregation.

1 Introduction

It has been shown in the past that the use of decomposition and aggregation techniques (DATs) is of outstanding importance for the analysis of complex performance models. Especially techniques that aggregate a submodel independent of its environment (environment independent aggregation techniques (IDATs)) provide a base for the analysis of large scale hierarchically structured models. In contrast to techniques which decompose the Markov chain underlying a complete model, IDATs are more efficient and can handle larger models. The basic technique for the aggregation of isolated submodels is the short-circuit pre-analysis and the substitution of the submodel by a flow-equivalent service center (FESC) (also denoted as flow-equivalent aggregation) as developed in [6, 2]. The technique is exact, in the sense that stationary performance quantities can be determined without an error, in product-form models and yields a good approximation in models violating product-form assumptions only slightly. Using the famous results of Courtois [8] concerning decomposition and aggregation in nearly completely decomposable systems, we further know that the results are good approximations whenever the coupling between the submodel to be aggregated and its environment is loose.

If none of the above conditions is satisfied, the use of submodel aggregation might become dangerous, because the approximation error potentially can be very large. Although decomposition and aggregation approaches are known for a long time, extensions of the flow-equivalent aggregation approach are rare and other environment

---

* Part of this work has been supported by the CEC under the Esprit II contract no. 2143 (IMSE)

independent aggregation techniques are only known for special model types. However, a technique is needed that extends flow equivalent aggregation by reducing the resulting approximation errors, can be used for a broad model class with multiple entity types and can be automized to be accepted also by non expert users. In this paper we present an aggregation approach going in this direction. The paper results from the outcome of our contribution to the IMSE project [13]. The new DAT has been completely implemented and allows the automatic aggregation of submodels which have been specified as queueing networks, generalized stochastic petri nets or stochastic automata.

The outline of the remainder of the paper is as follows. In the next section submodels and the underlying state spaces and transition matrices are introduced. Section 3 describes the pre-analysis of submodels which is based on numerical techniques for absorbing Markov chains. Aggregate construction is considered in section 4. In the following section the automization of the approach and the integration in a modelling tool environment are considered very briefly. Two example models are analysed in section 6 and the paper ends with the conclusions.

2 Submodel structures

Submodel structures are introduced here on two levels. The first level covers the high level description of a submodel as a queueing network or coloured GSPN. The second level describes the underlying matrix structures that do not depend on the specific high level description.

2.1 Submodel specification

It has been shown in [4] that a broad class of Markovian submodels, specified using various paradigms like queueing networks (QNs), GSPNs, stochastic automata, special state transition languages etc., can be mapped on a unique matrix structure, which is independent of the concrete specification technique. With this result specification and analysis of models can be divided into two parts; the specification part using one or various paradigms for the submodels, and the analysis part using the underlying matrices. In this paper we consider in particular the aggregation of submodels that are specified as QNs or GSPNs. However, the use of other specification paradigms is rather straightforward.

Submodels are specified as extended QNs or coloured GSPNs. Let K be the set of entity types. Entity types can be interpreted as customer chains in QNs or as sets of colours, which are reachable from one another, in coloured GSPNs. To each entity type k belongs a set of subtypes (or classes adopting the QN terminology) $\{k_1...k_X\}$. The behaviour of an arriving entity in a submodel depends only on its type identity and the internal state of the submodel and not on external states or events. An entity of type k belongs inside the submodel to one subtype $k_x \in \{k_1...k_X\}$, when leaving the submodel, the identity changes back to type k.

Additionally the submodel might include local entity types. Entities belonging to these types do not enter or leave the submodel and are therefore not visible from the "outside". The population of local types must be finite to guarantee a finite state space.

To specify a submodel, the description is extended by a so called "pseudo environment", realized, independent of the real environment, by a finite capacity source per entity type. Entities are generated by the source with an exponentially distributed interarrival time with some fictive rate $\lambda > 0$. Entities leaving the submodel are absorbed by a sink. Submodels are analysed up a finite limit of entities for each type. Let N_k the limit for type k. If the submodel contains N_k type k entities, the source for type k is switched off until a type k entity has left the submodel. Let $\underline{N} \in \mathbf{N}^{\|K\|}$ be a vector including the limits for all entity types. For the purposes of aggregation, the model including submodel and pseudo environment has to observe the following conditions:

- The model has to be mapped on a time homogeneous, finite and irreducible Markov chain.
- Simultaneous departures from the pseudo environment and arrivals to the pseudo environment are not allowed.
- The number of type $k \in K$ entities has to be constant i.e., an entity cannot change its type identity.

Other restrictions on the level of the submodel transition matrices are introduced in the following section. Nevertheless, the above restrictions are not very hard and are normally observed in realistic and correctly specified submodels.

2.2 Matrix structures

The previously introduced specification of a submodel is used for the generation of the submodel state space and transition matrix. Let Z be the state space of submodel and pseudo environment. The state space can be decomposed in disjoint subspaces $Z(\underline{n})$ $(\underline{0} \leq \underline{n} \leq \underline{N})$ according to the population inside the submodel. Different types of transitions affect the state of a submodel. Assuming the submodel is in a state $z \in Z(\underline{n})$, the following types of transitions can occur and change the state to a successor state z'.

If z' is in the same subset $Z(\underline{n})$, then the transition is caused by an internal event in the submodel (e.g., an entity changing the station in a QN submodel). The rates of such transitions are collected as non-diagonal elements in a matrix $Q^{\underline{n}}$, which contains in the main diagonal the negative rate out of the actual state.

$$Q^{\underline{n}} \in \mathbf{R}^{\|Z(\underline{n})\| \times \|Z(\underline{n})\|} \qquad Q^{\underline{n}}\underline{e}^T \leq \underline{0}$$
$$Q^{\underline{n}}(z, z') \geq 0 \text{ for } z \neq z', \ Q^{\underline{n}}(z, z) \leq - \sum_{z' \in Z(\underline{n})} Q^{\underline{n}}(z, z') \tag{1}$$

The second transition type describes the departure of a type k entity. The departure changes the state from $z \in Z(\underline{n})$ to $z' \in Z(\underline{n} - \underline{e}_k)$. Departure rates of type k entities leaving the submodel are collected in a matrix $S^{\underline{n}-k}$.

$$S^{\underline{n}-k} \in \mathbf{R}_+^{\|Z(\underline{n})\| \times \|Z(\underline{n}-\underline{e}_k)\|} \qquad \text{for all } n(k) > 0 \tag{2}$$

Since a transition originated in the submodel either results in a local change of the state or in the departure of an entity, the following equation holds.

$$Q^{\underline{n}}\underline{e}^T + \sum_{k \in K} S^{\underline{n}-k}\underline{e}^T = \underline{0}^T \tag{3}$$

The last transition type describes the arrival of an entity. The state changes from $z \in Z(\underline{n}-\underline{e}_k)$ to $z' \in Z(\underline{n})$. The rate of an entity arrival is not known in the submodel since it depends on the environment. Transitions are quantified with conditional probabilities in the matrix $U^{\underline{n}-k}$. Element $U^{\underline{n}-k}(z, z')$ represents the probability that the state is changed from z to z', if the submodel is in state z at the arrival instants of a type k entity.

$$U^{\underline{n}-k} \in \mathbf{R}_+^{\|Z(\underline{n}-\underline{e}_k)\| \times \|Z(\underline{n})\|} \qquad U^{\underline{n}-k}\underline{e}^T = \underline{e}^T \qquad \text{for all } n(k) > 0 \qquad (4)$$

For purposes of pre-analysis we define for each entity type k and population vector $\underline{n}$ a matrix including the transitions of the submodel with all other types short-circuited.

$$Qk^{\underline{n}} = Q^{\underline{n}} + \sum_{l \in K, l \neq k, n(l) > 0} S^{\underline{n}-l} U^{\underline{n}-l} \quad \text{for all } k \in K \text{ with } n(k) > 0 \qquad (5)$$

To perform pre-analysis as described below each matrix $Qk^{\underline{n}}$ has to be either a conservative matrix (i.e., $S^{\underline{n}-k} = \underline{0}$), or the inverse of $Qk^{\underline{n}}$ hs to exist (i.e., the matrix contains no traps, see [11]). The latter assumption is, in terms of the submodel behaviour, not too restrictive. It says that, independent of the actual state $z \in Z(\underline{n})$, a type k entity can either leave the submodel with the short-cut of the other types, or that type k entities cannot leave the submodel before an entity of another type departs and stays for some time outside in the environment.

3 Pre-analysis of submodels

Pre-analysis performed here is an extension of short-circuit pre-analysis. In short-circuit analysis the submodel is analysed according to the first moment of the inter-departure time through the short-circuit and the aggregate is constructed to match this quantity. We still measure the interdeparture time of the submodel, but we do not restrict the measurement to the first moment and we take other situations and not only the short-cut into account and try to match these measurements with aggregates as well. This idea of pre-analysis is general and not restricted to the quantities introduced below and also not restricted to Markovian submodels and numerical pre-analysis. However, to develop a usable approach we restrict the general view to the numerical pre-analysis of the class of submodels introduced previously.

Like in short-circuit pre-analysis we analyse the submodel for each possible population and each entity type separately. This can be done by means of the matrix $Qk^{\underline{n}}$ for type k and population $\underline{n}$, which describes, after introduction of an artificial absorbing state, an absorbing Markov chain. Using this matrix, for each state z the moments of the time to absorption starting in z can be calculated. The resulting vector of absorption time moments, multiplied with probability vectors describing the state of the submodel in different situations, yields conditional interdeparture time moments for the submodel. The use of the matrix $Qk^{\underline{n}}$ implies that we analyse the interdeparture time of a single type according only to the behaviour of this type. Entities of other types are assumed to behave like in short-circuit.

3.1 Calculation of con of conditional distributions

The first step of pre-analysis is the computation of appropriate probability distributions defining the state of the submodel in various situations. There are many possibilities to define and compute conditional distributions in submodels. Especially we are interested in distributions that occur immediately after the population in the submodel has changed due to the arrival or departure of an entity and in the stationary short-circuit distribution of the submodel. The stationary short-circuit distribution with population $\underline{n}$ is denoted by $\underline{p}_S^n$ and is calculated as solution of the following equation.

$$\underline{p}_S^n(Q^n + \sum_{l \in K, n(l) > 0} S^{\underline{n}\text{-}l} U^{\underline{n}\text{-}l}) = \underline{0} \quad \text{and} \quad \underline{p}_S^n \underline{e}^T = 1.0 \tag{6}$$

Other distributions considered here should be calculated from the short-circuit distribution without too much effort, to allow an efficient pre-analysis and should be matched by the aggregates to be constructed. Therefore we restrict ourselves to very few types of distributions. However, additional distributions and more complicated aggregates can be estimated following the same ideas. The remaining distributions are all computed with respect to a specific type, therefore we denote them by $\underline{pk}_X^n$ for distribution X, type k and population $\underline{n}$ in the submodel.

Distribution $\underline{pk}_{AS}^n$ specifies the state of the short-circuited submodel immediately after the arrival of a type k entity, $\underline{pk}_{DS}^n$ specifies the state of the short-circuited submodel immediately after the departure of a type k entity (the population in the submodel is $\underline{n}$ after the departure). Both distributions can be interpreted as embedded distributions before/after a transition specified in the the matrix $S^{\underline{n}\text{-}k} U^{\underline{n}\text{-}k}$ in a Markov process with a generator matrix as defined in (6).

$$\underline{pk}_{AS}^n = \underline{p}_S^n S^{\underline{n}\text{-}k} U^{\underline{n}\text{-}k} / (\underline{p}_S^n S^{\underline{n}\text{-}k} \underline{e}^T) \qquad \text{for all } \underline{0} < \underline{n} \le \underline{N} \text{ with } n(k) > 0$$
$$\underline{pk}_{DS}^n = \underline{p}_S^{\underline{n}+\varepsilon_k} S^{(\underline{n}+\varepsilon_k)\text{-}k} / (\underline{p}_S^{\underline{n}+\varepsilon_k} S^{(\underline{n}+\varepsilon_k)\text{-}k} \underline{e}^T) \quad \text{for all } \underline{0} \le \underline{n} < \underline{N} \text{ with } n(k) < N(k) \tag{7}$$

The following distribution describes the situation, where the submodel with a fixed population is short-circuited and an entity of type k has immediately arrived at an arbitrary time (viewpoint of the random observer seeing the stationary distribution of the short-circuited submodel with one type k entity less). The distribution is denoted by $\underline{pk}_{AM}^n$.

$$\underline{pk}_{AM}^n = \underline{pk}_S^{\underline{n}-\varepsilon_k} U^{\underline{n}\text{-}k} \qquad \text{for all } \underline{0} < \underline{n} \le \underline{N} \text{ with } n(k) > 0 \tag{8}$$

All distributions introduced above can be computed from the stationary short-circuit distribution by vector matrix multiplications.

3.2 Calculation of conditional moments

The moments of interdeparture time starting in a specific state can be computed as the moments of absorption time of an absorbing Markov chain, which is generated by introducing an artificial absorbing state to the set $Z(\underline{n})$. The new matrix of the absorbing Markov chain for type k and population $\underline{n}$ is given in the following equation.

$$\begin{pmatrix} Qk^{\underline{n}} & S^{\underline{n}-k}\underline{e}^T \\ \underline{0} & 0 \end{pmatrix} \tag{9}$$

The absorption of the above process describes at the level of the submodel the first departure of a type k entity. Due to the previous assumptions two situations are possible; the matrix $S^{\underline{n}-k}$ can be $\underline{0}$ or $n(k) = 0$, then the moments of absorption time are assumed to equal all ∞, otherwise an absorption is possible from each state, the moments of absorption time starting from a state $z \in Z(\underline{n})$ are finite and can be computed from the following equation [10].

$$-Qk^{\underline{n}}(\underline{mk_i^n})^T = i(\underline{mk_{i-1}^n})^T \text{ and } \underline{mk_0^n} = \underline{e} \tag{10}$$
where $\underline{mk_i^n}$ is the vector of the i-th moment of absorption time.

In the remainder we need the first moments of interdeparture time, which will be denoted by $\underline{mk^n}$ instead of $\underline{mk_1^n}$.

Arbitrary conditional moments of the interdeparture time are calculated by multiplying the vector of interdeparture time moments with a conditional distribution vector. We are mainly interested in the first moments, which are computed for the various distributions as shown in the following equation.

$$\begin{aligned} Ek_S^{\underline{n}} &= \underline{p_S^n}(\underline{mk^n})^T & Ek_{AS}^{\underline{n}} &= \underline{pk_{AS}^n}(\underline{mk^n})^T \\ Ek_{DS}^{\underline{n}} &= \underline{pk_{DS}^n}(\underline{mk^n})^T & Ek_{AM}^{\underline{n}} &= \underline{pk_{AM}^n}(\underline{mk^n})^T \end{aligned} \tag{11}$$

Higher order moments are estimated using the vector containing higher order moments of absorption time. Notice that the calculation of $Ek_{AS}^{\underline{n}}(T)$ and $Ek_S^{\underline{n}}(T)$ implicitly determines the second moment of short-circuit interdeparture time for type k, which equals $2.0 * Ek_{AS}^{\underline{n}}(T) * Ek_S^{\underline{n}}(T)$ as shown in [4].

4 Aggregate construction

For aggregate construction characteristics of interdeparture time are reflected by the aggregate. The first characteristic is the mean short-circuit interdeparture time which is the only value considered in standard flow equivalent aggregation. Other characteristics approximate the "deviation from the arrival theorem" for product form networks. The deviation of a submodel from product-form is measured here by three quantities:

- In product-form submodels the arrival theorem holds (see [12]) i.e., $\underline{pk_{AS}^n} = \underline{pk_{AM}^n}$ and therefore also $Ek_{AS}^{\underline{n}}(T) = Ek_{AM}^{\underline{n}}(T)$.
- In product-form submodels the departure theorem holds (see [12]) i.e., $\underline{p_S^n} = \underline{pk_{DS}^n}$ for all k with $n(k) < N(k)$ and therefore also $Ek_S^{\underline{n}}(T) = Ek_{DS}^{\underline{n}}(T)$.
- For the mean interdeparture time of product-form submodels in short-circuit the relation $Ek_{AS}^{\underline{n}-\underline{e}_l}(T)/Ek_{AS}^{\underline{n}}(T) = El_{AS}^{\underline{n}-\underline{e}_k}(T)/El_{AS}^{\underline{n}}(T)$ holds for all combinations of entity types where the mean values are defined (see [9]).

We distinguish product-form and non-product-form behaviour of a submodel according to the arrival theorem. New aggregates are generated by matching the behaviour of the submodel according to the mean interdeparture time in short-circuit and under Markovian arrivals. It is known that both quantities are equal for product-form submodels and differ normally for non-product-form submodels. If we use the aggregates introduced in this section for submodels where the above mean values are equal, the simple FESC is constructed anyhow. In [5] new aggregate types for product form submodels matching the second moment of short-circuit interdeparture time are also introduced. Here we only consider FESCs and extended FESCs which are described by a more complex state dependent service time distribution for the different entity types.

4.1 Simple FESCs

FESCs are characterized by a single parameter per population vector and entity type to specify the state dependent service rate. Let $sk(\underline{n})$ be the state dependent service rate for type k with population $\underline{n}$. The mean service time has to match the mean interdeparture time of the submodel in short-circuit.

$$sk(\underline{n}) = \begin{cases} 0.0 & \text{if } Ek_{AS}^{n} = \infty \\ (Ek_{AS}^{n})^{-1} & \text{else} \end{cases} \tag{12}$$

Of course, constructing the FESC we do not care about the difference between Ek_{AS}^{n} and Ek_{AM}^{n}, which measures here the difference of the submodel from product-form. Therefore, the FESC constructed for a non-product-form submodel might have product-form, if the relation between the speeds of the various types satisfies the product-form condition as described above (this is always the case for submodels containing only a single entity type).

4.2 FESCs with Coxian distribution

A FESC with Coxian service time distribution is characterized by the state dependent speeds, as introduced for the simple FESC in (12), and the Coxian service time distribution, which is assumed to be of the type described in the appendix. Since the mean service time is determined by the state dependent speeds, the mean service time of the Coxian distribution for type k $Ek(T^1)$ is fixed to 1. Let $Ek(T^2)$ be the second moment of the Coxian distribution for type k. The parameters of the distribution are denoted by μk_1, μk_2, mk and ak_1. If we analyse the FCFS server with Coxian service time distribution with the methods introduced in section 3, we get the following results for $\widetilde{Ek}_{AS}^{n}$ and $\widetilde{Ek}_{AM}^{n}$[2].

$$\widetilde{Ek}_{AS}^{n} = \begin{cases} sk(\underline{n})^{-1} & \text{if } sk(\underline{n}) > 0.0 \\ \infty & \text{else} \end{cases} \qquad \widetilde{Ek}_{AM}^{n} = \begin{cases} \infty & \text{if } \widetilde{Ek}_{AS}^{n} = \infty \\ Ek(T^2)/(2.0\, sk(\underline{n})) & \text{else} \end{cases} \tag{13}$$

---

[2] The ˜ is used here to distinguish the values determined for the aggregate from the values determined for the submodel (without ˜).

Since only one value per type k can be selected for $Ek(T^2)$, this value should be chosen to approximate Ek_{AM}^n as good as possible. One possibility is to use an average value to be matched, as shown in the following equation.

$$Ek(T^2) = \frac{2.0}{\theta(\underline{N})} \sum_{\underline{0} < \underline{n} \leq \underline{N}, \, n(k) > 0, \, sk(\underline{n}) < \infty} Ek_{AM}^n sk(\underline{n})$$

$$\text{where } \theta(\underline{N}) = \sum_{\underline{0} \leq \underline{n} \leq \underline{N}, \, sk(\underline{n}) < \infty} \delta(n(k)), \ \delta(i) = 1 \text{ if } i > 0 \text{ and } 0 \text{ else} \tag{14}$$

The aggregate matches Ek_{AM}^n quite well, if the values do only slightly vary with the population, in other cases the aggregate type is not flexible enough. However, we still have two quantities per type to fix, the number of Coxian phases mk and the probability ak_1. The number of phases is set to the possible minimum and the probability ak_1 is chosen to yield equal occupied phases (the computation is described in the appendix).

4.3 FESCs with state dependent Coxian distribution

A natural extension of the FESC with fixed Coxian service time distribution and state dependent speeds is the FESC with a Coxian service time distribution depending on the population. However, to define usable aggregates, some restrictions have to be introduced for the state dependencies. Namely, the number of Coxian phases has to be equal for all population vectors and all phases are equal occupied. Therefore the parameter mk is fixed for all populations, whereas the remaining parameters $\mu k_1(\underline{n})$, $\mu k_2(\underline{n})$ and $ak_1(\underline{n})$ are determined depending on the population.

The mean service time is fixed by the load dependent service rates $sk(\underline{n})$, the mean of the Coxian service time distribution for type k and population $\underline{n}$ ($Ek^{\underline{n}}(T^1)$) equals 1. The second moment $Ek^{\underline{n}}(T^2)$ is computed according to

$$Ek^{\underline{n}}(T^2) = \begin{cases} \infty & \text{if } Ek_{AM}^n = \infty \\ 2.0 Ek_{AM}^n sk(\underline{n}) & \text{else} \end{cases} \tag{15}$$

The number of phases for the different types k is chosen as the minimum value allowing the construction of Coxian distributions with the above first and second moments.

$$mk = \begin{cases} \max(\lceil \frac{Ek^{\underline{n}}(T^1)^2}{Ek^{\underline{n}}(T^2) - Ek^{\underline{n}}(T^1)^2} \rceil) \text{ if } Ek^{\underline{n}}(T^2) < 2Ek^{\underline{n}}(T^1)^2 \text{ for some } \underline{n} \\ 2 \qquad\qquad\qquad\qquad\qquad\qquad \text{else} \end{cases} \tag{16}$$

The values $ak_1(\underline{n})$ are computed as described in the appendix. With the above formulas FESCs with state dependent Coxian service time distributions can be computed directly from the pre-analysis results with a very low effort.

5   Integration in a modelling tool environment

To gain acceptance DATs have to be automized because the manual use of the techniques is often very time consuming and will not be done by a non expert user analysing realistic systems. The new IDAT has been completely implemented in the IMSE modelling tool environment [13]. For the lack of space we cannot introduce here the structure of IMSE and the integration of the techniques in detail, for a comprehensive description the reader is referred to [13] and [5], respectively. However, we will sketch very briefly the main ideas of the implementation. The following steps have to be performed:

- Specification of submodels and the construction of the submodel matrices.
- Pre-analysis of the submodel.
- Computation of the aggregate parameters.
- Integration of the aggregate in an environment.

The key steps of aggregation as described here are the steps 2 and 3 above. However, the automatic use of DAT relies also on the possibility of specifying submodels and embedding aggregates in an upper level model. This, of course, can be summarized as hierarchical modelling. A module which computes submodel matrices from the specification of submodels can be integrated in a performance modelling tool with numerical solution facilities without too much effort. In the IMSE the queueing network tool QNAP2 [14] and the GSPN tool GreatSPN1.5 [7] provide numerical solutions. Both have been extended to generate matrices for submodels specified in isolation with an appropriate "pseudo environment" (see section 2.1). The aggregation module reads the (sparse) submodel matrices and computes the aggregate parameters. All objects (matrices, aggregate parameters, etc.) are handled by an object management system underlying the IMSE. Pre-analysis is performed on sparse matrix structures using direct or iterative solution techniques to compute the distributions (see section 3.1) and conditional moments (see section 3.2). The integration of aggregates in an environment is performed in two different ways. The manual specification as needed for QNAP2 and GreatSPN1.5 requires the specification of an appropriate aggregate structure and the input of the generated parameters in the aggregate structure. However, predefined aggregate structures which only have to be filled with the parameters and embedded in their environment can be defined a priori for both tools. The simulation tool PIT [13] allows an automatic use of aggregates and submodels by defining a submodel in a hierarchical model and specifying a simple parameter which describes if the submodel is represented by the detailed submodel or one of the aggregates. The latter solution is, of course, the ideal way which should be striven for in all performance modelling tools. Obviously the approach builds bridges between the different modelling tools and modelling paradigms and is, of course, one step towards multi-paradigm modelling and analysis.

Another approach of embedding the new aggregates is to describe the aggregates by means of matrices as done for submodels and use this matrix description in recently developed techniques for the numerical analysis of hierarchical Markovian models (see [4]). This approach allows the numerical analysis of rather large models on a standard workstation.

Nevertheless, the automization of DATs which do not provide exact aggregation includes also some danger. A user has to be aware that the solution is only an approximation and might become worse. However, our experience indicates that results are often acceptable and guidance based on heuristics can be given which submodels should be aggregated and which might yield larger errors (see [5]).

6 Examples

The first example is a simple single class queueing network model. The submodel to be aggregated is realized by two parallel stations with two phase Coxian service time distribution and coefficient of variation 10.0 each. The submodel is aggregated into a standard FESC (AGG0), a FESC with Coxian distribution (AGG1) and a FESC with state dependent Coxian service time distribution (AGG2). To compare the aggregates the submodel is combined with an environment consisting of a station with a 2-phase Coxian service time distribution and a coefficient of variation varying between 0.5 and 10.0. The population is 5, thus the original and aggregated models can be analysed using a direct numerical solution technique which provides exact results. In figure 1 the relative errors in the computed throughputs for the three aggregate types are shown. Obviously the simple FESC yields the largest errors, whereas the FESC with state dependent Coxian distribution gives the smallest errors.

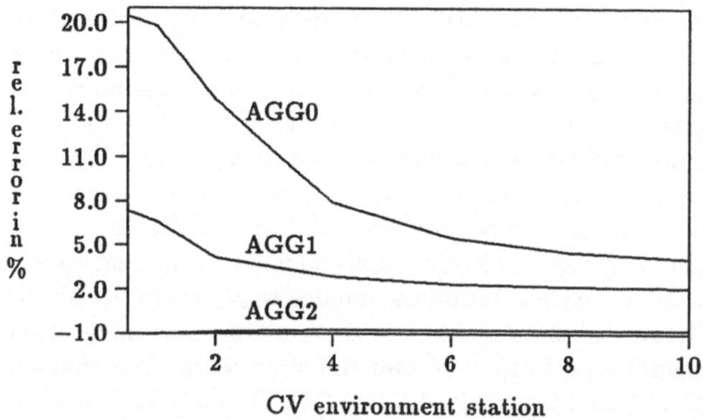

Fig. 1. Relative error Throughput

The simple model has been analysed for various parameter sets. However, we can only give a short summary of the results. In all configurations the standard FESC yields the largest errors. The gain due to the new aggregates is a reduction of the resulting error by a factor between 2 and 30 depending on the model parameters. The FESC with state dependent Coxian service time distribution is normally better than the FESC with fixed Coxian service time distribution. However, the last result depends on the model parameters and the performance quantity which is considered.

The second example (see figure 2) is an extended version of a combined queueing network - GSPN model presented in [1]. The environment is realized by an IS station modelling the *Terminals* and a PS station modelling the *CPU*. Both stations have exponentially distributed service times. The subnet to be aggregated describes the IO system and is realized by a coloured GSPN. The IO system includes two disks and a single shared channel. Entities enter the submodel and choose one of the disks by firing t_{11} or t_{12}. Afterwards an entity needs its disk and for a short amount of time the channel to initiate the seek operation (transitions t_get_1, t_get_2). Then the entity has to wait for positioning the disk, the end of positioning is realized by firing t_pos_1 or t_pos_2, respectively. To transfer data from/to the disk the channel is needed, thus the entity has to wait in place w_chan_i to get access to the channel. Afterward the

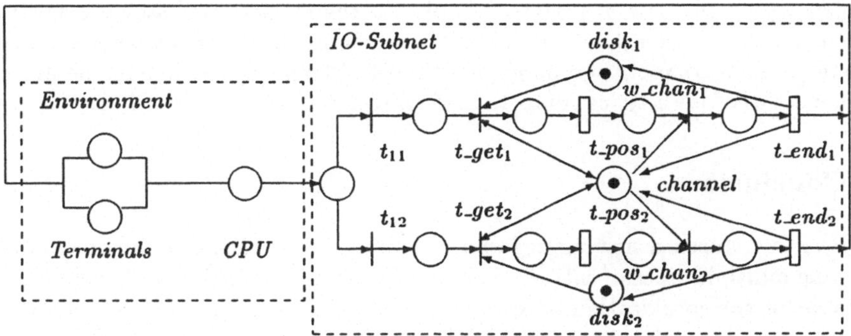

Fig. 2. Second example model

data transfer is performed holding the disk and the channel during this time. The end of data transfer is realized by firing transition t_end_i. The model includes 2 types of entities with population 3 each. We assume that both entity types behave totally equivalent except for the amount of data to be transferred.

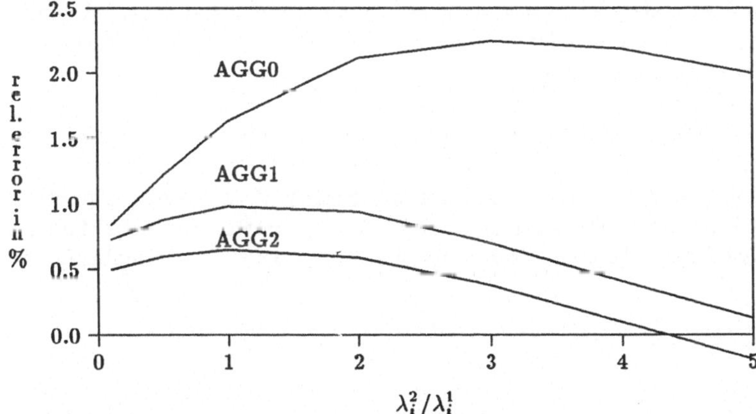

Fig. 3. Relative error Population of Type 2

Let λ_i^j be the firing rate of transition t_end_i $(i = 1, 2)$ for entity type $j = 1, 2$. Experiments have been performed varying λ_i^2 between $0.1\lambda_i^1$ and $10\lambda_i^1$. All three aggregate types have been computed and used instead of the original submodel in combination with the environment. As an example the relative errors of the class 2 population in the subnet and aggregates are shown in figure 3. The new aggregate types yield smaller errors, however, the difference to the standard FESC is smaller than in the single type case. The results conform with other examples and performance quantities, most times' results are improved (although this is not as strict as in the single class case), but the improvement is sometimes rather small. The problem seems to be that we analyse the behaviour of one entity type according to entities of the same type very detailed, but the behaviour of entities of other types is assumed to be as in short-circuit. In reality there are stronger relations between entities of different types. Thus, results for multi-type models are improved significantly by the new aggregates (similar to the single type case) whenever the dependency between entities of different types is loose and improvements are smaller if there is much competition among entities of different types, like in the example where entities of both types compete in getting access to the channel and the disks.

7 Conclusions

We have introduced a new aggregation technique for a general class of submodels including multiple types of entities. Submodels can be specified in various techniques available for the specification of Markov models. The new approach is environment independent (i.e., only information about the submodel and not about the environment is used for aggregate construction). The effort for pre-analysis is comparable with the effort for a numerical short-circuit pre-analysis. On contemporary workstations submodels including several thousands of states per population can be aggregated. Additionally pre-analysis can be performed in parallel by computing conditional distributions and moments for different population vectors on different processors. Since several calculations are completely independent, analysis can also be distributed on a workstation cluster with larger communication delays. Usually the sets of equations to be solved for pre-analysis are small compared with the size of a model composed of the submodel and an environment (see [4]).

The new approach can be used automatically in an appropriate modelling environment like the IMSE. Nevertheless, the technique is based on heuristics, like most of the known environment independent aggregation techniques. This has, of course, the consequence that formal proofs for the quality of the results cannot be given. However, examples show significantly smaller aggregation errors for the new aggregates compared with standard flow-equivalent aggregation in particular in the single type case.

References

1. G. Balbo, S.C. Bruell, S. Ghanta; Combining Queueing Networks and Generalized Stochastic Petri Nets for the Solution of Complex Models of System Behavior; *IEEE Trans. on Comp., Vol. 37, No 10, 1988, pp. 1251-1268.*

2. G. Balbo, S.C. Bruell; Computational Aspects of Aggregation in Multiple Class Queueing Networks; *Performance Evaluation, Vol. 3, 1983, pp. 177-185.*

3. G. Balbo, G. Serazzi (ed.), Computer Performance Evaluation - Modelling Techniques and Tools; *North Holland 1992.*

4. P. Buchholz; The Structured Analysis of Markovian Models (in German); *IFB 282, Springer 1991.*

5. P. Buchholz, M. Sczittnick; DAT Final Report; *IMSE Deliverable D5.4-2, 1992.*

6. K.M. Chandy, U. Herzog, L. Woo; Parametric Analysis of Queueing Networks; *IBM Jour. Res. and Dev. Vol. 19, No. 1, January 1975, pp. 36-42.*

7. G. Chiola; GreatSPN 1.5 Software Architecture; *in [3]*

8. P.J. Courtois; Decomposability: Queueing and Computer System Application; *Academic Press 1977.*

9. J.P. Hong, G. Kim; Class dependent queueing disciplines with product form solutions; *in A.K. Aggrawalla, S.K. Tripathi (ed.), Performance 83; North Holland 1983.*

10. P.J. Kuehn; Analysis of busy periods and response times in queueing networks by the method of first passage times; *in A.K. Aggrawalla, S.K. Tripathi (ed.), Performance 83, North Holland 1983.*

11. R. Lal, U.N. Bhat; Reduced Systems in Markov Chains and their Application in Queueing Theory; *Queueing Systems, Vol. 2, 1987, pp. 147-172.*

12. S.S. Lavenberg, M. Reiser; Stationary State Probabilities at Arrival Instants for Closed Queueing Networks with Multiple Types of Customers; *J. Appl. Prob., vol. 17, 1980, pp. 1048-1061.*

13. R. Pooley; The Integrated Modelling Support Environment a new generation of performance modelling tools; *in [3].*

14. M. Veran, D. Potier; A Portable Environment for Queueing Systems Modelling; *in D. Potier (ed.); Modelling Techniques and Tools for Performance Analysis, North Holland 1984.*

A A brief survey on Coxian distributions

As service time distribution for the new aggregates we use a special type of a Coxian distribution. Parameter estimation for these distributions is very briefly introduced in this appendix, more detailed results and proofs can be found in [4]. The used Coxian distributions consist of m (≥ 2) exponential phases, phase 1 has a rate μ_1, the remaining phases $2..m$ all have the same rate μ_2. An entity enters phase 2 after leaving phase 1 with probability a_1 or leaves the distribution with probability $1 - a_1$. After entering phase 2 the entity has to pass through all phases $2 \ldots m$ (i.e., $a_i = 1$ for all $1 < i < m$, $a_m = 0$). The class contains all Coxian distributions with 2 phases and a subclass of Coxian distributions with more than 2 phases. The first and second moment of the distribution $E(T^1)$ and $E(T^2)$ are calculated as

$$E(T^1) = \frac{1}{\mu_1} + \frac{(m-1)a_1}{\mu_2} \qquad E(T^2) = \frac{2E(T^1)}{\mu_1} + (m-1)m\frac{a_1}{\mu_2^2} \tag{17}$$

The minimal number of phases m needed to match a given second moment equals

$$m = \begin{cases} \lceil \frac{E(T^1)^2}{E(T^2)-E(T^1)^2} \rceil & \text{if } E(T^2) \leq 2E(T^1)^2 \\ 2 & \text{else} \end{cases} \tag{18}$$

The parameter a_1 can be chosen in the following intervals:

- if $E(T^2)/E(T^1)^2 > 2.0$: $0 < a_1 < mE(T^1)^2/((m-1)E(T^2))$
- if $E(T^2)/E(T^1)^2 = 2.0$: $a_1 = 0$
- if $E(T^2)/E(T^1)^2 < 2.0$: $m(2E(T^1)^2 - E(T^2))/((m-1)E(T^1)^2 \leq a_1 \leq 1.0$

If the phases of the distribution should be equally occupied, then

$$a_1 = \frac{(m-1)E(T^1)^2}{mE(T^2) - 2E(T^1)^2} \tag{19}$$

After the values for a_1 and m have been fixed in an appropriate way, the remaining service rates are computed using the following equations.

$$\mu_2 = \frac{\pm\sqrt{2m(m-1)a_1 E(T^2)+a_1((m-1)^2 a_1 - 2m(m-1))E(T^1)^2} - (m-1)a_1 E(T^1)}{E(T^2)-2E(T^1)} \tag{20}$$
$$\mu_1 = \frac{\mu_2}{E(T^1)\mu_2 - a_1}$$

For μ_2 only positive solutions are allowed. With the above formulas Coxian distributions matching the first and second moment can be generated, the free parameter a_1 can be varied inside the allowed interval.

This article was processed using the LaTeX macro package with LLNCS style

Random Quantum Allocation: A new approach to waiting time distributions for M/M/N processor sharing queues

Jens Braband*   Rolf Schaßberger

Institut für Mathematische Stochastik

Technische Universität Braunschweig

Pockelsstraße 14

D–38106 Braunschweig

Abstract

Several variants of multiple server queues with Poisson input, exponentially distributed service demands and processor sharing discipline are considered. These queues are approximated by sequences of models featuring a new natural discipline called Random Quantum Allocation (RQA) operating in discrete time. This approach can be used for the numerical approximation of waiting and response time distributions for processor sharing queues. In the particular case of the M/M/1–RQA model we derive the generating function of the waiting time distribution of a tagged customer conditioned on service demand and number of customers in the system and the corresponding first two moments. The results are compared with the results for the M/M/1 processor sharing queue. Additionally we discuss the effect of the number of parallel processors on the response time distribution under the condition of fixed total service capacity.

Keywords: Processor sharing, multiple server queues, waiting time distributions.

1   Introduction

Queueing models with processor shared service have attracted considerable interest as models of time sharing computer systems. If there are n customers present in a single server processor sharing (PS) model each customer receives service at a rate of $\frac{1}{n}$ of the total service rate. The main performance measure of such a computer model is a customers response or waiting time either conditioned on the state of the system at his arrival and/or his total service demand or under stationary conditions.

While several single server PS models have been studied, relatively little is known about multiple server PS models (see [5] for stationary distributions and the survey [8] as

---

*Since 1st February 1993 the first author is with Siemens AG, Bereich Verkehrstechnik, Ackerstraße 22, D–38126 Braunschweig

a general reference). Multiple server PS models are of particular interest because the usual way to increase the performance of a computer system is to use a faster processor. But as faster processors become very expensive, a natural way to overcome this bottleneck is to use parallel processors.

The common approach to PS queueing models is via an approximating sequence of Round Robin (RR) models in discrete time, see for example [2] for the M/M/1–PS model or [7] for the M/G/1–PS model. From the practical point of view this is a realistic and natural approach because PS models are idealizations of RR queues. But if we are mainly interested in PS models, RR models have two major drawbacks: Firstly in the PS model there is no overt queueing at all, and secondly the description of RR models is much more complicated.

We have asked the question whether there exists a natural approach in the above sense. Our answer is the Random Quantum Allocation (RQA) model, which in contrast to the RR model gives up the ordering of the customers in the queue. The basic idea is to select the next customers to be served at random. This results in an improved numerical approximation of the PS model.

The paper is organized as follows: We define the M/M/N–RQA model which serves as an approximation for the M/M/N–PS model and show how the waiting time distributions for the RQA model can be determined numerically. We choose this model because there exist no results [8] about the waiting time distributions in the M/M/N–PS model. Our methods can easily be adapted to several variants and generalizations of the M/M/N–RQA model. Unfortunately exact analytical results for the waiting time distributions of most of the PS models discussed here are unknown. The M/M/1–RQA and M/M/1–PS models seem to be the only models where waiting time distributions and moments can be analysed in detail. We derive the waiting time distribution and moments for the M/M/1–RQA model and compare the results with the results for the M/M/1–PS model. We discuss the effect of the number of parallel processors on the response time distribution for fixed total service capacity.

2 The M/M/N–RQA model

Consider a system with $N \geq 1$ identical servers and an unbounded waiting room for customers. Let the system operate in discrete time as follows:

1. Arrivals and departures of customers occur only at multiples tq, $t \in \mathbb{N}$, of the time slice length $q > 0$.

2. There is at most one arrival at tq. The probability of an arrival is $\lambda q < 1$ independent of all other events in the system.

3. A newly arriving customer at tq is being served by one of the N servers during the next time slice $[tq, (t+1)q)$.

4. If there are $n \leq N$ customers already in the waiting room at tq and there is no arrival, all customers are being served in the next time slice by one server, the other servers remaining idle. If there are at least $N + 1$ customers present without a new

customer arriving, N customers are selected at random for service during the next time slice. If there is an arrival at tq, only the remaining $N-1$ service positions are distributed among the waiting customers in the above manner.

5. Each customer that has been served during the time slice $[tq, (t+1)q)$ leaves the system with probability $\mu q < 1$ after his service, independent of all other events in the system.

The M/M/N–RQA model is obviously a discrete approximation for the M/M/N–PS model with Poisson input stream with intensity λ and customers having exponentially distributed service demands with mean $\frac{1}{\mu}$. The weak convergence of the waiting time distributions in the M/M/N–RQA model to the corresponding waiting time distributions in the M/M/N–PS model can be proved along the same lines of reasoning as in [7], for details see [1].

We remark that the servicing of newly arriving customers simplifies the analysis of the M/M/1–RQA model. Other possible choices are to treat arriving customers in the same way as waiting customers or to serve no customer at all if there is a new arrival. We remark that the service behaviour of the model can be changed for time slices immediately after the arrival of new customers without changing the weak convergence properties.

3 Waiting time distributions in the M/M/N–RQA model

Consider a tagged customer with a remaining service demand of k time slices. Let $p_{k,m}(n)$ be the probability that the tagged customer remains in the system for exactly $k+m$ time slices, conditioned on his remaining service demand k and the number n of competing customers in the system (not including the tagged customer). Then $\{p_{k,m}(n), m \in \mathbb{N}\}$ is the conditioned waiting time distribution. This distribution is completely determined by the following set of recursive equations, which we can derive by conditioning on the events that occur during the next time slice (the details are given above in the description of the model)

$$
\begin{aligned}
p_{0,m}(n) &= \delta_{m,0} \\
p_{k,m}(n) &= \lambda q \left(\sum_{i=0}^{n+1} \mu_i^{n+1} p_{k-1,m}(n+1-i) \right) + (1-\lambda q) \left(\sum_{i=0}^{n} \mu_i^{n} p_{k-1,m}(n-i) \right) \\
&\qquad n < N-1 \\
p_{k,m}(n) &= (1-\lambda q) \left\{ \frac{N}{n+1} \sum_{i=0}^{N-1} \mu_i^{N-1} p_{k-1,m}(n-i) \right. \\
&\qquad \left. + \left(1 - \frac{N}{n+1} \right) \sum_{i=0}^{N} \mu_i^{N} p_{k,m-1}(n-i) \right\} \\
&\quad + \lambda q \left\{ \frac{N-1}{n+1} \sum_{i=0}^{N-1} \mu_i^{N-1} p_{k-1,m}(n+1-i) \right. \\
&\qquad \left. + \left(1 - \frac{N-1}{n+1} \right) \sum_{i=0}^{N} \mu_i^{N} p_{k,m-1}(n+1-i) \right\}, n \geq N-1
\end{aligned}
\tag{1}
$$

$$p_{k,m}(-1) = p_{k,-1}(n) = 0$$

where $\mu_i^n = \binom{n}{i}(\mu q)^i(1-\mu q)^{n-i}$ denotes the probability that among n customers that have been served i leave the system and δ the Kronecker symbol. The first recursion formula states that the tagged customer leaves the system immediately after receiving the last service time slice. The second formula stands for the case where all customers are being served during the next time slice, while the last represents the case where we have $n+1$ customers (including the tagged one) are competing for service. Note that the tagged customer cannot leave the system before his fixed service demand is completed and that the maximal number of the customers who can leave the system depends on whether the tagged customer is being served during the time slice or not.

The conditioned waiting time distributions for the M/M/N–RQA model can be evaluated numerically via (1) with reasonable computational effort for moderate values of q. The computational effort can be further reduced by the introduction of further approximations:

1. For small time slice length q we have $\mu_i^n = o(q)$ for $i \geq 2$ and a reasonable approximation for this case is $\mu_0^n = 1 - \mu nq$, $\mu_1^n = \mu nq < 1$ and $\mu_i^n = 0$ for $i \geq 2$.

2. If there is no arrival no customer at all is being served in the next time slice. This reduces the complexity of (1) significantly but alters the waiting time distributions for small q only very little.

In the same manner we can find recursions for the waiting time distribution $\{p_m(n), m \in \mathbb{N}\}$ conditioned on the number n of competing customers only. The only difference is that now the tagged customer himself is allowed to leave the system after each service with probability μq. As an example we give the recursion for the waiting time distribution $\{p_m(n), m \in \mathbb{N}\}$ modified by the two approximations proposed above. Using the abbreviation $\varphi(n) = \min\{n+1, N\}$, which simply stands for the number of customers which can be served during the next time slice, we have

$$p_0(n) = (1 - \lambda q)\frac{\varphi(n)}{n+1} \tag{2}$$
$$\{\mu q + (1 - \mu q)\left((\varphi(n) - 1)\mu q p_0(n-1) + (1 - (\varphi(n) - 1)\mu q)p_0(n)\right)\}$$

$$p_m(n) = \lambda q p_{m-1}(n+1) \tag{3}$$
$$+(1 - \lambda q)\left\{\frac{\varphi(n)}{n+1}(1 - \mu q)\left((\varphi(n) - 1)\mu q p_m(n-1) + (1 - (\varphi(n) - 1)\mu q)p_m(n)\right)\right.$$

$$\left. + \left(1 - \frac{\varphi(n)}{n+1}\right)\left(\varphi(n)\mu q p_{m-1}(n-1) + (1 - \varphi(n)\mu q)p_{m-1}(n)\right)\right\}, m > 0,$$

$$p_m(-1) = p_{-1}(n) = 0.$$

We remark that due to the first approximation all sums that appeared in (1) are reduced to just two terms, which is a significant advantage for the analysis and numeric evaluation of the recursions. We notice that the corresponding recursion for the response time distribution $\{\hat{p}_m(n), m \in \mathbb{N}\}$ can be obtained in a simpler form

$$\hat{p}_1(n) = (1 - \lambda q)\frac{\varphi(n)}{n+1}\mu q \tag{4}$$

$$\hat{p}_m(n) = \lambda q \hat{p}_{m-1}(n+1) \tag{5}$$

$$+(1-\lambda q)\left\{ \frac{\varphi(n)}{n+1}(1-\mu q)\left((\varphi(n)-1)\mu q \hat{p}_{m-1}(n-1) + (1-(\varphi(n)-1)\mu q)\hat{p}_{m-1}(n)\right) \right.$$

$$\left. + \left(1 - \frac{\varphi(n)}{n+1}\right)\left(\varphi(n)\mu q \hat{p}_{m-1}(n-1) + (1-\varphi(n)\mu q)\hat{p}_{m-1}(n)\right) \right\}, m > 1,$$

$$\hat{p}_m(-1) = \hat{p}_{-1}(n) = 0,$$

where m now stands for the discrete response time, which, in contrast to the waiting time, is being reduced during each time slice by one.

We remark that the waiting time distributions for M/M/N–PS models are unknown [8], except for the classical case $N = 1$ [2] where their Laplace–Stieltjes transforms have been found. Additionally an integral representation for the distribution function of the equilibrium response time has been given [6]. For this reason we concentrate in the following sections on the M/M/1–PS respectively RQA model, where analytical solutions exist and can be compared.

4   Analysis of the M/M/1–RQA model

In this particular case we can determine the generating function of the waiting time distributions by analytic methods. We consider the case $q = 1$ to simplify the notation. We get the results in the general case by substitution of λ and μ by λq and μq in the results for $q = 1$.

Theorem 1 *Let $x, y, z, \lambda, \mu \in (0,1)$. The transform*

$$G(x,y,z) := \sum_{k=0}^{\infty}\sum_{n=0}^{\infty}\sum_{m=0}^{\infty} p_{k,m}(n) z^m y^n x^k - \frac{1}{1-y} \tag{6}$$

of the waiting time distribution in the M/M/1–RQA model satisfies the first order linear differential equation

$$\alpha(y,z)\frac{\partial G}{\partial y} = \beta(x,y,z)G + \gamma(x,y) \tag{7}$$

where

$$\begin{aligned}
\alpha(y,z) &= -(1-\lambda)\mu z y^2 + (1-\lambda\mu z - (1-\lambda)(1-\mu)z)y - \lambda(1-\mu)z \\
\beta(x,y,z) &= (1-\lambda)\mu z y - (1-\lambda\mu z) + (1-\lambda)x \\
\gamma(x,y) &= \frac{(1-\lambda)x}{1-y}
\end{aligned}$$

Proof: The recursion (1) reduces in the case $N = 1$ to

$$p_{k,0}(n) = \left(\frac{1-\lambda}{n+1}\right)^k \quad \text{and} \quad p_{0,m}(n) = \delta_{m,0}$$

and

$$p_{k,m}(n) = (1-\lambda)\left\{\frac{1}{n+1}p_{k-1,m}(n) + \frac{n}{n+1}\left(\mu p_{k,m-1}(n-1) + (1-\mu)p_{k,m-1}(n)\right)\right\}$$

$$+\lambda\left\{(1-\mu)p_{k,m-1}(n+1) + \mu p_{k,m-1}(n)\right\}.$$

For the generating function of the waiting time distribution $f_{k,n}(z) = \sum_{m=0}^{\infty} p_{k,m}(n)z^m$ we find $f_{0,n}(z) = 1$ and for $k \geq 1$

$$((n+1)(1-\lambda\mu z) - (1-\lambda)(1-\mu)nz)\, f_{k,n}(z) =$$
$$(1-\lambda)f_{k-1,n}(z) + (1-\lambda)\mu nz f_{k,n-1}(z) + \lambda(1-\mu)(n+1)z f_{k,n+1}(z).$$

We remark that $f_{k,n}(z)$ is not determined by the equation above because $f_{k,0}(z)$ is unknown. Straightforward application of the transformations with respect to y and x yields (7). ∎

(7) implies a boundary condition at the points (y,z) with $\alpha(y,z) = 0$. Simple calculus shows

Lemma 2 *For all* $\lambda \in (0,1), \mu \in (0,1), y \in [0,1], z \in (0,1)$ *the polynomial* $\alpha(y,z)$ *possesses two real roots*

$$y_1(z) \;=\; \frac{1 - \lambda\mu z - (1-\lambda)(1-\mu)z - \sqrt{D(z)}}{2\mu(1-\lambda)z}$$

$$y_2(z) \;=\; \frac{1 - \lambda\mu z - (1-\lambda)(1-\mu)z + \sqrt{D(z)}}{2\mu(1-\lambda)z}$$

$$D(z) \;=\; (\lambda\mu - (1-\lambda)(1-\mu))^2 z^2 - 2(\lambda\mu + (1-\lambda)(1-\mu))z + 1 > 0.$$

satisfying $0 < y_1(z) < 1 < y_2(z)$.

Lemma 2 and (7) provide the boundary condition

$$G(x, y_1(z), z) = -\frac{(1-\lambda)x}{(1 - y_1(z))(\beta(y_1(z), z) + (1-\lambda)x)}. \tag{8}$$

Now the solution of (7) can be given in terms of the hypergeometric function [3]

$$F(a, b; c; z) = \sum_{i=0}^{\infty} \frac{(a)_i (b)_i}{(c)_i\, i!} z^n \tag{9}$$

or the generalized Zeta function [3]

$$\Phi(z, s, \nu) = \sum_{i=0}^{\infty} (\nu + i)^{-s} z^n$$

where $(x)_i$ denotes the Pochhammer symbol

$$(x)_i = \frac{\Gamma(x+i)}{\Gamma(x)}.$$

We define the auxiliary functions

$$c_1(y, z) \;=\; (y - y_1(z))(y_2(z) - 1)$$
$$c_2(y, z) \;=\; (y_2(z) - y)(1 - y_1(z))$$
$$\Delta(x, z) \;=\; \frac{1}{2} - \frac{(1-\lambda)x + \frac{1}{2}(z(\lambda + \mu - 1) - 1)}{\sqrt{D(z)}}.$$

Theorem 3 *The differential equation (7) possesses for all $x, y, z, \lambda, \mu \in (0,1)$ satisfying*

$$\left| \frac{c_1(y,z)}{c_2(y,z)} \right| < 1$$

a unique solution which can be stated explicitly as

$$G(x,y,z) \;=\; \frac{x}{\mu z c_2(y,z)} \Phi\left(\frac{c_1(y,z)}{c_2(y,z)}, 1, \Delta(x,z) \right) \tag{10}$$

$$=\; \frac{x}{\mu z} \int_0^\infty \frac{e^{-\Delta(x,z)t}}{c_2(y,z) - c_1(y,z)e^{-t}} dt \tag{11}$$

$$=\; \frac{x}{\mu z c_2(y,z)\Delta(x,z)} F\left(1, \Delta(x,z); 1 + \Delta(x,z); \frac{c_1(y,z)}{c_2(y,z)} \right) \tag{12}$$

$$=\; \frac{x}{\mu z} \int_0^1 \frac{t^{\Delta(x,z)-1}}{c_2(y,z) - c_1(y,z)t} dt. \tag{13}$$

Proof: We remark that we have $\Delta(x,z) > 0$ for all $x \in [0,1]$ and $z \in [0,1)$ and that a sufficient condition for $\left|\frac{c_1(y,z)}{c_2(y,z)}\right| < 1$ is given by $\frac{\lambda}{\mu} \leq 1$.

(7) can be solved by standard methods for the integration of linear ordinary differential equations of the first order. This gives for $\alpha(y,z) \neq 0$ the general solution

$$G(x,y,z) = M(x,y,z)^{-1}\left(\int \frac{(1-\lambda)x}{(1-y)\alpha(y,z)} M(x,y,z)\,dy + C(x,z) \right)$$

where $C(x,z)$ is an arbitrary function and

$$M(x,y,z) = \exp\left(-\int \frac{\beta(x,y,z)}{\alpha(y,z)} dy \right).$$

Integration and a geometric series expansion with respect to t yields

$$G(x,y,z) \;=\; \frac{(1-\lambda)x}{(1-\lambda)\mu z c_2(y,z)} \sum_{i=0}^\infty \left(\frac{c_1(y,z)}{c_2(y,z)} \right)^i \frac{1}{i + \Delta(x,z)} + \frac{C(x,z)}{M(x,y,z)}$$

$$=\; \frac{x}{\mu z c_2(y,z)} \Phi\left(\frac{c_1(y,z)}{c_2(y,z)}, 1, \Delta(x,z) \right) + \frac{C(x,z)}{M(x,y,z)},$$

and

$$M(x,y,z) = \sqrt{(1-\lambda)\mu z}\, \frac{|y - y_1(z)|^{\Delta(x,z)}}{|y - y_2(z)|^{\Delta(x,z)-1}}.$$

Now the boundary condition (8) implies $C(x,z) = 0$ because of

$$\lim_{y \to y_1(z)} \frac{x}{\mu z c_2(y,z)} \Phi\left(\frac{c_1(y,z)}{c_2(y,z)}, 1, \Delta(x,z) \right) \;=\; \frac{(1-\lambda)x}{(1-\lambda)\mu z(1 - y_1(z))(y_2(z) - y_1(z))\Delta(x,z)}$$

$$=\; \frac{(1-\lambda)x}{(1 - y_1(z))(\beta(y_1(z),z) + (1-\lambda)x)}$$

$$=\; G(x, y_1(z), z)$$

and $M(x, y_1(z), z) = 0$. The representations (11), (12) and (13) of the solution (10) result from well known properties of the generalized Zeta and hypergeometric function [3]. ∎

We now calculate an explicit representation for the generating function of the waiting time distribution in the M/M/1–RQA model.

Theorem 4 *Let the conditions of Theorem 3 be fulfilled. Then we have for $k > 0$*

$$f_{k,n}(z) = \frac{1}{\mu z(k-1)!} \left(\frac{1-\lambda}{\sqrt{D(z)}} \right)^{k-1} \int_0^\infty t^{k-1} e^{-\Delta(0,z)t} \frac{(1 - y_1(z) + (y_2(z) - 1)e^{-t})^n}{(y_2(z) - r + (r - y_1(z))e^{-t})^{n+1}} dt,$$

$$(14)$$

where $r = \frac{\lambda(1-\mu)}{\mu(1-\lambda)}$.

Proof: Choosing the representation (11) for the solution of (7), we can show that in (11) differentiation with respect to y and the limit for $y \to 0$ may be interchanged with the integration with respect to t. A Taylor expansion of $G(x, y, z) = \sum_{n=0}^\infty G_n(x, z)y^n$ gives

$$G_n(x, z) = \frac{x}{\mu z} \int_0^\infty e^{-\Delta(x,z)t} \frac{(1 - y_1(z) + (y_2(z) - 1)e^{-t})^n}{(y_2(z) - r + (r - y_1(z))e^{-t})^{n+1}} dt.$$

Repeating the same argument with respect to x leads to the result (14). ∎

From (14) we compute the moments of the waiting time distribution.

Theorem 5 *Let $E_{k,n}$ be the expected value and $V_{k,n}$ the variance of the waiting time distribution (14) in the M/M/1–RQA model. For $\varrho = \lambda/\mu < 1$ and $r = \varrho\frac{1-\mu}{1-\lambda}$ we have*

$$E_{k,n} = \frac{1}{1-\lambda} \left\{ \frac{\lambda}{\mu(1-r)}k + \frac{n(1-r)-r}{\mu(1-r)^2} \left(1 - \left(\frac{1-\lambda}{1+\mu-2\lambda} \right)^k \right) \right\} \tag{15}$$

and

$$V_{k,n} = \frac{\alpha_0 + \alpha_1 \left(\dfrac{1-\lambda}{1+\mu-2\lambda} \right)^k + \alpha_2 \left(\dfrac{1-\lambda}{1+2\mu-3\lambda} \right)^k + \alpha_3 \left(\dfrac{1-\lambda}{1+\mu-2\lambda} \right)^{2k}}{\mu^2(1-\varrho)^4} \tag{16}$$

with

$$\begin{aligned}
\alpha_0 &= n\left(1 - \varrho^2 - \mu(1-\varrho)(1+\varrho^2)\right) + k\lambda(1-\varrho)\left(2 - (\lambda+\mu)\right) \\
&\quad - \varrho(\varrho+4) - \lambda\mu(\varrho^2 + 3\varrho - 1) + \lambda(\varrho^2 + 4\varrho + 5) \\
\alpha_1 &= n\mu(1-\varrho)^3 + \varrho\left(4 + \mu^2(1+\varrho)^2 - \mu(\varrho^2 + 2\varrho + 5)\right) \\
&\quad + 2k\mu(1 - \varrho^2)(1-\mu)\frac{\varrho(1-\mu) - n(1-\varrho)}{1+\mu-2\lambda} \\
\alpha_2 &= n^2(1-\varrho)^2 + n(1-\varrho)(4\lambda - 3\varrho - 1) + 2\varrho^2(1-\mu)^2 \\
\alpha_3 &= -\left(n(1-\varrho) + \lambda - \varrho\right)^2
\end{aligned}$$

Proof: The straightforward but lengthy and tedious computations have been carried out with the help of the symbolic algebra package REDUCE [4] and will be omitted. ∎

5 Comparing M/M/1–RQA and PS models

First we show the consistency of our results with the corresponding results for the M/M/1–PS model. Let $w(s; \tau, n)$ be the Laplace–Stieltjes transform of the waiting time distribution in the M/M/1–PS model conditioned on the service demand τ of the tagged customer and the number n of competing customers [2].

Substituting λ and μ in (10) by λq and μq, we have the results for arbitrary time slice length q. As in [7] we get the Laplace–Stieltjes transform of the waiting time distribution in the M/M/1–PS model by substituting k by $k(\tau, q) = \lceil \frac{\tau}{q} \rceil$ and z respectively x by e^{-sq} respectively e^{-tq}, and performing the limiting procedure for $q \to 0$. For (10) this yields after some algebra and rearrangement of terms

$$\lim_{q \to 0} qG(e^{-tq}, y, e^{-sq}) = \frac{r}{\varrho(1 - \varrho r)(1 - ry)} \Phi\left(\frac{(1 - r)(y - \varrho r)}{(1 - ry)(1 - \varrho r)}, 1, \frac{r(t + \lambda(1 - r))}{\varrho(1 - \varrho r^2)}\right)$$

with

$$r = \frac{\lambda + \mu + s - \sqrt{(\lambda + \mu + s)^2 - 4\mu\lambda}}{2\lambda}.$$

Using the integral representation [3]

$$\Phi(z, s, \nu) = \frac{1}{\Gamma(s)} \int_0^\infty \frac{t^{s-1} e^{-\nu t}}{1 - ze^{-t}} dt$$

for the generalized Zeta function and a Taylor expansion with respect to y we get the classical results of [2]. Similarly we can show the convergence of $qE_{k,n}$ and $q^2V_{k,n}$ for $q \to 0$ to the corresponding formulae for the mean and variance of the conditioned waiting time in the M/M/1–PS model.

A comparision of the means and variances for the waiting time distributions in the M/M/1–RQA and M/M/1–PS models shows the quick convergence of these performance measures. The figures 1 and 2 show for an example with $\mu = 1$, $n = 0$, $\tau = 5$, $q = 2^{-i}, i = 1, \ldots, 8$, $k = \lceil \tau/q \rceil$ the relation between the load ϱ and the means $E(q, n) = qE_{k,n}$ and standard deviations $S(q, n) = q\sqrt{V_{k,n}}$. The dashed lines stand for the M/M/1–RQA model, whereas the solid lines represent the corresponding M/M/1–PS model. We notice that in all examples we studied a time slice length $q \approx 0.01$ yielded sufficiently good approximation results.

Additionally we can compute the distribution of the equilibrium response time V in the M/M/1–RQA model via (4), (5) and the stationary distribution of customers in the M/M/1–RQA model. For the M/M/1–PS model an integral representation for the equilibrium response time distribution is known [6], which can be evaluated numerically. For time slice length $q = 0.01$ respectively $q = 0.001$ the absolute differences between the RQA approximation and the numerical results from [6] in our examples were less than 1.5×10^{-3} respectively 2×10^{-4}, the plots of the response time distributions cannot be distinguished in the scale of the following figures. We show in figure 3 and 4 the complementary response time distribution $P(V > t)$ for M/M/1–RQA and M/M/2–RQA models for the same load in logarithmic scale. In particular the parameters are $\lambda = 0.1, 0.2, \ldots, 0.9$ and $\mu = 1$ respectively $\mu = \frac{1}{2}$.

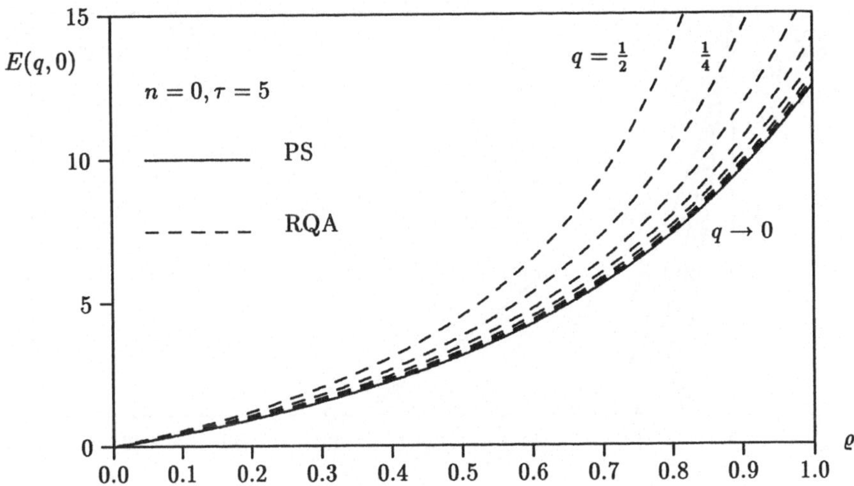

Figure 1: Comparision of expected waiting times

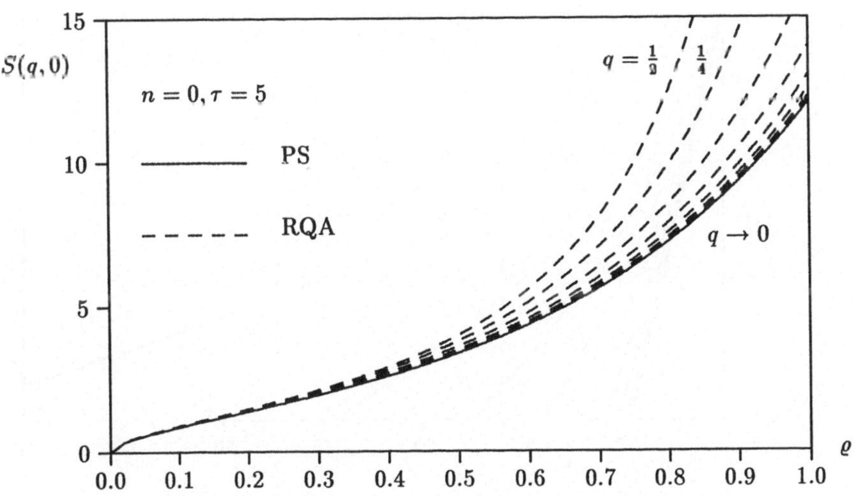

Figure 2: Comparision of standard deviations of waiting times

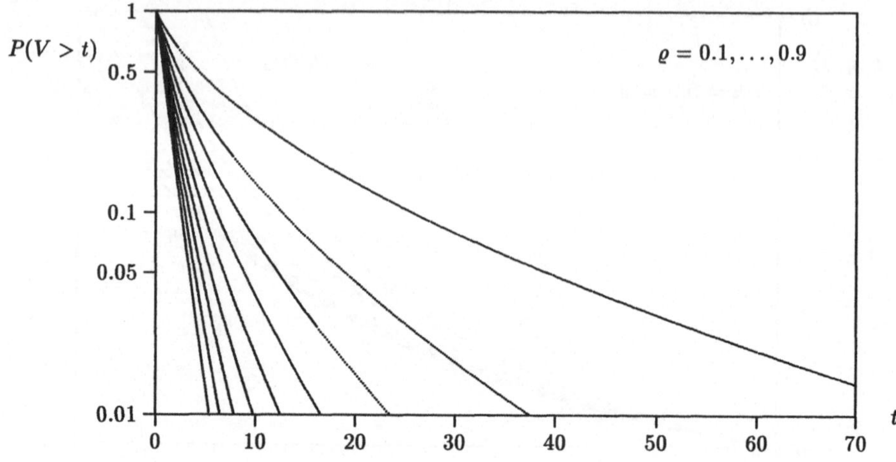

Figure 3: Response time distributions for the M/M/1–RQA model

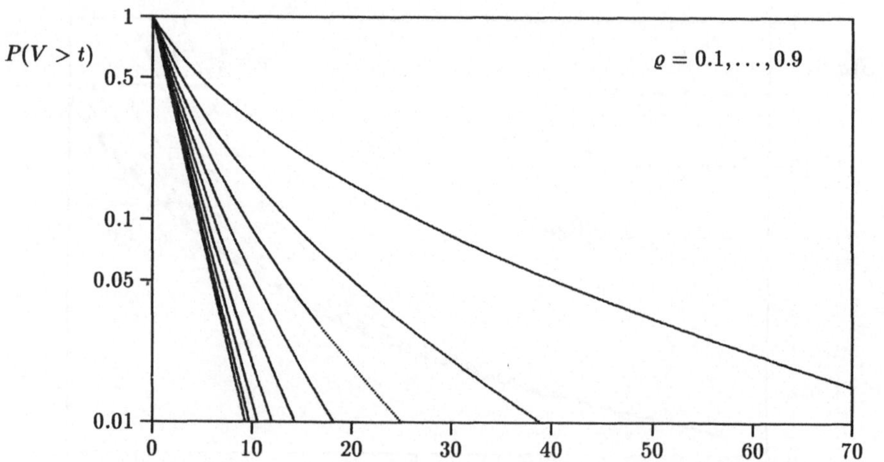

Figure 4: Response time distributions for the M/M/2–RQA model

The largest absolute error between the distribution functions for the RQA approximations with $q = 0.01$ and $q = 0.001$ in the numerical examples below was less than 1.2×10^{-3}. The results show that the response time increases with the number of processors and the effect is larger for small load. For high load the response times are practically identical because almost no processor is idle at any time.

6 Conclusion

We showed in this paper that the RQA approach is useful for the numerical and analytical approximation of the waiting and response time distributions of the M/M/1–PS model. The weak convergence of the waiting and response time distributions of the M/M/N–RQA model to the corresponding quantities of the M/M/N–PS model is known [1], but up to now no explicit representations for transforms like (14) for the M/M/N–RQA model have been found. Nevertheless the efficient numerical computation of the waiting and response time distributions of the M/M/N–RQA model allows the determination of the waiting and response time distributions of the M/M/N–PS model with high accuracy, which seems to be sufficient for practical purposes.

In the same fashion as above we can approximate closed M/M/N–PS models with a fixed number of customers or gated M/M/N–PS models. Other possible generalizations might be models with arrival rates $\lambda = \lambda(n)$ depending on the number n of waiting customers or varying service capacity $N = N(n)$ where only approximations for the moments of the waiting time distributions have been found. Here the numerical evaluation of the corresponding recursions should be more difficult than in the case discussed in this paper.

We can also give recursions for waiting time distributions for more general models, e. g. M/G/1–RQA, but due to the high dimension of the state space we cannot evaluate the recursions efficiently. The RQA approach fails completely for models allowing group arrivals because $p_{k,m}(n)$ may depend on all $p_{k,m-1}(n + i)$, $i \in \mathbb{N}$, and we no longer have a recursive structure.

References

[1] J. Braband. *Wartezeitverteilungen für M/M/N–Processor–Sharing–Modelle*. Dissertation, Technische Universität Braunschweig, Braunschweig, 1992.

[2] E. G. Coffman, R. Muntz, and H. Trotter. Waiting time distributions for processor-sharing systems. *J. Ass. Comp. Mach.*, 17:123–130, 1970.

[3] A. Erdélyi, editor. *Higher Transcendental Functions*, volume 1 of *Bateman Manuscript Project*. McGraw Hill, New York, 1953.

[4] A. C. Hearn. *REDUCE User's Manual Version 3.2*. Rand Publication CP 78, 1985.

[5] F. P. Kelly. *Reversibility and Stochastic Networks*. Wiley, Chichester, 1979.

[6] J. A. Morrisson. Response time distribution for a processor–sharing system. *SIAM J. Appl. Math.*, 45:152–167, 1985.

[7] R. Schaßberger. A new approach to the M/G/1 processor sharing queue. *Adv. Appl. Prob.*, 16:202–213, 1984.

[8] S. F. Yashkov. Processor–sharing queues: Some progress in analysis. *Queueing Systems*, 2:1–17, 1987.

Mean Waiting Time Approximations
for Symmetric and Asymmetric Polling Systems
with Time-Limited Service

Michael Tangemann*
Alcatel SEL Research Centre
Lorenzstr. 10, D-7000 Stuttgart 40

Abstract

Cyclic polling systems are frequently used as models for the performance evaluation of token passing Local Area Networks (LANs) such as Token Ring or Token Bus and High Speed Local Area Networks (HSLANs), e.g., FDDI (Fiber Distributed Data Interface). The model is characterized by Poisson arrival processes, general independent packet service and switchover times and infinite buffer lengths. Frequently, the service disciplines exhaustive service or limited service are considered, because many results for these disciplines are available in the literature [14, 15]. However, they are not always appropriate for modeling the time-limited service disciplines defined in the standards for Token Ring, Token Bus and FDDI.

In this paper, we concentrate on these time-limited service disciplines to which little attention has been payed due to the complexity they impose on the mathematical model. Both the synchronous service discipline (fixed maximum service time) and the asynchronous service discipline (cycle time dependent maximum service time) are considered. Our approach is based on the use of the pseudo-conservation law, for which new approximate expressions for the mean unfinished work left behind by the server in a queue will be derived. With these expressions new pseudo-conservation laws for the weighted sum of the mean waiting times are obtained. They are used to determine the mean waiting times in symmetric systems. With additional assumptions relating the mean waiting times to the second moment of the cycle time solutions for asymmetric systems are obtained. Finally, the results of the analysis are validated by comparison to simulation results.

1 Introduction

An important class of Local Area Networks (LANs) and High Speed Local Area Networks (HSLANs) employs a token passing mechanism as the media access control (MAC) protocol for packet switched traffic. These networks are based on an either logical or physical ring topology. Since a ring represents a single medium shared by all stations, a MAC protocol is required to control the access of the stations to the medium. This can be achieved by passing a token from station to station which represents the access right. A

*This work was done while the author was with the Institute of Communications Switching and Data Technics of the University of Stuttgart, Germany. It was supported in part by the NATO under grant CRG 900108.

station that wants to transmit packets must first wait until the next token arrival and can then remove the token from the medium, transmit the packets and issue a new token which is passed to the next station on the ring.

One characteristic all standardized versions of Token Passing LANs and HSLANs, i.e. ANSI X3T9.5 FDDI [5], IEEE 802.4 Token Bus [21] and IEEE 802.5 Token Ring [22], have in common is the use of time-limited service disciplines. Two variations of these time-limited service disciplines exist:

1. Synchronous service: If queue i receives synchronous service, it may be served up to a fixed time threshold $\tau_{s,i}$ independently of the traffic load of the system. If the cycle time is limited (which happens if time-limited service disciplines are employed for all stations), this also means that limits for the access time (defined as the interval between the packet arrival instant and the next token arrival) and the minimum bandwidth available for this station exist. This is the reason why the name synchronous service has been chosen though service does not occur periodically for constant service times, as this name might perhaps imply.

2. Asynchronous service: A queue i with asynchronous service is assigned a time limit $\tau_{a,i}$ for the sum of the service time and the preceding cycle time. This service discipline can be implemented by using a token rotation timer that is reset and started on every token arrival. Upon token arrival, the token rotation timer therefore contains the measured value of the cycle (token rotation) time. This value is transferred into a token holding timer which is incremented while packets are transmitted and expires upon reaching the threshold $\tau_{a,i}$. However, if the cycle time itself exceeds $\tau_{a,i}$, queue i may not be served and the token must be passed to the next station (late token arrival). This kind of control makes the service time limit load-dependent: Under light load the cycle times will be small and the service time limit is large. On the other hand, as load increases, the cycle times also increase and queue i will be assigned a smaller service time maximum.

Additionally, two cases can be distinguished for both disciplines, depending on whether so-called overrun is permitted or not. If overrun is allowed, packet transmissions are always finished even if the timer elapses during a packet's service time. Since this could result in a performance degradation for the other stations, some protocols prohibit overrun.

The IEEE 802.5 Token Ring [22] uses synchronous service without overrun. Both IEEE 802.4 Token Bus [21] and ANSI X3T9.5 FDDI [5] offer a synchronous and multiple asynchronous traffic classes per station. The Token Bus standard permits overrun for all traffic classes, whereas FDDI allows overrun only for asynchronous traffic. Since the standards do not specify how overrun can be avoided, we assume that this is achieved by reducing the thresholds by the maximum packet service time and then permitting overrun, i.e., the reduced threshold may be exceeded, but the timer values are always smaller than the original thresholds. Thus it is sufficient to consider systems with overrun in the analysis.

Several analytic approaches for the analysis of token passing systems with time-limited service disciplines have been suggested in the literature. Yue and Brooks [24] developed the asymptote shifting method based on an idea by Fuhrmann [6]. The extended walk time method has been invented by Karvelas and Leon-Garcia [9]. An overview and a comparison of the two methods is given in [13]. Finally, Karvelas and Leon-Garcia developed the extended service time method [10]. However, a major drawback of these methods is that they do not take into account the pseudo-conservation law [1] which has been developed for cyclic polling systems with switchover times and is therefore applicable to FDDI. In this paper, a pseudo-conservation law for FDDI is derived and used for the analysis of the waiting times in symmetric and asymmetric systems.

The rest of this paper is organized as follows. After a description of the model used for the analysis and the pseudo-conservation laws for cyclic polling systems in Sec. 2 and 3, first the stability conditions for queues with synchronous or asynchronous service will be derived (Sec. 4). In Sec. 5, approximate expressions for the mean unfinished work for both synchronous and asynchronous service are derived. They are then used for a general formulation of a pseudo-conservation law with mixed time-limited service disciplines in Sec. 6, from which the mean waiting times in symmetric systems are derived (Sec. 7.1). An extension for asymmetric systems is given in Sec. 7.2. Finally, some results of the analysis are discussed and compared to simulation results.

2 Modeling

In this paper, we consider a cyclic polling system with N queues with infinite buffer space, Poisson arrivals at rate λ_i, and general service times $T_{B,i}$ with the first and second moments b_i and $b_i^{(2)}$ (cf. Fig. 1). The ring latency $T_{C,0}$ with the first two moments c_0 and $c_0^{(2)}$ is defined as the sum of the switchover times $T_{R,i}$

$$T_{C,0} = \sum_{i=1}^{N} T_{R,i} \tag{1}$$

The offered load at queue i is given by

$$\rho_i = \lambda_i \cdot b_i \ , \tag{2}$$

and the total offered load is

$$\hat{\rho} = \sum_{i=1}^{N} \rho_i \ . \tag{3}$$

The cycle time $T_{C,i}$ is defined as the interval between subsequent arrivals of the server at station i. Independently of the service discipline and the station number, the mean cycle time is given by [12]

$$c = \frac{c_0}{1 - \hat{\rho}} \ . \tag{4}$$

Each queue i can receive either synchronous or asynchronous service. The corresponding thresholds are $\tau_{s,i}$ or $\tau_{a,i}$, respectively. Overrun is taken into account by using the virtual thresholds $\tau_{s,i}^*$ and $\tau_{a,i}^*$ which represent the mean timer values at the instants when the

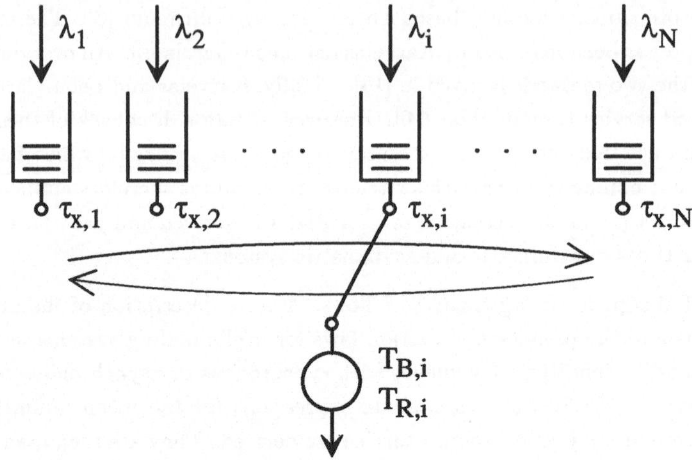

Figure 1: Modeling token passing systems with a cyclic polling system

server leaves the queue. They can be obtained by adding the age-dependent mean forward recurrence time of a packet service time to the thresholds [18]. Since this forward recurrence time depends on the age of the service process, the following limits exist:

$$\lim_{\tau_{s,i}\to 0} \tau_{s,i}^* = b_i \ , \tag{5}$$

$$\lim_{\tau_{x,i}\to\infty} (\tau_{x,i}^* - \tau_{x,i}) = \frac{b_i^{(2)}}{2b_i} \ , \tag{6}$$

where $x = s$ and $x = a$ stand for synchronous and asynchronous service, respectively. The same notation is used for the mean waiting times $w_{x,i}$ as well as the mean unfinished work at service completion $u_{x,i}$, where additionally $x = e$ is used for exhaustive service.

3   Pseudo-Conservation Laws

A general framework for pseudo-conservation laws has been provided by Boxma and Groenendijk [1, 8], who extended the laws found by Watson [23] using a stochastic decomposition approach similar to that one introduced by Fuhrmann and Cooper [6, 7]. Boxma and Groenendijk obtained an extension of the well-known conservation law for the M/G/1 queue [11] which includes switchover times and is therefore applicable to the cyclic polling model introduced in the previous section.

The pseudo-conservation law provides the following expression for the weighted sum of the mean waiting times $w_{x,i}$

$$\sum_{i=1}^{N} \rho_i w_{x,i} = \sum_{i=1}^{N} \rho_i w_{e,i} + \sum_{i=1}^{N} u_{x,i} \ . \tag{7}$$

As the switchover times are included, this expression now depends on the service discipline of each queue. However, the only quantity in eq. (7) which is influenced by the service discipline of queue i is the mean unfinished work $u_{x,i}$ the server leaves behind in queue i. In case of exhaustive service, we have $u_{x,i} = u_{e,i} = 0$ and $w_{x,i} = w_{e,i}$, in which case the pseudo-conservation law is explicitly given by [1]

$$\sum_{i=1}^{N} \rho_i w_{e,i} = \hat{\rho} \cdot \frac{\sum_{i=1}^{N} \lambda_i b_i^{(2)}}{2(1-\hat{\rho})} + \hat{\rho}\frac{c_0^{(2)}}{2c_0} + \frac{c_0}{2(1-\hat{\rho})}\left[\hat{\rho}^2 - \sum_{i=1}^{N} \rho_i^2\right] \ . \tag{8}$$

If one or more queues are not served exhaustively, the weighted sum of the mean waiting times is increased by the mean unfinished work, and equation (7) is obtained. This also includes the possibility of considering systems with mixed service disciplines.

If the polling system is symmetric, i.e., the system and traffic parameters as well as the service discipline are the same for each queue, the mean waiting times are also the same for each queue because of the inherent symmetry of the system, and they can be obtained directly from the pseudo-conservation law (7) as follows:

$$w_x = w_e + \frac{u_x}{\rho} \ , \tag{9}$$

where

$$w_e = \frac{N\lambda b^{(2)}}{2(1-\hat{\rho})} + \frac{c_0^{(2)}}{2c_0} + \frac{\rho c_0(N-1)}{2(1-\hat{\rho})} \ . \tag{10}$$

For several service disciplines such as gated service, limited-1 service, decrementing service, Bernoulli service and binomial service, exact expressions for the mean unfinished work have been found [1, 8, 20]. Furthermore, for limited-k service an exact expression including the unknown second factorial moment of the number of customers served per server arrival is given in [4]. However, time-limited service disciplines have not been considered in this context. The purpose of this paper is to derive approximate expressions for the mean unfinished work for both synchronous and asynchronous service.

4 Stability Conditions

A necessary condition for the stability of the system is [1]

$$\hat{\rho} < 1 \ . \tag{11}$$

However, this condition is not sufficient for the stability of the individual queues. For each queue, an additional stability condition exists, which depends on the system and traffic parameters as well as the service discipline.

Queue i with synchronous service approaches the stability boundary, when the mean service time for this queue given by $\rho_i c$ approaches the corresponding threshold [16, 17]. Therefore,

$$\rho_i c < \tau_{s,i}^* \tag{12}$$

is a sufficient condition for the stability of queue i.

In order to determine the stability boundary for queues with asynchronous service, the workload to be served during both the service time of queue i and the preceding cycle time must be taken into account. In a stable system, $\hat{\rho}c$ is the mean total service time during a cycle, and $\rho_i c$ is the mean service time of queue i. Asynchronous service means that the maximum mean service time available at queue i is $\tau_{a,i}^* - c = \tau_{a,i}^* - \hat{\rho}c - c_0$ [16, 17]. Therefore, the stability condition for queue i is

$$(\rho_i + \hat{\rho})c < \tau_{a,i}^* - c_0 \ . \tag{13}$$

5 Mean Unfinished Work

5.1 Queues with Synchronous Service

The mean unfinished work $u_{s,i}$ is defined as the sum of the service times of all customers that are left behind by the server when he leaves queue i. If the mean number of customers left behind is $n_{t,i}$, the mean unfinished work is given by

$$u_{s,i} = n_{t,i} \cdot b_i \ . \tag{14}$$

Our approach to derive an expression for $n_{t,i}$ is to regard the service process at queue i. The customers are served in batches of variable size K_i with the first two moments k_i and $k_i^{(2)}$. The time instants at which the service of a batch is started are arrival instants of the server to queue i. However, queue i is served only if it is not empty upon server arrival, which occurs with a certain probability, say $p_{B,i}$. If the queue is served, the mean number $n_{l,i}$ of customers left behind in queue i by the last customer of a batch is the unknown quantity $n_{t,i}$. On the other hand, if queue i is found empty, the server immediately moves to the next queue and $n_{t,i}$ is zero. This yields

$$n_{t,i} = p_{B,i} \cdot n_{l,i} + (1 - p_{B,i}) \cdot 0 = p_{B,i} \cdot n_{l,i} \ . \tag{15}$$

The mean number of customers an arbitrary customer leaves behind in queue i is given by

$$n_{b,i} = \lambda_i(w_{s,i} + b_i) \ , \tag{16}$$

where $(w_{s,i} + b_i)$ is the sojourn (waiting plus service) time in queue i. After the arbitrary customer, another

$$k_i^V = \frac{k_i^{(2)} - k_i}{2k_i} \tag{17}$$

customers are served in the same batch, i.e., $n_{b,i}$ is reduced by k_i^V. During service of these customers, new customers arrive. Their mean number is given by $\lambda_i \cdot (k_i^V b_i) = \rho_i k_i^V$. Therefore, the mean number left behind by the last customer of a batch can be derived from $n_{b,i}$ as

$$n_{l,i} = n_{b,i} - (1 - \rho_i)k_i^V \ . \tag{18}$$

Combining equations (14) - (18) yields

$$u_{s,i} = p_{B,i} \cdot \left[\lambda_i(w_{s,i} + b_i) - (1 - \rho_i)k_i^V\right] \cdot b_i \ . \tag{19}$$

This result is exact so far. However, it still contains some unknown quantities, namely $w_{s,i}, k_i^V$ and $p_{B,i}$. The mean waiting time $w_{s,i}$ is the final result of the analysis and therefore unknown. However, if the other unknown quantities are determined, a pseudo-conservation law for the unknown $w_{s,i}$ is obtained by using eq. (7). It directly yields an expression for the mean waiting times in symmetric systems, whereas for the analysis of the mean waiting times in asymmetric systems additional assumptions are required.

The number of customers served in a cycle is given by G_i. G_i and the batch size K_i are related by

$$P\{K_i = n\} = \begin{cases} \dfrac{P\{G_i = n\}}{1 - P\{G_i = 0\}} & n \geq 1 \\ 0 & n = 0 \ . \end{cases} \tag{20}$$

This yields

$$k_i^V = g_i^V = \frac{g_i^{(2)} - g_i}{2g_i} \ , \tag{21}$$

where $g_i = E[G_i] = \lambda_i c$ is the mean number of customers served per cycle. For the second moment $g_i^{(2)} = E[G_i^2]$, two different cases are considered. If the service discipline were exhaustive service,

$$g_i^{(2)} = g_{e,i}^{(2)} = g_i + \frac{2g_i \lambda_i (w_{s,i} + b_i)}{1 - \rho_i} \tag{22}$$

would be obtained from $n_{l,i} = 0$. On the other hand, assuming a binomial distribution with the (approximate) maximum

$$g_{s,i,max} = k_{s,i,max} = \frac{\tau_{s,i}^*}{b_i} \tag{23}$$

yields

$$g_i^{(2)} = g_{b,i}^{(2)} = g_i^2 + g_i \frac{k_{s,i,max} - g_i}{k_{s,i,max}} \ . \tag{24}$$

Here, the linear combination

$$g_i^{(2)} = p_{e,i} \cdot g_{e,i}^{(2)} + (1 - p_{e,i}) \cdot g_{b,i}^{(2)} \tag{25}$$

will be used, where $p_{e,i}$ is the probability for exhaustive service. With this assumption,

$$u_{s,i} = p_{B,i}(1 - p_{e,i}) \left[\lambda_i(w_{s,i} + b_i) - (1 - \rho_i)\frac{\lambda_i c}{2} \left(1 - \frac{1}{k_{s,i,max}} \right) \right] b_i \tag{26}$$

is obtained for the mean unfinished work.

In order to determine $p_{B,i}(1 - p_{e,i})$, the following two cases are considered. For $\tau_{s,i} \to \infty$ or $\rho_i \to 0$ queue i will be served exhaustively, i.e. $p_{e,i} = 1$ and $p_{B,i}(1 - p_{e,i}) = 0$. For $\lambda_i c \to k_{s,i,max}$, queue i approaches the stability boundary (cf. eq. (12)) and the probability that it is empty is zero. Therefore, $p_{e,i} \to 0$ and $p_{B,i} \to 1$, which yields $p_{B,i}(1 - p_{e,i}) = 1$. This behaviour can be achieved by using the approach

$$p_{B,i}(1 - p_{e,i}) = \frac{\lambda_i c}{k_{s,i,max}} = \frac{\rho_i c}{\tau_{s,i}^*} \ . \tag{27}$$

This finally yields the following approximate expression for the mean unfinished work:

$$u_{s,i} = \frac{\rho_i c}{\tau_{s,i}^*}\left[\lambda_i(w_{s,i}+b_i) - (1-\rho_i)\frac{\lambda_i c}{2}\left(1 - \frac{b_i}{\tau_{s,i}^*}\right)\right]b_i \ . \tag{28}$$

Though this solution is approximate, it behaves correctly in various limiting cases. For $\tau_{s,i} \to \infty$ or $\rho_i \to 0$, e.g., exhaustive service and $u_{s,i} = 0$ is obtained. For very small thresholds, i.e. $\tau_{s,i} \to 0$ and $\tau_{s,i}^* \to b_i$ because of overrun, equation (28) yields the correct result for limited-1 service. Furthermore, for constant service times the case of limited-k service with the limit $k_{s,i,max}$ is obtained. In this case, the same solution as equation (28) is obtained by inserting a binomial approximation for $g_i^{(2)}$ in Everitts result[1] for limited-k service [4].

5.2 Queues with Asynchronous Service

The derivation of the mean unfinished work for stations with asynchronous service is an extension of the analysis presented in the previous section, taking into account the main differences between synchronous and asynchronous service. In case of asynchronous service

1. the service limit $\tau_{a,i}$ limits the sum of the station service time <u>and</u> the cycle time

2. the possibility of late token arrivals exists, i.e. $T_{C,i} > \tau_{a,i}$, and therefore station i may not be served during this cycle.

Under light and medium load, the probability for late token arrivals is small and can be neglected. If the load approaches the stability boundary, this probability is increased, which leads to an increased amount of unfinished work left in the queue. In this case, neglecting late token arrivals results in underestimating the unfinished work. However, since the unfinished work itself has an asymptotic behaviour for high load due to the limitation of the service times, the error caused by neglecting late token arrivals again is small. Therefore, late token arrivals will be neglected in the following analysis.

The other difference mentioned above influences both the stability condition and the distribution of the size of the batches in which the customers are served. For the batch size, the same approximations are used as above, except that now

$$k_{a,i,max} = \frac{\tau_{a,i}^* - c_0}{b_i} \tag{29}$$

is used for the maximum batch size.

Using the same arguments as in the previous section and the stability condition for queues with asynchronous service derived in Sec. 4, the approximation

$$p_{B,i}(1-p_{e,i}) = \frac{(\rho_i + \hat{\rho})c}{\tau_{a,i}^* - c_0} \ . \tag{30}$$

---

[1]Note that Everitt used $g_i^{(2)}$ for the second factorial moment $E[G_i(G_i - 1)]$ instead of $E[G_i^2]$.

can be used. With these assumptions, the expression

$$u_{a,i} = \frac{(\rho_i + \hat{\rho})c}{\tau_{a,i}^* - c_0} \left[\lambda_i(w_{a,i} + b_i) - (1 - \rho_i)\frac{\lambda_i c}{2}\left(1 - \frac{b_i}{\tau_{a,i}^* - c_0}\right)\right] b_i \tag{31}$$

is obtained for the mean unfinished work of a queue with asynchronous service.

6 An Approximate Pseudo-Conservation Law for Polling Systems with Time-Limited Service

An approximate pseudo-conservation law can now be obtained by substituting the results for the mean unfinished work according to eq. (28) and (31) into eq. (7), which yields

$$\sum_{i \in \mathcal{S}} \rho_i w_{s,i}\left(1 - \frac{\rho_i c}{\tau_{s,i}^*}\right) + \sum_{i \in \mathcal{A}} \rho_i w_{a,i}\left(1 - \frac{(\rho_i + \hat{\rho})c}{\tau_{a,i}^* - c_0}\right)$$
$$= \sum_{i=1}^{N} \rho_i w_{e,i} + \sum_{i \in \mathcal{S}} \frac{\rho_i c}{\tau_{s,i}^*}\left[\rho_i - (1 - \rho_i)\frac{\lambda_i c}{2}\left(1 - \frac{b_i}{\tau_{s,i}^*}\right)\right] b_i$$
$$+ \sum_{i \in \mathcal{A}} \frac{(\rho_i + \hat{\rho})c}{\tau_{a,i}^* - c_0}\left[\rho_i - (1 - \rho_i)\frac{\lambda_i c}{2}\left(1 - \frac{b_i}{\tau_{a,i}^* - c_0}\right)\right] b_i \quad , \tag{32}$$

where $\mathcal{A}$ is the set of queues with asynchronous service and $\mathcal{S}$ the set of queues with synchronous service. This form of the pseudo-conservation law is especially suitable for the analysis of Token Ring, Token Bus or FDDI due to the fact that they use time-limited service disciplines. For general purposes, the mean unfinished work expressions for further service disciplines can also be included.

7 Mean Waiting Time Approximations

7.1 Symmetric Systems

As mentioned in Sec. 3, the pseudo-conservation law includes the solution for the mean waiting times in symmetric systems. The results for symmetric systems with either synchronous or asynchronous service will be discussed in this section.

In a symmetric system with synchronous service, the mean unfinished work is

$$u_s = \frac{\rho c}{\tau_s^* - \rho c} \cdot \left[\lambda(w_e + b) - (1 - \rho)\frac{\lambda c}{2}\left(1 - \frac{b}{\tau_s^*}\right)\right] \cdot b \; . \tag{33}$$

Therefore, the pseudo-conservation law yields the following expression for the mean waiting time

$$w_s = \frac{w_e(1 - \hat{\rho}) + \dfrac{c_0 b}{\tau_s^*}\left[\rho - \dfrac{(1 - \rho)\lambda c_0}{2(1 - \hat{\rho})} \cdot \left(1 - \dfrac{b}{\tau_s^*}\right)\right]}{1 - \hat{\rho} - \dfrac{\rho c_0}{\tau_s^*}} \quad , \tag{34}$$

where w_e is given by eq. (10). This expression is not exact due to the approximations in the derivation of $u_{s,i}$. However, it is correct for $\tau_s \rightarrow \infty$, which means that the queues are served exhaustively. If $\rho \to 0$ or $c_0 \to 0$, the mean waiting time is independent of the service discipline (in the latter case this is true since polling systems without switchover times are work conserving). In both cases, eq. (34) yields the correct result $w_s = w_e$. For very small thresholds ($\tau_s^* \to b$), limited-1 service and the corresponding exact mean waiting time are obtained. Finally, w_s increases asymptotically if the offered load approaches the stability boundary derived in Sec. 4.

For symmetric systems with asynchronous service, eq. (31) yields

$$u_a = \frac{(N+1)\rho c}{\tau_a^* - (1+\rho)c} \cdot \left[\lambda(w_e + b) - (1-\rho)\frac{\lambda c}{2}\left(1 - \frac{b}{\tau_a^* - c_0}\right)\right] \cdot b \ . \tag{35}$$

Hence,

$$w_a = \frac{w_e(1-\hat{\rho}) + \dfrac{(N+1)c_0 b}{\tau_a^* - c_0}\left[\rho - \dfrac{(1-\rho)\lambda c_0}{2(1-\hat{\rho})}\cdot\left(1 - \dfrac{b}{\tau_a^* - c_0}\right)\right]}{1 - \hat{\rho} - \dfrac{(N+1)\rho c_0}{\tau_a^* - c_0}} \ . \tag{36}$$

is obtained. Again this is an approximate expression, which is correct for $\tau_a \to \infty$, $\rho \to 0$ or $c_0 \to 0$, where $w_a = w_e$ is obtained. Additionally it takes into account the stability condition derived in Sec. 4.

7.2 Asymmetric Systems

The pseudo-conservation law itself only yields one equation for N unknown mean waiting times. Therefore, additional equations are required to determine the mean waiting times in asymmetric systems. Analogously to the approach suggested in [8] this can be achieved by expressing the mean waiting times as a function of the second moment of the cycle time $c^{(2)}$, which is assumed to be approximately independent of the station index i. The pseudo-conservation law is then used to determine $c^{(2)}$, from which the mean waiting times can be obtained. This will be done first for synchronous and then for asynchronous systems.

7.2.1 Synchronous Service

For asymmetric systems with synchronous service, we use the heuristic approach

$$w_{s,i} = \frac{x_i}{1 - y_i} \cdot \frac{c^{(2)}}{2c} \ . \tag{37}$$

The stability condition derived in Sec. 4 is taken into account by choosing

$$y_i = \frac{\rho_i c}{\tau_{s,i}^*} \ . \tag{38}$$

For the choice of x_i well-known limits are considered. For $\tau_{s,i}^* \to \infty$, queue i is served exhaustively, and

$$\lim_{\tau_{s,i}^* \to \infty} \frac{x_i}{1 - y_i} = 1 - \rho_i \tag{39}$$

is required to obtain the approximate solution suggested in [3]. On the other hand, $\tau_{s,i} \to 0$ (i.e., $\tau_{s,i}^* \to b_i$) leads to limited-1 service. In this case,

$$\lim_{\tau_{s,i}^* \to b_i} \frac{x_i}{1-y_i} = \frac{1-\hat{\rho}+\rho_i}{1-\hat{\rho}-\lambda_i c_0} \quad . \tag{40}$$

yields the solution derived in [2]. Both limits can be taken into account by using a linear approach which yields

$$x_i = 1 - \rho_i \cdot \left(1 - \frac{b_i}{\tau_{s,i}^*} \cdot \frac{2-\hat{\rho}}{1-\hat{\rho}}\right) \quad . \tag{41}$$

Now the pseudo-conservation law can be used to determine $c^{(2)}$, and with (37) finally

$$w_{s,i} = \frac{1 - \rho_i \cdot \left(1 - \dfrac{b_i}{\tau_{s,i}^*} \cdot \dfrac{2-\hat{\rho}}{1-\hat{\rho}}\right)}{1 - \dfrac{\rho_i c}{\tau_{s,i}^*}}$$

$$\cdot \frac{\displaystyle\sum_{i=1}^{N} \rho_i w_{e,i} + \sum_{i=1}^{N} \frac{\rho_i c}{\tau_{s,i}^*}\left[\rho_i - (1-\rho_i)\frac{\lambda_i c}{2}\left(1 - \frac{b_i}{\tau_{s,i}^*}\right)\right] b_i}{\displaystyle\sum_{i=1}^{N} \rho_i\left[1 - \rho_i \cdot \left(1 - \frac{b_i}{\tau_{s,i}^*} \cdot \frac{2-\hat{\rho}}{1-\hat{\rho}}\right)\right]} \tag{42}$$

is obtained as an approximate solution for the mean waiting times.

7.2.2 Asynchronous Service

For queues with asynchronous service, the same approach as before will be used, i.e.,

$$w_{a,i} = \frac{x_i}{1-y_i} \cdot \frac{c^{(2)}}{2c} \tag{43}$$

However, x_i and y_i have to be adapted to the asynchronous service discipline. With

$$y_i = \frac{(\rho_i + \hat{\rho})c}{\tau_{a,i}^* - c_0} \quad , \tag{44}$$

again the stability condition is taken into account. For the derivation of x_i, $k_{s,i,max}$ is replaced by $k_{a,i,max}$, which yields

$$x_i = 1 - \rho_i \cdot \left(1 - \frac{b_i}{\tau_{a,i}^* - c_0} \cdot \frac{2-\hat{\rho}}{1-\hat{\rho}}\right) \quad . \tag{45}$$

Finally,

$$w_{a,i} = \frac{1 - \rho_i \cdot \left(1 - \dfrac{b_i}{\tau_{a,i}^* - c_0} \cdot \dfrac{2-\hat{\rho}}{1-\hat{\rho}}\right)}{1 - \dfrac{(\rho_i + \hat{\rho})c}{\tau_{a,i}^* - c_0}}$$

$$\cdot \frac{\displaystyle\sum_{i=1}^{N} \rho_i w_{e,i} + \sum_{i=1}^{N} \frac{(\rho_i + \hat{\rho})c}{\tau_{a,i}^* - c_0}\left[\rho_i - (1-\rho_i)\frac{\lambda_i c}{2}\left(1 - \frac{b_i}{\tau_{a,i}^* - c_0}\right)\right] b_i}{\displaystyle\sum_{i=1}^{N} \rho_i\left[1 - \rho_i \cdot \left(1 - \frac{b_i}{\tau_{a,i}^* - c_0} \cdot \frac{2-\hat{\rho}}{1-\hat{\rho}}\right)\right]} \tag{46}$$

is obtained as an approximate solution for the mean waiting times.

7.2.3 Mixed Service Disciplines

In the same manner as explained in the previous two subsections, also mixed systems can be considered which contain both stations with synchronous service and stations with asynchronous service. The mean waiting times are obtained by substituting the approaches according to eq. (37) and (43), respectively, into the pseudo-conservation law given by eq. (32) and solving for $c^{(2)}$. As soon as $c^{(2)}$ is known, eq. (37) and (43) yield the desired mean waiting times. Furthermore it is possible to take into account stations with limited-1, gated or exhaustive service by using the corresponding relationships given in [8].

8 Examples and Validation

In this section, first some results for a symmetric system are given. We assume $N = 10$ stations and the constant ring latency $c_0 = 0.1$ ms. For the purpose of comparisons between synchronous and asynchronous service, the thresholds are chosen such that the stability boundary is the same for both disciplines, i.e.,

$$\tau_a^* = c_0 + (N+1)\tau_s^* \ . \tag{47}$$

For negative-exponentially distributed packet service times with a mean value of $b_i = 0.01$ ms and the synchronous threshold $\tau_s = 0.1$ ms this yields the virtual thresholds $\tau_s^* = 0.11$ ms and $\tau_a^* = 1.31$ ms and thus $\tau_a = 1.3$ ms for the asynchronous threshold.

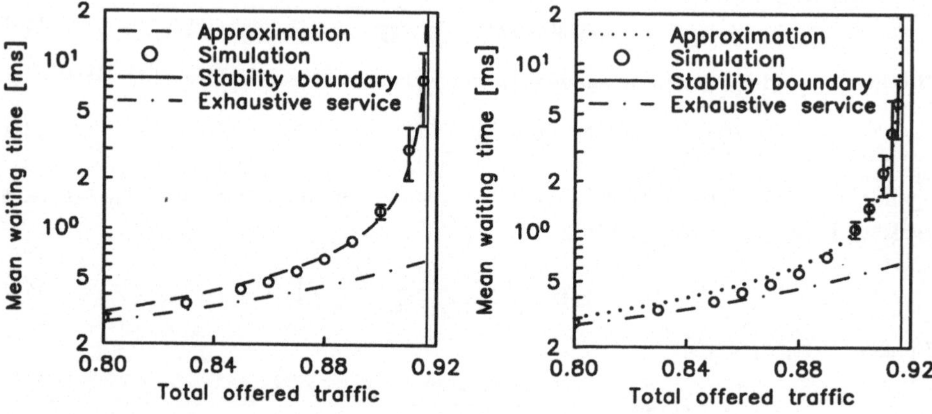

Figure 2: Symmetric system with synchronous service

Figure 3: Symmetric system with asynchronous service

In Fig. 2 the mean waiting time in a symmetric system with synchronous service are depicted for total offered traffic values $\hat{\rho}$ ranging from 0.8 to 0.92 which is the most critical load range due to the limitation of the service times. Simulation results are provided for a validation of the approximations. It can be seen that the approximation for the mean waiting time is quite accurate for the whole load range. The approximation tends to overestimate the mean waiting times because of the approximations in the derivation of $u_{s,i}$, but the error is small. As the load approaches the stability boundary, the mean waiting times increase asymptotically, and the results of the analysis are within the 95% confidence intervals of the simulation. For smaller load values than considered in Fig. 2, the approximation behaves even better, since the unfinished work becomes negligible and the queues are served almost exhaustively.

Fig. 3 shows the corresponding results for a symmetric system with asynchronous service. Again, the approximation slightly overestimates the mean waiting times.

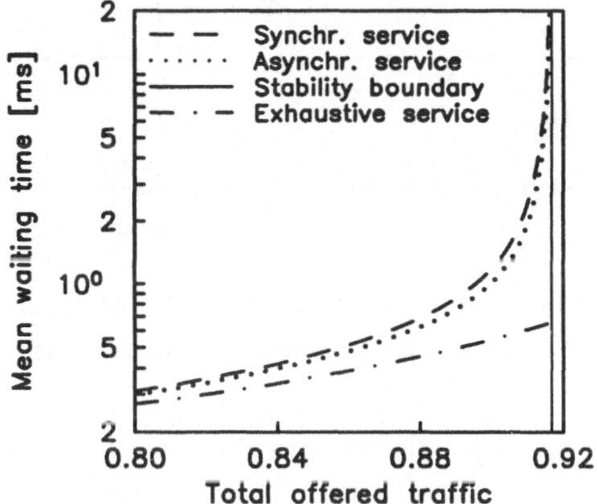

Figure 4: Comparison of synchronous, asynchronous and exhaustive service

A comparison between the mean waiting times for synchronous, asynchronous and exhaustive service is given in Fig. 4. It can be seen that for $\hat{\rho} = 0.8$ (and below) the differences between the service disciplines are small. Under high load, the mean waiting times for both time-limited service disciplines are much larger than for exhaustive service. In systems with exhaustive service, the stability boundary is $\hat{\rho} = 1$, whereas for time-limited systems the stability boundary is smaller and depends on the system parameters. Finally, it can be seen that the asynchronous service discipline is slightly more efficient due to its capability to adapt quickly to changing load patterns, i.e., with the asynchronous service discipline a statistical multiplexing gain can be achieved.

In Figs. 5 and 6 asymmetric systems are considered, where the arrival rates are chosen such that station 1 generates 50% of the total offered load, and the rest of the load is distributed equally among stations 2 through 10. The other parameters remain the same, except that the thresholds are adapted to accommodate the high load of station 1.

In order to achieve the same maximum total throughput as before, we choose for the synchronous system $\tau_{s,1} = 0.54$ ms and $\tau_{s,i} = 0.0511$ ms for $i = 2,...,N$. Fig. 5 shows the results for 80% and 88% total offered traffic. The mean waiting time of station 1 is smaller than for the other stations. The analysis overestimates the mean waiting time of station 1, whereas the waiting times of the other stations are underestimated. These errors are caused by the heuristic approach in eq. (37), which may be improved in further studies. However, even for 88% total offered traffic, the approximation can be used as a

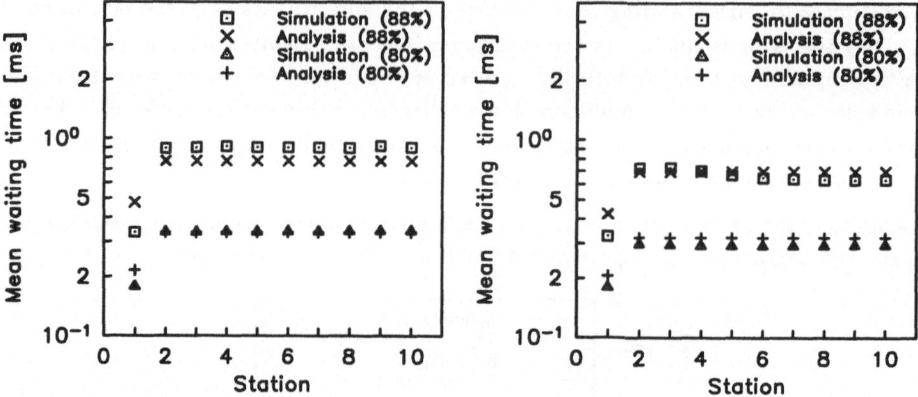

Figure 5: Asymmetric system with synchronous service

Figure 6: Asymmetric system with asynchronous service

first result which is obtained very much faster than the simulation results. For smaller load values, the accuracy of the results increases since the unfinished work becomes more and more negligible.

The adaptation of the thresholds for the asynchronous system according to the rules derived in [17] yields $\tau_{a,1} = 1.74$ ms and $\tau_{a,i} = 1.251$ ms for $i = 2,...,N$. With these thresholds, the results in Fig. 6 are obtained. For 88% total offered load, the mean waiting times of stations $2,...,N$ are not the same due to the physical ordering of the stations. Though the approximation does not capture this effect, it provides an average value which is quite accurate. Analogously to the results of the synchronous system, the mean waiting times of station 1 are overestimated. Again, the accuracy will increase further for smaller total offered traffic values.

9   Conclusion

In this paper, new approximations for the mean waiting times in symmetric and asymmetric polling systems with time-limited service have been derived. Since both the synchronous and the asynchronous service discipline have been taken into account, the analysis is applicable to token passing systems such as Token Ring, Token Bus and FDDI. The approximations are based on the well-known pseudo-conservation laws for polling systems in conjunction with new approximate expressions for the mean unfinished work the server leaves behind in a queue. A general formulation of the pseudo-conservation law as well as the mean waiting times for symmetric systems have been obtained. With additional assumptions relating the mean waiting times to the second moments of the cycle time approximations for the mean waiting times in asymmetric systems have been derived. A comparison to simulation results has shown that even for high load the results are reasonably accurate despite several approximations. The fact that explicit closed-form expressions have been obtained opens a wide range of applications for these new solutions.

The framework presented in this paper has been used for a case study of an FDDI system, where various configurations and the influence of several system parameters on the quality of the results have been studied. The results of this case study will be published in a future paper [19].

10   Acknowledgement

The author would like to thank Professor P.J. Kühn (University of Stuttgart) and Professor Vernon Rego (Purdue University) for many stimulating discussions on this topic. The comments of the anonymous referees are greatly appreciated.

References

[1] O.J. Boxma, W.P. Groenendijk, "Pseudo-Conservation Laws in Cyclic Service Systems," *Journal of Applied Probability*, Vol. 24, No. 4, Dec. 1987, pp. 949-964.

[2] O.J. Boxma, B.W. Meister, "Waiting-Time Approximations for Cyclic-Service Systems with Switchover Times," *Performance Evaluation*, Vol. 7, No. 4, Nov. 1987, pp. 299-308.

[3] D. Everitt, "Simple Approximations for Token Rings," *IEEE Transactions on Communications*, Vol. 34, No. 7, July 86, pp. 719-721.

[4] D. Everitt, "A Note on the Pseudoconservation Laws for Cyclic Service Systems with Limited Service Disciplines," *IEEE Transactions on Communications*, Vol. 37, No. 3, July 1989, pp. 781-783.

[5] "FDDI Token Ring Media Access Control (MAC)," ANSI X3.139 - 1987, ISO 9314-2: 1989.

[6] S.W. Fuhrmann, "Symmetric Queues Served in Cyclic Order," *Operations Research Letters*, Vol. 4, No. 3, Oct. 1985, pp. 139-144.

[7] S.W. Fuhrmann, R.B. Cooper, "Stochastic Decompositions in the M/G/1 Queue with Generalized Vacations," *Operations Research*, Vol. 33, No. 5, Sept.-Oct. 1985, pp. 1117-1129.

[8] W.P. Groenendijk, *Conservation Laws in Polling Systems*, Dissertation, Centrum voor Wiskunde en Informatica (CWI), Amsterdam, 1989.

[9] D. Karvelas, A. Leon-Garcia, "Performance Analysis of the Medium Access Control Protocol of the FDDI Token Ring Network," *Proc. GLOBECOM 88*, Ft. Lauderdale, Fl., USA, Nov. 1988, pp. 1119-1123.

[10] D. Karvelas, A. Leon-Garcia, "A General Approach to the Delay Analysis of Symmetric Token Ring Networks," *Proc. INFOCOM 91*, Bel Harbour, Fl., USA, April 1991, pp. 181-190.

[11] L. Kleinrock, *Queueing Systems,* Vol. 2: Computer Applications, John Wiley & Sons, New York, USA, 1976.

[12] P.J. Kühn, "Multiqueue Systems with Nonexhaustive Cyclic Service," *The Bell System Technical Journal,* Vol. 58, No. 3, March 1979, pp. 671-698.

[13] R.O. LaMaire, E.M. Spiegel, "FDDI Performance Analysis: Delay Approximations," *Proc. GLOBECOM 90,* San Diego, Ca., USA, Dec. 1990, Vol. 3, Paper 903.1, pp. 1838-1845.

[14] H. Takagi, *Analysis of Polling Systems,* The MIT Press, Cambridge, Mass., USA, 1986.

[15] H. Takagi, "Queueing Analysis of Polling Models: An Update," *Stochastic Analysis of Computer and Communication Systems,* H. Takagi (Ed.), Elsevier Science Publishers B.V. (North-Holland), Amsterdam, The Netherlands, 1990, pp. 267-318.

[16] M. Tangemann, "A Mean Value Analysis for Throughputs and Waiting Times of the FDDI Timed Token Protocol," *Proc. 13th International Teletraffic Congress,* Copenhagen, Denmark, June 1991, pp. 173-179.

[17] M. Tangemann, "Timer Threshold Dimensioning and Overload Control in FDDI Networks," *Proc. INFOCOM 92,* Florence, Italy, May 1992, pp. 363-371.

[18] M. Tangemann, *Modelling and Analysis of High-Speed Local Area Networks with Time-Limited Token Passing Media Access Protocols,* (german), Dissertation, Institut für Nachrichtenverarbeitung und Datenverarbeitung, Universität Stuttgart, 1993.

[19] M. Tangemann, "Mean Waiting Time Approximations for FDDI," submitted for publication.

[20] Tedijanto, "Exact Results for the Cyclic-Service Queue with a Bernoulli Schedule," *Performance Evaluation,* Vol. 11, No. 2, July 1990, pp. 107-115.

[21] *Token-Passing Bus Access Method and Physical Layer Secifications,* IEEE Std 802.4 - 1990, ISO/IEC 8802-4 : 1990.

[22] *Token Ring Access Method and Physical Layer Specifications,* IEEE Std 802.5 - 1989, ISO/IEC DIS 8802-5.2 : 1990.

[23] K.S. Watson, "Performance Evaluation of Cyclic Service Strategies - A Survey," *Proc. Performance 84,* E. Gelenbe (Ed.), North-Holland, pp. 521-533.

[24] O. Yue, C.A. Brooks, "Performance of the Timed Token Scheme in MAP," *IEEE Transactions on Communications,* Vol. 38, No. 7, July 1990, pp. 1006-1012.

Optimal Transient Service Strategies for Adaptive Heterogeneous Queuing Systems

Hermann de Meer and Kishor S. Trivedi
Department of Electrical Engineering, Duke University, Durham, NC – 27708, U.S.A.

Gunter Bolch and Fridolin Hofmann
Institute of Mathematical Machines and Data Processing IV,
FA University Erlangen-Nuernberg, Martensstr. 1, 91058 Erlangen, Germany
e-mail: bolch@informatik.uni-erlangen.de

Abstract

In this study we investigate heterogeneous queuing systems. Transient evaluation and control
is performed with regard to various performance measures. We choose the throughput, the mean
number of customers in the system, and the utilization as the measures of performance. Strategies
and performance functions are computed for finite capacity queuing systems. Both interruptive and
non-interruptive service strategies are considered. Results are provided for systems with two and for
systems with three heterogeneous servers. As the method of computation we use Extended Markov
Reward Models (EMRMs).
Keywords: Heterogeneous Queuing Systems, Extended Markov Reward Models, optimal strategies,
throughput, utilization, sojourn time, transient evaluation

1 Introduction

In [7] a queuing system with two heterogeneous servers is investigated. It is shown that the optimal
policy which minimizes the *mean sojourn time* of customers in the queue is of threshold type. The faster
server should be fed a customer from a common buffer whenever it becomes available for service, but
the slower server should be utilized if and only if the queue length exceeds a readily computed threshold
value. Note that the sojourn time equals waiting time in buffer plus service time. By Little's theorem,
minimizing mean sojourn time is equivalent to minimizing the *mean number of customers* in the system.
A restriction is imposed that a customer has to complete all its service at just one server.

In [7] *policy iteration* on the discounted cost problem is used to prove the existence of a threshold
type optimal *stationary* policy. The authors show that for a queuing system with infinite capacity and two
heterogeneous servers there exists some number n such that the optimal policy is to use the fast server
all the time and to send a customer to the slow server if and only if the number of customers in the queue
at that time is at least n. The average cost problem is taken as the limit of the discounted cost problem.
Intermediate results are obtained by using value iteration. The original continuous-time problem is
converted into an equivalent discrete-time problem by sampling the system at certain random instances
of time. "Dummy" customers are introduced to consider the case of idle servers [13]. In [10, 13] it is
shown that the discrete and continuous time problems are equivalent in that for the infinite-horizon cost
criteria the optimal policies for the two formulations coincide. Further stationary results are presented in
[1]. Approximative analysis of heterogeneous queuing systems are pursued in [3].

Such models can be applied to the dynamic routing problem in computer systems or communication
networks. A server may model a communication line over which messages are sent. The service time is
then the time taken for message transmission. Messages arriving at the buffer have to be routed over one
of several communication lines, each with a different mean transmission delay. And the goal now is to
choose among the several alternatives in such a way as to minimize the average overall message delay,
or to maximize the network throughput, for example. Other areas of application are found in modelling
manufacturing networks. Here also routing is important [5, 14]. More results are found in [4].

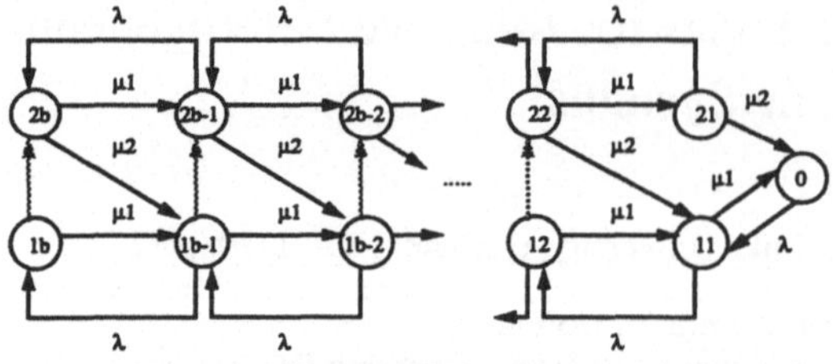

symbol	meaning
λ	arrival rate
μ_1	larger service rate
μ_2	smaller service rate
b	buffer size
$(1.)$	*only* server unit 1 busy
$(2.)$	*at least* server unit 2 busy
$(.j)$	j customers in system

Fig. 1 EMRM for evaluation and control of heterogeneous $M/M/2/b$-queueing systems with $\mu_1 \mu_2$

Optimal stationary policies, as investigated in [1, 3, 7], are not adequate for many practical problems. Realistic constraints on buffer space and the system usage time have to be considered. Thus, *transient* evaluation and control techniques of finite buffer queuing systems are of fundamental interest. This is the type of problem we pursue in the current study. Examples of applications are widely found in the manufacturing context, where typically finite planning horizons are extensively used. We study the dynamic properties of heterogeneous $M/M/m/b$ queuing systems with respect to different performance measures.

In section 2 we introduce the basic model and motivate our modeling approach. In section 3 our modeling approach, based on Extended Markov Reward Models (EMRMs), is briefly introduced. We apply EMRMs for the optimization of throughput, the mean number of customers in the system, and the utilization of the server units in sections 4, 5, and 6, respectively. By investigating various scenarios we show that the transient optimization of different performance measures results in different types of control strategies. In section 7 we extend the results to the interesting case of three heterogeneous servers. Concluding remarks are presented in section 8.

2 The Basic Model

We investigate a finite capacity heterogeneous queuing system. Finite capacity queues are often used as a method to limit congestion, and hence to bound the response time. We consider a system with b buffer units and m servers, such that the service rate at server i is μ_i. Customer arrival process is assumed to be Poisson with rate λ. Service strategy is assumed to be non interruptive.

In Fig. 1 the underlying EMRM is shown for the case of $m = 2$ servers. In state (ij) if $i = 1$ then only the faster server (unit 1) is active. If $i = 2$ then both servers are active, *unless* there is only a single customer in the system. In this case, i.e., in state (21) *only* the slower server is active. In state (0) no customer is present. A poor system performance results if the slower server is active while the faster one is idle. An optimal use of the servers should minimize the risk of being in state (21).

Our model includes the options *to use the slow server* or *not to use the slow server* whenever it is idle and a customer has not yet been assigned to a server. In Fig. 1 the decision options are represented by *shaded* arcs. Furthermore, whenever there remain customers to be served, and the fast server is idle, the next customer is immediately fed to the fast server. An appropriate *reward structure* is superimposed over this baseline model. The assigned reward rates will reflect the different measures of interest for the optimization. We will discuss the definition of the reward rates in detail later on.

EMRMs form the core of the software tool PENELOPE.[1] Here we discuss only those features that are of importance to the current study. Other features, algorithms, and the graphical user interface (currently being developed) will be introduced elsewhere.

---

[1] dePENdability EvaLuation and the Optimization of PErformability

3 Extended Markov Reward Models

3.1 Motivation

The main features of EMRMs are already informally introduced above. We will briefly sketch the concept here. EMRMs provide a unifying framework for the combined *evaluation and optimization* of *adaptive* systems. The method is the result of a marriage between Markov decision processes and performability modeling techniques. This marriage is encouraged by the fact that both fields are based on Markov reward models. Both stationary and transient measures and strategies may be computed. In this paper we emphasize the computation of transient results. Stationary results will only be mentioned, without going into detail, in order to complete the picture. The expected accumulated reward over a finite time horizon is used as the optimization criterion if transient measures are investigated. Time averaged reward rates are used in the stationary case.

The most important feature of EMRMs is the *optimization abstraction* that is provided. A potential user does *not* have to be familiar with the underlying Markov decision theory. The concept of *dynamic reconfiguration* that can be represented and optimized by EMRMs is fundamental to adaptive systems. Systems may be reconfigured to improve system performance as a response to some external events, e.g., arrivals of customers to a system or the passage of time. EMRMs have also been used for controlling reconfiguration optimally to preserve service in the presence of component failures and repairs [8].

3.2 The Fundamental Equations

Let the transition rate from state j to state i be denoted by $q_{j,i}$. Thus, the holding time in state j is exponentially distributed with parameter $\sum_{i=1}^{n} q_{j,i} = q_j$. The probability of transition from state j to i is given by $p_{j,i} = \frac{q_{j,i}}{q_j}$. Associating real valued reward rates with the Markov states leads to the concept of *Markov reward models*. The behavior of a system over time is characterized by the stochastic process $\{Z : \Re^+ \longrightarrow S\}$, where S comprises the finite set of all possible states. $\{Z(t); t \geq 0\}$ is often called the *structure state process* . The random variable $Z(t)$ denotes the state of the underlying process at time t. To indicate the *instantaneous reward rate* at time t and the *accumulated reward* in the interval $(0, t)$, we use the random variables $X(t)$ and $Y(t)$. $Z(t), X(t)$, and $Y(t)$ are non-independent random variables. $X(t) = r(Z(t))$, where r denotes the reward rate associated with the current state $Z(t)$, and $Y(t) = \int_0^t X(\tau)d\tau$. $P(Y(t) \leq y)$ is called the *performability* [11].

We are interested in computing $E[Y_j(t)]$, the expected accumulated reward conditioned on the initial state j, for EMRMs. Later in this paper we will use this measure as a criterion of optimization. $E[Y_j(t)]$ can be computed for all states j by the following system of integral equations. We define $E[Y_j(0)] \equiv 0$ for all $j \in S$.

$$E[Y_j(t)] = r(j)te^{-q_j t} + \int_0^t q_j e^{-q_j \sigma}(r(j)\sigma + \sum_{i=1}^{n} p_{j,i}E[Y_i(t - \sigma)])d\sigma \tag{1}$$

Here, $e^{-q_j t}$ is the probability that the system, started in state j, will not make a transition out of that state during $(0, t)$. Thus, the total reward gained is $r(j) \times t$. This is reflected by the first term of the equation. The integral indicates the other event, namely that a state change occurs during the interval $[\sigma, \sigma + d\sigma], 0 \leq \sigma, \sigma + d\sigma < t$. In this case the mean accumulated reward is composed of two weighted parts: the reward gained in the state j, $r(j) \times \sigma$, plus the mean reward achieved in the remaining mission time, $t - \sigma$, depending on the successor states of the transition.

3.3 The Method of Computation

The solution method is based on discretization of the finite time horizon. The interesting measures are computed backwards in time. The accuracy of the algorithm depends on the size of the time step $\Delta \hat{t}$. We choose $\Delta \hat{t}$ so that the probability of more than one state transition in $\Delta \hat{t}$ approaches zero. As a default value, $\Delta \hat{t}$ is chosen to be one hundredth of the mean state holding time. Since $\Delta \hat{t}$ can be chosen adaptively, the computational overhead can be reduced to a minimum at each step.

For all time steps and for all states the following basic computations are performed. We define the vector $\underline{E}[Y_j(\hat{t})] = (E[Y_j(\hat{t})], E^1[Y_j(\hat{t})], \ldots, E^m[Y_j(\hat{t})])$, where $E^m[Y_j(\hat{t})]$ denotes the m-th derivative of $E[Y_j(\hat{t})]$. For each time step $\underline{E}[Y_j(\hat{t} + \Delta \hat{t})]$ is computed iteratively by using the quotient of differences as an approximation:

$E^m[Y_j(\hat{t} + \Delta\hat{t})] \approx \frac{E^{m-1}[Y_j(\hat{t}+\Delta\hat{t})]-E^{m-1}[Y_j(\hat{t})]}{\Delta\hat{t}}$, where $m \geq 1$ and $E^0[Y_j(\hat{t})] = E[Y_j(\hat{t})]$. Assume that $E[Y_j(\hat{t})]$ has already been computed for all $j \in S$ and a certain $\hat{t} < T$, where T denotes the finite time horizon. Now using *Taylor polynomials* of order m as a method of approximation the further evaluation of $E[Y_j(\hat{t})]$ in a small time interval $\Delta\hat{t}$ can be interpolated. Thus, the above recursive integrals are transformed such that they can be computed easily. Concerning the current time step, Equation 1 can be rewritten as Equation 2 below.

$$E[Y_j(\hat{t} + \Delta\hat{t})] = e^{-q_j\Delta\hat{t}}(r(j)\Delta\hat{t} + E[Y_j(\hat{t})]) +$$
$$\int_0^{\Delta\hat{t}} q_j e^{-q_j\sigma}(r(j)\sigma + \sum_{i=1}^{n} p_{j,i} E_{pol}[Y_i(\hat{t} + \Delta\hat{t} - \sigma)])d\sigma \qquad (2)$$

We use the Taylor polynomial to define: $E_{pol}[Y_j(\hat{t} + \tau)] = E[Y_j(\hat{t})] + E^1[Y_j(\hat{t})]\tau + \cdots + E^m[Y_j(\hat{t})]\frac{\tau^m}{m!}$, $0 \leq \tau \leq \Delta\hat{t}$.

Observe that normally Taylor polynomials of first order, i.e, $m = 1$, yield satisfying results for our application. This results in an efficient algorithm. The largest models we investigated with a reasonable computation time were in the order of hundreds of thousands of states. A sparse storage technique and an adaptive selection of $\Delta\hat{t}$ makes the computation efficient for both large and stiff models.

Decision Points:

Now let us assume a given state j with optimization options $i_1, i_2, \ldots, i_n$. In other words, $i_1, i_2, \ldots, i_n$ are all states to which the system can be reconfigured whenever it is in state j. Then the optimization is performed by determining the solution θ of Equation 3 at each time step $\Delta\hat{t}$.

$$E[Y_\theta(\hat{t} + \Delta\hat{t})] = \max\{E[Y_y(\hat{t} + \Delta\hat{t})] | y \in \{j, i_1, \ldots, i_n\}\} \qquad (3)$$

In [9] it is shown how the solution of Equation 3 corresponds to the theory of Markov decision processes. We avoid the lengthy discussion of this topic here. The effect of an optimization decision can be thought of as a transformation of j into an immediate and deterministic transition to y, i.e., $p_{j,y} = 1$, if y is found to maximize Equation 3 and $y \in \{i_1, \ldots, i_n\}$. If $y = j$ maximizes Equation 3 the possibilities of reconfiguration are simply neglected. Note that by choosing larger time steps the interpolation scheme above allows a fast approximate computation of the expected accumulated reward and the optimal strategy with a high accuracy.

4 Transient Maximization of the Throughput

4.1 The Strategy

We investigate a queuing system where $n = 10$ buffers and $m = 2$ servers are available. The service rates are fixed at $\mu_1 = 1$ and $\mu_2 = 0.1$. Any lost customer due to buffer overflow reduces the throughput equivalently. As the parameter of interest the arrival rate λ of the customers is chosen.

To maximize the throughput we assign the *total service completion rate* as the *reward rate* to each state of the model in Fig. 1. $E[Y_j(t)]$ evaluates to the mean total number of customers served in the time interval $(0, t)$, conditioned on the initial state $j \in S$. The reward rates are summarized in the table attached to Figure 3. With the short hand notation $(i.)$ we denote all states which are not explicitly mentioned in the table, where the first index is i.

Recall from the earlier description of our baseline model that the shaded arcs $'(ij) \rightarrow (kl)'$ can be rephrased as to "reconfigure the system from state (ij) to state (kl) in order to improve system performance". If $i = k$ and $j = l$ then no reconfiguration is performed. The results are represented as a function of the *remaining time* $\hat{t} = T - t$, where t, $0 \leq t \leq T$ is the elapsed time and $[0, \ldots, T]$ the finite time horizon. A *strategy* is the assignment of a decision to each state where an option is available for given time point. Since we want to show the optimal strategy at every instant of time in the chosen time horizon, we have to represent an infinite number of strategies. To make this feasible we do not represent the strategies directly, but rather indirectly by indicating only where a stategy *switches* from

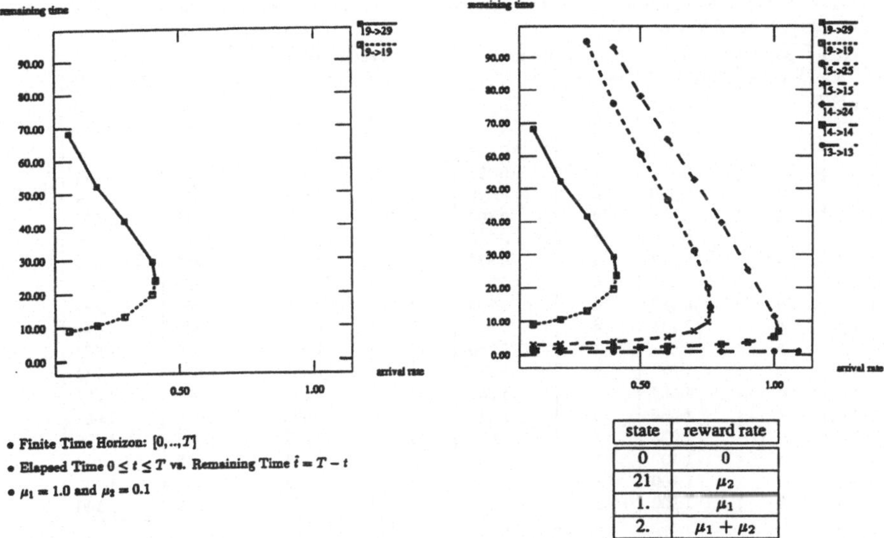

• Finite Time Horizon: $[0, ..., T]$

• Elapsed Time $0 \leq t \leq T$ vs. Remaining Time $\hat{t} = T - t$

• $\mu_1 = 1.0$ and $\mu_2 = 0.1$

state	reward rate
0	0
21	μ_2
1.	μ_1
2.	$\mu_1 + \mu_2$

Fig. 2 Optimal transient strategy to maximize the throughput of an adaptive heterogeneous $M/M/2/10$ queueing system for a single state only

Fig. 3 Optimal transient strategy to maximize the throughput of an adaptive heterogeneous $M/M/2/10$ queueing system given $\mu_1 = 1.0$ and $\mu_2 = 0.1$

one decison to another for each state. This allows us to use a very compact way to depict the optimal strategies graphically.

To give an example of the representation, we discuss the optimal control strategy for a single state only. In Fig. 2 the transient strategy that maximizes the throughput for our model is shown for state (19). Since in the long run the optimal decision is to use both servers, we fix the decision '(19) $\rightarrow$ (29)' as the *default* assumption. But, for a certain range of the interesting parameter λ, as time elapses there exists an instant of time where the strategy switches from using both servers to using the fast server only. The switching of the strategy is indicated by the curve to which the symbol '(19) $\rightarrow$ (29)' is attached. Hence, the curve marks the end of the denoted decision. As time elapses further, the strategy finally switches back from '(19) $\rightarrow$ (19)' to '(19) $\rightarrow$ (29)'. The two curves enclose the region where the optimal strategy is to use the fast server only. Outside that region both servers should be used. Recall that the time elapses from the top of the figure to the bottom. The strategy which is indicated by the label applies as long as the current situation is located "above" the respective curve. If no curve exists for a certain parameter value then the default strategy holds.

We are now ready to generalize our results according to Fig. 3 where the strategy is shown for some more states. The labels used in the legend of the figure characterize the strategy. The curves in Fig. 3 to which a corresponding label is attached represent the state dependent instants of time where the strategy changes with respect to the *remaining mission time*. Hence, we call them *switching curves*. In the legend we use the following notation: The curve which is associated with the label '$1j \rightarrow 2j$', $j \in \{2, ..., b\}$, denotes the instants of time where the strategy changes from *do use the slow server* to *do not use the slow server* whenever the system is in state $(1j)$. Similarly, the curve to which the label '$1j \rightarrow 1j$' is attached denotes the instants of time where the strategy changes from *do not use the slow server* to *do use the slow server*. In other words: If, with respect to the interesting parameter λ and time t, the current situation is located "above" the state dependent switching curve then the denoted decision should be made. "Underneath" the switching curve the opposite is true. The strategies may change several times as a function of time. Note that the time axis shows at every instant the remaining time.

Consider, for example, the case where three customers are in the system. Whenever the slow server is empty it should be kept switched off nearly till the end of the mission time. Nearly always the current

Table 1 Optimal strategies and maximum time averaged throughput of a heterogeneous $M/M/2/10$ queueing system in steady state given $\mu_1 = 1.0$ und $\mu_2 = 0.1$.

λ	strategy-iteration		value-iteration		transient optimization			SHARPE
	strategy	$E[X(\infty)]$	strategy	$E[X(\infty)]$	strategy	$\frac{E[Y_0(300)]}{300}$	$\frac{E[Y_{10}(300)]}{300}$	$E[X(\infty)]$
0.2	4	0.200	4	0.200	4	0.199	0.232	0.200
0.3	4	0.299	4	0.299	4	0.299	0.331	0.300
0.4	4	0.399	4	0.399	4	0.398	0.429	0.400
0.5	4	0.499	4	0.499	4	0.497	0.527	0.499
0.6	4	0.599	4	0.599	4	0.595	0.624	0.599
0.7	4	0.696	4	0.696	4	0.690	0.718	0.696
0.8	4	0.789	4	0.788	4	0.780	0.806	0.789
0.9	4	0.872	4	0.872	4	0.862	0.885	0.871
1.0	4	0.941	4	0.941	4	0.930	0.950	0.941
1.1	4	0.993	4	0.994	4	0.983	1.000	0.994
1.2	4	1.031	4	1.031	4	1.021	1.035	1.031
1.3	4	1.057	4	1.056	4	1.046	1.059	1.056
1.4	4	1.073	4	1.073	4	1.063	1.074	1.073
1.5	4	1.083	4	1.083	4	1.075	1.083	1.083
1.6	4	1.089	4	1.089	4	1.082	1.089	1.089
2.0	3	1.098	3	1.098	3	1.093	1.098	1.098
3.0	3	1.100	3	1.100	3	1.098	1.100	1.100
4.0	3	1.100	3	1.100	3	1.099	1.100	1.100
5.0	3	1.100	3	1.100	3	1.099	1.100	1.100

situation is located "above" the switching curve '$(13) \rightarrow (13)$'. The corresponding decision is, not to reconfigure and remain in state (13). Only if the remaining time is less than a very small amount, e.g., one unit of time, the second server may be admitted into service. The switching curve '$(13) \rightarrow (13)$' is hardly sensitive to the arrival rate λ. It is nearly parallel and very close to the abscissa. According to the threshold proposition above, the second server should also be turned off if two customers are in the system. Note that this is not shown in the figure.

So far the extensions due to transient evaluations as compared to the stationary strategy, i.e., the existence of a threshold $n = 3$ for the investigated model, seem to have little impact on the results. But this changes substantially if one considers the states where at least 4 customers are waiting for service. While in the infinite time case the slow server would always be used, this is not true from a time dependent point of view. Interestingly, the strategies change twice. In the long run the slow server is used according to the stationary strategy, the situation is located "above" '$(14) \rightarrow (24)$'. Also for relatively short remaining time periods the second server is admitted to service, since the situation is located "underneath" '$(14) \rightarrow (14)$' in this case. But, if the arrival rate λ is small enough, for each fixed value of λ there exists a state dependent time interval where only the fast server is used, i.e., the current situation is located "underneath" '$(14) \rightarrow (24)$' and "above" '$(14) \rightarrow (14)$'. Note that the smaller λ, the larger this interval becomes. For state (14) such an interval exists if λ is less than 1.02. For state (15) the upper bound for λ evaluates to 0.77 and for (19) to 0.412.

The figure indicates a reasonable monotonicity of the strategies. Whenever the slow server is kept turned off for a fixed λ if there are n customers present it is also turned off if $n - m$, $m \leq n$, customers are present.[2] Hence, the threshold property is not only valid in the infinite time case but at all instants of time! Since time and space are usually finite in practice it is quite useful to know about these time dependent monotonicities.

The double switching remains to be interpreted. If a relatively small time interval is left it is reasonable to use both servers. The chance that the fast server serves all present and possibly further arriving customers becomes eventually smaller than the chance by serving one less customer by the fast server and the remaining customer by the slow server.

For the time interval enclosed by corresponding switching curves the single server 1 will be fast enough to serve all customers. This outperforms the risk inherent in the slower server 2. It may not finish service in the remaining time horizon. If time increases further than the risk inherent in the slow server reduces more and more. Hence it is eventually worthwile to use the capacity of the second server. Of

---

[2]Note that only some selected switching curves are depicted in Fig. 3.

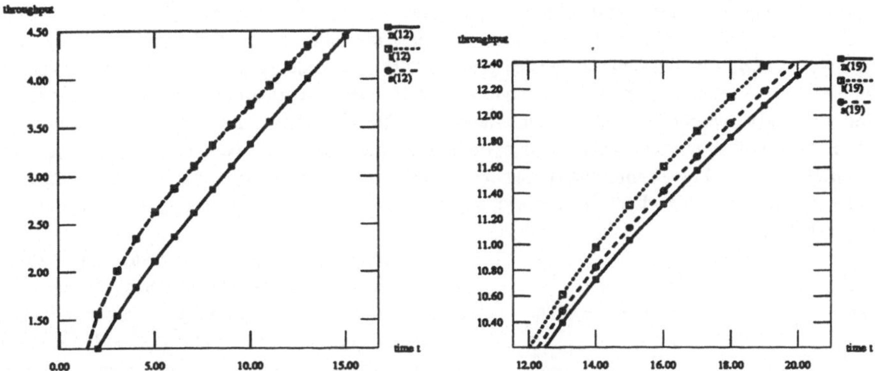

Fig. 4 *Stationary optimized, transient optimized, and non optimized throughput for initial states (12) und (19) given $\lambda = 0.2$*

course this is dependent on the number of customers present as we conclude from Fig. 3.

Interestingly, the stationary results are independent of λ for realistic values of λ. In the long term the average throughput is maximized when both servers are used provided at least four customers are in the system. This can be seen in Table 1. Here the optimal stationary strategy, which has been computed in three different ways, is depicted as a function of λ. In the strategy columns the requested minimum number of customers in the system to use the slow server is shown according to the threshold type strategy. The results verify that the strategies computed with our algorithm converge nicely to those, computed with the well-known algorithms called *value iteration* and *policy iteration*. The resulting reward rates are also verified by comparison with the results obtained by using the independently implemented tool SHARPE [12]. In this case, the earlier computed optimal stationary strategy was applied to specify the input model to SHARPE. Note that $E[Y_0(300)]/300$ and $E[Y_{10}(300)]/300$ are lower and upper bounds on $E[X(\infty)]$. The numbers in the table also indicate that the transient optimization can indeed improve the stationary optimal reward rates, i.e., results in a higher time averaged throughput.

4.2 The Throughput

In the following we investigate the impact of the control on the throughput. The influence depends on the state and on the values of the parameters. Two cases are shown in Fig. 4. In any case, the throughput of the controlled system surpasses the one of the non-optimized model.

The transient strategies always yield the highest improvement. Often, the effective throughput of the system controlled by a steady state or a transient strategy are relatively close together compared to the non-optimized case. This can be seen in the left part of Fig. 4. The right part of Fig. 4, on the other hand, shows a scenario where the transient strategy has a relatively higher impact on the performance than the stationary one has. In both figures steady-state (s), transient (t), and the non optimized case (n) are compared. The results depend on the initial state, e.g., (12) or (19).

5 Transient Minimization of the Mean Number of Customers

5.1 No Interruption of Service

In this section we choose the same model parameters as before. Instead of maximization of the throughput, the mean number of customers in the system is minimized. This is the most commonly used performance measure for the kind of optimization problem we investigate. As before, the underlying assumption is that service is non-interruptive. The *reward rate* assigned to state (ij) equals j, the number of customers in the system in this state. They are summarized in the table attached to Figure 5.

In Fig. 5 the major results for this example are shown. Again, the curves in the figure indicate the state dependent time instants of a strategy switch as a function of the arrival rate λ.

From the figure it is evident that both transient and steady state strategies are strongly dependent on λ. This was not the case in the previous section, where throughput was maximized. Now we observe a *different structure* of the optimal service strategy. Still the strategy tends to use both servers if the remaining time is relatively small. But in contrast to the throughput maximization case, the second server is not eventually switched in again as time increases. The switching curves indicate for each state the range of values of λ for which a single server optimal solution exists. This comprises exactly the interval of λ which is covered by a switching curve corresponding to the interesting state. The curves themselves indicate the time instants where the transient strategies switch. The switching curves approach infinity asymptotically.

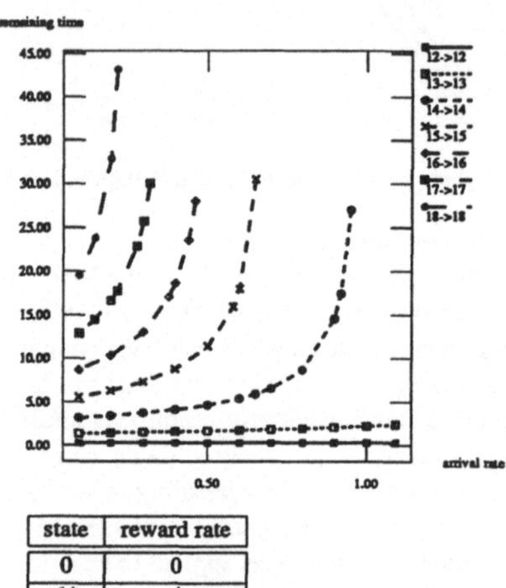

state	reward rate
0	0
1j	j
2j	j

Fig. 5 Optimal transient strategy to minimize the mean number of customers in a heterogeneous $M/M/2/10$ queueing system given $\mu_1 = 1.0$ and $\mu_2 = 0.1$

If there are no more than 3 customers present, the slow server should always be switched off except in case the remaining time is very small. This is indicated by the switching curves of the states (12) and (13) in Fig. 5. These curves are close to the abscissa, and therefore the current situation is nearly always located "above". The switching curves of the other states are much more sensitive to λ. For example, if there are 8 customers in the system, then the second server is *not* kept switched off if $\lambda \geq 0.3$. For all larger values of λ the situation has to be interpreted as "underneath" '(18) $\rightarrow$ (18)'. Only if the traffic intensity is even less a single server configuration is preferable to a double server configuration. Note that the switching curve is very susceptible to the arrival rate λ in this case.

In summary, the strategy is sensitive to the current load in the system and to the traffic intensity λ. Choosing the throughput or the number of customers in the system as a measure of optimization leads to different structures of the optimal strategy. The available processing power is more qutilized in the former case than in the latter case. Minimizing the mean number of customers in the system leads to a significantly reduced usage of the slow server in the long term average. Whereas in the "throughput case" a switch off was only performed if no more than three customers were present, in the "number case" even if 8 customers were present a steady state optimal switch off strategy exists for small values of λ. The strategy for the throughput optimization is more complicated. In any case, the following monotonicity holds **for each instant of time**, including steady state (infinity). **Whenever a server is switched off if there are k customers in the system it is also switched off if there are $k - 1$ customers present.** In Table 2 the optimal stationary strategies are compared by using different algorithms. As the optimization criterion the time averaged mean number of customers in the system is chosen.

5.2 With Interruption of Service

Now we change the assumptions made earlier and allow interruption of the service. In order to make the strategy non-trivial, we assume that switching a job from the slow to the fast server incurs a small delay. We assume this delay to be negative exponentially distributed with rate δ. δ is chosen as the parameter of interest in this section. The question which immediately arises is whether it is worthwhile to interrupt service of a customer when it is fed to the slow server and the fast server has become idle meanwhile. Furthermore, it is interesting to study the possible dependence of the strategy, i.e. whether to include the second server, on the delay suffered from switching over.

The baseline model from Fig. 1 has been extended appropriately to capture the problem of interest. An additional decision option has been included to switch over from state (21) to state (11) via a newly introduced state (01). The only possible transitions from (01) are to (11) with rate δ and to (22) with rate λ. In this example we choose $\lambda = 0.6$, $\mu_1 = 1.1$, and $\mu_2 = 0.1$. No service is received in state (01).

Table 2 Stationary optimal strategies and *minimum number* of customers in a heterogeneous $M/M/2/10$ queueing system given $\mu_1 = 1.0$ und $\mu_2 = 0.1$.

	strategy-iteration		value-iteration		transient optimization		SHARPE
λ	strategy	$E[X(\infty)]$	strategy	$E[X(\infty)]$	strategy	$\frac{E[Y_0(500)]}{500}$	$E[X(\infty)]$
0.2	9	0.250	9	0.250	9	0.248	0.250
0.3	8	0.429	8	0.429	8	0.426	0.429
0.4	7	0.665	7	0.665	7	0.660	0.665
0.5	6	0.986	6	0.986	6	0.978	0.986
0.6	6	1.419	6	1.419	6	1.402	1.419
0.7	5	1.986	5	1.987	5	1.960	1.987
0.8	5	2.695	5	2.695	5	2.652	2.695
0.9	5	3.529	5	3.529	5	3.466	3.529
1.0	4	4.422	4	4.422	4	4.337	4.422
1.1	4	5.300	4	5.300	4	5.188	5.299
1.2	4	6.072	4	6.072	4	5.958	6.072
1.3	4	6.732	4	6.732	4	6.614	6.732
1.4	4	7.266	4	7.266	4	7.148	7.266
1.5	4	7.689	4	7.689	4	7.575	7.690
1.6	4	8.023	4	8.023	4	7.913	8.023
2.0	3	8.800	3	8.800	3	8.715	8.800
3.0	3	9.421	3	9.421	3	9.370	9.421
4.0	3	9.621	3	9.621	3	9.584	9.620
5.0	3	9.718	3	9.718	3	9.690	9.718

Because one customer is in the system, the reward rate attached to (01) equals one. State (21) represents the only case where the slow server is active while the fast one is not.

In Fig. 6 the major results are depicted. The curve with the label '21 → 01' attached signifies the instants of time where the strategy switches from *do interrupt* to *do not interrupt* as a function of δ. In the long run, interruption is performed if δ0.12. But the decision is quite time dependent. The epoch of the decision switch decreases from approximately 18 units to 1 unit of remaining time as δ increases from 0.13 to 0.4.

Interestingly, the strategy for two customers in the system, i.e., being in state (12) is hardly responsive to an increase of δ. Further computations have shown that δ has to exceed 5.5 before the second server is considered as useful in this case. On the other hand, the switching time in state (15) already increases from 9.49 to 18.50 while δ increases to 0.27. In the former case no interruption is performed because interruption is excluded a priori, or $\delta \leq 0.12$. A further slight increase of δ results in the decision to include the slow server independently of time. Hence, the strategy is susceptible to a delay due to switch ove if interruption is admissible. But the intensity of this responsiveness depends strongly on the state, i.e., the number of customers in the system. Furthermore, there always exists a relatively small range of values where the strategy is responsive to even a small change of δ. Initially the curves are flat, followed by a sharp increase.

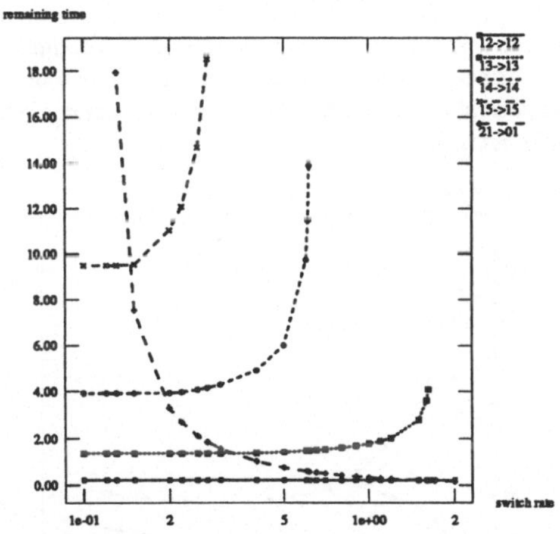

Fig. 6 On the impact of delay overhead due to interruption and switchover

5.3 On the Service Rate Ratio

In this section we investigate the impact the ratio of the service rates has on the mean number of customers in the system. No interruption of service is allowed. The optimized case $(o.)$ is compared with the non-optimized case $(n.)$. In the left part of Fig. 7 the mean number of customers in the system is shown as a function of the ratio of the service rates. The rates of the servers are assumed to add to 1.2. The

168

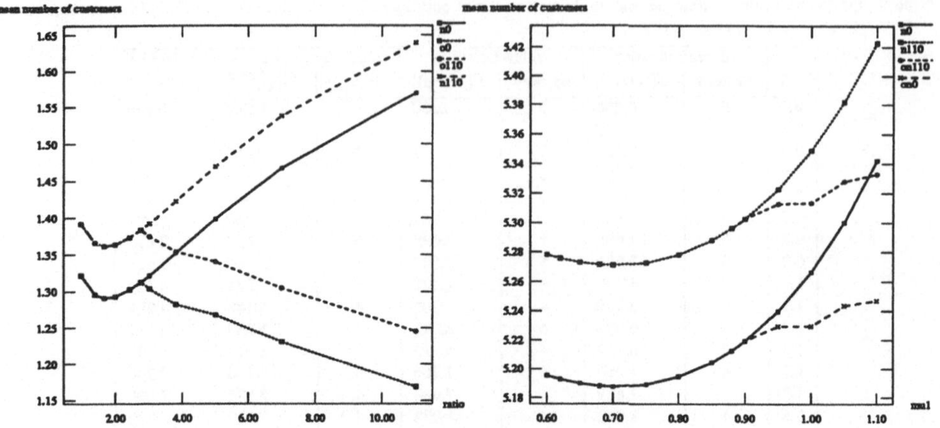

Fig. 7   On the impact of the service rate ratio given $\lambda = 0.6$ (left part) and $\lambda = 1.2$ (right part)

arrival rate λ is fixed at 0.6. Upper and lower bounds on the mean number of customers are given by the initial states (.110) and (.0), respectively. The results are evaluated for 1000 units of time. Steady state is nearly reached.

Interestingly, it is only considered worthwhile to leave the slow server idle if the ratio of μ_1 and μ_2 exceeds 2.75. The larger this ratio, the higher is the resulting improvement due to the optimization procedure. While in the non-optimized case the mean number of customers in the system increases nearly linearly with an increase of the ratio, in the optimized case it decreases inverse proportionally! The best performance characteristics are obtained when the system is optimized and the ratio is chosen as high as possible. On the contrary, the worst measures result when the most unbalanced configuration is used without control.

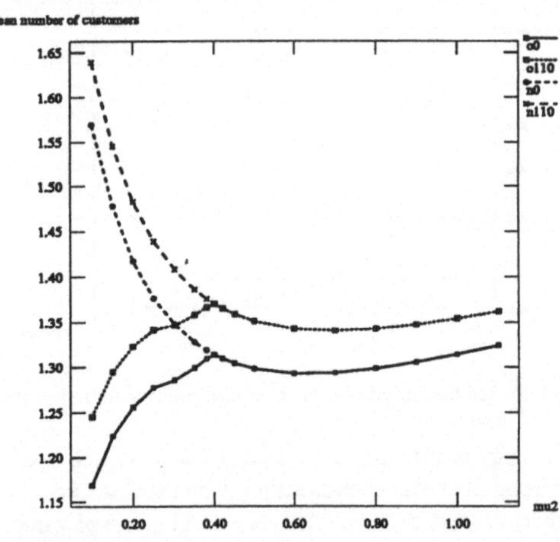

Fig. 8   On the impact of the service rate ratio given $\lambda = (\mu_1 + \mu_2)/2$

Furthermore, it is to be noted that the balanced system, i.e. $\mu_1 = \mu_2$, is **not** the best configuration, as might have been suspected. Even if no optimization is incorporated the system is improved if it is *moderately unbalanced*. The ratio for this optimum evaluates in the current example to approximately 1.7. The higher the utilization of the servers, the smaller this value becomes. Increasing, for example, the traffic intensity to $\lambda = 1.2$ results in the reward functions depicted in the right part of Fig. 7. Here we show the mean number of customers in the system. The minimum has decreased to a ratio of 1.4, which is equivalent to a service rate of $\mu_1 = 0.7$. Though the reward functions have shifted in relation to both the ordinate and the abscissa, the structure is preserved in the non-controlled case. This outcome is confirmed by the results shown in Fig. 8. Here the service rate μ_1 is fixed at 1.1. μ_2 is varied between 0.1 and 1.1. The arrival rate is adjusted according to $\lambda = 0.5 * (\mu_1 + \mu_2)$. Again the reward functions are quite similar to the ones discussed earlier. Also the improvement by applying control appears to be close to the results as presented in the left part of Fig. 7.

6 The Utilization

Subsequently we examine the utilizations of the servers under different assumptions. In our first study we assume that *no optimization* is performed. Whenever a customer remains to be served and a server becomes idle, the customer is immediately fed to the idle server, independent of its capacity. If a customer arrives to an empty system it will be served by the fast server. No decision option is included. All states $(1j)$, $j \geq 2$, are omitted from the model. To all states $(2j)$, $j \geq 2$, a *reward rate* of one is assigned. To state (0) reward rate of zero is assigned. Whether a reward rate of one or of zero is assigned to states (21) and (11) depends on the aim of analysis, i.e., the utilization of the fast or the slow server, or of both servers (see Table 3).

In our second study we investigate the impact of the throughput optimization strategy on the utilizations. First, the reward structure of the EMRM shown in Fig. 1 is changed to reflect the utilizations of the servers analogously as discussed in this chapter. Then, we use the optimal policies from above and compute the utilizations. Of course, now the states $(1j)$, $j \geq 2$, are readmitted to the model. The reward structure is adjusted according to the aim of analysis, i.e., utilization of the slow or of the fast server.

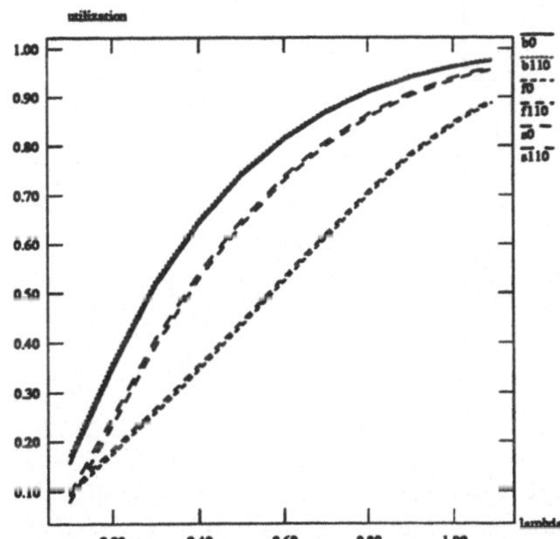

Fig. 9 Comparing utilizations of the servers without optimization

Fig. 10 Optimized vs. non-optimized utilizations of fast and slow servers separately

state	reward rate
0	0
21	1 or 0
11	1 or 0
2.	1

Table 3: The Reward Rates Denoting the Utilization of the Servers

Fig. 10 depicts the utilizations of the slow $(.s.)$ and the fast server $(.f.)$ under the condition that the *throughput* is maximized. The notation used for the optimized case is $(o..)$ while that for the non-optimized case is $(n..)$. Results for the non-optimized case are given in Fig. 9. The model is evaluated for 1000 units of time. Fig. 9 indicates that the slow server is continuously *"overutilized"*. For example, assuming an arrival rate $\lambda = 0.6$ yields a utilization of approximately 73 percent for the slow server whereas the fast server is only utilized for 53 percent of the time, a total difference of more than 20 percent! The relation is worst for medium traffic intensity. Note that only for a very low traffic intensity, i.e., $\lambda \leq 0.1$, the fast server is more utilized than slow one. This is reasonable because under this assumption the probability that there is only one or no customer in the system increases. In that case only the fast server or none will be busy.

The curves reveal that the utilization of the fast server slightly increases under the impact of the optimization strategy. But the slow server is much less used. The relation of the usage of the servers is inverted. The fast server is clearly more often used. This coincides with intuition. For a relatively low traffic intensity, i.e. $\lambda \leq 0.3$, the slow server is hardly used. Further studies have shown that the slow server is even less used if the mean number of customers in the system is to be minimized.

7 A Queuing System with Three Heterogeneous Servers

We now extend our results to the case of three heterogeneous servers. Without loss of generality we assume $\mu_1 \geq \mu_2 \geq \mu_3$. Again we choose the mean number of customers as the measure to be minimized. Including a third server in the baseline model in Fig. 1 results in a straight forward extension. To save space we do not show the model.

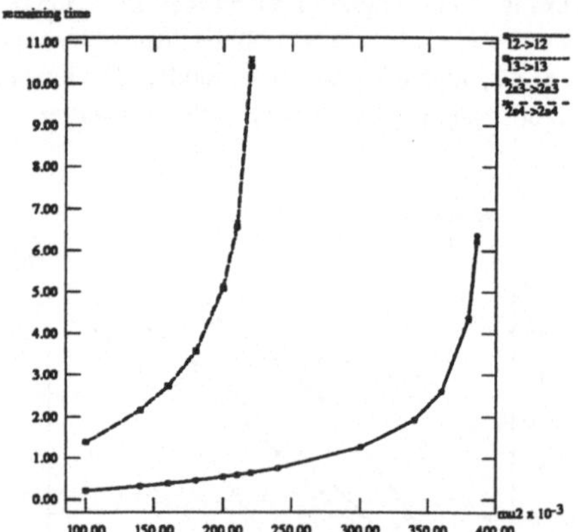
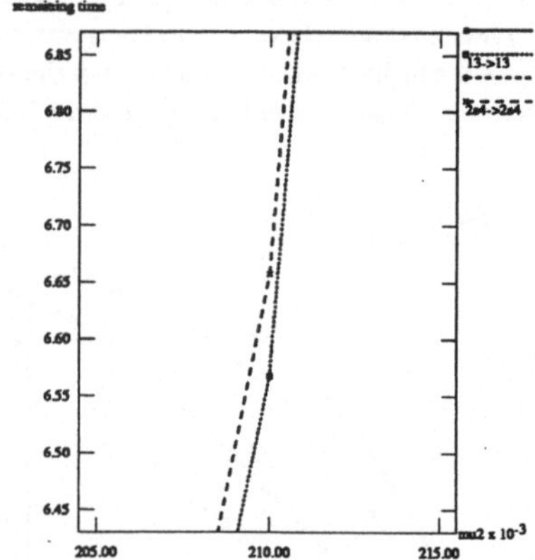

Fig. 11 To use the medium server or not to use the medium server?

We are now faced with a situation where a medium fast server has to be evaluated in the context of the existence of both a faster and a slower additional server. It is interesting to know how the strategies are affected by this relatively complicated relation. In particular, how does the strategy to feed a customer to the second server depend on the state of the third server? We conclude the answer to this question from the left part of Fig. 11. In this example μ_1 is fixed at 1.1, μ_3 at 0.1, while μ_2 is varied between 0.1 and 1.1. λ is adjusted according to the relation $2 * \lambda = \sum_i \mu_i$.

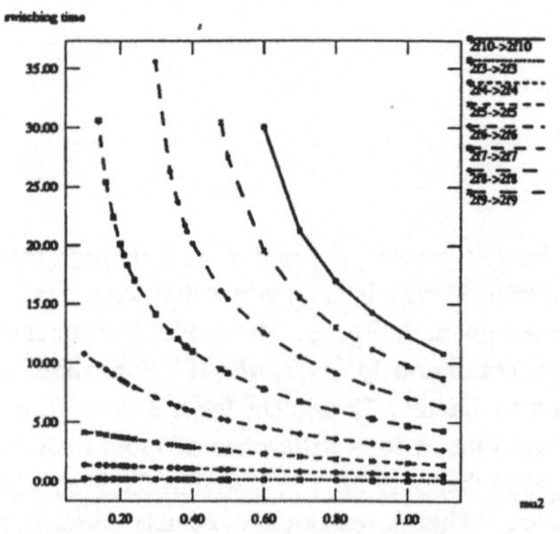

Fig. 12 To use the slow server or not to use the slow server?

The above mentioned problem translates to the two following cases. First, whenever only the fast server is active while there are $j, j \geq 2$, customers present, should the second server be admitted to service or not? The epochs of a change of the decision are represented by the switching curve to which the symbol '$1j \rightarrow 1j$' in the figure is attached. Hence at the denoted time instants the strategy switches from *do not use the second server* to *do use it* with respect to the remaining time horizon. If no curve exists for a given δ this has to be interpreted as to *do use* the medium server. Second, the other case is equivalently labelled with '$2sj \rightarrow 2sj$'. This denotes the occasion where a *slow two*-server configuration is active while there are $j, j \geq 3$, customers in the system. "Slow" ($.s.$) means that the first and the third server are active. The other situation, namely that and the first and the second servers are active while the third is idle, will be denoted by the "fast" ($.f.$) two-server configuration.

From the left part of Fig. 11 we conclude that the strategies for states $(1j)$ and $(2sj + 1)$ are nearly identical. This means that given there are j customers in the system and only the fastest server is active, the second (medium speed) server is admitted to service nearly under the same conditions as if $j + 1$ customers were in the system and both the fastest and the slowest servers were active. A closer look at the results in the right part of Fig. 11 reveals that the strategy for $1j$ is slightly more conservative with respect to the admission of the medium server. **Whenever the second server is admitted to service, given that only the first server is active and there are j customers in the system, the second server is also admitted if the first and the third server are active and $j + 1$, $j \geq 2$, customers are present.** These conclusions hold for all states of the investigated model. Furthermore, the strategies are identical in the long run, i.e., stationary, case. The differences between the corresponding decision epochs are very small. The structures of the decision strategies are qualitatively identical.

Figure 12 shows the impact of the speed of the second server on the decision to include the third (the slowest server) into the service process. It is assumed that the fast two-server configuration is already active. The larger the value of μ_2, the less likely that the server 3 is used. If μ_2 exceeds 0.6 the slow server is not used in the long run, even if 10 customers are in the system. The situation is always located "above" the switching curves. Furthermore, the third server is only used in the *whole mission time* if at least 7 customers are present. For state $(2f7)$ this is only the case if μ_2 is very close to 0.1, i.e, μ_2 approaches μ_3.

8 Conclusion

We have investigated the transient evaluation and optimization of adaptive heterogeneous queuing systems. We chose the throughput, the mean number of customers in the system, and the utilization as optimization criteria and compared the results. Each measure led to a significantly different transient optimal strategy. Transient strategies can improve system performance more than stationary strategies are able to. Furthermore, often short term performance functions are of significant interest in practice.

Extended Markov Reward Models were applied as the method of analysis. EMRMs are the result of a marriage between performability modeling techniques and Markov decision theory. The marriage resulted in a modeling tool to support the design and dynamic control of adaptive, reconfigurable systems. Reconfiguration options can be explicitly included into a model representation without the need of any knowledge of the underlying Markov decision theory.

References

[1] Baer, M., K. Fischer, G. Hertel, "Leistungsfaehigkeit-Qualitaet-Zuverlaessigkeit Kapitel 4: Modelle und Formeln fuer Bedienungssysteme mit nichtidentischen Kanaelen," *Transpress Verlagsgesellschaft* mbh, Berlin, (1988).

[2] Bellman, R., *Dynamic Programming*, Princeton University Press, (1957).

[3] Bolch, G., A. Scheuerer, "Analytische Untersuchung asymmetrischer prioritaetsgesteuerter Wartesysteme," *Proc. of the DGOR-Conf.*, Stuttgart-Hohenheim, (Sept. 1991).

[4] Crabill, T., D. Gross, M.J. Magazine, "A classified bibliography of research on optimal control of queues," *Operat. Res.*, Vol. 25, (1977), 219–232.

[5] Hahne, E.L., "Dynamic routing in an unreliable manufacturing network with limited storage," Mass. Inst. Technol., Cambridge, Rep. LIDS-TH-1063, (1981).

[6] Howard, R.A., *Dynamic Probabilistic Systems*, Vol. II: *Semi-Markov and Decision Processes*, John Wiley & Sons, New York, (1971).

[7] Lin, W., P.R. Kumar, "Optimal control of a queuing system with two heterogeneous servers," *IEEE Trans. Aut. Control*, AC-29, (1984), 696–705.

[8] de Meer, H., H. Mauser, "A Modeling Approach for Dynamically Reconfigurable Systems," *Proc. of the Second Intern. Workshop on Responsive Computer Systems*, Kamifukuoka, Saitama, Japan, (Oct. 1–2 1992), pp.149–158. Also to appear in the Springer Verlag Series on *Dependable Computing and Fault Tolerance*, (1993).

[9] de Meer, H., "Transiente Leistungsbewertung und Optimierung rekonfigurierbarer fehlertoleranter Rechensysteme," *Arbeitsberichte des IMMD*, Vol. 25, No. 10, FA University Erlangen-Nuernberg, Erlangen, (Oct. 1992).

[10] Rosberg, Z., P. Varaiya, J. Walrand, "Optimal Control of service in tandem queues," *IEEE Trans. Automat. Control*, Vol. AC-27, (1982), 600–610.

[11] Meyer, J.F., "On Evaluating the Performability of Degradable Computer Systems,," *IEEE Trans. on Computers*, Vol. 29, No. 8, (1980), 720–731.

[12] Sahner, R.A., K.S. Trivedi, "A Software Tool for Learning About Stochastic Models", *IEEE Transactions on Education*, Vol. 36, No. 1, (Feb. 1993).

[13] Serfozo, R.F., "An equivalence between continuous and discrete time Markov decision processes," *Operat. Res.* Vol. 27, (1979), 616–620.

[14] Tsitsiklis, J.N., "Convexity and characterization of optimal policies in a dynamic routing problem," Mass. Inst. Technol., Cambridge, Rep. LIDS-R-1178, (1982).

Wartezeiten für Pollingsysteme mittels numerischer Modelle

Theodor Heinrichs, Berthold Bärk, Johann Christoph Strelen

Rheinische Friedrich-Wilhelms-Universität Bonn
Institut für Informatik II, Römerstr. 164, 5300 Bonn 1

Zusammenfassung

Pollingsysteme können mit numerischen Modellen im allgemeinen genauer analysiert werden als mit analytischen Modellen, allerdings nicht unmittelbar ihre
Warte- und Verweilzeiten. Die zusätzlich verfügbaren Systemkenngrößen ermöglichen jedoch neue exakte Verfahren bei der Strategie Gated und die Verbesserung
bekannter Methoden. Für Systeme mit der Strategie Gated-limited und Batch-
Ankünften wird ein numerisch nutzbares Pseudoerhaltungsgesetz angegeben und
für Wartezeitberechnungen angewendet.

Schlüsselwörter: Pollingsystem, Wartezeit, Pseudoerhaltungsgesetz, numerische Analyse

1   Einleitung

Zyklische Bediensysteme mit mehreren Warteschlangen und einem Bediener (Pollingsysteme) kommen in Daten- und Kommunikationssystemen vor; genannt seien Rechnernetze und Token-Passing-Systeme. In ihnen bringen Ankunftsprozesse die Arbeit zu den
Stationen in Form von Aufträgen (Nachrichten); häufig werden dafür Poisson-Prozesse
angenommen. Ein Auftrag kann im allgemeinen aus mehreren Kunden (Paketen) bestehen; dann liegen Batch-Ankünfte vor. Die Stationen mit beschränkten oder unbeschränkten Warteschlangen für die Aufträge werden zyklisch vom Bediener abgefragt,
ob Arbeit anliegt. Diese wird dann gemäß einer Strategie ausgeführt; verbreitet sind die
Strategien Gated, Exhaustive und Limited. Wird nach der Strategie Gated vorgegangen, werden nur solche Aufträge ausgeführt, die der Bediener bei der Abfrage vorfindet.
Aufträge, die danach eintreffen, werden erst in einem späteren Durchgang (Zyklus) des
Bedieners bearbeitet. Bei der Strategie Exhaustive wird jede Station solange bedient, bis
kein Auftrag mehr vorhanden ist. Ist die Strategie Limited, dann gibt es ein Bedienungslimit ξ: nach einer Anfrage werden höchstens ξ Kunden bedient. Ist das Bedienungslimit
eins, heißt die Strategie 1-limited, Nonexhaustive oder Ordinary cyclic. Hat der Bediener

die Arbeit in einer Station beendet oder dort keinen Auftrag vorgefunden, geht er zur nächsten Station. Dazu benötigt er im allgemeinen eine gewisse Umschaltzeit.

Für die Bewertung eines Pollingsystems sind folgende Leistungsmaße von Bedeutung: Die Auslastung des Bedieners und der Warteschlangen (Pufferspeicher), Verlustwahrscheinlichkeiten durch beschränkte Puffer, Durchsätze, Wartezeiten von Paketen und Nachrichten auf Bearbeitung, Verweilzeiten von Nachrichten in dem System. Takagi ([23, 24]) gibt eine Übersicht über die Analyse von Pollingsystemen. Uns interessieren hier insbesondere Warte- und Verweilzeiten. Die wichtigsten Arbeiten dazu werden im Literaturverzeichnis noch einmal zusammengestellt. Von großer Bedeutung sind dafür Erhaltungsgesetze und Pseudoerhaltungsgesetze ([3, 4, 12]).

In der vorliegenden Arbeit berichten wir von der meist näherungsweisen Berechnung von Wartezeiten und Verweilzeiten in Pollingsystemen, wenn diese mit numerischen Modellen analysiert werden ([1, 20, 21]). Damit gelingt es in der Regel, mehr Systemkenngrößen zu berechnen und somit detailliertere Kenntnis des Systemverhaltens zu bekommen als mit analytischen Modellen, deren Auswertung in der Angabe von einfachen, übersichtlichen Formeln besteht. So eröffnen sich neue Möglichkeiten für die Berechnung von Warte- und Verweilzeiten.

Die zusätzlich bekannten Systemparameter können genutzt werden, um in bekannten Näherungsverfahren für Wartezeiten heuristisch geschätzte Größen zu ersetzen. Damit werden die Ergebnisse besser. Dies wurde an vielen Methoden erprobt ([15]); in Abschnitt 5 berichten wir exemplarisch davon.

Es ist kein vollwertiges Pseudoerhaltungsgesetz für Systeme mit allgemeiner Strategie Gated-limited, d. h. mit einem Sendelimit größer eins, bekannt. Wir geben in Abschnitt 4 eines an, das Batch-Ankünfte berücksichtigt; es ist zumindest bei der numerischen Analyse der Systeme verwendbar. In dem Sonderfall, daß die Batches immer nur ein Paket enthalten, reduziert es sich auf einen Vorschlag von Everitt in [13].

Für Pollingsysteme mit der Strategie Gated, positiven Umschaltzeiten und Batch-Ankünften in Poisson-Strömen geben wir in Abschnitt 6 Formeln für Warte- und Verweilzeiten an, die exakte Resultate liefern, falls die verwendeten Kenngrößen aus der numerischen Analyse fehlerfrei sind. Für diese Systeme mit Batch-Ankünften sind uns für die Verweilzeiten von Nachrichten keine anderen Verfahren bekannt.

Für Systeme mit allgemeiner Stategie Gated-limited und Batch-Ankünften geben wird in Abschnitt 7 (positive Umschaltzeiten) und in Abschnitt 8 (keine Umschaltzeiten) approximative Formeln für Warte- und Verweilzeiten an.

In Abschnitt 2 beschreiben wir das Pollingmodell, und in Abschnitt 3 skizzieren wir seine numerische Analyse mit eingebetteten Markovketten.

2 Pollingsysteme

Ein Bediener bediene in zyklischer Reihenfolge die Stationen $Q_1, \ldots, Q_K$ mit je einer unbeschränkten Warteschlange. Die Bedienstrategie sei

- *Gated*: es werden genau die vom Bediener angetroffenen Aufträge ohne Unterbrechung bedient,

- *1-limited* (auch *Nonexhaustive*, *Ordinary cyclic service*, *Limited service* genannt): findet der Bediener Aufträge vor, so bedient er genau einen Kunden oder

- *Gated-limited* : findet der Bediener in Station Q_k Kunden vor, so bedient er diese, jedoch höchstens ξ_k Stück.

Für alle Stationen Q_k, $k \in \mathcal{K} \triangleq [1 : K]$, bestehe ein *Auftrag* (eine *Nachricht*) im allgemeinen aus L_k Kunden (Paketen) ($l_k \triangleq E[L_k]$, $l_k^{(2)} \triangleq E[L_k^2]$), es finden also Batch-Ankünfte statt. Diese bilden einen Poisson-Prozeß mit der Rate λ_k. Die Bedienzeit für ein Paket sei B_k ($b_k \triangleq E[B_k]$, $b_k^{(2)} \triangleq E[B_k^2]$). Damit seien die Auslastungen $\rho_k \triangleq \lambda_k b_k l_k$, $k \in \mathcal{K}$, und $\rho \triangleq \rho_1 + \ldots + \rho_K$.

Die Warteräume in den Stationen für die Pakete können beliebig groß oder endlich sein; im letzten Fall kommt es zu Verlusten. Wir betrachten in dieser Arbeit unbeschränkte Warteräume.

Der Wechsel von Station Q_k zur nächsten benötige eine Umschaltzeit S_k ($s_k \triangleq E[S_k]$, $s_k^{(2)} \triangleq E[S_k^2]$), und es sei $S \triangleq S_1 + \ldots + S_K$ ($s \triangleq E[S]$, $s^{(2)} \triangleq E[S^2]$); bei Systemen *ohne Umschaltzeiten* ist $S = 0$.

Alle Zwischenankunftszeiten, Batchgrößen, Bedienzeiten und Umschaltzeiten seien unabhängig.

Eine Nachricht aus im allgemeinen mehreren Paketen, die in Station Q_k ankommt, wartet W_{Nk} Zeiteinheiten auf Übertragung (Bedienung), die *Nachrichtenwartezeit*, und bis zu ihrer vollständigen Übertragung vergeht $\widetilde{W}_{Nk}$, die *Nachrichtenverweilzeit* ($w_{Nk} \triangleq E[W_{Nk}]$, $\widetilde{w}_{Nk} \triangleq E[\widetilde{W}_{Nk}]$). Für ein Paket vergeht bis zum Beginn der Übertragung die *Paketwartezeit* W_k und bis zum Ende die *Paketverweilzeit* $\widetilde{W}_k = W_k + B_k$ ($w_k \triangleq E[W_k]$, $\widetilde{w}_k \triangleq E[\widetilde{W}_k]$).

Die *Zykluszeit* Z_k ist die Zeit zwischen zwei aufeinanderfolgenden Ankünften des Bedieners in Station Q_k ($z_k \triangleq E[Z_k]$). Sie ist im statistischen Gleichgewicht unabhängig von k ([16]).

3   Numerische Analyse

Die genannten Pollingsysteme können mit einer eingebetteten Markovkette mit den Zuständen

$$\mathbf{V}^{(t)} = (V_1^{(t)}, \ldots, V_K^{(t)}, C^{(t)}), \quad t \in I\!N,$$

analysiert werden ([1, 21]). Die Einbettungszeitpunkte t sind definiert durch das Eintreffen des Bedieners bei den Stationen. Er besucht zum Zeitpunkt t die Station $Q_{C^{(t)}}$ und findet dort $V_k^{(t)}$ Pakete vor.

Der Zustandsraum ist unendlich. Es werden jedoch nur stabile Systeme ([16]) betrachtet. Daher kann die Markovkette beliebig genau durch eine solche mit endlichem Zustandsraum approximiert werden. Dieser kann jedoch sehr groß sein; wie damit approximativ umgegangen werden kann, wird in [1, 20, 21] behandelt. Für die Zahlenbeispiele in der vorliegenden Arbeit wurden die letztgenannten Näherungen nicht benutzt, um nicht zwei Arten von Approximationsfehlern zu überlagern; nur so kann die Güte der hier vorgestellten Methoden beurteilt werden. Unbeschadet dessen ist es natürlich möglich und beabsichtigt, beide Vorgehensweisen zusammen zur Analyse großer Pollingsysteme zu verwenden.

Neben den Zustandswahrscheinlichkeiten werden bei der numerischen Analyse auch andere wichtige Systemparameter errechnet; hier seien nur die Zykluszeiten genannt, die von besonderer Wichtigkeit für die Wartezeiten sind.

Von Interesse sind auch die stationären Zustandswahrscheinlichkeiten zu beliebigen Zeitpunkten, also die für einen zufälligen Beobachter maßgeblichen; die entsprechenden Zufallsvariablen seien $\mathbf{V}^* = (V_1^*, \ldots, V_K^*, C^*)$. Bei der Analyse mit eingebetteten Markovketten kann ihre Verteilung im allgemeinen nicht angegeben werden.

4 Erhaltungsgesetze und Pseudoerhaltungsgesetze

Die Anwendung von Erhaltungsgesetzen (EG) und Pseudoerhaltungsgesetzen (PEG) hat das Problem, Wartezeiten in Pollingsystemen zu bestimmen, einer Lösung ein gutes Stück näher gebracht.

Wir benutzen das von Boxma in [3] angegebene PEG für Pollingsysteme in der Form [1]

$$\sum_k \rho_k w_k = \frac{\rho}{2(1-\rho)} \sum_k \lambda_k l_k b_k^{(2)} + \frac{1}{2(1-\rho)} \sum_k \lambda_k b_k^2 l_{Fk}$$

$$+ \rho \frac{s^{(2)}}{2s} + \frac{s}{2(1-\rho)} \left(\rho^2 - \sum_k \rho_k^2 \right) + \sum_k m_k' \tag{1}$$

mit $l_{Fk} \triangleq l_k^{(2)} - l_k$. M_k' ist bei Systemen mit positiven Umschaltzeiten die Menge Arbeit, die der Bediener in Station Q_k zurückläßt, wenn er sie verläßt ($m_k' \triangleq E[M_k']$). Das ist der einzige strategieabhängige Term; wir kommen darauf zurück.

Dieses PEG geht von Batch-Ankünften aus, die an den Stationen Poisson-Prozesse bilden.

In [3] werden die m_k' für verschiedene Strategien angegeben; hier interessieren

$$m_k' = \frac{\rho_k^2}{1-\rho} s \quad \text{für Gated} \tag{2}$$

---

[1] $\sum_k$ steht kurz für $\sum_{k=1}^{K}$

und

$$m'_k \;=\; \frac{\rho_k}{1-\rho}\lambda_k l_k s w_k + \frac{\rho_k^2}{1-\rho}s + \frac{1}{2(1-\rho)}\lambda_k s b_k l_{Fk} \quad \text{für 1-limited.} \tag{3}$$

Für die Strategie Gated-limited wird keine entsprechende Formel angegeben, weil keine bekannt ist, in der nur leicht verfügbare Systemkenngrößen vorkommen.

Hier eröffnen sich bei numerischer Analyse neue Möglichkeiten, da man in der Lage ist, die zurückgelassene Arbeit M'_k anzugeben. Sie besteht aus zwei Anteilen. Der erste Anteil ist N_k, die Anzahl von Paketen, die der Bediener bei Ankunft in der Station Q_k vorfand, die aber gemäß der Strategie im aktuellen Zyklus nicht mehr zur Bearbeitung vorgesehen sind. R_k sei die Anzahl von Paketen, die bearbeitet werden. Nachrichten, die während der Bearbeitung dieser R_k Pakete ankommen, bleiben ebenfalls unbearbeitet zurück und bilden den zweiten Anteil. Damit hat man die Erwartungswerte

$$m'_k \;=\; n_k b_k + \lambda_k r_k l_k b_k \tag{4}$$

($n_k \triangleq E[N_k]$, $r_k \triangleq E[R_k]$). Die Verteilungen von N_k und R_k werden bei der numerischen Analyse berechnet.

Everitt gibt in [13] eine entsprechende Lösung an, allerdings nicht für Batch-Ankünfte. Dabei schlägt er vor, die nicht bekannte Größe durch eine Heuristik zu ermitteln.

Für Systeme ohne Umschaltzeiten erhält man das entsprechende EG, wenn man in (1) die Umschaltzeiten und die m'_k null setzt:

$$\sum_k \rho_k w_k \;=\; \frac{\rho}{2(1-\rho)}\sum_k \lambda_k l_k b_k^{(2)} + \frac{1}{2(1-\rho)}\sum_k \lambda_k b_k^2 l_{Fk} \;. \tag{5}$$

Dieses EG gilt für alle arbeitserhaltenden Strategien.

In symmetrischen Systemen, also solchen, in denen alle Stationen und ihre Ankunftsprozesse identisch sind, können EG und PEG unmittelbar angewendet werden: man erhält damit Erwartungswerte für Wartezeiten.

Näherungsverfahren für die Berechnung von Wartezeiten in unsymmetrischen Pollingsystemen werden meistens folgendermaßen entwickelt: Es wird eine Formel für den Erwartungswert von Wartezeiten angegeben, in der jedoch unbekannte Kenngrößen des Pollingsystems vorkommen. Für diese Kenngrößen werden Heuristiken eingesetzt; daraus resultiert dann eine Näherungsformel für Wartezeiten.

Zwei Möglichkeiten gibt es, ein passendes Erhaltungsgesetz (EG) oder Pseudoerhaltungsgesetz (PEG) bei solchen Näherungsverfahren nutzbringend zu verwenden. Entweder wird die Näherungsformel mit einem freien Parameter versehen, z. B. einem Faktor, und dieser wird dann so festgelegt, daß das EG bzw. PEG erfüllt ist; wir nennen diese Vorgehensweise *mit dem EG (PEG) normieren*. Alternativ kann man eine der unbekannten Kenngrößen aus dem EG bzw. PEG bestimmen statt mit einer Heuristik. In der Regel bewirkt beides eine Verbesserung der Genauigkeit.

5 Anpassung bekannter Wartezeitapproximationen an die numerische Analyse

Am Ende des vorangehenden Abschnitts wurde skizziert, wie Näherungsformeln für Wartezeiten entwickelt werden. Ein wesentliches Problem sind dabei unbekannte Systemkenngrößen.

Gegenüber analytischen Modellen, bei denen Leistungsgrößen durch einfache, übersichtliche Formeln berechnet werden, können Systeme mit numerischer Analyse im allgemeinen genauer und detaillierter untersucht werden, so daß zusätzliche Systemkenngrößen verfügbar sind. Die Anpassung von Wartezeitapproximationen an die numerische Analyse besteht nun darin, Heuristiken durch solche zusätzlich berechneten Größen zu ersetzen. Ist das nicht für jede Heuristik möglich, kann man wieder wie oben besprochen ein EG bzw. PEG benutzen.

Wurden auf diese Weise alle Näherungen und Heuristiken beseitigt, werden die Erwartungswerte der Wartezeiten exakt berechnet. Wenn dies nicht gelingt, dann darf man doch erwarten, daß die Resultate genauer sind als ohne die zusätzlich durch die numerische Analyse verfügbaren Systemkenngrößen. Diese These wird durch unsere Untersuchungen bestätigt.

Wir haben zahlreiche Näherungsmethoden angepaßt, von Boxma [3], Boxma und Meister [5, 6], Everitt [13, 10], Fuhrmann und Wang [14], Kühn [16], de Moraes und Fuhrmann [17] und Watson [25]. Dabei wurden Resultate der Originalvorschläge denen der angepaßten Methoden gegenübergestellt, um die vermutete Verbesserung zu verifizieren.

In diesem Abschnitt berichten wir exemplarisch davon. Die zahlreichen Einzelheiten der Untersuchung finden sich in [15].

Für die Berechnung von Wartezeiten sind die Zykluszeiten Z_k wichtig und folgende *bedingte Zykluszeiten* $Z_{x,k}$: das ist die Dauer eines Zyklus, innerhalb dessen die Station Q_k genau x Pakete sendet ($z_{x,k} \triangleq E[Z_{x,k}]$, $z_{x,k}^{(2)} \triangleq E[Z_{x,k}^2]$). Üblicherweise werden für diese Momente Heuristiken benutzt; bei der numerischen Analyse dagegen sind die Verteilungen verfügbar.

Bei den Zahlenbeispielen, die im folgenden vorgestellt werden, wird immer davon ausgegangen, daß die Anzahl L_k von Paketen in einer Nachricht einer Gleichverteilung genügt. Die Länge eines Pakets und damit seine Übertragungsdauer B_k ist konstant, also einpunktverteilt. Ebenso sind die Umschaltzeiten zwischen den Stationen konstant.

Die Genauigkeit der Zahlenergebnisse wurde durch Vergleich mit Simulationen beurteilt.

5.1 Die Methode von KÜHN

In [16] wird für Pollingsysteme mit Umschaltzeiten und der Strategie 1-limited eine Näherung für Paketwartezeiten angegeben,

$$w_k \;\approx\; \frac{z_{0,k}}{2z_{0,k}} + \frac{\lambda_k l_k z_{1,k}^{(2)} + z_{1,k} l_k'}{2(1 - \lambda_k l_k z_{1,k})}, \quad k \in \mathcal{K}, \tag{6}$$

mit $l_k' \triangleq l_k^{(2)}/l_k - 1$.

Die Anpassung bestand darin, für die Momente der bedingten Zykluszeiten $Z_{0,k}$ und $Z_{1,k}$ die Resultate der numerischen Analyse zu übernehmen.

Es wurden 31 unterschiedliche Systeme auf diese Weise untersucht. Die Ergebnisse sind sehr genau, die relativen Fehler bleiben unter 5%, meistens unter 1%. Das ist noch besser als mit den ursprünglichen Heuristiken aus [16].

5.2 Die Näherung für Gated-limited Systeme von EVERITT

In [13] werden Wartezeiten in Pollingsystemen mit der Strategie Gated-limited und Nachrichten, die aus einem Paket bestehen, untersucht. Grundlage ist dort die Näherung

$$w_k \;\approx\; \frac{1}{\lambda_k r_k}\left(\xi_k(v_k - r_k) + \frac{1+\rho_k}{2} r_{Fk}\right), \quad k \in \mathcal{K}, \tag{7}$$

in der die Anzahlen V_k der vom Bediener in Station Q_k vorgefundenen Pakete vorkommen und die Anzahlen R_k der während eines Zyklus von der Station übertragenen Pakete ($v_k \triangleq E[V_k]$, $r_k \triangleq E[R_k]$, $r_{Fk} \triangleq E[R_k^2] - E[R_k]$). In [13] werden für die Ermittlung dieser Momente Heuristiken angegeben, die positive Umschaltzeiten voraussetzen.

Numerische Analyse dagegen macht diese Momente unmittelbar verfügbar. Sie wurden in (7) eingesetzt, und es wurde mit dem PEG ((1) mit dem strategieabhängigen Term (4)) normiert. Damit verbessern sich die Wartezeitnäherungen wesentlich, die relativen Fehler blieben in den 77 durchgeführten Versuchen unter 3%. Darüberhinaus spielt es hier keine Rolle, ob das System positive Umschaltzeiten aufweist oder nicht, d. h. die Näherungsmethode hat in diesem Kontext einen erweiterten Anwendungsbereich. Die Genauigkeit ist bei Systemen ohne Umschaltzeiten ebenso gut. Das ist insofern von besonderer Bedeutung, als sich in der Literatur nur wenige Ergebnisse für diese Systeme finden.

5.3 Die Näherungen von DE MORAES und FUHRMANN

In [17] werden Pollingsysteme mit der Strategie 1-limited und positiven Umschaltzeiten betrachtet. In den Stationen kommen Nachrichten aus im allgemeinen unterschiedlich vielen Paketen als Poisson-Strom an. Es werden genaue Schätzungen für die Wartezeiten w_k von Paketen und für die Verweilzeiten $\tilde{w}_{Nk}$ ganzer Nachrichten gegeben; letzteres ist das Besondere daran:

$$w_k \approx \frac{w_{0k} + z_{1,k} l'_k/2}{1 - \lambda_k l_k z_{1,k}},$$

$$\tilde{w}_{Nk} \approx \frac{w_{0k} + z_{1,k} l'_k/2}{1 - \lambda_k l_k z_{1,k}} + \frac{z_{1,k}}{2}\left(\frac{2l_k^2 - l_k^{(2)}}{l_k} - 1\right) + b_k, \quad k \in \mathcal{K}, \tag{8}$$

wobei

$$w_{0k} = \frac{z_k^{(2)}}{2z_k}$$

aus der Erneuerungstheorie bekannt ist, wenn W_{0k} die Zeit vom Eintreffen einer Nachricht in Station Q_k ist bis zu dem Zeitpunkt, in dem der Bediener das nächste Mal dort ankommt ($w_{0k} \triangleq E[W_{0k}]$).

In [17] werden nun die unbekannten Momente in (8) mit Hilfe zweier Approximationsannahmen und dem PEG ((1) mit dem strategieabhängigen Ausdruck (3)) ersetzt.

Die numerische Analyse stellt diese Momente wieder unmittelbar bereit; mit dem PEG wird normiert. Die resultierenden Näherungen für die Paketwartezeiten und die Nachrichtenverweilzeiten sind damit genauer; die relativen Fehler lagen bei den 31 untersuchten Systemen meistens um 1%, maximal um 4%.

6 Warte- und Verweilzeiten bei der Strategie Gated

In Pollingsystemen mit positiven Umschaltzeiten, der Strategie Gated und Ankünften in Poisson-Strömen von Nachrichten ermöglicht es die numerische Analyse, Warte- und Verweilzeiten einfach zu berechnen.

Für die Wartezeit einer Nachricht gilt hier

$$w_{Nk} = (1 + \rho_k)w_{0k}, \quad k \in \mathcal{K};$$

das kann etwa bei Takagi ([23]) nachgelesen werden. w_{0k} kann wie in (8) ersetzt werden, und

$$w_{Nk} = (1 - \rho_k)\frac{z_k^{(2)}}{2z_k}, \quad k \in \mathcal{K}, \tag{9}$$

ist damit eine Formel für die Nachrichtenwartezeiten. Für die Verweilzeiten folgt damit

$$\tilde{w}_{Nk} \;=\; w_{Nk} + l_k b_k\,, \quad k \in \mathcal{K}. \tag{10}$$

Nun betrachten wir die Wartezeit eines Pakets. Ein markiertes Testpaket kommt in einer Nachricht an, deren Größe den Erwartungswert $l_k^{(2)}/l_k$ hat, siehe z. B. [17]. In dieser Nachricht hat das Testpaket mit gleicher Wahrscheinlichkeit eine der Positionen $1, 2, \ldots, L_k$; daher ist der Erwartungswert für die Anzahl vor ihm liegender Pakete $(l_k^{(2)}/l_k - 1)/2$. Mit (9) ist deswegen

$$w_k \;=\; (1 + \rho_k)\frac{z_k^{(2)}}{z_k} + b_k \left(\frac{l_k^{(2)}}{l_k} - 1 \right) /2\,, \quad k \in \mathcal{K}, \tag{11}$$

der Erwartungswert für die Paketwartezeit.

Diese Gleichungen sind exakt, Näherungsfehler können nur entstehen, wenn die Zykluszeiten nicht fehlerfrei sind; das wurde in Abschnitt 3 angesprochen. Es ist daher selbstverständlich, daß die Rechenergebnisse für diese Untersuchung praktisch fehlerfrei waren.

7 Paketwartezeiten bei der Strategie Gated-limited und positiven Umschaltzeiten

Für den allgemeinen Fall der Strategie Gated-limited mit einem Sendelimit größer als eins ist die Wartezeitberechnung offenbar besonders schwierig. Uns sind dazu keine Vorschläge aus der Literatur bekannt, und auch ein PEG, das gleichartig den PEGs für andere Strategien wäre, ist dafür nicht vorhanden.

Das PEG (1) mit dem strategieabhängigen Term (3) kann unmittelbar für die Wartezeitberechnung in symmetrischen Systemen benutzt werden.

Für unsymmetrische Pollingsysteme mit Batch-Ankünften und positiven Umschaltzeiten machen wir einen heuristischen Vorschlag für die näherungsweise Berechnung von Paketwartezeiten:

$$w_k \;\approx\; \frac{1 - \rho + \rho_k - \rho\rho_k + \rho\rho_k/\xi_k}{1 - \rho - \lambda_k l_k s/\xi_k} \frac{z_k^{(2)}}{2z_k} + \frac{s + \xi_k b_k}{2(\xi_k - \rho - \lambda_k l_k s)} l_k'\,, \quad k \in \mathcal{K}. \tag{12}$$

Diese Heuristik ist für $\xi_k = 1$ die Näherung von de Moraes und Fuhrmann für die Strategie 1-limited und für $\xi_k \to \infty$ die exakte Gleichung (11). Sie beruht auf folgenden Überlegungen. Die Wartezeit eines zufällig ausgewählten Paketes einer Nachricht besteht aus drei Anteilen ([14]), $W_k = W_{0k} + W_{1k} + W_{2k}$. W_{0k} wurde oben besprochen, W_{1k} besteht aus einer Anzahl von Zyklen, in denen vorangehende Pakete aus Station $\mathcal{Q}_k$ bearbeitet werden, und W_{2k} ist der Zeitraum unmittelbar vor der Bearbeitung des betrachteten Paketes, während dessen Pakete aus Q_k bearbeitet werden. Damit ist

$$w_k \ \approx \ w_{0k} + E\left[\lfloor (V_k^* + \tilde{L}_k)/\xi_k\rfloor\right] z_{\xi_k,k} + E\left[(V_k^* + \tilde{L}_k) \bmod \xi_k\right] b_k \,; \qquad (13)$$

hier ist $\tilde{L}_k$ die Anzahl von Paketen, die dem betrachteten in seiner Nachricht vorangehen. Heuristische Überlegungen sowie $w_{0k} = z_k^{(2)}/(2z_k)$ und $z_{\xi_k,k} \approx (s + \xi_k b_k)/(1 - \rho + \rho_k)$ ([14]) führen damit zu (12).

Für die Berechnungen wird die Formel (12) noch mit dem PEG ((1) mit (4)) normiert.

Die Näherung erwies sich bei den 96 Rechenversuchen als gut, wenn die Sendelimits ξ_k verglichen mit der Nachrichtengröße nicht zu groß waren: bei Nachrichten gleichverteilt zwischen 1 und β Paketen und ξ_k bis ungefähr β^2 waren die relativen Fehler unter $3,6\%$.

Es ist bedauerlich, daß die Resultate bei großen Sendelimits in wenigen Fällen nicht genau waren, und daß wir keine ebenso gute Heuristik für Nachrichtenverweilzeiten gefunden haben.

8 Wartezeiten bei Systemen ohne Umschaltzeiten und mit der Strategie Gated-limited

Für Pollingsysteme ohne Umschaltzeiten, mit der Strategie Gated-limited und mit Batch-Ankünften schlagen wir als Näherung für die Paketwartezeiten vor:

$$w_k \approx \frac{1}{1 - \rho}\left(w_{0k}(1 - \rho + \rho_k) + b_k l_k'/2\right)$$

mit

$$w_{0k} \ \approx \ \frac{\rho \sum_i \lambda_i l_i b_i^{(2)} + \sum_i \lambda_i b_i^2 l_{Fi} - \sum_i \rho_i b_i l_i'}{2 \sum_i \rho_i (1 - \rho + \rho_i)}. \qquad (14)$$

Das ergibt sich wieder wie in Abschnitt 7 aus (13) mit heuristischen Überlegungen und $z_{\xi_k,k} \approx \xi_k b_k/(1 - \rho + \rho_k)$. Hier wird w_{0k} aber folgendermaßen ersetzt: Wie in [5] wird angenommen, daß die w_{0k} alle gleich sind. Ihr Wert wird mit dem EG (5) berechnet.

Falls die Stationen nicht zu unterschiedlich ausgelastet sind, d. h. die Auslastungen sich um weniger als einen Faktor 10 für verschiedene Stationen voneinander unterscheiden, und falls die Sendelimits nicht zu groß werden, wie in Abschnitt 7, haben wir für (14) ein gutes Fehlerverhalten beobachtet; die relativen Fehler blieben in allen Fällen unter $7,5\%$.

Auch hier muß wieder angemerkt werden, daß bei anderen Systemkenngrößen, d. h. extreme Unsymmetrie der Stationen oder große Sendelimits, die Ergebnisse nicht immer so genau waren.

Für die Nachrichtenverweilzeiten schlagen wir

$$\tilde{w}_{Nk} \approx w_{0k} + \frac{\lambda_k l_k w_k + l_k - 1}{1 - \rho + \rho_k} b_k + b_k, \quad k \in \mathcal{K}, \tag{15}$$

vor, wobei w_{0k} und w_k gemäß (14) eingesetzt werden.

Diese Näherung wird wie folgt hergeleitet. Man schreibt (13) für das letzte Paket einer Nachricht auf, indem man $\tilde{L}_k$ durch $L_k - 1$ ersetzt, also die Nachrichtenlänge um eins vermindert, und b_k addiert. Damit hat man einen Ausdruck für die Verweilzeit, der wie für (14) umgewandelt wird.

Die Näherung (15) zeigte bei den 81 Versuchen ein gutes Fehlerverhalten unter denselben Voraussetzungen wie die Näherung (14); die relativen Fehler blieben unter 8%.

9 Schlußbemerkung

Es wurde gezeigt, wie die numerische Analyse mit Nutzen bei der Berechnung von Warte- und Verweilzeiten in Pollingsystemen verwendet werden kann. Bei den unsymmetrischen Systemen mit der Strategie Gated limited blieben Wünsche offen; hier ist weiterzuarbeiten. Wir versprechen uns viel von einem Ansatz, der mit numerischer Analyse die Wahrscheinlichkeitsverteilung der Systemzustände zu beliebigen Zeitpunkten verfügbar machen soll. An (13) sieht man, daß dies unmittelbar nützlich wäre.

Literatur

[1] B. Bärk, M. Schmitz und J. Ch. Strelen, Globale Zustände bei der numerischen Analyse von Pollingsystemen, Interner Bericht II/91/4, Institut für Informatik, Universität Bonn, 1991.

[2] O.J. Boxma und W.P. Groenendijk, Waiting times in discrete-time cyclic-service systems, *IEEE Trans. Comm* **36**(2) (Feb. 1988) 164–170.

[3] O.J. Boxma, Workloads and waiting times in single-server systems with multiple customer classes, *Queueing Systems* **5** (1989) 185–214.

[4] O.J. Boxma und W.P. Groenendijk, Pseudo-conservation laws in cyclic service systems, *J. Appl. Prob.* **24**(4) (1987) 949–964.

[5] O.J. Boxma und B.W. Meister, Waiting-time approximations in multi-queue systems with cyclic service, *Performance Evaluation* **7** (1987) 59–70.

[6] O.J. Boxma und B.W. Meister, Waiting-time approximations for cyclic service systems with switchover times, *Performance Evaluation* **7** (1987) 299–308.

[7] O.J. Boxma und J.A. Weststrate, Waiting times in polling systems with Markovian server routing, in: G. Stiege und J.S. Lie, Hrsg., *Messung, Modellierung und Bewertung von Rechensystemen und Netzen*, IFB 218 (Springer, Berlin, 1989) 90–104.

[8] W. Bux und H.L. Truong, Mean-delay approximation for cyclic-service queueing systems, *Performance Evaluation* **3** (1983) 187–196.

[9] G.L. Choudhury und H. Takagi, Comments on "Exact results for nonsymmetric token ring systems", *IEEE Trans. Comm.* **38**(8) (Aug. 1990) 1125–1127.

[10] D. Everitt, Simple approximations for token rings, *IEEE Trans. Comm.* **34**(7) (July 1986) 719–721.

[11] D. Everitt, Approximations for asymmetric token rings with a limited service discipline, *Br. Telecom. Technol. J.* **6**(3) (July 1988) 46–51.

[12] D. Everitt, A note on the pseudoconservation laws for cyclic service systems with limited service disciplines, *IEEE Trans. Comm.* **37**(7) (July 1989) 781–783.

[13] D. Everitt, An approximation procedure for cyclic service queues with limited service, *Performance Evaluation*, 1989, 141–156.

[14] S.W. Fuhrmann und Y.T. Wang, Analysis of cyclic service systems with limited service: bounds and approximations, *Performance Evaluation* **9** (1988) 35–54.

[15] T. Heinrichs, Erhaltungsgesetze in zyklischen Pollingsystemen, Diplomarbeit, Universität Bonn, 1991.

[16] P.J. Kühn, Multiqueue systems with nonexhaustive cyclic service, *Bell Syst. Tech. J.* **58** (1979) 671–699.

[17] L.F.M. de Moraes und S.W. Fuhrmann, Mean delay approximations for polling systems with batch Poisson input, *Performance Evaluation* **12** (1991) 147–156.

[18] J.W.M. Pang und R.W. Donaldson, Approximate delay analysis and results for asymmetric token-passing and polling networks, *IEEE J. Sel. Areas in Comm. SAC-4* (1986), 783–793.

[19] M.M. Srinivasan, An approximation for mean waiting times in cyclic server systems with nonexhaustive service, *Performance Evaluation* **9** (1988) 17–33.

[20] J.Ch. Strelen, Iterative Analyse von Markov-Modellen mit alternierender Aggregation und Disaggregation, in: A. Lehmann und F. Lehmann, Hrsg., *Messung, Modellierung und Bewertung von Rechensystemen*, IFB 286 (Springer, Berlin, 1991) 320–336.

[21] J.Ch. Strelen und B. Bärk, An approach to the numerical analysis of multiple-queue, cyclic service systems, Interner Bericht II/88/4, Institut für Informatik, Universität Bonn, 1988.

[22] H. Takagi, Mean message waiting time in a symmetric polling system, in: E. Gelenbe, Hrsg., *Performance 84* (North Holland, Amsterdam, 1984) 293–302.

[23] H. Takagi, *Analysis of polling systems* (MIT Press, Cambridge, MA, 1986).

[24] Hideaki Takagi, Queueing analysis of polling systems: an update, in : H. Takagi, Hrsg., *Stochastic Analysis of Computer and Communication Systems* (North Holland, Amsterdam, 1990) 267–318.

[25] K.S. Watson, Performance evaluation of cyclic service strategies – a survey, in: E. Gelenbe, Hrsg., *Performance 84* (North Holland, Amsterdam, 1984) 521–533.

A Comparison of Priority Strategies
for ATM Switching

Frits C. Schoute[1,2] and Ellen G. Janssens[2]

[1] Philips Communication Systems
P.O. Box 32
1200 JD Hilversum
The Netherlands
[2] Delft University of Technology
P.O. Box 5031
2600 GA Delft
The Netherlands

Abstract. The different QoS requirements of different classes of traffic ask for priority strategies. In this paper we compare several priority schemes that have been proposed in literature. The QoS requirements are often complementary: some traffic classes require a low cell loss probability, others demand low cell delay jitter. The delay-loss plane is introduced to compare priority schemes in the case of two priority classes. Comparisons are made for stationary and time-varying traffic. It shows that the so called LDOLL threshold policies are optimal among the class of work conserving policies.

1 Introduction

The Asynchronous Transfer Mode (ATM), and fast packet switching in general, must be fast and therefore simple. So, initially, many argued that no priority classes should be introduced. However as the ideas of fast packet switching mature, it turns out to be feasible and desirable to have different priorities for different kinds of traffic. We shall show that already a wide spectrum of priority strategies has been proposed and compare the alternatives.

In this paper we concentrate on the Asynchronous Transfer Mode (ATM), as a specific form of fast packet switching. With ATM, the fixed length cells are switched by sending them to the appropriate output channel of the switching element. Somewhere in the switching element, the cell must be buffered. Output buffering is the most favored approach [1]. We consider here the case of one (or possibly more) output buffer(s) for one ATM output channel. In this context we want to discuss alternative priority strategies.

Not all kinds of traffic have the Quality of Service (QoS) requirement of, say, a cell loss probability less than 10^{-9}. Some kinds of traffic may require low delay jitter while allowing higher loss probabilities. We denote the ATM cells that require a low loss probability as LL (Low Loss) cells. As we consider the case of two priority classes, we have LL cells and non-LL cells. The non-LL cells are denoted LD cells. LD comes from Low Delay. It is used here as a general designation; arguments will be presented to let the non-LL cells be Low Delay cells indeed. To accommodate those different traffic streams and let them beneficially share switching and transmission resources, priorities must be applied.

Traditionally, in queueing theory, 'priority' for customers (e.g. ATM cells) means that customers with high priority are served before customers with a lower priority. We call this time priority (also the terms retrieval priority or service priority are used, as the high priority cells are retrieved from the cell buffer before others). For ATM switching elements, space priority may be of greater importance. A specific form of space priority is that low priority cells are pushed out from the buffers (without being transmitted on the outgoing link) to make room for high priority cells. Synonyms are: storage priority and input priority.

There are many ways in which time and space priorities can be exercised. Cheng and Akyildiz [2] consider reserved buffers with push-out as space priority strategy. As time priority strategy they use the following scheduling disciplines: Head Of Line priority (HOL), Shortest Line First (SLF), Longest Line First (LLF) and Random Scheduling (RS). To be noted is that in their paper class 1 can push-out class 2, and also gets priority in the scheduling disciplines (e.g. the HOL policy always gives class 1 priority over class 2, and in SLF and LLF class 1 has priority when the lines are equally long).

Lin and Sylvester [3] describe a number of space priority strategies, which differ in the degree of resource sharing, namely complete partitioning, complete buffer partitioning (separate buffers) but complete bandwidth sharing (here they use First Come First Serve with respect to the order of service), partial buffer sharing (which strategy is also known as reserved buffers), and complete sharing with push-out (and HOL priority).

Ohnishi, Okada and Noguchi [4] present 4 performance control mechanisms, which they call variable and fixed method A and B. These methods are listed below:

- variable priority method A: LD cells always have time priority, LL cells have space priority with push-out;
- variable priority method B: the same as the variable method A, except that when LL cells wait within the buffer for longer than a determined threshold period, output priority is changed from the LD cells to the LL cells;
- fixed priority method A: cells are either of priority or normal class. The priority class always has priority in both input and output control (i.e. space and time priority);
- fixed priority method B: again cells are either of priority or normal class, but now there is no input control (no space priority); there is only time priority for the priority class.

Kröner, Hébuterne, Boyer and Gravey [5] also describe a number of space priority strategies. They compare the push-out scheme, partial buffer sharing and route separation, using FIFO (First In First Out) as time priority strategy.

Bonomi, Fratta, Motagna and Paglino [6] study the performance of three priority mechanisms for an ATM switch with two traffic classes. The policies they compare are:

- Threshold(T): the output line has a shared buffer of size K. Incoming cells of low priority are admitted if the total number of cells in the buffer is less than or equal to S. High priority cells are admitted as long as buffer space is available. There is no priority in accessing the output line (service priority), and the service discipline is FCFS. This is the same strategy as described by Lin and Silvester [3], which they call partial buffer sharing;
- Separate Buffers with Service Priority (SBSP): the output line has a separate buffer space for the two cell classes. High priority cells have non-preemptive service priority over low priority cells. Within each service class the service discipline is FCFS;
- Threshold Access plus Service Priority (TSP): the output line has a shared buffer. Incoming cells of low priority are admitted if the total number of cells in the buffer is less than or equal to S. The service priority strategy is equal to that of SBSP.

They also suggest to give the cells with high access priority low service priority.

Awater and Schoute [7] conjecture that LDOLL (Low Delay or Low Loss) threshold policies are optimal in the sense of minimizing as well delay for LD cells as loss for LL cells. The LDOLL threshold policy always gives space priority to the LL cells, that is, if the buffer is full with LL and LD cells, and an LL cell arrives, then one of the LD cells will be pushed out. The LD cells receive a conditional time priority, conditioned on the number of LL cells. If the number of LL cells is equal to or larger than a threshold value n, then the LL cells receive time priority.

In the remainder of this paper we shall discuss first the loss and delay requirements for different traffic classes in section 2. In section 3 the two dimensional state space model is presented. This model allows a unified presentation of priority alternatives (section 4) and enables analysis of the performance of the alternatives (section 5). The performance analysis in section 5 includes as well stationary as non-stationary analysis. In section 6 we introduce the delay-loss-plane, which is then used to display the relative merits of different alternatives, leading to the conclusions of section 7.

2 Loss and delay

Loss and delay are the two factors that predominate any QoS consideration. Loss occurs principally due to (temporary) shortage of buffer space; queueing in the same buffer adds to the delay that a cell encounters on its way from source to destination. Enlarging the size of the buffer reduces the loss probability but at the same time increases the delay.

Given the transmission speeds of fast packet switching, one can argue that queueing delay is insignificant compared to propagation delay. However, as the fixed propagation delay is a given fact that can be coped with, the variable queueing delay is a component that for some applications should be reduced to a minimum. This variation, or delay jitter, is undesirable for traffic flows for which the time relation between cells needs to be restored after passage through the network.

In [7] it is stated that generally a minimization of queueing delay is accompanied by a reduction of delay jitter. So, if not a (slight) reduction of delay is of importance, then still the reduction of delay jitter may be the objective. In all cases, we shall just consider the minimization of delay as it also encompasses reduction of jitter.

The objective of a low cell loss probability exists for all kinds of traffic. For most data communication traffic and for compressed real time traffic with little redundancy the specification can ask for a loss probability as low as 10^{-9}. Other traffic classes, notably voice, will have less stringent requirements.

The combination of both performance objectives leads in the first instance to four classes of traffic as depicted below. The most demanding class is best

Low Delay and Low Loss	Low Delay don't mind loss
Low Loss don't mind delay	don't mind delay don't mind loss

Fig. 1. The full matrix of delay and loss requirements leads in first instance to four traffic classes.

handled by giving it reserved peak bandwidth, protected from the rest, and handled separately in that sense. The non demanding class can be used just to fill up any spare capacity. As is the case in most priority systems, the higher priority classes will hardly, if ever, notice the non demanding lowest priority class. In this way, we are left only with two classes of traffic, the ones that are off-diagonal in the matrix in figure 1.

The two classes are denoted LL and LD respectively. LL is the Low Loss class, for which delay, or rather, delay variation, is not an important performance measure. LD is the Low Delay class, for which in the first place minimization of delay jitter is sought and for which much higher loss probabilities can be tolerated than for the LL class.

3 State space model

Since we consider two classes of traffic, we use the tuple (n_{LD}, n_{LL}) to represent the state of the output buffer (which may be partitioned in some cases). Here n_{LD} is the number of LD cells in the buffer and n_{LL} the number of LL cells. Arrivals into the buffer occur according to a random process that is assumed to be memoryless. Any possible auto-correlation in the arrival process will be modelled by having the cell arrival probability change from high to low, and vice versa, for designated periods of time. This way the state is simply determined by (n_{LD}, n_{LL}) together with a parameter that quantifies the arrival process.

Consider time to proceed in discrete steps: $t = 0, 1, 2, \ldots$, where one unit of time is equal to the time needed to transmit one cell on an ATM channel. A total of N channels may contribute cells to the buffer. For time slot t, the arrival probability at inlet channel $i, i = 1, \ldots, N$, is $p_i(t)$. Given that an arrival takes place, it is of class LD with probability $r_i(t)$ or of class LL with probability $1 - r_i(t)$.

Once the arrival process is specified, the possible states of the buffer are indicated by the points in the state space which is illustrated in figure 2. The triangular shape for the non-partitioned buffer is induced by the constraint $n_{LD} + n_{LL} \leq Q$, where Q is the number of cells that the buffer can hold. This state space illustration can also very conveniently be used to depict alternatives in time priority (i.e. the cell retrieval policies). By way of example we show the *LDOLLn policy with n = 5* of [7] for a buffer with $Q = 10$.

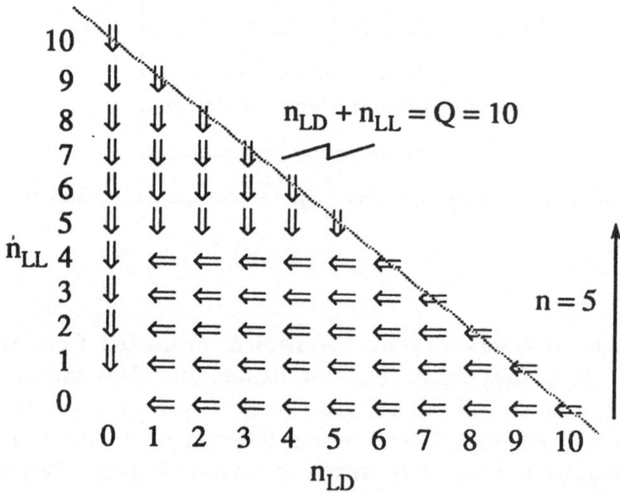

Fig. 2. State space of buffer contents (vertically n_{LL} and horizontally n_{LD}) and indication of time priority ($\Leftarrow$ means: serve an LD cell; $\Downarrow$ means: serve an LL cell). The diagram represents the *LDOLL policy with n = 5*.

Cell retrieval is assumed to take place at the beginning of a time slot; cell arrivals take place during a time slot. The state transition that occurs between t and $t + 1$ is then described as one step *down* or *left* (as dictated by the policy) followed by up to N steps *up* or *right*. As long as no blocking or push-out occurs, each inlet channel that brings an LD cell causes a step *right*; for an LL cell this becomes a step *up*.

The space priority is exerted by the storage policy. For example, when the buffer is full an LL cell arrival may push-out an LD cell (in the state space this is one step *north-west*). Or the storage policy may prescribe that LD cells are blocked when less than F buffer places are free.

4 Alternatives in time and space priority

As we saw in the preceding section, many space and time priority strategies can be formulated in terms of the two dimensional state space model. A drawback of this state space presentation is that information on the order of arrival is lost. Thus a plain FIFO strategy does not exactly fit into the model of section 3. However, when we nevertheless use the model to analyse the performance of FIFO, retrieving an LD cell with probability $n_{LD}/(n_{LD} + n_{LL})$ and an LL cell with probability $n_{LL}/(n_{LD} + n_{LL})$, we find exact results for the performance measures that we want to calculate. Because of this drawback it is also not possible to exactly fit the variable priority method B into this model. Because we assume that LL cells keep arriving with a predefined probability, whenever LL cells stay in the buffer longer than a certain threshold value, the number of LL cells will also reach the LDOLL threshold value. Therefore we use the LDOLL results as an approximation of this method.

Below we make a list of the space and time priority strategies that we have analysed.

Space priority strategies:

RBn: Reserved Buffers, LD cells can only be stored in the buffer if the number of cells in the buffer is less than n, i.e. $Q - n$ places are reserved for exclusive use by LL cells.
This is the same strategy as the partial buffer sharing strategy described in [3] and [5] and the threshold access strategy described in [6];

SBn: Separate Buffers, the buffer space is devided into two parts with n places for LL cells and $Q - n$ places for LD cells; this strategy has been described by Bonomi et al.[6], it is also the same policy as described by Lin and Sylvester in [3], which they call complete partitioning;

SBPOn: Separate Buffers with Push-Out; because in the separate buffer strategy cells may be lost even though there are still empty places, we have also analysed this strategy, where each cell type has push-out priority in its own buffer. If e.g. the LD buffer is full with LD cells and the LL buffer isn't completely filled, then an arriving LD cell may use the empty LL buffer spaces, but can be pushed out by arriving LL cells;

CSPO: Complete Sharing with Push-Out, when the buffer is full, an arriving LL cell is allowed to push-out an LD cell; described by Kröner et al. in [5]; the LDOLL threshold policies [7] also use this form of space priority.

Time priority strategies:

LDF: Serve LD cells First (only when there are no LD cells left to serve, then LL cells will be served); Cheng and Akyildiz call this strategy HOL;

THn: Threshold strategy, if there are n or more LL cells in the buffer, then the LL cells will be served first; this is the time priority strategy used by Awater and Schoute in [7].

Other strategies, which combine both types of priorities:

FIFO: The ordinary First In First Out policy, with no distinction between LD or LL cells;

LDOLLn: Serve LD cells first unless there are n or more LL cells; storage priority for LL cells (as in [7]), can also be written as CSPO-THn;

SpTi: Space priority for LL cells and time priority for LD cells.
   This strategy is equal to the variable priority method A mentioned in [4] and also equal to the LDOLLn strategy with $n = Q$;

FixedB: Fixed method B, as described in Ohnishi et al. [4].

5 Performance analysis

The performance measures of interest are: loss and delay. More precisely, we want to calculate the loss probability for LL cells and the expected delay for LD cells. As said before, expected delay generally gives a relative indication of delay jitter.

To reduce the variety in the parameter space, some choices must be made. The buffer size is set to $Q = 40$, equal to the largest buffer size considered in [2] (the corresponding state space has then already 861 states). Cell loss can only occur when the number of inlets, N, is larger than one. Four inlets is already more than sufficient to show the effects of temporary input excess; so we set the number of inlets $N = 4$. Assuming an equal mix of LD and LL cells we let $r_i(t) = 0.5$ for all t and all $i = 1, \ldots, N$. Other choices of parameters will lead to other absolute performance measures but it will turn out that the conclusions about the relative merits of the different priority strategies remain the same.

We want to analyse the performance for both stationary and time-varying traffic. In the stationary case, the arrival probability per inlet is set to $p_i(t) = 0.225$ resulting in a offered load of $\rho = 0.9$. In the non-stationary analysis, we have $p_i(t) = 0.2$ if $t \bmod 8000 < 4000$ and $p_i(t) = 0.25$ otherwise. This way the offered load jumps from $\rho = 0.8$ to $\rho = 1.0$, and back, every 4000 cell times.

For each strategy, the matrix of transition probabilities can be filled in by skillful bookkeeping. The equilibrium distribution (for the stationary analysis) is then found by repeatedly multiplying with the transitionmatrix. Of course, there are other methods, but this one is convenient in the light of the non-stationary analysis that is also done.

From the equilibrium distribution we get the expected number of cells of either type and thereby the expected delay using Little's result. For the type LD this becomes:

$$\text{E}\{LD\ delay\} \approx \frac{\displaystyle\sum_{n_{LD}+n_{LL}\leq Q} P(n_{LD},n_{LL})\cdot n_{LD}}{\displaystyle\sum_{n_{LD}+n_{LL}\leq Q} P(n_{LD},n_{LL})\cdot\gamma(n_{LD},n_{LL})} \tag{1}$$

where $P(n_{LD},n_{LL})$ is the equilibrium probability of being in state (n_{LD},n_{LL}) and $\gamma(n_{LD},n_{LL})$ is the probability that in state (n_{LD},n_{LL}) an LD cell is retrieved, as prescribed by the time priority strategy (generally the value will be 0 or 1).

In (1) the *approximately equal symbol* '$\approx$' is used since the formula gives a slight overestimation of the expected delay. Namely, the numerator also includes the contribution of LD cells that will be pushed out, whereas the denominator, as it should be, only considers retrieved LD cells. With push-out probabilities of less than 0.01, the introduced error is correspondingly small.

The loss probability, also for either type, is found by considering for each state and each possible arrival pattern the number of cells lost under the prevailing strategy. For the type LL this is written as:

$$\text{Pr}\{LL\ Loss\} = \frac{\displaystyle\sum_{n_{LD}+n_{LL}\leq Q} P(n_{LD},n_{LL})\cdot \Lambda(n_{LD},n_{LL})}{\displaystyle\sum_{i=1}^{N} p_i\cdot(1-r_i)} \tag{2}$$

$$\begin{aligned}
\Lambda(n_{LD},n_{LL}) = \ &\text{E}\{\#\ \text{LL losses}\,|\,(n_{LD}-1,n_{LL})\}\cdot\gamma(n_{LD},n_{LL})\ + \\
&\text{E}\{\#\ \text{LL losses}\,|\,(n_{LD},n_{LL}-1)\}\cdot(1-\gamma(n_{LD},n_{LL})) \\
&\hspace{6cm}(n_{LD},n_{LL})>(0,0)
\end{aligned} \tag{3}$$

Where $\Lambda(n_{LD},n_{LL})$ is the expected number of LL cells lost per time slot, which is found by evaluating—for all arrivals patterns and weighted with the probability of the arrival patterns—the number of LL cells lost under the current space priority strategy.

For the non-stationary case the probability distribution at time t is given by $P_t(n_{LD},n_{LL})$. By starting at t sufficiently negative, we can be sure that any start-up effects are extinct at $t = 0$. We apply here the theory of simputation, which was presented in [8], with an $80\% - 100\%$ load pattern simulated at the BURST time scale and computation at the CELL time scale. The only difference is that here we simulate a deterministic load pattern whereas in [8] Monte-Carlo simulation was discussed.

Let $T = 8000$ be the cycle time of the periodic load. Then

$$\mathrm{E}\{LD\ delay\} \approx \frac{\sum\limits_{t=0}^{T-1} \sum\limits_{n_{LD}+n_{LL}\leq Q} P_t(n_{LD},n_{LL}) \cdot n_{LD}}{\sum\limits_{t=0}^{T-1} \sum\limits_{n_{LD}+n_{LL}\leq Q} P_t(n_{LD},n_{LL}) \cdot \gamma(n_{LD},n_{LL})} \tag{4}$$

and

$$\mathrm{Pr}\{LL\ loss\} \approx \frac{\sum\limits_{t=0}^{T-1} \sum\limits_{n_{LD}+n_{LL}\leq Q} P_t(n_{LD},n_{LL}) \cdot \Lambda_t(n_{LD},n_{LL})}{\sum\limits_{t=0}^{T-1} \sum\limits_{i=1}^{N} p_i(t) \cdot (1 - r_i(t))} \tag{5}$$

6 Results

To make a handy comparison of all alternatives, we introduce the delay-loss-plane. In this plane, the abscissa quantifies the expected delay for LD cells and the vertical axis measures (on a logarithmic scale) the loss probability for LL cells. Thus, each alternative shows up as a mark in the delay-loss-plane.

The objective to minimize loss probability for LL cells and variable delay for LD cells can be translated as the goal to be as far as possible in the southwest corner of the delay-loss-plane.

In figure 3 the delay-loss-plane is shown for a constant load of $\rho = 0.9$ and in figure 4 for a load that alternates between $\rho = 0.8$ and $\rho = 1.0$. In these graphs the following combinations of the alternatives indicated at the end of section 4 have been plotted, using the formulas of section 5:

- The LDOLLn strategies, with n ranging from 1 to 40. Because the FixedB strategy has an only slightly higher loss probability than and the same delay as the SpTi (or equal: the LDOLL40 strategy) this point is not plotted separately.
- The ordinary First In First Out (FIFO) strategy.
- The Reserved Buffer strategy (RBn), with n having the values 1 to 40, combined with the following time priority strategies:
  - Threshold strategy (THm): Because it turned out that for the plotted values this strategy gives the same results as the LDF strategy, for values of $m \geq n$, and less optimal results for $m \leq n$, this strategy also hasn't been plotted separately;
  - The LD cells First (LDF) strategy;
  - The First In First Out policy, only used with respect to the order of service.

- The Separate Buffers strategy (SBn), using the Threshold time priority policy (THm): this strategy has been plotted for n equal to 35, and m taking on the values between 1 and 40.
- The Separate Buffers with Push-Out strategy (SBPOn), also using the Threshold time priority policy (THm): with $n = 35$ with m ranging from 1 to 40. For n is 40 this strategy is equal to the LDOLL strategy.

The values of the SB35THm strategy for constant load are less optimal than those for the LDOLL strategy; this in contrast to the graph for the variable load.

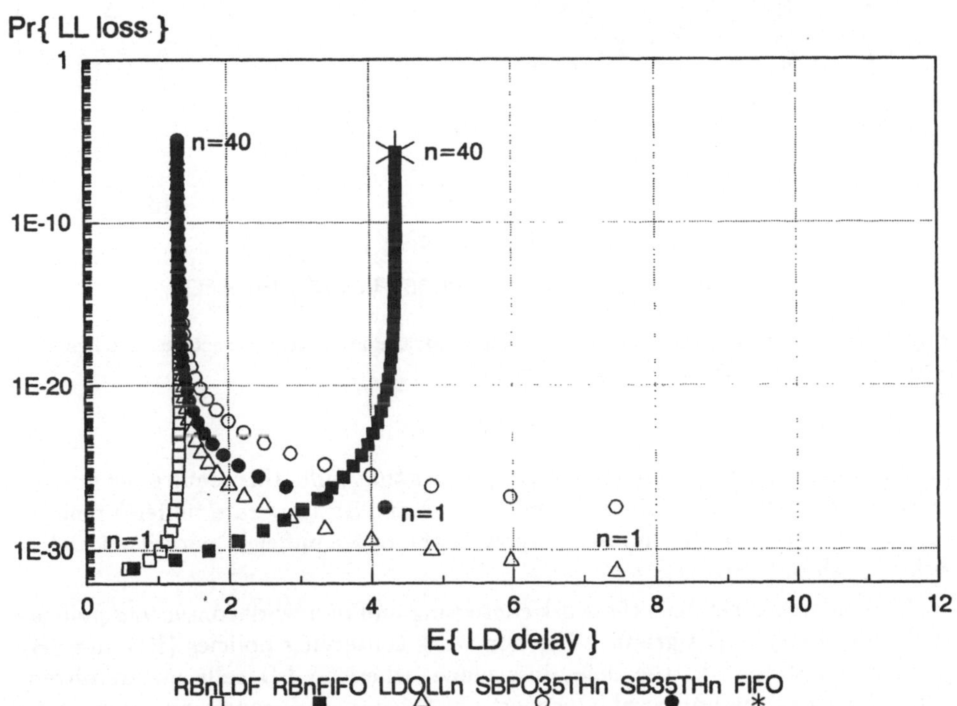

Fig. 3. Delay-loss performance of the priority strategies listed in section 4, at a stationary load of $\rho = 0.9$.

What is not shown in this delay-loss-plane is the delay of LL cells and the loss probability for LD cells. Especially the latter can be quite high for some policies. For example the SB35TH1 policy, which has only $40 - 35 = 5$ places for LD cells and which only serves LD cells when there is less than 1 LL cell in the buffer, throws away a large fraction of the LD cells. This observation leads to the requirement that a policy should not throw away cells when there are still buffer

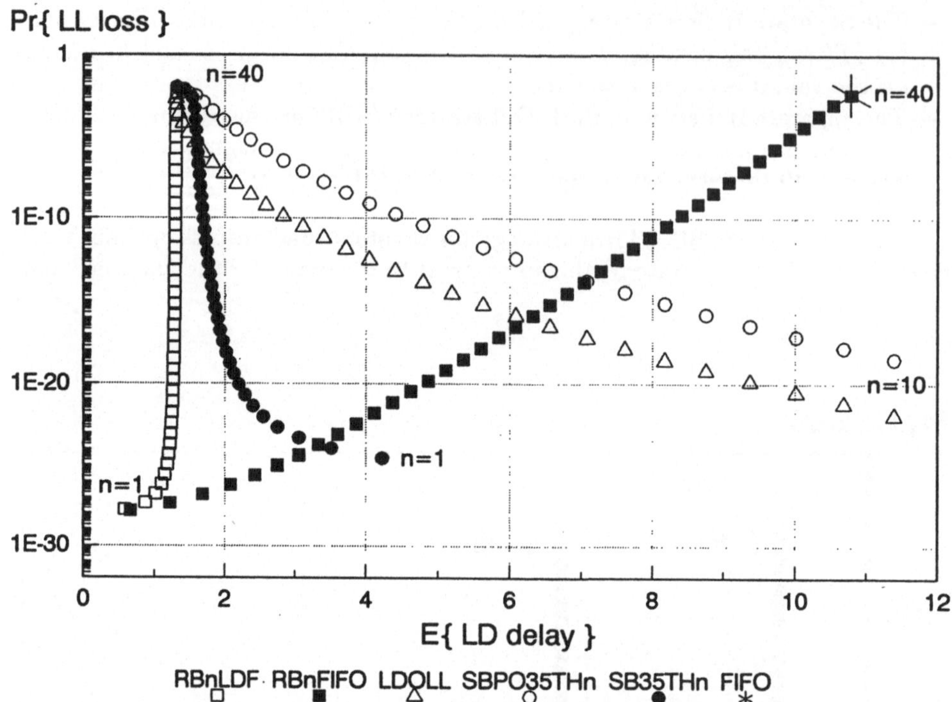

Fig. 4. Delay-loss performance of the priority strategies listed in section 4, when the load alternates between $\rho = 0.8$ and $\rho = 1.0$.

places available. Inspired by [3], we call policies that fulfill this requirement: work conserving policies. The RB (reserved buffers) and SB (separate buffers) policies are not work conserving unless overflow in the other buffer is permitted at the risk of push out (SBPO).

The difference between the work conserving and non work conserving policies is shown clearly in the graphs. The non work conserving policies (RB and SB) give their optimum in the delay-loss plane, when no LD cells are admitted. This illustrates the undesirable property of the not work conserving policies to achieve the optimum at the cost of unexceptable loss probabilities (even equal to 1) for LD cells. To indicate the impact the different policies have on the loss probability of the LD cells in table 1 an indication of the LD loss probabilities has been given.

It turns out that indeed the LDOLL threshold policies are the best in the class of work conserving policies. Moreover, with the threshold parameter n one can trade off loss for LL against delay for LD cells, e.g. by going from LDOLL5 to LDOLL10 the loss probability for LL increases from 10^{-29} to 10^{-26} while the mean delay lessens from 3.4 to 1.8 cell times.

Space priority	Service priority	Maximum LD loss probability	Minimum LD loss probability
LDOLL threshold		3.81E-6(1)	3.06E-6(40)
Separate Buffers (35) with Push-Out	Threshold	3.81E-6(1)	1.37E-8(40)
Reserved Buffers	All	0.43(1)	1.91E-6(40)
Separate Buffers (35)	Threshold	5.52E-2(1)	1.12E-4(40)
First In First Out		1.91E-6	

Table 1. LD loss probabilities in case of a stationary load $\rho = 0.9$

Although the absolute performance measures for a load alternating between 80% and 100% are quite different from the stationary case of 90% load, the observations above remain valid in the time varying case.

7 Conclusions

The utilization of ATM links, and thereby the efficiency of ATM networks, can be greatly enhanced by exploiting the complementary requirements of low delay and low loss traffic. Dealing with those complementary requirements asks for priority strategies. The graphs of the preceding section demonstrate that indeed, at a load as high as $\rho = 0.9$, it is possible to have, contrary to the high loss probability without priorities, for Low Loss traffic a loss probability below 10^{-9} and at the same time a mean delay for Low Delay traffic that is significantly less than the delay in the case of plain FIFO queueing. The latter observation suggests that also the delay jitter can be significantly reduced (compared to FIFO).

A complete ordering of alternatives is not possible in a multi-objective context. However, most priority alternatives improve on both objectives when compared with plain FIFO. There are policies that perform better (in the delay-loss plane) than the 'optimal' LDOLL threshold policies. Reserved Buffers with FIFO is a simple strategy that seems to perform well. However, policies of the Reserved Buffer or Separate Buffers type are not work conserving, i.e. they refuse cells even when not all buffer places are occupied. The price to be paid is a very high loss probability for LD cells which does not show up in the delay-loss plane. Within the set of work conserving policies the LDOLL policies form an 'optimal' family (no other policy can give a lower loss probability for LL cells **and** lower delay for LD cells). Within the LDOLL family, there is one parameter by which the tradeoff between LL-loss and LD-delay can be chosen at will.

Since in real networks the load will never be stationary, it was useful to evaluate the performance of alternative priority strategies also for non- stationary cell arrival statistics. A load that alternates between 80% and 100% induces a performance that is strikingly different from the performance at 90% loading: in the examples computed, the loss probabilities increased with more than two orders of magnitude and the delays increased with much more than a factor of two for the varying load case. Nevertheless, the main conclusions: improvement by priorities and optimality of LDOLL threshold policies, showed to remain valid.

Further research will be focused at a more direct evaluation and minimization of delay jitter. The extension of the analysis to the case of one shared buffer for more than one output channel will be a challenging subject of future research.

Acknowledgement

We thank Geert Awater for the substantial help he offered, ranging from down to earth coding support to mathematical wisdom. We also thank Albert Swart for being our LaTeX wizard.

References

1. Y. Sakurai, N. Ido, S. Gohara, and N. Endo, "Large-scale ATM multistage switching network with shared buffer memory switches," *IEEE Comm. Mag.*, vol. 29, Jan. 1991.
2. X. Cheng, and I.F. Akyildiz, "A finite buffer two class queue with different scheduling and push-out schemes," in *Proc. INFOCOM '92*, Florence, Italy, May 1992, pp. 231–241.
3. A.Y.-M. Lin, and J.A. Silvester, "Priority queueing strategies and buffer allocation protocols for traffic control at an ATM integrated broadband switching system," *IEEE J. Select. Areas Commun.*, vol. SAC-9, no. 9, pp. 1524–1535, Dec. 1991.
4. H. Ohnishi, T. Okada, and K. Noguchi, "Flow control schemes and delay/loss tradeoff in ATM networks," *IEEE J. Select. Areas Commun.*, vol. SAC-6, no. 9, pp. 1609–1615, Dec. 1988.
5. H. Kröner, G. Hébuterne, P. Boyer, and A. Gravey, "Priority management in ATM switching nodes," *IEEE J. Select. Areas Commun.*, vol. SAC-9, no. 3, pp. 418–427, Apr. 1991.
6. F. Bonomi, L. Fratta, S. Motagna, and R. Paglino, "Priority on cell service and cell loss in ATM Switching," in *Proc. 7th ITC Sem.*, Morristown, NJ, Oct. 1990, paper 7.2.
7. G.A. Awater, and F.C. Schoute, "Optimal queueing policies for fast packet switching of mixed traffic," *IEEE J. Select. Areas Commun.*, vol. SAC-9, no. 3, pp. 458–466, Apr. 1991.
8. G.A. Awater, and F.C. Schoute, "Performance improvement of fast packet switching by LDOLL queueing," in *Proc. INFOCOM '92*, Florence, Italy, May 1992, pp. 562–568.

A Performance Model for Statistical Multiplexing of correlated ATM Traffic Superpositions

Christoph Herrmann

Communication Networks, Aachen University of Technology
Kopernikusstr.16, D-52056 Aachen, Germany
E-Mail: chh@dfv.rwth-aachen.de

Abstract. Models for ATM statistical multiplexing must involve bursty (i.e. several cell arrivals are possible at a time instant) and correlated input processes. Correlation is important, since ATM networks will carry VBR video sources, the cell streams of which are typically correlated. In addition, the superposition of individual sources (e.g. in an ATM multiplexer), which are renewal (and non-Poisson), shows correlations.
This paper extends recent results on queues with deterministic service times (greater or equal to the time-unit) and Semi-Markovian input processes (SMP's) to the $SMP^{[X]}/D/1/s$ queue. The SMP generates arrival instants, and the independent process X of i.i.d. random variables "modulates" the batch size. The solution provides the probability functions of the number of cells in the system and of the waiting time of a test-cell, the loss probability of a test-cell and the conditional cell loss probability. A possible extension allowing one batch input stream and one single cell stream is outlined; it can serve as a model for Connection Admission Control (CAC) in ATM.

KEYWORDS: discrete-time queue, finite buffer queue, Semi-Markovian input, correlated input, ATM statistical multiplexing.

1 Introduction

There are two important reasons, why ATM networks will have to deal, in each switch, with correlated input processes: Some individual sources have a typically correlated structure, e.g. video sources [7]. The superposition of sources, which are renewal, but non-Poisson, is known to result in a process with interarrival times, which are not mutually independent [16]. The usual assumption (in other fields of modelling) that correlations can be ignored is not justified, since Quality of Service (QOS) parameters are very sensitive in ATM. In an ATM switch, several input lines are switched to the same output line. As long as the output line is occupied by the transmission of a cell, incoming cells are buffered; this gives rise to a queueing system with deterministic service time due to the constant cell length for all connections. The queue sees a batch of size v ("v-batch"), when v input lines produce a cell simultaneously and these cells are switched to the same output line. So the maximum number b_{max} of the batch size is given by the number of input lines producing cells, that are switched to the same output line. Modelling ATM switches is usually done by means of discrete-time queueing systems [1][2][8][4], since the switches are assumed to work synchronously [14], and so there is a smallest time unit, which all time interalls of interest refer to. Furthermore, superimposing continuous time processes does not provide batch arrivals: e.g. superimposing two Markovian Arrival processes (MAPs) still provides a MAP and no Batch Markovian Arrival process (BMAP) [12]. The event that both processes generate an arrival simultaneously has zero probability. However, the probability is positive, if two DMAPs are superimposed [9][1]. In most cases, the service time is set equal to the time unit. As long as the input process is a superposition of several sources, and the individual sources cannot be identified in the superposition, the approach of "service time equal to the time unit" is sufficient, even if the output bitrate is lower than the input bitrate (and this must happen somewhere in the network close to the receiving terminal equipment). Assuming a deterministic service time D higher than the time unit yields smaller batches and a finer division of the time axis on the input side, thus coming closer to the actual discrete-time nature of the input process. As soon as there is an individual source recognizable within the superposition, it can be necessary to use higher values for D, especially if the output bitrate is lower than that of the input lines.

This paper extends [8] to the $SMP^{[X]}/D/1/s$ finite buffer queue; the discrete-time Semi-Markov process (SMP) produces correlated interarrival times, and the independent process $X := \{X_n; n \in \mathbb{N}_0\}$ (X_n independent identically distributed (i.i.d.)) "modulates" the batch size at the n-th arrival. The assumption of the independence and the i.i.d.-property of X seems to be justified, since the input lines produce independent cell-streams; it has already been used in [13]. The extension has the advantage, that the batch size can be modelled separately, whereas batches are generated in [8] by allowing zero interarrival times of the SMP. The solution is based on the "method of unfinished work", which was applied in [15] for renewal inputs. It provides loss probability and moments of the waiting time of a test-cell, which account for QOS parameters loss probability, mean delay and delay jitter, as well as conditional loss probability.

2 Semi-Markov Processes

According to [3], Semi-Markov processes can be described by an (embedded) Markov chain (MC, with transition probability matrix $\mathbf{p} = (p_{ij})_{i,j \in E}$) with the state space $E = \{1, 2, \ldots, m\}$ and a set of state sojourn time distribution functions $F_{ij}(t)$, $i, j \in E, t \in \mathbb{R}_0$. We only consider discrete-time SMPs, therefore: $t \in \mathbb{N}_0$. We use the state sojourn time probability functions

$$f_{ij}(t) = P\{A_{n-1} = t | S_n = j, S_{n-1} = i\},$$

where $A_{n-1} := T_n - T_{n-1}$ is the sojourn time in state S_{n-1} until changing to state S_n at time instant T_n. The independence of n in $f_{ij}(t)$ implies the further assumption of time homogeneity [3]. An SMP is completely described by the

Semi-Markov kernel given as the matrix $\mathbf{q}(t) = (q_{ij}(t))_{i,j \in E}$, with

$$q_{ij}(t) = p_{ij} \cdot f_{ij}(t) = P\{S_n = j, A_{n-1} = t | S_{n-1} = i\}.$$

We also need distribution functions $Q_{ij}(k) = \sum_{\ell=0}^{k} q_{ij}(\ell)$, $\mathbf{Q}(k) = (Q_{ij}(k))_{i,j \in E}$. Using an SMP as an input process of a queue, the state sojourn times correspond to the interarrival times. An interarrival time of length zero leads to a batch arrival. Because of the MC the state sojourn times are, in general, not independent. The joint probability function is:

$$P\{A_n = t_n, \ldots, A_{n+\nu} = t_{n+\nu}\} = \underline{P}^{(n)} \cdot \mathbf{q}(t_n) \cdot \ldots \cdot \mathbf{q}(t_{n+\nu}) \cdot \underline{e}, \quad \nu \in \mathbb{N}, \quad (1)$$

where $\underline{P}^{(n)}$ denotes the state probability of the MC after n steps, $\underline{e} = (1, 1, \ldots, 1)^T$ with m components. In order to get joint probability functions of the state sojourn times, which are invariant to an arbitrary shift of the index n, stationary state probabilities are assumed for the embedded MC.

Whenever the SMP enters a state i, the next state j to be visited is chosen according to p_{ij} and the sojourn time in state i until changing to j according to $f_{ij}(t)$. The time instant of entering a next (possibly the same) state is interpreted as an arrival instant.

3 Analysis of the discrete-time $\text{SMP}^{[X]}/\text{D}/1/\text{s}$ finite buffer queue

We consider a discrete-time $\text{SMP}^{[X]}/\text{D}/1/\text{s}$ queue with FIFO service strategy: The (positive) interarrival times correspond to the state sojourn times $T_{n+1} - T_n$ of a Semi-Markov process, the buffer size is s, and the service time process $\{B_n; n \in \mathbb{N}_0\}$ is deterministic: $B_n = D$. $X := \{X_n; n \in \mathbb{N}_0\}$ determines the batch size: At arrival instant T_n the batch size is given by $X_n \in \mathbb{N}$; $P\{X_n = v\} =: x(v), x(v) = 0$ for $v > b_{max}$, $P\{X_n \leq v\} =: X(v), X^c(v) := P\{X_n \geq v + 1\} = 1 - X(v)$. Since X accounts for the batches we only assume positive interarrival times for the SMP. Whenever a batch arrival occurs, as many cells as possible are buffered.

The central approach to the solution is the "unfinished work $U(t)$ in the system at time instant t". In continuous-time systems, this is the amount of work to be done from t on (with ignoring future arrivals), until the system is empty. At the n−th arrival instant T_n we consider $U_n :=$ *unfinished work at T_n with ignoring the arrival* and $U_n^+ :=$ *unfinished work at T_n taking the arrival into account*. In case of continuous time systems, U_n equals the unfinished work *immediately before* the n-th arrival instant, and U_n^+ refers to that *immediately after* the arrival instant.

3.1 The waiting room policies Arrival First (AF) and Departure First (DF)

Describing the development of a discrete-time queueing system by means of the unfinished work can be done by step-functions, which are constant for a time unit and change their values at discrete-time instants. The step-functions can be continuous from the right or from the left. It turns out (see Fig. 1) that in terms of the waiting room policies explained in [6], right-continuous step-functions correspond to the case "departure first" (**DF**), which means that in the case of simultaneity of an arrival and a departure, the arriving cell enters the system immediately after the departing one has left. The other policy "arrival first" (**AF**) refers to the case that the arriving cell still sees the departing cell, when arrival and departure happen simultaneously. In an earlier publication, DF equals the "early arrival system", AF the "late arrival system" [10], p.193. More formally it is (see Fig. 1):

$$U(T+0) := \lim_{t \downarrow T} U(t), \ \ U(T-0) := \lim_{t \uparrow T} U(t), \ \ U_0 := 0$$

$$\text{AF:} \quad \begin{aligned} U_n &= U(T_n) \\ U_n^+ &= U(T_n + 0) \end{aligned} \qquad \text{DF:} \quad \begin{aligned} U_n &= max(U(T_n - 0) - 1, 0) \\ U_n^+ &= U(T_n) \end{aligned} \tag{2}$$

Continuous-time queueing systems do not show these two alternatives, since the simultaneous occurence of an arrival and a departure has zero probability [6].

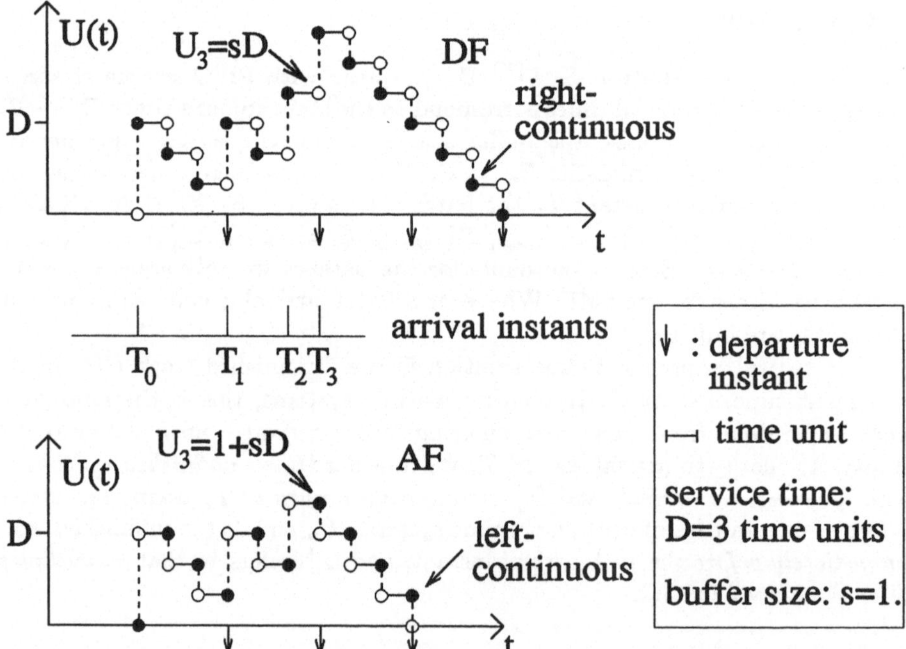

Fig. 1 *Paths of the unfinished work $U(t)$ for DF and AF with buffer size $s = 1$: The cell arriving at T_3 is lost in case of AF, since it still sees the cell having arrived at T_1.*

3.2 Unfinished work at arrivals

There are the following relations between U_{n-1} and U_{n-1}^+ for DF:

$$U_{n-1}^+ = \begin{cases} \begin{rcases} U_{n-1} + X_{n-1}D & 0 \le U_{n-1} \le (s - X_{n-1} + 1)D, \\ U_{n-1} + \xi D & 1 + (s - \xi)D \le U_{n-1} \le (s - \xi + 1)D \\ & \text{for each } \xi \text{ with } 0 \le \xi \le X_{n-1} - 1 \end{rcases} 1 \le X_{n-1} \le s, \\[2mm] \begin{rcases} U_{n-1} + sD + D & U_{n-1} = 0, \\ U_{n-1} + \xi D & 1 + (s - \xi)D \le U_{n-1} \le (s - \xi + 1)D \\ & \text{for each } \xi \text{ with } 0 \le \xi \le s \end{rcases} 1 + s \le X_{n-1}. \end{cases} \tag{3}$$

Between U_n and U_{n-1}^+ the following holds [15]:

$$U_n = \begin{cases} U_{n-1}^+ - A_{n-1} & \text{for } U_{n-1}^+ > A_{n-1} \\ 0 & \text{else.} \end{cases} \tag{4}$$

AF is given by:

$$U_{n-1}^+ = \begin{cases} \begin{rcases} U_{n-1} + X_{n-1}D & U_{n-1} = 0, \\ U_{n-1} + X_{n-1}D - 1 & 1 \le U_{n-1} \le (s - X_{n-1} + 1)D, \\ U_{n-1} + \xi D - 1 & 1 + (s - \xi)D \le U_{n-1} \le (s - \xi + 1)D \\ & \text{for each } \xi \text{ with } 0 \le \xi \le X_{n-1} - 1 \end{rcases} 1 \le X_{n-1} \le s, \\[2mm] \begin{rcases} U_{n-1} + sD + D & U_{n-1} = 0, \\ U_{n-1} + \xi D - 1 & 1 + (s - \xi)D \le U_{n-1} \le (s - \xi + 1)D \\ & \text{for each } \xi \text{ with } 0 \le \xi \le s \end{rcases} 1 + s \le X_{n-1}. \end{cases} \tag{5}$$

and

$$U_n = \begin{cases} U_{n-1}^+ - A_{n-1} + 1 & \text{for } U_{n-1}^+ \ge A_{n-1} \\ 0 & \text{else.} \end{cases} \tag{6}$$

An important argument is the following

Lemma 1 *For all $n \in \mathbb{N}$ it is:*
$$P\{S_n = j, A_{n-1} = t | S_{n-1} = i, U_{n-1} = k, X_{n-1} = v\} =$$
$$= P\{S_n = j, A_{n-1} = t | S_{n-1} = i\}.$$

Proof: We recall the central defining property of SMPs[3]:
$$P\{S_{n+1} = j, T_{n+1} - T_n \le t | S_n, \cdots, S_0, T_n, \cdots, T_0\} =$$
$$= P\{S_{n+1} = j, T_{n+1} - T_n \le t | S_n\}. \tag{7}$$

Note that $A_n := T_{n+1} - T_n$. Any realization $((t_0, i_0, v_0), \ldots, (t_{n-2}, i_{n-2}, v_{n-2}))$ of the probability vector $((T_0, S_0, X_0), \cdots, (T_{n-2}, S_{n-2}, X_{n-2}), (T_{n-1}, S_{n-1}, \cdot))$ determines one path of the process of the unfinished work at an arbitrary discrete-time instant up to the $(n-1)$th arrival and thus one realization k of U_{n-1}. The set of all realizations falls into classes C_k, the elements of which determine paths with the same realization k of U_{n-1}. With $C_k^i := \{(t_0, i_0, v_0, \ldots, t_{n-2}, i_{n-2}, v_{n-2}, t_{n-1}) | (t_0, i_0, v_0, \ldots, t_{n-2}, i_{n-2}, v_{n-2}, t_{n-1}, i) \in C_k\}$ it is:

$$\{S_{n-1} = i, U_{n-1} = k, X_{n-1} = v\} =$$

$$= \bigcup_{\substack{(t_0, i_0, v_0, \cdots, \\ t_{n-2}, i_{n-2}, v_{n-2}, t_{n-1}) \in C_k^i}} \{(T_0, S_0, X_0) = (t_0, i_0, v_0), \cdots, \\ (T_{n-2}, S_{n-2}, X_{n-2}) = (t_{n-2}, i_{n-2}, v_{n-2}), \\ (T_{n-1}, S_{n-1}, X_{n-1}) = (t_{n-1}, i, v)\}. \tag{8}$$

By (7), (8) and the independence of $\{X_n; n \in \mathbb{N}_0\}$ we get:
$$P\{S_n = j, A_{n-1} = t, S_{n-1} = i, U_{n-1} = k, X_{n-1} = v\} =$$
$$= P\{S_n = j, A_{n-1} = t | S_{n-1} = i\} \cdot P\{S_{n-1} = i, U_{n-1} = k, X_{n-1} = v\} \qquad \square$$

By Lemma 1 two relations are obtained, which are important in what follows:

$$P\{S_n = j | S_{n-1} = i, U_{n-1} = k, X_{n-1} = v\} = p_{ij} \tag{9}$$

$$P\{A_{n-1} = t | S_n = j, S_{n-1} = i, U_{n-1} = k, X_{n-1} = v\} =$$

$$= P\{A_{n-1} = t | S_n = j, S_{n-1} = i\} = f_{ij}(t) \tag{10}$$

For DF they lead to:

Lemma 2 *For all* $n \in \mathbb{N}$, $k, \ell \in \{0, \cdots, sD + D\}$, $i, j \in E$, $v \in \mathbb{N}$ *the conditional probability* $P\{U_n = \ell, S_n = j | U_{n-1} = k, S_{n-1} = i, X_{n-1} = v\}$ *can be expressed by the Semi-Markov kernel* $\mathbf{q}(t)$ *alone, and it is for DF:*
$$P\{U_n = \ell, S_n = j | U_{n-1} = k, S_{n-1} = i, X_{n-1} = v\} =$$

$$= \begin{cases} \left. \begin{cases} q_{ij}(k - \ell + vD) & 0 \le k \le (s + 1 - v)D, \\ q_{ij}(k - \ell + \xi D) & 1 + (s - \xi)D \le k \le (s-\xi+1)D \\ & \text{for each } \xi \text{ with } 0 \le \xi \le v - 1, \end{cases} \right\} 1 \le v \le s \\ \left. \begin{cases} q_{ij}(k - \ell + \xi D) & 1 + (s - \xi)D \le k \le (s-\xi+1)D \\ & \text{for each } \xi \text{ with } 0 \le \xi \le s, \\ q_{ij}(-\ell + sD + D) & k = 0, \end{cases} \right\} 1 + s \le v \end{cases} \quad \ell > 0, \\ \\ \left. \begin{cases} p_{ij} - Q_{ij}(k - 1 + vD) & 0 \le k \le (s + 1 - v)D, \\ p_{ij} - Q_{ij}(k - 1 + \xi D) & 1 + (s - \xi)D \le k \le (s-\xi+1)D, \\ & \text{for each } \xi \text{ with } 0 \le \xi \le v - 1, \end{cases} \right\} 1 \le v \le s \\ \left. \begin{cases} p_{ij} - Q_{ij}(k - 1 + \xi D) & 1 + (s - \xi)D \le k \le (s-\xi+1)D, \\ & \text{for each } \xi \text{ with } 0 \le \xi \le s, \\ p_{ij} - Q_{ij}(-1 + sD + D) & k = 0, \end{cases} \right\} 1 + s \le v \end{cases} \quad \ell = 0. \end{cases}$$

Proof: X_n, X_{n-1} and the SMP are independent, i.e. (S_n, A_n) and X_n, X_{n-1} are independent. However, U_n and X_{n-1} are not independent, as the batch size at the $(n - 1)$th arrival affects the unfinished work U_n at the following arrival; but (S_n, U_n) and X_n are independent. Together with (9), we have:

$$P\{U_n = \ell, S_n = j | U_{n-1} = k, S_{n-1} = i, X_{n-1} = v\} =$$

$$= P\{U_n = \ell | S_n = j, U_{n-1} = k, S_{n-1} = i, X_{n-1} = v\} \cdot p_{ij} \tag{11}$$

For the conditional probability $P\{\cdot | S_n = j, S_{n-1} = i, U_{n-1} = k, X_{n-1} = v\}$ we write $P_{ijkv}\{\cdot\}$. We use an indicator function $1_{k=a}^b = \begin{cases} 1 \text{ for } a \le k \le b \\ 0 \text{ else.} \end{cases}$

First we state with the help of (4):

$$P_{ijkv}\{U_n = \ell\} = \begin{cases} P_{ijkv}\{U^+_{n-1} - A_{n-1} = \ell\} & \text{for } \ell > 0 \\[2mm] P_{ijkv}\{U^+_{n-1} \leq A_{n-1}\} & \text{for } \ell = 0. \end{cases} \tag{12}$$

Now we investigate the set $\{U^+_{n-1} = \ell', S_{n-1} = i, X_{n-1} = v\}$. As an example, we explain the case $1 \leq v \leq s$: If $\ell' \leq sD$, all the cells of a v-batch were admitted (there is still room for at least one more cell in the queue); in addition $\ell' \geq vD$ (no loss!). If $1 + sD \leq \ell' \leq D + sD$, there were $v, v-1, \ldots,$ or 0 cells lost, and U_{n-1} was so large that (together with the admitted cells) U^+_{n-1} takes a value between $1 + sD$ and $D + sD$. The other cases are reasoned similarly (see also (3)). Using the abbreviation $\{ \ \cdot \ \}_{iv} := \{ \ \cdot \ , S_{n-1} = i, X_{n-1} = v\}$ we have for all $i \in E$:

$$\{U^+_{n-1} = \ell'\}_{iv} =$$

$$= \begin{cases} \left. \begin{array}{ll} \bigcup_{\xi=0}^{v} \{U_{n-1} = \ell' - \xi D\}_{iv} & \text{for } 1 + sD \leq \ell' \leq sD + D \\ \{U_{n-1} = \ell' - vD\}_{iv} & \text{for } vD \leq \ell' \leq sD \end{array} \right\} & 1 \leq v \leq s, \\[4mm] \left. \begin{array}{ll} \bigcup_{\xi=0}^{s+1} \{U_{n-1} = (s+1-\xi)D\}_{iv} & \text{for } \ell' = sD + D \\ \bigcup_{\xi=0}^{s} \{U_{n-1} = \ell' - \xi D\}_{iv} & \text{for } 1 + sD \leq \ell' \leq sD + D - 1 \end{array} \right\} & 1 + s \leq v. \end{cases} \tag{13}$$

With the disjoint unions in (13), we can go on in (12), noting that $P_{ijkv}\{U_{n-1} = \ell, \ \cdot \ \} = 0$ for $k \neq \ell$. **In the case $\ell > 0$:**
a) For $1 \leq v \leq s$:

$$P_{ijkv}\{U^+_{n-1} - A_{n-1} = \ell\} = \sum_{\ell'=vD}^{sD+D} P_{ijkv}\{U^+_{n-1} = \ell', A_{n-1} = \ell' - \ell\} =$$

$$= 1_{k=0}^{(s-v+1)D} P_{ijkv}\{A_{n-1} = k - \ell + vD\} + \sum_{\xi=0}^{v-1} 1_{k=1+(s-\xi)D}^{(s-\xi+1)D} P_{ijkv}\{A_{n-1} = k - \ell + \xi D\} =$$

$$\overset{by\,(10)}{=} 1_{k=0}^{(s-v+1)D} f_{ij}(k - \ell + vD) + \sum_{\xi=0}^{v-1} 1_{k=1+(s-\xi)D}^{(s-\xi+1)D} f_{ij}(k - \ell + \xi D)$$

b) For $1 + s \leq v < \infty$:

$$P_{ijkv}\{U^+_{n-1} - A_{n-1} = \ell\} = \sum_{\ell'=1+sD}^{D+sD} P_{ijkv}\{U^+_{n-1} = \ell', A_{n-1} = \ell' - \ell\} =$$

$$= \sum_{\xi=0}^{s} 1_{k=1+(s-\xi)D}^{(s+1-\xi)D} P_{ijkv}\{A_{n-1} = k - \ell + \xi D\} + 1_{k=0}^{0} P_{ijkv}\{A_{n-1} = sD + D - \ell\} =$$

$$\overset{by\,(10)}{=} \sum_{\xi=0}^{s} 1_{k=1+(s-\xi)D}^{(s+1-\xi)D} f_{ij}(k - \ell + \xi D) + 1_{k=0}^{0} f_{ij}(sD + D - \ell)$$

The expressions for $\ell = 0$ are found by calculating

$$P_{ijkv}\{U^+_{n-1} \leq A_{n-1}\} = 1 - \sum_{\ell=1}^{sD+D} P_{ijkv}\{U^+_{n-1} - A_{n-1} = \ell\}. \qquad \square$$

Because of (3), (4), $\{(U_n, S_n, X_n); n \in \mathbb{N}_0\}$ is a MC with the transition probabilities $P\{U_n = \ell, S_n = j, X_n = w | U_{n-1} = k, S_{n-1} = i, X_{n-1} = v\} = P\{U_n = \ell, S_n = j | U_{n-1} = k, S_{n-1} = i, X_{n-1} = v\} \cdot x(w)$ according to Lemma 2. The next section shows, that the stationary state probabilities $P\{U_n = \ell, S_n = j, X_n = w\} = P\{U_n = \ell, S_n = j\} \cdot x(v)$ of the chain can be calculated by means of a matrix with $m(sD + D + 1)$ rows and columns, thus reducing the number of computations. For AF similar expressions hold.

3.3 Transient equations (DF)

Because of the Markov property, $u_n(\ell, j, w) := P\{U_n = \ell, S_n = j, X_n = w\}$ can be calculated from $u_{n-1}(k, i, v)$. With the abbreviation $P_{ikv}\{U_n = \ell, S_n = j\} := P\{U_n = \ell, S_n = j | U_{n-1} = k, S_{n-1} = i, X_{n-1} = v\}$ it is, as usual:

$$u_n(\ell, j, w) = x(w) \cdot \sum_{k=0}^{sD+D} \sum_{i=1}^{m} \sum_{v=1}^{b_{max}} u_{n-1}(k, i, v) \cdot P_{ikv}\{U_n = \ell, S_n = j\}$$

Since $P\{U_n = \ell, S_n = j, X_n = w\} = P\{U_n = \ell, S_n = j\} \cdot x(w)$, the equations can be reduced to relations between $u_n(\ell, j) := \sum_{w=1}^{\infty} u_n(\ell, j, w)$ and $u_{n-1}(k, i) := \sum_{v=1}^{\infty} u_{n-1}(k, i, v)$: Given the vector $\underline{u}_n = (u_n(0, 1), \ldots, u_n(0, m), \ldots, u_n(sD + D, m))$, the resulting equations $\underline{u}_n = \underline{u}_{n-1}F$ define a stochastic matrix

$$F = \begin{pmatrix} \mathbf{F}_0^0 & \cdots \mathbf{F}_0^{sD+D} \\ \vdots & \vdots \\ \mathbf{F}_{sD+D}^0 & \cdots \mathbf{F}_{sD+D}^{sD+D} \end{pmatrix} \quad \text{with}$$

$$\mathbf{F}_k^0 = \begin{cases} \mathbf{p} - \sum_{v=1}^{s} x(v)\mathbf{Q}(-1 + vD) - X^c(s)\mathbf{Q}(-1 + sD + D) & \text{for } k = 0 \\ \mathbf{p} - \sum_{v=1}^{\xi-1} x(v)\mathbf{Q}(k - 1 + vD) - X^c(\xi - 1)\mathbf{Q}(k - 1 + \xi D) \\ \qquad \text{for } 1 + (s - \xi)D \leq k \leq (s + 1 - \xi)D, \text{for each } \xi \text{ with } 2 \leq \xi \leq s \\ \mathbf{p} - \mathbf{Q}(k - 1 + D) & \text{for } 1 + sD - D \leq k \leq sD \\ \mathbf{p} - \mathbf{Q}(k - 1) & \text{for } 1 + sD \leq k \leq sD + D \end{cases}$$

and for $\ell > 0$

$$\mathbf{F}_k^{\ell} = \begin{cases} \sum_{v=1}^{s} x(v)\mathbf{q}(-\ell + vD) + X^c(s)\mathbf{q}(-\ell + sD + D) & \text{for } k = 0 \\ \sum_{v=1}^{\xi-1} x(v)\mathbf{q}(k - \ell + vD) + X^c(\xi - 1)\mathbf{q}(k - \ell + \xi D) \\ \qquad \text{for } 1 + (s - \xi)D \leq k \leq (s + 1 - \xi)D, \text{for each } \xi \text{ with } 2 \leq \xi \leq s \\ \mathbf{q}(k - \ell + D) & \text{for } 1 + sD - D \leq k \leq sD \\ \mathbf{q}(k - \ell) & \text{for } 1 + sD \leq k \leq sD + D \end{cases}$$

Since $\mathbf{F}$ is stochastic, the algorithms of Grassmann et al. [5] or Kramer [11] are applicable in order to calculate (if existing) the stationary state probabilities gathered in $\underline{u}$. (By Kramer's algorithm the partitioning of $\mathbf{F}$ in submatrices can be used to advantage.)

3.4 Number of cells in the system, waiting time, loss probabilities

In contrast to [8], the event of loss is ambiguous: losing at least one cell, losing a test-cell, mean number of lost cells; the waiting time is defined here as that of a test-cell marked among the cells of an arriving batch. The expressions refer to the stationary case $(n \to \infty)$.

Number L_n of cells in the system:

$$P\{L_n = \mu\} = \begin{cases} \displaystyle\sum_{j=1}^{m} u(0,j) & \text{for } \mu = 0 \\ \displaystyle\sum_{j=1}^{m} \sum_{\ell=1+(\mu-1)D}^{\mu D} u(\ell,j) & \text{for } 1 \le \mu \le s+1 \end{cases} \tag{14}$$

Probability of losing at least one cell: Loss does not only depend on the number of cells in the system, but also on the size of the batch arriving:

$$P_{loss} = P\{X_n \ge 2+s\}P\{L_n = 0\} + \sum_{\mu=1}^{s+1} P\{X_n \ge 2+s-\mu\}P\{L_n = \mu\} =$$

$$= 1 - \sum_{j=1}^{m}\left[u(0,j)X(s+1) + \sum_{\mu=1}^{s+1} X(s+1-\mu) \sum_{k=1+(\mu-1)D}^{\mu D} u(k,j) \right] \tag{15}$$

Loss probability of a test-cell: In an arriving w–batch the sequence of admission of its cells is chosen randomly. The probability of a test-cell of being chosen ν–th ($\nu < w$) is therefore $\frac{1}{w}$, and the test-cell is lost, if ν exceeds the number of admitted cells of the batch:

$$P_{loss\ test-cell} = \sum_{i=1}^{m}\sum_{\mu=1}^{s+1}\sum_{w=s+2-\mu}^{s+1} x(w) \cdot \frac{w-(s+1-\mu)}{w} \sum_{k=1+(\mu-1)D}^{\mu D} u(k,i) +$$

$$+ \sum_{i=1}^{m}\sum_{w=s+2}^{\infty} x(w) \cdot \left[\frac{w-(s+1)}{w} u(0,i) + \sum_{\mu=1}^{s+1} \frac{w-(s+1-\mu)}{w} \sum_{k=1+(\mu-1)D}^{\mu D} u(k,i) \right] \tag{16}$$

The same expression is obtained for the expected number of lost cells.

Waiting time of a test-cell: A test-cell, chosen ν–th and not lost, sees a waiting time, which is the sum of the unfinished work at the arrival instant and the service time of those cells of the same batch, which are admitted before. (N is a normalizing constant: $N := \sum_{\ell=0}^{sD} P\{W_n = \ell\}$):

$$N \cdot P\{W_n = \ell\} = 1_{\ell=0}^{sD} \cdot \sum_{i=1}^{m}\left[\sum_{w=1}^{s+1}\sum_{\nu=1}^{w} \frac{x(w)}{w} \cdot u(\ell-(\nu-1)D,i) + \right.$$

$$\left. + \sum_{w=s+2}^{\infty}\sum_{\nu=1}^{s+1} \frac{x(w)}{w} \cdot u(\ell-(\nu-1)D,i) \right] \tag{17}$$

3.5 Conditional loss probability

In [1] with the service time equal to the time unit, as an important performance measure of a multiplexer, the probability of the following event is discussed: "Given a cell is lost at the n-th arrival, the multiplexer also loses cells at the $(n+r)$-th arrival." Since $\{(U_n, S_n, X_n); n \in \mathbb{N}_0\}$ is a MC, this conditional loss probability can be calculated here also for $D > 1$:

$$P_{cond.loss} = P\{\Gamma_{n+r} = 1 | \Gamma_n = 1\}$$

with $\Gamma_n = \begin{cases} 1 & \text{if at least one cell is lost at the } n\text{-th arrival} \\ 0 & \text{if no cell is lost at the } n\text{-th arrival.} \end{cases}$

$$P\{\Gamma_{n+r} = 1, \Gamma_n = 1\} = \sum_{w=s+2}^{\infty} \sum_{j=1}^{m} x(w) P\{U_{n+r} = 0, S_{n+r} = j, \Gamma_n = 1\} +$$

$$+ \sum_{\mu=1}^{s+1} \sum_{\ell=1+(\mu-1)D}^{\mu D} \sum_{w=s+2-\mu}^{\infty} \sum_{j=1}^{m} x(w) P\{U_{n+r} = \ell, S_{n+r} = j, \Gamma_n = 1\}$$

with $P\{U_{n+r} = \ell, S_{n+r} = j, \Gamma_n = 1\} =$

$$= \sum_{k'=0}^{sD+D} \sum_{i'=1}^{m} \left[\mathbf{F}^{r-1}\right]_{(k',i'),(\ell,j)} P\{U_{n+1} = k', S_{n+1} = i', \Gamma_n = 1\}$$

with $\left[\mathbf{F}\right]_{(k',i'),(\ell,j)} := \left[\mathbf{F}^{\ell}_{k'}\right]_{i',j}$ and $[\mathbf{q}(\,\cdot\,)]_{i',j} := q_{i'j}(\,\cdot\,)$ and

$P\{U_{n+1} = k', S_{n+1} = i', \Gamma_n = 1\} =$

$$= \sum_{v=s+2}^{\infty} \sum_{i=1}^{m} u(0, i) x(v) P_{i0v}\{U_{n+1} = k', S_{n+1} = i'\} +$$

$$+ \sum_{\mu=1}^{s+1} \sum_{k=1+(\mu-1)D}^{\mu D} \sum_{v=s+2-\mu}^{\infty} \sum_{i=1}^{m} u(k, i) x(v) P_{ikv}\{U_{n+1} = k', S_{n+1} = i'\}$$

For $P\{\Gamma_n = 1\}$ see (15); $P_{ikv}\{\,\cdot\,\}$ is defined in section 3.3.

$P\{\Gamma_{n+r} = 1 | \Gamma_n = 1\}$ is used in [1] (with $D = 1$) as an estimate for the conditional cell loss probability of an individual source, where r is chosen to be the cell interarrival time for that particular source. A high conditional loss probability means that a connection is likely to lose two or more consecutive cells. This can reduce the QOS, even if loss probability is quite low.

3.6 Numerical results (for stationary probabilities)

We consider an SMP with 2 states and the state sojourn time probability functions: $f_{11}(k) = f_{12}(k) = (1 - q_1)q_1^{k-1}$, $f_{21}(k) = f_{22}(k) = (1 - q_2)q_2^{k-1}$, $k \geq 1$. The batch size is assumed to have a truncated geometrical probability function: $x(v) = \frac{1-q_b}{1-q_b^{b_{max}}} q_b^{v-1}$, $1 \leq v \leq b_{max}$. p is determined by the assumed coefficient of correlation as explained below. $\underline{P} = (0.3, 0.7)$. $\underline{P} \cdot \mathbf{p} = \underline{P}$ yields $P_1 p_{12} = P_2 p_{21}$.

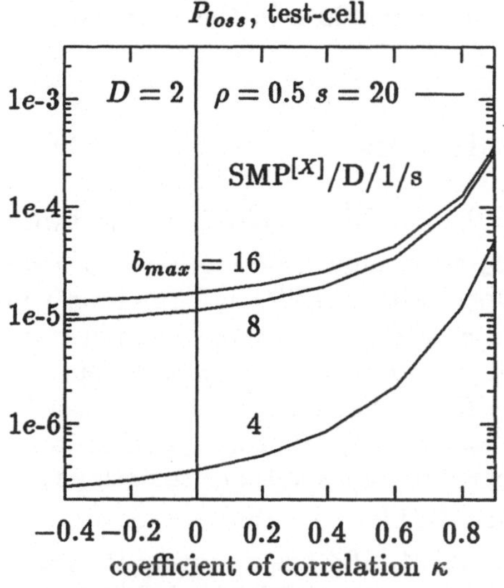

Fig. 2 *Loss probability of a test-cell over coefficient of correlation for different values of b_{max}.*

Fig. 3 *Conditional loss probability over steps r for various values of κ.*

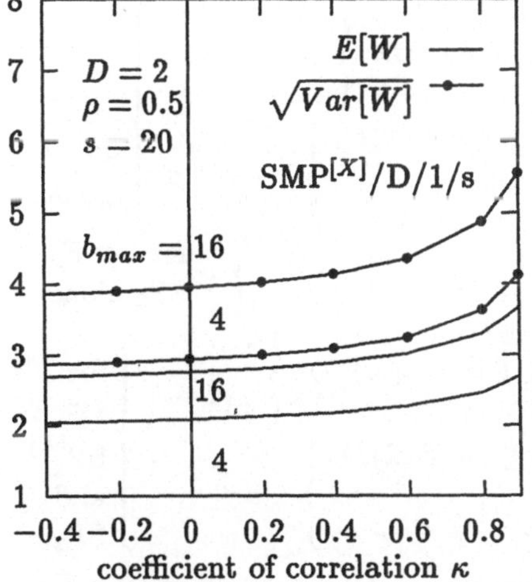

Fig. 4 *Mean value and deviation of the waiting time (test-cell) over coefficient of correlation for two values of b_{max}.*

The first-order coefficient of correlation of the interarrival times $(A_n)_{n \in \mathbf{N}_0}$ is given by: $Corr(A_{n+1}, A_n) = \kappa \cdot \left(1 + \frac{P_1 Var[A^{(1)}] + P_2 Var[A^{(2)}]}{P_1 P_2 (E[A^{(1)}] - E[A^{(2)}])^2}\right)^{-1}$, $\kappa = 1 - p_{12} - p_{21} = 1 - \frac{p_{12}}{P_2}$ being the coefficient of correlation of the embedded Markov chain, $E[A^{(i)}]$, $Var[A^{(i)}]$ denoting the mean value, respectively variance of the sojourn time of state $i = 1, 2$. By (1) it is $E[A] = P_1 E[A^{(1)}] + P_2 E[A^{(2)}]$. Given $E[A]$, q_1, q_2, which determine $E[A^{(1)}]$ and $E[A^{(2)}]$, are fixed. $P_1 E[A^{(1)}] = 0.2 \cdot P_2 E[A^{(2)}]$ was used. By choosing $p_{12} \in [0, min(1, \frac{P_2}{P_1})]$ κ can be fixed. The resulting offered traffic is given by $\rho = D \cdot E[X]/E[A]$. For a mean value of the batch size of about 1.6 for $b_{max} = 4, 8, 16$, we used $q_b = 0.4$.

Fig 2 and 4 reveal the effect of correlation in the interarrival times on the QOS parameters cell loss, mean delay and delay jitter (estimated by the mean deviation of the waiting time). Conditional loss probability (Fig. 3) increases with growing κ. Mean value and deviation of the waiting time are less sensitive to correlation than loss probability. In view of the fact that a single source may be renewal whereas the superposition becomes correlated, the results reflect the negative influence, which is possible due to correlations in the superimposed input stream.

4 Extension for two separate streams

Combining the results presented here with those of [9], it is possible to deal with a superposition of two streams $\mathrm{SP}_1^{[X]}+\mathrm{SP}_2$ as an input (SP: stochastic process generating arrival instants), if only the superposition of SP_1 and SP_2 results in an SMP. SP_1 generates arrival instants of a batch stream (X_n determines the batch size) and SP_2 those of a single cell-stream. The state space E must be given as a decomposition $E = E_1 \cup E_2 \cup E_3$ so that QOS parameters can be calculated for each stream separately, the states of E_1 [E_2] corresponding to arrivals due to SP_1 [SP_2] and those of E_3 representing arrivals due to both (X_n is ignored, if $S_n \in E_2$). Hence, the $\mathrm{SP}_1^{[X]}+\mathrm{SP}_2/D/1/s$ queue can serve as a model for connection admission control (CAC) in ATM, $\mathrm{SP}_1^{[X]}$ representing the existing traffic, SP_2 a new connection. The resulting state transition probabilities (for DF) analoguous to Lemma 2 are given as follows (for $\ell > 0$):

$$P\{U_n = \ell, S_n = j | U_{n-1} = k, S_{n-1} = i, X_{n-1} = v\} =$$

$$
= \begin{cases}
\begin{rcases}
\begin{rcases}
q_{ij}(k - \ell + vD) \text{ for } 0 \leq k \leq sD - vD + D \\
q_{ij}(k - \ell + \xi D) \text{ for } 1 + (s-\xi)D \leq k \leq (s-\xi+1)D, \\
\qquad 0 \leq \xi \leq v - 1,
\end{rcases} 1 \leq v \leq s, \\
\begin{rcases}
q_{ij}(k - \ell + \xi D) \quad \text{for } 1 + (s-\xi)D \leq k \leq (s-\xi+1)D, \\
\qquad 0 \leq \xi \leq s, \\
q_{ij}(-\ell + sD + D) \text{ for } k = 0
\end{rcases} 1 + s \leq v
\end{rcases} \begin{array}{l} \text{for} \\ i \in E_1, \\ \mathrm{SP}_1^{[X]} \\ \text{alone,} \end{array} \\[2ex]
\begin{rcases}
q_{ij}(k - \ell + D) \quad \text{for } 0 \leq k \leq sD \\
q_{ij}(k - \ell) \qquad \text{for } 1 + sD \leq k \leq sD + D
\end{rcases} 1 \leq v , \quad \begin{array}{l} \text{for } i \in E_2, \\ \mathrm{SP}_2 \text{ alone,} \end{array} \\[2ex]
\begin{rcases}
\begin{rcases}
q_{ij}(k - \ell + vD + D) \text{ for } 0 \leq k \leq sD - vD \\
q_{ij}(k - \ell + \xi D) \qquad \text{for } 1 + (s-\xi)D \leq k \leq (s-\xi+1)D, \\
\qquad 0 \leq \xi \leq v,
\end{rcases} \begin{array}{l} 1 \leq v \\ v \leq s-1 \end{array} \\
\begin{rcases}
q_{ij}(k - \ell + \xi D) \quad \text{for } 1 + (s-\xi)D \leq k \leq (s-\xi+1)D, \\
\qquad 0 \leq \xi \leq s, \\
q_{ij}(-\ell + sD + D) \text{ for } k = 0
\end{rcases} s \leq v,
\end{rcases} \begin{array}{l} \text{for} \\ i \in E_3, \\ \mathrm{SP}_1^{[X]} \\ \text{and} \\ \mathrm{SP}_2. \end{array}
\end{cases}
$$

According to [9], the superposition of two DMAPs results in an SMP.

5 Conclusion

The analysis of the $\mathrm{SMP}^{[X]}/D/1/s$ queue (given here in detail for DF) allows to compute, for the waiting room policies AF and DF, several performance measures for service times greater or equal to the time unit: probability functions of the number of cells in the system and of the waiting time of a test-cell, loss probability of a test-cell, conditional loss probability. The probability function of the batch size can be fixed separately, whereas in [8] the batches occur, when the state sojourn time becomes zero. The solution is extendable to the case that a batch stream and a single stream are superimposed, if the superimposed processes, generating the arrival instants of both streams, result in an SMP.

Acknowledgement. The author would like to thank the reviewers for their helpful remarks.

References

1. C. Blondia and O. Casals. *Statistical multiplexing of VBR sources: A matrix-analytic approach.* Perf. Eval., Vol. 16, No. 1-3, pp. 5–20, Nov. 1992.
2. U. Briem, T.H. Theimer, H. Kröner. *A General Discrete-Time Queueing Model: Analysis and Applications.* In *ITC-13, Vol. 14, Copenhagen*, pp. 13–19, June 19-26 1991.
3. E. Cinlar. *Introduction to Stochastic Processes.* Prentice Hall, New Jersey, 1st edition, 1975.
4. W. Ding and P. Decker. *Waiting time distribution of a discrete SSMP/G/1 queue and its implications in ATM systems.* In *7th ITC Spec. Sem.*, paper 9.2, Morristown, USA, Oct. 9-11 1990.
5. W. Grassmann, M. Taksar, D. Heyman. *Regenerative Analysis and Steady State Distributions for Markov Chains.* Opns. Res., Vol. 33, No. 5, pp. 1107–1116, 1985.
6. A. Gravey, J. Louvion and P. Boyer. *On the Geo/D/1 and Geo/D/1/n Queues.* Perf. Eval., Vol. 11, No. 2, pp. 117–125, July 1990.
7. R. Grünenfelder J.P. Cosmas, S. Manthorpe, A. Odinma-Okafor. *Characterization of Video Codecs as Autoregressive Moving Average Processes and Related Queueing System Performance.* J. Sel. Areas Com, Vol. 9, No. 3, pp. 284–293, April 1991.
8. C. Herrmann. *Analysis of the Discrete-time SMP/D/1/s Finite Buffer Queue with Applications in ATM.* In *IEEE INFOCOM'93, San Francisco, March 28-April 1, 1993, Session 2a.3, pp. 160 - 167.*
9. C. Herrmann. *Correlation Effect on Per-stream QOS Parameters of ATM Traffic Superpositions relevant to Connection Admission Control.* In *IEEE ICC'93, Geneva, May 23-26, 1993, pp. 1027 - 1031.*
10. J. J. Hunter. *Mathematical Techniques of Applied Probability, Vol. 2, Discrete Time Models: Techniques and Applications.* Academic Press, New York, 1983.
11. M. Kramer. *Computational Methods for Markov Chains occuring in Queueing Theory.* In *Messung, Modellierung und Bewertung von Rechnersystemen, Informatik Fachberichte 154, Springer*, pp.164-175, 1987.
12. D.M. Lucantoni, M.F. Neuts and K.S. Meier-Hellstern. *A single server queue with server vacations and a class of non-renewal arrival processes.* Adv. Appl. Prob., Vol. 22, pp. 676–705, Sept. 1990.
13. M. Murata, Y. Oie, T. Suda, H. Miyahara. *Analysis of a Discrete-Time Single-Server Queue with Bursty Inputs for Traffic Control in ATM Networks.* IEEE J-SAC, Vol. 8, No. 3, pp. 447–458, April 1990.
14. J.W. Roberts, editor. *COST 224, Performance Evaluation and design of multiservice networks.* Information technologies and sciences. France Telecom, 1991.
15. P. Tran-Gia, Hamid Ahmadi. *Analysis of a discrete-time $G^{[X]}/D/1$-S queueing system with applications in packet-switching systems.* In *IEEE INFOCOM'88*, paper 9A.1.10, March 27-31, 1988.
16. W. Whitt. *Approximating a point process by a renewal process, I.: two basic methods.* Operations Research, Vol. 30, No. 1, pp. 125–147, 1982.

Call and Burst Blocking in Multi-Service Broadband Systems with CBR and VBR Input Traffic

F. Hübner, M. Ritter

Institute of Computer Science, University of Würzburg,
Am Hubland, D-8700 Würzburg, Federal Republic of Germany
Tel.: +49/931/8885511, Fax: +49/931/8884601,
e-mail: huebner@informatik.uni-wuerzburg.dbp.de

Keywords: Multi-service systems, Connection acceptance control, ON/OFF sources, Equivalent bandwidth, Multi-dimensional Markov chains

Abstract

We consider a multi-service broadband system in which the services form different traffic classes. The superimposed traffic is carried by a link of fixed bit-rate. The services are of constant bit-rate (CBR) as well as of variable bit-rate (VBR). The VBR services are characterized as ON/OFF sources. We derive approximate algorithms for the computation of blocking probabilities at call and at burst level. The algorithms consist of two phases using a product-form solution. The computational complexity of the approximations is low and allows the investigation of large numbers of traffic classes. Comparison of numerical results with simulation results and results from an exact iterative algorithm indicate that the approximation is of excellent accuracy. It can be concluded from numerical results that the burst blocking probability is strongly dependent on the estimation of the required bit-rate of the VBR calls.

1   Introduction

In B-ISDN several different types of traffic will be transmitted on the same medium. Since the traffic types differ not only in their peak and mean transmission bandwidths but also in their bandwidth variances, the Connection Acceptance Control (CAC) has to be designed very carefully. To guarantee a certain Grade of Service (GoS) for accepted calls, several CAC mechanisms (e.g. by peak bandwidth allocation, equivalent bandwidth allocation or using the trunk reservation operation mode) have been proposed. In [12] the equivalent bandwidth is calculated using an estimation of the bandwidth variance. Another approach also based on mean and peak bit-rate was presented in [1]. In [2] also the burst length was taken into account for the determination of the equivalent bandwidth. Estimates for the equivalent bandwidth of so-called ON/OFF sources have been proposed in [4]. The trunk reservation operation mode was analyzed e.g. in [9], [11]. In this paper we do not focus on a particular CAC but investigate the blocking behavior of traffic mixes from CBR and VBR sources to derive a basis for the discussion of CAC methods for these traffic mixes.

The state probabilities for the queueing model if only CBR sources are taken into account are derived in product-form (see [3]). Also for the case of a finite number of traffic sources the state probabilities have been given in a product-form. A simpler recursive solution for the state probabilities was proposed in [6] and [8] independently of each other. In [6] the assumption upon the holding time was extended from a negative exponential distribution to distributions with rational Laplace transform. A general distribution for the holding time was assumed in [8]. For larger and more realistic numbers of traffic classes the numerical complexity can be reduced by using the recursive solution. Another algorithm for the computation of the state probabilities if the arrival process is a state dependent Poisson process and the holding times are generally distributed was given in [5].

In [7] it was assumed that blocked calls can retry immediately to be admitted to the system with a smaller bit-rate requirement. To fulfill their total bit-rate requirement, the product of bit-rate and holding time is kept constant, i.e. the holding time increases proportional to the bit-rate decrease. The results are approximate and based on the recursive algorithm proposed in [6] and [8]. In [10] it was assumed that calls which can not be admitted to the system at a certain time instant are lost with probability p and retry to be admitted with probability $1 - p$ after being delayed. It should be noted that the latter two policies are only useful if delay insensitive traffic is concerned.

In this paper we investigate the blocking behavior if CBR and VBR calls are taken into account. The paper is organized as follows. In the next section we describe the traffic model. The product-form solution which forms a basis for further analysis is shortly recapitulated in Section 3. In Section 4 we present an approximate analysis for the blocking probabilities of calls on call and burst level. In Section 4.1 we consider only VBR input traffic, whereas mixes of VBR and CBR input traffic are taken into account in Section 4.2. To show the accuracy of the approximation, we present in Section 5 some numerical examples and compare the approximate analytic results with simulation results and results from an exact iterative algorithm. Section 6 concludes the paper and contains a short outlook on further research activities.

2 Traffic model

We consider a broadband system transmission link with a fixed transmission speed C. The input traffic consists of the superposition of the traffic from N different traffic classes with some classes containing CBR and others containing VBR traffic. The CBR calls are considered only at call level whereas the VBR calls are examined at call and burst level. The arrival traffic of service class i is assumed to follow a Poisson process with rate λ_i. The holding time T_{H_i} of a call of class i is assumed to be negative exponentially distributed with mean $1/\mu_i$.

CBR calls of class i generate a constant bit-rate C_i during their holding time. VBR calls (class j) are modeled as ON/OFF sources, i.e. they generate a constant bit-rate C_j in times of activity (ON phase) and nothing in times of silence (OFF phase). The distribution of the time in the ON or OFF phases is negative exponential with means $1/\beta_j$ and $1/\gamma_j$ respectively. When an ON/OFF call is accepted by the CAC, it can start with an active or a silent phase. Calls which start in the ON (OFF) phase arrive with rates $\lambda_{j_{ON}}$ ($\lambda_{j_{OFF}}$). Any choice of $\lambda_{j_{ON}}$ and $\lambda_{j_{OFF}}$ that sum up to λ_j can be made, but for the numerical examples in Section 5 we take into account the mean times in the ON and OFF phases during a call and define $\lambda_{j_{ON}}$ and $\lambda_{j_{OFF}}$ by

$$\lambda_{j_{ON}} = \lambda_j \cdot \frac{1/\beta_j}{1/\beta_j + 1/\gamma_j} \tag{1}$$

and

$$\lambda_{j_{OFF}} = \lambda_j \cdot \frac{1/\gamma_j}{1/\beta_j + 1/\gamma_j}. \tag{2}$$

The basic system environment is shown in Fig. 1.

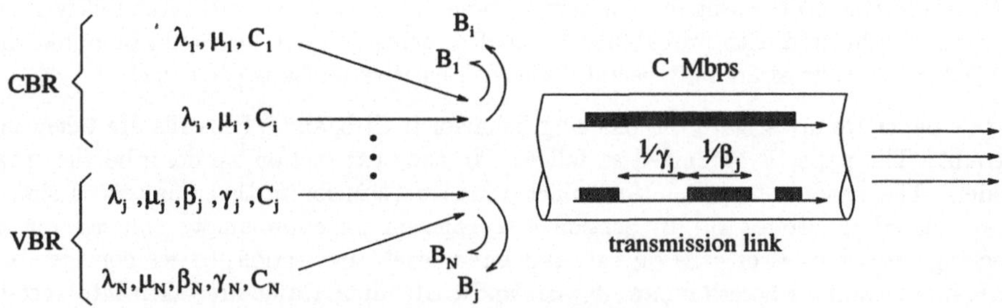

Figure 1: *Basic link model.*

The CAC and blocking behavior is basically different for CBR and VBR calls:

1. CBR calls (class i) are accepted if their required bandwidth C_i is available at call and burst level, i.e. that

   - the sum of the bandwidths of already accepted CBR and the equivalent bandwidths $\tilde{C}_j$ of already accepted VBR calls[1] on **call level** must be less or equal than $C - C_i$

   and

   - the sum of the bandwidths of already accepted CBR and the sum of the bandwidths of currently active VBR calls on **burst level** must be less or equal than $C - C_i$.

2. VBR calls (class j) are accepted if their equivalent bandwidth $\tilde{C}_j$ is available at call level, i.e. that the sum of the bandwidths of already accepted CBR calls and the sum of the equivalent bandwidths of already accepted VBR calls is less or equal than $C - \tilde{C}_j$.

Calls of class i or j are blocked at call level with probability B_i^c and B_j^c respectively, and influence the system not any longer. VBR calls can also be blocked on burst level (with probability B_j^b), since too many VBR calls can be in the ON phase at a certain time instant so that the sum of their bandwidths and the bandwidths from the accepted CBR calls can exceed the link capacity. If burst blocking occurs, the affected burst is not transmitted and the VBR source remains in the OFF phase.

The normalized offered bit-rate traffic from CBR (VBR) calls α_i (α_j) is defined by

$$\alpha_i = \frac{\lambda_i}{\mu_i}\frac{C_i}{C} \qquad \alpha_j = \frac{\lambda_j}{\mu_j}\frac{\tilde{C}_j}{C}. \tag{3}$$

The overall offered bit-rate traffic α is:

$$\alpha = \sum_{k=1}^{N} \alpha_k. \tag{4}$$

3 Product-form solution

When only CBR input traffic is considered, an exact product-form solution for the state probabilities can be given as proposed in [3]. First, we give an example state space to illustrate the structure of the solution and the numerical complexity. We consider a transmission link of capacity $C = 10$ Mbps and $N = 2$ traffic classes with bit-rate requirements of $C_1 = 2$ Mbps and $C_2 = 4$ Mbps. The states in Fig. 2 denote the number of accepted calls from each class (n_1, n_2) and the state space has thus as much dimensions as different traffic classes are considered.

---

[1] The equivalent bandwidth $\tilde{C}_j$ should be chosen between the mean bandwidth $C_j \cdot \frac{\gamma_j}{\gamma_j + \beta_j}$ and the maximum bandwidth C_j and can be determined by algorithms as proposed e.g. in [1], [2], [12].

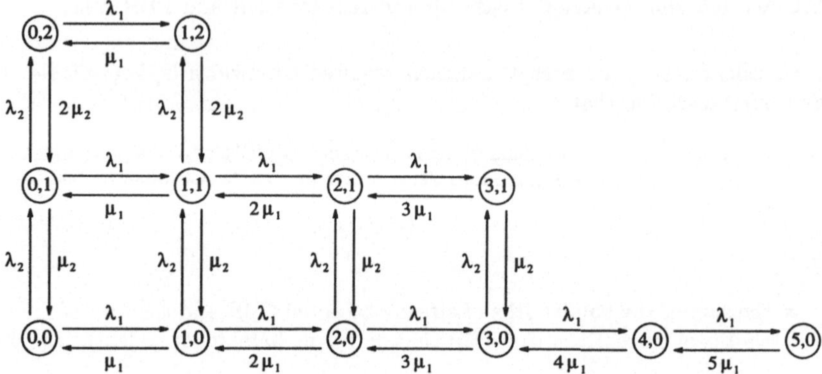

Figure 2: *Example state space for two CBR traffic classes.*

First, the unnormalized state probabilities $\tilde{p}(n_1, ..., n_N)$ can be given as:

$$\tilde{p}(n_1, ..., n_N) = \begin{cases} \prod\limits_{i=1}^{N} \frac{(\lambda_i/\mu_i)^{n_i}}{n_i!} & : \quad \sum\limits_{i=1}^{N} n_i C_i \leq C \\ 0 & : \quad \sum\limits_{i=1}^{N} n_i C_i > C \end{cases} \tag{5}$$

We arrive then at the state probabilities by normalization:[2]

$$p(n_1, ..., n_N) = \tilde{p}(n_1, ..., n_N) \cdot \left(\sum_{n_1=0}^{\lfloor C/C_1 \rfloor} \cdots \sum_{n_N=0}^{\lfloor C/C_N \rfloor} \tilde{p}(n_1, ..., n_N) \right)^{-1} . \tag{6}$$

With these state probabilities the probability of blocking an arriving call of class i is:

$$B_i = \sum_{(n_1,...,n_N) \in S_i} p(n_1, ..., n_N) \tag{7}$$

with the set of blocking states S_i defined by:

$$S_i = \{(n_1, ..., n_i, ..., n_N) \mid (n_i + 1)C_i + \sum_{\substack{k=1 \\ k \neq i}}^{N} n_k C_k > C\}. \tag{8}$$

In Fig. 2 the call blocking probabilities for class-1 calls are

$$B_1 = p(1, 2) + p(3, 1) + p(5, 0) \tag{9}$$

and for class-2 calls we arrive at

$$B_2 = p(0, 2) + p(1, 2) + p(2, 1) + p(3, 1) + p(4, 0) + p(5, 0). \tag{10}$$

In general, calls with higher bandwidth requirements experience higher blocking probabilities (see e.g. [11]).

---

[2] $\lfloor x \rfloor$ denotes the largest integer less or equal x

4 Approximate analysis

In this section we present approximate analytical approaches to derive the blocking probabilities for the model described in Section 2. Section 4.1 deals only with VBR sources, whereas CBR and VBR sources are considered in Section 4.2.

4.1 VBR input traffic

To illustrate the structure of the state space for the model if only VBR sources are considered, we show in Fig. 3 a simple example state space for only **one** VBR traffic class. The system states $(\tilde{n}_1, n_1, \ldots, \tilde{n}_N, n_N)$ are defined by the number $\tilde{n}_j$ of accepted calls of class j and by the number n_j of class-j calls which are in the ON phase. Thus, the state space has the dimension of twice the number of considered traffic classes. In our example a transmission link with $C = 12$ Mbps serves one class of VBR sources with a bandwidth requirement of $C_1 = 4$ Mbps while being in the ON phase. The ratio of mean active and silent times is assumed to be $3\beta_1 = \gamma_1$. This results in an equivalent bandwidth $\tilde{C}_1 = 3$ Mbps, if the mean bandwidth is used for CAC.

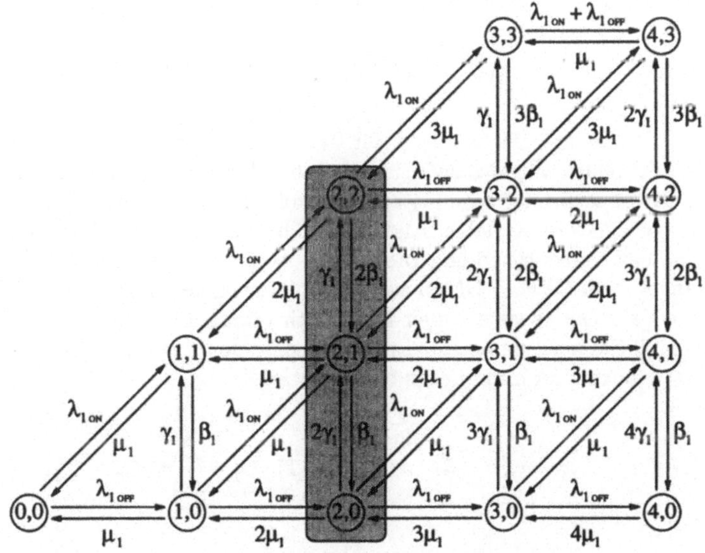

Figure 3: *Example state space for one VBR traffic class.*

The structure of the state space contains an irregularity between states (3,3) and (4,3). In state (3,3) an arriving call which wants to start in the ON phase is accepted at call level but blocked at burst level. This causes a change of the transition rate from $\lambda_{1_{OFF}}$ to $\lambda_{1_{ON}} + \lambda_{1_{OFF}} = \lambda_1$.

4.1.1 Blocking probabilities

A product-form solution for a state space like in Fig. 3 does not exist. In principle, an exact computation, at least for smaller state spaces, can be performed by resolving the system of state equations, e.g. with an iterative algorithm. For realistic parameters, which lead to larger state spaces, this possibility is however numerically intractable. Thus, we first focus on the calculation of the blocking probabilities and present in Section 4.1.2 a simple algorithm to derive approximate state probabilities.

If the state probabilities $p(\tilde{n}_1, n_1, \ldots, \tilde{n}_N, n_N)$ are known, the call and burst blocking probabilities can be derived as follows. The call blocking probability B_j^c is given by:

$$B_j^c = \sum_{(\tilde{n}_1, n_1, \ldots, \tilde{n}_N, n_N) \in S_j^c} p(\tilde{n}_1, n_1, \ldots, \tilde{n}_N, n_N). \tag{11}$$

The set S_j^c is composed of those states, in which the available capacity on call level is less than the equivalent bandwidth of an arriving class-j call:

$$S_j^c = \{(\tilde{n}_1, n_1, \ldots, \tilde{n}_j, n_j, \ldots, \tilde{n}_N, n_N) \mid (\tilde{n}_j + 1) \cdot \tilde{C}_j + \sum_{\substack{k=1 \\ k \neq j}}^{N} \tilde{n}_k \tilde{C}_k > C\}. \tag{12}$$

For the example in Fig. 3 the call blocking probability B_1^c is:

$$B_1^c = p(4, 0) + p(4, 1) + p(4, 2) + p(4, 3). \tag{13}$$

Burst blocking for class-j calls can occur for two reasons. First, an already accepted call being in the OFF phase wants to switch to the ON phase but the required bandwidth is not available at the switching time instant. Second, an arriving call can not start in the ON phase due to a lack of available bandwidth. The resulting burst blocking probability B_j^b can not be calculated by adding the corresponding state probabilities, because the rates for changes from OFF to ON phases are not the same for all states. Additionally, arrivals of new calls can cause a higher bandwidth utilization on burst level. Therefore, the state probabilities must be weighted with the corresponding rates. The set S_j^b of states in which burst blocking for class-j calls can occur is:

$$S_j^b = \{(\tilde{n}_1, n_1, \ldots, \tilde{n}_j, n_j, \ldots, \tilde{n}_N, n_N) \mid (n_j + 1) \cdot C_j + \sum_{\substack{k=1 \\ k \neq j}}^{N} n_k C_k > C\}. \tag{14}$$

For the example in Fig. 3 we obtain:

$$S_1^b = \{(3, 3), (4, 3)\}. \tag{15}$$

If S denotes the set of all existing states, B_j^b can be derived using the weighted state probabilities:

$$B_j^b = \frac{\sum\limits_{\vec{n} \in S_j^b} p(\vec{n}) \cdot \gamma_j \cdot (\tilde{n}_j - n_j) + \sum\limits_{\vec{n} \in S_j^b / S_j^c} p(\vec{n}) \cdot \lambda_{j_{ON}}}{\sum\limits_{\vec{n} \in S} p(\vec{n}) \cdot \gamma_j \cdot (\tilde{n}_j - n_j) + \sum\limits_{\vec{n} \in S / S_j^c} p(\vec{n}) \cdot \lambda_{j_{ON}}}. \tag{16}$$

The variable $\vec{n}$ is an abbreviation for the state vector $(\tilde{n}_1, n_1, \ldots, \tilde{n}_N, n_N)$. The first part of the sum in the numerator of eqn. (16) denotes the weighted state probabilities for state transitions, representing that an already accepted call switches from the OFF to the ON phase. The weighted state probabilities, representing state transitions for arriving calls which want to start in the ON phase, are denoted by the second part of this sum. The denominator in eqn. (16) plays the role of a normalizing constant. An approximate computation of the state probabilities which are needed for the calculation of the blocking probabilities is described in the next section.

4.1.2 State probabilities

Considering the model with VBR sources, we can distinguish between two different processes. The first one is given by the arrival and the departure of calls and the second one is the switching of accepted calls between ON and OFF phases. State transitions of the first process are independent of the present state of the second process. Due to this independence, we can calculate the **exact** state probabilities for the macro states, which represent the number of accepted calls of each class, by the product-form solution mentioned before. In Fig. 3 the macro state for two accepted calls is shaded. The unnormalized state probabilities of the macro states $\tilde{Q}(\tilde{n}_1, \ldots, \tilde{n}_N)$ are given by:

$$
\tilde{Q}(\tilde{n}_1, \ldots, \tilde{n}_N) = \begin{cases} \prod_{k=1}^{N} \frac{(\lambda_k/\mu_k)^{\tilde{n}_k}}{\tilde{n}_k!} & : \quad \sum_{k=1}^{N} \tilde{n}_k \tilde{C}_k \leq C \\ 0 & : \quad \sum_{k=1}^{N} \tilde{n}_k \tilde{C}_k > C \end{cases} \tag{17}
$$

After normalization we arrive at the macro state probabilities $Q(\tilde{n}_1, \ldots, \tilde{n}_N)$:

$$
Q(\tilde{n}_1, \ldots, \tilde{n}_N) = \tilde{Q}(\tilde{n}_1, \ldots, \tilde{n}_N) \cdot \left(\sum_{\tilde{n}_1=0}^{\lfloor C/\tilde{C}_1 \rfloor} \cdots \sum_{\tilde{n}_N=0}^{\lfloor C/\tilde{C}_N \rfloor} \tilde{Q}(\tilde{n}_1, \ldots, \tilde{n}_N) \right)^{-1}. \tag{18}
$$

An approximate distribution of the state probabilities within the macro states can also be obtained by a product-form solution. The solution is approximate since burst blocking can occur within the macro states. The unnormalized state probabilities $\tilde{q}(\tilde{n}_1, n_1, \ldots, \tilde{n}_N, n_N)$ within the macro state $(\tilde{n}_1, \ldots, \tilde{n}_N)$ are given by

$$
\tilde{q}(\tilde{n}_1, n_1 \ldots, \tilde{n}_N, n_N) = \begin{cases} \prod_{k=1}^{N} \frac{\tilde{n}_k!}{(\tilde{n}_k - n_k)!} \cdot \frac{(\gamma_k/\beta_k)^{n_k}}{n_k!} & : \quad \sum_{k=1}^{N} n_k C_k \leq C \\ 0 & : \quad \sum_{k=1}^{N} n_k C_k > C \end{cases} \tag{19}
$$

and by normalization we arrive at the state probabilities $q(\tilde{n}_1, n_1, \ldots, \tilde{n}_N, n_N)$

$$
q(\tilde{n}_1, \ldots, n_N) = \tilde{q}(\tilde{n}_1, \ldots, n_N) \cdot \left(\sum_{n_1=0}^{\min\{\tilde{n}_1, \lfloor C/C_1 \rfloor\}} \cdots \sum_{n_N=0}^{\min\{\tilde{n}_N, \lfloor C/C_N \rfloor\}} \tilde{q}(\tilde{n}_1, \ldots, n_N) \right)^{-1}. \tag{20}
$$

Finally, the approximate state probabilities $p^*(\tilde{n}_1, n_1, \ldots, \tilde{n}_N, n_N)$ are computed by multiplying the state probabilities within the macro states with the probabilities for the corresponding macro states:

$$p^*(\tilde{n}_1, n_1, \ldots, \tilde{n}_N, n_N) = q(\tilde{n}_1, n_1, \ldots, \tilde{n}_N, n_N) \cdot Q(\tilde{n}_1, \ldots, \tilde{n}_N). \tag{21}$$

Thus, the approximate calculation of the state probabilities consists of a two-phase product-form solution. In the first phase the exact probabilities of the macro states are derived. In the second phase an approximate calculation of the probability distribution in the macro states is carried out. Using the state probabilities from eqn. (21) the call and burst blocking probabilities (see eqns. (11) and (16)) can be determined. As indicated above the burst blocking probabilities are approximate but the call blocking probabilities are exact.

4.2 CBR and VBR input traffic

If mixes of CBR and VBR sources are considered, the blocking probabilities could also be computed with the results of Section 4.1. To make use of these results, the CBR sources could be considered as VBR sources with time in the ON phase tending to infinity and time in the OFF phase tending to zero. But the dimension of the resulting state space is twice the number of considered traffic classes. The dimension can be reduced by the number of CBR traffic classes if the CBR traffic is considered only on call level since no burst blocking for CBR calls can occur.

4.2.1 Blocking probabilities

Again, we first focus on the computation of the blocking probabilities if the state probabilities are known. Without loss of generality, we assume that traffic classes 1 to k consist of CBR sources and the other $N - k$ classes consist of VBR sources. The system states $(\tilde{n}_1, \ldots, \tilde{n}_N, n_{k+1}, \ldots, n_N)$ are then defined by the number $\tilde{n}_i$ of accepted class-i calls and by the number n_i of active calls of class i. For the CBR classes no dimension n_i for the number of calls in ON phases exists, since they are always active. To get a simpler notation for the following equations, we use the equivalent bandwidth $\tilde{C}_i$ for the CBR sources too ($\tilde{C}_i = C_i$ for $i = 1, \ldots, k$).

The call blocking probability B_i^c is again the sum of the probabilities for the call blocking states S_i^c:

$$B_i^c = \sum_{(\tilde{n}_1, \ldots, \tilde{n}_N, n_{k+1}, \ldots, n_N) \in S_i^c} p(\tilde{n}_1, \ldots, \tilde{n}_N, n_{k+1}, \ldots, n_N). \tag{22}$$

The set of blocking states S_i^c for CBR calls of class i ($i = 1, \ldots, k$) is given by the states in which either more than $C - C_i$ Mbps of the transmission link capacity are reserved on call level **or** the available bandwidth on burst level is less than C_i:

$$S_i^c = \{(\tilde{n}_1, \ldots, \tilde{n}_N, n_{k+1}, \ldots, n_N) \mid (\tilde{n}_i + 1) \cdot \tilde{C}_i + \sum_{\substack{j=1 \\ j \neq i}}^{N} \tilde{n}_j \tilde{C}_j > C\} \quad \cup$$

$$\{(\tilde{n}_1, \ldots, \tilde{n}_N, n_{k+1}, \ldots, n_N) \mid (\tilde{n}_i + 1) \cdot \tilde{C}_i + \sum_{\substack{j=1 \\ j \neq i}}^{k} \tilde{n}_j \tilde{C}_j + \sum_{j=k+1}^{N} n_j C_j > C\}. \qquad (23)$$

The set of blocking states for VBR calls of class i ($i = k+1, \ldots, N$) is given by the states in which more than $C - C_i$ Mbps of the transmission link capacity are reserved on call level:

$$S_i^c = \{(\tilde{n}_1, \ldots, \tilde{n}_N, n_{k+1}, \ldots, n_N) \mid (\tilde{n}_i + 1) \cdot \tilde{C}_i + \sum_{\substack{j=1 \\ j \neq i}}^{N} \tilde{n}_j \tilde{C}_j > C\}. \qquad (24)$$

The blocking probabilities B_i^b on burst level for the $N - k$ VBR classes can be computed as shown in Section 4.1.1. For VBR calls of class i the burst blocking probability B_i^b can be calculated by eqn. (16). The parameter $\vec{n}$ is now an abbreviation for the system states $(\tilde{n}_1, \ldots, \tilde{n}_N, n_{k+1}, \ldots, n_N)$. The set S_i^b of burst blocking states is given for traffic classes $i = k+1, \ldots, N$ by:

$$S_i^b = \{(\tilde{n}_1, \ldots, \tilde{n}_N, n_{k+1}, \ldots, n_N) \mid (n_i + 1) \cdot C_i + \sum_{\substack{j=k+1 \\ j \neq i}}^{N} n_j C_j + \sum_{j=1}^{k} \tilde{n}_j \tilde{C}_j > C\}. \qquad (25)$$

4.2.2 State probabilities

An approximate calculation of the state probabilities can be done as described in Section 4.1.2. The macro state probabilities $Q(\tilde{n}_1, \ldots, \tilde{n}_N)$ for the number of accepted calls of each class, are computed according to the product-form solution (cf. eqns. (17) and (18)). The calculation is approximate since the process on call level is not independent of the burst level process. The dimension of the state space within the macro states is equal to the number of VBR classes. The probability distributions within the macro states can also be derived by a product-form solution. For the unnormalized state probability $\tilde{q}(\tilde{n}_1, \ldots, \tilde{n}_N, n_{k+1}, \ldots, n_N)$ within the macro state $(\tilde{n}_1, \ldots, \tilde{n}_N)$ we obtain:

$$\tilde{q}(\tilde{n}_1, \ldots, n_N) = \begin{cases} \prod_{i=k+1}^{N} \frac{\tilde{n}_i!}{(\tilde{n}_i - n_i)!} \cdot \frac{(\gamma_i/\beta_i)^{n_i}}{n_i!} & : \quad \sum_{i=1}^{k} \tilde{n}_i \tilde{C}_i + \sum_{i=k+1}^{N} n_i C_i \leq C \\ 0 & : \quad \sum_{i=1}^{k} \tilde{n}_i \tilde{C}_i + \sum_{i=k+1}^{N} n_i C_i > C \end{cases}. \qquad (26)$$

By normalization like in eqn. (20) we arrive at the approximate state probabilities within the macro states $q(\tilde{n}_1, \ldots, \tilde{n}_N, n_{k+1}, \ldots, n_N)$. By multiplying the state probabilities within the macro states with the corresponding macro state probabilities, the state probabilities $p^*(\tilde{n}_1, \ldots, \tilde{n}_N, n_{k+1}, \ldots, n_N)$, which are also approximate, are finally given as:

$$p^*(\tilde{n}_1, \ldots, \tilde{n}_N, n_{k+1}, \ldots, n_N) = q(\tilde{n}_1, \ldots, \tilde{n}_N, n_{k+1}, \ldots, n_N) \cdot Q(\tilde{n}_1, \ldots, \tilde{n}_N). \qquad (27)$$

5   Numerical examples

In this section we present numerical results to show the accuracy of the approximate algorithms presented in Section 4. To compare the approximate results with exact ones, the first example deals with one VBR traffic class with $C_1 = 20$ Mbps and a transmission link of capacity $C = 150$ Mbps. The mean times in ON and OFF phases are assumed to be equal ($\beta_1 = \gamma_1$) and the equivalent bandwidth is chosen in this example as the mean bandwidth $\tilde{C}_1 = 10$ Mbps. For the computation of the exact solution we solved the complete system of state equations by an iterative algorithm. In case of the exact solution the results for the burst blocking probabilities depend on the ratio β_i/μ_i which represents the mean number of ON phases per call duration.

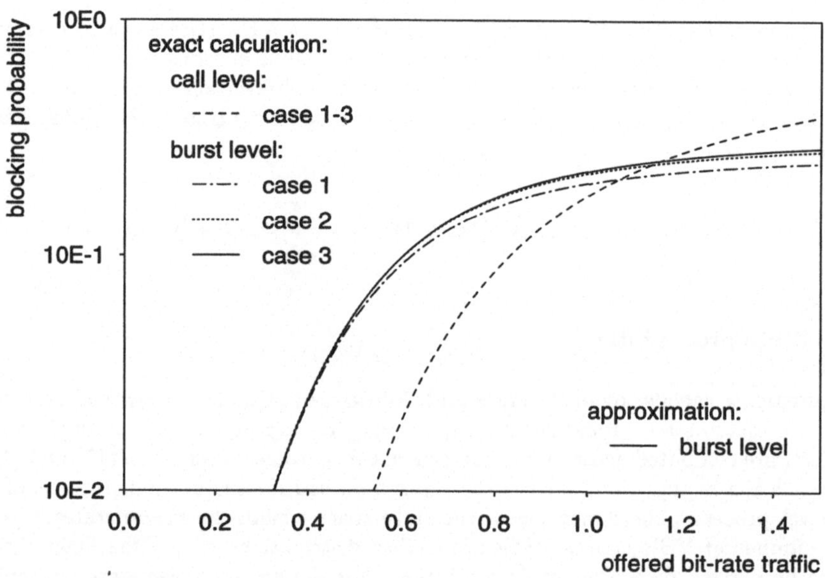

Figure 4: *Approximation accuracy of burst blocking probabilities.*

Fig. 4 shows the call and burst blocking probabilities in dependence on the offered bit-rate traffic[3] α for three different ratios of β_i/μ_i. We have chosen β_1/μ_1 as 1 (case 1), 5 (case 2), and 50 (case 3). Note that $\beta_1/\mu_1 = 1$ means that the VBR sources behave like CBR sources since there is only one ON phase per call in equilibrium. It can be seen that the curves of the exact call blocking probabilities are the same for each of the cases. This is due to the fact that the blocking process on call level is independent of the burst level process. If we look at the burst blocking probability, we can observe a slight difference between the curves of the exact iterative solution and the curve of the approximate solution, which is the same for all three cases and constitutes an upper bound. The difference between the curves becomes smaller the larger the ratio β_1/μ_1 is.

---

[3]Numerical tests have shown that the blocking probabilities depend only on the ratio of λ and μ but not on their individual values although the corresponding state space does not allow for a product-form solution.

This effect is due to the fact that most state changes take place inside the macro states if the ratio is large and therefore the exact probability distribution within the macro states is closer to the one calculated approximately. The ratio $\beta_1/\mu_1 = 1$ (case 1) can be seen as worst case for the approximation. For realistic parameter sets the ratio β_1/μ_1 is in the order of 10^2 and so the approximation provides numerical results which are very close to the exact ones.

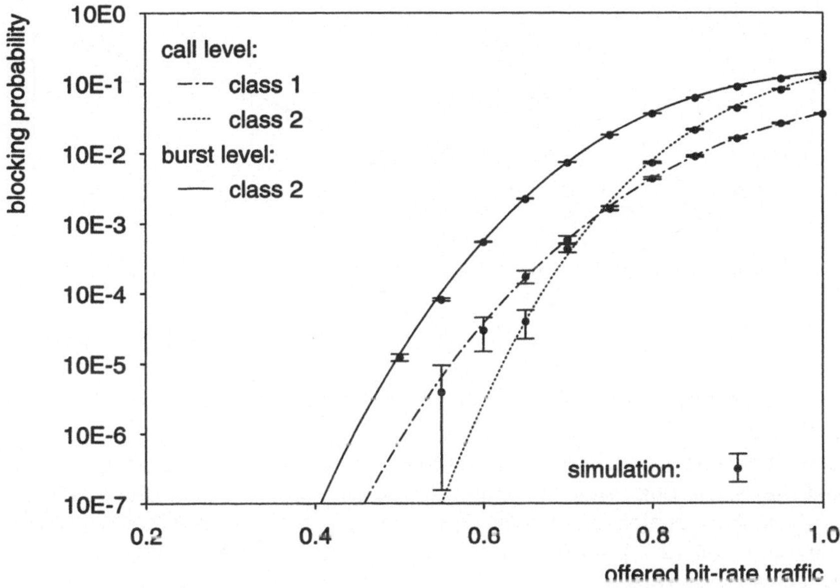

Figure 5: *Blocking probabilities for mean bit-rate as equivalent bandwidth.*

In Figs. 5 and 6 we depict the influence of the choice of the equivalent bandwidth on the blocking behavior if one CBR and one VBR traffic class are taken into account. We consider a transmission link with capacity $C = 600$ Mbps while CBR calls require $C_1 = 2$ Mbps and VBR calls have a peak bit-rate of $C_2 = 20$ Mbps. The mean times in the ON and OFF phases are assumed to be equal ($\beta_2 = \gamma_2$) and the offered bit-rate from both traffic classes is equal ($\alpha_1 = \alpha_2$). The mean bit-rate is chosen as equivalent bandwidth $\tilde{C}_2 = 10$ Mbps for the curves in Fig. 5. It should be noted that an iterative algorithm, as used for only one traffic class, is not appropriate if more than one traffic class is considered. This is due to the huge number of states that must be taken into account.

As has been mentioned in Section 3, calls with higher bandwidth requirements experience higher blocking probabilities if only CBR calls are considered. Considering mixes of CBR and VBR traffic classes, it turns out (cf. Fig. 5) that CBR calls of lower bit-rate than VBR calls can be blocked with higher probability depending on the offered bit-rate traffic. Moreover it can be observed in Fig. 5 that the burst blocking probability of the VBR calls is unacceptable high ($> 10^{-2}$). Therefore we consider in Fig. 6 a higher equivalent bandwidth of $\tilde{C}_2 = 17.5$ Mbps for CAC of VBR calls.

It can be observed that increasing the equivalent bandwidth leads to lower burst blocking probability for VBR calls ($< 10^{-4}$). In contrast, the call blocking probabilities for the

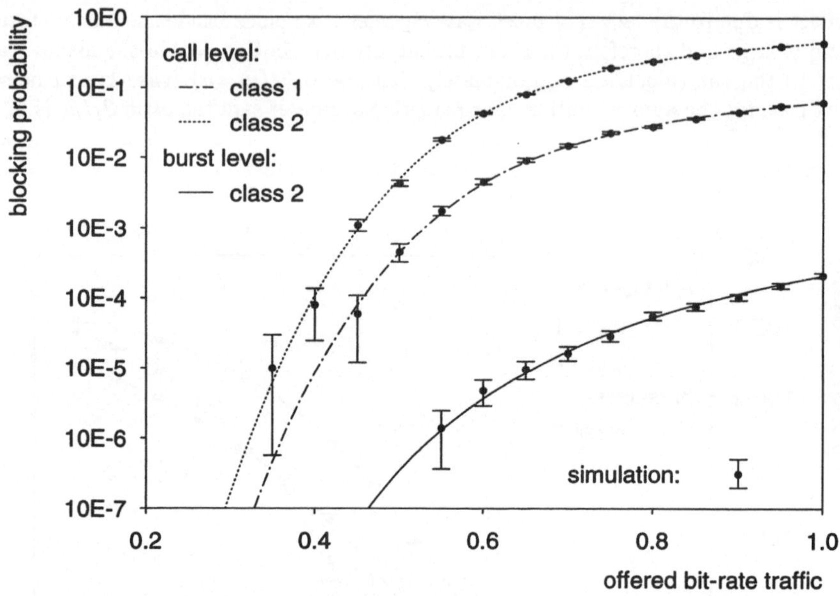

Figure 6: *Blocking probabilities for increased equivalent bandwidth.*

CBR and VBR classes are higher compared to the numerical results from Fig. 5. It should be noted that simulation results are quite close to the approximate results obtained with the algorithm from Section 4.2. The investigation of larger numbers of traffic classes does not imply any numerical problems and the requirements on memory effort and run time are not increased considerably.

6   Conclusion

In this paper we considered a multi-service broadband system with different CBR and VBR service classes. The transmission link was assumed to have a fixed bit-rate and VBR services were characterized as ON/OFF sources. We derived approximate algorithms for the calculation of the call and burst level blocking probabilities which allow the investigation of large numbers of traffic classes. We compared our numerical results with simulation results and exact results derived by an iterative algorithm which needs much more time effort than the approximation and is numerically intractable for larger numbers of traffic classes. It turned out that the approximation is of excellent accuracy for each of the numerical examples. From numerical results it can be concluded that the burst blocking probability is strongly dependent on the estimation of the required bit-rate of the VBR calls.

Acknowledgement

The authors would like to thank Prof. P. Tran-Gia for fruitful discussions during the course of this work.

References

[1] COST[4] 224 Final Report, *"Performance Evaluation and Design of Multiservice Networks"*, J. W. Roberts (ed.), Paris, October 1991.

[2] M. Decina, L. Faglia, T. Toniatti, *"Bandwidth Allocation and Selective Discarding for Variable Bit Rate Video and Bursty Data Calls in ATM Networks"*, IEEE INFOCOM, 1991, pp.1386-1393.

[3] O. Enomoto, H. Miyamoto, *"An Analysis of Mixtures of Multiple Bandwidth Traffic on Time Division Switching Networks"*, Proceedings of the 7th International Teletraffic Congress, Stockholm 1973, pp. 635.1-635.8.

[4] R. Guérin, H. Ahmadi, M. Naghshineh, *"Equivalent Capacity and Its Application to Bandwidth Allocation in High-Speed Networks"*, IEEE Journal on Selected Areas in Communications, Vol. 9, No. 7, September 1991, pp. 968-981.

[5] V. B. Iversen, *"A Simple Convolution Algorithm for the Exact Evaluation of Multi-Service Loss Systems with Heterogeneous Traffic Flows and Access Control"*, COST[4] 214 Technical Document (084), 1987.

[6] J. S. Kaufman, *"Blocking in a Shared Resource Environment"*, IEEE Transactions on Communications, Vol. 29, No. 10, 1981, pp. 1474-1481.

[7] J. S. Kaufman, *"Blocking with Retrials in a Completely Shared Resource Environment"*, Performance Evaluation 15, June 1992, pp. 99-113.

[8] J. W. Roberts, *"A Service System with Heterogeneous User Requirements - Application to Multi-Service Telecommunications Systems"*, Proc. Performance of Data Communication Systems and their Applications, G. Pujolle (ed.), North Holland, 1981, pp. 423-431.

[9] J. W. Roberts, *"Teletraffic Models for the Telecom 1 Integrated Services Network"*, Proceedings of the 10th International Teletraffic Congress, Montreal 1983, paper 1.1.2.

[10] P. Tran-Gia, *"Modelling Overload Control in SPC Switching Systems"*, 36th Report on Studies in Congestion Theory, University of Stuttgart, 1982.

[11] P. Tran-Gia, F. Hübner, *"An Analysis of Trunk Reservation and Grade of Service Balancing Mechanisms in Multiservice Broadband Networks"*, IFIP Workshop TC6, Modelling and Performance Evaluation of ATM Technology, La Martinique, January 1993.

[12] E. Wallmeier, *"A Connection Acceptance Algorithm for ATM Networks Based on Mean and Peak Bit Rates"*, Int. Journal on Digital and Analog Communication Systems, Vol. 3, 1990, pp.144-153.

---

[4]COST: European Cooperation in the Field of Scientific and Technical Research

BANDWIDTH MANAGEMENT OF VIRTUAL PATHS
- PERFORMANCE VERSUS CONTROL ASPECTS -

Manfred N. Huber, Volker H. Tegtmeyer
Siemens AG
Hofmannstr.51
D-8000 München 70

Abstract

In the B-ISDN the asynchronous transfer mode is used, which is subdivided into the virtual path (VP) level and the virtual channel (VC) level. For an efficient network operation, economic resource management at both levels is required. In our paper we will focus on VP management. We will evaluate the performance of different bandwidth allocation strategies for VPs (e.g. loss probability for VC connections) and their influence on the processing load for the VP bandwidth manager, which is part of the VP management. These investigations show that an improvement in performance, relating to decreased loss probability and/or increased offered traffic, is possible by using virtual path bandwidth management based on a partial-sharing strategy with two limits. It is shown that these limits of an optimal strategy can easily be determined in a totally symmetric system (i.e. all VPs and VCs on a link are of the same kind and the same bandwidth demand, all VPs have the same offered traffic) . The evaluations for an asymmetric system show that it is very difficult to determine the optimal strategy because there are too many variable, correlating parameters. This paper elaborates some rules to obtain a strategy for improved performance despite these difficulties.

1. Introduction

In the B-ISDN the asynchronous transfer mode, which is subdivided into the virtual path (VP) level and the virtual channel (VC) level, is used. In our opinion the VP level is under control of network management (VP management) whereas the VC level is controlled by signalling. For efficient network operation, economic resource management at both levels is required [1], [2]. In our paper we will focus on VP management. A lot of research has been done for the VC level, whereas for the VP level only a few studies are known [4]. We will evaluate the performance of different bandwidth allocation strategies for VPs (e.g. loss probability for VC connections) and their influence on the processing load for the VP bandwidth manager, which is part of the VP management.

The following four bandwidth allocation strategies are discussed in this paper:

1. *non-sharing*
2. *multi-hour engineering*
3. *complete-sharing*
4. *partial-sharing*

The probability that a new VC connection (VCC) is refused, the probability of demand to change the VP bandwidth and the probability of bandwidth change (relating to required control efforts) are evaluated with a traffic model. We consider one link which contains several VPs and each VP is shared by some VCCs simultaneously. The sum of the bandwidths of the VPs in this link cannot exceed the link capacity. A VCC is refused, if there is not enough unused bandwidth on the VP, and a change to a higher bandwidth is not possible for the VP, as the VP bandwidth is already at the upper limit, or an increase would exceed the link capacity.

2. Bandwidth Allocation Strategies

A number of bandwidth allocation strategies exist and these are described in detail in the literature. In this paper we distinguish between the following four bandwidth allocation strategies.

1. *non-sharing (ns)*
The VP bandwidth manager allocates an amount of bandwidth to the VP during the set-up procedure. This VP bandwidth is fixed and constant until the VP is released. The processing load for the VP management is very low. This strategy normally only allows a low link bandwidth utilisation.

2. *multi-hour engineering*
For this strategy VP bandwidth allocation is based on traffic measurements in periods of hours, days, weeks and months. The VP bandwidth is not changed at every VCC set-up / release but over a period of time. In comparison to non-sharing, the performance (relating to loss probability of a VCC) is improved without overloading the network manager.

3. *complete-sharing (cs)*
For this strategy the unused bandwidth on a link is completely shared by all VPs on the link. An advantage is the optimal utilisation of the link bandwidth. The drawback is the required bandwidth change for a VP at every VCC set-up and release which causes a high processing load for the VP manager.

4. *partial-sharing (ps)*
This strategy allows the partial-sharing of the unused link bandwidth in different ways. One approach proposes a VP bandwidth allocation in multiple, load-dependent steps [4]. In contrast to that approach, we will keep the processing load of the network management at a reasonable level. We provide only two bandwidth values for a VP. Changes of the VP bandwidth are performed in a load-dependent manner. With our strategy the probability of VP bandwidth change is lower than in case of multiple steps. The processing load on the network manager is low but the performance behaviour is very good.

As the multi-hour engineering needs a lot of information about the traffic from traffic measurements, it is not discussed in detail in this paper. However it must be mentioned since it is an important and interesting alternative to the other strategies. In comparison to the partial-sharing strategy, non-sharing and complete-sharing are regarded as upper and lower boundaries for processing load and performance. The non-sharing strategy only allows a low - not the lowest- link utilization, coupled with a minimum of processing load. The complete-sharing strategy requires the highest processing load and achieves as the best link utilization.

3. The Traffic Model

The probability of a new VCC being refused, the probability of a demand for bandwidth change and the probability of bandwidth change (related to control efforts required) are evaluated with a traffic model. We consider one link which contains several VPs where each VP is shared by a number of VCCs simultaneously. The sum of the bandwidths of the VPs in this link cannot exceed the link capacity. A VCC is refused if there is not enough unused bandwidth on the VP and a change to a higher bandwidth is not possible for the VP, as the VP bandwidth is already at the upper limit, or if an increase would exceed the link capacity. For the VCCs a Poisson Arrival process with an infinite number of sources is assumed. The loss probability of VCC calls, the probability of bandwidth change (change probability) and the probability of a demand for a bandwidth change (demand probability) are calculated as follows:

The state distribution corresponding to a resource sharing policy Ω (relating to the two bandwidths determined) is determined by the multidimensional Erlang-loss formula (1) as described by Kaufmann [3]. The loss probability is the sum of state probabilities where a new VCC arrives and is refused as described above. The probability of bandwidth change is the sum of state probabilities where a new VCC arrives and the VP bandwidth is at the lower level which is insufficient and a change to the upper bandwidth limit is possible. The demand probability is the sum of state probabilities where a new VCC arrives and the VP bandwidth is at the insufficient lower limit and has to be changed.

$$P(n) = \prod_{i=1}^{k} \frac{a_i^{n_i}}{n_i!} G^{-1}(\Omega) \qquad \text{all } n \in \Omega \tag{1}$$

$$G(\Omega) = \sum_{n \in \Omega} \left(\prod_{i=1}^{k} \frac{a_i^{n_i}}{n_i!} \right) \tag{2}$$

$$n = (n_1, n_2, ..., n_i, ... n_k)$$

$P(n)$: state probability of n
n: state vector
Ω: set of allowable states (determined by the resource-sharing policy in effect)
n_i: number of used channels in path i
a_i: traffic offered to path i
k: number of virtual paths on the link

For this calculation the capacities, bandwidths and boundaries of the strategies are normalized to the capacity of the smallest channel, for example with a bitrate of 2 Mbit/s.

4. Symmetric Traffic Model

The first model consists of several VCCs which are bundled into seven VPs. All VCCs are of the same kind and require the same bandwidth. The offered load is identical for every VP, related to the number of VCC calls. The link capacity contains 35 channels, in the following written as 35. Using the non-sharing strategy each VP has a bandwidth of 5. The determination of the VP bandwidth limits is more complicate for the partial-sharing strategy and will be described below. The lower boundary has to be less than 5 channels otherwise there will be no profit compared to the non-sharing strategy. Also this boundary should be not too low, because this would result in a high processing load, caused by frequent bandwidth change requests. The demand probability which is related to VP bandwidth limit can be estimated with the Erlang-table. For this the lower bandwidth limit has to be regarded as a fixed limit and the change probability is assumed to be a loss probability. The result has to be seen as an estimation, because these state distributions of both systems are not exactly the same. The estimated value is higher than the real value because the number of possible states is smaller than in the real system. This means that the estimation yields a higher bandwidth than the real limit.

With this estimation the lower boundary should not be lower than 3 in this model. The upper boundary is not allowed to exceed the link capacity and has to be higher than the non-sharing capacity. All possible combinations of boundaries which meet these rules are listed in Table 1. The maximum number of VPs which can be switched to the upper boundary at the same time is listed in the third column. In a group of strategies with the same lower boundary and the same maximum number of VP at the upper boundary, the strategy with the highest upper boundary achieves the lowest loss probability. The other strategies will be worse because they produce more unused link capacity. These considerations lead to a selection of seven strategies which are of interest for subsequent calculations.

The relation between the offered traffic and loss probability is shown in Figure 1 for these partial-sharing strategies and the non-sharing strategy. The loss probability of complete-sharing is below 0,01 percent with an offered traffic of 2,5 Erl per VP which is far below the other strategies and therefore not shown in Figure 1. These results show that the offered traffic can be increased by about 50 percent using an optimal ps-strategy (partial-sharing strategy). It also shows the performance deterioration by using sub optimal strategies. By using inappropriate lower and upper VP bandwidth limits, the performance is worse, compared to the non-sharing strategy. Inappropriate values are the combination of extreme lower VP bandwidth limits and very high upper VP bandwidth limits because the VP reserves more bandwidth than it needs when it switches to the upper limit. See strategy ps3:17 in Figure 1. This strategy does not utilize all the allocated bandwidth as much as the other VPs demand it. Therefore it is possible to reduce the value for the upper boundary so that more VPs get the opportunity to enlarge their bandwidth. This example demonstrates the fact that the partial-sharing strategy does not automatically imply an improvement in performance.

The relation between demand probability and offered traffic is shown in Figure 2. The probabilities fall into two groups, depending on the lower bandwidth limit. The slight differences within each group are the effect of normalization of state probabilities because in formula (2) Ω depends on the strategy. The most important result is that the demand probability primarily depends on the lower bandwidth limit. The estimation of the bandwidth limit with the Erlang-table, which was done above, yields a bandwidth limit which is slightly higher than the real limit. But this deviation is acceptable as very small values are inappropriate.

In Figure 3 the relation between offered traffic and change probability is shown. For a low offered traffic, which causes a low loss probability, the demand probability is equal to the change probability. At high offered traffic the change probability decreases with an increase in loss probability. This is because some VPs switched to the upper bandwidth limit and hold this as their load does not fall below the lower bandwidth limit.

There is no explicit formula to determine the optimal bandwidth limits. Hence the following

lower boundary	upper boundary	maximum number of VP at the upper boundary at the same time	interesting strategy for calculation
4	11	1	X
4	10	1	
4	9	1	
4	8	1	
4	7	2	X
4	6	3	X
3	17	1	X
3	16	1	
3	15	1	
3	14	1	
3	13	1	
3	12	1	
3	11	1	
3	10	2	X
3	9	2	
3	8	2	
3	7	3	X
3	6	4	X

Table 1: Selection of strategies for further calculations

paragraphs describe an iteration to find the optimal boundaries for a symmetric traffic model. Initially the lower limit can be estimated in the way described above. With this a lot of strategies lose their interest for further calculations as their demand probability will be too high and the high number of possible strategies is reduced. The second step reduces the remaining strategies by selecting the limit combinations of interest as has been done for Table 1. In this example these two steps reduce the high number of 60 possible strategies to 7 strategies. In the next step the maximum loss probability which is acceptable for network operation has to be determined. There is an offered traffic value which causes this loss probability using the non-sharing strategy. With this offered traffic the loss probability and change probability are calculated for the selected partial-sharing strategies. All strategies with loss probabilities above the chosen limit values are refused. Then these probabilities are calculated again for the remaining strategies with increased offered traffic. This step is continued until only one strategy is left.

Figure 4 shows the relation between change probability and loss probability. Points of the same strategy are connected by the fine line and points of the same offered traffic are connected by the bold line. This figure demonstrates how the optimal strategy changes with the chosen limit values for change and loss probability. It also demonstrates the significant interdependency of change probability and lower bandwidth limit.

5. Asymmetric Traffic Model

This model also consists of several VCCs and VPs. In distinction to the symmetric model the VCCs have non-uniform bandwidth demands as they belong to different service classes. The VCCs are bundled into seven VPs and each VP contains only VCCs of one service class. The offered traffic to every VP is identical. The VP bandwidth limits of VPs with the same service class are of the same size. Other models are conceivable (e.g. VPs containing different service classes) but not discussed in this paper. With this model it is possible to evolve a feeling for the correlation between performance and service class. The chosen system parameters are very important for these investigations, because they significantly influence the results.

In this section three different service classes are studied in combinations of 2 service classes which are bundled into seven VPs on one link. In every combination one service class contains a service with a bandwidth demand of 2 Mbit/s per VCC. The second class contains a service with a bandwidth demand of either 4 or 8 Mbit/s. The total link capacity varies with the number of service classes. It is dimensioned to be utilized by 100 percent if the non-sharing strategy would be used. According to this and to the symmetric model a normalized capacity of 5 (5 channels, each of 2 Mbit/s) is assigned to each VP with services of 2 Mbit/s. A proportional increased normalized bandwidth of 10 or 20 (10 corresponds to 5 channels with 4 Mbit/s each, 20 corresponds to 5 channels with 8 Mbit/s each) is assigned to VPs with service classes of 4 and 8 Mbit/s. The bandwidth limits of the partial-sharing strategies are based on the symmetric model results. The lower and upper normalized limits are 4 to 7, 8 to 14 and 16 to 28, according to the service classes. All ratios of the number of 2 Mbit/s service classes to the number of second service classes are calculated. The offered traffic varies from 1 Erl per VP to 2,5 Erl. The calculated results are described below:

- Link with 2 Mbit/s and 4 Mbit/s service classes (see Figures 5 and 6)
  In comparison to the non-sharing strategy the offered traffic of the 2 Mbit/s service class can be increased by 48 percent to 65 percent, depending on the ratio of service class, without exceeding the loss probability of 1 percent. The 4 Mbit/s service class behaves differently. For this class the offered traffic can only be increased by 22 percent up to 58 percent depending on ratio of service classes.

- Link with 2 Mbit/s and 8 Mbit/s service classes (see Figures 7 and 8)
  In this combination the offered traffic to the 2 Mbit/s service class can be increased by 45 percent to 82 percent. The offered traffic of the 8 Mbit/s service class can be increased up to 58 percent. But, if there are not enough VPs of this service class on this link, it is impossible for these VPs to change to the upper bandwidth limits, because this would exceed the link capacity. This problem will be explained in detail later. The demand probability normally depends on the lower bandwidth limit more than on service class.

Although there is an improvement in performance, relating to decreased loss probability and/or increased offered traffic, there is that significant problem of impossible changes to the upper bandwidth limits. In these cases it is impossible to replace the non-sharing strategy by the partial-sharing strategy, as there will be no improvement, but a deterioration for these prejudice strategies. Investigation is needed into whether these bandwidth limits may be optimized for asymmetric models, due to the fact that these limits have been determined for the symmetric model. Characteristic parameters of the strategies are listed in Table 2 and 3 for this investigation.

2Mbit/s service ps 4:7	4Mbit/s service ps 8:14	link capacity	shared link capacity	maximum number of VPs at the upper limit 2Mbit/s	4Mbit/s	unused link capacity
0	7	70	14	0	2	2
1	6	65	13	0	2	1
				1	1	4
2	5	60	12	0	2	0
				2	1	0
3	4	55	11	1	1	2
				3	0	2
4	3	50	10	1	1	1
				3	0	1
5	2	45	9	1	1	0
				3	0	0
6	1	40	8	0	1	2
				2	0	0
7	0	35	7	2	0	1

Table 2: Characteristic parameters in a system with 2 Mbit/s and 4 Mbit/s service classes

These parameters are the number of VPs with dedicated service classes, link capacity, shared common link capacity, maximum number of VPs switched to the upper limit at the same time and unused link capacity. Table 2 does not reveal anything of significance. All VPs are able to change to the upper bandwidth limit and all VPs are sharing the common bandwidth.

However, 2 strategies are significant in Table 3 . The strategy with 2 VPs of 2 Mbit/s service classes has no restriction for these VPs to change to the upper limit. In this case the bandwidth management could be relieved of management functions if a fixed bandwidth would be allocated to this VPs. There also is a lot of unused link capacity which may be better utilized. The second remarkable strategy has 6 VPs with 2 Mbit/s service classes. There it is not possible for the VP with 8 Mbit/s service class to change to the upper bandwidth limit, because this would exceed the link capacity.

To solve these problems and to optimize the utilization of link capacity, there has to be either an increase in link capacity, which is not possible in this model as it should be 100 percent allocated with the non-sharing strategy, or there has to be a decrease of the upper bandwidth limits. A decrease of limits is practicable if the limit is still above the limit of the non-sharing strategy. In this case a bandwidth change will become possible for more VPs.

This step is studied in the next 2 systems, shown in Table 4 and 5. The limits of the VPs with 2 Mbit/s service classes are unchanged.

In system no.1 the upper limit was decreased to allow the possibility of bandwidth change. With this the loss probability increases for the 2 Mbit/s service classes as expected, because the VP with 8 Mbit/s service classes starts to compete with the other VPs for the shared link capacity, see Fig.9. The loss probability of the 8 Mbit/s service classes decreases significantly and for these VPs the offered traffic can be increased by 14 percent related to the non-sharing strategy without exceeding the loss probability of 1 percent, see Fig.10.

2Mbit/s service PS 4:7	8Mbit/s service PS 16:28	link capacity	shared link capacity	maximum number of VPs at the upper limit		unused link capacity
				2Mbit/s	8Mbit/s	
0	7	140	28	0	2	4
1	6	125	25	0	2	1
				1	1	10
2	5	110	22	2	1	4
3	4	95	19	2	1	1
				3	0	10
4	3	80	16	1	1	1
				4	0	4
5	2	65	13	0	1	1
				4	0	1
6	1	50	10	3	0	1
7	0	35	7	2	0	1

Table 3: Characteristic parameters in a system with 2 Mbit/s and 8 Mbit/s service classes

no.	number of system classes	lower and upper limits symmetric optimized		intention
1	6x2 Mbit/s 1x8 Mbit/s	16 : 28	16 : 24	possibility of bandwidth change
2	2x2 Mbit/s 5x8 Mbit/s	16 : 28	16 : 24	improved utilization of link capacity

Table 4: Intention for optimizing the strategies

Before system no.2 was optimized only one VP with 8 Mbit/s service class was able to change the bandwidth at one time. Now two VPs are able to change their bandwidth. The loss probability of these VPs, compared to the non optimized strategy, increases for an offered traffic below 1.4 Erl respectively 0,26 percent loss probability, see Fig. 10. Above this point the performance is improved. The optimized strategy causes a stronger increase of loss probability at the upper bandwidth limit for low offered traffic, as it reduces the loss at the lower bandwidth limit with one additional VP which is able to jump to the upper limit. The opposite behaviour can be seen above an offered traffic of 1.4 where the loss probability decreases. The possibility for an additional VP being able to jump decreases the loss probability at the lower bandwidth limit. For the VPs with 2 Mbit/s service classes there is no change in performance because they are still able to change the bandwidth all the time, see Fig. 9.

VPs with service classes 2 Mbit/s and 8Mbit/s		link capacity	shared capacity	maximum number of VPs at the upper limit at the same time		unused link capacity
				2Mbit/s	8Mbit/s	
2 (PS4:7)	5 (PS16:24)	110	22	2 ☞	2	0 ☺
6 (PS4:7)	1 (PS16:24)	50	10	0	1 ☺	2
				3	0	1

Table 5: Characteristic parameters of optimized strategies

6. Conclusion

These investigations show that an improvement in performance, related to decreased loss probability and/or increased offered traffic, is possible in most cases by using bandwidth limits which are determined for symmetric models. Problems may occur if there are service classes with bandwidth demands of very different dimensions. In these cases a bandwidth change may be impossible, if a change would exceed the link capacity. This paper shows that this problem can be solved by decreasing the upper bandwidth limits. In some cases a part of the link capacity remains unused if the partial-sharing strategy is used. This capacity can be utilized in a better manner by increasing upper bandwidth limits or establishing new VPs. There is in some cases no restriction in bandwidth change for VPs with service classes of small bandwidth demand. A fixed bandwidth could be allocated to these VPs if they are always able to change the bandwidth simultaneously. With this the bandwidth manager would be relieved of processing power. Another potentiality to reduce the required processing power is a loss-dependent change of bandwidth. In this paper a VP bandwidth request occurs if the VC call exceeds the lower bandwidth limit. The loss-dependent bandwidth request occurs if VC calls exceed a predetermined loss probability at the lower bandwidth limit. VP bandwidth is decreased if the lower bandwidth limit was sufficient for a predetermined time Δ.

7. References

[1] BURGIN J., DORMAN D.: Broadband ISDN Resource Management: The Role of Virtual Path. *IEEE Communication Magazine*, pp.44-48, Sept.91.

[2] HÄNDEL, R., HUBER, M.N.: Integrated Broadband Networks - *An Introduction to ATM-Based Networks*. Addison-Wesley Publishers Limited, Wokingham, 1991.

[3] KAUFMANN J.S.: Blocking in a Shared Resource Environment. *IEEE Transactions on Communications*, vol.29, no.10, pp.1474-1480, Oct. 1981.

[4] SATO K., OHTA S., TOKIZAWA S.: Broad-Band ATM Network Architecture Based on Virtual Paths. *IEEE Transactions on Communications*, vol.38, no.8, pp.1212-1222, August 1990.

[5] OHTA S., SATO K.: Dynamic Bandwidth Control of the Virtual Path in an Asynchronous Transfer Mode Network. *IEEE Transactions on Communications*, vol.40, no.7, pp.1239-1247, July 1992.

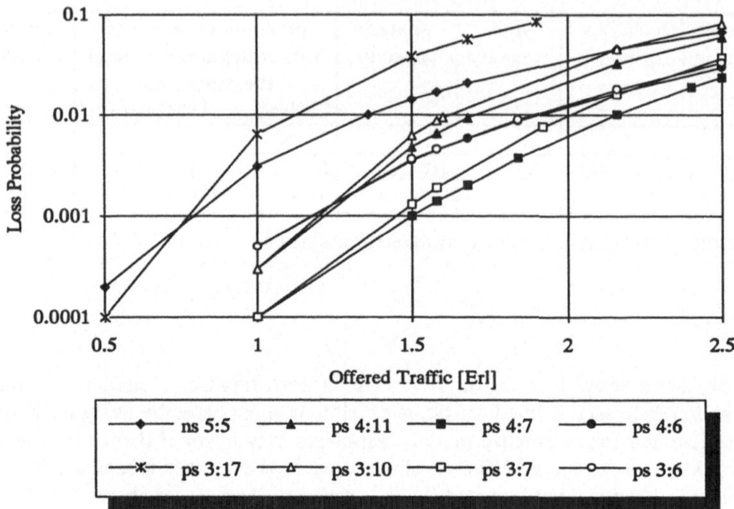

Figure 1: Loss probability in the symmetric model

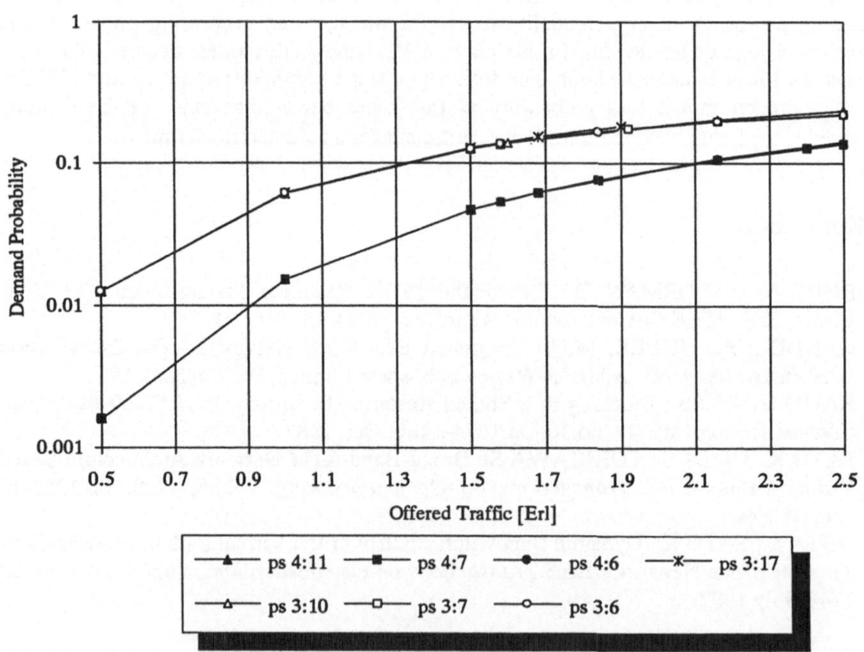

Figure 2: Demand probability in the symmetric model

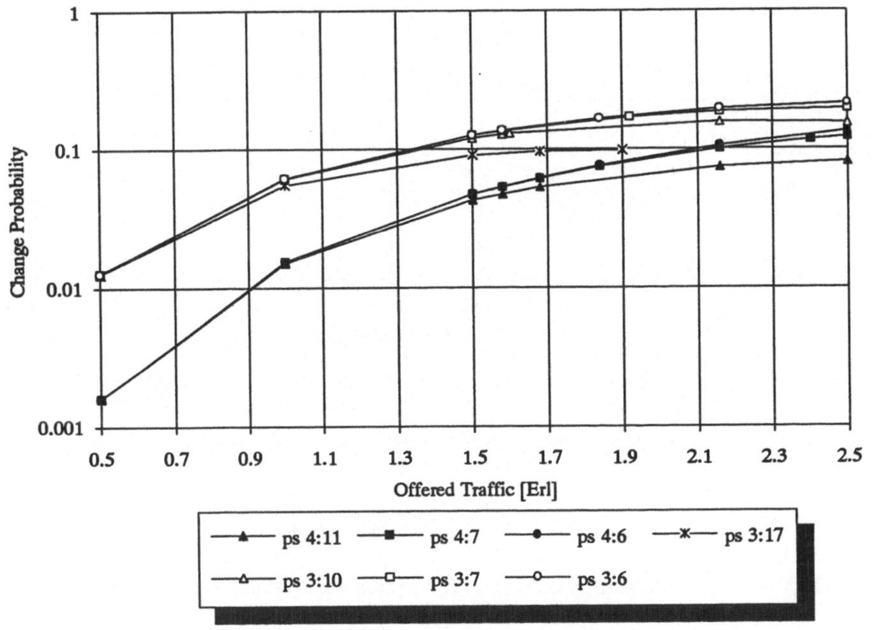

Figure 3: Change probability in the symmetric model

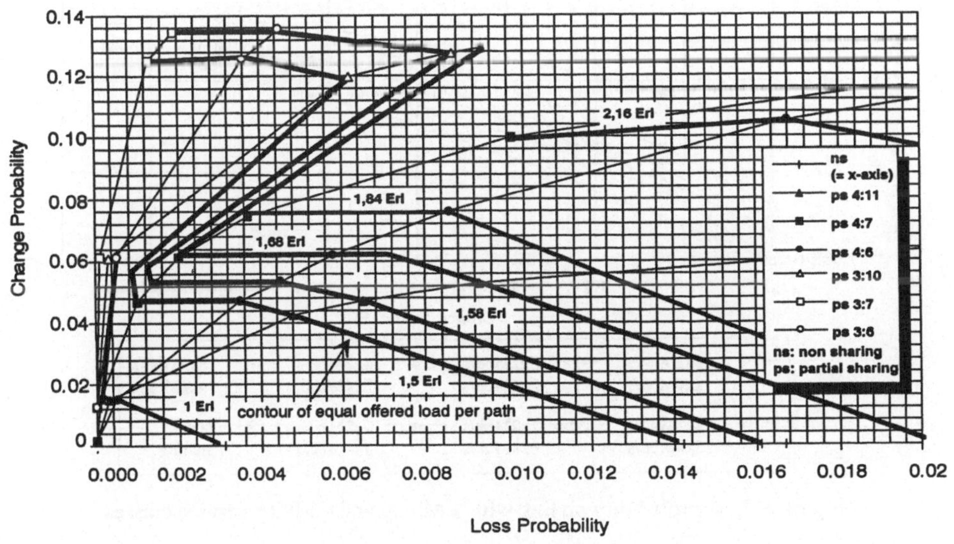

Figure 4: Change probability versus loss probability in the symmetric model

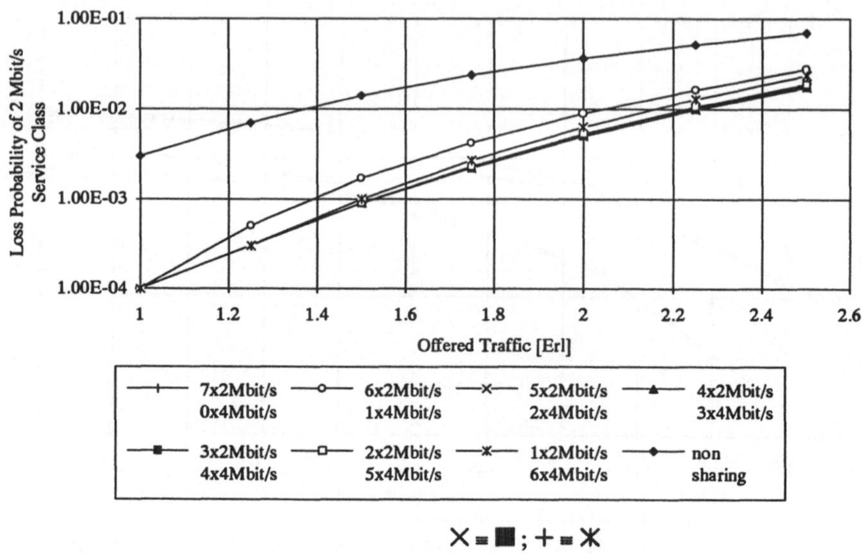

Figure 5: Loss probability on link with 2 Mbit/s and 4 Mbit/s service classes

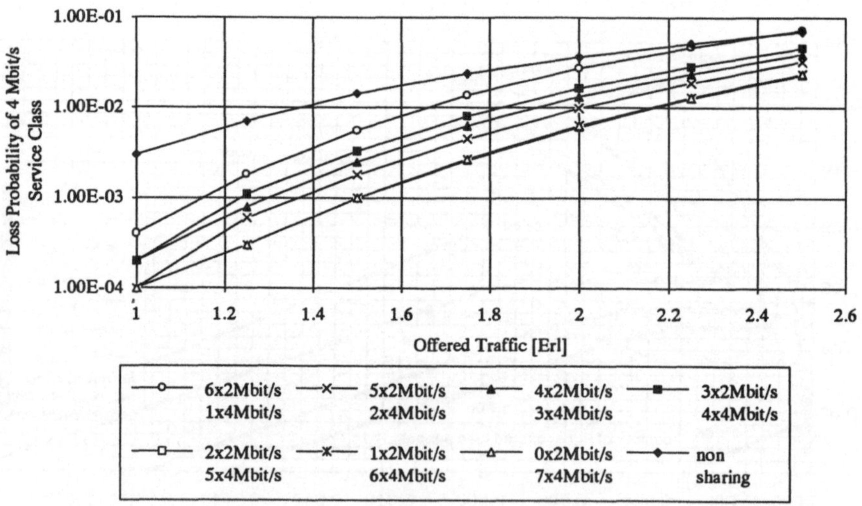

Figure 6: Loss probability on link with 2 Mbit/s and 4 Mbit/s service classes

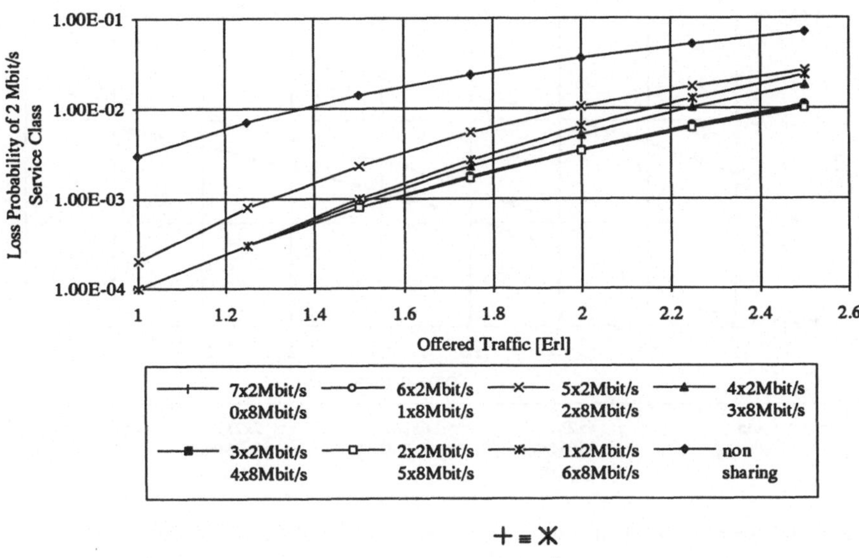

Figure 7: Loss probability on link with 2 Mbit/s and 8 Mbit/s service classes

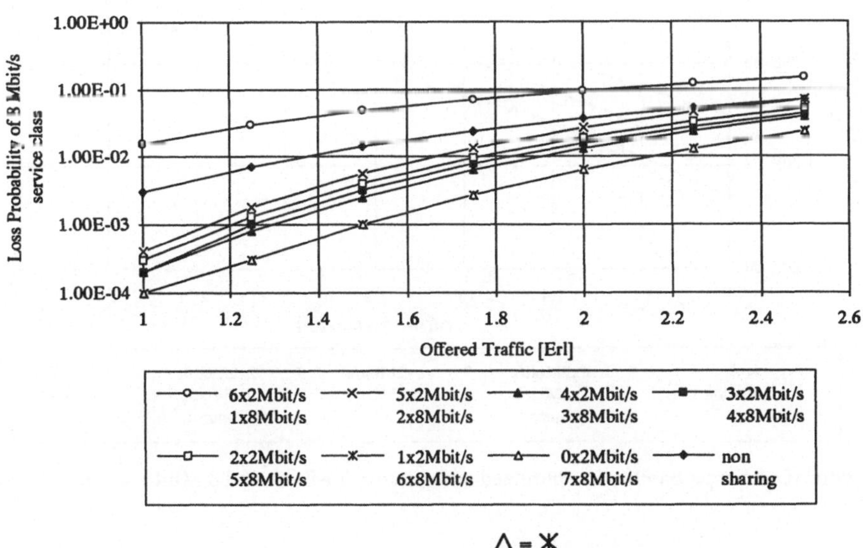

Figure 8: Loss probability on link with 2 Mbit/s and 8 Mbit/s service classes

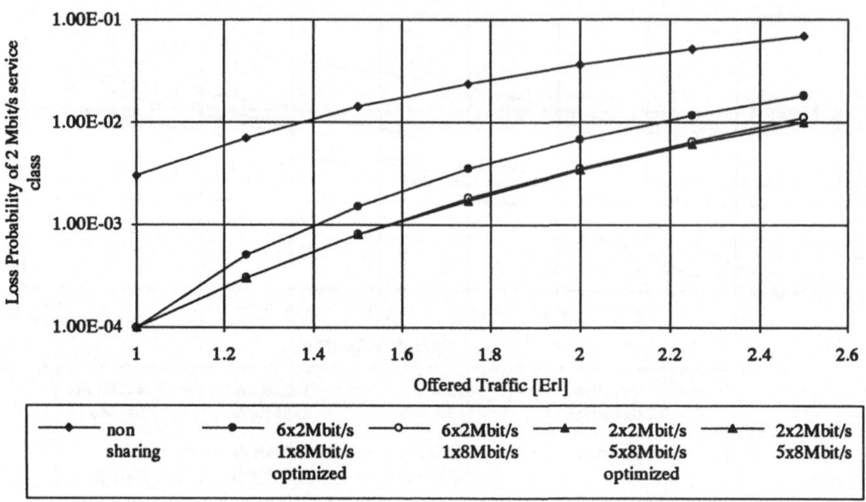

Figure 9: Loss probability in optimized system with 2 Mbit/s and 8 Mbit/s service classes

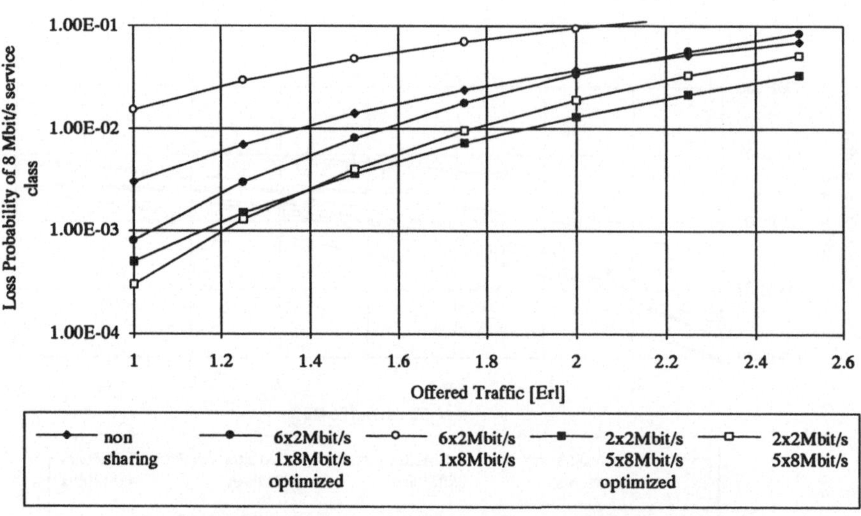

Figure 10: Loss probability in optimized system with 2 Mbit/s and 8 Mbit/s service classes

Capacity and Performance Analysis for Signalling Networks Supporting UPT

M. Bafutto * , P.J. Kühn

University of Stuttgart
Institute of Communications Switching and Data Technics
Seidenstraße 36, D – 70174 Stuttgart, Federal Republic of Germany

Abstract. This work yields a generic modelling approach for the signalling load as a result of the various communications services, especially new services like UPT. A tool has been developed which provides the distinct loading of all hard- and software signalling network resources and on which a hierarchical performance analysis and planning procedures are based. The results of the analysis are used to evaluate the end-to-end performance of the call scenarios under consideration. A numerical example, including ISDN and PLMN scenarios, outlines the application of the tool to a hypothetical network.

1 Introduction

The Universal Personal Telecommunication (UPT) is a new service concept that improves subscriber mobility by deattaching the subscriber identity from the terminal identity. A UPT subscriber is identified by a unique Personal Telecommunication Number (PTN) and can register on specific access points across different networks (PSTN, ISDN, or PLMN). In an access point the UPT subscriber can initiate or receive calls and the charge is provided on the basis of the PTN.

The efforts to produce international standards for UPT has recently begun in CCITT and also in ETSI. According to the CCITT view [4, 5], the elements of the UPT functional architecture comprises a Registration Point (RP) for storage of dynamic and static data, a Call Routing Point (CRP) for UPT call handling, and an Access Point (AP) through which the subscriber utilizes the service.

The Intelligent Network (IN) concept [3, 8, 16, 17] offers a possibility for a fast and flexible UPT service deployment [6, 7, 19]. The CCITT has already started a study concerning the mapping of the UPT architecture onto Intelligent Network architecture, and an initial approach may be found in [5].

The implementation of the UPT service depends on the capabilities and restrictions of the support network. In the signalling domain, for example, some aspects of the user and network signalling may be considered. The fixed wired

---

* Under contract with Telegoias and supported by CAPES Brazil, grant 9532/88-15.

networks have different user signalling structure, e.g., the "in-band" user signalling of PSTN, the "out-band" ISDN user signalling. In the mobile networks a user signalling protocol adjustment is necessary, and in some mobile networks, like GSM, the use of a smart card as a Subscriber Identity Module requires new terminal functions [11]. On the network signalling plane, it was concluded that the Mobile Application Part (MAP) of CCITT Signalling System No. 7 was not in line with current MAP specifications in practical use, thus representing an obstacle for the UPT service implementation, this fact led to a proposal of updating or even deleting the recommendation CCITT Q.1051 [4].

Despite of the support network, the deployment of the UPT procedures related to mobility, call handling and service management require additional information to be transported by the signalling network. The introduction of the UPT service increases the signalling network load, and may lead to a performance degradation of the signalling network, therefore affecting not only the UPT quality of service parameters, but also the services already offered by the network.

In this article, a modelling approach is used to develop a tool concept which is suitable to support the planning of new signalling networks according to given service, load, and grade of service figures, or to detect bottlenecks or possible deficiencies in case of resource outages.

2 The Signalling Network

A signalling network [2, 12, 13] is composed of signalling points (SP), service control points (SCP) and signalling transfer points (STP) interconnected by links, and supports the exchange of information related to call/connection control, distributed application processing, and network management.

In the signalling network domain, a telecommunication service can be viewed as a number of packets transmitted to and from the related nodes. Changes in the traffic intensity of a particular service, introduction of new services or temporary outages usually cause variations of the network load and, therefore, of the quality of service parameters. The various network components are typically affected in the following way:

- *Links:* The offered signalling link load per call may change drastically with the introduction of new services.
- *Signalling Points:* The increasing signalling traffic load requires more processing capacity from the network elements. Since this additional load may not be homogeneously distributed over all processes within an SP, only some processors may become overloaded.
- *Service Control Points:* Since the capacity of an SCP is determined by the number and types of transactions and by the offered functionality, the effect of the introduction of a new service can be estimated by the resource capacity required to process the related transactions.

The functional structure of Signalling System No. 7 is divided into the Network Service Part (NSP) and the User Parts (UPs). The NSP consists of the Message Transfer Part (MTP) and the Signalling Connection Control Part (SCCP), while the UPs are the Telephone User Part (TUP), the Integrated Services Digital Network User Part (ISUP), the Data User Part (DUP), and the Transaction Capabilities (TC). The TC can be further subdivided into the Transaction Capabilities Application Part (TCAP) and the Intermediate Service Part (ISP), which is still empty.

The MTP provides a simple datagram service, and its addressing capabilities are limited to the identification of a certain UP in one specific node. The SCCP extends the MTP capabilities in order to identify a subsystem of a UP or to translate an address that does not contain MTP routing information (e.g., a Global Title).

The ISUP offers the signalling functions that are necessary to support voice and non-voice applications in an ISDN network. The TUP and DUP functions are assumed as part of the ISUP and are not considered in the rest of this work. Finally, the TC provide a set of capabilities in a transaction-based and connectionless environment that support applications which require remote procedure calls or database queries.

3 Modelling Framework

The modelling methodology presented in [20] is used as baseline. Each submodel is derived directly from the CCITT functional specifications with consideration of internal mechanisms such as segmenting/forking of messages and scheduling strategies, thus, reflecting the internal behavior of the underlying blocks. Hence, this approach is relatively independent of specific implementations leading to a generic model of the signalling network composed of generic submodels. The generic submodels are finally transformed into realistic models where the actual assignment of functional processes to real processors are taken into account.

The principles of this methodology can be explained using the TCAP block as an example of derivation of a generic submodel. According to [2, Figure A-2a/Q.774], the TCAP is composed of two subblocks: the Transaction Sub-layer (TSL) and the Component Sub-layer. The Component Sub-layer consists of the Dialog Handling (DHA) and Component Handling. The Component Handling is further subdivided into the Component Coordinator (CCO) and the Invocation State Machine (ISM). From this, a processor model comprising four distinct processing phases (TSL, DHA, CCO, and ISM) and four message input queues is derived. Inside this submodel, there are different message routing paths, i.e., message chains. As an example, the message chain corresponding to an outgoing Dialogue Begin message containing two Invoke components is described bellow and depicted in Figure 1.

- The primitive "TC-BEGIN req" received from the TC User is processed by DHA. Any Invoke components with the same Dialogue ID (in this case two

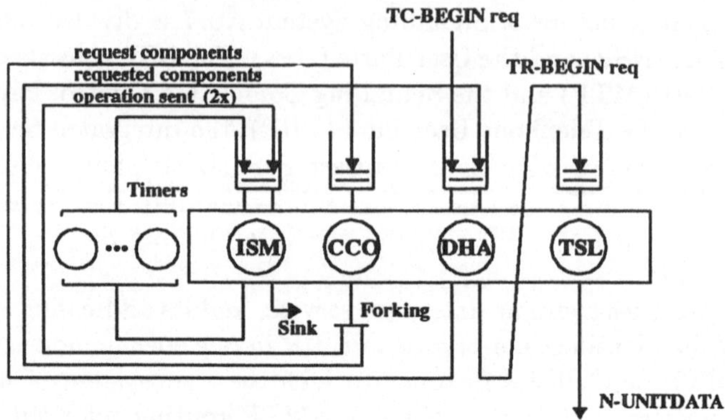

Fig. 1. Message chain for the Dialogue Begin message

components) are then requested from the CCO through a "request components" signal;
- The CCO processes the "request components" signal and generates three
  outputs signal (fork): two "operation sent" signals to the ISM (one for each
  Invoke component) and then one "requested components" signal to the DHA;
- Under reception of each of the two "operation sent" signals, the ISM starts
  an invocation timer. No output is generated (sink). The case of time-out can
  be modelled by a message branching with the branching probability given
  by the time-out probability;
- When the DHA receives the "requested components" signal, it composes a
  "TR-BEGIN req" primitive to the TSL;
- The TSL processes the "TR-BEGIN req" and requests the service of the
  Signalling Connection Control Part (SCCP) through an "N-UNITDATA"
  primitive.

The TCAP functional block is not restricted to the Dialogue Begin message, and comprises a set of messages consisting of a combination of all possible
types for the transaction portion and component portion. The representation of
all these message chains requires the extension of the model depicted in Figure 1 through additional chains. The full model, which is depicted in Figure 2,
is obtained by considering the set of all possible message chains for the TCAP
functional block.

The models for the functional blocks of the Levels 3 and 4 of the signalling
network protocol architecture (MTP Level 3, SCCP, and ISUP) are obtained in
the same way. The reader interested in more detail about these models is refered
to [20].

MTP Level 1 is simply modelled as an infinite server with a service time
representing the signalling link propagation delay. The modelling approach described before cannot be applied to the MTP Level 2 entities, because they are
closely coupled via the error correction and flow control mechanisms on Level 2.

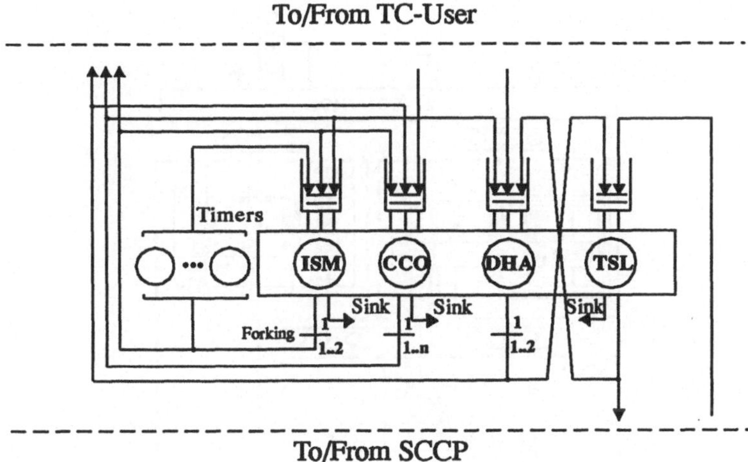

Fig. 2. Generic submodel for the TCAP block

Therefore, the approach included in the CCITT recommendations is adopted, where the corresponding queueing delay formulas are given explicitly.

In order to embed all these models in a realistic environment, it is necessary to extend the model by adding traffic sources representing the traffic generated by the users, traffic sinks, response times of exchanges and users, database access delays, etc..

A better overview of a complete model for the Levels 3 and 4 can be obtained by representing the individual submodels in a reduced form, as depicted in Figure 3. In that case it was assumed that each functional block is implemented in a single real processor. In the MTP the identified processes are the Message Discrimination (HMDC), Message Distribution (HMDT), and Message Routing (HMRT). The ISUP contains the Call Processing Control Incoming (CPCI), Call Processing Control Outgoing (CPCO), Message Distribution Control (MDSC), and Message Sending Control (MSDC). The processes of the SCCP are the Connection Oriented Control, Connectionless Control and Routing Control and since they are used in both directions, transmitting and receiving, they were split in one processing phase for each direction.

4   Analysis Outline

The complete model for the entire signalling network includes extended queueing network elements like, e.g., full duplex flow controlled links, priority processors, multiple-chain multiple-class traffic streams, segmenting and reassembling of messages, etc. The exact analysis of such a large and complex system is far beyond the current knowledge, and an approximation based on a combined decomposition and aggregation technique is used.

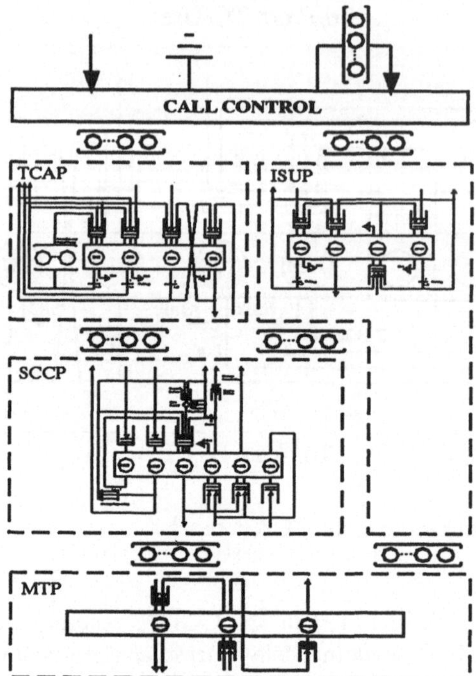

Fig. 3. Submodels for the functional blocks in a signalling point

The principle of decomposition is to break up a complex system into its subsystems in order to achieve a reduction in the complexity of the whole system. This assumption is valid if the interactions between the subsystems are largely dominated by the local interactions inside each subsystem. This can be assumed to be sufficiently satisfied in our case. The network is decomposed into link sets, SPs, and STPs. Then, in the second decomposition step, the link sets are further decomposed into single signalling links, whereas the SPs and STPs are decomposed into their submodels, i.e., MTP Level 3, SCCP, ISUP, and TCAP.

The basic idea behind the signalling traffic aggregation is the observation that a particular subsystem is shared by a large number of connections, and, because of this, message streams belonging to individual connections need not be distinguished from the corresponding aggregate traffic streams. The aggregate arrival processes to each subsystem are approximated by suitable point processes, e.g., Poisson processes.

The application of the principles above allow the analysis of each system in isolation. For the MTP Level 2 the formulas given in the CCITT recommendations are used. The performance of models for the upper Levels depends on additional factors like, e.g., the priority and the distribution of the message processing times of each process.

An exact analysis of the models of Level 3 and 4 may become quite complex, but mean value analysis is still possible in most cases. Previous work has been done in the analysis of priority queue systems in which a message may feedback and change priority after having been served [9, 14, 18]. An algorithm considering also bulk arrivals, forking and branching of messages, and different preemption strategies is available in [15]. The application of this algorithm results in a system of linear equations for the mean sojourn times of all message chains in each process. The global performance results, e.g., message transfer time or a call setup delay is obtained by composition of the submodel results.

5 A Planning Tool

Using this methodology, a signalling network planning tool has been implemented. Its input data are the topology, the sequence of processing phases visited by a message when passing through a signalling point (message chains) with the corresponding processing times, the scenario descriptions, the traffic matrix, and the routing strategy. The execution of the tool can be divided into two main steps:

- *Message Flow* – For the analysis of the signalling network, we just start with a message flow analysis from given data about the network configuration, routing plan, mix of services types, and a traffic origination-destination matrix. This message flow analysis yields the message flow rates on each transmission or processing resource partitioned to all message types. From message length and processing time distributions, the resource utilization follows straightforwardly. In order to provide a better survey on the impact of the introduction of a new service, the load information is already given with respect to each scenario at this stage of the analysis.

- *Performance Analysis* – The performance analysis for all nodes of a large network may represent a considerable expense of computer resources and the network designer is usually interested in the performance characteristic of some critical paths. With these considerations, the analysis is carried out for chosen paths. Low traffic approximations, such those presented in [1], may be used as an approach for the cases where the results for all nodes of a large network are desired.

  In a multivendor environment, the implementation of the functional blocks among the processors may not be the same for all SPs and STPs. For example, in a distributed SP architecture each functional block may be implemented in isolated processors, while in a centralized one, various functional blocks may share the same processor. The tool provides the user with the flexibility of defining his own architecture with arbitrary distribution of functional blocks among processors.

  The priority assignment for the processing phases is one of the parameters that determine the sojourn time for a message type. According to the priority assignment and traffic load, the differences between the sojourn time for distinct message types can be significant, in such a way that for one of them the processor can be considered as overloaded.

With the remarks above, the user is required to provide for each SP, SCP, and STP along the path the number of processors and the distribution of the functional blocks between them. For each processor, the number of units and the priority assignment of the processing phases are also necessary.

These input data and the individual message arrival rates for each submodel obtained from the traffic flow study are used to carry out a performance analysis for the submodels. In the cases where there are more than one processing unit available, it is assumed that the incoming traffic is homogeneously distributed between the units. The mean sojourn time for the individuals message chain are calculated using the algorithm contained in [15] as baseline.

The end-to-end transfer time of a particular message is computed by the summation of the individual transfer times, sojourn times and other delays along the path through the network. As in the message flow phase, this is again done by routines working with the network topology and routing strategy. With the end-to-end transfer time of a particular message sequence, it is possible to evaluate response delay parameters, such as connection set-up delay, data transfer delay and database query delay.

6 UPT Case Study

A simplified case study is provided to demonstrate the capabilities of the described planning tool. In order to not increase the complexity and the size of the traffic matrix a network with few nodes was chosen as an example. This fact does not represent a hindrance for the analysis of a real network containing a much larger number of nodes, in that case the traffic matrix data could be read from a magnetic media.

The topology of the Figure 4 is considered. On the highest hierarchical level (level 1) there are three interconnected STPs. The next hierarchical level (level 2) contains 2 transit SPs of the ISDN subnetwork and 1 Gateway Mobile Switching Center (GMSC) for the PLMN. Under the transit SPs there are three SPs of the lowest level (level 3). Three Mobile Switching Centers MSCs are linked to the GMSC. Each link set consists of 4 links in the highest level and 2 links in the remainder of the network. The transmission capacity of each link is 64 kbit/s, and the propagation delay is 5 ms. The routing is assumed to be strictly hierarchical.

The information related to the UPT Registration Point (RP) functionality is stored in an SCP connected to the STP identified by the code "100". For the PLMN, the Visitor Location Register (VLR) is integrated in the MSC and the Home Location Register is centralized in an SCP linked to the STP with code "300".

The ISDN and PLMN voice services are in operation in the example network. The typical scenarios for these services can be classified into three subgroups: normal call, subscriber busy, and no answer. Each service comprises 70% successful calls, 20% subscriber busy, and 10% no answer. The PLMN total traffic

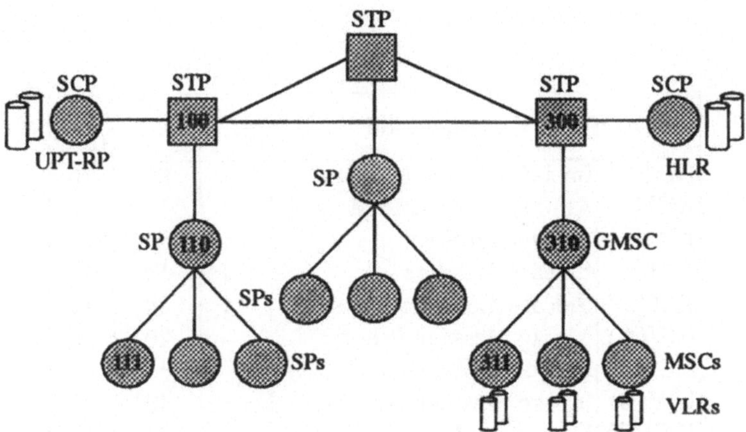

Fig. 4. Structure of the example network

corresponds to 10% of the ISDN total traffic.

The composition of the mobility related signalling scenarios in the PLMN requires some assumptions to be made, e.g., at location update the user is identified by his International Mobile Subscriber Identity (IMSI) instead by the Temporary Mobile Subscriber Identity (TMSI) avoiding an additional query to the old VLR, the VLR has the necessary information to manipulate an outgoing call, the HLR knows the Mobile Station Roaming Number (MSRN), etc. The consideration of all transactions produces a spectrum of messages generally with different message lengths. In order to simplify the example, the transaction related messages were divided into two subgroups, i.e., short and long messages, according to the amount of information. A database query in one of the SCPs consumes 200 ms. The message types and their corresponding lengths are listed in Table 1.

The traffic between the ISDN and PLMN subnetworks is assumed to be unbalanced and characterized as follow: 5% of the ISDN traffic is directed to the PLMN and 95% of the PLMN traffic is homogeneously distributed between the ISDN nodes.

The generated traffic corresponding to the support of the mobility procedures is a function of some network characteristics, e.g., cell size, ground topology, subscriber moving speed, etc. In this example a simplified stationary approach is considered, with a PLMN subscriber generating a location update request for each call and a handover being performed in 30% of the calls. Subsequent handovers are not taken into account.

With the introduction of the UPT concept, it is also necessary to differentiate between the calls destined to from those originated from a UPT user currently registered in an ISDN or PLMN terminal. A percentage of the ISDN or PLMN traffic is substituted by the UPT service. The traffic between UPT users is considered to be negligible.

Table 1. Messages considered in the example

Message	Designation	Length [byte]		
		ISUP	PLMN	UPT
IAM	Initial Address Message	59	65	70
ACM	Address Complete Message	17	17	17
ANM	Answer Message	15	15	15
REL	Release Message	19	19	19
RLC	Release Complete Message	14	14	14
INV(A)	Invoke Message (Short)	-	20	25
RES(A)	Response Message (Short)	-	30	35
INV(B)	Invoke Message (Long)	-	40	45
RES(B)	Response Message (Long)	-	60	65

It is assumed that the UPT functions are merged into normal ISDN/PLMN call setup, e.g. by including new UPT information in the related messages. The user is authenticated on registration, deregistration, incoming and outgoing calls. The storage of the UPT authentication information is centralized in the UPT-SCP.

The comparison between the different possibilities of physical implementation of the SS7 functionalities is beyond the scope of this work. In this example we have arbitrarily chosen an architecture where the MTP and SCCP are implemented in a single processor. The ISUP and TCAP functions are assumed to be performed by isolated processors.

The priority strategy of the processors is non-preemptive. The priority assignment for the processes in a decreasing order of priority is:

- ISUP processor: MSDC, CPCO, CPCI, and MDSC.
- TCAP processor: TSL, DHA, CCO, and ISM.
- MTP/SCCP processor: HMDC, HMDT, HMRT, SCLR, SCLT, SCRR, and SCRT.

The database query is performed using the TC. The processing times in the TCAP block of an SP are assumed to be 2 ms for the DHA, and 1.5 ms, 1 ms, and 0.5 ms for the CCO, TSL and ISM, respectively. All processes of the SCCP have a processing time of 1 ms. For the ISUP, the processing time is 1 ms for the CPCI and CPCO, and 0.5 ms for the MSDC and MDSC. In the MTP, the delay for a message in the HMDT and HMRT is 1 ms and in the HMDC 0.5 ms.

Before the evaluation of the network parameters it is interesting to check the accuracy of the adopted modelling approach through a simulation study. A good agreement between analysis and simulation results suggests that the assumptions of the analysis do not introduce significant errors. Simulations were performed with 10 subsequent replications simulating 90 seconds of a MSC. The warm-up phase comprised 60 seconds. The input data was obtained from the output data of the message flow phase. This information was taken as the boundary conditions for the signalling point analysis, i.e., the arrival rate of all messages destined to, originated from, and passing through the underlying node. The analysis and simulation results for the sojourn time in a MSC of an incoming TCAP Begin Message with an Invoke Component and an incoming TCAP End Message with a Result Component is shown in Figure 5. The results are depicted with the call attempt loading normalized with respect to the maximum call attempt loading of the underlying MSC.

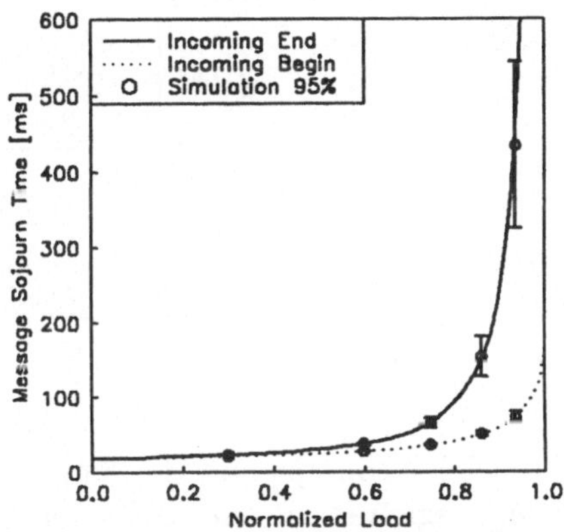

Fig. 5. Analysis and simulation results for a MSC

The difference between the sojourn times of the messages result from the fact that the incoming TCAP Begin Message is not processed by the ISM process. The assignment of the lowest priority to the ISM implies that a message in the ISM must wait until the queues of all the remaining processes are empty, and the probability that it occurs decreases with the increase of the load. This example illustrates a case where a processor is practically considered as overloaded for a particular message type, while for other message types it continues to operate normally.

The total CPU time for the simulation run of a single load case was about 75 minutes, contrasting with the 50 seconds consumed for the analysis. The computer resources required by the simulation highlights the constraints involved with application of the simulation technique to large signalling networks.

Firstly, the impact of the introduction of the UPT concept on both networks is studied. The UPT concept is introduced in a limited basis and the parameter of interest is the connection setup time between ISDN and PLMN. The results for a substitution of 3% and 5% of the voice service of the ISDN and PLMN are depicted in Figure 6. The call attempt loading is normalized with respect to the maximum call attempt loading of the network carrying only ISDN and PLMN voice services.

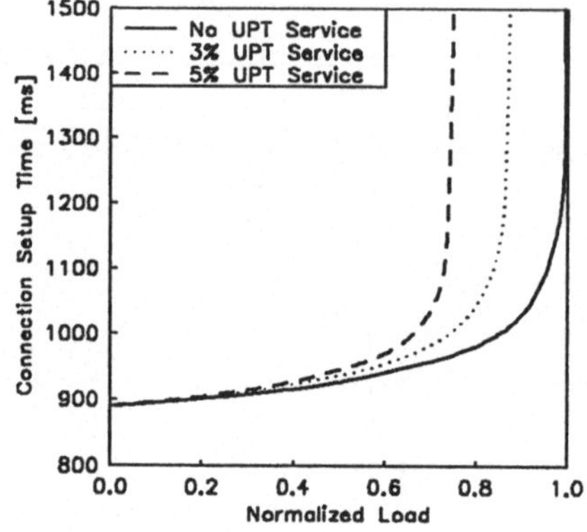
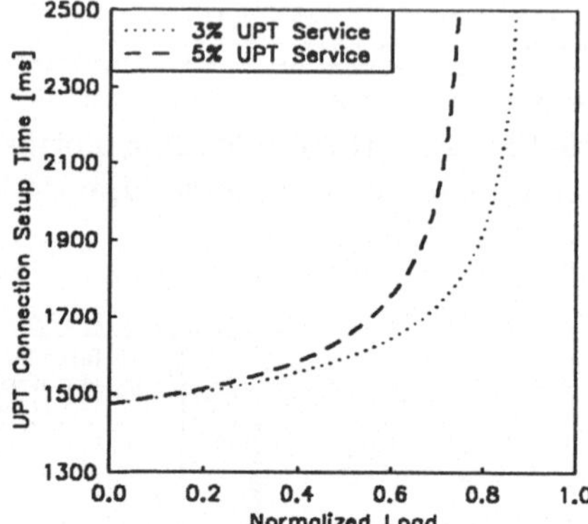

Fig. 6. Influence of the UPT concept on the ISDN–PLMN call setup delay

Fig. 7. Connection setup delay from an UPT user in ISDN to an PLMN user

The introduction of the UPT concept and the support of the mobility functions like, e.g., call routing, registration, authentication, etc., represent an additional load for the signalling network in the form of transactions to retrieve the necessary information. This load is not homogeneously distributed on the network and varies with the amount of introduced UPT services. In the cases of no UPT and 3% UPT service, the bottlenecks are located in the ISUP block of the transit ISDN-SP and in the ISUP block of the GMSC, respectively. For an introduction of 5% UPT traffic, however, the overload situation is observed in the TCAP block of the UPT-SCP. The quality of service parameters of the existing ISDN and PLMN services are also affected by the UPT introduction.

The complexity of these new scenarios and the corresponding effect on the call routing, the number of data base queries, the signalling network load, and the setup times suggest the use of alternative architectures considering factors like, e.g., data base to data base interactions, integration of data bases, allocation of IN functionality into the MSC [10].

The individual message transfer time between two nodes yields the computation of the delay involved in the exchange of any message sequence. With this information, there are various parameters of interest that can be evaluated. The results corresponding to the connection setup time for a call originated from a UPT user registered in the ISDN to a PLMN user is shown in Figure 7.

The shape of the graphics in Figure 7 differs from those obtained for the connection setup between ISDN and PLMN. This difference is explained by the larger number of elements involved in the UPT scenario.

7 Conclusion

The results show that quality of service parameters of future networks will be strongly influenced by the performance of the signalling network. The introduction of new services which require database interactions, such as UPT services and mobile communication services, will impact the signalling network performance, e.g., the processing load of signalling points and the end-to-end message transfer delays.

The presented modelling approach, with the consideration of physical implementation aspects, like distribution of the processes among processors and priority assignment, cover important characteristics present in a multivendor environment. This modelling framework has been implemented in a tool suitable to support the planning of new signalling networks according to given service, load and grade of service figures, or to detect bottlenecks or possible deficiencies in case of resource outages.

References

1. M. Bafutto, P.J. Kühn, G. Willmann, J. Zepf, "A Capacity and Performance Planning Tool for Signalling Networks based on CCITT Signalling System No. 7", in *Intelligent Networks – The Path to Global Networking*, (Ed. Paul W. Bayliss), IOS Press, Washington, pp. 368–379, 1992.

2. CCITT, *Blue Book, Volume IV, Fascicles VI.7–VI.9*, "Specifications of Signalling System No. 7", Recommendations Q.700–Q.795, International Telecommunication Union, Geneva, 1989.

3. CCITT Intelligent Network Capability Set 1 — Draft Recommendations, *Study Group XI, Report COM XI-R 207-218*, Meeting Held in Geneva on 9–20 March 1992.

4. CCITT, *Study Group XI, Report COM XI-R 60*, Meeting Held in Geneva on 8–12 April 1991.

5. CCITT, *Study Group XI, Report COM XI-R 262-E*, Meeting Held in Geneva on 21–25 September 1992.

6. M.C. Ciancetta, R. Lavagnolo, T. di Stefano, "An Approach to Universal Personal Telecommunication (UPT) Implementation in Intelligent Networks", *Proceedings of the 1992 International Zurich Seminar on Digital Communications – Intelligent Networks and their Applications*, Zurich, Switzerland, pp. 333–347, March 1992.

7. J.C. Dang, C. Vernhes, B. Chatras, "IN as Platform for UPT: Constrains and Requirements", *Proceedings of the 2nd International Conference on Intelligence in Networks*, Bordeaux, France, pp. 79–82, March 1992.

8. J.M. Duran, J. Visser, "International Standards for Intelligent Networks", *IEEE Communications Magazine*, vol. 30, no. 2, pp. 34–42, February 1992.

9. D.H.J. Epema, "Mean Waiting Times in a General Feedback Queueing Model with Priorities", *Performance '90*, (Editors P.J.B. King, I. Mitrani, and R.J. Pooley), North-Holland Publishing Company, Amsterdam, pp. 221–235, 1990.

10. E. Guarene, M.C. Ciancetta, T.D. Stefano, "IN and GSM Integration for Personal Communication Services Provision", in *Intelligent Networks – The Path to Global Networking*, (Ed. Paul W. Bayliss), IOS Press, Washington, pp. 290–299, 1992.

11. H.P.J. Hecker, J. Hegeman, W.R. Mol, M.J.J. van Nielen, "The Application of the IN-concept to Provide Mobility in Underlying Networks", *Proceedings of the 2nd International Conference on Intelligence in Networks*, Bordeaux, France, pp. 95–100, March 1992.

12. B. Jabbari, "Common Channel Signalling System Number 7 for ISDN and Intelligent Networks", *Proceedings of the IEEE*, vol. 79, no. 2, pp. 155–169, February 1991.

13. A.R. Modarressi, R.A. Skoog, "Signaling System No. 7: A Tutorial", *IEEE Communications Magazine*, vol. 28, no. 7, pp. 19–35, July 1990.

14. M. Paterok, O. Fischer, "Feedback Queues with Preemption-Distance Priorities", *ACM SIGMETRICS Performance Evaluation Review*, vol. 17, no. 1, pp. 136–145, May 1989.

15. M. Paterok, "Warteschlangensysteme mit Rückkopplung und Prioritäten", *Arbeitsberichte des Instituts für Mathematische Maschinen und Datenverarbeitung*, Band 23, no. 12, Erlangen, Germany, October 1990.

16. P.S. Richards, "Rapid Service Delivery and Customization in a Developing Network Infrastructure", *Performance Evaluation*, vol. 25, no. 10, pp. 1031–1039, May 1993.

17. R.B. Robrock, "The Intelligent Network — Changing the Face of Telecommunications", *Proceedings of the IEEE*, vol. 79, no. 1, pp. 7–20, January 1991.

18. B. Simon, "Priority Queues with Feedback", *Journal of the ACM*, vol. 31, no. 1, pp. 134–149, January 1984.

19. J. Vandenameele, J.B. Thieffry, H. Decuypere, "UPT, a New Dimension in Telecommunications provided by IN", *Proceedings of the 1992 International Zurich Seminar on Digital Communications - Intelligent Networks and their Applications*, Zurich, Switzerland, pp. 41–54, March 1992.

20. G. Willmann, P.J. Kühn, "Performance Modeling of Signaling System No. 7", *IEEE Communications Magazine*, vol. 28, no. 7, pp. 44–56, July 1990.

Geschlossene Optimierung symmetrischer Referenznetze mit nichthierarchischer Verkehrslenkung

von

Harro L. Hartmann, Hucang He und Zhe Bai
Institut für Nachrichtensysteme
der
Technischen Universität Braunschweig

1. Einleitung

Die Verkehrslenkung beinhaltet im allgemeinen eine statische und dynamische Flußzuweisung auf Ursprungs-Ziel-Wege, so daß die Kosten bzw. Ende zu Ende Blockierungen (EEB) minimal werden. Man minimiert daher bei der statischen Flußzuweisung die erforderlichen Kanalzahlen unter der Nebenbedingung EEB = const. und minimiert bei der dynamischen Flußzuweisung die EEB bei installierten, d.h. Kapazitäten = const, [HAR 91a]. Die meisten Orts- und Fernnetze sind nicht vollvermascht, so daß deren Ursprungs-Ziel-Knoten zumindest teilweise nicht durch direkte Verbindungsleitungen (Links) gekoppelt sind. Auch die Verkehrsangebote differieren räumlich und zeitlich. Zu einem symmetrischen Referenznetz gelangt man, indem unter Beibehaltung der Netzknotenzahl eine Vollvermaschung mit mittleren Bündelkapazitäten und Ursprungs-Ziel-Verkehrsangeboten gebildet wird, welche in der Summe der Gesamtkapazität des Netzes bzw. dem Gesamtverkehrsangebot in einer relevanten Lastperiode entspricht.

Im Fachschrifttum wurden symmetrische Netze bisher unter dem Aspekt der Modellierung und Performance-Auswertung betrachtet. Den ausschlaggebenden Anstoß hierzu lieferte ein Beitrag von R. S. Krupp in [KRU 82], wobei insbesondere die Ursachen für hochlastbedingte Durchsatzeinbußen und Richtwerte für deren Einebnung im Vergleich zu Simulationen betrachtet wurden. T.-K. G. Yum und M. Schwartz berechneten hierauf aufbauend die Call Processing Load bei Hochlast und die Auswirkung einer externen Routing-Abschaltung auf die Processing Load-Minderung, [YUM 87]. In beiden Beiträgen werden symmetrische Netze mit fest installierten Linkkapazitäten und der entsprechende Durchsatz bei variablem Angebot mit Trunk-Reservierung betrachtet.

Im vorliegenden Beitrag werden demgegenüber die gleichen Netze erstmalig einer Kapazitäts- und Fluß-Optimierung unterworfen. Dabei erlaubt die Symmetrie-Annahme eine kompakte systemtheoretische Beschreibung. Die Abhängigkeit der Zielfunktionen von den Vorgaben und Nebenbedingungen erscheint in geschlossener Form, so daß selbst bei sehr großen Netzen kürzeste Rechenzeiten erreicht werden.

Zunächst werden die Rahmenbedingungen der Modellierung und Problemformulierungen erörtert. Im nächsten Hauptabschnitt erfolgt eine Kapazitätszuweisung bei Vorgabe des Verkehrsangebotes auf den Planungshorizont (Engineered Load) sowie der Ende zu Ende Blokkierung (EEB) als grundlegende Restriktion. Im dritten Hauptabschnitt erfolgt dann die Flußzuweisung bei außerplanerischen, insbesondere hohen Verkehrsangeboten unter der Nebenbedingung fester, z. B. installierter Kapazitäten. Im vierten Hauptabschnitt werden sodann die EEB-Steigerungen bei hochlastbedingten Anrufwiederholungen und Prozessorlasten infolge des Absuchens potentieller Alternativwege erörtert. Der Beitrag schließt mit konzeptionellen Folgerungen und Hinweisen zur restlichen Optimierung für den Wirkbetrieb nichthierarchischer Netze.

Wir behandeln hier nur den Fall der dynamischen, nichthierarchischen Verkehrslenkung unter der grundlegenden Beschränkung auf symmetrische Referenznetze mit maximal zwei Linkabschnitten zwischen allen Ursprungs- und Zielvermittlungen. Solche symmetrischen Netze genügen folgenden Bedingungen:

   (i) Sie sind vollvermascht,

   (ii) alle Ursprungs-Ziel-Verkehrsangebote sind gleich groß,

   (iii) alle Linkkapazitäten haben den gleichen Wert und die Links werden doppelt
        gerichtet betrieben.

Die Bedingung (i) beinhaltet, daß ein Netz mit N Vermittlungen (Knoten) N(N-1)/2 Kanten bei N(N-1) Verkehrspaaren umfaßt. Jede Kante beinhaltet eine kommend und gehend betriebene Verbindungsleitung (Link) mit n Kanälen (Trunks). Dann unterstellt (ii) einfach gerichtete Verkehrsangebote A/2, welche gemäß (iii) in der Summe das Angebot A pro Link mit n Kanälen oder Trunks ergeben.

Die nichthierarchische Verkehrslenkung wird unter folgenden Bedingungen betrachtet:

   (j)   Steuerung der Verkehrslenkung vom Ursprungsamt aus (Originating Office Control-
         OOC) mit der Routing-Vorschrift: Direktweg zuzüglich $M \leq (N-2)$ Zweilink-Alternativwege,

   (jj) wechselseitiger, nichthierarchischer Verkehrsüberlauf (Mutual Overflow),

   (jjj) Rufrückholung (Crankback) bei Blockierung im zweiten Linkabschnitt bei weiteren
         Überlaufmöglichkeiten in der steuernden Ursprungsvermittlung.

2. Kostenoptimierung (Capacity Assignment with Mutual Overflow-CAMO)

Gegeben: Symmetrisches Netz mit nichthierarchischer Verkehrslenkung und einem Verkehrsangebot A/2 für alle gerichteten Verkehrspaare. Grade of Service (GOS).

Problemformulierung:

   Min{n(LB)/[A(1-EEB)]} mit der Linkblockierung (LB) als Systemvariable.

Optimale LB = LB*, n* = Min{n}, und optimaler Wegefächerumfang M*
Nebenbedingungen:

EEB = GOS und Flußerhaltungsrelationen für alle Netzknoten und Links.

Infolge der Symmetrie besteht auf jeder Link das gleiche fiktive Verkehrsangebot $a \geq A$ in Erlang, welches sowohl den Direktverkehr als auch den induzierten Überlaufverkehr anderer Verkehrspaare umfaßt. Der Zugang von sehr vielen Rufankünften zu jeder Link oder Bündel mit n Kanälen bzw. Trunks erfolgt über ein ggf. mehrstufiges, jedoch von inneren Blockierungen freies Koppelnetzwerk, welches als Verlustsystem modelliert wird. Im Falle Poissonscher Rufankünfte und stationärer Verhältnisse gilt dann die Erlangsche Wahrscheinlichkeitsverteilung der Belegungszustände jedes Abnehmerbündels

$$p_j = \frac{a^j/j!}{\sum_{i=0}^{n} a^i/i!} \quad \text{mit } 0 \leq j \leq n \tag{1a}$$

und der Blockierungswahrscheinlichkeit oder Erlangschen Formel 1. Art, $E1(n, a)$

$$E1(n,a) = p_n = \frac{a^n/n!}{\sum_{i=0}^{n} a^i/i!} = p. \tag{1b}$$

Die Auflösung dieser Relation nach dem Argument n wird im Folgenden als Invertierte Erlangsche Formel 1. Art (IE1) bezeichnet, so daß $n = IE1(p, a)$ folgt.

Weiterhin gilt für $M \leq (N\,2)$ Zweilink-Alternativwege für die EEB des entstehenden Serien-Parallel-Graphen die von der Reihenfolge der Alternativwege unabhängige EEB-Relation

$$EEB(M, p) = p\,(1-q^2)^M = p\,[1-(1-p)^2]^M \tag{2}$$

wobei $q = 1-p$ die Wahrscheinlichkeit dafür ist, daß der betreffende Linkabschnitt nicht blockiert, also wenigstens ein Kanal frei ist.

Diese Relation definiert die präzisierbare Funktion des Routingverfahrens. Insbesondere unterstellt Gl. (2), daß sowohl der Direktweg als auch M Zweilink-Alternativwege blockiert sind. Jedes Verfahren, das den vollen Wegefächer des Umfanges M+1 verlustfrei nutzt, erfüllt zunächst Gl. (2). Eine besonders einfache Implementierung ermöglicht dabei der sequentielle, blockierungsbedingte, jedoch wechselseitige, also nichthierarchische Überlauf nach **Bild 1**(a), der beim jeweiligen Direktweg beginnt. Falls der zweite Linkabschnitt eines Alternativweges blockiert ist und weitere Alternativwege zur Verfügung stehen, wird der Ruf von der steuernden Ursprungsvermittlung zurückgeholt (OCC and Crankback). Bei anderen Routingverfahren ändert sich Gl. (2). Wird z. B. auf Crankback verzichtet, so treten zusätzliche Verluste in den Zweitlinks mit der Folge größerer EEB-Werte und Optimalitätseinbußen auf. Im vorliegenden Referenznetz wird nun jeder Link zu n Kanälen das fiktive Verkehrsangebot a angeboten, welches die Grundlast A zzgl. Überlaufeinströmungen a-A umfaßt. Die Belastung

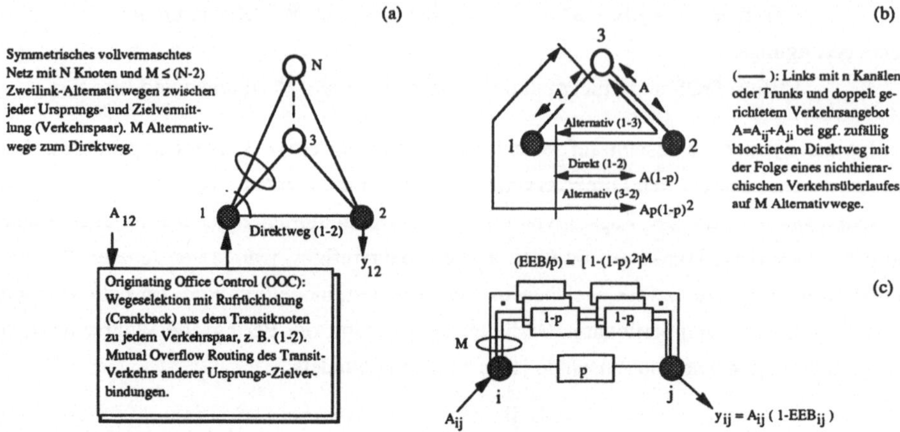

Bild 1. Das Prinzip der nichthierarchischen Verkehrslenkung. (a) OOC-Routing im exemplarisch ausgewählten Netzknoten 1, (b) 'Traffic carried'-Überlagerungen auf der Link 1-2, (c) Blockierungen des Direktweges und der parallelen Alternativwege.

(traffic carried) K jeder Link ist dann nach R. S. Krupp [KRU 82] und **Bild 1 (b)** einerseits

$$K = [A + (a - A)] \, (1 - p) = a(1-p) \tag{3a}$$

und andererseits

$$K = A(1-p) + 2Ap \, (1-p)^2 = A(1-p) + 2Ap \, [1-EEB(1, p)/p], \tag{3b}$$

bzw. allgemeiner nach Bild 1 (c)

$$K = A(1-p) + 2Ap \, [1-EEB(M, p)/p], \tag{3c}$$

mit der EEB(M, p) bei wirksamem Crankback gemäß Gl. (2). Insbesondere ist A(1-p) die carried load des Direktverkehrs und 2Ap[1-EEB(M,p)/p] der erfolgreich induzierte Überlaufverkehrsanteil der übrigen Verkehrspaare des Alternativwege-Parallelnetzes mit der Blockierung EEB[M, p]/p nach **Bild 1(c)**. Der Faktor 2 bringt dabei die Überlauf-Induktion von jeweils zwei Verkehrspaaren der M Zweilink-Alternativwegabschnitte zum Ausdruck. Z. B. haben in Bild 1(b) beide Alternativweg-Belastungen den gleichen für das Verkehrspaar (3-2) angegebenen Wert. Hingegen gelangt man zu den Verkehrsangebotswerten, z. B. vor der Link (1-2) durch Multiplikation der Belastungsanteile mit [1/(1-p)].

Löst man die Gleichungen (3a) und (3c), so folgt die Bestimmungsgleichung für a bei gegebenem Verkehrsangebot A

$$a = A \, [1+p-2 \, EEB(M, p)]/(1-p) = a(A, p, EEB). \tag{3d}$$

Führt man nun p als Systemvariable ein, so folgt aus Gl. (3d) mit Gl. (1b) die zugehörige Linkkapazität n = IE1(p,a). Diese fällt mit wachsendem p und steigt mit wachsendem a. Ihr Minimum sei n* = IE1(p*, a*). Der Verkehrsüberlauf von a* hat dann den Mittelwert m und die Varianz v gemäß

$$m = a^* p^* \quad \text{bzw.} \qquad v = m\left(1 - m + \frac{a^*}{n^* + 1 + m - a^*}\right) , \tag{4a}$$

so daß das fiktive Angebot unter Vernachlässigung von Überlaufeinströmungen von höherer als erster Ordnung in p die Spitzigkeit $z^* \approx$ (relevante Varianz / relevanter Mittelwert) gemäß

$$z^* \approx \frac{A + 2(1 - p^*)(A/a^*)v}{A[1 + 2p^*(1 - p^*)]} = \frac{1 + 2p^*(1 - p^*)v/m}{1 + 2p^*(1 - p^*)} \geq 1. \tag{4b}$$

aufweist. Man beachte, daß der Arbeitspunkt der Links durch die Parameter a^*, p^* und n^* gegeben ist und v nur nach Maßgabe zweier nichtblockierter Überläufe 1. Ordnung wirkt. Der Equivalent Random Method (ERM) von R. I. Wilkinson entsprechend, kann man die Parameter x und a′ eines virtuellen Gesamtbündels der Kapazität x+n′ mit dem Angebot a′ der Spitzigkeit 1 bestimmen, so daß n′ $\geq$ n* aus x+n′ = IE1[E1(x, a′)p*, a′] folgt. E1(x, a′)p* definiert dabei die Blockierung des virtuellen Poisson-Angebotes a′ am Bündel x+n′ und n′-n* den Spitzigkeitszuschlag, [WIL 70]. Im Punkt Min{n′} = n** gilt dann z = z**.

Die optimierende Kapazitätszuweisung erfolgt unter der Nebenbedingung

$$EEB(M, p) = GOS = \text{const.} \tag{5a}$$

Weiterhin gilt noch für den erfolgreichen Verkehr jedes Verkehrspaares nach Bild 1(c)

$$y = A(1 - GOS) \text{ in Erl carried.} \tag{5b}$$

Dann folgt für die normierte Kapazität unmittelbar

$$[n (p, a)/y] = IE1[p, a(A, p, GOS)]/A(1-GOS) \tag{6}$$

in Trunks per Erlang carried als zu optimierender Kostenwert des Netzes. Da die Restriktion (5a) in Gl. (3d), (5b) und (6) eingesetzt wird, formuliert Gl. (6) mit a(A, p, GOS) aus Gl. (3d) ein unbeschränktes, nichtlineares Optimierungsproblem in der Variablen p mit einer nachträglichen eindeutigen Festlegung von M aus p und GOS gemäß Gl. (2) bzw. (5a). Unter Berücksichtigung der nachzuschaltenden Durchsatzoptimierung führt jedoch ein einheitlicher Bezug auf M zu durchgängigen Vergleichsmöglichkeiten. Man beachte, daß Gl. (6) sogar eine explizite Lösung für p* impliziert, wenn IE1 nach p und a(A, p, GOS) in Form einer Reihenentwicklung vorliegt. Dies ist nach [WIL 70] tatsächlich möglich, und n(p, a) erweist sich als eine konvexe Funktion über p.

Für die angestrebten weiten Linkblockierungs- und Angebotsbereiche wurde jedoch eine genaue algorithmische Enumeration der IE1[p, a] gewählt. Das so implementierte CAMO-Verfahren beinhaltet dann in Anlehnung an **Bild 2** die folgenden Lösungsschritte:

1. Ermittle den interessierenden Bereich der Systemvariablen $p \in (p_{min}, p_{max})$ aus
   $EEB(0, p_{min}) = GOS$ und $EEB(10, p_{max}) = GOS$,

2. Suche das Minimum der Zielfunktion nach Gl. (6) über p bei mitlaufendem a gemäß
   Gl. (3d), z. B. mit Hilfe des Fibonacci-Suchverfahrens, [BAZ 79]. Hierfür gelte $p =$
   p^* und $Min\{n/y\} = [n(p^*, a^*)/y] = n^*/y$,

3. Ermittle den optimalen Wegefächerumfang $M = M^*$ aus Gl. (2) mit Gl. (5a).

Die folgenden Schritte beinhalten die präzisierende Ermittlung von Spitzigkeitszuschlägen
der Größenordnung einiger Prozent:

4.1. Berechne die Spitzigkeit z in der Umgebung von n^*, a^* und p^* nach den
   Gleichungen (4a) und (4b) sowie die neuen Linkkapazitäten n' nach der ERM.

4.2. Wiederhole die Schritte 2. und 3. für n' mit $Min\{n'/y\}=n^{**}/y$ und $M'= M^*$.

Bild 2 veranschaulicht den Verlauf von
n/y für A=100 Erl. und desweiteren
sowohl den auf A normierten totalen
und ersten Angebotssüberlauf $(a/A-1)=$
$= 2(p-GOS)/(1-p)$ bzw. $2p(1-p)$ nebst
$p(M, GOS)$ für GOS=0,001 als Funktion von M. Da bei Mittelwert-Refe-
renznetzen auch kontinuierliche M-
Werte existieren, werden die Kurven-
punkte unter einführender Vernachlässigung präzisierender Stützwerte verbunden. Für M=2 resultiert als ´Eco-
nomic High Linkblocking (EHLB)´
p^*=6,4% und das Kapzitätsminimum
von n^*/y = 1,15 Trunks pro Erl carried.
Daher werden in diesem Optimum
beim vorgenannten GOS = 0,1% $y/n^*=$
0,87 Erl/Trunk erfolgreich transportiert
oder n^*/y = 1,15 Trunks/Erl benötigt.

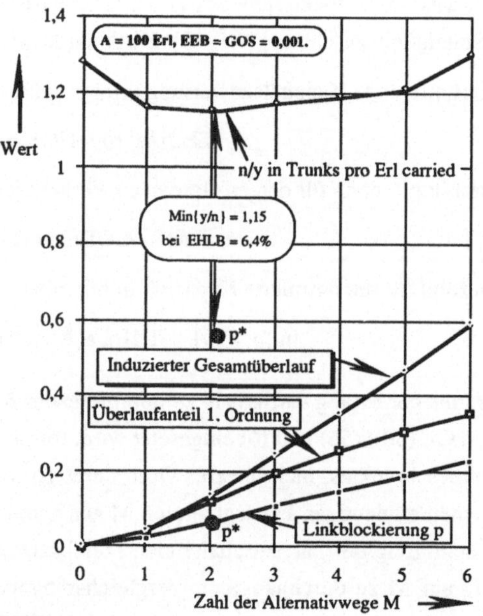

Bild 2.
Normierte Kosten, induzierte Verkehrsüberläufe und Linkblockierungen als Funktion der Alternativwegezahl M.

Der Serien-Parallelgraph aller OD-Paare des Netzes ermöglicht bei GOS-Vorgabe mit zu-
nehmenden Wegefächerumfang M wachsende Linkblockierungen p. Zugleich steigt aber das
fiktive Verkehrsangebot a. Daher resultiert aus dieser Gegenläufigkeit über die IE1-Relation
ein Minimum der normierten Kosten. Diejenige Blockierung, welche dieses Minimum definiert, heißt daher Economic High Link Blocking. Das Attribut "High" resultiert aus dem

Sachverhalt EHLB >> GOS. Die optimierende Zuweisung von n bei gegebenem A und GOS wird zur Verdeutlichung der Methode als Capacity Assignment with Mutual Overflow (CAMO) bezeichnet. Eine Verallgemeinerung des Bildes 2 für verschiedene Verkehrsangebote, jedoch gleichem Grade of Service erfolgt in **Bild 3**.

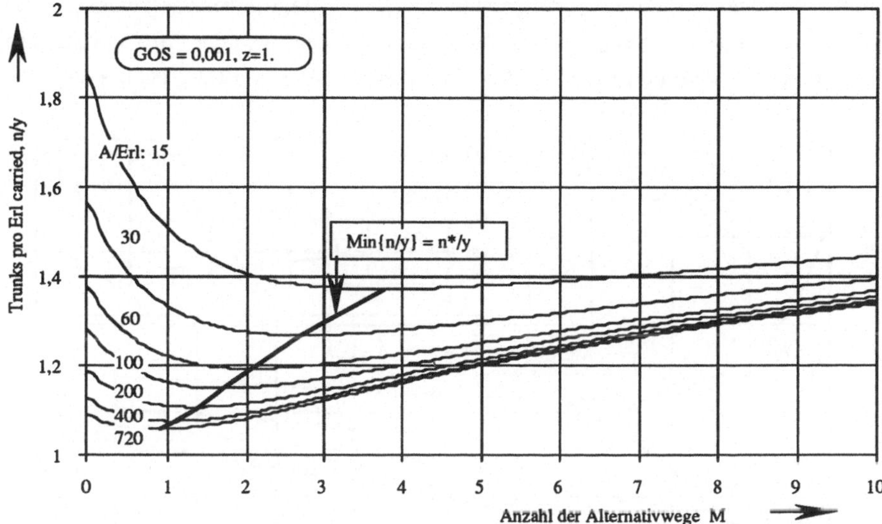

Bild 3. Normierter Kapazitätsbedarf als Funktion des Wegefächerumfanges bei unterschiedlich planerischen Verkehrsangeboten und vorgeschriebenem Grade of Service (GOS).

In jedem Falle beinhaltet $M = 0$ das ungesteuerte Netz oder eine volle Reservierung der Links zu Gunsten des Direktverkehrs. Die Kostenminima zeigen, daß insbesondere Netze mit relativ kleinen Angebotswerten infolge ihrer geringen Trunk-Effizienz von einem größeren Planwegefächer profitieren. Bei großen Angebotswerten und entsprechenden Bündelkapazitäten wird jedoch, vorbehaltlich der anschließenden Betrachtungen zur Durchsatzoptimierung bei außerplanerischen Lasten, die Optimierungswirkung des statischen Routings geringer, weil die Links über soviele Trunks verfügen, daß nur eine relativ geringe Aushilfe durch einen Alternativweg die Kostenminderung begünstigt. **Bild 4** veranschaulicht desweiteren den Verlauf von n^{**}, wenn die Spitzigkeit z^* näherungsweise berücksichtigt wird. Für $A = 60$ Erl. folgt z. B. aus Bild 3 $M^* = 2$ und aus Gl. (2) $p^* = 0,064$, so daß gemäß Gl. (3d) $a^* = 68,1$ Erl und mit $n^* = 71$, $z = 1,38$. Weiterhin resultiert aus Bild 4: $n^{**} \approx 1,22 \cdot 59,4 = 72,5$, so daß der Spitzigkeitszuschlag $n^{**}-n^* \approx 1,5$ Trunks beträgt. Ferner gilt in diesem neuen Arbeitspunkt $z^{**} \approx 1,33$.

Die minimalen Kapazitäten erhöhen sich im Prozentbereich und verschieben sich bei flachem Verlauf zu etwas kleineren M-Werten. Im oberen Fenster des Bildes werden z und die erforderlichen Trunkzuschläge pro Erl carried wiedergegeben. Erst diese Zuschläge sichern eine Bestätigung des GOS-Wertes durch Simulationen bei gegebenen Linkkapazitäten. Die zu n^{**} und den weiteren Parametern a^{**}, p^{**} gehörenden z^{**}-Werte liegen nun zwischen z**=1,34 bis 1,31. Schließlich kann Bild 4 der erzielbare Trunk- und Port-Gewinn (TG bzw. PG) gegenüber dem ungesteuerten Referenznetz gemäß

$$TG = \{[n(0) - n^{**}]/n(0)\} = \{2[n(0) - n^{**}]/2n(0)\} = PG \tag{7}$$

entnommen werden. Der absolute Portgewinn 2n(0)PG beträgt dabei das zweifache des Trunk-Gewinns, da jede Leitung zwei vermittlungsseitige Zugänge oder Ports umfaßt. Die vorgenannten Gewinne betragen z. B. für A = 100 Erlang mit M = 1,4: TG = PG = 8,3%.

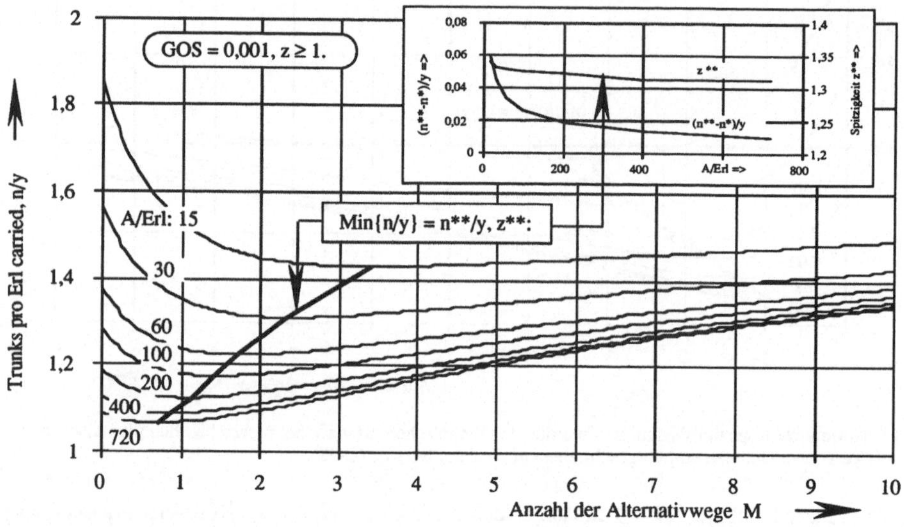

Bild 4. Normierter Kapazitätsbedarf als Funktion des Wegefächerumfanges bei unterschiedlich planerischen Verkehrsangeboten und vorgeschriebenem Grade of Service (GOS) für z** > 1.

3. Durchsatzoptimierung (Flow Assignment with Mutual Overflow-FAMO)

Zur Veranschaulichung des erzielbaren Durchsatzes werden wiederum Netze mit beliebiger Knotenzahl, jedoch n fest installierten Trunks pro Link betrachtet. Das netzweit koinzidente Verkehrsangebot betrage A/n in Erl offered pro Trunk für jedes Verkehrspaar und sei variabel. Auf jeder Link werden TR Kanäle für den direkten Verkehr reserviert, um diesen bei Hochlast nicht kostenträchtig auf Umwege abzudrängen. Rufankünfte, welche in den Zweitlinks der Alternativwege nicht vermittelt werden können, werden zurückgeholt (Crankback) und falls vorhanden, weiteren Alternativwegen angeboten. Beobachtet wird der erfolgreiche Durchsatz y/n in Erl carried pro Trunk in Abhängigkeit von der Zahl der Alternativwege M und bei festem TR. Für feste Werte von M und TR gelten nach R. S. Krupp, [KRU 82] grundlegende Relationen, welche im Unterschied zum CAMO zu einem Flow Assignment with Mutual Overflow (FAMO) führen.

Gegeben: Symmetrisches Netz, Trunkreservierung (TR), Crankback (CB). Verkehrsangebot A und Linkkapazität n pro doppelt gerichtetem Verkehrspaar.

Problemformulierung: Min {End to End Blocking} = Min {EEB} oder

$$\text{Max}\{y/n\} = \text{Max }\{\text{Erl carried/Trunk}\}.$$

Nebenbedingungen:

Feste Linkkapazitäten in Trunks pro Link sowie

Flußerhaltungsrelation für jede Link.

Für die Verteilung der Belegungszustände mit Trunk Reservation (TR) gegenüber induziertem Verkehrsüberlauf aus zunächst M Zweilink-Alternativwegen gilt z. B. nach [YUM 87] mit A = a(1-r) oder dem gesamten Verkehrsüberlauf ra = a - A die Verteilung

$$p_j = \begin{cases} \dfrac{a^j}{j!}\,p_0 & \text{für } 0 \le j \le n - TR \quad \text{sowie} \\[2ex] p_{n-TR}\,\dfrac{A^{j-(n-TR)}}{j(j-1)..(n-TR+1)} = \dfrac{a^j(1-r)^{j-(n-TR)}}{j!}\,p_0 & \text{für } n - TR < j \le n. \end{cases} \tag{8a}$$

Die Wahrscheinlichkeit p_0 dafür, daß das Abnehmerbündel frei ist, folgt aus der Normierungsrelation gemäß

$$\sum_{j=0}^{n} p_j = p_0\left(\sum_{j=0}^{n-TR} \frac{a^j}{j!} + \sum_{j=n-TR+1}^{n} \frac{a^j(1-r)^{j-(n-TR)}}{j!} \right) = 1. \tag{8b}$$

Desweiteren ist die Blockierungswahrscheinlichkeit für den Direktverkehr

$$\hat{p} \equiv p_n = \frac{a^n(1-r)^{TR}}{n!}\,p_0 \tag{9a}$$

und die Wahrscheinlichkeit dafür, daß der Überlaufverkehr nicht blockiert wird

$$\hat{q} = P\{J < n - TR\} = \sum_{j=0}^{n-TR-1} \frac{a^j}{j!}\,p_0 = 1 - \sum_{j=n-TR}^{n} p_j \le (1 - \hat{p}). \tag{9b}$$

Für die Knoten-und Linkflüsse gilt: "Interner Direkt- plus durchgelassener fiktiver Überlaufverkehr pro Link = angebotsbedingter direkter Fluß plus induzierter Überlauf aus allen Zweilink-Alternativwegen pro Link":

$$A(1-\hat{p}) + (a - A)\hat{q} = A(1-\hat{p}) + 2A\hat{p}[1 - EEB(\hat{p},\hat{q},M)\,/\,\hat{p}] \tag{10a}$$

oder

$$A = a\hat{q}\,/\,[\hat{q} + 2\hat{p} - 2EEB(\hat{p},\hat{q},M)]. \tag{10b}$$

Die neuen Zielfunktionen lauten nun

$$EEB(\hat{p},\ \hat{q},\ M) = \hat{p}\left(1-\hat{q}^2\right)^M \quad \text{bzw.} \tag{11a}$$

$$(y/n) = (A/n)\left[1 - EEB(\hat{p},\ \hat{q},\ M)\right], \tag{11b}$$

wobei gemäß Abschnitt 2 (CAMO) insbesondere n = n** sein kann, nun jedoch A z. B. vom Planungswert abweichen kann, so daß EEB ≠ GOS eintritt und die Problemformulierung gilt. Ferner trägt gemäß Gl. (8a) auf den reservierten Trunks nur noch A < a zur Zustandswahrscheinlichkeit bei, was die Blockierung des Direktverkehrs p_n und gleichzeitig die Spitzigkeit des Gesamtangebotes a mindert. Simulationen bei außerplanerischen Hochlasten zeigen, daß hierbei eine EEB-Überschneidung zu Berechnungen mit z = 1 auftritt. Zur Vereinfachung der folgenden Betrachtungen wird daher bei TR > 0 in guter Näherung mit z ≈ 1 gerechnet.

Bild 5 veranschaulicht den Verlauf des normierten erfolgreichen Verkehrsdurchsatzes y/n bei festen Linkkapazitäten n = 100 und TR = 4 als Funktion des normierten Verkehrsangebotes A/n in jeweils Erlang pro Trunk für verschiedene Wegefächergrößen M. Man erkennt, daß für die exemplarisch ausgewählten Wegefächergrößen M=0 (ungesteuertes Netz) bis M=14 unterschiedliche Bereiche maximalen Durchsatzes existieren. Der Eckpunkt in der Charakteristik M=14 signalisiert zugleich den Ansatz eines sichelförmigen Durchsatzeinbruches, welcher durch eine geringfügige Erhöhung der TR mit der Folge einer ausgeprägteren Verrundung des Durchsatzes eingeebnet werden könnte. Daher folgt nun die wichtige Adaptionsregel: Großer Wegefächer bei planerischer und kleiner Wegefächer bei hoher Last. Ferner gilt

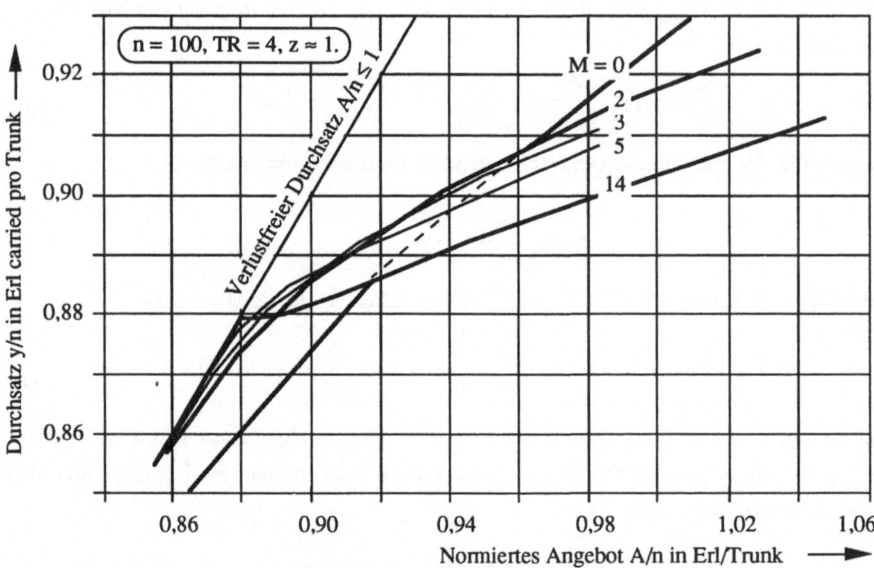

Bild 5. Normierter erfolgreicher Verkehrsdurchsatz als Funktion des normierten, außerplanerischen Verkehrsangebotes bei festen Kapazitäten incl. Reservierung und verschiedenen Werten M.

nach Gl. (11b) [(A - y)/A] = EEB und Bild 5 zeigt, daß die EEB eine konvexe Funktion über M ist. FAMO verwendet daher M als Systemvariable und beinhaltet die lastadaptierende Optimierung des wechselseitigen Überlaufs auf genau M** Zweilink-Alternativwege zu jedem Angebot A bei zunächst willkürlicher Reihenfolge der Wege, mit weiteren Rangzuweisungs-Möglichkeiten nach Abschnitt 5. Das algorithmisch implementierte FAMO-Verfahren umfaßt daher die folgenden Lösungsschritte:

1. Initialisiere mit einem definierten Wert M,
2. schätze einen Anfangswert von a für das gegebene Angebot A,
3. berechne die Blockierung des Direktverkehrs mit r = (a-A)/a gemäß Gl. (9a) und die Wahrscheinlichkeit $\hat{q}$ dafür, daß wenigstens ein Trunk der Alternativweg-Links frei ist nach Gl. (9b),
4. kalkuliere $EEB(\hat{p},\hat{q},M)$ gemäß Gl. (11) sowie A nach Gl. (10b) als A´,
5. variiere a und iteriere 3. bis 4. so, daß $|A-A´| \leq \Delta A$, z. B. mit $\Delta A \approx 0,1$ Erl.,
6. variiere M und wiederhole 2 bis 5, bis M=M** für Max{y/n, M} oder Min{EEB(M)} gefunden ist (FAMO).

Bild 6 verdeutlicht in Präzisierung des Bildes 5 als Optimierungsergebnis die minimale EEB als Funktion des normierten Angebotes mit unterschiedlichen Linkkapazitäten und Alternativwegzahlen M** als Parameter. Z. B. gilt für A/n = 0,88 Erl/Trunk und n = 100 Trunks/Link: Min{EEB}-> 0 (Steilabfall bei hier nicht wiedergegebener logarithmischer Darstellung von

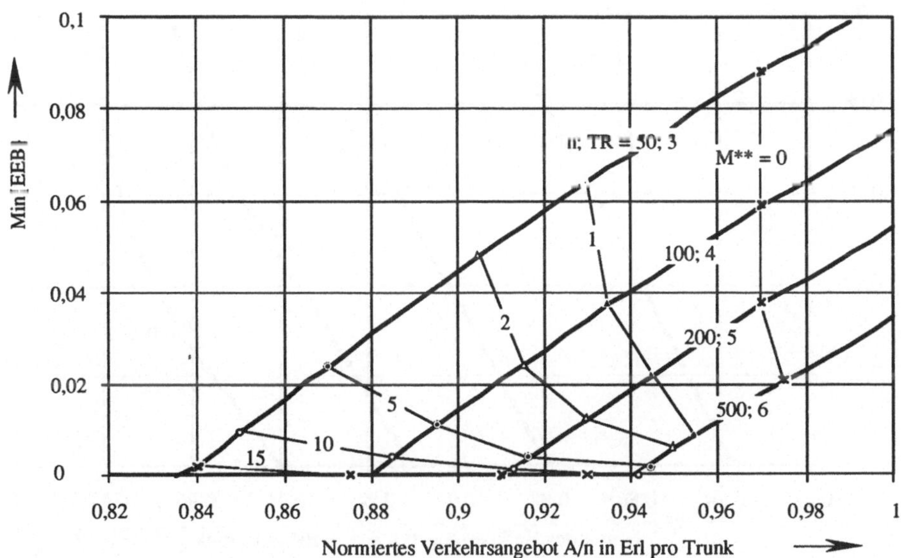

Bild 6. Minimale Ende zu Ende Blockierung als Funktion des außerplanerischen normierten Verkehrsangebotes bei verschiedenen Linkkapazitäten n und TR-Werten.

Min{EEB}) wenn M** ≈ 15 gewählt wird. Bei (A/n) = 0,92 Erl/Trunk gilt M** ≈ 2 für n ≈ 130 und 1 < M** < 15 für abweichende Linkkapazitäten. Schließlich folgt für A/n ≥ 0,97 ERL/Trunk Min{EEB} ≥ 8% ...9% mit M** ≈ 0.

4. Hochlastbedingte Anrufwiederholungen (Retries) und Route Processing Load

Bei den außerplanerischen Hochlasten nach Abschnitt 3 und 4 kehren erfahrungsgemäß ein großer Teil der erfolglosen Rufankünfte wieder. Bezeichnet nun R die Anzahl der 'Retries', so erzeugen diese ein zusätzliches Verkehrsangebot A'-A, wobei A' der Relation

$$A' = A \sum_{j=0}^{R} EEB^{j}(n, A') = A \frac{1 - EEB^{R+1}}{1 - EEB} \leq \frac{A}{1 - EEB} \tag{12a}$$

folgt. Die Obergrenze von A' oder Näherung für EEB << 1 und R ≥ 1 folgt dann der Gleichung

$$A' [1\text{-}EEB(n, A')] = A \tag{12b}$$

und liefert zugleich die neue 'Worst Case EEB with Retries'.

In Verbindung zum relevanten Bild 6 ermittelt man für ausgewählte Angebotswerte, die als A' bezeichnet seien, den neuen Wert A gemäß Gl. (12b) und trägt sodann EEB(n,A') über A auf. Hieraus resultiert dann die Darstellung nach **Bild 7**. Z. B. erreicht dann das Maximum der minimalen EEB für n = 50 breits bei A/n ≈ 0,892 den Wert 0,1, während ohne Retries nach Bild 6 A/n = 0,99 betragen könnte. Da im Wirkbetrieb R selbst eine Zufallsvariable mit

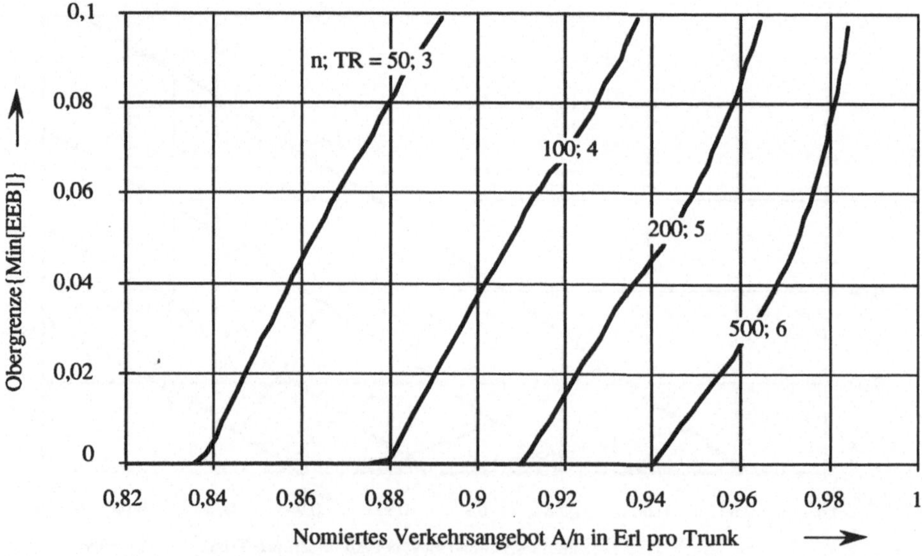

Bild 7. Obergrenzen der minimalen EEB bei blockierungsbedingten Retries.

signifikanten Wahrscheinlichkeiten bei R = 1...3 ist und äußerst seltene netzweite Hochlasten oberhalb 0,85 Erl/Trunk von zusätzlichen Abwehrmechanismen begleitet werden, liegen die wirklichen EEB-Werte deutlich unter ihren Obergrenzen. Trotzdem verdeutlichen die EEB-Erhöhungen, weshalb man unter Einbeziehung der vorausgesetzten Rufrückholungsmechanismen unter allen Umständen bemüht bleibt, die Netzblockierungen durch Crankback so klein wie möglich zu halten. Schließlich bindet jeder partielle Verbindungsaufbau bis zum Transfer im nichthierarchischen Netz vorlaufende Prozessorleistungen, die im Retry-Fall vom Netzbetreiber finanziert werden müssen.

Die Implementierbarkeit selbst eines einfachen Routing-Verfahrens mit wechselseitigem, blockierungsbedingtem Überlauf in weitere Alternativwege wird durch sein spezifisches Processing Load Ratio (PRLR) pro eingehendem Ruf, die benötigte Database pro Vermittlung sowie ggf. erforderlichen CCS-Transfers in Message Signalling Units pro Sekunde und allen Verkehrspaaren entscheidend bestimmt. Das PRLR definiert den erforderlichen Call- und Route-Processing-Aufwand in einer wie auch immer gewählten Maschinen-Umgebung (Soft- oder Hardware). Für symmetrische Netze kann das PRLR (unter Ausklammerung von Ziffernbewertungen, zustandsbedingte Entscheidungen etc.) verschiedener Routing Verfahren bei festem M nach G. Yum und M. Schwartz, [YUM 87] in Form der "expected number of attempted links" berechnet werden. Hiernach erfolgt zunächst der Belegungsversuch des Direktweges mit einer Processing Unit (U), die erste Link des ersten Alternativweges erfor-

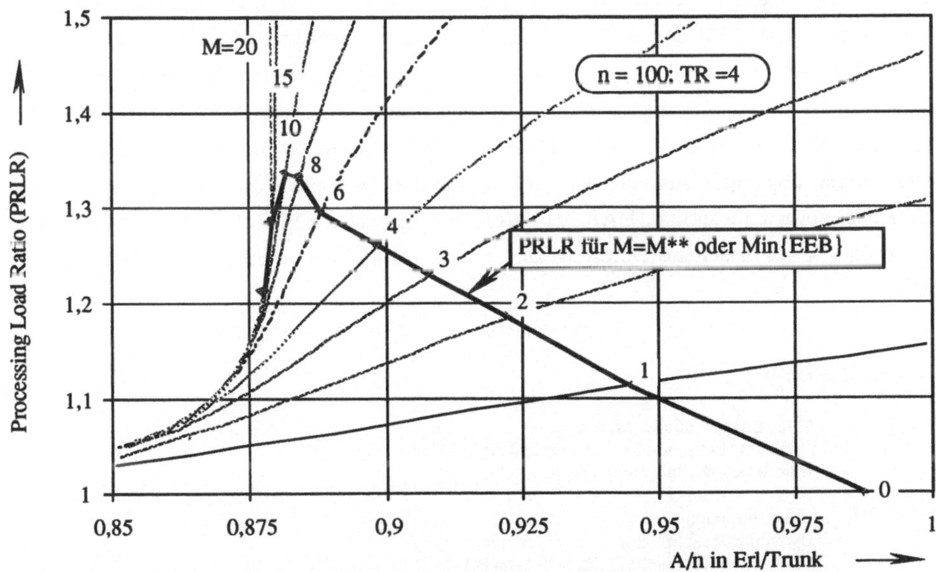

Bild 8. Processing Load Ratio ohne und mit Wegefächeroptimierung als Funktion des normierten Verkehrsangebotes bei exemplarisch fester Linkkapazität n und Trunkreservierung TR.

dert die Lasteinheiten $\hat{p}U$ und der erste Crankback der zweiten Link $\hat{q}\hat{p}U$. Der M-te Alternativweg wird abgesucht, wenn M-1 seqentielle Vorgänger-Wege blockiert waren und fordert daher den Arbeitsanteil $(1-\hat{q}^2)^{(M-1)}(\hat{p}+\hat{p}\hat{q})U$. Daher erhält man die auf U normierte Summe über alle Lasteinheiten zu

$$PRLR(M) = 1 + \hat{p}(1+\hat{q})\sum_{j=0}^{M-1}(1-\hat{q}^2)^j = 1 + \hat{p}(1+\hat{q})\frac{1-(1-\hat{q}^2)^M}{1-(1-\hat{q}^2)} \quad \text{oder}$$

$$PRLR(M) = \left\{1 + (1 + 1/\hat{q}) \left[\hat{p} - EEB(M)\right] / \hat{q}\right\} = 1 + RPRL. \tag{13}$$

Für die normierte Route Processing Load (RPRL) gilt daher einfach PRLR(M)-1. **Bild 8** zeigt, daß bei hoher Verkehrslast und insbesondere größeren Wegefächern indiskutable Prozessing-Lasten entstehen, wenn die optimierende Wegefächer-Adaption nicht berücksichtigt wird. Daher liegt der potentielle PRLR-Bereich innerhalb der zu M** gehörenden Grenzkurve, denn die RPPL mindert sich nach Maßgabe einer erfolgreichen Selektion vorrangiger Alternativwege.

5. Folgerungen

Symmetrische Netze mit nichthierarchischer Verkehrslenkung sind geschlossen modellierbar. Die entwickelten Zielfunktionen verdeutlichen den Einfluß der Verkehrs- und Netzparameter. Bei planerischer Last und strikter Vorgabe EEB = GOS = 0,1% liegt die wirtschaftliche Linkblockierung bei 5% und führt daher gegenüber ungesteuerten Netzen zur Einsparung von Trunks bzw. Ports der Größenordnung 10%. Bei außerplanerischen Lasten und zumindest semipermanent festen Kapazitäten des Wirkbetriebes minimiert ein adaptiver Wegefächerumfang die netzweite EEB und das RPRL. Weiterführende Arbeiten betreffen die erfolgsorientierte Reihenfolge der Alternativwege, so daß die RPRL unter der Nebenbedingung Min{EEB} = const. minimiert wird. Die zweckmäßige Rangfolge der Wege kann im getakteten Betrieb entweder aus der Anzahl durchgängig freier Kanäle oder vorlaufenden Erfolgserfahrungen abgeleitet werden. Man gelangt dann zu einem echtzeitigen, zustands- bzw. ereignisgesteuerten Routing, [HAR 91b]. Während sich dabei RPLR drastisch mindert, bleibt insbesondere der erzielbare Durchsatz davon unbetroffen, denn die EEB-Werte ändern sich nicht.

6. Quellenhinweise

[BAZ 79]   M. S. Bazaraa and C. M. Shetty
Nonlinear Programming: Theory and Algorithms
John Wiley & Sons 1979, 560 p.

[HAR 91a]   H. L. Hartmann
Dynamische nichthierarchische Verkehrslenkung.
Nachrichtentechnische Zeitschrift (ntz) Bd. 44 (1991), Heft 10, S. 724 - 732.

[HAR 91b]   H. L. Hartmann
Verfahren zur nichthierarchischen Verkehrslenkung in einem Kommunikationsnetz,
Patentanmeldung, Europäisches Patentamt Den Haag (Netherlands), 15.10.1991.

[KRU 82]   R. S. Krupp
Stabilization of Alternate Routing Networks.
ICC, Philadelphia, June 1982, pp. 31.2.1 - 31.2.5.

[WIL 70]   Roger I. Wilkinson
Nonrandom Traffic Curves and Tables.
Traffic Studies Center Bell Telephone Laboratories, 1970, pp. 1-211.

[YUM 87]   T.-K. G. Yum and M. Schwartz
Comparison of Routing Procedures for Circuit Switched Traffic in Non-hierarchical Networks.
IEEE Transaction on Communications, Vol. COM-35, No. 5, May 1987, pp. 535 - 544.

SPRACHÜBERTRAGUNG ÜBER ISPNs: MESSUNG UND MODELLIERUNG

Bernd Heinrichs, Raschid Karabek

Lehrstuhl für Informatik IV; RWTH Aachen
Ahornstr. 55, 52056 Aachen
Tel.: +241/80-21410; FAX: +241/80-21429
e-mail: heibelraschid@informatik.rwth-aachen.de

KURZFASSUNG

Zusätzlich zur klassischen Datenkommunikation müssen künftige paketvermittelnde Netze (ISPNs, Integrated Services Packet Networks) in der Lage sein, Audio- und Videodatenströme gemäß ihrer harten zeitlichen Anforderungen zu übertragen. Zur Entwicklung, Optimierung und Bewertung von ISPNs werden Simulationen eingesetzt. Ausschlaggebend für die Qualität der erzielten Ergebnisse sind realistische Lastgeneratoren für Audio-, Video- sowie herkömmliche Datenströme. Bisherige Audio-Lastgeneratoren basieren auf Untersuchungen aus dem Bereich der Telekommunikation, die sich nicht auf ISPNs übertragen lassen. Zur Modellierung von Sprachdatenströmen existieren zahlreiche Studien, die sich mit statistischen Analysen der Längen von Sprach- (Talkspurts) und Stillephasen (Silence) beschäftigen. Herkömmliche sprachaktivitäts-erkennende Systeme ermitteln diese Längen unter Verwendung relativ kurzer Analyseintervalle (5-10 ms). Die Talkspurt- und Silencelängen können dabei durch geometrische Verteilungen angenähert werden. Dieser Artikel beschäftigt sich mit der Modellierung von Sprachdatenströmen für die veränderten Gegebenheiten paketvermittelnder Netze. Dazu wurde ein experimentelles Sprachaktivitäts-Erkennungssystem, bestehend aus Digitalisierungshardware, Benutzeroberfläche und interruptgesteuerter Analyse erstellt. Die Ergebnisse zeigen, daß sich beim Übergang auf Pakete als kleinste Analyseintervalle völlig andere Verteilungen ergeben. Hierzu bieten wir einen Erklärungsansatz anhand von Korrelationsbetrachtungen. Dieser deckt eine statistische Abhängigkeit zwischen Talkspurt- und Silence-Längen insbesondere bei kurzen Analyseintervallen auf. Desweiteren wurden die während aktiver Sprachphasen auftretenden Stilleperioden zwischen Phrasen, Wörtern bzw. Silben in die Modellierung integriert.

1 MOTIVATION

Zukünftige Netzwerke müssen in der Lage sein, zusätzlich zum herkömmlichen Datenverkehr auch isochronen Verkehr wie Audio- und Videodatenströme effizient zu übertragen. Insbesondere müssen strikte zeitliche Schranken eingehalten werden. Mit der fortschreitenden Verbreitung von Hochgeschwindigkeitsnetzen und dem Einsatz geeigneter Protokollmechanismen (Reservierung, Multicasting etc.) wird die adäquate Unterstützung von Applikationen mit gehobenen Leistungs- und Funktionalitätsanforderungen möglich.

Für die Forschung und Entwicklung im Bereich Hardware, Algorithmen und Protokolle sind Simulationen unerläßlich. Die Güte der Ergebnisse solcher Simulationen ist in erster Linie von der Realitätsnähe der verwendeten Lastgeneratoren abhängig. Dieser Artikel beschäftigt sich mit der Erstellung eines Lastgenerators für Audiodatenströme in paketvermittlenden Netzen.

Teile der Arbeit wurden im Rahmen des von der Deutschen Forschungsgemeinschaft finanzierten Projektes "**PIKOM** - Parallelität in **Kom**munikationsprotokollen" durchgeführt.

2 SPRACHAKTIVITÄTSERKENNUNG IN TELEKOMMUNIKATIONS-SYSTEMEN

Bereits in den 50er Jahren hatten Telefongesellschaften die Idee, Stillephasen von Telefongesprächen zu nutzen. Bei einem normalen Telefongespräch benötigt jeder der beiden Teilnehmer seinen Kommunikationskanal zu weniger als der Hälfte der Zeit. Zusätzlich legt ein Teilnehmer, wie in Abb. 2.1 angedeutet, Pausen zwischen Phrasen, Wörtern oder gar einzelnen Silben ein.

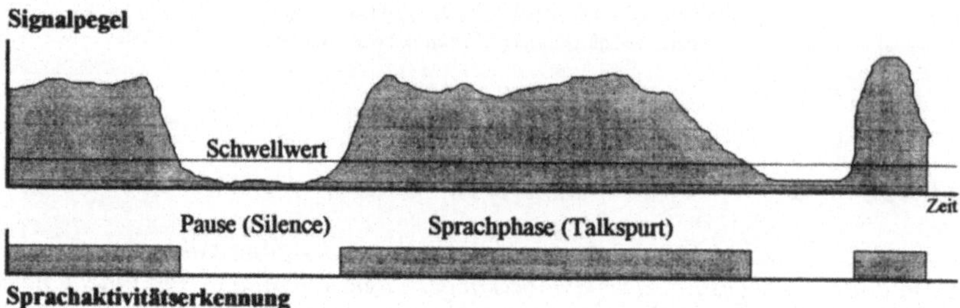

Abb. 2.1: Prinzip der Sprachaktivitätserkennung

Mit der Einführung digitaler Telekommunikationsnetze und zur optimalen Ausnutzung teurer physikalischer Verbindungen wie Tiefseekabel und Satellitenstrecken haben sprachaktivitätserkennende Systeme an Bedeutung gewonnen, da sie bei Einsatz von statistischem Multiplexen mehr Verbindungen zulassen als Kanäle vorhanden sind (TASI[1], DSI[2]).

Die sich bei der Sprachaktivitäts-Erkennung ergebenden Ein/Aus-Muster (Abb. 2.1) sind in vielen Studien analysiert worden. Beispielhaft seien hier die grundlegenden Arbeiten von Paul Brady [3,4,5] angeführt. Darin wurde ein sehr komplexes Sprachmodell entwickelt, das vielen nachfolgenden Arbeiten als Ausgangspunkt gedient hat. Brady ermittelte u.a. durchschnittliche Längen und Verteilungen von folgenden Sprachzuständen während Telefongesprächen:

- Talkspurt (Sprachphase eines Sprechers),
- Silence (Stillephase eines Sprechers),
- Double Talk (beide Teilnehmer sprechen gleichzeitig),
- Mutual Silence (keiner der beiden Teilnehmer spricht),
- Alternation Silence (Stillephase beim Wechseln von einem Sprecher zum anderen),
- etc.

Im folgenden Kapitel wird die Funktionsweise von Sprachaktivitäts-Erkennungssystemen erläutert und auf einige Schwierigkeiten bei der Übertragung der Ergebnisse auf Audio-Kommunikation in paketvermittelnden Systemen eingegangen.

3 VERFAHREN DER SPRACHAKTIVITÄTSERKENNUNG

Brady verwendete bei seinen Analysen ein analoges Spracherkennungssystem: Das Audiosignal wird gleichgerichtet und ungefiltert an einen Schwellwertschalter geleitet. Dieser wird gesetzt, wenn der Schwellwert überschritten wird. Der Zustand des Schalters wird alle 5 ms abgefragt, aufgezeichnet und anschließend zurückgesetzt. Die Schaltung liefert eine Folge von Nullen (*Silence*) und Einsen (*Talkspurts*), die den jeweiligen Aktivitätszustand des Sprachsignals beschreiben. Alle Talkspurts, die kürzer als 15 ms sind, werden ignoriert (nullgesetzt), um Impulsstörungen auszuschalten. Folgen von Nullen, die kürzer als 200 ms sind, werden durch Einsen ersetzt, um kurzzeitige Unterbrechungen zu eliminieren.

Bei modernen digitalen Telekommunikationssystemen mit Sprachaktivitätserkennung erfolgt die Unterscheidung von Stille, Hintergrundrauschen und Sprache in algorithmischer Form. Das analoge Signal wird gefiltert und digitalisiert. Der sich ergebende Strom von Abtastwerten (Samples) S wird in Intervalle (Frames) fester Länge k eingeteilt. Typischerweise liegt die Zeitdauer dieser Intervalle um 5 ms, was bei einer Abtastrate von 8 kHz und einer Auflösung von 8 Bits pro Abtastwert einer Intervall-Länge von k = 40 Bytes entspricht. Für jedes Intervall wird anhand verschiedener Kriterien ermittelt, ob es Sprache enthält oder nicht. Die meisten Verfahren nutzen dazu eines oder mehrere der folgenden Charakteristika:

- **Kurzzeit-Signalpegel** (Short-Time Signal Magnitude, Short-Time Signal Energy):

  Die Signalstärke (gemessene Spannung am Eingang des A/D-Wandlers) innerhalb eines Intervalls wird folgendermaßen ermittelt:

  $$a = \frac{1}{k} \sum_{j=1}^{k} | S_j | \qquad \text{mit Sj : j-ter Abtastwert im aktuellen Abtastintervall}$$

  Überschreitet **a** einen bestimmten Wert, wird das Intervall einem Talkspurt zugerechnet. Mit diesem Kriterium lassen sich stimmhafte Laute (Vokale, Nasale) zuverlässig erkennen, da sie einen hohen Signalpegel liefern. Zischlaute, die einen hohen Rauschanteil enthalten, werden jedoch durch die für die Digitalisierung unumgängliche Tiefpassfilterung zum Teil soweit abgesenkt, daß sie sich durch dieses Kriterium nicht zuverlässig vom Hintergrundrauschen unterscheiden lassen.

- **Variation des Kurzzeit-Signalpegels**:

  Da der Kurzzeit-Signalpegel von Sprachsignalen im Gegensatz zum Leitungsrauschen Schwankungen unterliegt, läßt sich die Pegeldifferenz jeweils aufeinanderfolgender Intervalle zur Detektion von Talkspurts heranziehen. Überschreitet diese Differenz einen gewissen Schwellwert, wird von einem Sprachsignal ausgegangen. Zu bedenken ist jedoch, daß auch kurze Störgeräuschspitzen zu Signalpegelschwankungen und somit zu einem unerwünschten Ansprechen des Systems führen.

- **Nulldurchgangsrate** (Zero-Crossing Rate):

  Bei diesem Verfahren wird die Anzahl von Nulldurchgängen des Signals innerhalb eines Intervalls gemessen. Die Nulldurchgangsrate ist für stimmhafte Laute niedrig. Stimmlose Sprachbestandteile enthalten jedoch hohe Frequenzanteile, so daß hier häufig Nulldurchgänge erwartet werden können. Etwas niedriger liegt die typische Nulldurchgangsrate des Leitungsrauschen [6]. Die Unterscheidung zwischen stimmlosen Lauten und Hintergrundrauschen ist jedoch von der Qualität der Audioelektronik und der Intensität und Färbung des Leitungsrauschens abhängig.

Da Audiosignale starke Pegel-Schwankungen aufweisen, sollten für auf Schwellwerten basierende Kriterien zwei Schwellwerte, ein oberer und ein unterer, definiert werden (s. Abb. 3.1).

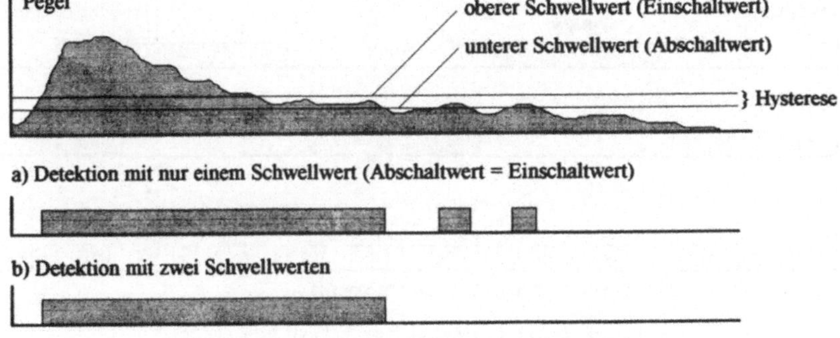

Abb. 3.1: Schwellwertschalter mit Hysterese

Der obere Schwellwert gibt dabei die Einschaltschwelle an, der um einen gewissen Betrag (Hysterese) unter diesem liegende untere Schwellwert die Ausschaltschwelle. Dieser Mechanismus verhindert bei Signalen, deren Pegel ständig im Bereich einer der beiden Schwellwerte liegt, ein mehrfaches Ansprechen ('Flattern'). Problematisch bei der Realisierung von zuverlässigen und effektiven Sprachaktivitäts-Erkennungssystemen ist die Bestimmung der einzelnen Schwellwerte. Sind sie zu niedrig, spricht das System zu häufig auf Störsignale an. Zu hohe Schwellwerte führen zur Verminderung der Sprachverständlichkeit. Insbesondere am Anfang und am Ende eines Talkspurts liegende Sprachanteile, die eine geringere Lautstärke aufweisen, werden abgeschnitten (Front-End-/Back-End-Clipping). Möglichkeiten zur Reduzierung dieser Effekte stellen neben der optimalen Wahl der Schwellwerte Fill-In- und Hangover-Verfahren dar. Beim Fill-In werden, wie in Abb. 3.2 angedeutet, Pausen, die eine bestimmte Länge unterschreiten, eliminiert. D.h. es werden für eine gewisse Zeit weitere Audio-Pakete übertragen, obwohl eine Pause erkannt wurde. Beim Hangover wird ebenfalls eine bestimmte Anzahl von Audio-Paketen übertragen.

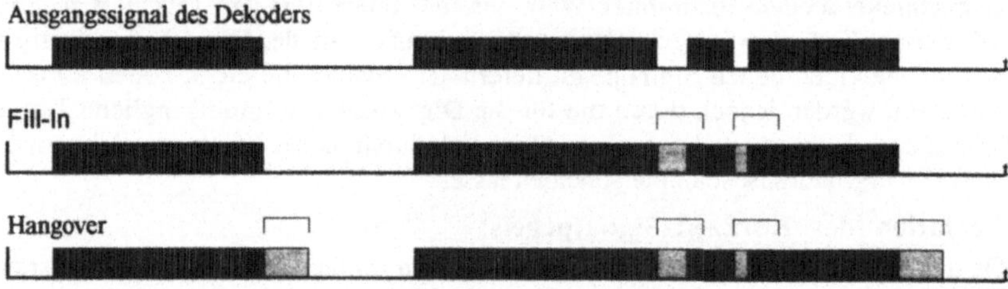

Abb. 3.2: Hangover und Fill-In

Fill-In läßt sich aufgrund des Realzeitcharakters telekommunikativer Anwendungen nur für sehr kurze Pausen einsetzen, da erst beim Beginn des nachfolgenden Talkspurts oder nach dem Verstreichen der Fill-In-Zeit entschieden werden kann, ob weitere Pakete übertragen werden sollen oder nicht. Dies bedingt eine Verzögerung der Ausgabe der Audiosignale auf den Kommunikationskanal, die bei Realzeitkommunikation nur sehr klein sein darf [7].

Bei modernen digitalen Kommunikationssystemen treten Störsignale, die zu einem unerwünschten Ansprechen des Sprach-Erkennungssystems führen, weitaus seltener auf als bei analogen Systemen. Dadurch lassen sich die Schwellwerte erheblich empfindlicher einstellen und somit Clipping-Effekte reduzieren. Dies ermöglicht eine drastische Senkung der Hangoverzeiten [6]. Dadurch bedingt treten allerdings vermehrt kurze Pausen zwischen Phrasen, Worten und Silben (z.B. bei Stoppkonsonanten oder stimmlosen Lauten) während der Sprachphase eines Sprechers auf (siehe Abb. 3.3).

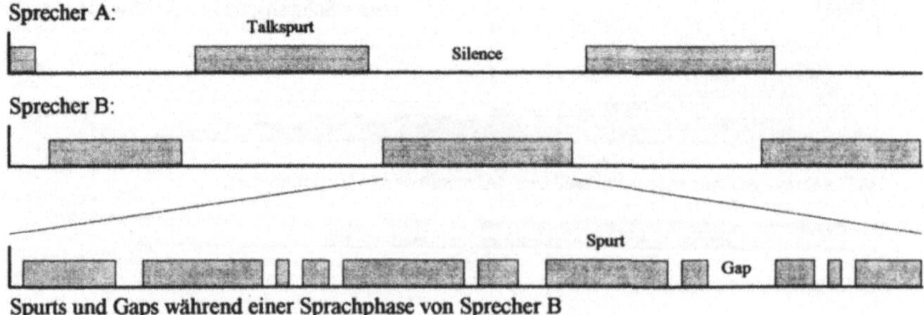

Abb. 3.3: Ein/Aus-Muster während Sprechphasen

4 Analyse und Modellierung von Ein/Aus-Mustern während Sprechphasen

Zur Modellierung von Sprachdatenströmen in modernen digitalen Kommunikationssystemen ist eine Modellierung des Verhaltens des Sprachaktivitäts-Erkennungssystems nötig. Für die Entwicklung entsprechender Lastgeneratoren ist die realistische Modellierung dieser Ein/Aus-Muster auch innerhalb von Sprachphasen aus verschiedenen Gründen wichtig:

- Die Längen von Sprech- und Zuhörphasen sind stark abhängig von der Gesprächssituation sowie der Anzahl der Teilnehmer. So ist bei Videokonferenz-Anwendungen pro Teilnehmer mit erheblich längeren Zuhörphasen zu rechnen als bei ausschließlicher Audiokommunikation. Bei der Modellierung und Bewertung von Kommunikationssystemen und deren Komponenten kommt es i.a. die Anzahl der aktiven Verbindungen an. Diese Anzahl läßt sich unter Verwendung von Angaben über die erwartete Teilnehmeranzahl pro Verbindung und die erwarteten Sprach- und Zuhörphasen unter Berücksichtigung der Ergebnisse von Brady ermitteln.

- Bei der Simulation von sehr komplexen Kommunikationsszenarien sind je nach zur Verfügung stehender Rechenleistung nur kurze Simulationszeiträume realisierbar. Liegt der simulierte Zeitraum in oder wenig oberhalb der Größenordnung einzelner Sprech- und Zuhörphasen, also im Bereich von Sekunden oder wenigen Minuten, ist es günstiger, insbesondere das Geschehen während Sprachphasen möglichst genau abzubilden.

Viele aus der Literatur bekannte Analysen lassen sich für die Modellierung von Ein/Aus-Mustern nicht heranziehen, da dort Sprachaktivitäts-Erkennungssysteme mit großen Fill-In- oder Hangover-Werten eingesetzt wurden. Studien, bei denen auf Hangover oder Fill-In völlig verzichtet wird, zeigen, daß die Längen von Talkspurts und Silences durch geometrische Verteilungen oder die Kombination zweier geometrischer Verteilungen angenähert werden können [7,8]. Danach hat die weitaus größte Anzahl von Talkspurts und Silences eine Länge von wenigen Analyse-Intervallen (z.B. 40 % aller Talkspurts sind kürzer als 50 ms [8]).

5 Sprachaktivitätserkennung in ISPNs

Seit Mitte der 70er Jahre ist mit Systemen zur Übertragung von Sprachdaten über Paketnetzen experimentiert worden. Paketvermittlung stellt ein leistungsfähiges Konzept für die effektive Verteilung von Netzressourcen dar, da die Gesamtübertragungsbandbreite dynamisch den Anwendungen mit unterschiedlichem und stark variierendem Bandbreitenbedarf zugeteilt wird. Andererseits entstehen durch die Paketisierung und Pufferung in Zwischenknoten Verzögerungen, die für Realzeit-Audioanwendungen einen gewissen Wert (400-600 ms [9,10]) nicht überschreiten dürfen. Um die Paketisierungsverzögerung gering zu halten, dürfen Audiopakete nicht zu groß sein. Zu kleine Pakete hingegen führen zu großem Overhead (Paket-Header etc., [13]). Realistisch sind Paketisierungsintervalle von 15-30 ms [10,11,12]. Im folgenden werden wir Pakete mit einer Länge von 30 ms betrachten, was bei einer Abtastrate von 8 kHz und einer Auflösung von 8 Bits pro Abtastwert (entsprechend CCITT G.711 PCM-Kodierung) 240 Bytes pro Paket ergibt. Beim Einsatz von ADPCM-Verfahren reduziert sich die Paketgröße auf 120 Bytes gemäß CCITT G.721 bzw. 90 Bytes nach CCITT G.713 (24 KBit/s).

Die Feststellung, daß die in Kapitel 3 beschriebenen Kriterien zur Sprachaktivitätserkennung nicht einfach auf die bei Paketnetzwerken größer gewordenen Betrachtungs-Intervalle übertragen werden können, soll hier anhand des Kriteriums 'Kurzzeitsignalpegel' kurz erläutert werden. Eine Berechnung des Signalpegels über den gesamten Paketisierungszeitraum von 30 ms erschwert eine günstige Festlegung der Schwellwerte. So würden zum Beispiel Audiosignale, wie sie in Abb. 5.1 a) und b) angedeutet sind, etwa denselben Wert a liefern, da in beiden Fällen der Pegel über das gesamte Paket-Intervall im Durchschnitt über dem Schwellwert liegt. D.h. sowohl für kurze Störimpulse, als auch für schwache Sprachsignale ergeben sich knapp über dem Schwellwert liegende Werte a.

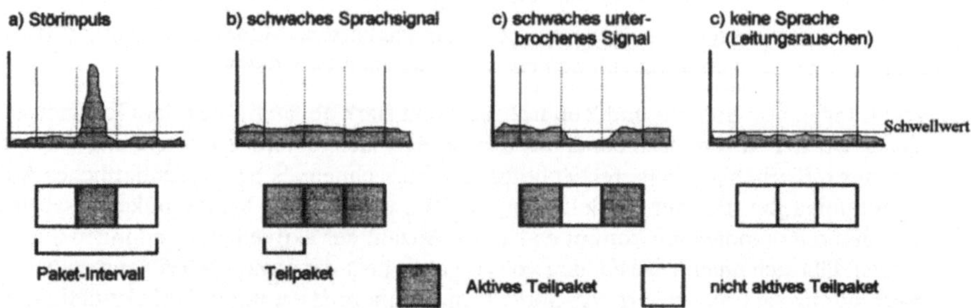

Abb. 5.1: Kritische Sprachsituationen

Es erweist sich daher als günstiger, das Paket-Intervall in mehrere (z.B. drei) Teilpakete aufzuteilen, für die unabhängig voneinander anhand obiger Kriterien entschieden wird, ob es sich bei ihnen um 'aktive' oder 'nicht aktive' Teilpakete handelt. Sind nun z.B. weniger als zwei von drei Teilpaketen 'aktiv', so kann von einem Störimpuls ausgegangen werden. Die untere Zeile in Abb. 5.1 zeigt grafisch, wie in a) und b) zwischen Störung und schwachem Sprachsignal unterschieden werden kann. Ähnlich verhält es sich bei kurzen Unterbrechungen innerhalb schwacher Sprachphasen, wie unter c) in Abb. 5.1 angedeutet. Wird hier der Kurzzeit-Signalpegel über das ganze Paket ermittelt, wird dieser sehr nah am entsprechenden Wert für knapp unterhalb des Schwellwertes liegende Störgeräusche (Rauschen etc.) liegen. Auch hier hilft die Unterteilung des Pakets in Teilpakete, wie in der zweiten Zeile grafisch verdeutlicht ist. Entsprechendes gilt für die anderen in Kapitel 3 angeführten Kriterien. Offensichtlich ist, daß bei obigem Verfahren alle kurzen Silence-Phasen (in der Größenordnung einer Teilpaketlänge) unberücksichtigt bleiben, was zu im Durchschnitt längeren Talkspurts führt.

6 VERSUCHSAUFBAU

Das verwendete Sprachmaterial wird unter Verwendung eines Rauschunterdrückungssystems (dbx) auf Tonband aufgezeichnet. Vor der Analog/Digital-Wandlung wird das Signal durch einen Tiefpassfilter mit einer Eckfrequenz von 3,4 kHz und einer Flankensteilheit von 24 db pro Oktave geleitet. Frequenzen unterhalb 100 Hz werden um etwa 6 db abgesenkt, um Brummstörungen zu vermeiden. Digitalisiert wird das Signal mit einem linearen 8 Bit-Wandler mit einer Abtastrate von 8 kHz. Grenzfrequenz der Filter, Abtastrate und Wandlereigenschaften entsprechen dabei prinzipiell der CCITT-Empfehlung G.711 für PCM-Kodierung des Stimmfrequenzbereichs. Der resultierende Audiodatenstrom wird in Teilpakete mit je 80 Bytes=10 ms unterteilt. Je drei aufeinanderfolgende Teilpakete werden zu einem Paket zusammengefaßt und mittels eines Interrupt-Handlers in Echtzeit analysiert. Für jedes Teilpaket wird der Kurzzeit-Signalpegel und die Nulldurchgangshäufigkeit ermittelt und in einem Datensatz gespeichert, so daß auch ohne erneute Digitalisierung Analysen mit verschiedenen Parametern (Schwellwerte, Teilpakete pro Paket, Teilpaketlänge, Hangover) durchgeführt werden können. Da die Analyse in Echzeit erfolgt, können Pakete, die zu Talkspurts gehören, über eine D/A-Wandlerstufe mit darauffolgendem Filter an eine Mithörschaltung ausgegeben werden. Daher ist eine subjektive Beurteilung der Qualität der Sprachaktivitätserkennung möglich. Da die Entscheidung, ob ein Paket zu einem Talkspurt gehört, erst nach der Analyse eines kompletten Pakets, also nach Bearbeitung des letzten Abtastwerts des Pakets gefällt werden kann, erfolgt die Ausgabe mit einer Verzögerung von 30 ms. Eine Blockdarstellung des Versuchsaufbaus zeigt Abb. 6.1.

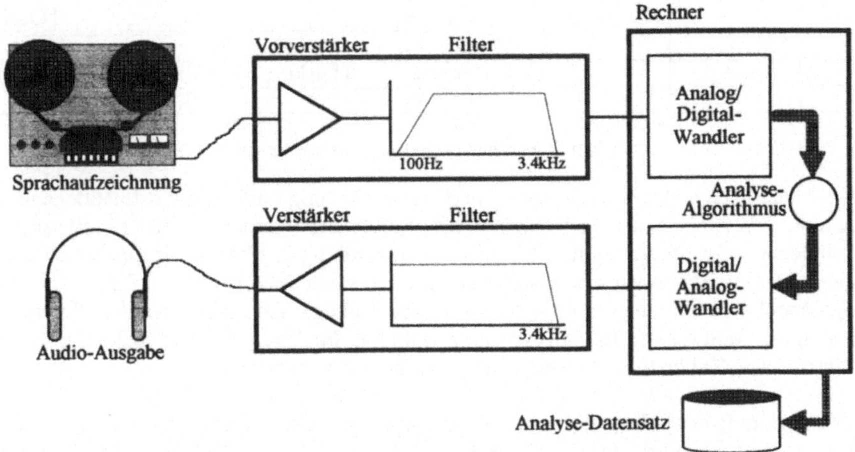

Abb. 6.1: Versuchsaufbau

Die Entscheidung, ob ein Paket zu einem Talkspurt gehört oder nicht, d.h. ob sich das System im Zustand TALKSPURT oder SILENCE befindet, erfolgte nach dem folgenden Algorithmus:

Wird im Zustand SILENCE bei zwei der drei Teilpakete der obere Signalpegel-Schwellwert oder der Schwellwert der Nulldurchgangshäufigkeit überschritten, wird in den Zustand TALKSPURT übergegangen. Werden in diesem Zustand die unteren Schwellwerte unterschritten, wird das System in den Zustand SILENCE zurückgesetzt. Wurde ein Hangover definiert, dann wird das System nach einem Talkspurt mit einer entsprechenden Verzögerung in den Zustand SILENCE zurückgesetzt.

Während der Messungen werden die Längen der einzelnen Talkspurts und Silences in zwei Tabellen erfaßt, die Aufschluß über die Häufigkeitsverteilung der Talkspurt- bzw. Silence-Längen geben. Zur Erfassung von Zusammenhängen zwischen Talkspurts und Silences bestimmter Längen werden die gemessenen Längen weiterhin in zwei zweidimensionalen Listen erfaßt. In diesen Listen wird während der Analyse die Anzahl der auf einen Talkspurt (bzw. eine Silence) mit bestimmter Länge folgenden Silence- (bzw. Talkspurt-) Längen eingetragen. So läßt sich anhand dieser Listen feststellen, wie häufig eine Silence-Phase der Länge x auf einen Talkspurt der Länge y folgt (s. Kap. 7). Weiterhin werden die folgenden Kennwerte erfaßt:

- **Sprachaktivität:** Das Verhältnis der Anzahl der zu Talkspurts bzw. zu Silences gehörenden Pakete wird erfaßt. Mit Hilfe dieses Kennwerts kann unter anderem die Auswirkung verschiedener Hangover-Werte verglichen werden.

- **Talkspurts pro Minute:** Mit wachsendem Hangover und steigender Empfindlichkeit der Sprachaktivitätserkennung (niedrige Schwellwerte) nimmt, da mehr und mehr kurze Silence-Phasen überbrückt werden, die Anzahl der Talkspurts ab.

- **Signalverluste durch Front-End- bzw. Back-End-Clipping:** Durch die Ermittlung der durchschnittlichen Pegelwerte der Teilpakete unmittelbar vor und nach einem Talkspurt lassen sich näherungsweise Aussagen über das Ausmaß von Clipping-Verlusten machen.

7. ERGEBNISSE

Als Ausgangsmaterial für die folgenden Experimente dienen drei Testserien mit den in Tabelle 7.1 angeführten Eigenschaften. Bei den Serien 1 und 3 waren alle Sprecher männlichen Geschlechts, während bei Serie 2 sowohl männliche als auch weibliche Sprecher aktive waren.

	Länge	# Sprecher	Sprache	Typ	Quelle
Serie 1	100 min	8	deutsch	Monolog, gelesen	1
Serie 2	45 min	5	deutsch	Diskussion, 5 Teilnehmer	2
Serie 3	47 min	5	englisch	Frei gesprochen, Dialoge	3

Tab. 7.1: Verwendetes Sprachmaterial

Dieses Material ist nicht als repräsentativ und allgemeingültig für Gesprächssituationen in Kommunikationssystemen anzusehen. Dazu wären weitaus umfangreichere Studien mit sehr vielen verschiedenen Sprechern, unterschiedlichen anwendungstypischen Gesprächssituationen, weitaus längeren Testserien sowie Serien in verschiedenen Sprachen nötig. Eine solche Studie würde jedoch den Umfang dieser Arbeit sprengen. Bei den hier durchgeführten Untersuchungen steht die Analyse von Ein/Aus-Mustern während *Sprachphasen* und nicht wie bei Brady das Sprech- und Zuhör-Verhalten einzelner Sprecher im Vordergrund.

Zur Verifizierung der in Kap. 6 gemachten Aussagen über die Reduzierung von Front-End- und Back-End-Clipping-Verlusten durch die Aufteilung der Pakete in Teilpakete wurden zunächst vier Testläufe mit der Testserie 1 durchgeführt. Die Länge der Pakete betrug dabei 30 ms und jedes Paket wurde in 3 Teilpakete der Länge 10 ms unterteilt. Beim Testlauf *A* mußten die Schwellenwerte in allen 3 Teilpaketen über- bzw. unterschritten werden, um in den Zustand *TALKSPURT* bzw. *SILENCE* überzugehen. Bei Testlauf *B* reichten dafür je zwei von drei Teilpaketen. In Testlauf *C* wurde bereits bei einem die Schwellenwerte überschreitenden Teilpaket in den Zustand *TALKSPURT* übergegangen, während für ein Zurücksetzen zu *SILENCE* in allen drei Teilpaketen der Schwellwert unterschritten werden mußte. In Testlauf *D* wurde auf eine Aufteilung in Teilpakete verzichtet. Tabelle 7.2 zeigt die Parameter und Ergebnisse der Testläufe. Die Clipping-Werte geben die durchschnittlichen Kurzzeit-Signalpegel (s. Kap 3.2) der jeweils vor Beginn eines Talkspurt befindlichen Teilpakete an. Die in der letzten Zeile angegebene Sprachaktivität stellt, da sie unmittelbar vom verwendeten Sprachmaterial abhängt, keinen absoluten Wert dar, sondern dient hier nur zum Vergleich der Effektivität der Sprachaktivitätserkennung.

Testlauf:	A	B	C	D
Parameter:				
Abtastwerte pro Paket	240	240	240	240
Teilpakete pro Paket	3	3	3	1
Kurzzeit-Sinalpegel				
unterer Schwellwert	2	2	2	2
oberer Schwellwert	4	4	4	4
Schwelle der Nulldurchgangsrate	28	28	28	84
Ergebnisse:				
Front-End-Clipping	9.91	4.09	1.75	1.85
Back-End-Clipping	1.72	2.48	1.72	1.78
mittlere Talkspurt-Länge	1016 ms	756 ms	979 ms	715 ms
mittlere Silence-Länge	218 ms	158 ms	175 ms	152 ms
Talkspurt-Rate (min^{-1})	39.1	59.8	41.5	65
Sprachaktivität	84 %	81 %	86 %	80 %

Tab. 7.2: Ergebnisse der Testläufe

Ein Vergleich der Ergebnisse der Testläufe zeigt, daß beim ersten Testlauf Back-End-Clipping zwar so weit unterdrückt werden konnte, daß auf Hangover nahezu vollständig verzichtet wer-

---

1 ARD, ZDF Presseschau
2 ARD Presseclub
3 CNN, SkyNews: aktuelle Berichterstattung und Gespräche mit Korrespondenten

den könnte, im Front-End-Bereich treten jedoch deutlich zu hohe Werte auf. Auch bei der subjektiven Beurteilung trat häufig zu Beginn von Talkspurts ein verspätetes Einschalten des Systems auf, so daß häufig Anfangsphasen von Silben und Worten abgeschnitten wurden. Dieses Verhalten ist bei der vorgenommen Parameterwahl auch zu erwarten: Das System geht nur dann in den Zustand *TALKSPURT* über, wenn für drei Teilpakete die entsprechenden Schwellwerte überschritten werden. Beginnt nun ein Talkspurt mit dem zweiten Teilpaket eines Pakets, so wird dieses Paket nicht als 'aktiv', erkannt. Dies bedeutet, daß bis zu 20 ms zu Beginn eines Talkspurts verstreichen, bis dieser vom System erkannt wird. Weiterhin fällt die im Vergleich zu den anderen Testläufen recht hohe Aktivität auf. Dies ist darauf zurückzuführen, daß nur wenn alle Teilpakete die Abschalt-Schwellwerte unterschreiten ein *TALKSPURT/SILENCE* - Zustandswechsel erfolgt. Leise Hintergrund- und Störgeräusche können somit das System auch dann im Zustand *TALKSPURT* halten, wenn keine Sprache übertragen wird. Dies erklärt die geringen *'Back-End-Clipping'*-Verluste sowie die außergewöhnlich hohe mittlere Talkspurt-Länge, die von zu einem Talkspurt verschmolzenen Talkspurt-Paaren herrührt. Auch bei Testlauf *B* waren *'Front-End-Clipping'*-Effekte zu beobachten, wenn auch in deutlich geringerem Ausmaß. Hinzu kamen geringe, aber in einigen Fällen deutlich hörbare *'Back-End-Clipping'*-Verluste. Die Sprachaktivität fiel bei diesem Testlauf relativ gering aus, da hier Pausen in Phasen erkannt wurden, die bei Testlauf *A* als durchgehender Talkspurt registriert wurden. Sehr gute Ergebnisse wurde beim dritten Testlauf beobachtet. Bei der subjektiven Beurteilung waren nahezu keine Clipping-Effekte hörbar. Auch dieses Verhalten ist bei genauer Betrachtung der gewählten Parameter zu erwarten: Das System geht bereits dann in den Zustand *TALKSPURT* über, wenn nur bei einem der drei Teilpakete die Schwellwerte überschritten werden. Ein Zustandswechsel nach *SILENCE* erfolgt jedoch nur dann, wenn wie bei Testlauf *A* alle Teilpakete die Voraussetzungen dafür erfüllen. Aufgrund dieser Übereinstimmung mit dem ersten Testlauf gelten auch hier dieselben Beobachtungen zur Aktivität und mittleren Talkspurt-Länge. Überraschend sind die Ergebnisse für Testlauf *D*. Hier wurde auf die Unterteilung in Teilpakete verzichtet. Es ergab sich der geringste Sprachaktivitätswert und die geringste durchschnittliche Talkspurt-Länge, obwohl die beiden Clipping-Kennwerte auf den ersten Blick in der Großenordnung der Werte von Testlauf *C* liegen. Diese Kennwerte geben jedoch den durchschnittlichen Kurzzeit-Signalpegel der **Teilpakete** unmittelbar vor Beginn von Talkspurts wieder! Ein direkter Vergleich der Werte ist nicht möglich. Trotzdem stellt dieses einfachere Verfahren bei störungsarmen Übertragungskanälen eine sehr gute Alternative zu den komplexeren, auf Teilpaketen basierenden Verfahren dar. Da auch bei der subjektiven Beurteilung des Verfahrens nur sehr selten Clipping-Verluste auftraten, wurde bei den folgenden Untersuchungen auf die Benutzung von Teilpaketen verzichtet und mit den Parametern von Testlauf *D* gearbeitet. Tab. 7.3 zeigt die Ergebnisse der Serien 1 bis 3, wobei die letzten beiden Zeilen die Parameter für die Approximation der Talkspurt-Längenverteilungen durch Lognormalverteilungen darstellen. Diese Verteilungen und ihre Approximationen sind in Abb. 7.1 bis Abb. 7.3 für die jeweiligen Serien dargestellt. Abb. 7.4 zeigt die entsprechenden Verteilungen der Silence-Längen.

	Serie 1	Serie 2	Serie 3
Front-End Clipping	1.85	1.98	1.79
Back-End Clipping	1.78	1.89	1.73
Aktivität	80 %	84 %	73 %
Anzahl der Talkspurts	3941	2794	5156
Talkspurt-Rate (min.$^{-1}$)	65	63	110
Mittlere Talkspurt-Länge	715 ms	715 ms	418 ms
Mittlere Silence-Länge	152 ms	125 ms	117 ms
Parameter σ	0.991	1.022	0.789
Parameter μ	2.675	2.677	2.191

Tabelle 7.3: Ergebnisse der verschiedenen Testserien

Auffällig ist die Übereinstimmung der Ergebnisse der Serien 1 und 2. Obwohl hier verschiedenste Gesprächssituationen vorlagen (Monologe vs. Diskussion) sind die mittleren Talkspurt-Längen identisch und es ergeben sich ähnliche Talkspurt-Raten. Eine sehr viel größere Rate und entsprechend kleinere mittlere Talkspurt-Länge weist Serie 3 auf. Inwieweit diese Unterschiede von der Sprache abhängen oder sprechertypisch sind, kann nur mit sehr umfangreichen Untersuchungen bei einem Vielfachen des hier eingesetzten Sprachmaterials geklärt werden.

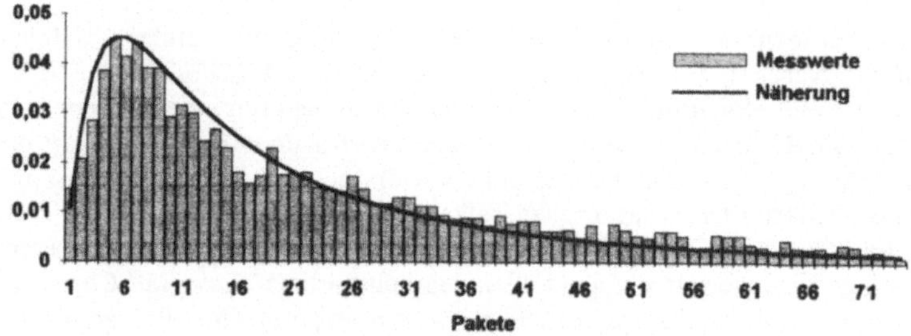

Abb. 7.1: Verteilung der Talkspurt-Längen für Serie 1

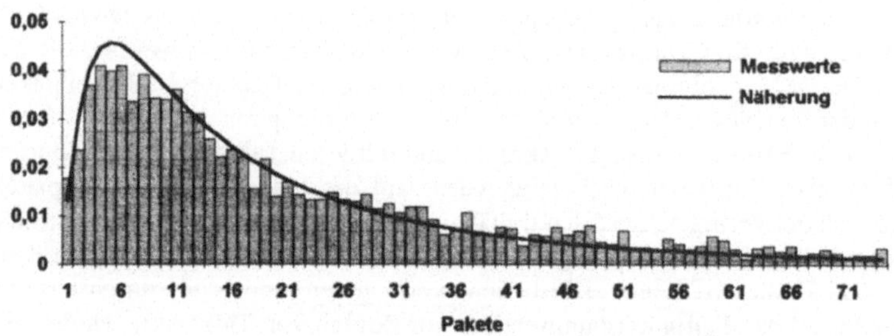

Abb. 7.2: Verteilung der Talkspurt-Längen für Serie 2

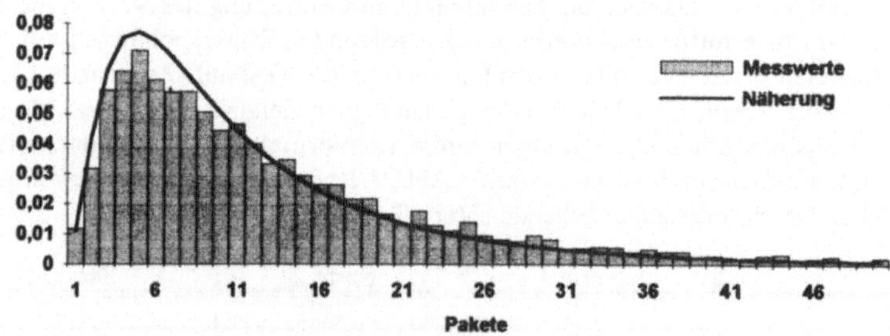

Abb. 7.3: Verteilung der Talkspurt-Längen für Serie 3

Es zeigt sich im Gegensatz zu früheren Untersuchungen, daß die Talkspurt-Längenverteilung besser durch eine Lognormalverteilung als durch (zusammengesetzte) geometrische Verteilungen annäherbar ist. Dies bedeutet, daß kurze Talkspurts, die bei früheren, auf kurzen Analyseintervallen basierenden Untersuchungen dominierten, hier weitaus seltener vorkommen. Dies kann nicht allein durch den Übergang auf größere Analyseintervall (Pakete) erklärt werden, da sich falls von der Unabhängigkeit des Vorkommens von Talkspurts und Silences ausgegangen wird, ebenfalls wieder eine Dominanz kurzer Talkspurts einstellen würde.

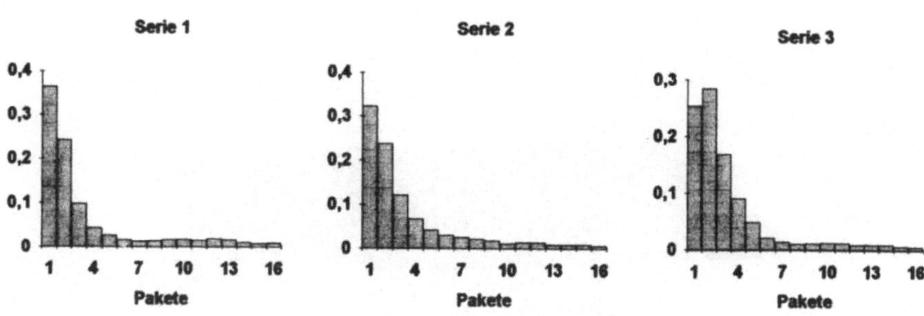

Abb. 7.4: Verteilung der Silence-Längen

Eine kritische Betrachtung der üblichen Modellierung von Talkspurt- und Silencelängen durch geometrische Verteilungen wirft die Frage auf, inwieweit die Dominanz kurzer Längen auf unerwünschte 'Flatter-Effekte' bei der Sprachaktivitätserkennung zurückzuführen sind, zumal offensichtlich sein dürfte, daß Talkspurts mit einer Länge der Größenordnung 5-10 ms kaum komplette phonetische Einheiten enthalten. Um dies zu prüfen, wurde ein Testlauf mit kurzen Paketlängen (1 Paket = 1 Teilpaket = 10 ms) durchgeführt und zusätzlich zu den Talkspurt- und Silence-Längen (wie oben erwähnt) auch aufeinanderfolgende Talkspurt/Silence und Silence/ Talkspurt-Längenpaare in zweidimensionalen Listen erfaßt. Die sich ergebenden zweidimensionalen Verteilungen wurden errechneten Längenpaar-Verteilungen gegenübergestellt, bei denen die gemessenen Verteilungen für Talkspurt- und Silence-Längen als Randfunktionen dienten und von Unabhängigkeit zwischen Talkspurt- und Silence-Längen ausgegangen wurde. Die Abb. 7.5 und 7.6 zeigen die gemessenen Verteilungen für Talkspurt/Silence- und Silence/Talkspurt-Längenpaare. Abb. 7.7 zeigt die errechnete Verteilung.

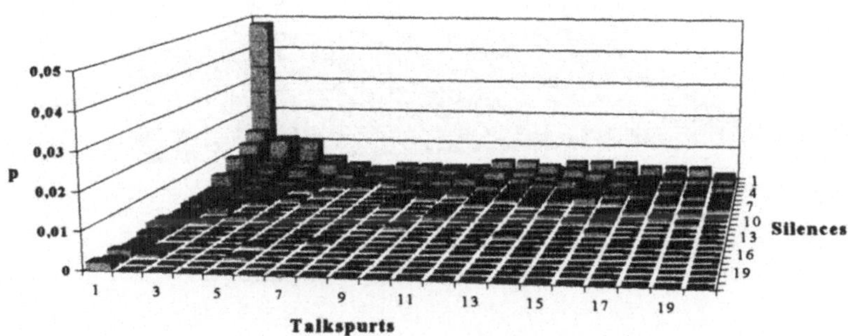

Abb. 7.5: Talkspurt/Silence-Längenpaare

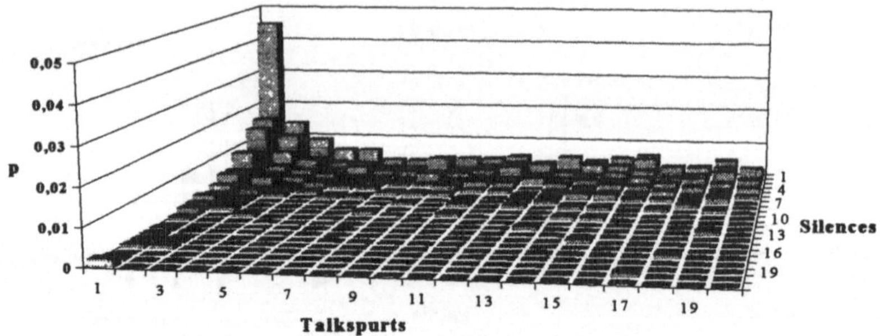

Abb. 7.6: Silence/Talkspurts-Längenpaare

Während die gemessene Paar-Verteilung in Abb.7.5 eine Wahrscheinlichkeit von 4,8 % für das Aufeinanderfolgen einer Silence der Länge 1 auf einen Talkspurt gleicher Länge angibt (bzw. 4,5 % im umgekehrten Falle, Abb.7.6), besitzen beide Kombinationen bei der Annahme der statistischen Unabhängigkeit (Abb.7.7) die weitaus niedrigere Wahrscheinlichkeit von 3.1 %. Diese Abweichung weist auf das Vorhandensein aufeinanderfolgender Talkspurts und Silences mit sehr kurzen Längen hin. Beim Übergang von Betrachtungsintervallen, die in der Größenordnung dieser kurzen Talkspurts und Silences liegen, auf größere Einheiten, werden diese Folgen zu wenigen Talkspurts zusammengeschmolzen, die ihrerseits nur noch von Pausen, die größer als eine Paketlänge sind, unterbrochen werden.

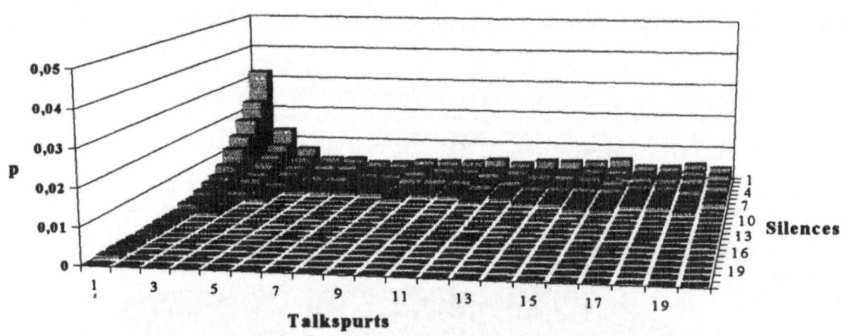

Abb. 7.7: Errechnete Längenpaare

7 ZUSAMMENFASSUNG UND AUSBLICK

In diesem Artikel wurden die Grundlagen für die Erstellung realistischer Lastgeneratoren für Audiodatenströme in paketvermittelnden Netzen herausgearbeitet. Solche Lastgeneratoren sind für die simulative Analyse multimedialer Realzeit-Anwendungen und Systemkomponenten in Paketnetzwerken unerläßlich. Desweiteren sind die Untersuchungsergebnisse für die Entwicklung von Strategien zur Ressourcenreservierung einsetzbar, da sich aus einer realistischen Modellierung von Sprachquellen Kriterien zur Zulassung bzw. Verweigerung von Verbindungsaufbauwünschen (Call-Blocking) herleiten lassen.

Zur Entwicklung eines statistischen Modells für die Talkspurt- und Stillephasen wurde ein experimenteller Sprachaktivitätserkennungs-Prototyp erstellt, mit dessen Hilfe statistische Daten über *Talkspurt-* und *Silence*-Längen erfaßt werden können. Weiterhin liefert das System Angaben über statistische Zusammenhänge zwischen *Talkspurts* und *Silences* bestimmter Längen. Zusätzlich wurde ein auf Teilpakete basierendes Verfahren zur Steigerung der Zuverlässigkeit der Sprachaktivitätserkennung vorgestellt.

Beim experimentellen Einsatz des Systems ergaben sich grundlegende Unterschiede zu ähnlichen Untersuchung im Telekommunikationsbereich. Die Gründe für diese Unterschiede wurden untersucht und erklärende Ansätze aufgezeigt. Mittels Korrelationsbetrachtungen wurde offengelegt, daß insbesondere bei den in Telekommunikationsanwendungen üblichen Analyseintervallen (in der Größenordnung von 5-10 ms) mit aufeinanderfolgenden kurzen Talkspurts und Silences zu rechnen ist. Dieser Effekt stellt die Hauptursache für die extremen Unterschiede der Verteilungen von Talkspurt- und Silence-Längen in den verschiedenen Szenarien (Telekommunikation/Leitungsvermittlung und Datenkommunikation/Paketvermittlung) dar. Weiterhin wurden die Auswirkungen verschiedener *Hangover*-Werte auf die Längen-Verteilungen untersucht. Dabei zeigte sich, daß für Testläufe mit *Hangover*-Werten die Länge des vorliegenden Audiomaterials nicht ausreicht. Daher werden Untersuchungen mit umfangreicherem Audiomaterials folgen.

In einer auf die Ergebnisse dieser Arbeit aufbauenden Studie werden wir einen Lastgenerator für Audioanwendungen entwickeln. In weitergehenden Arbeiten werden dann mit Hilfe dieses Generators verschiedene Komponenten von Paketnetzwerken auf ihre Eignung für multimediale Echtzeitanwendungen untersucht werden. Ein besonderes Augenmerk wird dabei auf die Bewertung verschiedener Bedienstrategien in Netzknoten liegen.

LITERATUR

[1] K. Bullington, J. M. Fraser: *'Engineering Aspects of TASI*, Bell System Technical Journal, Vol. 38, pp. 353-364, 1959

[2] E. Lyghounis, I. Poretti, G. Monti: *'Speech Interpolation in Digital Transmission Systems'*, IEEE Transactions on Communications, Vol. 22, No. 9, September 1974

[3] P. T. Brady: *'A Technique for Investigating On-Off Patterns of Speech'*, Bell System Technical Journal, Vol. 44, pp. 1-22, January 1965

[4] P. T. Brady: *'A Statistical Analysis of On-Off Patterns in 16 Conversations'*, Bell System Technical Journal, Vol. 47, pp. 73-91, 1968

[5] P. T. Brady: *'A Model for Generating On-Off Speech Patterns in Two-Way Conversations'*, Bell System Technical Journal, Vol. 48, pp. 2245-2472, 1969

[6] Y. Yatsuzuka: *'Highly Sensitive Speech Detector and High-Speed Voiceband Data Discriminator in DSI-ADPCM'*, IEEE Transactions on Communications, Vol. 30, No. 4, pp. 739-750, April 1982

[7] J. G. Gruber: *'A Comparison of Measures and Calculated Speech Temporal Parameters Relevant to Speech Activity Detection'* IEEE Transaction on Communications, Vol. 30, No.4, pp. 728-738, April 1982

[8] H. H. Lee, C. K. Un: *'A Study of On-Off Characteristics of Conversational Speech'*, IEEE Transactions on Communications, Vol. 34, No. 6, pp. 630-637, June 1986

[9] CCITT Recommendation G.114, *'Mean One-Way Propagation Time'*, Malaga-Torremolinos, Oktober 1984

[10] Thomas M. Chen, Jean Walrand, David G. Messerschmitt: *'Dynamic Priority Protocols for Packet Voice'*, IEEE Journal on Selected Areas in Communications, Vol. 7, Nr. 5, Juni 1989

[11] J. G. Gruber, L Strawczynski: *'Subjective Effects of Variable Delay and Speech Clipping in Dynamically Managed Voice Systems'*, IEEE Transactions on Communications, Vol. 33, pp. 801-808, August 1985

[12] D. Minoli: *'Optimal Packet Length for Packet Voice Communication'*, IEEE Transaction on Communication, Vol. 27, pp. 607-611, März 1979

[13] A.S. Dhillon, L.O. Barbosa: *'Study of multimedia variable bit rate video and audio sources over FDDI Networks'*, Proc. 2nd International Conference on Broadband Islands, Athens, Greece, June 15-16, 1993

XOR-Selective-Repeat : Ein neues effizientes Selective-Repeat-Verfahren für die Multicast-Kommunikation

M. Aghadavoodi Jolfaei, S.C. Martin, J. Mattfeldt*, U. Quernheim
Lehrstuhl für Informatik IV
RWTH Aachen
Ahornstraße 55 • W-5100 Aachen • Germany
Tel. +49 241 80 21413
* Institut für Statistik und Wirtschaftsmathematik
Tel. +49 241 80 4610
E-mail masoud@informatik.rwth-aachen.de

Kurzfassung

In diesem Beitrag untersuchen wir Selective-Repeat-ARQ-Fehlersicherungsverfahren für die Punkt-zu-Mehrpunkt-Kommunikation über eine Broadcast-Verbindung. Hierfür wird eine neue XOR-Strategie vorgeschlagen, die auf der Selective-Repeat-Strategie (SR-Strategie) basiert und zur Kapazitätssteigerung von Kommunikationskanälen dient. Die Idee der XOR-SR-Strategie beruht auf der Kombination von mehreren Blöcken, die von verschiedenen Empfängern negativ quittiert wurden, mittels der XOR-Verknüpfung (d.h. modulo-2-Addition). Hierdurch wird eine Reduzierung der Anzahl der Wiederholungen und Erhöhung des Durchsatzes erreicht. Wir vergleichen die XOR-Strategie mit der SR-Strategie analytisch bzgl. des Durchsatzes für die beiden Fälle, daß die Empfängerstationen über eine unbegrenzte oder eine begrenzte Pufferkapazität verfügen. Die analytischen Resultate zeigen, daß die XOR-Strategie bzgl. des Durchsatzes wesentlich bessere Ergebnisse erzielt als die normale SR-Strategie.

1. Einleitung

Bei der Broadcast-Kommunikation kann eine einfache Übertragung einer Sendestation gleichzeitig von verschiedenen Zielstationen empfangen werden. Beispiele hierfür sind Satellitenkanäle und Paket-Radio-Netzwerke.

Eine häufig benutzte Technik zur Behandlung von Übertragungsfehlern auf dem Data Link Layer in Datenkommunikationssystemen stellen die Automatic-Repeat-Request (ARQ) Fehlersicherungsverfahren dar, die durch eine Wiederholung fehlerhaft empfangener Blöcke eine hohe Zuverlässigkeit erreichen. Man unterscheidet folgende drei Klassen von ARQ-Verfahren: 1) Stop-and-Wait, 2) Go-Back-N und 3) Selective-Repeat .

Viele Arbeiten haben sich bereits mit der Analyse dieser Protokolle [BeF 64], [BrM 86], [BuS 72] und ihrer Varianten beschäftigt [Sas 75], [ToM 87], [YuL 81], [Wel 82]. Eine Grundidee dieser Varianten besteht aus dem Senden mehrerer Kopien eines Blocks anstelle einer einzigen Kopie.

Gopal und Jaffe [GoJ 84] haben drei verschiedene Go-Back-N ARQ-Schemata für die Punkt-zu-Mehrpunkt-Kommunikation vorgestellt. Wang und Silvester [WaS 88] analysierten eine Reihe verschiedener adaptiver Go-Back-N ARQ-Protokolle für die Punkt-zu-Mehrpunkt-Kommunikation. Weitere Untersuchungen wurden u.a. von Aghadavoodi [AgB 92] und Quernheim [Que 93] durchgeführt.

In Kapitel 2 diskutieren wir das Systemszenarium und die getroffenen Voraussetzungen. Eine Beschreibung der Protokolle enthält Kapitel 3. Einige XOR-Strategien werden in Kapitel 4 präsentiert. Das Selective Repeat Protokoll (SR) und das XOR-Selective-Repeat (XOR-SR) Protokoll für Punkt-zu-Mehrpunkt-Kommunikation werden in Kapitel 5 für eine unbeschränkte bzw. beschränkte Empfängerpufferkapazität, d.h. für den "idealen" bzw. "realen" Fall analysiert. Abschließend werden in Kapitel 6 die Verfahren anhand der analytischen Ergebnisse verglichen.

2. Das System-Szenario

Das zu betrachtende Szenario besteht aus einem Sender und K Empfängern. Die Kommunikation zwischen dem Sender und den Empfängern verläuft über einen Broadcastkanal, z.B. einen Satelliten- oder terrestrischen Funkkanal. Der Sender überträgt Nachrichten als Datenblöcke fester Länge, welche gleichzeitig von allen K Empfängern empfangen werden können. Die Zeit ist eingeteilt in Slots fester Länge, wobei die Slotdauer der Übertragungszeit eines (normalen) Datenblocks entspricht. Jeder Datenblock enthält redundante Informationen wie z. B. einen Cyclic Redundancy Check (CRC) zur Fehlerentdeckung durch den Empfänger. Ein Empfänger überprüft einen Datenblock zunächst auf Fehlerfreiheit und sendet auf einem Feedbackkanal entweder eine positive Quittung (ACK) zum Sender zurück, falls der Block erfolgreich dekodiert wurde, oder eine negative Quittung (NACK), falls die Dekodierung des Datenblocks mißlingt. Der Feedbackkanal wird als fehlerfrei vorausgesetzt. Wir nehmen außerdem einen saturierten Sender an. Wir setzen fest, daß die Time-Out-Periode dem Round-Trip-Delay (RTD) entspricht. Während eines Round-Trip-Delays können S Datenblöcke gesendet werden. Nach einem Round-Trip-Delay wird immer ein ACK oder NACK empfangen (bzw. tritt ein Time-Out ein). Die Datenblöcke werden fortlaufend numeriert.

Für die Fehlerprozesse einer Verbindung treffen wir die einfache Annahme, daß Bitfehler voneinander unabhängig auftreten (Burstfehler werden nicht betrachtet) [AgQ 92] und daß es zwei Arten von Fehlern gibt: Blockfehler auf dem Uplinkkanal mit der Wahrscheinlichkeit p_u bewirken, daß ein Datenblock von allen Empfängern fehlerhaft empfangen wird. Auf dem Downlinkkanal wird ein Block vom Empfänger l ($1 \leq l \leq K$) mit Wahrscheinlichkeit p_l fehlerhaft empfangen. Weiterhin nehmen wir an, daß die Downlink-Fehlerprozesse für alle Empfänger unabhängig voneinander sind.

3. Protokolle

Selective-Repeat-Retransmission-Strategie
Beim SR Protokoll überträgt der Sender fortlaufend Datenblöcke zu den Empfängern und behält von jedem übertragenen Block eine Kopie in seinem Sendepuffer, bis von allen Empfängern eine positive Quittung für diesen Block empfangen wurde.
Die Empfänger (siehe Abb. 1) überprüfen die Korrektheit jedes empfangenen Blocks, und jeder sendet entweder ein ACK oder ein NACK zum Sender. In Abb. 1 stellt ein ACK die positive Quittung aller Empfänger dar, während ein NACK bedeutet, daß mindestens einer der Empfänger eine negative Quittung übertragen hat. Nach einem Round-Trip-Delay kann der Sender überprüfen, ob alle Empfänger den Datenblock erfolgreich empfangen haben. Falls nicht, überträgt der Sender den Datenblock erneut.

XOR-Selective-Repeat-Retransmission-Strategie
Beim XOR-SR wiederholt der Sender negativ quittierte (NACKed) Blöcke nicht sofort nach Erhalt des NACKs, sondern sammelt XWindow-Anzahl von ACK/NACK Quittungen und entscheidet dann über die Wiederholung negativ quittierter Blöcke. Unser Ansatz besteht aus einer XOR-Verknüpfung verschiedener negativ quittierter Blöcke (d. h. Modulo-2-Addition),

um die Anzahl der zu wiederholenden Blöcke zu minimieren und den Durchsatz zu erhöhen. Der so entstehende Block heißt X-Block. Natürlich muß ein Empfänger, der einen bestimmten Block erwartet, in der Lage sein, diesen aus dem X-Block zu rekonstruieren, d. h. er muß alle anderen am X-Block beteiligten Blöcke kennen. Durch nochmaliges Anwenden der XOR-Operation auf den X-Block und alle daran beteiligten und korrekt empfangenen Blöcke erhält der Empfänger den erwarteten Block. Somit besteht die Hauptschwierigkeit dieser Strategie darin, soviele negativ quittierte Blöcke wie möglich zu einem X-Block zusammenzufassen und dabei sicherzustellen, daß jeder gewünschte Empfänger alle bis auf einen der beteiligten Blöcke kennt.

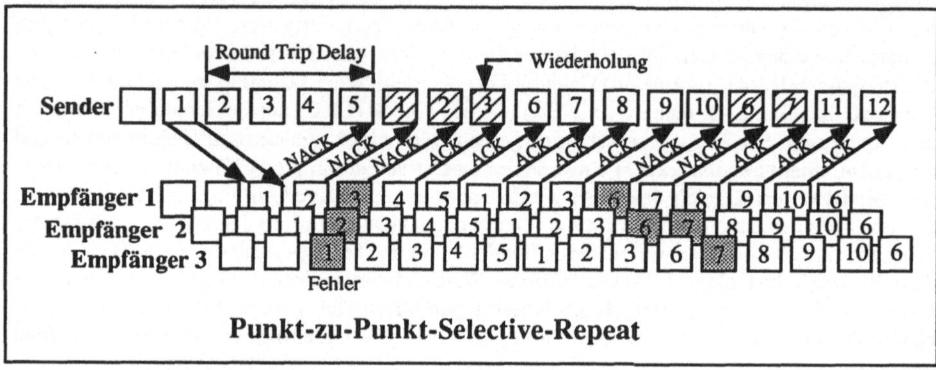

Abbildung 1: Punkt-zu-Punkt-Selective-Repeat-Strategie

Abb. 2 zeigt ein Beispiel für XOR-SR. Die Größe des XWindows beträgt 3 Datenblöcke. Der Sender addiert die negativ quittierten Blöcke 1, 2 und 3 durch Modula 2 Addition (XOR) zu einem X-Block und überträgt diesen X-Block anstelle der einzelnen Blöcke 1, 2 und 3.

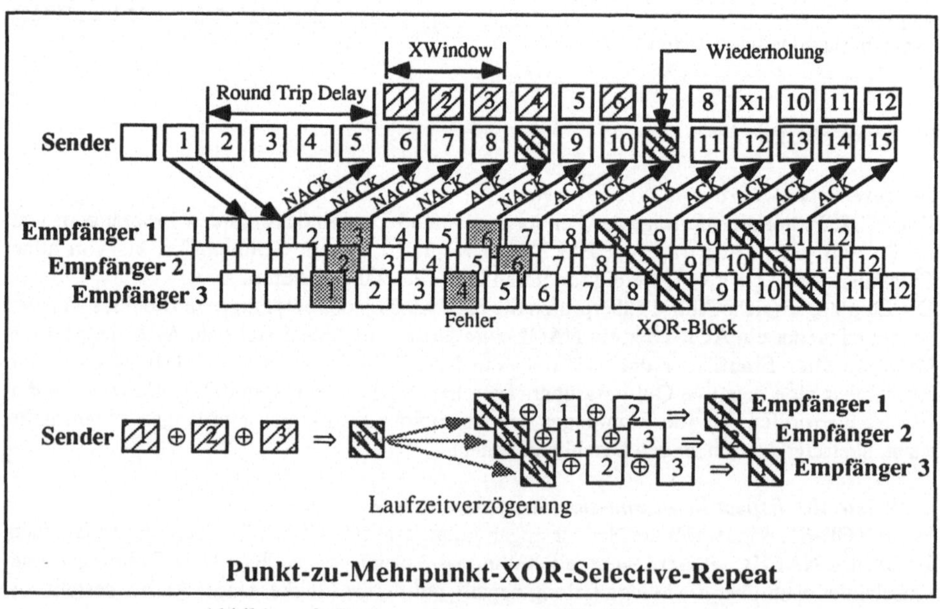

Abbildung 2: Punkt-zu-Mehrpunkt-XOR-SR-Strategie

Nach einem fehlerfreien Empfang des X-Blocks überprüft jeder Empfänger den Header des X-Blocks und bestimmt die Sequenznummern der am X-Block beteiligten Datenblöcke. Mit dieser Information kann der Empfänger den erwarteten Block in der oben beschriebenen Art aus dem X-Block zurückgewinnen. Z. B. ist es für Empfänger 1 Block 3, der durch Modulo-2-Addition aus dem X-Block und den Blöcken 1 und 2 extrahiert werden kann.

4. Die XOR Methode

Für die Analyse unserer Strategie müssen wir eine mathematische Beschreibung der von den verschiedenen Stationen angeforderten Blöcke festlegen. Dazu benutzen wir Fehlermatrizen, die nach XWindow-Quittungen erzeugt werden. Wenn das Matrixelement (i,j) gesetzt ist $(=1)$, bedeutet dies, daß Station i den Block mit der Nummer j fehlerhaft empfangen/quittiert hat, ansonsten ist das Element (i,j) mit Null besetzt. Wir interpretieren diese Matrix als Inzidenzmatrix eines Hypergraphen. Dadurch verbinden wir das Problem der Erzeugung von X-Blöcken aus einer gegebenen Fehlermatrix mit dem Kantenfärbungsproblem für Hypergraphen in der Graphentheorie. In diesem Zusammenhang werden wir Methoden für die Lösung des Kantenfärbungsproblems für Hypergraphen angeben, die zu Heuristiken für die Erzeugung von X-Blöcken führen.

Wir beginnen mit einigen Definitionen. Seien $V = \{v_1,...,v_K\}$ und $E = \{e_1,...,e_m\}$ mit $e_i \subseteq V$ und $i = 1,...,m$, endliche Mengen, dann wird das Tupel (V,E) als Hypergraph H bezeichnet [Ber 89]. Die Elemente aus V werden als Ecken und die Elemente aus E als Kanten aus H bezeichnet. H kann durch eine Inzidenzmatrix $J = (a_{ij})_{i=1,...,K, j=1,...,m}$ repräsentiert werden, wobei jedes Element aus J aus der Menge $\{0,1\}$ stammt. Hierbei stellen die Spalten aus J die Kanten und die Zeilen die Ecken aus H dar. Ferner gilt $a_{ij}=1$ bzw. $a_{ij}=0$ falls $v_i \in e_j$ und $v_i \notin e_j$. Zwei Kanten e und e' aus H werden als adjazent (benachbart) bezeichnet, wenn diese eine gemeinsame Ecke besitzen. Zwei Ecken $v \neq v'$ heißen adjazent, wenn beide Elemente einer Kante $e \in E$ sind. Der Grad $\Delta(v)$ einer Ecke wird wie folgt definiert:

(1) $\Delta(v) := |\{v'; v' \text{ adjazent zu } v\}|.$

Der Eckengrad von H wird als $\Delta(H) := \max_{v \in V} \Delta(v)$ definiert. Ferner bezeichnen wir mit

(2) $\Delta(e) := \sum_{v \in e} \Delta(v)$

den Kantengrad von $e \in E$. Der chromatische Index $\mathcal{X}(H)$ von H gibt die kleinste Anzahl von Farben an, die für die Färbung von H notwendig sind, und zwar derart, daß zwei benachbarte Kanten verschiedene Farben besitzen. Das Problem der Bestimmung des chromatischen Indexes eines Hypergraphen ist NP-vollständig [Ho 81]. Für einfache Graphen besagt ein Theorem von Vizing, daß $\mathcal{X}(G) \in \{\Delta(G), \Delta(G)+1\}$. Es ist möglich, eine Kantenfärbung mit $\Delta(G)+1$ Farben in $O(|V|^4)$ Schritten zu bestimmen. In allgemeinen Hypergraphen scheint solch ein effizienter Algorithmus nicht möglich zu sein. Bei Betrachtung der Farben als X-Blöcke stellt $\mathcal{X}(H)$ die optimale (d.h. kleinste) Anzahl von X-Blöcken für eine gegebene Fehlermatrix J dar. In unserem Fall ist das Problem der Minimierung der Anzahl von notwendigen Übertragungen mit Hilfe der XOR-Strategie also äquivalent zum Problem des Findens einer optimalen Kantenfärbung in einem Hypergraph H, der durch eine Fehlermatrix dargestellt wird. Dieses Problem ist NP-schwer. Zur Implementierung der XOR-Strategie betrachten wir Verfahren zur effektiven Bestimmung einer möglichst guten Kantenfärbung. Wir haben mehrere Heuristiken für die Lösung dieses Problems implementiert. Bei den folgenden Algorithmen zur Zuweisung von Farben zu den Kanten eines Hypergraphen werden die Farben mit natürlichen Zahlen identifiziert.

Input: Hypergraph $H=(V,E)$ mit $V = \{v_1,...,v_K\}$ und $E = \{e_1,...,e_m\}$.

Output: Kantenfärbung von H.

Algorithmus:

```
begin
        Weise Farbe1 e1 zu;
        col:=1;
        for i:=2 to m do
        begin
                Weise ei die kleinste mögliche Farbe c mit 1 ≤ c ≤ col+1 zu;
                if c = col+1 then col := col + 1;
        end;
end;
```

Bevor der obige Algorithmus angewendet werden kann, muß die Inputsequenz der Kanten bestimmt werden, d.h. die Indizierung der Elemente aus E. Die Indizierung ist entscheidend für die Effektivität des Algorithmus. Wir haben verschiedene Methoden zur Indizierung der Kanten aus H betrachtet; Beispiele hierfür sind:

Heuristik 1:   Degree

Bestimme eine Indizierung von E, welche die Bedingung $|e_1| \geq |e_2| \geq ... \geq |e_m|$ erfüllt.

Heuristik 2:   Random

Bestimme die Indizierung von E zufällig.

Weitere Heuristiken wurden in [AMM 93] vorgestellt und simulativ deren Leistungsfähigkeit bzgl. der mittleren Anzahl der kombinierten Basisblöcke in XOR-Blöcken und bzgl. der Bearbeitungszeit untersucht.

5. Durchsatzanalyse von XOR-Selective-Repeat

5.1 Unbeschränkte Empfängerpufferkapazität

Bei der Durchsatzanalyse des idealen Falls wird zur Vereinfachung der Analyse die Größe des Headers vernachlässigbar klein vorausgesetzt.

Für die Analyse des Durchsatzes beschreibt die Zufallsvariable (ZV) X_i, $i=1,...,K$ die Anzahl der Übertragungen für einen bestimmten Block bis zu seinem korrekten Empfang beim Empfänger i. Wenn wir annehmen, daß keine Uplink-Fehler auftreten und voraussetzen, daß in unserem Modell die ZV'en voneinander unabhängig sind, dann wird ein Block nach $X = \max_{1 \leq i \leq K} X_i$ Übertragungen von allen Empfängern korrekt bestätigt. Der Durchsatz ergibt sich dann nach üblicher Definition zu:

$$T = \frac{1}{E[X]} = \frac{1}{1 + \sum_{x=2}^{\infty} (x - 1)\, P(X = x)} \cdot \quad (I)$$

Dieser Ausdruck muß für die Analyse unserer XOR-Strategie verallgemeinert werden. Der Grund hierfür wird anhand des folgenden Beispiels für K=2 demonstriert (Tab. 1).
Jeder der Blöcke 1 und 2 benötigt zwei Übertragungen, aber insgesamt sind nur drei statt vier Übertragungen notwendig. Um diese mehrfachen Zählungen zu verhindern, muß eine gewichtete Zählung für die Übertragung von XOR-Blöcken einführt werden.

Übertragungen	1.	2.	3.
Blocknummer	1	2	1 XOR 2
Station 1	1	0	0
ACK/NACK			
Station 2	0	1	0

Tab. 1) Blockkorrektur-Möglichkeiten durch XOR-Block

Deshalb weisen wir der ZV X die ZV'en $(Y_{ix-1})_{1\leq i\leq x-1, x-1\in N}$ zu. Y_{ix-1} beschreibt die Anzahl der XORten Blöcke in der i-ten Wiederholung des betrachteten Blocks, wobei x die Anzahl der Übertragungen angibt, die für den korrekten Empfang dieses Blocks bei allen K Stationen notwendig sind. Wenn beim obigen Beispiel X den ersten Block beschreibt, dann ist $Y_{11}=2$, weil bei der ersten Wiederholung von Block 1 zwei Blöcke im X-Block mittels XOR-Verknüpfung zusammengefaßt wurden. Im verallgemeinerten Fall ergibt sich für den Durchsatz:

$$T = \frac{1}{1 + \sum_{x=2}^{\infty} \left(\sum_{i=1}^{x-1} \frac{1}{E[Y_{i\,x-1}]} \right) P(X = x)} \cdot \qquad \text{(II)}$$

Offensichtlich gilt bei üblichen SR-Verfahren $E[Y_{ix}] = 1$ für alle i,x, also:

$$\sum_{i=1}^{x-1} \frac{1}{E[Y_{i\,x-1}]} = x - 1 .$$

Die Beziehung (I) stellt einen Spezialfall der obigen Formel (II) dar. Bei Verwendung des XOR-SR-Verfahrens gilt $E[Y_{ix}] \geq 1$. Wir analysieren nun den Durchsatz der XOR-Strategie und vergleichen diese mit der SR-Strategie.

SR:
Aus der Literatur ([GoJ 84], [Dav 70]) ist bekannt:

$$E[X] = \sum_{x=1}^{\infty} x\, P(X = x) = \sum_{x=0}^{\infty} (1 - P(X \leq x)) = 1 + \sum_{x=1}^{\infty} (1 - \prod_{i=1}^{K} (1 - p_i^x))$$

Mit der Uplink-Blockfehlerwahrscheinlichkeit p_u und der Downlink-Blockfehlerwahrschein-lichkeit p_i für Station i gilt [AMM 93]:

$$T_{SR} = \frac{1 - p_u}{1 + \sum_{x=1}^{\infty} (1 - \prod_{i=1}^{K} (1 - p_i^x))} \cdot$$

XOR:

Es scheint keinen allgemeinen Weg zur Bestimmung von $E[Y_{ix}]$ zu geben, da dieser Wert stark von der verwendeten Heuristik abhängt. Deshalb nehmen wir für eine erste Analyse $E[Y_{ix}] = M \geq 1$ (unabhängig von i,x) an, falls der übertragene Block ein XOR-Block ist, dann erhält man (p_u = Uplink- und p_i = Blockfehlerwahrscheinlichkeit)[AMM 93]:

$$E[X] = \frac{1}{1-p_u}\left(1 + \frac{1}{M}\sum_{x=1}^{\infty}(1 - \prod_{i=1}^{K}(1 - p_i^x))\right)$$

daher

$$T_{XOR} = \frac{1 - p_u}{1 + \frac{1}{M}\sum_{x=1}^{\infty}(1 - \prod_{i=1}^{K}(1 - p_i^x))}\,.$$

Man beachte, daß M eine Funktion von den Blockfehlerwahrscheinlichkeiten p_i und der Empfängeranzahl K ist. Da stets $E[Y_{ix}] \leq K$ gilt, erhalten wir somit

$$T_{XOR} \leq \frac{1 - p_u}{1 + \frac{1}{K}\sum_{x=1}^{\infty}(1 - \prod_{i=1}^{K}(1 - p_i^x))}\,,$$

als obere Schranke für den Durchsatz im XOR-Fall.
Hierbei ist die größere Blockfehlerwahrscheinlichkeit eines XOR-Blockes noch nicht berücksichtigt, vgl. Kapitel 5.2.

5.2 Beschränkte Empfängerpufferkapazität

Wir verallgemeinern den Ansatz von Weldon [Wel 82] für die Point-to-Point Kommunikation auf die Multicast-Kommunikation.
Jeder Empfänger besitze einen Empfängerpuffer für L*S Blöcke. Hierbei bezeichne S die Anzahl der Blöcke, die innerhalb eines Round-Trip-Delays (RTD) übertragen werden können. Im folgenden nehmen wir $p_u = 0$ an, und die Wahrscheinlichkeit p_i seien gleich für alle i ($1 \leq i \leq K$). Blockfehler seien unabhängig voneinander.
Bei der Analyse wird davon ausgegangen, daß am Anfang alle Empfängerpuffer leer sind und die erste Übermittlung eines Blockes mit der Wahrscheinlichkeit $P(X=1) = (1-p)^K$ erfolgreich ist. Falls bei dieser Übertragung ein Fehler auftritt, wird der Block wiederholt übertragen, und alle darauffolgende Blöcke können bei korrekter Wiederholung in den Empfängerpuffer gerettet werden. Benötigt der Block nun mehr als L+1 Wiederholungen bis zu seinem korrekten Empfang, so führt dies ab der L+1-ten Übertragung zu einem Pufferüberlauf. Dadurch müssen jeweils S Blöcke zusätzlich wiederholt werden. Diese Annahme ist jedoch pessimistisch: Der maximale Wert von S verlorengegangenen Blöcken wird nur dann erreicht, wenn diese S Blöcke alle korrekt übertragen wurden. Während diese Analyse für niedrige Blockfehlerraten eine relative gute Annährung des realen Durchsatzes erzielt, nimmt deren Abweichung mit steigender Blockfehlerwahrscheinlichkeit zu.
Für L = 1 sieht dann die Analyse wie folgt aus:

$$P(X=1) = (1-p)^K.$$

$$P(X=2) = \sum_{i=1}^{K} \binom{K}{i} \, p^i \, (1-p)^{K-i} \, (1-p)^i = (1-p)^K \, [(1+p)^K -1].$$

$$P(X=2+1+S) = \sum_{i=1}^{K} \binom{K}{i} \, p^i \, (1-p)^{K-i} \, [\sum_{j=1}^{i} \binom{i}{j} \, p^j \, (1-p)^{i-j} \, (1-p)^j]$$

$$= (1-p)^K [(1+p+p^2)^K - (1+p)^K].$$

$$P(X=2+2(1+S)) =$$

$$= \sum_{i=1}^{K} \binom{K}{i} \, p^i \, (1-p)^{K-i} \, \{ \sum_{j=1}^{i} \binom{i}{j} \, p^j \, (1-p)^{i-j} \, [\sum_{l=1}^{j} \binom{j}{l} \, p^l \, (1-p)^{j-l} \, (1-p)^l]\}$$

$$= (1-p)^K [(1+p+p^2+p^3)^K - (1+p+p^2)^K].$$

Allgemein ergibt sich also:

$$P(X=2+i(1+S)) = (1-p)^K \, [(\sum_{j=0}^{i} p^j)^K - (\sum_{m=0}^{i-1} p^m)^K].$$

Für den Erwartungswert erhält man dann:

$$E[X] = (1-p)^K + (1-p)^K \sum_{i=1}^{\infty} [2+(i-1)(1+S)] \, [(\sum_{j=0}^{i} p^j)^K - (\sum_{m=0}^{i-1} p^m)^K]$$

$$= (1-p)^K + (1-p)^K \sum_{i=1}^{\infty} [2+(i-1)(1+S)] \, [\left(\frac{1-p^{i+1}}{1-p}\right)^K - \left(\frac{1-p^i}{1-p}\right)^K].$$

Analog ergibt sich bei einer Empfängerpuffergröße L*S:

$$E[X] = (1-p)^K + (1-p)^K \sum_{i=1}^{L} [2+(i-1)] \, [\left(\frac{1-p^{i+1}}{1-p}\right)^K - \left(\frac{1-p^i}{1-p}\right)^K]$$

$$+ (1-p)^K \sum_{i=L+1}^{\infty} [2+(i-L)(1+S)] \, [\left(\frac{1-p^{i+1}}{1-p}\right)^K - \left(\frac{1-p^i}{1-p}\right)^K].$$

Der Durchsatz der XOR-SR-Strategie hängt sehr stark von der mittleren Anzahl der beteiligten Basisblöcke, die in einem XOR-Block enthalten sind, ab. Wie im idealen Fall (alle Stationen besitzen unendlichen Puffer) gehen wir auch hier von einer mittleren Anzahl der beteiligten Basisblöcke in XOR-Blöcken aus, die mit M bezeichnet wird (siehe unendlichen Fall). Wir gehen davon aus, daß bei der Wiederholung eines fehlerhaften Blockes dieser als XOR-Block (als XOR-Summe der M beteiligten Blöcke) übertragen wird und daß XOR-Blöcke bei einem Übertragungsfehler unverändert wiederholt werden. Bei der Analyse der XOR-SR-Strategie wird angenommen, daß der Sender ab der ersten Wiederholung den Block nicht wie in der SR-Strategie als Einzelblock, sondern als XOR-Block überträgt. Dies bedeutet, daß pro Wiederholung nicht ein Block, sondern M Blöcke gleichzeitig übertragen werden. Aber jeder XOR-Block benötigt einen zusätzlichen Overhead zur Kennzeichnung der beteiligten Basisblöcke für die Empfänger. Während sich die Blocklänge der Basisblöcke aus Datenteil und Header in Bits ergibt, setzt sich der XOR-Block aus Datenteil, Headerteil und (M-1) * Blockidentifier (Sequenznummer eines Blocks, eine Sequenznummer ist immer im Overhead vorhanden) in Bits zusammen. Da XOR-Blöcke aufgrund des zusätzlichen Overheads länger als die Basisblöcke sind, muß die Analyse bei der Wiederholung von XOR-Blöcken dies berücksichtigen. Dies geschieht durch eine Normierung. Das bedeutet für die Analyse, daß die Basisblöcke bei der Übertragung als eine Blockübertragung gezählt werden, während die XOR-Blöcke als

$$1_{XOR} = \frac{\text{Datenteil (bits)} + \text{Overhead(bits)} + (M - 1) * \text{Blockidentifier (bits)}}{M * (\text{Datenteil (bits)} + \text{Overhead (bits)})}$$

betrachtet werden (mit M=1 folgt 1_{XOR} = Basisblock). Damit ist ein direkter Vergleich beider Verfahren gewährleistet. Es ist zu beachten, daß aufgrund der größeren Länge der XOR-Blöcke diese einer höheren Blockfehlerwahrscheinlichkeit (p_{XOR}) als die Basisblöcke unterliegen. Zur Vereinfachung der XOR-SR-Analyse gehen wir im folgenden davon aus, daß die Wiederholung eines Basisblocks als Bestandteil der XOR-Blöcke mit dem konstanten Parameter M durchgeführt wird. Analog ergibt sich nach einigen Umformungen [ABB 93] für XOR-SR Strategie bei einer Empfängerpuffergröße L*S:

$$E[X]_{XOR} = (1-p)^K$$
$$+ \sum_{i=1}^{L} [1+1_{XOR}+(i-1)\, 1_{XOR}]\, [(1-p+p(1-(1-p_{XOR})^i))^K-(1-p+p(1-(1-p_{XOR})^{i-1}))^K]$$
$$+ \sum_{i=L+1}^{\infty} [1+1_{XOR}+(i-L)(1_{XOR}+S)][(1-p+p(1-(1-p_{XOR})^i))^K-(1-p+p(1-(1-p_{XOR})^{i-1}))^K].$$

Setzt man in der obigen Gleichung S gleich Null, d.h. man weist dem Empfänger einen unendlichen Puffer zu, und geht man in beiden Strategien von gleicher Blocklänge aus, so erhält man für den Idealfall die gleichen Durchsatzterme wie im vorigen Kapitel.

Die Definition des Durchsatzes wird nun bei dem realen Fall nicht mehr auf Anzahl der korrekt übertragenen Blöcke pro Zeiteinheit bezogen [MLi 81], sondern auf Datenbits. Dies basiert darauf, daß nun das System unterschiedlich lange Blöcke und Overheads (Basis- und XOR-Blöcke) überträgt. Der effektive Durchsatz wird dann wie folgt definiert:

$$T_{eff} = \frac{\text{Datenteil (bits)}}{\text{Datenteil (bits)} + \text{Overhead (bits)}} \frac{1}{E[X]}$$

6. Ergebnisse

Die vorgestellte XOR-SR-Strategie ist besonders nützlich in Netzwerken mit vielen Teilnehmern, z.B. VSAT-Netzwerken [AgQu 92]. Weiterhin werden wir sehen, daß in einem weiten Bereich der Blockfehlerwahrscheinlichkeit, der abhängig von K und M ist, der Durchsatz der XOR-SR-Strategie erheblich höher ist als bei der SR-Strategie.

6.1 Unbeschränkte Empfängerpufferkapazität

Um Resultate und Formeln für XOR-SR mit SR vergleichen zu können, setzen wir einfach M gleich 1 für SR, da hier keine XORung verwendet wird. Im Gegensatz zu Abschnitt 6.2 wird hier der zusätzliche Overhead eines XOR-Blockes nicht berücksichtigt.

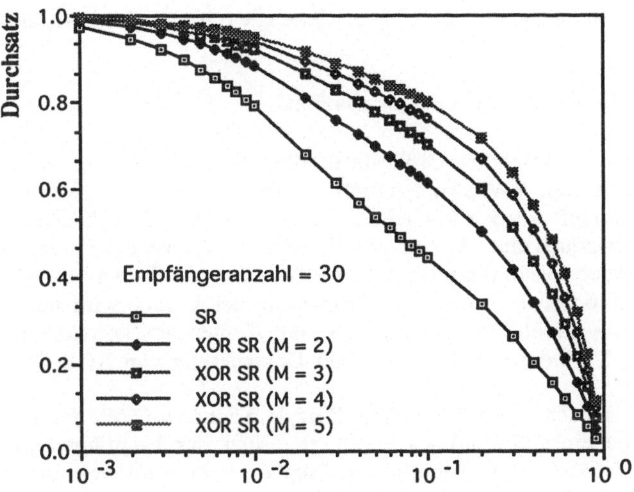

Abbildung 3: Durchsatz als Funktion der Blockfehlerwahrscheinlichkeit für unterschiedliche M-Werte.

Der analytische Vergleich des Durchsatzes zwischen der SR- und XOR-SR-Strategie in Bezug auf Blockfehlerwahrscheinlichkeiten zeigt (siehe Abb. 3), daß die XOR-SR-Strategie einen höheren Durchsatz für M = 2 und 5 erreicht, und daß der Unterschied im Durchsatz zwischen der SR und XOR-SR-Strategie mit ansteigendem M anwächst.

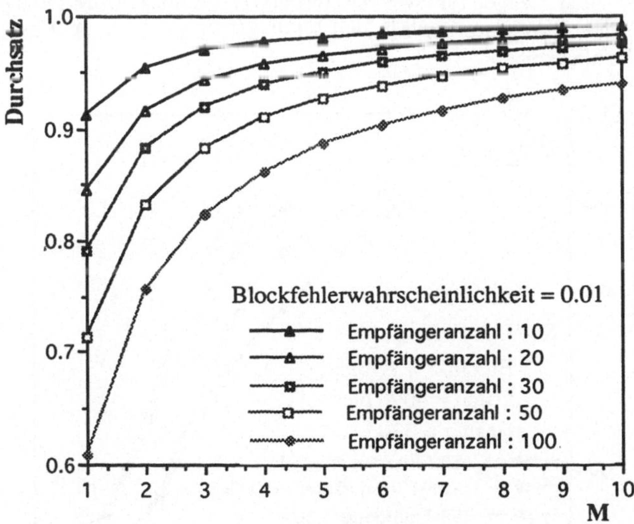

Abbildung 4: Durchsatz als Funktion von M für verschiedene Empfängeranzahlen.

Dies liegt darin begründet, daß die Anzahl der X-Blöcke mit wachsendem M abnimmt, d.h. die mittlere Anzahl von beteiligten Blöcken an einem X-Block ansteigt und die Anzahl der notwendigen Wiederholungen größer wird. Abb. 4 zeigt, daß der Unterschied im Durchsatz zwischen der SR-Strategie und der XOR-SR-Strategie mit M und der Anzahl der Empfänger zunimmt.

6.2 Beschränkte Empfängerpufferkapazität

Der Sender trifft in XWindow-Größe-Intervallen die Entscheidung, welche Basisblöcke innerhalb des aktuellen XWindows mittels einer der XOR-Heuristiken (siehe Kapitel 4) miteinander verknüpft werden können. Dazu führt er eine Liste über die eingetroffenen ACKs/NACKs innerhalb eines XWindows. Er behält die Basisblöcke in seinem Sendepuffer. Ferner überträgt der Sender die fehlerhaften Blöcke die zum dritten Mal wiederholt werden direkt als Basisblöcke, d. h. eine Komprimierung der Blöcke wird nur nach der ersten Wiederholung angestrebt. Der Empfänger behält Kopien von korrekt erhatenen Blöcken innerhalb eines XWindows zwecks etwaiger Dekodierung von XOR-Blöcken in seinem Empfängerpuffer.

Da der Sender erst nach einem Round-Trip-Delay + Xwindow-Größe die betreffenden XOR- und Basisblöcke eines XWindows überträgt, erhält der Empfänger diese nach einer Signallaufzeit (0,5*S). Somit benötigt ein Empfänger eine Mindestpuffergröße von S + 3*XWindow-Größe. Im folgenden Szenario gehen wir von einer Empfängerpuffergröße von 2 * S aus, wobei die Analysen zeigen, daß mit der Zunahme der Puffergröße die Differenz des erzielten Durchsatzes zwischen SR- und XOR-SR drastisch zunimmt. Da wir hier den zusätzlichen Overhead in XOR-Blöcken und damit auch deren höhere Fehlerwahrscheinlichkeit berücksichtigen, geben wir nun den effektiven Durchsatz als Funktion der Bitfehlerwahrscheinlichkeit an. In Simulationen wurden entsprechend bei der Übertragung der XOR-Blöcke den zusätzlichen Overhead miteinbezogen. Dadurch bleibt im Gegensatz zu reiner SR-Strategie die Anzahl der übertragenen Blöcke (Basis und XOR-Blöcke) in einem Round-Trip-Delay (in SR-Fall: S=128) nicht mehr konstant.

Die Abbildungen 5 und 6 zeigen für zwei verschiedene Datenblock-Größen und gleiche Header-Größe (in bits) den Durchsatz der SR und XOR-SR-Strategie in Abhängigkeit von der Bitfehlerwahrscheinlichkeit.

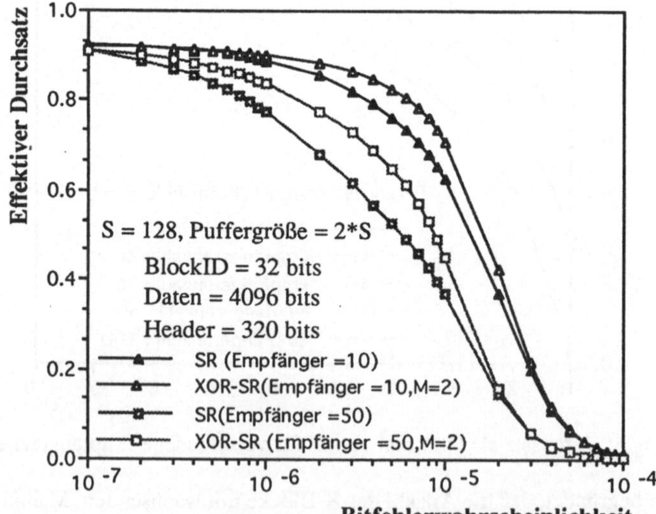

Abbildung 5: Durchsatz der SR und XOR-SR-Strategie in Abhängigkeit von Bitfehlerwahrscheinlichkeit für verschiedene Empfängeranzahlen.

Eine Zunahme der Empfängeranzahl führt wie es auch im Idealfall (unbegrenzte Pufferkapazität) gezeigt wurde, bis zu einer gewissen Bitfehlerwahrscheinlichkeit zu einem höheren Durchsatzgewinn der XOR-SR-Strategie.

Abbildung 6 zeigt, daß eine Erhöhung von M (die Anzahl der beteiligten Basisblöcke in XOR-Blöcken) ebenfalls zu einem höheren Durchsatzgewinn beiträgt. Durch Erhöhung der Puffergröße steigt ebenfalls der Durchsgewinn der XOR-SR-Strategie gegenüber SR-Strategie.

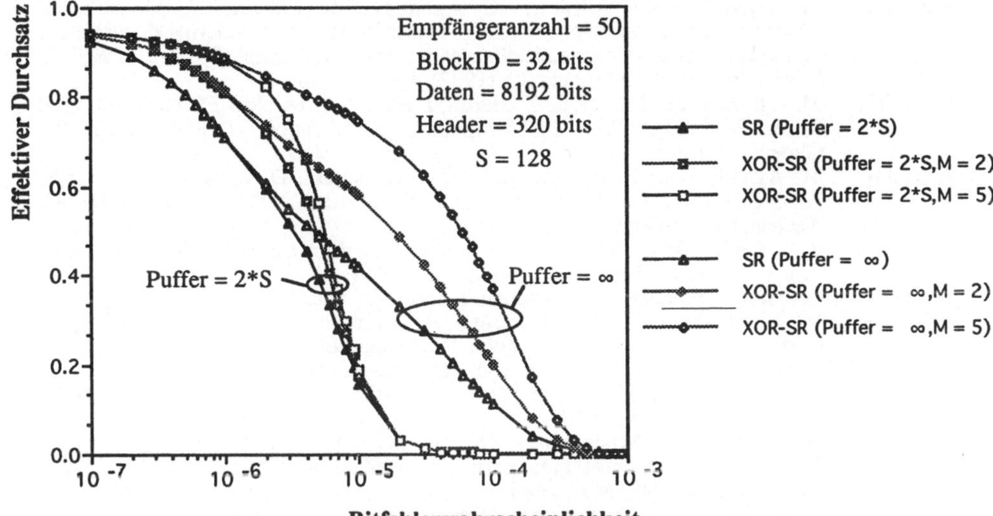

Bitfehlerwahrscheinlichkeit

Abbildung 6: Durchsatz der SR und XOR-SR-Strategie in Abhängigkeit der Bitfehlerwahrscheinlichkeit für M=2 und 5.

Da bei niedrigen Bitfehlerwahrscheinlichkeiten fehlerhafte Blöcke seltener wiederholt werden, tragen die zusätzlichen Overheads der XOR-Blöcke zur Reduzierung des Durchsatztes bei. Ferner zeigt der Vergleich beider Abbildungen 5 und 6, daß der Durchsatzgewinn mit der Erhöhung des Datenanteils und somit Verringerung des Overheadanteils ebenfalls zunimmt.

7. Zusammenfassung

In dieser Arbeit haben wir eine neue SR-Strategie für die Punkt-zu-Mehrpunkt-Kommunikation, XOR-SR-Strategie genannt, vorgestellt. Bei dieser Strategie wiederholt der Sender negativ quittierte (NACKed) Blöcke nicht sofort nach dem Empfang eines NACKs, sondern faßt XWindow ACK/NACKs zusammen und entscheidet dann über die neu zu übertragenden Blöcke. Die Idee der XOR-SR-Strategie basiert auf der XOR-Verknüpfung (d. h. Modulo-2-Addition) verschiedener negativ quittierter (NACKed) Blöcke durch XORung , um die Anzahl der Wiederholungen zu minimieren und den Durchsatz zu erhöhen. Die XOR-SR-Strategie weist einen höheren Durchsatz auf als Selective-Repeat. Die analytischen Ergebnisse bei beschränkter und unbeschränkter Empfängerpufferkapazität für die SR-Strategie zeigen, daß der Durchsatzgewinn der XOR-SR-Strategie mit wachsendem M und wachsender Anzahl der Teilnehmerstationen gegenüber dem normalen SR-Verfahren mit zunehmender Blockfehlerwahrscheinlichkeit bis zu einer gewissen Grenze ansteigt.

Literatur

[AgB '92]   M. Aghadavoodi Jolfaei, S. Baucke, A. Bernatzki, D. Kreuer, "Verbesserte ARQ-Strategien für Kanäle mit hohen Fehlerraten", Tagungsband MMB '92, Aachen.

[AgQ 92]   M. Aghadavoodi Jolfaei, D. Kreuer, O. Maly, U. Quernheim, " Two Time Variant Models for Satellite Channels", Proceeding Supercom/Icc '92, Chicago, USA, pp. 314.31.1- 314.3.5

[AgQu 92]   M. Aghadavoodi Jolfaei,, K. Aghadavoodi Jolfaei, U. Quernheim, "Performance Comparison of VSAT Access Protocols considering disturbances on the link", Space Communications an international journal (Special Issue), IOS Press, Volume 10, Numbers 2,3 (1992), pp. 151-156

[AMM 93]   M. Aghadavoodi Jolfaei, S. C. Martin, J. Mattfeldt, "A New Efficient Selective Repeat Protocol for Point-To-Multipoint Communication", Proceeding ICC '93, Geneva, Schweiz

[ABB 93]   M. Aghadavoodi Jolfaei, S. Baucke, A. Bernatzki, D. Kreuer, "Verbesserte ARQ-Strategien für Kanäle mit hohen Fehlerraten", Proceeding MMB '93, Aachen, Deutschland

[BeF 64]   R. J. Benice, Jr. A. H. Frey, "An Analysis of Retransmission System", IEEE Trans. Commun. Technol., 135-145, Dec. 1964

[Ber 89]   C. Berge, Hypergraphs, Amsterdam: North-Holland, 1989

[BHMN 81]   V. K. Bhargava, D. Haccoun, R. Matyas, P. P. Nuspl, "Digital Communications by Satellite", John Wiley and Sons, USA, 1981

[Bol 79]   B. Bollobás, Graph Theory, New York: Springer, 1979

[Bre 79]   D. Brelaz, "New Method to color the Vertices of a Graph", Comm. ACM, vol.22, pp. 251-256, 1979

[BrM 86]   H. Bruneel, M. Moeneclaey,"On the Throughput Performance of Some Continuos ARQ Strategies with Repeated transmissions", IEEE Trans, Commun., 244-249, Mar. 1986

[BuS 72]   H. O. Burton, D. D. Sullivan, "Errors and Error Control", Proc. IEEE, pp. 1293-1303, Nov. 72

[CaE 86[S. R. Chandran, S. Lin," A Selective-Repeat ARQ Scheme fot Point-To-Multipoint Communications and It´s Throughput Analysis" Proc. ACM SIGCOM Conference, pp. 292-301, Stowe, VT, Aug. 1984

[Dav 70]   M. A. David, Order Statistics, New York: Wiley, 1970

[GoJ 84]   I. S. Gopal, J. M. Jaffe,"Point-To-Multipoint Communication Over Broadcast Links", IEEE Trans. Commun., Com-3, pp. 1034-1044, Sep. 1984

[Ho 89]   I. Hoyer, "The NP-Completeness of the Edge-Coloring", SIAM J. Comput., vol. 10, pp. 718-720, Nov. 1981

[MLi 81]   M. J. Miller, s. Lin, "The Analysis of Some Selective-Repeat ARQ Schemes with Finite Receiver Buffer", IEEE Trans. Commun., pp. 1307-1315, Sep. 1981

[Que 93]   U. Quernheim,"Satellitenkommunikation-Kanalmodellierung und Protokoll-bewertung", Augustinus-Buchhandlung, Aachen, 1993.

[Sas 75]   A. R. K. Sastry, "Improving Automatic Repeat-Request (ARQ) Performance on Satellite Channels under High Error Rate Conditions", IEEE Trans. Commun. Electron., pp. 224-231, Apr. 1975

[ToM 87]   D. Towsley, S. Mithal., "A Selective Repeat ARQ Protocol for a Point to Multipoint Channel", Proc. INFOCOM, pp. 521-526, San Franscisco, CA, Mar. 1987

[WaS 88]   J. L. Wang, J. A. Silvester, "Optimal Adaptive ARQ Protocols for Point-To-Multipoint Communication", P. S. Yu, S. Lin, "An efficient Selective Repeat ARQ Scheme for Satellite Channels and Its Throughput Analysis", IEEE Trans. Commun., 353-363, Mar. 1981 IEEE INFOCOM, pp. 704-713, LA, 1988

[Wel 82]   E. J. Weldon, "An Improved Selective-Repeat ARQ Strategy", IEEE Trans. Comm., vol. COM-30, pp. 480-486, Mar. 1982

[YuL 81]   P. S. Yu, S. Lin, "An Efficint Selective Repeat ARQ Scheme for Satellite Channels and Its Throughput Analysis", IEEE Trans. Commun., pp. 353-363, Mar. 1981

Verbesserte ARQ-Strategien für Kanäle mit hohen Fehlerraten

M. Aghadavoodi Jolfaei, S. Baucke, A. Bernazki, D. Kreuer
RWTH Aachen
Lehrstuhl für Informatik IV
Ahornstr. 55 • W-5100 Aachen • Deutschland • Tel. +49-241-80 21413
e-mail: masoud@informatik.rwth-aachen.de

Kurzfassung

In den letzten Jahren wurde die Qualität und Leistungsfähigkeit von Satellitenstrecken ständig verbessert, wodurch die Einführung von VSATs (Very Small Aperture Terminals) und anderen Satellitensystemen mit niedrigem Link-Budget und begrenzter Speicherkapazität ermöglicht wurde. Durch Kopplung von paketorientierten Netzen (LANs, HSLANs und ATM/BISDN) über VSAT-Stationen treten sowohl Paketverluste durch Pufferüberläufe in Brücken und Routern im terrestischen Netz, als auch Bitfehler auf der Satellitenstrecke auf. Die resultierenden hohe Fehlerraten erfordern Verfahren zur Fehlerkorrektur, die einfach und effizient in Bezug auf Durchsatz und benötigten Speicherplatz sind. Es wurde eine Reihe von ARQ-Fehlersicherungsverfahren (Automatic Repeat Request) zur paketorientierten Kommunikation entwickelt, die zwar mit beschränktem Speicherplatz auskommen, jedoch entweder nur einegeringe Sicherheit bei hohen Blockfehlerraten aufweisen, oder durch den geringen Durchsatz eine große Bandbreite erfordern. In diesem Beitrag stellen wir eine einfache und effiziente Strategie (genannt Stutter-XOR-Strategie, SXOR) zur Erhöhung des Durchsatzes bekannter Verfahren vor. Im Gegensatz zu herkömmlichen hybriden Verfahren (Kombination von ARQ und Forward-Error-Correction) kann diese nicht nur Bitfehler sondern auch Blockverluste korrigieren. Wir haben mehrere Varianten dieser Strategie entwickelt. Zwei von ihnen sollen hier analytisch und simulativ bewertet werden.

1. Einleitung

In dieser Einführung umreißen wir zunächst das unseren Betrachtungen zugrundeliegende Kommunikationsmodell. In Kapitel 2 betrachten wir ein existierendes Multicopy-ARQ-Verfahren, die Weldon-Strategie [Wel 82]. Die SXOR-Strategie und ihre Anwendungsmöglichkeiten werden in Kapitel 3 vorgestellt. In Kapitel 4 wird eine Analyse verschiedener Varianten der Stutter-XOR-Strategie hergeleitet, deren Ergebnisse in Kapitel 5 präsentiert werden. Kapitel 6 gibt schließlich einen Überblick über die erzielten Resultate.

Die Zeit, die von der Aussendung des ersten Bits eines Blocks bis zum Eintreffen der zum Block gehörenden Quittung beim Sender vergeht, wird als *Round-Trip-Delay* (Umlaufverzögerung) bezeichnet. Sie beträgt das Doppelte des *Link-Propagation-Delays* (Signallaufzeit des Kanals). Während die Roundtrip-Zeit der Satellitenstrecke stets konstant ist, muß diese Bedingung für terrestrische Netze aufgrund alternierender Wegwahl nicht immer erfüllt sein. Wir setzen hier voraus, daß die Round-Trip-Zeit auf der gesamten Strecke vom Sender zum Empfänger und zurück konstant ist. Das Round-Trip-Delay kann als maximale Anzahl S von Blöcken ausgedrückt werden, die vom Sender übertragen werden können, bis eine Quittung für den ersten Block eintrifft. Zur Vereinfachung nehmen wir an, daß der Rückkanal (mit derselben Signallaufzeit wie der Datenkanal), auf dem die Quittungen für empfangene Blöcke übertragen werden, fehlerfrei ist, d.h. die Quittungen werden nach einem Round-Trip-Delay korrekt empfangen und tragen nicht zur Auslastung des Datenkanals bei.

Mit jedem Block werden Paritäts-Bits, genannt CRC (Cyclic Redundancy Check), übertragen, durch die der Empfänger die Möglichkeit hat, Übertragungsfehler zu erkennen. Ein *Blockfehler* tritt auf, wenn mindestens ein Bit des Blocks fehlerhaft übertragen wird. Die Möglichkeit, daß Blockfehler durch die CRC nicht erkannt werden, wird hier nicht mit einbezogen. Weiterhin wird angenommen, daß die Blockfehler gleichverteilt und unabhängig voneinander auftreten. Ein Block wird mit einer Wahrscheinlichkeit p von einem Blockfehler betroffen (Bündelfehler werden hier nicht betrachtet) [AgQ 92]. Bei einer gegebenen Bitfehlerrate p_b ist für Blöcke der Länge L Bits die Blockfehlerrate $p = 1 - (1-p_b)^L$. Im Falle der Punkt-zu-Mehrpunkt-Kommunikation besitzen alle Empfänger die gleiche Blockfehlerwahrscheinlichkeit.

Die Art der Wiederholung von fehlerhaften Blöcken hängt von der benutzten ARQ-Strategie ab. Bei den für uns in Frage kommenden Continuous-ARQ-Strategien überträgt der Sender ununterbrochen neue Blöcke und der Empfänger akzeptiert jeden fehlerfrei empfangenen Block und sendet eine positive Quittung (ACK) hierfür. Trifft nun ein fehlerhafter Block beim Empfänger ein, so überträgt er eine negative Quittung (NACK) zum Sender. Der Sender stoppt nach Erhalt eines NACKs die Übertragung neuer Blöcke. Im Falle der Go-Back-N-Strategie überträgt der Sender nicht nur den negativ quittierten Block, sondern auch alle darauffolgend gesendeten Blöcke neu. Das sind diejenigen Blöcke, die innerhalb eines Round-Trip-Delays übertragen wurden. Im Falle der Selective-Repeat-Strategie überträgt der Sender nur den negativ quittierten Block [BrM 86], [BuS 72], [ToM 87], [YuL 81]. Diese Strategien werden auch für die Punkt-zu-Mehrpunkt-Kommunikation eingesetzt. Hierbei wird ein Block nur dann als korrekt (positiv quittiert) betrachtet, wenn alle Empfänger diesen Block korrekt empfangen haben. Demgemäß entscheidet der Sender nach Erhalt der Quittungen von allen K Empfängern für einen bestimmen Block, ob dieser wiederholt werden muß oder nicht [CaE 86], [GoJ 84], [WaS 88], [AgM 92].

Eine andere Methode zur Korrektur fehlerhaften Blöcke stellt die vorausschauende Fehlerkorrektur (FEC, Forward Error Correction) dar. Hierbei versucht man durch Übertragung redundanter Information die empfängerseitige Korrektur fehlerhafter Blöcke zu ermöglichen. Dieses Verfahren kann sowohl auf Bits innerhalb eines Datenblocks als auch auf ganze Blöcke angewandt werden. Während das Ziel der herkömmlichen FEC-Verfahren (z.B. BCH- oder Viterbi-Codes) die Korrektur von Bitfehlern ist, zielt die Stutter-XOR-Strategie (SXOR) auf die Korrektur ganzer Blöcke ab. Diese Anforderung basiert darauf, daß in den pakertorientierten Netzen die Paketverlustraten in Brücken, Routern und Empfängern durch Pufferüberlauf wesentlich höher sind als die Bitfehlerraten auf den Netzen. Dies ist einer der Gründe warum heutige Transportprotokolle (z.B. ISO-OSI-TP4, TCP/IP, XTP) die Automatic-Repeat-Request-Strategien (ARQ), welche durch Wiederholung die fehlerhaften Blöcke Blockfehler korrigieren, als Fehlerkorrekturtechnik verwenden.

Im Bereich der Korrektur von Paketverlusten sind in den letzten Jahren wenige Untersuchungen durchgeführt worden [Bier 92], [LaEf 91], wobei diese sich nur auf die Korrektur von zeitsensitven Datenübertragungen beziehen (delay sensitve, wie z.B. Videoübertragung oder Sprache), bei denen eine Wiederholung der verlorengegangenen Blöcke, also eine ARQ-Strategie, aus Zeitgründen nicht in Frage kommt. Das SXOR-Schema kann sowohl als reine vorausschauende Fehlerkorrektur als auch in Kombination mit jedem der normalen ARQ-Verfahren als hybrides Verfahren eingesetzt werden. Hier betrachten wir als hybride Methode eine Variante der Stutter- oder Multicopy-Selective-Repeat-Strategien [Sas 75], [Tows 79], das Weldon-Verfahren [Wel 82], kombiniert mit der SXOR-Strategie.

2. Weldon-Strategie

In [Wel 82] schlägt E.J. Weldon ein weiterentwickeltes Multicopy-Schema vor. Dabei wird angenommen, daß der Empfänger eine auf q·S Blöcke begrenzte Puffer-Kapazität besitzt, wobei S die Anzahl der Blöcke bezeichnet, die während eines Round-Trip-Delays gesendet werden können, und q eine feste Ganzzahl ist. Im Puffer ist also Platz für q komplette Umläufe. Wenn der Sender nun ein NACK erhält, wiederholt er den betroffenen Block nicht nur einmal, sondern $n_1 \geq 1$ Male. Falls jeder der wiederholten Blöcke wiederum gestört wird, werden diesmal $n_2 > n_1$ Wiederholungen gesendet. Das geht so weiter bis n_q, wobei n_1 ,..., n_q vom Benutzer definierte Werte sind. Wenn Stufe q erreicht wird, können maximal q·S Blöcke (neue und wiederholte) gesendet und im Empfängerpuffer abgelegt worden sein (tatsächlich wird die Anzahl durch begrenzte Auslastung, Wiederholungen und verworfene fehlerhafte Blöcke geringer sein). Der Sender muß nun mit der Möglichkeit eines Puffer-Überlaufs beim Empfänger rechnen. Bei den weiteren Übertragungsversuchen sendet er n_q Wiederholungen des fehlerhaften Blocks, sowie je eine Wiederholung eines jeden der S folgenden Blöcke, von denen angenommen werden muß, daß sie durch Puffer-Überlauf verloren gegangen sind. Abb. 2.1 zeigt ein Beispiel für $q = 2$, $n_1 = 2$ und $n_2 = 3$.

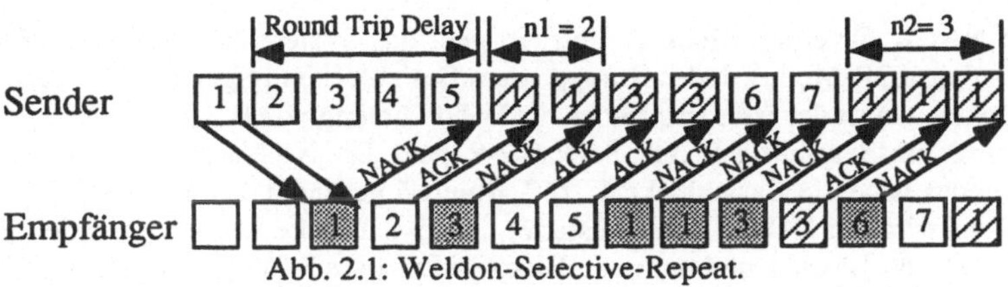

Abb. 2.1: Weldon-Selective-Repeat.

Bei $q=1$ und $n_1 = 1$ ergibt sich im wesentlichen das normale Selective-Repeat-Schema. Bei unseren Untersuchungen gehen wir im Falle der Weldon-Strategie auch für $q > 1$ von der konstanten Empfängerpuffergröße S aus.

3. Stutter-XOR-Strategie (SXOR)

Die verschiedenen ARQ-Verfahren unterscheiden sich in der Anzahl der zur Korrektur eines Blockfehlers gesendeten Wiederholungen. Multicopy-Verfahren verwenden eine große Anzahl von Wiederholungen, um einen hohen Grad an Sicherheit zu erreichen, was jedoch auf Kosten des Durchsatzes geht. Unsere neue SXOR-Strategie zielt auf eine Verringerung der Anzahl von Wiederholungen, die bei Verwendung geläufiger ARQ-Verfahren zur Korrektur einer bestimmten Anzahl von Fehlern nötig sind. Dies wird durch Zusammenfassung mehrerer wiederholter Blöcke durch Modulo-2-Addition (bitweises logisches Exklusiv-Oder, $\oplus$) erreicht. Die Strategie arbeitet wie folgt:
Wir definieren ein sogenanntes XOR-Fenster der Größe n. Solange keine Fehler auftreten, werden nacheinander neue Blöcke gesendet. Wenn jedoch ein oder mehrere NACKs beim Sender eintreffen, wird ein XOR-Fenster geöffnet, in dem neue Blöcke, wiederholte Blöcke, oder *XOR-Blöcke* auftreten können. Die XOR-Blöcke bestehen aus der Modulo-2-Summe der übrigen Blöcke des XOR-Fensters. Im folgenden werden wir die Blöcke, welche keine XOR-Blöcke sind, als *Basisblöcke* bezeichnen. Das XOR-Fenster bestimmt die Anzahl der Blöcke, die zu einem XOR-Block kombiniert werden können. Der auf einen bestimmten, bisher nicht korrekt empfangenen Block B wartende Empfänger kann nun entweder warten, bis B als Basisblock übertragen wird, oder er kann einen XOR-Block heranziehen, der aus B und einer Menge bereits korrekt empfangener Blöcke zusammengesetzt ist. Wenn der Empfänger beispielsweise die Blöcke A, C und D korrekt empfangen hat, nicht aber die Blöcke B und E, kann er Block B aus dem XOR-Block $X = A \oplus B \oplus C \oplus D$ gewinnen, indem er $X \oplus A \oplus C \oplus D$ berechnet. Durch Ersetzen von X und Umstellen erhält man

A⊕A ⊕ C⊕C ⊕ D⊕D ⊕ B = B, da die Summe eines Blocks mit sich selbst den Null-Block ergibt. Aus einem XOR-Block, der mehrere noch nicht korrekt empfangene Blöcke enthält, kann jedoch keiner davon zurückgewonnen werden: Der Block Y = B ⊕ C ⊕ E wäre beispielsweise nutzlos, da weder B noch E korrekt empfangen wurden (es sei denn, entweder B oder E könnten aus einem anderen Block rekonstruiert werden). Es ist wichtig, anzumerken, daß die Berechnung der Modulo-2-Summe direkt während der Übertragung erfolgen kann, ohne daß ein (im Vergleich zu Verfahren ohne XOR) zusätzlicher Zwischenspeicher nötig wäre. Dazu werden korrekt empfangene Blöcke eines XOR-Fensters unmittelbar in dem Puffer des Empfängers XOR-verknüpft, in dem die ankommenden Blocks zusammengesetzt werden.

3.1. SXOR-Selective-Repeat

Wenn ein NACK für einen Block B eintrifft, geht das System für die Dauer eines XOR-Fensters in den XOR-Modus. Jeder Gruppe von n Basisblöcken folgt ein XOR-Block aus den n Basisblöcken, wobei der erste Basisblock die Wiederholung von B ist.
Abb. 3.1 zeigt ein Bespiel für SXOR-Selective-Repeat. Die XOR-Fenstergröße betrage n=3, und der Sender habe die Basisblöcke 1, 2, 3, 4 und 5 gesendet, als ein NACK für Block 1 eintrifft. Nun wird ein XOR-Fenster gestartet und n=3 Blöcke werden gesendet: zuerst die Wiederholung von Block 1 und der neue Block 6. Zu diesem Zeitpunkt trifft ein NACK für Block 3 ein, und so wird dieser Block wiederholt, anstelle der Sendung des neuen Blocks 7. Damit ist die XOR-Fenstergröße erreicht. Das XOR-Fenster wird geschlossen und der dazugehörige XOR-Block X = 1 ⊕ 6 ⊕ 3 gesendet. Für diese vier Blöcke (Fenster und XOR-Block) sind nun 16 verschiedene Kombinationen von korrekten und fehlerhaften Blöcken möglich. Fünf davon (diejenigen mit 3 oder 4 korrekt empfangenen Blöcken) ergeben korrekte Versionen von 1, 3 und 6: 3, 6, X korrekt, 1, 6, X korrekt, 1, 3, X korrekt, 1, 3, 6 korrekt und 1, 3, 6, X korrekt. Bei den anderen Kombinationen (2, 1, oder gar kein Block korrekt) kann der XOR-Block nicht ausgenutzt werden.

Beim SXOR-SR unterscheidet sich der Austausch der Blockquittungen leicht von demjenigen beim Selective-Repeat. ACKs werden weiterhin unmittelbar nach dem korrekten Empfang abgeschickt, zur Implementation der NACKs gibt es jedoch zwei Möglichkeiten. Entweder werden sie unmittelbar nach Empfang eines fehlerhaften Blocks gesendet, oder sie werden bis zum Ende des XOR-Fensters zurückgestellt. Im ersten Fall muß der Sender aus den empfangenen Quittungen ableiten, ob der Empfänger in der Lage war, die fehlenden Blöcke zu korrigieren. Das bedeutet auch, daß ein ACK oder NACK für den XOR-Block gesendet werden muß. Im zweiten Fall wird das erste NACK zurückgehalten, bis entweder das XOR-Fenster beendet ist (wenn der Block dann durch den XOR-Block korrigiert werden konnte, wird er schließlich doch noch geACKt), oder ein zweites NACK auftritt. Wenn mehr als ein fehlerhafter Block in einem XOR-Fenster auftritt, ist der XOR-Block auf jeden Fall nutzlos und fehlerhafte Blöcke können sofort negativ quittiert werden, um eine schnellere Reaktion durch den Sender zu ermöglichen.

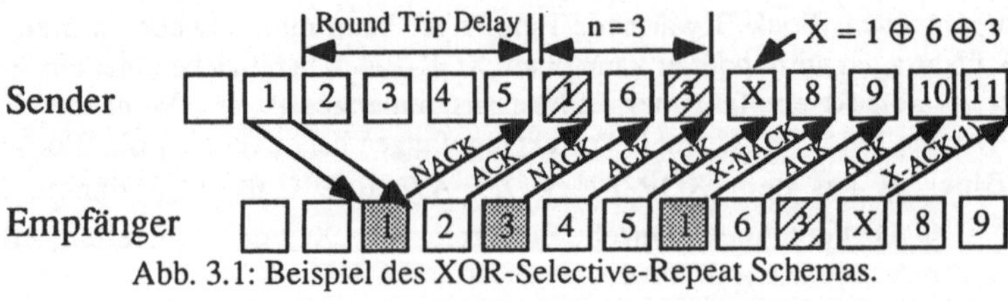

Abb. 3.1: Beispiel des XOR-Selective-Repeat Schemas.

3.2. SXOR-Weldon

Wie beim normalen Weldon-Schema treten Wiederholungen in q Stufen auf, wobei auf der i-ten Stufe n_i Wiederholungen gesendet werden. Es wird jedoch jetzt statt eines einzelnen Blocks ein komplettes XOR-Fenster n_i mal gesendet. Das heißt, während der Wiederholungen treten sowohl Basisblöcke als auch XOR-Blöcke auf. Ein XOR-Fenster besteht aus dem zu wiederholenden Block plus n-1 anderen Basisblöcken, gefolgt von einem XOR-Block des gesamten Fensters (analog zu XOR-Selective-Repeat).
Ein Beispiel für diese Strategie zeigt Abb. 3.2. Seien n=2 und $n_1 = 2$. Die Blöcke 1, 2, 3, 4 und 5 seien gesendet, als ein NACK für 1 eintrifft. Nun tritt Stufe q=1 in Kraft, d.h. es finden $n_1 = 2$ Übertragungen eines XOR-Fensters der Größe n=2 statt. Das erste Fenster besteht aus den Blöcken 1 und 6, gefolgt von X1 = 1 $\oplus$ 6. Das zweite besteht aus den Blöcken 1 und 3, da in der Zwischenzeit ein NACK für Block 3 eingetroffen ist (sonst würde Block 7 gesendet werden), gefolgt von X2 = 1 $\oplus$ 3. Stufe q=2 würde n_2 XOR-Fenster ergeben, jedes mit 2 Basisblöcken und einem XOR-Block des gesamten Fensters, und so weiter.

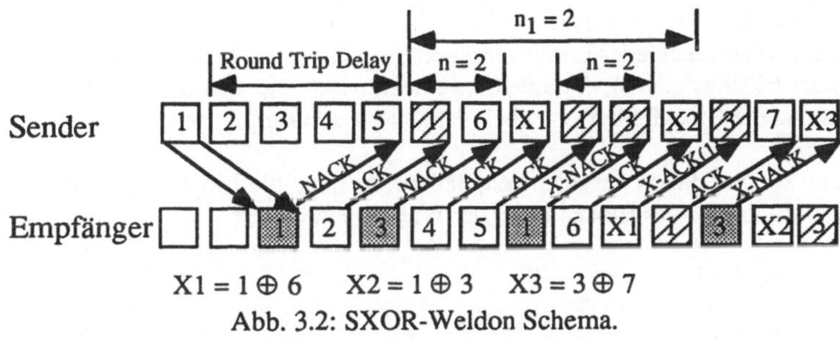

X1 = 1 $\oplus$ 6   X2 = 1 $\oplus$ 3   X3 = 3 $\oplus$ 7
Abb. 3.2: SXOR-Weldon Schema.

4. Analyse der SXOR-Strategien

Für die Durchsatzanalyse der XOR-Strategie haben wir zwei verschiedene Ansätze in Betracht gezogen: den Ansatz von Weldon [Wel 82] und den Ansatz von Lin und Yu [YuL 81]. Die Simulationen und Analysen haben gezeigt, daß der Ansatz von Weldon trotz seiner Einfachheit eine gute Annährung der Simulationergebnisse darstellt, jedoch nur bis zu einer bestimmten Blockfehlerwahrscheinlichkeit. Der erweiterte Ansatz von Lin und Yu ist zwar komplizierter, liefert aber auch für hohe Blockfehlerwahrscheinlichlichkeiten eine gute Approximation der Simulationergebnisse. Im folgenden wird beispielhaft nur der weniger aufwendige Ansatz von Weldon demonstriert.
Wir setzen hier voraus, daß der Sender immer saturiert ist und daß der zur Implementierung der SXOR-Strategien zusätzlich benötigte Overhead vernachlässigbar ist.
Man betrachtet einen repräsentativen Block vom Zeitpunkt seiner ersten Übertragung bis zum korrekten Empfang beim Empfänger. Für die Durchsatzanalyse beschreibe die Zufallsvariable X die Anzahl der Übertragungen, die für den korrekten Empfang eines bestimmten Blocks benötigt werden. Der Erwartungswert E[X] gibt dann die im Mittel benötigte Zahl von Sendungeversuchen eines jeden Blocks an. Der Durchsatz ergibt sich damit bei einem Continuous-ARQ-Verfahren zu:

$$T = \frac{1}{E[X]} \tag{1}$$

Definition (1) muß für eine Analyse der XOR-Strategie noch verallgemeinert werden, wie am Beispiel der Situation aus Abb. 3.1 deutlich wird:

Übertragung		6te	7te	8te	9te
Blocknummer		1	6	3	$X=1\oplus6\oplus3$
ACK Szenarien	1)	NACK	ACK	ACK	ACK
	2)	ACK	NACK	ACK	ACK
	3)	ACK	ACK	NACK	ACK

Bei einzelnen Blockfehlern im XOR-Fenster wird Block X in 1/3 aller Fälle zur Rückgewinnung der Basisblöcke 1, 3 oder 6 benötigt. Daher gewichten wir diesen Block beim Zählen der Übertragungsversuche für jeden der drei Basisblöcke mit 1/3. Bei der Bestimmung der Summe aller Übertragungen ergeben 3 mal 1 für die Basisblöcke und 3 mal 1/3 für Block X die korrekte Anzahl von 4 Block-Gewichten. Ganz allgemein ordnen wir bei Beschränkung der Betrachtung auf einen repräsentativen Block jedem aus n Basisblöcken zusammengesetzten XOR-Block ein Gewicht von 1/n zu.

Wir gehen davon aus, daß jeder Emfänger einen Empfängerpuffer der Größe S besitzt, wobei S die Anzahl der Blöcke darstellt, die innerhalb einer Round-Trip-Zeit übertragen werden können. Desweiteren hat die Blockfehlerwahrscheinlichkeit für alle Empfänger unabhängig voneinander den Betrag p.

Bei der Analyse wird davon ausgegangen, daß am Anfang alle Empfängerpuffer leer sind und die erste Übermittlung eines Blocks B mit der Wahrscheinlichkeit

$$P(X=1) = (1-p)$$

erfolgreich ist. Falls bei dieser Übertragung ein Fehler auftritt, werden L Kopien des Blocks B wiederholt übertragen und alle darauffolgenden Blöcke können bei korrekter Übertragung in den Empfängerpuffer abgelegt werden. Die Wahrscheinlichkeit, daß dieser Übertragungsversuch erfolgreich ist, beträgt

$$P(X=1+L) = p\, Q(p,L)$$

Hierbei stellt Q(p,L) die Wahrscheinlichkeit dar, daß bei der Übertragung der L Kopien des Blocks mindestens eine dieser Kopien fehlerfrei übertragen wird. Die Anzahl der pro Wiederholung gesendeten Blöcke hängt von der verwendeten Strategie ab. Für die Weldon-Strategie werden einfach L Kopien des fehlerhaften Blocks gesendet. Dabei wird mit einer Wahrscheinlichkeit von $Q(p,L) = 1 - p^L$ mindestens ein Block korrekt übertragen. Bei der SXOR-SR-Strategie setzt sich L aus dem wiederholten Basisblock und seinem Anteil an dem zusätzlich übertragenen XOR-Block zusammen, also $L = 1 + \frac{1}{n}$. Die Wahrscheinlichkeit, daß der fehlerhafte Block B bei diesem Versuch dekodiert werden kann, ergibt sich zu:

$$Q(p,L) = (1-p)^{n+1} + (n+1)p(1-p)^n + (1-p)\,(1-(1-p)^n - n\,p\,(1-p)^{n-1})$$

Dies ist die Summe der Wahrscheinlichkeiten, daß entweder alle Blöcke des Fensters korrekt empfangen werden, oder genau ein Blockfehler innerhalb des Fensters auftritt, oder aber B korrekt und mindestens zwei andere Blöcke fehlerhaft sind. Man beachte, daß sich diese drei Fälle gegenseitig ausschließen.

In analoger Weise ergeben sich Terme für L und Q(p,L) bei den anderen Verfahren.

- Selective-Repeat:
  $L = 1$
  $Q(p,1) = 1-p$

- Weldon (q=1):
  $L = n_1$
  $Q(p,n_1) = 1 - p^{n_1}$

- SXOR-Selective-Repeat:
  $$L = 1 + \frac{1}{n}$$
  $$Q_{XOR-SR} = Q(p, 1+\frac{1}{n}) = (1-p)^{n+1} + (n+1)p(1-p)^n + (1-p)\,(1-(1-p)^n - n\,p\,(1-p)^{n-1})$$

- SXOR-Weldon:
  $$L = n_1(1+\frac{1}{n})$$
  $$Q(p, n_1(1+\frac{1}{n})) = 1 - (1-Q_{XOR-SR})^{n_1}$$

Falls noch ein dritter Übertragungsversuch nötig ist, haben wir bereits 1+L Blöcke bei den ersten beiden Versuchen gesendet und übertragen nun zusätzlich L+S Blöcke, denn wir nehmen an, daß zwischen dem ersten und zweiten Versuch B zu übertragen S neue Blöcke gesendet wurden und den Empfängerpuffer gefüllt haben. Wenn die dritte Übertragung von B den Empfänger erreicht, sind bereits S weitere Blöcke gesendet worden, die jedoch durch den Überlauf des Empfängerpuffers verloren gehen und somit ebenfalls wiederholt werden müssen. Damit ergibt sich

$$P(X=1+L+L+S) = p\,(1-Q(p,L))\,Q(p,L)$$

Diese Annahme ist jedoch pessimistisch: Der maximale Wert von S verlorengegangenen Blöcken wird nur dann erreicht, wenn auch S Blöcke korrekt übertragen wurden. Während diese Analyse für niedrige Blockfehlerraten eine relative gute Annäherung des realen Durchsatzes erzielt, nimmt die Abweichung davon mit steigender Blockfehlerwahrscheinlichkeit zu.
Diese Situation gilt auch bei weiteren Übertragungsversuchen. Damit ergibt sich für die m-te Wiederholung (m ≥ 2)

$$P(X=1+L+m(L+S)) = p\,(1-Q(p,L))^{m-1}\,Q(p,L)$$

Durch Summierung der gewichteten Zählergebnisse erhalten wir den erwarteten Wert für die Anzahl der Übertragungsversuche von dem repräsentativem Block B:

$$E[X]=(1-p)+\sum_{i=1}^{\infty} (1+L+(i-1)(L+S))\,p\,(1-Q(p,L))^{i-1}\,Q(p,L) = 1 - pS + \frac{p(L+S)}{Q(p,L)} \qquad (2)$$

Setzt man in obiger Formel (2) $L=1$ und $Q(p,L)=1-p$, so führt dies zu der mittleren Anzahl von Übertragungsversuchen, die nötig sind, um bei der Selective-Repeat-Strategie einen Block korrekt zu übertragen [MiSh 81], [Weld 82]:

$$E[X] = \frac{1+Sp^2}{(1-p)} \qquad (3)$$

Möchte man den Durchsatz der Weldonstrategie für $q=1$ und n_1 bestimmen, so ersetzt man in der obigen Formel $L = n_1$ und $Q(p,n_1) = 1 - p^{n_1}$. Dies führt zu Weldon $(q=1)$ nach [Wel 82]:

$$E[X] = 1 + n_1 p + \frac{(n_1 + S)p^{1+n_1}}{1 - p^{n_1}} \tag{4}$$

5. Ergebnisse

Im Selective-Repeat-Verfahren wiederholt der Sender nur negativ quittierte Blöcke. Der Empfänger weist solche Blöcke zurück, die entweder von einem Übertragungsfehler betroffen sind, oder nicht im Empfängerpuffer abgespeichert werden können. Für die Simulation erfolgt die Speicherung im Empfängerpuffer nach folgender Strategie: Sei i_0 der kleinste vom Empfänger noch nicht korrekt empfangene Block. Dann wird für alle Blöcke mit einer Sequenznummer $i < i_0 + S$ ein Platz im Empfängerpuffer reserviert, der nicht durch neuere Blöcke belegt wird. Auf diese Weise wird sichergestellt, daß für diese Blöcke, die zur Weiterleitung der Daten in korrekter Reihenfolge benötigt werden, bei einem korrekten Empfang auch Platz vorhanden ist [YuL 81].

Die Abbildungen 5.1 und 5.2 bzw. 5.3 und 5.4 zeigen die Ergebnisse von Simulation und Analyse im Vergleich.

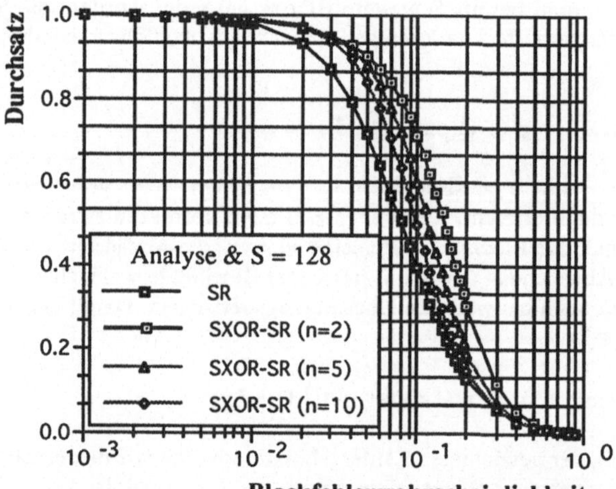

Abb. 5.1: Analyse für die Selective-Repeat- und die XOR-SR-Strategie bei verschiedenen XOR-Fenstergrößen (n=2, 5 und 10)

Bei höheren Blockfehlerwahrscheinlichkeiten ist die Analyse zu pessimistisch. Das simulierte System weist nun eine geringere Wahrscheinlichkeit eines Puffer-Überlaufs auf, als bei der Analyse angenommen wird. Mit steigender Blockfehlerwahrscheinlichkeit beginnt dieser Effekt zu dominieren, so daß die Ergebnisse von Analyse und Simulation zunehmend voneinander abweichen. Diese Tendenz tritt bei Punkt-zu-Mehrpunkt-Kommunikation durch die höhere Empfängeranzahl noch stärker in Erscheinung, weshalb wir für diesen Fall nur simulative Ergebnisse präsentieren.

Bei der Punkt-zu-Punkt-Kommunikation und einem XOR-Fenster von n=2 weist XOR-Selective-Repeat ab einer gewissen Blockfehlerrate den besten Durchsatz auf (Abb. 5.1 und 5.2). Bei größerem XOR-Fenster steigt die Wahrscheinlichkeit, daß mehr als ein Blockfehler innerhalb eines XOR-Fensters auftritt. Da in solchen Fällen der zusätzliche XOR-Block nutzlos ist, nähern sich die Ergebnisse bei steigenden Fenstergrößen denen von Selective-Repeat.

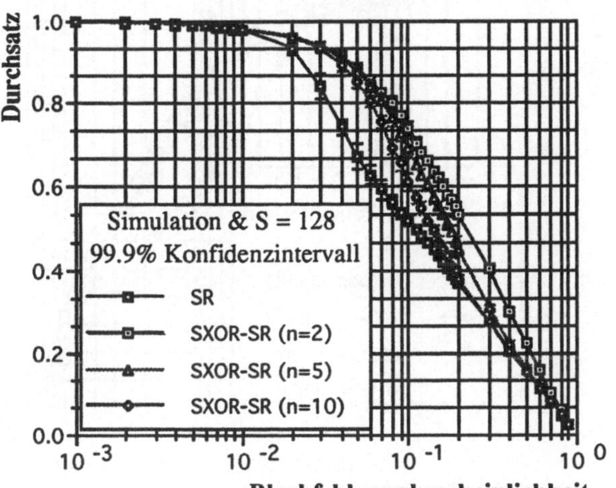

Abb. 5.2: Simulation der Selective-Repeat- und SXOR-SR-Strategie mit verschiedenen XOR-Fenstergrößen (n=2, 5 und 10; 99.9% Konfidenzintervall)

In Abb. 5.3 und 5.4 werden die Selective-Repeat-, Weldon-, SXOR-Selective-Repeat- und SXOR-Weldon-Strategien verglichen.

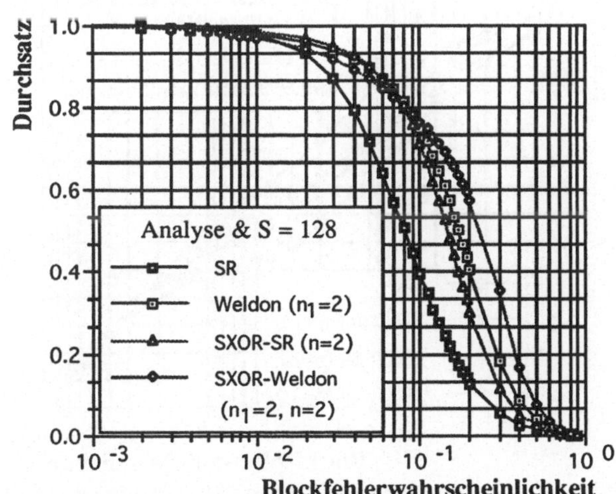

Abb. 5.3: Analytischer Durchsatzvergleich der Selective-Repeat, SXOR-SR und SXOR-Weldon-Strategien.

Selective-Repeat weist den niedrigsten Durchsatz aller Verfahren auf. Zudem zeigt sich, daß der Durchsatz der SXOR-SR-Strategie (n=2) geringfügig schlechter als derjenige der Weldon-

302

Strategie (q=1, n_1=2) ist. SXOR-Weldon (q=2, n=2) erreicht durch die höhere Anzahl von Wiederholungen erst bei hohen Blockfehlerraten einen besseren Durchsatz als Weldon und SXOR-SR. Da SXOR-Weldon mit n_1 = 1 dem SXOR-SR-Verfahren entspricht, würde ein adaptives Verfahren über n_1 das beste Ergebnis liefern.

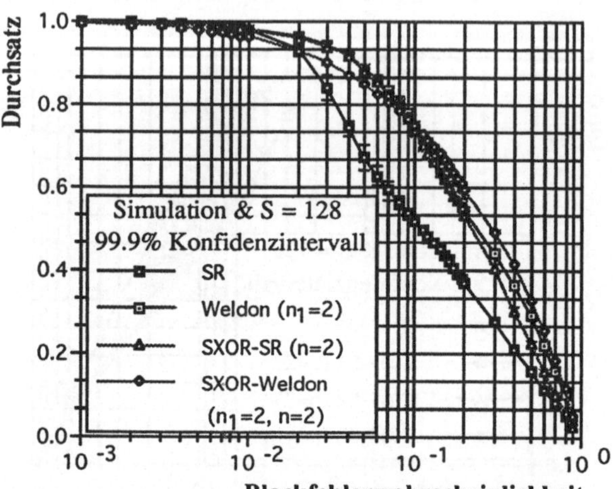

Abb. 5.4: Simulativer Durchsatzvergleich der Selective-Repeat, SXOR-SR und SXOR-Weldon-Strategien (99.9% onfidenzintervall).

Abb. 5.5. zeigt die simulativen Ergebnisse der Verfahren SR-, Weldon- und SXOR-SR-Strategie für Punkt-zu-Mehrpunkt-Kommunikation mit 50 Empfängern.

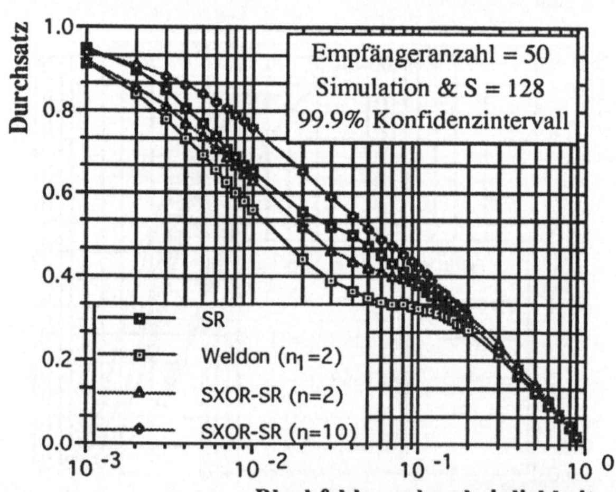

Abb. 5.5: Simulativer Durchsatzvergleich von SR-, Weldon und SXOR-SR für Punkt-zu-Mehrpunkt-Kommunikation

Im Gegensatz zur Punkt-zu-Punkt-Kommunikation erweisen sich bei höheren Empfänger-anzahlen größere XOR-Fenster als vorteilhaft. Hierbei tritt die Situation auf, daß verschiedene Empfänger unterschiedliche Blöcke korrekt empfangen. Dadurch sind bei der Wiederholung in einem XOR-Fenster häufig Blöcke enthalten, die einige Empfänger bereits vorher korrekt empfangen haben. Diese Blöcke können ggf. zur Dekodierung eines gewünschten Blocks aus dem XOR-Fenster eingesetzt werden, auch wenn die entsprechenden Basisblöcke bei der neuen Wiederholung fehlerhaft empfangen wurden, so daß auch die Störung mehrerer Basisblöcke den XOR-Block nicht nutzlos macht. Andererseits wird durch die größeren XOR-Fenster der Overhead verringert.

Die SXOR-Strategie kann auf solchen Kanälen vorteilhaft angewendet werden, auf denen sowohl Bitfehler (z. B. auf Satellitenstrecke oder Mobilfunk) als auch Blockverluste (z.B. durch Pufferüberläufe in Brücken oder Gateways) auftreten. Dies wird in Abb. 5.6 demonstriert, in der wir die Ergebnisse in Abhängigkeit von der Bitfehlerwahrscheinlichkeit bei einer zusätzlichen konstanten Blockverlustwahrscheinlichkeit P(Blockverlust) von 0.05 betrachten. Nach Ergebnissen aus [Bier 92] können bei hoher Last derartige Blockverlustraten auftreten. Es wird angenommen, daß die Blockverluste gleichverteilt und unabhängig voneinander und von Bitfehlern auftreten. Die betrachteten Strategien können auch mit herkömmlicher FEC kombiniert werden. Hier haben wir eine (1023,1013)-BCH-Kodierung [LiCo 83] verwendet, mit der 1-Bit-Fehler korrigiert werden können. Die FEC-Kodierung wird auf jeden Datenblock angewendet, so daß sich dabei durch den zusätzlichen Overhead die Anzahl der Blöcke, die innerhalb eines Round-Trip-Delays gesendet werden können (S), etwas verringert (S'). Ferner haben wir bei den SXOR-Strategien einen weiteren Overhead von 8 Bits an Protokolldaten angenommen.

Die Definition des Durchsatzes wird nun nicht mehr auf die Anzahl der korrekt übertragenen Blöcke pro Zeiteinheit bezogen [MLi 81], sondern auf Datenbits, damit die unterschiedliche Blocklänge der verschiedenen Verfahren keinen Einfluß hat. Der effektive Durchsatz wird dann wie folgt definiert:

$$T_{eff} = \frac{\text{Datenteil (bits)}}{\text{Datenteil (bits) + Overhead (bits)}} \cdot \frac{1}{E[X]}$$

Die Ergebnisse zeigen, daß in diesem Szenario das SXOR-SR-Verfahren sowohl mit als auch ohne FEC-Kodierung einen deutlich höheren Durchsatz erzielt, als die anderen Verfahren.

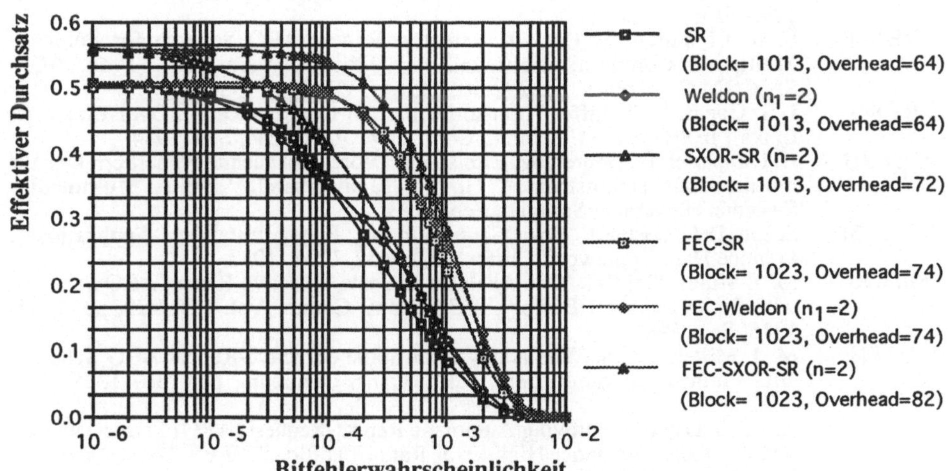

Abb. 5.6: Selective-Repeat-, Weldon- und SXOR-SR-Strategie mit und FEC.

6. Zusammenfassung

Es wurde demonstriert, daß der Durchsatz bestehender ARQ-Fehlersicherungsverfahren durch Kombination mehrerer Blöcke in XOR-Blöcke verbessert werden kann. Diese Methode kann auf jedes ARQ-Verfahren angewendet werden und bewirkt im allgemeinen eine Leistungssteigerung, insbesondere auf Übertragungsstrecken, auf denen Blockverluste in Kombination mit Bitfehlern auftreten. Bei Anwendung auf das Selective-Repeat-Verfahren ist die Verbesserung deutlich. Selbst die bekannte Weldon-Strategie, die bislang als eine der besten Strategien bei hohen Fehlerraten gilt, kann so noch verbessert werden. Auch in Kombination mit FEC kann die SXOR-Methode vorteilhaft angewendet werden. Die Stutter-XOR-Strategie kann effizient durch Software implementiert werden; im Gegensatz zu FEC-Dekodern ist keine spezielle Hardware nötig. Daher kann sie leicht in existierende Transportprotokolle oder Satelliten-Controller und preiswerte Systeme, wie etwa VSATs, integriert werden.

Literatur

[AgM 93]   M. Aghadavoodi Jolfaei, S.C. Martin, J. Mattfeldt, U. Quernheim, "XOR-Selective-Repeat: Ein neues effizientes Verfahren für die Multicast-Kommunikation", Tagungsband MMB '93, Aachen.

[AgQ 92]   M. Aghadavoodi Jolfaei, D. Kreuer, O. Maly, U. Quernheim, "Two Time Variant Models for Satellite Channels", Proceeding Supercom/Icc 92, Chicago, USA, pp. 314.31.1- 314.3.5.

[AgQu 92] M. Aghadavoodi Jolfaei, K. Aghadavoodi Jolfaei, U. Quernheim, "Performance Comparison of VSAT Access Protocols considering disturbances on the link", Space Communications an international journal (Special Issue), IOS Press, Volume 10, Numbers 2,3 (1992), pp. 151-156

[BeF 64]   R. J. Benice, Jr. A. H. Frey, "An Analysis of Retransmission System", IEEE Trans. Commun. Technol., 135-145, Dec. 1964.

[BHMN 81] V. K. Bhargava, D. Haccoun, R. Matyas, P. P. Nuspl, "Digital Communications by Satellite", John Wiley and Sons, USA, 1981.

[BrM 86]   H. Bruneel, M. Moeneclaey, "On the Throughput Performance of Some Continuous ARQ Strategies with Repeated Transmissions", IEEE Trans, Commun., 244-249, Mar. 1986.

[BuS 72]   H. O. Burton, D. D. Sullivan, "Errors and Error Control", Proc. IEEE, pp. 1293-1303, Nov. '72.

[CaE 86]   S. R. Chandran, S. Lin, "A Selective-Repeat ARQ Scheme for Point-to-Multipoint Communications and Its Throughput Analysis", Proc. ACM SIGCOM Conference, pp. 292-301, Stowe, VT, Aug. 1984.

[GoJ 84]   I. S. Gopal, J. M. Jaffe, "Point-to-Multipoint Communication Over Broadcast Links", IEEE Trans. Commun., Com-3, pp. 1034-1044, Sep. 1984.

[LaEf 91] B. Lamparter, O. Böhrer, W. Effelsberg, "Vorausschauende Fehlerkorrektur für multimediale Datenströme", GI/ITG-Tagungsband Verteilte Multimedia-Systeme, Universität Stuttgart, Feb. 1993.

[LiCo 83] S. Lin, D.J. Costello, "Error Control Coding: Fundamentals and Applications", Prentice Hall, Englewood Cliffs, N.J. 07632, USA, 1983.

[MiSh 81] M. J. Miller, Shu Lin, "The Analysis of Some Selective-Repeat ARQ Schemes with Finite Receiver Buffer", IEEE Trans. Comm., vol. COM-29, pp. 1307-1315, Sep. 1981.

[MLi 81]   M. J. Miller, s. Lin, "The Analysis of Some Selective-Repeat ARQ Schemes with Finite Receiver Buffer", IEEE Trans. Commun., pp. 1307-1315, Sep. 1981

[Sas 75]   A. R. K. Sastry, "Improving Automatic Repeat-Request (ARQ) Performance on Satellite Channels under High Error Rate Conditions", IEEE Trans. Commun. Electron., pp. 224-231, Apr. 1975.

[ToM 87]   D. Towsley, S. Mithal, "A Selective Repeat ARQ Protocol for a Point to Multi-point Channel", Proc. INFOCOM, pp. 521-526, San Franscisco, CA, Mar. 1987.
[Tows 79]   D. Towsley "The Stutter Go Back-N ARQ Protocol", IEEE Trans. Comm., vol. COM-27, pp. 869-875, Jun. 1979.
[WaS 88]   J. L. Wang, J. A. Silvester, "Optimal Adaptive ARQ Protocols for Point-To-Multipoint Communication", P. S. Yu, S. Lin, "An efficient Selective Repeat ARQ Scheme for Satellite Channels and Its Throughput Analysis", IEEE Trans. Commun., 353-363, Mar. 1981 IEEE INFOCOM, pp. 704-713, LA, 1988
[Wel 82]   E. J. Weldon, "An Improved Selective-Repeat ARQ Strategy", IEEE Trans. Comm., vol. COM-30, pp. 480-486, Mar. 1982.
[YuL 81]   P. S. Yu, S. Lin, "An Efficient Selective Repeat ARQ Scheme for Satellite Channels and Its Throughput Analysis", IEEE Trans. Commun., pp. 353-363, Mar. 1981.

Quelle-Ziel-Durchsätze in Multihop-Paketfunknetzen

Klaus Gotthardt
FernUniverstät-GH-Hagen, Fachbereich Elektrotechnik
Elberfelder Str. 95, 58084 Hagen

Zusammenfassung

In paketvermittelten Mobilfunknetzen, die bei sehr hohen Frequenzen arbeiten, haben die einzelnen Stationen eine stark begrenzte Sendereichweite. Es entsteht das Problem der Weitervermittlung von Paketen zu weiter entfernten, über die Sendereichweite hinausgehende, Zielstationen. Für eine Quelle-Ziel-Übertragung sind u.U. mehrere One-Hop-Übertragungen (Hops) notwendig. Die Zahl der benötigten Hops hängt ab vom Abstand zwischen Quell- und Zielstation und dem pro Hop zurückgelegten Fortschritt in Richtung Ziel. Sie ist die entscheidende Größe bei der folgenden Systemanalyse. Um qualitative Leistungsvergleiche der betrachteten teil- mit voll-vermaschten Netzen anstellen zu können, wird in diesem Beitrag der Quelle-Ziel-Durchsatz an Paketen für verschiedene Kanalzugriffsprotokolle (S-ALOHA, S-ALOHA unter Berücksichtigung von Capture, CSMA) analytisch untersucht.

Schlüsselwörter
Multihop-Packetfunknetze, Zugriffsprotokolle, Modellierung, Leistungsanalyse.

1 Einleitung

Wenn mobile Stationen untereinander Daten austauschen sollen, sind Funksysteme die einzige Alternative. Von besonderem Interesse sind paketvermittelte Funksysteme, da diese mit sehr wenig zentraler Koordination auskommen. Sie sind prinzipiell mit lokalen Netzen vergleichbar, über die angeschlossene Stationen meist per Zufallszugriff kommunizieren, sind jedoch an die besonderen Randbedingungen der Funkumgebung gebunden. Derzeit im Betrieb befindliche Paketfunksysteme sind überwiegend voll-vermascht, d.h. jede Station kann jede andere Station direkt erreichen. Der Sende-/Empfangsbereich jeder Station ist so ausgelegt, daß das Netz vollständig überdeckt wird.

Zuküftige Kommunikationsnetze für mobile Stationen werden, mangels verfügbarer Funkfrequenzen, in den heute kaum genutzten Frequenzbereichen mm-Wellen benutzen. Dort vorherrschende Übertragungsbedingungen und die geringe Sende-/Empfangsreichweite ergeben schwierige Randbedingungen: Die Stationen des Netzes sind funktechnisch nicht voll-, sondern nur teil-vermascht. Die Konnektivität ändert sich infolge der Mobilität ständig, bestehende Funkkontakte werden getrennt und neue entstehen [11].

Sollen nun Datenpakete zu entfernteren Stationen des Netzes außerhalb der eigenen Reichweite einer Station (Sendebereich) gesendet werden, so kann dies nur durch eine Weitervermittlung der Datenpakete über dazwischenliegende Stationen, welche die Pakete jeweils empfangen und wieder übertragen, erfolgen. Die Pakete müssen evtl. mehrmals erfolgreich übertragen werden bevor sie ihr Ziel erreichen, für eine Quelle-Ziel-Übertragung sind mehrere One-Hop-Übertragungen (Hops) notwendig. Die Zahl der benötigten Hops hängt ab vom Abstand zwischen Quell- und Zielststation und dem pro Hop zurückgelegten Fortschritt in Richtung Ziel. Diese Art der Übermittlung von Paketen bezeichnet man als Multihop-Paketdatenfunk. Da Stationen nur eine begrenzte kleine Zahl anderer Stationen erreichen, können Stationen in entfernt liegenden Teilen des Netzes gleichzeitig den Kanal für erfolgreiche Übertragungen nutzen. Dies bezeichnet man als räumliche Kanalwiederverwendung.

Paketdatenfunksysteme benutzen sog. Zufallszugriffsprotokolle, weil eine zentralisierte Kanalvergabe aufgrund der Stationsmobilität oder ihrer Funkreichweite oft nicht möglich ist. Zufallszugriff benötigt keine Koordination der Stationen untereinander, bringt aber das Problem von Kollisionen.

Von Interesse bei der Untersuchung solcher Systeme sind Leistungsgrößen wie der Durchsatz in Paketen pro Zeiteinheit und die dabei auftretende Paketverzögerung.

Grundsätzlich ist bei Multihop-Systemen zwischen dem One-Hop-Durchsatz und dem Quelle-Ziel-Durchsatz zu unterscheiden. Der One-Hop-Durchsatz ist die Zahl erfolgreich empfangener Pakete einer Station pro Zeit.

Der Quelle-Ziel-Durchsatz ist die Zahl erfolgreich empfangener Pakete zwischen Quelle und Ziel bezogen auf eine Station und ist daher die bedeutendere Größe. Er ist insbesondere von Interesse, da er eine quantitative Aussage, bzw. einen direkten Vergleich mit voll-vermaschten Systemen ermöglicht. Den Quelle-Ziel-Durchsatz erhält man, indem man den One-Hop-Durchsatz durch die Zahl der notwendigen One-Hop-Übertragungen (Hops) einer Quelle-Ziel-Übertragung dividiert, was sich bei der Analyse als schwierig erweist, da beides Zufallsgrößen sind.

Insbesondere ist in Netzen mit mobilen und damit quasi zufällig verteilten Stationen die Anzahl benötigter Hops eine schwer bestimmbare Zufallsgröße, was sich im folgenden noch zeigen wird.

One-Hop-Durchsatz

In den bisher veröffentlichten Analysen [10],[8] wurden die Leistungsgrößen mittlerer One-Hop-Durchsatz und mittlerer Fortschritt pro Slot (Paketlänge) in Richtung Ziel betrachtet. Der mittlere Fortschritt $E[F]$ eines Paketes in Richtung Ziel pro Slot ergibt sich aus dem mittleren One-Hop-Durchsatz $E[S_1]$ und dem mittleren Fortschritt $E[Z]$ pro Übertragung. Bei Unabhängigkeit von $E[S_1]$ und $E[Z]$ gilt:

$$E[F] = E[S_1] \cdot E[Z]$$

Dabei werden die zwei wichtigen gegenläufige Effekte, die den Quelle-Ziel-Durchsatz bestimmen, berücksichtigt: Ein kleiner Sendebereich (wenige Nachbarstationen zu einer gegebenen Station), bedeutet ein hohe Wahrscheinlichkeit einer erfolgreichen Übertragung, bewirkt aber einen kleinen Fortschritt in Richtung Ziel. Ein großer Sendebereich bringt einen großen Fortschritt pro Übertragung, aber auch eine hohe Kollisionswahrscheinlichkeit.

Der Fortschritt pro Slot in Richtung Ziel ist damit als Maß zum Leistungsvergleich verschiedener Kanalzugriffs-Protokolle, verschiedener Routingverfahren und zur Bestimmung des Einflusses des Capture-Effektes (Fähigkeit eines Empfängers sich auf den stärksten Sender zu synchronisieren) in Multihop-Netzen geeignet.

Quelle-Ziel-Durchsatz

Zur Berechnung des Quelle-Ziel-Durchsatzes ist die Zahl erforderlicher Hops einer Route notwendig. Diese Größe wurde bisher nur für Multihop-Netze mit ortsfesten Stationen bestimmt. Bei mobilen Stationen ist die Berechnung erheblich schwieriger, da die Stationen in der Ebene zufällig verteilt sind.

In [8] und [9] wurde der Quelle-Ziel-Durchsatz für S-ALOHA berechnet. Dazu wurde der Erwartungswert $E[d]$ des Abstandes zweier Stationen einer zufällig ausgewählten Quelle-Ziel-Beziehung und der Erwartungswert $E[Z]$ des Fortschritts in Richtung Ziel pro Hop berechnet. Zur Berechnung der Anzahl Hops wurden die beiden Erwartungswerte durcheinander dividiert, eine Vorgehensweise, die auch durch möglicherweise abweichende Modellannahmen nicht begründbar ist und dementsprechend stark abweichende Ergebnisse liefert. Die Gleichung (1) zeigt bereits daß aus der Division zweier Zufallsvariablen nicht auch die Division der Erwartungswerte folgt.

Im folgenden wird die Verteilungsfunktion $H(x)$ der Zahl benötigter Hops einer Quelle-Ziel-Route berechnet. Die Kenntnis der Verteilungsfunktion ist notwendig, um den Erwartungswert $E[1/H]$ ausrechnen. Sie ist aber auch von Bedeutung bei der Berechnung weiterer wichtiger Leistungskenngrößen. Dazu gehören die Wartezeit in den Stationen auf Kanalzugriff vor dem ersten Übertragungsversuch eines Paketes und die Länge der Paketwarteschlange in den Stationen. Die Paketverzögerungszeit von der Quelle zum Ziel ist nur bestimmbar, wenn $H(x)$ bekannt ist. Außerdem sind nicht nur die Mittelwerte der bisher betrachteten Leistungsgrößen von Interesse, sondern auch deren Verteilungen.

Im folgenden Abschnitt werden zuerst die bei Multihop-Netzen allgemein verwendeten Modellannahmen beschrieben. Danach folgt in einem weiteren Abschnitt die vollständige Analyse mit der Herleitung des One-Hop-Durchsatzes bei S-ALOHA, S-ALOHA unter Berücksichtigung von Capture und CSMA, sowie die Berechnung der Verteilung der Anzahl Hops pro Quelle-Ziel-Übertragung. Mit den beiden Größen wird der Quelle-Ziel-Durchsatz bestimmt. Für verschiedene Fälle und unterschiedliche Parameter werden numerische Auswertungen durchgeführt und die Ergebnisse diskutiert.

2 Modellannahmen

Zur Modellierung wird angenommen, daß die Stationen gleichmäßig in der Ebene verteilt sind: Die Anzahl Stationen in einer Fläche F ist Poisson-verteilt mit Mittelwert λF, wobei λ die Dichte der Stationen ist. Die zufällige Anordnung modelliert bei mobilen Stationen eine Momentaufnahme eines tatsächlichen Netzes. Der Sendebereich einer Station i wird kreisförmig angenommen. Der Radius R ist dabei eine harte Grenze. Stationen innerhalb eines Kreises mit Radius R um Station i haben Funkkontakt zu i, Stationen außerhalb nicht. Die mittlere Zahl Nachbarn einer Station ist $W = \lambda \pi R^2$. Real ist der Sendebereich eine sich stetig ändernde geschlossene Funktion, für die Analyse ist aber nur die überdeckte Fläche von Bedeutung.

Die Quelle-Ziel-Verkehrsbeziehungen sind gleichverteilt angenommen. Enthält das Netz n Stationen, dann sendet jede zu allen anderen $(n-1)$ Stationen der gleicher Wahrscheinlichkeit $1/(n-1)$. Diese Annahme trifft in den meisten Anwendungen nicht zu, z.B. werden Stationen in der näheren Umgebung meist häufiger angesprochen als weiter entfernte, so daß der tatsächliche Durchsatz besser sein dürfte als der berechnete. Randeffekte werden vernachlässigt, es wird angenommen, daß die Netzausdehnung entsprechend groß genug ist. Die betrachteten Kanalzugriffsprotokolle sind S-ALOHA und CSMA. Das Verkehrsaufkommen pro Station wird durch die Übertragungswahrscheinlichkeit p eines Paketes pro Slot modelliert.

Beim des Vorwärtsroutens sind zwei Verfahren von Interesse: das sog. Most-Forward-Routing (MFR) und das Routen zu einer zufällig ausgewählten Nachbarstation in Vorwärtsrichtung. Die beiden Verfahren sind von Bedeutung, weil sie sich hinsichtlich der benötigten Routing-Information extrem unterscheiden. Während beim zufälligen Vorwärtsrouten lediglich die grobe Richtung der Zielstation (linker oder rechter Halbkreis) als bekannt vorausgesetzt wird, ist bei MFR der Weg durch das Netz (Zwischenstationen) aufgrund von Routing-Tabellen vorherbestimmt. Der dazu notwendige Aufwand für die ständige Aktualisierung der Routing-Information wird sehr groß sein, soll aber hier nicht betrachtet werden.

Die Anzahl benötigter Hops eines Datenpaketes von einer Quelle zum Ziel ist von sehr vielen Annahmen abhängig. Neben der Abhängigkeit von den geometrischen Gegebenheiten des Netzes wie flächenmäßige Netzausdehnung, Dichte und Verteilung der Stationen, ist sie eine Funktion des Kanalzugriffsverfahrens und des angewandten Routing-Verfahrens, sowie der Verkehrsmatrix. Einen weiteren Einfluß bilden spezielle Funkausbreitungsbedingungen, wie z.B. der Capture-Effekt. Dieser bewirkt, daß eine nahe beim Empfänger befindliche Station erfolgreich ist gegenüber weiter entfernten. Dadurch wird zwar der One-Hop-Durchsatz vergrößert, die zurückgelegten Wege sind jedoch insgesamt kleiner.

3 Die wichtigsten Schritte der Analyse

Teile der folgenden Analyse wurden in früheren Beiträgen bereits veröffentlicht. In diesem Abschnitt sind die wichtigsten Schritte der Analyse zusammengefaßt, Details können in den entsprechenden Literaturstellen nachgelesen werden.

Der Quelle-Ziel-Durchsatz S_{QZ} ergibt sich aus dem One-Hop-Durchsatz S_1 und der Anzahl benötigter Hops H, wobei sowohl S_1 als auch H Zufallsvariablen sind:

$$S_{QZ} = \frac{S_1}{H} \qquad E[S_{QZ}] = E\left[\frac{S_1}{H}\right]$$

Man hat also den Erwartungswert einer Division von Zufallsvariablen zu bilden. Allgemein gilt für beliebige unabhängige Verteilungsdichtefunktion $f(x_1)$, $f(x_2)$:

$$E[Y] = E\left[\frac{X_1}{X_2}\right] = \int_{-\infty}^{+\infty} \int_{-\infty}^{+\infty} \frac{x_1}{x_2} f_{x1}(x_1) \cdot f_{x2}(x_2)\, dx_1\, dx_2 = E[X_1] \cdot E\left[\frac{1}{X_2}\right] \qquad (1)$$

Der Erwartungswert der ZV Y ergibt sich durch Multiplikation des Erwartungswertes von X_1 mit dem Erwartungswert des Kehrwertes von X_2. Für die Berechnung des Quelle-Ziel-Durchsatzes bedeutet dies, daß der Erwartungswert $E[S_1]$ des One-Hop-Durchsatzes mit dem Erwartungswert $E[1/H]$ der Anzahl Hops zu multiplizieren ist.

$$E[S_{QZ}] = E[S_1] \cdot E\left[\frac{1}{H}\right] \qquad (2)$$

3.1 One-Hop-Durchsätze $E[S_1]$

Für die Berechnung der One-Hop-Durchsätze gilt nach [5] folgender Ansatz:

$$E[S_1] = p \iint_{A_R} E[S_1 \mid \tilde{r} = r, \tilde{\vartheta} = \vartheta] \cdot P\{r < \tilde{r} \leq r + dr, \vartheta < \tilde{\vartheta} \leq \vartheta + d\vartheta\} \qquad (3)$$

p ist die Übertragungswahrscheinlichkeit des Senders, $E[S_1 \mid \tilde{r} = r, \tilde{\vartheta} = \vartheta]$ der One-Hop-Durchsatz einer Station unter der Bedingung, daß sich der Empfänger Q bei (r, ϑ) befindet. Zu integrieren ist über die Kreisfläche A_R um den Sender P, da der Empfänger Q alle Koordinaten innerhalb dieses Kreises annehmen kann. $P\{r < \tilde{r} \leq r + dr, \vartheta < \tilde{\vartheta} \leq \vartheta + d\vartheta\}$ ist die Wahrscheinlichkeit dafür, daß der Empfänger bei (r, ϑ) liegt.

3.1.1 Zugriffsprotokolle S-ALOHA und CSMA

Der One-Hop-Durchsatz einer Station in einem Multihop-System bei **S-ALOHA**, die außer dem Sender noch i weitere Stationen in ihrem Empfangsbereich hat, ist nach [2]

$$E[S_1|i+2] = (1 - e^{-W/2})\, p\, (1-p)(1-p)^i \qquad \text{mit} \quad W = \lambda \pi R^2$$

Der One-Hop-Durchsatz bei S-ALOHA ist offensichtlich unabhängig vom Routing-Verfahren, das Integral in Gl. (3) braucht hier nicht ausgewertet zu werden. Eine Übertragung in den Rückwärtshalbkreis ausgeschlossen, in der Gleichung ist daher noch der Faktor $(1 - e^{-W/2})$ berücksichtigt worden. Es folgt weiter:

$$E[S_1] = (1 - e^{-W/2})\, p\, (1 - p)e^{-pW} \tag{4}$$

Bei **CSMA** wird der Kanal vor dem Start einer Übertragung abgehört, um die Zahl der Kollisionen stark zu reduzieren. Da sich Sende- und Empfangsbereich der beteiligten Stationen in Abhängigkeit von ihrem Abstand mehr oder weniger unterscheiden, sind sog. verdeckte Stationen zu berücksichtigen [3]. Für $E[S_1 \mid \tilde{r} = r, \tilde{\vartheta} = \vartheta]$ gilt nach [5]:

$$E[S_1|\tilde{r} = r, \tilde{\vartheta} = \vartheta] = \frac{p'}{\nu}(1 - p')e^{-p'\lambda F_A}\left\{[1 - exp\,(-p'\lambda F_B)] \cdot exp\,[(1 - p')^{(1/\nu - 1)}\lambda F_B]\right.$$

$$\left. + exp\,[(1 - p')^{1/\nu}\lambda F_B]\right\} \cdot \frac{\nu\, e^{-\lambda F_B}}{\nu + (1 + \nu)[1 - e^{-p'\lambda F_B}]} \tag{5}$$

wobei $F_A = F_A(r) = 2R^2\left[\arccos\dfrac{r}{2R} - \dfrac{r}{2R}\sqrt{1 - (\dfrac{r}{2R})^2}\right], \quad F_B = F_B(r) = \pi R^2 - F_A(r)$

$$p' = p \cdot P_I = p\,\frac{\nu\,[1 - e^{-p'W}]}{\nu + (1 + \nu)[1 - e^{-p'W}]} \quad \text{mit} \quad W = \lambda\pi R^2$$

Da das CSMA-System nicht durch einen Takt synchronisiert werden muß, bezieht sich die Übertragungswahrscheinlichkeit p' hier auf eine Mini-Slot genannte Zeiteinheit der Länge ν, wobei ν der max. Signallaufzeit zwischen zwei Stationen in Funkreichweite entspricht. Bei CSMA ist der bedingte One-Hop-Durchsatz abhängig vom jeweiligen Abstand der beiden beteiligten Stationen (Sender-Empfänger), da beim Abhören des Kanals die Zahl der für den Sender versteckten Stationen mit zunehmendem Abstand (größerer Fortschritt) zunimmt. Es ist aber nur eine Abhängigkeit von r vorhanden und nicht von ϑ. Es gilt:

$$E[S_1] = \int_0^R E[S_1|\tilde{r} = r] \cdot P\{r < \tilde{r} \leq r + dr\} \tag{6}$$

3.1.2 S-ALOHA unter Berücksichtung von Capture

In Abschnitt 3.1.1 wurde angenommen, daß sich beim Empfänger überlappende Pakete nicht mehr detektieren lassen und damit zerstört sind. In der Praxis kann man jedoch abhängig vom Verhältnis der einzelnen Empfangsfeldstärken möglicherweise eine Sendung empfangen und den Rest als Rauschen eliminieren. Im Modell stellt sich dies folgendermaßen dar: Ein Empfänger Q befindet sich im Sendebereich zweier Stationen (S1,S2) mit den Empfangsleistungen P_1 (S1) und P_2 (S2) im Punkt Q. Bei Capture kann Q das Paket von S1 korrekt empfangen, wenn

$$\frac{P_1}{P_2} \geq c^2 \quad \Rightarrow \quad \frac{r_2}{r_1} \geq c \tag{7}$$

gilt, wobei c den Capture-Parameter bezeichnet. Geht man von omnidirektionalen Antennen und gleichen Sendeleistungen aller Stationen aus, dann kann man näherungsweise das Leistungsverhältnis in das Verhältnis der Abstände umwandeln. Um die weiteren Rechnungen zu vereinfachen, wurden dabei ideale Freiraum-Verhältnisse angenommen, wobei die empfangene Leistung in einem bestimmten Punkt proportional zu $1/r^2$ (r=Abstand vom **Sender**) ist. Außerdem wird nur der jeweils stärkste Störer berücksichtigt. Für

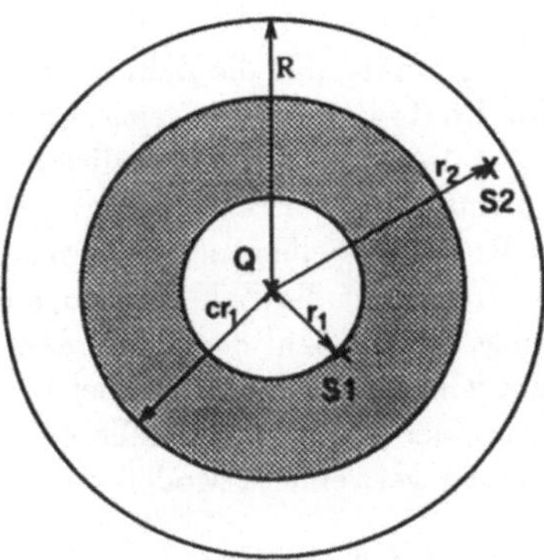

$c \rightarrow \infty$ ergibt sich der Fall ohne Capture, $c = 1$ bedeutet ideales Capture, praktische Werte liegen bei $c \cong 1,5$. Für $E[S_1 \mid \tilde{r} = r, \tilde{\vartheta} = \vartheta]$ in Gl. (3) gilt nach [8]:

$$E[S_1 \mid \tilde{r} = r, \tilde{\vartheta} = \vartheta] = \begin{cases} p(1-p)\, e^{-p\lambda\pi c^2 r^2} & \text{für} \quad cr \leq R \\ p(1-p)\, e^{-p\lambda\pi R^2} & \text{für} \quad cr \geq R \end{cases} \tag{8}$$

Auch hier ist nur eine Abhängigkeit vom Abstand Sender-Empfänger r gegeben. Damit folgt für den One-Hop Durchsatz bei S-ALOHA mit Capture:

$$E[S_1] = p(1-p)\pi \left[\int_0^{R/c} e^{-\lambda\pi c^2 r^2} + \int_{R/c}^{R} e^{-\lambda\pi R^2} \right] \cdot P\{r < \tilde{r} \leq r + dr\} \tag{9}$$

Berechenbar ist auch der One-Hop-Durchsatz für CSMA mit Capture. Wegen der Abhängigkeit der Erfolgswahrscheinlichkeit vom Abstand der betrachteten Stationen infolge der versteckten Stationen einerseits und des Capture-Effektes andererseits, sind die Gleichungen zu kompliziert und umfangreich um hier behandelt zu werden. Sie sind in [5] nachzulesen.

3.1.3 Routing-Verfahren

Zufälliges Vorwärtsrouten

In diesem Modell wird angenommen, daß bei Weitergabe eines Paketes in Zielrichtung eine beliebige Station gemäß einer Gleichverteilung aus der Halbebene des Sendekreises in Richtung Ziel ausgewählt wird. Liegen z.B. i Stationen aus Sicht des Senders P in Richtung Ziel, dann wählt P eine der i Nachbarstationen mit der Wahrscheinlichkeit $1/i$ aus. Daraus folgt nach [4] die zweidimensionale Verteilungsdichtefunktion in Polarkoordinaten:

$$P\{r < \tilde{r} \leq r + dr, \vartheta < \tilde{\vartheta} \leq \vartheta + d\vartheta\} = \frac{2\pi r \, dr \, d\vartheta}{\pi R^2} = \frac{2\, dA}{\pi R^2} \qquad dA = r\, dr\, d\vartheta \tag{10}$$

Umgerechnet in karthesischen Koordinaten mit $x = r\cos\vartheta$, $z = r\sin\vartheta$, $r\, dr\, d\vartheta = dz\, dx$ und Integration über x ergibt den Fortschritt pro Hop:

$$P\{z < \tilde{z} \leq z + dz\} = \frac{4\sqrt{R^2 - z^2}}{\pi R^2}\, dz = \frac{4}{\pi R}\sqrt{1 - (\frac{z}{R})^2}\, dz = f(z)\, dz \qquad 0 \leq z \leq R \tag{11}$$

MFR-Routing

Bei MFR-Routing ist die Route so gewählt, daß die Zahl benötigter Hops für eine Quelle-Ziel Beziehung minimiert ist. Die Route ist beispielsweise aufgrund sogenannter Konnektivitätstabellen [1], die von den Stationen ständig aktualisiert werden, vorherbestimmt. Das Verfahren ist theoretisch optimal, in der Praxis wird es jedoch infolge der Mobilität der Stationen mangels aktueller Routingtabellen möglicherweise nicht immer optimal arbeiten, so daß man eine untere Grenze für die Zahl der Hops erhält. Zufälliges Routen hingegen liefert eine obere Grenze für die Zahl der Hops, denn es setzt nur die Kenntnis der Richtung des Empfängers voraus. MFR-Routing ist wegen der Abhängigkeit der einzelnen Hops der Route voneinander kaum zu modellieren [7]. Simulationsergebnisse haben gezeigt, daß das im folgenden verwendete Modell des MFR-Routens fast äquivalente Aussagen liefert.

Im MFR-Modell wird angenommen, daß für ein gegebenes Ziel F bestimmte Pakete vorwärtsgeroutet werden, indem sie an diejenige erreichbare Station gesendet werden, die am weitesten in Richtung Ziel liegt. Damit gilt nach [5] für die Verteilung der Positionen des Empfängers Q in bezug auf den Sender P:

$$P\{r < \tilde{r} \leq r + dr \; \vartheta < \tilde{\vartheta} \leq \vartheta + d\vartheta\} = e^{-\lambda A_x}\lambda \, dA = e^{-\lambda A_x}\lambda r \, dr \, d\vartheta$$

Umwandlung in karthesische Koordinaten und Integration über x ergibt den Fortschritt pro Hop

$$P\{z < \tilde{z} \leq z + dz\} = 2\lambda\sqrt{R^2 - z^2}\, e^{-\lambda A_x}\, dz = f(z)\, dz \qquad -R \leq z \leq R \qquad (12)$$

$$\text{mit} \qquad A_x = R^2\left[\arccos \tfrac{z}{R} - \tfrac{z}{R}\sqrt{1 - (\tfrac{z}{R})^2}\right] \qquad (13)$$

3.1.4 Routen unter dem Einfluß von Capture

Der Capture-Effekt hat Einfluß auf das Routing, wenn zwei ungleich weit entfernte Sender denselben Empfänger adressieren. Wenn der Abstand der beiden Sender voneinander genügend groß ist, dann ist gemäß den oben gemachten Ausführungen immer der nähere erfolgreich. Übertragungen mit großem Fortschritt sind also weniger erfolgreich. Die Annahme von MFR bei starken Capture ist damit in Frage gestellt, denn die Routing-Vorgabe ist nur noch begrenzt erfüllt. Es ist nicht sinnvoll den Fortschritt zu optimieren, da man eine nicht zu vernachlässigende Rückwirkung auf den One-Hop-Durchsatz hat. Sinnvoll wäre es die Erfolgswahrscheinlichkeit als Funktion des Abstandes r zu bestimmen, mit r multiplizieren und diese Funktion bzgl. r zu optimieren. Daraus würde sich dann der optimal zu wählende Abstand Sender-Empfänger ergeben, der den Fortschritt $E[F]$ pro Slot in Richtung Ziel tatsächlich optimiert. Natürlich kann man nicht genau immer im Abstand r_{opt} einen Empfänger finden, man müßte einen Kreisring mit $\Delta r = r_{opt} \pm b$ definieren, in dem dann der richtungsoptimale Empfänger ausgesucht wird. Im folgenden wird daher bei Capture nur das Routen mit gleicher Wahrscheinlichkeit betrachtet, wobei die Rückwirkung entsprechend berücksichtigt wird. Bei zufälligem Vorwärtsrouten gilt für die Abstände zwischen Sender und ausgewähltem Empfänger nach Gl. (10)

$$P\{r < \tilde{r} \leq r + dr\} = \frac{2r}{R^2}dr$$

Unter Berücksichtigung der Erfolgswahrscheinlichkeit gilt für den tatsächlichlichen Abstand Sender-Empfänger

$$P\{r < \tilde{r} \leq r + dr | S\} = \frac{P\{r < \tilde{r} \leq r + dr, S\}}{P\{S\}} = \frac{p(1-p)(1-e^{-W/2})}{P\{S\}}\frac{2r}{R^2}\cdot e^{-p\lambda\pi[Min\{cr,R\}]^2}dr$$

Für die Erfolgswahrscheinlichkeit $P\{S\}$ bei S-ALOHA mit Capture gilt nach [8]:

$$P\{S\} = \frac{(1-p)(1-e^{-W/2})}{W}\left[\frac{1}{c^2}(1-e^{-pW}) + (1-\frac{1}{c^2})pW\,e^{-pW}\right]$$

mit $\quad \dfrac{p(1-p)(1-e^{-W/2})}{P\{S\}} = \dfrac{1}{s} \quad$ folgt nach einigen Umformungen

$$P\{r < \tilde{r} \le r + dr \,|\, S\} = \begin{cases} \dfrac{2r}{sR^2}e^{-p\lambda\pi(cr)^2}dr & 0 \le r \le \dfrac{R}{c} \\[2ex] \dfrac{2r}{sR^2}e^{-p\lambda\pi R^2}dr & \dfrac{R}{c} \le r \le R \end{cases} \tag{14}$$

Für die weiteren Berechnungen wird aber nicht der Abstand r, sondern der Fortschritt z in Richtung Ziel benötigt. Da die Stationen homogen in der Ebene verteilt sind, ist auch der Winkel ϑ gleichmäßig über der rechten Halbebene $[-\pi/2, +\pi/2]$ verteilt. Es folgt

$$P\{\tilde{z} > z\,|\,\tilde{r}\} = P\{\tilde{\vartheta} > \vartheta\} = \frac{2}{\pi}\vartheta \qquad \text{mit} \quad \vartheta = \arccos\frac{z}{r}$$

$$P\{\tilde{z} \le z\,|\,\tilde{r}\} = 1 - \frac{2}{\pi}\arccos\left(\frac{z}{r}\right)$$

$$f(z|r) = \frac{dP\{\tilde{z} \le z\,|\,\tilde{r}\}}{dz} = \begin{cases} 0 & r < z \\[2ex] \dfrac{2}{\pi}\dfrac{1}{\sqrt{r^2-z^2}} & 0 \le z \le r \le R \end{cases} \tag{15}$$

Hieraus läßt sich die Verteilungsdichtefunktion für den Fortschritt pro Hop berechnen:

$$f(z) = \int_0^R f(z|r)\cdot P\{r < \tilde{r} \le r + dr\,|\,S\} \tag{16}$$

$$f(z) = \frac{4}{s\pi R^2}\begin{cases} \displaystyle\int_z^{R/c} e^{-pW(c\frac{r}{R})^2}\frac{r\,dr}{\sqrt{r^2-z^2}} + e^{-pW}\left[\sqrt{r^2-z^2} - \sqrt{(\frac{R}{c})^2-z^2}\right] & r \le \dfrac{R}{c} \\[3ex] e^{-pW}\sqrt{r^2-z^2} & r \ge \dfrac{R}{c} \end{cases} \tag{17}$$

Eine äquivalente Gleichung läßt sich auch für CSMA mit Capture herleiten. Die Herleitung wäre aber zu umfangreich, um hier dargestellt zu werden.

3.2 Anzahl Hops zwischen Quell- und Ziel-Station

Da die Zielstationen einer Quelle zufällig verteilt sind, ist auch der Abstand zweier kommunizierender Stationen zufällig. Er ist hauptsächlich abhängig von der Dichte und Verteilung der Stationen in der Ebene, der Netzausdehnung und der Verteilung der Verkehrsbeziehungen. Die Lage der Stationen entspricht Punkten in einer unendlich ausgedehnten ebenen Kreisfläche, wobei angenommen wird, daß die Fläche genügend groß ist, um Randeffekte zu vernachlässigen. Nach [6] folgt für die Verteilungsdichtefunktion $f_x(x)$ des Abstandes einer zufälligen Quelle-Ziel Beziehung bei kreisförmiger Netzausdehnung (Radius ρ):

$$f_x(x) = \frac{4x}{\pi\rho^2}\arccos\frac{x}{2\rho} - \frac{x^2}{\pi\rho^2}\sqrt{(2\rho)^2-x^2} \qquad \bar{d} = E[X] = \int_0^{2\rho} x f_x(x)dx = \frac{128}{45\pi}\rho \tag{18}$$

Die Zahl benötigter Hops pro Quelle-Ziel Übertragung ergibt sich aus der Division der ZV Abstand X einer Quelle-Ziel Beziehung und der ZV Fortschritt Z pro Hop. Will man die zwei Zufallsvariablen X und Z dividieren und Momente oder die Verteilung der sich daraus ergebenden Zufallsvariablen H berechnen, dann werden dazu die Verteilungsdichtefunktionen der beiden bekannten Zufallsvariablen benötigt. Es gilt:

$$h(y) = \int_{-\infty}^{+\infty} |z|\, f_x(yz)\, f_z(z)\, dz \tag{19}$$

Aus der VDF $h(y)$ können durch Integration die Verteilungsfunktion (VF) und alle Momente berechnet werden. Für $E[1/H]$ gilt:

$$E[1/H] = \int_{-\infty}^{+\infty} \frac{1}{y} \cdot h(y)\, dy \tag{20}$$

Es muß ausgeschlossen werden, daß die VDF für den Fortschritt (Nenner) den Wert 0 annimmt, dazu wird der Beginn der VDF bei ϵR mit $\epsilon \to 0$ festgelegt.

(a) **Vorwärtsrouten mit gleicher Wahrscheinlichkeit:** Die Herleitung ist in [4] dargestellt. Danach folgt für die VDF $h(x)$ der Anzahl Hops

$$h(x) = \frac{64x}{\pi a^2} \frac{1}{\pi - 2[\epsilon\sqrt{1-\epsilon^2} + \arcsin \epsilon]} \int_{\epsilon}^{c_1} t^2 \sqrt{1-t^2} \{\arccos \frac{xt}{a} - \frac{xt}{a}\sqrt{1-(\frac{xt}{a})^2}\} dt \tag{21}$$

mit $z/R = t$, $2\rho/R = a$ und $c_1 = 1$ für $x \le a$ bzw. $c_1 = a/x$ für $x \ge a$.

Die betrachtete Funktion $h(x)$ ist eine kontinuierliche VDF. Die Verteilung der Zahl benötigter Hops für eine Quelle-Ziel-Übertragung ist real aber eine diskrete Zufallsvariable, denn die Zahl der Hops muß stets ganzzahlig sein. Die diskrete Verteilung erhält man aus der kontinuierlichen Verteilung, indem man jeweils die Wahrscheinlichkeitsdichte zwischen zwei benachbarten ganzen Zahlen integriert und diese der größeren der beiden ganzen Zahlen zuweist. Diese Maßnahme ist einfach zu begründen: Benötigt man rechnerisch gemäß der kontinuierlichen VDF X, x Hops für eine Quelle-Ziel-Übertragung, dann sind tatsächlich $(X+1)$ Hops zurückzulegen.

(b) **MFR-Routing:** Es gilt nach [4] für die VDF $h(x)$

$$h(x) = \frac{32xW}{(\pi a)^2} \frac{1}{1 - \exp\left(-\frac{W}{\pi}[\arccos \epsilon - \epsilon\sqrt{1-\epsilon^2}]\right)} \cdot \int_{\epsilon}^{c_1} t^2 \sqrt{1-t^2}$$

$$\left[\arccos \frac{xt}{a} - \frac{xt}{a}\sqrt{1-(\frac{xt}{a})^2}\right] \exp\left(-\frac{W}{\pi}[\arccos t - t\sqrt{1-t^2}]\right) dt \tag{22}$$

Die Funktion ist abhängig von der mittleren Anzahl Nachbarn W, die auch als Konnektivität bezeichnet wird, da sie ein Maß für die Vernetzung ist. Der Fortschritt bei MFR ist um so größer, je größer die Dichte der Stationen ist. Bei dem unter (a) betrachteten Routing hingegen war der Fortschritt unabhängig von W.

(c) **Routen bei Capture:**

$$f(z) = \int_0^R f(z|r) \cdot P\{r < \tilde{r} \le r + dr|S\}$$

$$f(z) = \frac{4}{s\pi R^2} \begin{cases} \int_z^{R/c} e^{-pW(c\frac{r}{R})^2} \dfrac{r\, dr}{\sqrt{r^2-z^2}} + e^{-pW}\left[\sqrt{r^2-z^2} - \sqrt{(\frac{R}{c})^2-z^2}\right] & r \le \dfrac{R}{c} \\[2ex] e^{-pW}\sqrt{r^2-z^2} & r \ge \dfrac{R}{c} \end{cases}$$

für $\quad r \leq R/c \quad P\{z \leq \epsilon R\} = \dfrac{4}{s\pi R^2} \left\{ \displaystyle\int_0^{\epsilon R} \int_z^{R/c} e^{-pW(c\frac{r}{R})^2} \dfrac{r\,dr\,dz}{\sqrt{r^2 - z^2}} + e^{-pW} \dfrac{R^2}{2} \left[\epsilon\sqrt{1 - \epsilon^2} \right. \right.$

$$\left. \left. + \arcsin\epsilon - \epsilon\sqrt{(\tfrac{1}{c})^2 - \epsilon^2} + (\tfrac{1}{c})^2 \arcsin(c\epsilon) \right] \right\}$$

für $\quad r \geq R/c \quad P\{z \leq \epsilon R\} = \dfrac{2}{s\pi} [\epsilon\sqrt{1 - \epsilon^2} + \arcsin\epsilon]$

$$h(x) = \int_a^b z\, f_x(xz)\, f_z(z)\,dz = \int_a^b z\, f_x(xz) \dfrac{f(z)\,dz}{1 - P\{z \leq \epsilon R\}}$$

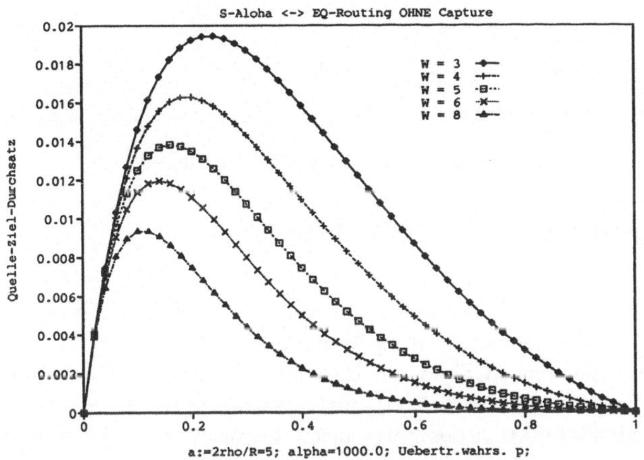

Abbildung 1: Quelle-Ziel-Durchsatz, S-ALOHA, Gleichwahrscheinliches Vorwärtsrouten

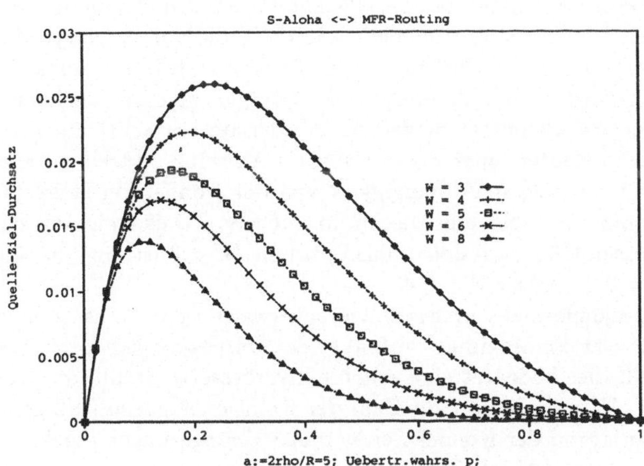

Abbildung 2: Quelle-Ziel-Durchsatz S-ALOHA, MFR-Routing

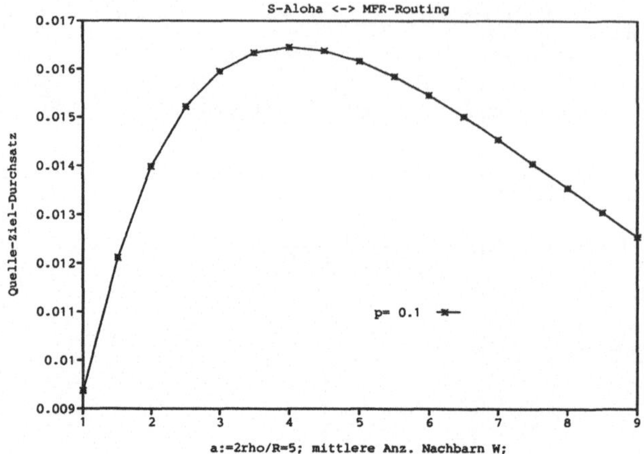

Abbildung 3: Quelle-Ziel-Durchsatz S-ALOHA, MFR-Routing

4 Zusammenfassung der Ergebnisse

Die Quelle-Ziel-Durchsätze ergeben sich durch Auswertung der Gl. (2). Dabei können die One-Hop-Durchsätze mit den entsprechenden Routing-Modellen kombiniert werden, z.B. CSMA mit MFR-Routing usw. aber nicht CSMA mit Routing bei Capture. Gemäß der Gleichung (2) ist der inverse Erwartungswert $E[1/H]$ des Fortschritts zu bilden. Es ist klar, daß dazu die Verteilungsdichtefunktion des Fortschritts benötigt wird, der Erwartungswert reicht nicht aus.

In Abb. 1 ist der Quelle-Ziel-Durchsatz für S-ALOHA und Vorwärtsrouten mit gleicher Wahrscheinlichkeit dargestellt, Abb. 2 zeigt den Quelle-Ziel-Durchsatz für S-ALOHA und MFR-Routing über dem Verkehrsaufkommen p. Der Parameter an den Kurven ist die mittlere Zahl Nachbarstationen oder die sog. Konnektivität W. Alle Kurven zeigen das gleiche Verhalten, der Durchsatz nimmt zu bis zu einem Maximum, bei dem auch die Stabilitätsgrenze überschritten wird, und fällt danach ab. Vergleicht man die beiden Routing-Verfahren miteinander, so erkennt man, daß der Durchsatz bei MFR um rund 25% besser ist, es lohnt sich beim Routen einen etwas größeren Aufwand zu treiben. Aus Abb. 3 erkennt man, daß der Durchsatz in Abhängigkeit von der Konnektivität W für ein bestimmtes Verkehrsaufkommen jeweils ein Maximum aufweist. Dies steht im Widerspruch zu früheren Ergebnissen [10], nach denen das optimale $W = 8$ ist, unabhängig vom Verkehr. Im Falle von $p = 0,1$ ist hier $W^* = 4$.

Bei CSMA (Abb. 4) zeigt der Quelle-Ziel-Durchsatz wie zu erwarten ein etwas anderes Verhalten. Die Kurven weisen zwar ein Maximum auf, aber der Durchsatz geht nach dem Überschreiten nicht gegen Null, dies bedeutet eine erheblich verbesserte Stabilität. Den max. Durchsatz erhält man bei $W = 2$, da dort die Zahl der Kollisionen gegen Null geht. Bei $W = 2$ können sich aber aufgrund der Konnektivität große Verzögerungen ergeben.

Aus den Kurven für S-ALOHA und CSMA bei MFR erkennt man aber auch, daß die Erfolgswahrscheinlichkeit einen stärkeren Einfluß auf den Quelle-Ziel Durchsatz hat als der Fortschritt pro Hop, denn dieser steigt mit fallendem W ständig an, obwohl mit fallendem W der Fortschritt pro Hop geringer wird.

Abb. 5 zeigt einen Vergleich zwischen einem teil-vermaschten S-ALOHA-System ($W = 4, a = 5$) und einem entsprechenden voll-vermaschten S-ALOHA-System. Dabei gilt:

$N = \lambda\pi\rho^2 = \lambda\pi(5R/2)^2 = (5/2)W$ Stationen

Aufgetragen ist der Durchsatz einer Station. Es ist schwer die Systeme zu vergleichen, da bei einem teil-vermaschten System weitere Parameter wie der S/E-Radius R und die Netzausdehnung ρ eingehen. Man erkennt, daß bei einem teil-vermaschten Netz mit $a = 2\rho/R = 5$ der Durchsatz gegenüber einem voll-vermaschten um ca. 25% größer ist, vor allem aber ergibt sich ein größerer Betriebsbereich (keine schmale Maximumspitze).

Abb. 6 zeigt, daß der Capture-Effekt den Quelle-Ziel-Durchsatz insgesamt weniger ver-

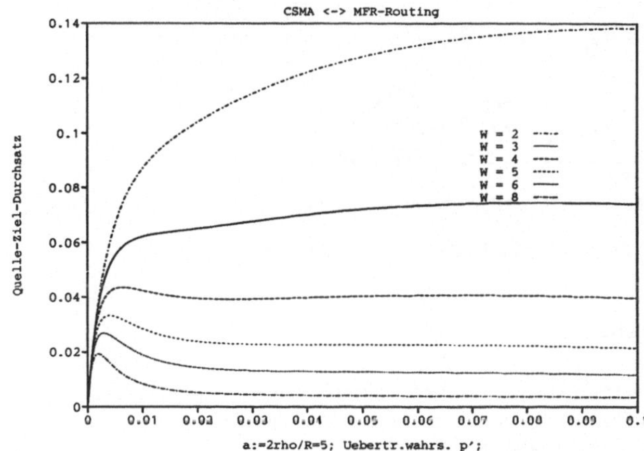

Abbildung 4: Quelle-Ziel-Durchsatz CSMA, MFR-Routing

bessert als erwartet. Der One-Hop-Durchsatz nimmt zwar stark zu, aber die Probleme beim Routen machen diesen Vorteil wieder zunichte. Der Quelle-Ziel Durchsatz nimmt

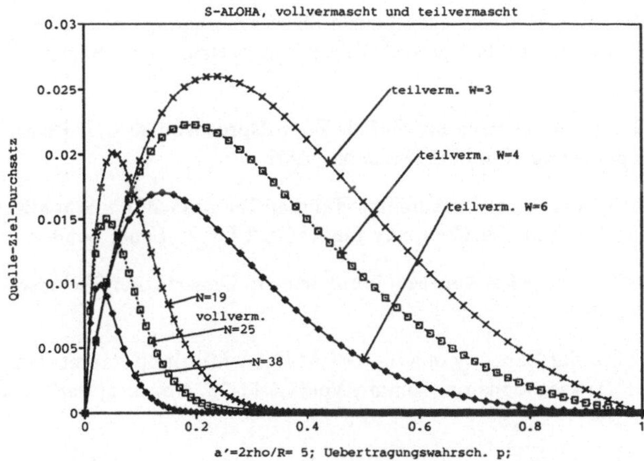

Abbildung 5: Durchsatzvergleich voll- und teil-vermaschtes S-ALOHA-System

nur geringfügig zu, da der Capture-Effekt bei kleineren Fortschritten die Kollisionswahrscheinlichkeit verringert.

Für seine Mitarbeit im Rahmen einer Diplomarbeit danke ich Herrn Georgios Nikolaidis.

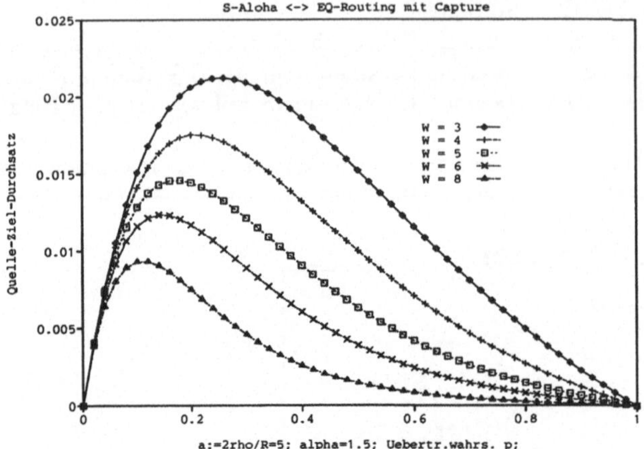

Abbildung 6: Quelle-Ziel-Durchsatz S-ALOHA, Capture

Literaturverzeichnis

[1] V. Brass: Ein Quittierungsverfahren für Multihop Paketfunknetze. Proc. ITG/GI-Tagung Messung, Modellierung und Bewertung von Rechensystemen", München, 1991, Informatik Fachberichte 286, Springer Verlag, Berlin, S. 167-181.

[2] K. Gotthardt, V. Brass: On Throughput and Delay in S-ALOHA Multihop Networks; Informatik-Fachberichte 154, Springer Verlag Berlin/Heidelberg, S. 236-249, 1987.

[3] K. Gotthardt: Durchsatz in CSMA-Multihop-Netzen; Informatik-Fachberichte 205, Springer Verlag Berlin/Heidelberg, S. 309-323, 1989.

[4] K. Gotthardt: Verteilung der Anzahl Hops einer Quelle-Ziel-Übertragung im Multihop-Paketfunknetz; Informatik-Fachberichte 286, Springer Verlag Berlin/Heidelberg, S. 182-195, 1991.

[5] K. Gotthardt: Analyse von Paket-Funknetzen mit Zufalls-Zugriffsprotokollen; UNI-PRESS Hochschulschriften Bd. 36, LIT-Verlag Hamburg/Münster, 1992.

[6] M.G. Kendall, P.A.P. Moran: Geometrical Probability, Number Ten of Griffin's Statistical Monongraphs & Courses; Charles Griffin & Company Limited, 42 Drury Lane, London.

[7] A. Mann: Funktion und Leistungsaspekte von Mobilfunknetzen; Dissertation Technische Hochschule Aachen, Aachen, 1990.

[8] R. Nelson, L. Kleinrock: The Spatial Capacity of a Slotted ALOHA Multihop Packet Radio Network with Capture; IEEE Transactions on Comm., Vol. COM-32, No. 6, pp. 684-694, 1984.

[9] J. Silvester, L. Kleinrock: Optimum Transmission radii for Packet Radio Networks or Why Six is a Magic Number; Conf. Rec., Nat. Telecommun. Conf., pp 4.3.1-4.3.5, 1978.

[10] H. Takagi, L. Kleinrock: Optimal Transmission Ranges for Randomly Distributed Packet Radio Terminals; IEEE Transactions on Comm., Vol. COM-32, No. 3, pp. 246-257, 1984.

[11] B. Walke, C.H. Rokitansky: Short-range mobile radio networks for road transport informatics; Proc. MRC'91 (Mobile Radio Conference), Nizza, France, Nov. 1991.

Leistungsanalyse von S-ALOHA Multihop-Netzen mit Diversitäts-Empfängern

Herbert Steffan
Lehrstuhl Kommunikationsnetze
RWTH Aachen
Kopernikusstr. 16
5100 Aachen
e-mail: hst@dfv.rwth-aachen.de

Abstract. Für teilvermaschte Stationen eines Paket-Datenfunknetzes mit slotted ALOHA Zugriffsprotokoll werden bei realistischer Modellierung des Funkübertragungsweges die Leistungskenngrößen Durchsatz und Fortschritt abgeleitet. Dazu werden bekannte Methoden aus der Analyse vollvermaschter Stationen aufgegriffen und hinsichtlich der Modellierung der Topologie erweitert. Die Verteilungsdichtefunktion des Abstandes des i-ten Störers bezüglich eines Empfängers bei Poisson-verteilten Stationen wird abgeleitet. Der Einfluß von verschiedenen Diversity-Techniken auf die Kenngrößen wird untersucht. Dabei zeigt es sich, daß diese Empfänger-Option Durchsatz und Fortschritt beträchtlich zu steigern vermag.

1 Einführung

Die Leistungsanalyse von Multihop-Netzen erfreute sich vor einigen Jahren besonderer Aufmerksamkeit, obwohl es zu dieser Zeit nur wenige reale Systeme gab. Bei der Analyse vollvermaschter Stationen konnten auch in jüngster Vergangenheit Fortschritte erzielt werden, indem die statistischen Eigenschaften des Funkübertragungsweges modelliert und in die Analyse einbezogen wurden, [KuAr82],[ArnBli87],[PraAr88].
Beim Mobilfunk kann nicht ohne Weiteres von dem stochastischen Modellprozeß, der aufgrund von Ausbreitungsmessungen der Funkwellen gebildet wurde, vgl. [KraWo90], [Okum68], auf die Fehlerrate eines übertragenen Datenpaketes geschlossen werden. Bei Annahme stochastischer Unabhängigkeit der Ereignisse, die das Verhalten einzelner Symbole beim Empfänger beschreiben, kann bei Analyse der Kommunikationsbeziehung ein geschlossener Ausdruck für die Paketfehlerrate abgeleitet werden. Dazu muß die stationäre Dichte des stochastischen Modellprozesses bekannt sein. Die Annahme der stochastischen Unabhängigkeit ist nur bei ausreichender Interleaving-Tiefe der Symbole

gerechtfertigt, da im allgemeinen der Funkübertragungsweg burstartig gestört ist. Dies äußert sich bezüglich des Modellprozesses in einer von Null verschiedenen Korrelation. Werden die Symbole nicht dem Interleaving unterworfen, ergeben sich bei der Analyse komplexe Strukturen. In [Wern91] wird die bivariate Fehlerwahrscheinlichkeit berechnet, indem die Korrelation zweier benachbarter Symbole berücksichtigt wird. Berechnungen der Fehlerwahrscheinlichkeit bei Berücksichtigung von Korrelationen aller in einem Datenpaket auftretenden stoch. Ordnungen sind dem Autor nicht bekannt. Um das Problem zu umgehen, wurde ein sog. Schwellenmodell entwickelt [KuAr82], das ein Paket genau dann als demodulierbar betrachtet, wenn der durchschnittliche Signalpegel bezogen auf die Paketübertragungsdauer oberhalb eines Schwellwertes liegt. Dies stellt bei im Vergleich zur Paketübertragungsdauer langsamen Variationen des Funkkanals eine gute Approximation dar. Der Schwellwert entspricht in etwa dem in realen Systemen geforderten durchschnittlichen Mindestpegel eines Datenpaketes, um es demodulieren zu können.

Bei diesem Ansatz wird jeweils die an der Antenne des Empfängers für die Demodulation verfügbare Leistung des Senders über dem Rauschen bestimmt, wobei die Beiträge der störenden Stationen als unkorreliert bezüglich des Nutzsignals angesehen und additiv der Rauschleistung hinzugefügt werden. In der bisherigen Modellierung von Multihop-Netzen wurden Störungen durch Capture-Abstände betrachtet, wobei jeweils nur der stärkste Störer berücksichtigt wurde, [GoPe89]. Hier sollen nun alle störenden Stationen einbezogen werden.

Für die Analyse eines Netzes mit Diversitäts-Empfängern muß die den Empfänger erreichende Leistung explizit berechnet werden. Mit den bisherigen Methoden ist dies nicht möglich.

Die Modellierung der Topologie des Netzes stellt ein besonderes Problem dar. Die übliche Annahme einer Poisson-verteilten Anzahl von Stationen kann auch hier übernommen werden. Jedoch kann nicht mit der daraus resultierenden Wahrscheinlichkeit, daß sich eine bestimmte Anzahl Stationen in einem Flächenelement befindet, gearbeitet werden, da eine realistische Modellierung des Funkkanals konkrete Abstände voraussetzt. Zu diesem Zweck wird in diesem Beitrag die Verteilungsdichtefunktion des Abstandes des i-ten Störers bezüglich eines Empfängers vorgestellt, vgl. Kap. 3, ohne die eine derartige Leistungsanalyse nur approximativ möglich ist. Damit läßt sich die Verteilungsdichtefunktion der Leistung des i-ten Störers an der Antenne eines Empfängers berechnen, Kap. 4. Diese Ergebnisse werden in Kap. 7 verwendet, um die Leistungskenngrößen Durchsatz und Fortschritt zu berechnen. In Kap. 8 werden Diversitäts-Empfänger in die Analyse einbezogen.

2   Eigenschaften des Funkkanals

Im Mobilfunk unterliegt die Empfangsfeldstärke während der Bewegung der Stationen starken Schwankungen, die 30dB - bezogen auf den Mittelwert - und mehr betragen können. Sind die Auswirkungen auf alle Frequenzanteile gleich, so spricht man von einem nicht frequenzselektiven Mobilfunkkanal. Dieser ist von drei statistisch nahezu unabhängige Ausbreitungsphänomene charakterisiert. Erreichen Funkwellen durch Reflexion und Beugung auf unterschiedlichen Wegen den Empfänger, wird dies Mehrwegeausbreitung genannt. Durch konstruktive und destruktive Überlagerung der auf verschiedenen Wegen und mit unterschiedlichen Verzögerungen und Dämpfungen den Empfänger erreichenden Signale entstehen Fadingeinbrüche im Signalpegel (multipath fading). Die Einhüllende dieses Signals kann unter bestimmten Umständen durch eine Rayleigh-Verteilung beschrieben werden (Rayleighfading), vgl. [Fleury92], wobei die stationäre Verteilungsdichtefunktion (VDF) des dem zeitlichen Verlauf der Leistung p_A entsprechenden Prozesses eine Exponential-Verteilung ist. Sie bezieht sich auf den lokalen Mittelwert $\overline{p}_A$, [Linn92],[ArnBli87].

$$f_{p_A}(p_A|\overline{p}_A) = \frac{1}{\overline{p}_A}\exp\left\{-\frac{p_A}{\overline{p}_A}\right\}$$
(1)

Neben diesen durch Mehrwegeausbreitung bedingten Schwunderscheinungen treten Signalschwankungen infolge von Abschattungen durch z.B. Gebäude oder Geländehindernisse, Hügel und

Waldflächen auf. Während der Rayleighprozeß die Schwankungen für kurze Zeiträume beschreibt, in denen sich die Umgebung der mobilen Station kaum ändert, werden die langsamen durch Abschattung bedingten Variationen in Bereichen von mehreren Sekunden durch einen zweiten Modellprozeß für die lokalen Mittelwerte $\overline{p}_A$ mit einer stationären Verteilungsdichte entspr. der Log-Normal-Verteilung beschrieben.

$$f_{\overline{p}_A}(\overline{p}_A|\overline{\overline{p}}_A) = \frac{1}{\sqrt{2\pi}\sigma\overline{p}_A}\exp\left\{-\frac{1}{2\sigma^2}\ln^2\frac{\overline{p}_A}{\overline{\overline{p}}_A}\right\} \tag{2}$$

Diese VDF bezieht sich auf den Langzeitmittelwert $\overline{\overline{p}}_A$. Die typischen Werte der Standardabweichung σ liegen für Stadtgebiete zwischen 6 und 12 dB. Der Schwund durch Abschattung wird als langsamer Schwund (slow fading, long-term fading) bezeichnet, [Turin72], [GuVis85]. Der Langzeitmittelwert dieses stochastischen Prozesses ist eine Funktion des Abstandes r zwischen Sender und Empfänger und wird allg. durch

$$\overline{\overline{p}}_A = \alpha r^{-\beta} \tag{3}$$

beschrieben, wobei $\beta = 2$ für Freiraumausbreitung gilt, und Werte bis 5 in stark bebauten Gebieten annehmen kann.

Für die Bewertung des Nah-Fern-Effektes, der u.U. den Durchsatz stark beeinflußt, ist die Kenntnis der Abstände der einzelnen Stationen von der Empfangsstation notwendig.

3 Abstand der i-ten Station

Die Verteilung der Stationen wird durch eine homogene stationäre zweidimensionale Poissonsche Punktfolge auf der Ebene mit der Intensität λ beschrieben:

$$Prob\{i\} = \frac{(\lambda F)^i}{i!}\exp(-\lambda F)$$

Die Wahrscheinlichkeit, i Stationen in der Fläche F anzutreffen, genügt nicht den Anforderungen von Gl. 3. Es müssen konkrete Abstände vom Sender bzw. Störer zum Empfänger vorliegen. Man erhält die Wahrscheinlichkeitsfunktion für den Abstand der i-ten Station zu einer betrachteten Station aus folgendem Gedankengang:

$$F_i(r) = Prob\{\text{ Abstand der i-ten Station } \leq r\} = Prob\{R_i \leq r\}$$

$$= Prob\{\text{ mindestens i Stationen in Kreisfläche } \pi r^2\}$$

$$= 1 - Prob\{\text{ keine Station in } \pi r^2\} - Prob\{\text{ eine Station in } \pi r^2\}$$

$$-Prob\{\text{ zwei Stationen in } \pi r^2\} - \cdots - Prob\{\text{ i-1 Stationen in } \pi r^2\}$$

$$= 1 - \exp(-\lambda\pi r^2) - \lambda\pi r^2\exp(-\lambda\pi r^2) - \frac{(-\lambda\pi r^2)^2}{2!}\exp(-\lambda\pi r^2) - \cdots$$

$$\cdots - \frac{(-\lambda\pi r^2)^{i-1}}{(i-1)!}\exp(\lambda\pi r^2)$$

$$F_i(r) = 1 - \sum_{k=0}^{i-1}\frac{a^k}{k!}\exp(-a) \qquad r \geq 0, \quad i \geq 1$$

mit $a = \lambda\pi r^2$. Die Verteilungsdichtefunktion (VDF) $f_i(r)$ berechnet sich mit $f_i(r) = \frac{dF_i(r)}{da}\frac{da}{dr}$ zu

$$f_i(r) = 2\lambda\pi r\frac{(\lambda\pi r^2)^{i-1}}{(i-1)!}\exp(-\lambda\pi r^2) = \frac{2(\lambda\pi)^i}{(i-1)!}r^{2i-1}\exp(-\lambda\pi r^2). \tag{4}$$

In Abb. 1 ist die VDF des normierten Abstandes für die ersten zehn Stationen dargestellt.

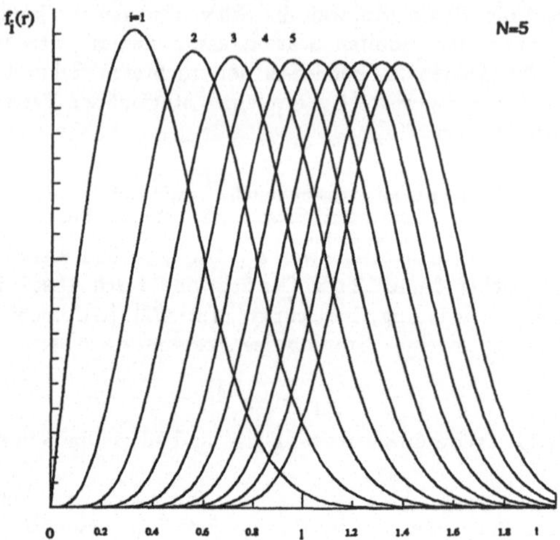

Fig. 1. Verteilungsdichtefunktion des Abstandes für verschiedene Stationen $i = 1$ bis 10

4   Leistung der i-ten Station

Die Empfangsleistung eines Signals, das von der i-ten Station ausgesandt wurde, ist abhängig von Mehrwegeausbreitung, Abschattung und der Entfernung des Empfängers von der i-ten Station. Die VDF der Leistung an der Empfangsantenne erhält man als Marginaldichte der Verbundverteilung mit

$$f_{p_A}(p_A|\overline{\overline{p}}_A) = \int_0^\infty f_{p_A}(p_A|\overline{p}_A) f_{\overline{p}_A}(\overline{p}_A|\overline{\overline{p}}_A)\, d\overline{p}_A.$$

Die Dichte des Langzeitmittelwertes der Leistung $\overline{\overline{p}}_A$ für einen Sender i bezogen auf einen Empfänger im Punkt (0,0) erhält man als Transformierte der Abstandsdichte der i-ten Station $f_i(r_i)$, vgl. Gl. (3).

$$f_{\overline{\overline{p}}_A}(\overline{\overline{p}}_A) = f_i(r(\overline{\overline{p}}_A)) \left| \frac{dr(\overline{\overline{p}}_A)}{dr} \right|$$

$$= \frac{2}{\beta}\, (\overline{\overline{p}}_A)^{-\frac{2i}{\beta}-1}\, \frac{N^i}{(i-1)!}\, \exp(-\overline{\overline{p}}_A{}^{\frac{2}{\beta}} N) \tag{5}$$

mit $N = R_s{}^2 \pi \lambda$ als die mittlere Anzahl der Stationen im Sendegebiet.

5   Nah-Fern-Effekt, Capture-Wahrscheinlichkeit und Schwellenmodell

Ein Datenpaket kann aufgrund des Nah-Fern-Effekts trotz zeitgleicher Übertragungen anderer Datenpakete korrekt empfangen werden. Voraussetzung ist, daß die mittlere Leistung p_S des Nutzsignals beim Empfänger über die Dauer des gewünschten Datenpaketes die Leistung der störenden Station p_{I_j} um eine gegebene Schwelle z_0 übersteigt. Das entspricht der Annahme eines Schwellenmodells für den Empfangs- bzw. Detektionsvorgang.

$$Prob_{cap} = Prob\{\frac{p_S}{p_{I_j}} > z_0\} = Prob\{z > z_0\} \tag{6}$$

Dabei bezeichnet $Prob_{cap}$ die Capture-Wahrscheinlichkeit. Ein Empfänger mit $z_0 = \infty$ (non capture) kann nur erfolgreich empfangen, wenn die Interferenzleistung gegen Null geht. Perfect Capture ($z_0 = 1$) bedeutet, das der Empfänger das gewünschte Datenpaket aus zwei sich überlagernden Signalen, die mit gleicher Leistung an der Antenne des Empfängers anliegen, herausfiltern kann. Die Leistungen am Empfänger werden durch ihre VDFs $f_{p_S}(P)$ und $f_{p_{I_j}}(P)$ beschrieben. Nach [Papo84] berechnet sich die VDF $f_z(z)$ der Zufallsvariablen z, die durch Division der Zufallsvariablen p_S und p_{I_j} entsteht und das Signal-zu-Störverhältnis (SIR) beschreibt, mit·

$$f_z(z) = \int\limits_0^\infty f_{p_S}(zw)\, f_{p_{I_j}}(w)\, w\, dw. \tag{7}$$

Die Wahrscheinlichkeit, daß der Schwellwert z_0 überschritten wird, ergibt sich mit:

$$Prob\{z > z_0\} = Prob\{\frac{p_S}{p_{I_j}} > z_0\} = \int\limits_{z_0}^\infty f_z(z)\, dz \tag{8}$$

Jede Mobilstation sei im Mittel von N Nachbarstationen umgeben. Nachbarn sind diejenigen Stationen, die mit einem bestimmten mittleren Mindestsignalpegel über dem Rauschpegel erreicht werden, wenn keine anderen Stationen die Übertragung stören. Da selbst sehr weit entfernte Stationen bei diesem Kanalmodell als Störer wirksam werden können steht diese Konsequenz im Gegensatz zu denen der einfachen Kanalmodelle, vgl. [TaKlei84], wo die Stationen außerhalb des Sende-/Empfangsgebietes mit dem Radius R_s um die empfangende Station die Übertragung nicht beeinträchtigen.

Nachdem die stochastischen Eigenschaften des Funkkanals kurz vorgestellt und aus Annahmen bezüglich der Topologie die VDFn der Abstände der Stationen hergeleitet wurden, sollen nun die Funktionen Routing und Kanalzugriff der mobilen Station erläutert und formal beschrieben werden.

6 Routing-Verfahren

In Multihop-Netzen darf eine Station P ein Datenpaket an eine Zielstation F senden, die außerhalb ihres Senderadius R_s liegt und deshalb nicht ihr Nachbar ist, vgl. Abb. 2. Wenn eine unmittelbare Übertragung des Paketes an die Zielstation F nicht möglich ist, werden zur Übertragung des Paketes die dazwischenliegenden Stationen Q_n als Relais benutzt. Der Festlegung der Wegewahl heißt Routing.

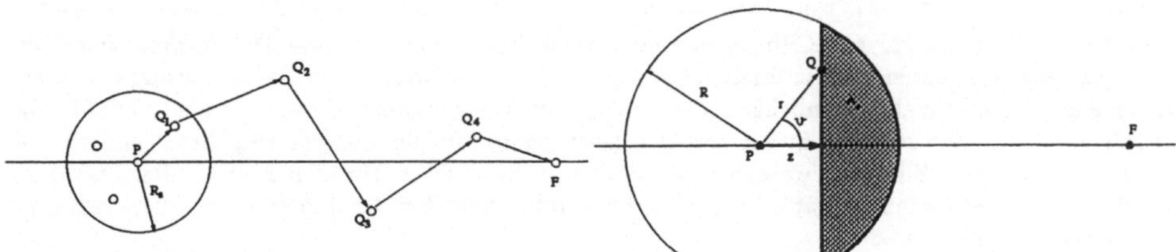

Fig. 2. Routing im Multihop-Netz

Fig. 3. Bestimmung von A_x

Aus der Literatur sind mehrere für die wahrscheinlichkeitstheoretische Analyse geeignete Routing-algorithmen bekannt. Hier wird das 'Most Forward within fixed Radius' (MFR) Routing betrachtet. Bei diesem Verfahren wird das Datenpaket an die Nachbarstation gesendet, die den größten Fortschritt in Richtung Zielstation ermöglicht. Ist keine Station näher am Ziel als die Station selbst, so wird rückwärts geroutet. Nach Abb. 3 läßt sich die VDF für den Abstand vom Sender zum Empfänger herleiten. Ausgehend von der Wahrscheinlichkeit, daß sich der Empfänger im Punkt (r, ϑ) befindet, gilt

$$Prob\{ \text{ der Empfänger befindet sich im Punkt } (r, \vartheta)\}$$

$$= Prob\{ \text{ keine Station in } A_x\} \cdot Prob\{ \text{ mindestens eine Station in } (r, \vartheta)\}$$

$$= Prob\{ r < \tilde{r} \le r + dr, \vartheta < \tilde{\vartheta} \le \vartheta + d\vartheta\}$$

$$= \exp(-\lambda A_x)\lambda dA.$$

In Polarkoordinaten läßt sich mit $dA = dx\, dy = r\, dr\, d\vartheta$ eine konkrete VDF für den Abstand vom Sender zum Empfänger angeben

$$f_{ra}\,(r)dr\, d\vartheta = \exp(-\lambda A_x)\,\lambda\, r\, dr\, d\vartheta \qquad 0 \le r \le R,\, 0 \le \vartheta \le 2\pi \tag{9}$$

$$\text{mit} \qquad A_x = R^2 \left[arccos(\frac{r}{R}\, cos\vartheta) - \frac{r}{R}\, cos\vartheta \sqrt{1 - (\frac{r}{R}\, cos\vartheta)^2} \right]$$

vgl. [TaKlei84], [GoPe89].

7 Berechnung der Leistungskenngrößen Durchsatz und Fortschritt

Zunächst sollen einige allgemein in der Literatur verwendete Annahmen erläutert werden. Der gemeinsame Übertragungskanal wird in äquidistante Zeitabschnitte entsprechend der Länge der Datenpakete eingeteilt unterstellt, sog. Slots. Nicht erfolgreiche Übertragungen werden auf einem (hier nicht betrachteten) verzögerungsfreien Quittungskanal angezeigt und erfordern Wiederholungen der Übertragungen. Ein neues, zu übertragendes Datenpaket wird für eine Station erst generiert, wenn das vorhergehende erfolgreich übertragen wurde, so daß eine Station immer genau ein Paket besitzt (heavy traffic Lastmodell). Alle Stationen senden mit der gleichen Übertragungswahrscheinlichkeit p. Als Kanal-Zugriffssprotokoll wird Slotted-Aloha verwendet.
Wenn ein Datenpaket erfolgreich übertragen werden soll, muß es eine bestimmte Station senden. Außerdem darf die Zielstation dieser Onehop-Übertragung nicht gleichzeitig senden. Dies tritt mit Wahrscheinlichkeit $1 - p$ ein. Zudem darf die Übertragung nicht mißlingen. Dies kann einerseits durch Kollisionen geschehen, andererseits kann durch nicht ideale Übertragungseigenschaften des Mobilfunkkanals das Datenpaket gestört werden. Mit dem hier verwendeten Schwellenmodell werden beide Phänomene erfaßt. An Kollisionen sind gemäß dieser Interpretation Datenpakete beteiligt, die wegen interferierender Pakete ihren Empfänger nicht mit ausreichender Signalleistung erreichen. Dieser Fall tritt mit Wahrscheinlichkeit $1 - Prob_{cap}$ ein. Die genannten Ereignisse sind unabhängig. Es soll nicht nur der stärkste Störer mit der Leistung p_{I_j} in die Analyse eingehen, sondern alle störenden Stationen. Zunächst werden $n + 2$ Stationen betrachtet. Um den Einfluß aller Stationen zu erfassen, ist der Grenzübergang $\lim_n \to \infty$ notwendig, bzw. bei der numerischen Auswertung ist n hinreichend groß zu wählen.
Nimmt man die Signale der verschiedenen Übertragungen als unkorreliert an [ArnBli87], addieren sich die an der Empfangsantenne anliegenden Leistungen aller sendenden Stationen, gewichtet mit der Wahrscheinlichkeit ihres Auftretens. Ein ähnlicher Ansatz ist in [Zand91] zu finden.

Es folgt für den bedingten Onehop-Durchsatz, der die mittlere Anzahl erfolgreich übertragener Pakete einer Station beschreibt

$$E[S|r] = p\,(1-p)\,Prob_{cap} = p\,(1-p)\,Prob\{\frac{ps(r)}{\overline{P}} > z_0\} \tag{10}$$

$$= p\,(1-p)\,Prob\{\frac{ps(r)}{p\sum\limits_{j=1}^{n}p_{I_j} + n_0} > z_0\}.$$

Dabei repräsentiert n_0 die spektrale Rauschdichte. Mit $z = \frac{ps(r)}{\overline{P}} = \frac{ps(r)}{p\sum\limits_{j=1}^{n}p_{I_j}+n_0}$ lassen sich die VDFs

wie abgeleitet berechnen. Mit $f_i(r_i)$ nach Gl. (4).

$$f_z(z|r) = \int\limits_0^\infty \int\limits_0^\infty \cdots \int\limits_0^\infty f_z(z|r\,r_1\,r_2\cdots r_n)\,f_1(r_1)\,f_2(r_2)\cdots f_n(r_n)\,dr_1\,dr_2\cdots dr_n \tag{11}$$

$$\text{mit} \qquad f_z(z|r\,r_1\,r_2\cdots r_n) = \int\limits_0^\infty f_{ps}(zw|r)\,f_{pI}(w|r_1\,r_2\cdots r_n)w\,dw$$

$$f_{pI}(w|r_1\,r_2\cdots r_n) = f_{pI_1}(w|r_1) * f_{pI_2}(w|r_2) * \cdots * f_{pI_n}(w|r_n)$$

Die Addition der Zufallsvariablen, die die Leistung der Störer beschreiben, ergibt eine Faltung der entsprechenden VDFn.

Um die Bedingung aufzulösen, wird die Verteilung der Position des Empfängers Q von dem Sender P benötigt. Diese wird durch den Routingalgorithmus festgelegt. Für den verwendeten MFR-Algorithmus erhält man, vgl. Kap. 6:

$$E[S] = \int\limits_0^{2\pi} \int\limits_0^R E[S|\,\tilde{r} = r]\,Prob\{r < \tilde{r} \le r+dr, \vartheta < \tilde{\vartheta} \le \vartheta + d\vartheta\}$$

$$= \int\limits_0^{2\pi} \int\limits_0^R E[S|\,\tilde{r} = r]\,\exp(-\lambda A_x)\,\lambda\,r\,dr\,d\vartheta \tag{12}$$

Der Onehop-Fortschritt berechnet sich aus der Projektion der Sendestrecke r auf die direkte Verbindungsline von der Quellstation zur Zielstation.

$$Z = r\cos(\vartheta).$$

Damit läßt sich der Erwartungswert des Fortschritts in Richtung der Zielstation berechnen. Es ist denkbar, daß eine Station nicht bis zur maximalen Reichweite R_s sendet, sondern sich auf

$$R = m\,R_s \qquad \text{mit} \qquad 0 < m \le 1$$

beschränkt, da die Erfolgswahrscheinlichkeit mit großen Übertragungsstrecken sinkt. Es wird sich zeigen, daß dies u.U. vorteilhaft sein kann. Die Übertragungsstrecke r soll wird auf die Sendereichweite R_s und der Fortschritt auf den mittleren Abstand zur ersten Nachbarstation normiert.

$$t = \frac{r}{R_s}$$

Damit lauten Durchsatz und Fortschritt

$$E[S] = \frac{2N}{\pi} \int\limits_0^{\pi} \int\limits_0^{m} t\, E[S|t]\, \exp(-B(t,\vartheta))\, dt\, d\vartheta \tag{13}$$

$$E[Z]\,\sqrt{\lambda} = 2\,\frac{N}{\pi}\,\sqrt{\frac{N}{\pi}} \int\limits_0^{\pi} \int\limits_0^{m} t^2 \cos\vartheta\, E[S|t]\, e^{-B(t,\vartheta)}\, dt\, d\vartheta \tag{14}$$

$$\text{mit} \quad B(t,\vartheta) = \frac{N}{\pi}\, m^2 \left[arccos(\frac{t}{m}\cos\vartheta) - \frac{t}{m}\cos\vartheta\sqrt{1 - (\frac{t}{m}\cos\vartheta)^2} \right].$$

Einige Integrale können nur für Sonderfälle der Parameter gelöst werden. Beispielsweise läßt sich das Integral von Gl. (7) für $\sigma = 0$ lösen und es bildet sich ähnlich [SheYu90], Gl. (3) eine Produktform der Wahrscheinlichkeiten, die das Capture-Verhalten beschreiben. Die Intergale über $f_i(r_i)$ lassen sich für $\beta = 4$ geschlossen lösen, s. Anhang. Numerisch lassen sich Fortschritt und Durchsatz problemlos visualisieren, s. Kap. 9. Doch soll zunächst der Einfluß der Empfänger-Option Diversität in die Analyse einbezogen werden.

8 Diversität in Multihop-Netzen

Unter Diversität versteht man dir Fähigkeit des Empfängers gesendete Signale von mindestens zwei unabhängig gestörten Ausbreitungspfaden zu empfangen. Der Empfänger verfügt dann über mehrere Empfangszweige. Diversität ist umso wirksamer, je geringer die Korrelation der Fadingprozesse in den Diversitäts-Zweigen ist. Man unterscheidet Frequenz-, Zeit-, Code-, und Raum-Diversität. Bei Antennen-Diversität, eine Form von Raum-Diversität, ist der Empfäger mit mindestens zwei Antennen ausgerüstet. Außerdem unterscheidet man Diversitäts-Empfänger nach der Ablösung bzw. Kombination der Signale, vgl. [Jakes74], [GuVis85].

8.1 Selektions-Diversität (SD)

Bei SD wird der Zweig mit dem besten Signal-zu-Störverhältnis (SIR) ausgewählt und das Signal zur Dekodierung verwendet. Für die Analyse wird zunächst ein Zweig betrachtet. Ein Empfänger, der das gewünschte Datenpaket zu dekodieren versucht, sei wieder von n anderen Stationen gestört, wobei alle Signale voneinander statistisch unabhängig seien. Die Leistungen der einzelnen Signale werden durch die Dichten $f_{ps_i}(ps_i)$ für das gewünschte Datenpaket und $f_{pI_{ij}}(pI_{ij})$ für das Paket des j-ten Störers im i-ten Zweig beschrieben. Die Wahrscheinlichkeit, daß das Verhältnis der Leistungen kleiner als z_0 ist, berechnet sich aus dem Komplement der Capture-Wahrscheinlichkeit.

$$1 - Prob_{capi} = or_i = Prob\{ \frac{ps_i}{p\sum\limits_{j=1}^{n} pI_{ij} + n_{0i}} < z_0 \}$$

$$= \int\limits_0^{z_0} \int\limits_0^{\infty} f_{ps_i}(zw)\, f_{pI_j}(w)\, w\, dw\, dz$$

Der Parameter *or* wird als outage-rate bezeichnet,[Linn92]. Für den Fall, daß die verschiedenen Zweige ideal unkorrelierte Signale liefern, sind die Wahrscheinlichkeiten für das Unterschreiten der Schwelle z_0 in den Zweigen unabhängig voneinander.

$$or = \prod_{i=1}^{K} or_i = \prod_{i=1}^{K} Prob\{\frac{ps_i}{p \sum_{j=1}^{n} pI_{ij} + n_{0i}} < z_0\} \tag{15}$$

Der Gewinn ist nach [Jakes71] selbst bei einem Korrelationskoeffizienten von 0.7 noch in der Größenordnung dessen, was bei ideal unkorrelierten Zweigen zu erwarten wäre.

Werden alle VDVn in den unterschiedlichen Zweigen durch die gleichen Parameter bestimmt, so ergibt sich

$$or = or_1^K = \left[Prob\{\frac{ps_i}{p \sum_{j=1}^{n} pI_{1j} + n_{01}} < z_0\} \right]^K$$

Damit läßt sich der bedingte Durchsatz für Selektions-Diversität mit n Störern und K Zweigen berechnen.

$$E[S_{SD}|t] = p(1-p)\, Prob_{cap_{SD}}(t) = p(1-p)(1 - or(t))$$

mit

$$or(t) = \int_0^\infty \int_0^\infty \cdots \int_0^\infty \left[\int_0^{z_0} f_z(z|t\, t_1 t_2 \cdots t_n)\, dz \right]^K f_1(t_1)\, f_2(t_2) \cdots f_n(t_n)\, dt_1\, dt_2 \cdots dt_n \tag{16}$$

Der Fortschritt läßt sich analog herleiten.

8.2 Maxumum-Ratio-Combining (MRC)

Wie in [Jakes74] abgeleitet, erhält man am Ausgang des MRC-Diversität-Empfängers ein resultierendes SIR, das der Summe der SIRs in den einzelnen Zweigen entspricht. Die VDF der Zufallsvariable z erhält man aus der Faltung der Dichten der z_i's.

$$z = \sum_{i=1}^{K} z_i \;\rightarrow\; f_z(z) = f_{z_1}(z) * f_{z_2}(z) * f_{z_3}(z) * \cdots * f_{z_k}(z)$$

Werden die VDFn in den einzelnen Zweigen durch die gleichen Parameter bestimmt, so entspricht das der K-fachen Faltung der Dichte von z_1. Die Wahrscheinlichkeit, daß ein Paket korrekt empfangen wird, entspricht der Wahrscheinlichkeit, daß SIR über dem Capture-Parameter z_0 liegt.

$$Prob\{z > z_0\} = \int_{z_0}^\infty f_z(z)\, dz = \int_{z_0}^\infty [f_{z_1}(z)]^{*K}\, dz \tag{17}$$

Dabei bezeichnet $*K$ die K-fache Faltung. Nun läßt sich der Durchsatz für MRC ableiten

$$E[S_{MRC}|t] = p(1-p)\, Prob_{cap_{MRC}}(t) = p(1-p) \int_{z_0}^\infty f_z(z|t)\, dz$$

mit

$$f_z(z|t) = \int_0^\infty \int_0^\infty \cdots \int_0^\infty [f_z(z|t\, t_1 t_2 \cdots t_m)]^{*K} f_1(t_1)\, f_2(t_2) \cdots f_m(t_m)\, dt_1\, dt_2 \cdots dt_m. \tag{18}$$

Der Fortschritt läßt sich analog herleiten.

9 Ergebnisse

Die abgeleiteten Gleichungen wurden teilweise numerisch ausgewertet. Die Abbildungen 4 bis 9 zeigen die Kurvenverläufe für Durchsatz E[S] und Fortschritt E[Z] über der Sendewahrscheinlichkeit p.
In Abb. 4 und 5 sind E[S] und E[Z] für unterschiedliche Nachbarschaftszahlen $N = 5$ bis 10 für Empfänger ohne Diversität dargestellt. Die Parameter $R = R_s$, $z_0 = 1$, $n_0 = 0$ werden konstant gehalten. Die Kurven fallen bei hohen Sendewahrscheinlichkeiten wegen zunehmender Kollisionen ab. Es zeigt sich, daß für Nachbarschaftszahlen um $N_{opt} = 9$ der Onehop-Fortschritt maximal wird. Dieser N_{opt} ist u.a. abhängig von dem die Signalabschwächung beschreibenden Parameter β. In [KleSy78] wurde $N_{opt} = 7$ abgeleitet.
Die Abhängigkeit des Durchsatzes von der Schwelle z_0 illustriert Abb. 6. Die Empfindlichkeit des Empfängers ist demnach eine den Durchsatz stark beeinträchtigende Größe. In der Leistungsanalyse wird fast ausnahmslos $z_0 = 1$ gewählt, obwohl $z_0 = 10$ realistischer ist.
In Abb. 7 wurde die maximale Routingdistanz auf $R = mR_s$ mit $m = 0.8$ beschränkt. Dies erweist sich für den Durchsatz als vorteilhaft, da die Erfolgswahrscheinlichkeit bei kürzeren Übertragungsstrecken höher ist. Für den Fortschritt stellt sich u.U. ein nachteiliger Effekt ein, da nicht bis zum maximal möglichen Senderadius gesendet wird.
Die Abbildungen 8 und 9 zeigen jeweils E[S] und E[Z] für die verschiedenen Diversität-Verfahren bei zwei und vier Zweigen, (SD2, SD4, MRC2, MRC4), im Vergleich zu den Kenngrößen von Stationen ohne Diversität. Das technisch schwer zu realisierende MRC liefert die besten Ergebnisse. Jedoch ist auch mit dem einfacheren SD bei entsprechender Anzahl der Zweige eine beträchtliche Leistungssteigerung zu verzeichnen. Die Parameter wurden mit $N = 7, z_0 = 1, m = 1$ gewählt.

Es konnte damit gezeigt werden, daß sich mit der vorgestellten Methodik eine Leistungsanalyse von Multihop-Netzen bei realistischer Modellierung der Funkübertragungswege möglich ist. Empfänger-Diversität ist offensichtlich geeignet, die Kenngrößen Durchsatz und Fortschritt beträchtlich zu erhöhen.

References

[ArnBli87] J. C. Arnbak W. v. Blitterswijk. *Capacity of Slotted ALOHA in Rayleigh-Fading Channels*, Vol. SAC-5, No. 2. pp. 263–269, February 1987.

[Fleury92] B. Fleury. *Charakterisierung von Mobil- und Richtfunkkanälen mit schwach stationären Fluktuationen und unkorrelierter Streuung.* Dissertation, ETH Zürich, 1990.

[GoPe89] C. Gotthardt H.J. Perz. *Maximum throughput and small delay, combined with an optimum degree of spatial reuse of channels.* In *2nd PROMETHEUS Workshop*, Stockholm, October 1989.

[Tables] I. S. Gradstein I. M. Ryshik. *Tables of Series, Produkts and Integrals.* Harri Deutsch, Thun Frankfurt /Main.

[GoSal87] D. J. Goodmann A. A. M. Saleh. *The Near/Far Effect in Local ALOHA Radio Communication.* *IEEE Transactions on Vehicular Technology*, Vol. VT-36, No. 1, pp. 19–27, February 1987.

[GuVis85] S. C. Gupta, R. Viswathan, R. Muammar. *Land Mobil Radio Systems, - a Tutorial Exposition.* *IEEE Communications Magazin*, Vol. 23, No. 6, pp. 34–45, June 1985.

[HanMe77] F. Hansen M. Finn. *Mobile Fading - Rayleigh and Lognormal Superimposed. IEEE Transactions on Vehicular Technology*, Vol. VT-26, No. 4, pp. 332–335, November 1971.

[HoLi86] T. C. Hou V. O. K. Li. *Transmission Range Control in Multihop Packet Radio Networks. IEEE Transactions on Communication*, Vol. COM-34, No. 1, pp. 38–44, January 1986.

[Jakes74] W.C Jakes. *Microwave Mobile Communications.* Wiley, New York, 1974.

[Jakes71] W. C. Jakes Jr. *A Comparison of Specific Space Diversity Techniques for Reduction of Fast Fading in UHF Mobile Radio Systems. IEEE Transactions on Vehicular Technology*, Vol. VT-20, No. 4, pp. 81–92, November 1971.

[KuAr82] F. Kuperus J. Arnbak. *Packet Radio in a Rayleigh Channel.* Electron Leters, Vol. 18, No. 12, June 1982.

[Koch90] Wolfgang Koch Jürgen Petersen. *Diversity und Frequenzsprungverfahren im D–Netz. PKI Technische Mitteilungen*, Vol. 2, pp. 13–19, 1990.

[KleSy78] L. Kleinrock J. Sylvester. *Optimum Transmission Radii for Packet Radio Networks or Why is Six a Magic Number.* Proc. IEEE Nat. Telecommun. Conf., Vol. 75, pp. 4.3.1 – 4.3.5, December 1978.

[KraWo90] A. Krantzik D. Wolf. *Statistische Eigenschaften von Fadingprozessen zur Beschreibung eines Landmobilfunkkanals.* Frequenz, Vol. 44, No. 6, June 1990.

[Linn91] J.-P. Linnartz. *Site Diversity in Land-Mobile Cellular Telephony Network with Discontinous Voice Transmission.* European Transactions on Telecommunications, Vol. 2, No. 5, 1991.

[Linn92] J.-P. Linnartz. *Exact Analysis of the Outage Probability in Multi-User Mobil Communication.* Proceedings of the IEEE, Vol. 2, No. 1, January 1992.

[LiPrAr88] J.-P. M. G. Linnartz, R. Prasad, J. Ch. Arnbak. *Spatial Distribution of Traffic in a Cellular ALOHA Network.* Archiv der Elektrischen Übertragung, Vol. AEÜ-42, No. 1, pp. 61–63, January 1988.

[Okum68] Y. Okumura, E. Ohmori, T. Kawano, K. Fukuda. *Field Strength and Its Variability in VHF and UHF Land Mobile Service.* Rev. Elec. Comm. Lab., Vol. 16, pp. 825 – 873, September 1968.

[PraAr88] R. Prasad J. C. Arnbak. *Enhanced Throughput in Packet Radio Channels with Shadowing.* Electronics Letters, Vol. 24, No. 16, pp. 986–988, August 1988.

[Papo84] Athanasios Papoulis. *Probability, Random Variables, and Stochastic Processes.* McGraw-Hill Book Company, *1984*, Vol. 29, No. 7, pp. 596–603, July 1980.

[PlaLin90] C. v. d. Plas J.-P. M. G. Linnartz. *Stability of Mobile Slotted ALOHA Network with Rayleigh Fading , Shadowing and Near-Far Effect.* IEEE Transactions on Vehicular Technology, Vol. VT-39, No. 4, pp. 359–366, November 90.

[ShoYu90] A. U. H. Sheikh, Y. Yao, X. Wu. *The ALOHA Systems in Shadowed Mobile Radio Channels with Slow or Fast Fading.* IEEE Transactions on Vehicular Technology, Vol. VT-39, No. 4, pp. 289–297, November 1990.

[Turin72] G. L. Turin, F. D. Clapp, T. L. Johnston, S. B. Fine, D. Lavry. *A Statistical Model of Urban Multipath Propagation.* IEEE Transactions on Vehicular Technology, Vol. VT-21, No. 1, pp. 1–9, February 1972.

[TaKlei84] H. Takagi L. Kleinrock. *Optimal Transmission Ranges for Randomly Distributed Packet Terminals.* IEEE Transactions on Communication, Vol. COM-32, No. 3, pp. 246–257, March 1984.

[TaKlei85] H. Takagi L. Kleinrock. *Throughput-Delay Characteristics of Some Slotted-ALOHA Multihop Packet Radio Networks.* IEEE Transactions on Communication, Vol. COM-33, No. 11, pp. 1200–1207, November 1985.

[Wern91] M. Werner. *Bit Error Correlation in Rayleigh-Fading Channels.* Archiv der Elektrischen Übertragung, Vol. AEÜ-45, No. 4, pp. 61–63, July 1991.

[Zand91] J. Zander. *Jamming in Slotted ALOHA Multihop Packet Radio Networks.* IEEE Transactions on Communication, Vol. COM-39, No. 10, October 1991.

A   Anhang

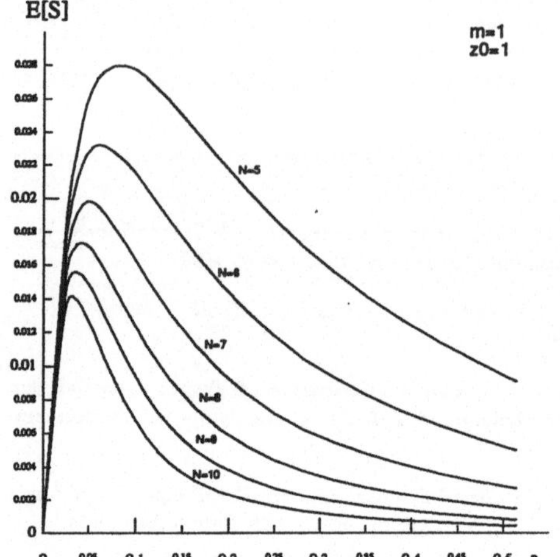

Fig. 4. Durchsatz ohne Diversität über p

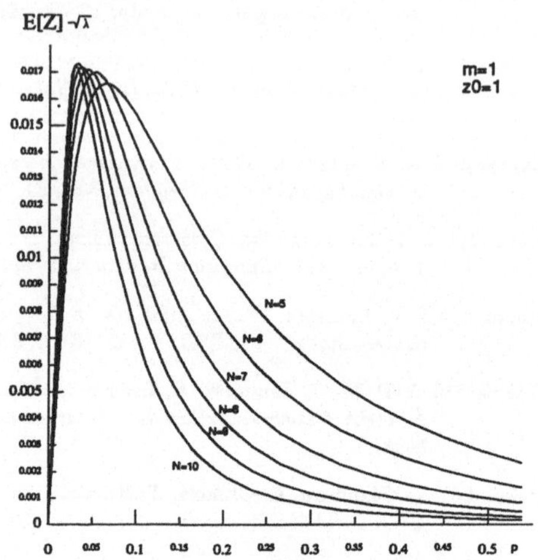

Fig. 5. Fortschritt ohne Diversität über p

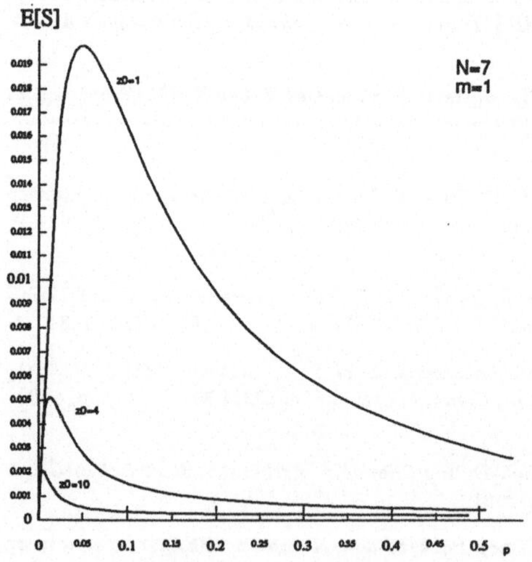

Fig. 6. Einfluß der Schwelle z_0 auf den Durchsatz

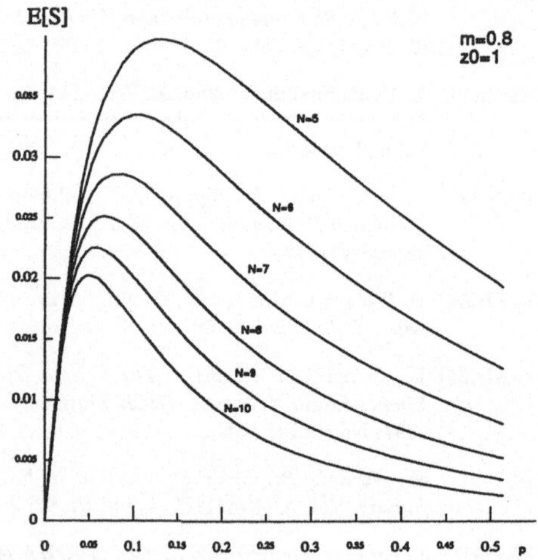

Fig. 7. Durchsatz bei $m = 0.8$ über p

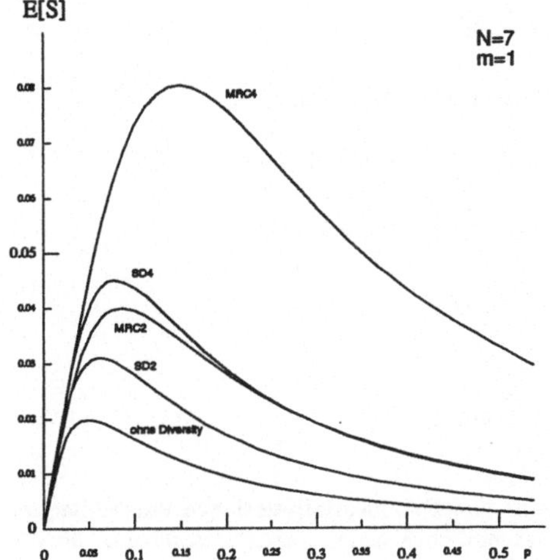

Fig. 8. Durchsatz bei Diversität über p

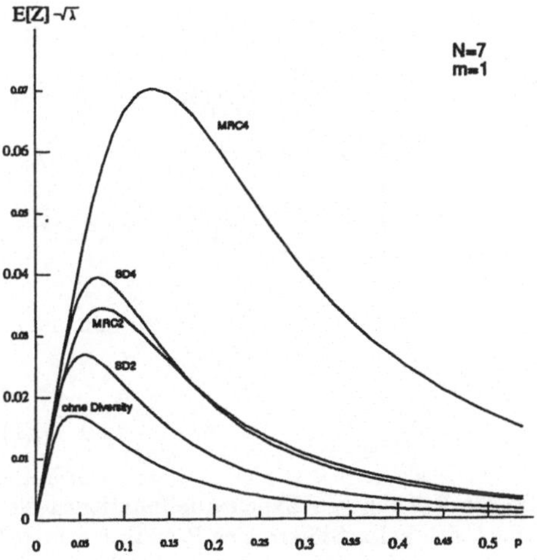

Fig. 9. Fortschritt bei Diversität über p

Mit (1) u. (8) , einem Störer j $(n = 1)$, $\sigma = 0$, folgt:

$$Prob\{z > z_0 \mid n = 1\,t, t_j\} = \int\limits_{z_0}^{\infty} f_{z\mid t, t_j}(z\mid t, t_j)dz = \int\limits_{z_0}^{\infty}\int\limits_{0}^{\infty} f_{ps\mid t}(zw\mid t)\, f_{p_{I_j}\mid t_j}(w\mid t_j)\, w\, dw\, dz$$

$$-\int\limits_{z_0}^{\infty}\int\limits_{0}^{\infty} t^{\beta} \exp(-t^{\beta} zw)\, t_j^{\beta} \exp(-t_j^{\beta} w)\, w\, dw\, dz = \frac{t_j^{\beta}}{t_j^{\beta} + z_0 t^{\beta}}$$

Mit (4) u. (11), $\beta = 4$ einem Störer j $(n = 1)$; $t_j^2 = x$, vgl. [Tables] S. 365, Gl. 1 u. 2,

$$Prob\{z > z_0 \mid n = 1\} = \int\limits_{0}^{\infty}\int\limits_{0}^{\infty} f_z(z\mid t\, t_j)\, f_{ra}(t)\, f_1(t_j)\, dt dt_j$$

$$= \int\limits_{0}^{\infty}\int\limits_{0}^{\infty} \frac{t_j^{\beta}}{t_j^{\beta} + z_0 t^{\beta}}\, \frac{2N^j}{(j-1)!}\, t_j^{2j-1} \exp(-t_j^2 N)\, f_{ra}(t)\, dt dt_j$$

$$= \int\limits_{0}^{\infty}\int\limits_{0}^{\infty} \frac{N^j\, x^{j+1} \exp(-xN)}{(j-1)!\, (x^2 + z_0 t^4)}\, f_{ra}(t)\, dt dx$$

$$
= \begin{cases}
\displaystyle\int_0^\infty (-1)^{\frac{j+1}{2}} (t^2\sqrt{z_0})^j \left[ci(Nt^2\sqrt{z_0})\sin(Nt^2\sqrt{z_0}) - si(Nt^2\sqrt{z_0})\cos(Nt^2\sqrt{z_0})\right] \\[2ex]
\qquad + \displaystyle\sum_{k=1}^{\frac{j+1}{2}} \frac{(j-2k+1)!}{(j-1)!} (-N^2 t^4 z_0)^{k-1} f_{ra}(t)\, dt \quad \text{für } j = 2n-1,\ n \in I\!N \\[3ex]
\displaystyle\int_0^\infty (-1)^{\frac{j}{2}-1} (t^2\sqrt{z_0})^j \left[ci(Nt^2\sqrt{z_0})\cos(Nt^2\sqrt{z_0}) + si(Nt^2\sqrt{z_0})\sin(Nt^2\sqrt{z_0})\right] \\[2ex]
\qquad + \displaystyle\sum_{k=1}^{j/2} \frac{(j-2k+1)!}{(j-1)!} (-N^2 t^4 z_0)^{k-1} f_{ra}(t)\, dt \quad \text{für } j = 2n,\ n \in I\!N
\end{cases}
$$

$$
\text{mit} \quad ci(x) = -\int_x^\infty \frac{\cos t}{t}\, dt
$$

$$
\text{und} \quad si(x) = -\int_x^\infty \frac{\sin t}{t}\, dt
$$

Da die Faltung von Exponentialfunktionen als Summe von Exponentialfunktionen darstellbar ist, bildet sich bei n Störern eine Produktform der Wahrscheinlichkeiten, die nach angegebenen Muster berechnet werden können.

$$
Prob\{z > z_0 \mid n\,t, t_1, t_2, \cdots t_n\} = \int_{z_0}^\infty f_z(z \mid t\, t_1\, t_2, \cdots t_n)\, dz
$$

$$
= \int_{z_0}^\infty \int_0^\infty t^\beta \exp(-t^\beta z w) \left[t_1^\beta \exp(-t_1^\beta w) * t_2^\beta \exp(-t_2^\beta w) * \cdots * t_n^\beta \exp(-t_n^\beta w)\right] w\, dw\, dz
$$

$$
= \frac{t_1^\beta}{t_1^\beta + z_0 t^\beta} \frac{t_2^\beta}{t_2^\beta + z_0 t^\beta} \cdots \frac{t_n^\beta}{t_n^\beta + z_0 t^\beta}
$$

Werden alle Stationen als potentielle Störer einbezogen, läßt sich schreiben

$$
Prob\{z > z_0\} = \lim_{n\to\infty} Prob\{z > z_0 \mid n\}.
$$

Gemeinsame Zeitskala für lokale Ereignisspuren

Richard Hofmann
Universität Erlangen
IMMD VII
Martensstr. 3
8520 Erlangen
email:rhofmann@informatik.uni-erlangen.de

Zusammenfassung

Zur Analyse des dynamischen Ablaufverhaltens von Software auf parallelen und verteilten Systemen bedient man sich immer mehr des Monitoring, weil es die genaueste Analysemethode ist. Viele Hardware-Monitore verfügen über einen globalen Zeitbezug; Hardware-Monitoren mit mehreren unabhängigen Meßstationen und Software-Monitoren, die in solchen Systemen eingesetzt werden, fehlt er jedoch. Um dennoch zeitliche Aussagen zu erhalten, die sich auf Zeitdistanzen zwischen Ereignissen auf verschiedenen Prozessoren beziehen, bedarf es aber einer global gültigen Zeitskala für die betrachteten Ereignisse. Hierzu werden in der vorliegenden Arbeit zwei aufeinander aufbauende Verfahren hergeleitet. Das erste liefert einen konstanten Korrekturterm, der es erlaubt die Zeitstempel eines Monitors auf diejenigen eines anderen zu beziehen. Dieses Verfahren liefert für die meisten Anwendungsfälle eine hinreichende Genauigkeit, und es wird ein Kriterium angegeben, wann es nicht mehr anwendbar ist. Das zweite Verfahren baut auf dem ersten auf, indem es das Datenmaterial gleichmäßig aufteilt, das erste Verfahren auf den Teilen jeweils separat anwendet und die Teilergebnisse einer Regressionsanalyse unterzieht.
Schlüsselwörter: *Monitoring, globale Zeit, Schätzverfahren, verteiltes System, Parallelrechner*

1 Einleitung

Die einzige Möglichkeit, den dynamischen Ablauf von Software in beliebigen Rechensystemen genau zu analysieren, ist das Monitoring. Es ermöglicht, die oft auf mehrere Rechner verteilten Aktivitäten innerhalb einer verteilten/parallelen Berechnung zueinander in Beziehung zu setzen und damit die Basis für ein Verständnis der Wechselwirkungen zwischen solchen Aktivitäten zu bilden. Aus diesem Verständnis heraus kann die dem gemessenen Ablauf zugrundeliegende Software verbessert und damit die Bearbeitung der ursprünglichen Aufgabe beschleunigt werden.

Es gibt verschiedene Wege, diese globale Sicht zu erzeugen. Eine Möglichkeit besteht darin, aus den Kommunikationsbeziehungen zwischen den Prozessen eine *Halbordnung* abzuleiten, die alle Vorgänger-/Nachfolgerbeziehungen zwischen den Ereignissen in allen Prozessoren im betrachteten System ergibt [Mat89], [Hof93]. Die daraus resultierende globale Sicht erlaubt Reihenfolgeaussagen für Debugging-Zwecke, jedoch keine Leistungsaussagen, da ihr der Bezug zur (physikalischen) Zeit fehlt.

Ein anderer Weg besteht darin, den Monitor so zu gestalten, daß er jedem Ereignis, das er aufzeichnet, einen *Zeitstempel aufprägt*. Da aber in verteilten und meist sogar in parallelen Systemen mit mehreren Monitoren gemessen werden muß, liegen den aufgeprägten Zeitstempeln auch verschiedenen Uhren zugrunde. Sind diese genau genug synchronisiert, dann können die

Zeitstempel als globales Ordnungskriterium eingesetzt werden. Dies ist z.B. bei eigens für diesen Zweck entwickelten Monitorsystemen der Fall, z.B. [HKLM87], [MCNR90], [ESZ90].

Eine Alternative hierzu bieten Software-Algorithmen zur Uhrensynchronisation, z.B. das *Network Time Protocol* von Mills [Mil90] oder das probabilistische Synchronisationsverfahren von Cristian [Cri89]. Diese Algorithmen sind zwar ausreichend genau, jedoch stehen sie bei nahezu keinem Rechensystem zur Verfügung, so daß sie erst implementiert werden müßten. Neben dem Implementierungsaufwand haftet einem solchen Vorgehen eine nicht vernachlässigbare Rückwirkung auf das damit ausgestattete System an.

Oft ist weder ein externer Hardware-Monitor nötig, noch bedarf es synchronisierter Uhren. Dies ist genau dann der Fall, wenn man über lokale Uhren mit einer ausreichenden Auflösung verfügt, und zusätzlich Ereignispaare existieren, die kausale Wirkungen zwischen Prozessen transportieren. Mit Hilfe solcher Ereignispaare und den ihnen aufgeprägten lokalen Zeitstempeln kann dann eine globale Zeit abeschätzt werden. Die Idee hierzu stammt von Duda u.a. [DHHB87], die zwei (ziemlich aufwendige) Verfahren zur Herstellung eines solchen globalen Zeitbezuges angeben.

In dieser Arbeit wird zunächst der Begriff des Ereignisses präzisiert, und es wird der Zusammenhang hergestellt zwischen Reihenfolgebeziehungen von zueinander in Kausalbeziehung stehenden Ereignissen und den daraus resultierenden Beziehungen zwischen deren Zeitstempeln. Im Anschluß daran werden zwei neue Verfahren zur Erzeugung einer gemeinsamen Zeitskala entwickelt, die bei gleicher Genauigkeit mit einem wesentlich geringeren Rechenaufwand auskommen als die bereits bekannten. Die Anwendung dieser Verfahren wird anschließend anhand eines einfachen, aber realistischen Beispiels erprobt.

2 Ereignisse, Reihenfolgen und Zeit

Das Ereigniskonzept basiert auf der Festlegung wesentlicher Stellen in einem zeitlichen Ablauf als Ereignisse und der Möglichkeit, das Durchlaufen solcher Stellen zu erkennen. Erreicht wird damit eine Abstraktion des realen Geschehens auf wenige, für dieses Geschehen charakteristische Ereignisse. Ein systematischer Weg zur Durchführung dieser Abstraktion und ein Verweis auf weiterführende Literatur finden sich bei Klar et al. [KQS92]. Zeichnet man das Verhalten eines Systems auf der Basis solchermaßen festgelegter Ereignisse auf, so erhält man eine Darstellung des realen Ablaufgeschehens, abstrahiert auf die zeitliche Abfolge dieser Ereignisse. Dieser Vorgang des Aufzeichnens heißt *Ereignisgesteuertes Monitoring*. Um aus den gemessenen Daten die Frage nach dem „Warum zeigt das System das beobachtete Verhalten?" beantworten zu können und daraus Hinweise in Richtung zur Beantwortung der Frage „Wie kann man das Verhalten gezielt verbessern?" geben zu können, müssen die Ereignisse so ausgewählt werden, daß sie Rückschlüsse auf die ursächlichen Zusammenhänge zwischen den verschiedenen Teilen des betrachteten Prozesses oder mehrerer Prozesse erlauben.

In Monoprozessorsystemen sind typischerweise bedingte Verzweigungen in einem Programm von besonderer Wichtigkeit, weil von ihnen abhängt, welche von u.U. sehr verschiedenen Möglichkeiten weiterverfolgt wird. Das Programm bestimmt also, in welcher Reihenfolge die vorher festgelegten Ereignisse eintreten können. Dadurch werden kausale Abhängigkeiten zwischen Ereignissen geschaffen. Die kausale Abhängigkeit des Ereignisses e_l vom Ereignis e_k wird im folgenden formal dargestellt durch

$$e_k \mapsto e_l , \tag{1}$$

wobei der Operator $\mapsto$ zu lesen ist als *wirkt kausal auf*. Gl. 1 ist also zu lesen e_k *wirkt kausal auf* e_l.

Dieselben Aussagen gelten auch für parallele und verteilte Systeme, also Systeme mit mehreren gleichzeitig aktiven Prozessen, die zur Lösung einer gemeinsam bearbeiteten Aufgabe miteinander in Wechselwirkung treten müssen. In solchen Systemen ergeben sich kausale Abhängigkeiten nicht nur durch die Bewertung lokaler Kriterien; vielmehr führen die Wechselwirkungen mit den anderen Prozessen zu kausalen Abhängigkeiten, die über die Prozessorgrenze hinaus wirken. Derartige Wechselwirkungen finden über die im Rechensystem realisierten Kommunikationsmechanismen statt. Diesen kommt eine große Bedeutung im Rahmen von Kausalitätsbetrachtungen zu, denn ein Ereignis e_k in einem Prozeß P_i kann nur dann auf das Ereignis e_l in einem anderen Prozeß P_j kausal wirken, wenn zwischen dem Eintreten von e_k und e_l ein Informationstransfer von P_i nach P_j stattfand.

Aus solchen Kausalbeziehungen kann man auf zeitliche Reihenfolgen schließen, denn ein kausal abhängiges Ereignis kann nur eintreten, wenn zuvor das für sein Eintreten ursächliche Ereignis bereits eingetreten war, also

$$e_k \mapsto e_l \;\Rightarrow\; t(e_k) < t(e_l)\,. \tag{2}$$

Dabei bedeutet $t(e_\nu)$ den Eintrittszeitpunkt des Ereignisses e_ν bezogen auf eine gemeinsame globale Zeitskala. Ein idealer Monitor würde für alle derartigen kausal abhängigen Ereignispaare Zeitstempel $C(t(e_\nu))$ liefern, welche ebenfalls Gl. 2 erfüllen. Dabei kann ein realer Monitor solange als ideal bezüglich dieser Aussage angesehen werden, wie die von ihm gebildeten (fehlerbehafteten) Zeitstempel Gl. 2 erfüllen.

Verfügt man nicht über eine geeignet hohe globale Zeitauflösung, sondern nur über nicht-synchronisierte lokale Uhren, deren jede für sich die Zeitstempel für die aufzuzeichnenden Ereignisse lokal bildet, dann fehlt den Zeitstempeln der globale Zeitbezug. Vergleiche zwischen Zeitstempeln, welche aus verschiedenen Uhren stammen, sind dann mit einem Fehler von im allgemeinen unbekannter Größe behaftet und daher sinnlos. Aber auch lokal betriebene Uhren sind Gebilde mit einem mathematisch beschreibbaren physikalischen Verhalten. Ein einfaches mathematisches Modell für die Anzeige $C(t)$ einer Uhr als Funktion der Zeit ist das folgende:

$$C(t) = t + \Delta t + \alpha \cdot t + R(t)\,. \tag{3}$$

Dabei bedeutet t die tatsächliche (globale) Zeit, Δt steht für den konstanten Teil der Abweichung vom Idealwert, welcher beliebig groß sein kann, Die durchschnittliche Rate, mit der die angezeigte Zeit von $t + \Delta t$ je Zeiteinheit wegdriftet, wird mit α bezeichnet; ihr Betrag liegt in der Größenordnung von $1 - 100\ \mu s/s$. $R(t)$ modelliert im wesentlichen Temperaturschwankungen in Form eines Zufallsprozesses, der die Uhr teils schneller, teils langsamer laufen läßt, im Durchschnitt aber ohne Wirkung bleibt. Diese Schwankungen sind in der Regel sehr klein gegenüber den anderen Einflüssen und können daher vernachlässigt werden.

3 Gemeinsame Zeitskala

3.1 Vorüberlegungen

Infolge der systembedingten Abweichungen realer Uhren vom Idealwert kann Gl. 2 nicht ohne Einschränkung auf deren Zeitstempel ausgedehnt werden. Die Einschränkung erfolgt nun durch einen korrigierten Wert $\tilde{C}_j(t(e_l))$, welcher von $C_j(t(e_l))$ abhängt und zusätzlich der Gl. 2 in der folgenden Form genügen muß:

$$P_i : e_k \mapsto P_j : e_l \;\overset{!}{\Rightarrow}\; C_i(t(e_k)) < \tilde{C}_j(t(e_l))\,. \tag{4}$$

Dabei bedeutet die Notation $P_\mu : e_\nu$, daß das Ereignis e_ν auf dem Prozessor P_μ stattgefunden hat. Um die Notation zu vereinfachen, wird statt $C_\nu(t(e_\mu))$ nur noch $C_\nu(e_\mu)$ geschrieben.

Für die Anwendbarkeit eines solchen Verfahrens genügt es nicht, von der kausalen Abhängigkeit beliebiger Ereignisse auf deren Reihenfolgen zu schließen. Vielmehr müssen solche Gesetzmäßigkeiten zwischen kausal abhängigen Ereignissen gefunden werden, die eine Paarbildung aus den unabhängig aufgezeichneten Ereignisspuren zulassen. Diese Ereignispaare bilden gewissermaßen die Finger eines Reißverschlusses, welcher je zwei Prozesse verbindet.

In Systemen, deren Kommunikation über Nachrichten erfolgt, ist dies bei geeigneter Ereignisfestlegung stets möglich: Das Empfangen einer Nachricht kann nur erfolgen, nachdem sie gesendet wurde. Hier gilt also

$$Send(N_k) \longmapsto Receive(N_k).$$

Mithilfe der Nummer k bei der Nachricht N ist es hier leicht möglich, zusammengehörige Paare kausal abhängiger Ereignisse auf verschiedenen Prozessoren zu identifizieren. An dieser Stelle sei angemerkt, daß die Anwendung der zu konstruierenden Verfahren nicht auf Systeme mit Nachrichten-Kopplung beschränkt sind; überall, wo eine Paarbildung zwischen unmittelbar kausal abhängigen Ereignissen auf zwei Prozessen möglich ist, kann auch eine gemeinsame Zeitskala aus lokal gemessenen Ereignisspuren abgeleitet werden.

3.2 Konstanter Korrekturterm

Aus den Messungen entstehen Ereignisspuren mit lokalen Zeitstempeln in jeder einzelnen Spur. Die Kausalitätsstruktur paralleler und verteilter Systeme erlaubt nun die Aussage, daß ein kausal abhängiges Ereignis e_l auf dem Prozessor P_j mit der Uhr C_j zu einem späteren Zeitpunkt eingetreten sein muß als seine Ursache e_k auf P_i mit C_i, also

$$P_i : e_k \longmapsto P_j : e_l \Rightarrow t(e_k) < t(e_l) \Rightarrow C_i(e_k) \overset{!}{<} C_j(e_l) + K_{ij}. \tag{5}$$

Die Aufgabe besteht nun darin, eine Bildungsvorschrift für den Korrekturwert K_{ij} abzuleiten, welcher obige Gl. 5 für alle Paare von kausal wirkenden Ereignissen zwischen den Prozessoren P_i und P_j mit verschiedenen Uhren erfüllt.

Bildet man die Menge

$$K_{ij}^+(e_{kl}) = \{C_i(e_k) - C_j(e_l) \mid P_i : e_k \longmapsto P_j : e_l\} \tag{6}$$

für alle Ereignispaare e_{kl}, die ihre Ursache e_k in P_i haben und ihre Wirkung e_l in P_j, und trägt man die Elemente von $K_{ij}^+(e_{kl})$ über $C_i(e_k)$ auf, dann entstehen im unteren Bereich z.B. die in Abb. 1 mit Kreuzen markierten Punkte. Dabei sagt der untere Index des Korrekturwertes aus, daß es sich um eine Verschiebung der Uhr C_j gegenüber der Uhr C_i handelt. Ein +-Zeichen im oberen Index signalisiert, daß die Richtung der kausalen Wirksamkeit von P_i nach P_j geht, entsprechend der Reihenfolge der unteren Indizes.

Die Wahl von

$$\overline{K_{ij}} = \max\left\{K_{ij}^+(e_{kl})\right\}, \tag{7}$$

erfüllt gerade Gl. 5. Die Addition von $\overline{K_{ij}}$ zu allen Zeitstempeln, welche von der Uhr C_j stammen, liefert die kleinsten Zeitstempel, welche alle kausalen Wirkungen von P_i auf P_j korrekt wiedergeben.

Der zur Übertragung der kausalen Wirksamkeit von P_i auf P_j stattfindende Kommunikationsvorgang benötige die Zeit T_{ij}, die als Mindestwert die geringste aufgetretene Nachrichtenlaufzeit

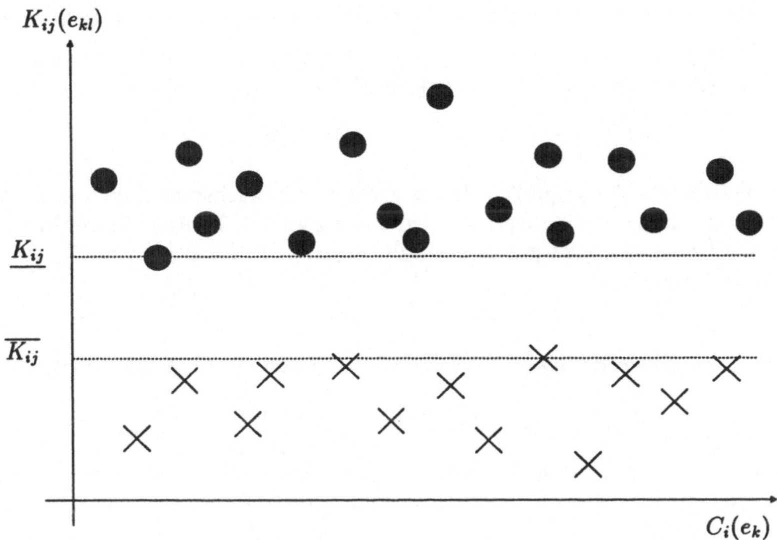

Abbildung 1: Korrekturwerte für lokale Uhren

aufweist. Für die Berechnung von $\overline{K_{ij}}$ wird aber nur vorausgesetzt, daß T_{ij} nicht negativ wird. Weil $T_{ij} = 0$ gesetzt wurde, führt die Wahl des minimal möglichen Korrekturwerts $\overline{K_{ij}}$ zu einer zu kleinen Korrektur. Was noch fehlt ist die Ermittlung eines möglichst realistischen Korrekturwertes.

Hier hilft folgende Überlegung weiter: Die beiden beteiligten Uhren C_i und C_j seien gleich und es gelte $C_i(t) - C_j(t) = t$. Dann kann die Nachrichtenlaufzeit T_{ij} direkt als Differenz der Zeitstempel zwischen Empfangs- und Sendeereignis ermittelt werden. Einsetzen dieser Werte in Gl. 6 für ein Ereignispaar

$$K_{ij}^{+}(e_{kl}) = C_i(e_k) - C_j(e_l) = t - (t + T_{ij}) = -T_{ij}$$

läßt erkennen, daß $K_{ij}^{+}(e_{kl})$ immer kleinere Werte annimmt je weiter die Übertragungszeit wächst, und daß unter diesen idealen Bedingungen die Anwendung von Gl. 7 das Minimum der aufgetretenen Übertragungsdauer ergibt. Es folgt, daß der ideale Wert für K_{ij} sich aus

$$K_{ij} = \overline{K_{ij}} + \min T_{ij} \tag{8}$$

ergibt. Im Falle der idealen Uhren wird der Korrekturwert dadurch wieder annulliert.

Im allgemeinen sind Kausalbeziehungen bidirektional, und dies kann genutzt werden, um den gesuchten Idealwert für die Korrektur näher einzugrenzen. Ein kausal abhängiges Ereignis e_l auf dem Prozessor P_i mit der Uhr C_i muß zu einem späteren Zeitpunkt eingetreten sein als seine Ursache e_k auf P_j mit C_j, also

$$P_j : e_k \mapsto P_i : e_l \Rightarrow t(e_k) < t(e_l) \Rightarrow C_j(e_k) + K_{ij} \overset{!}{<} C_i(e_l). \tag{9}$$

Bildung von

$$K_{ij}^{-}(e_{kl}) = \{C_i(e_l) - C_j(e_k) \mid P_j : e_k \mapsto P_i : e_l\} \tag{10}$$

und Eintragung in dasselbe Diagramm liefert die Punkte im oberen Teil der Abb. 1. Hier ergibt die Wahl von

$$\underline{K_{ij}} = \min\left\{K_{ij}^{-}(e_{kl})\right\} \tag{11}$$

den Korrekturwert für alle Zeitstempel der Uhr C_j für Ereignispaare mit der Ursache in P_j.

Analoge Überlegungen wie für den Fall der Übermittlung der kausalen Wirksamkeit von P_i nach P_j führen durch Einsetzen idealer Werte in Gl. 10

$$K_{ij}^-(e_{kl}) = C_i(e_l) - C_j(e_k) = (t + T_{ji}) - t = T_{ji}$$

zur Erkenntnis, daß $K_{ij}^-(e_{kl})$ größere Werte annimmt für wachsende Übertragungszeit, und daß unter diesen idealen Bedingungen die Anwendung von Gl. 11 ebenfalls das Minimum der aufgetretenen Übertragungsdauer ergibt. Damit folgt für den Idealwert von K_{ij} eine weitere Bestimmungsgleichung

$$K_{ij} = \underline{K_{ij}} - \min T_{ji}. \tag{12}$$

Gleichsetzen der beiden Bestimmungsgleichungen Gl. 8 und Gl. 12 für K_{ij} liefert

$$\underline{K_{ij}} - \overline{K_{ij}} = \min T_{ij} + \min T_{ji}. \tag{13}$$

Der Abstand zwischen Mindest- und Maximalwert setzt sich demnach zusammen aus den Minimalwerten der aufgetretenen Übertragungsdauern in beiden Richtungen. Die Mitte dieses Intervalls

$$K_{ij} = \frac{\overline{K_{ij}} + \underline{K_{ij}}}{2} \tag{14}$$

repräsentiert somit den *konstanten Korrekturterm* K_{ij}, der im folgenden Sinne optimal ist:

1. Alle Kausalbeziehungen zwischen P_i und P_j werden durch die korrigierten Zeitstempel $C_j + K_{ij}$ richtig dargestellt.

2. Die Wahl der Intervallmitte ergibt den geringsten Betrag des maximal möglichen Fehlers. Sind obendrein die Zeitdauern T_{ij} und T_{ji} gleich, dann verschwindet der Fehler ganz.

Gl. 13 kann auch zur Bestimmung eines Schätzwertes für die minimale Übertragungsdauer eingesetzt werden, denn mit der Intervallbreite $\underline{K_{ij}} - \overline{K_{ij}}$ ist deren Summe bestimmt. Sei weiterhin $2\epsilon = \min T_{ij} - \min T_{ji}$ die Differenz zwischen den beiden Laufzeit-Minima, dann gilt

$$\min T_{ij} - \epsilon = \min T_{ji} + \epsilon = \frac{\underline{K_{ij}} - \overline{K_{ij}}}{2}. \tag{15}$$

Setzt man das unbekannte $\epsilon = 0$, so erhält man eine Abschätzung, die umso genauer wird, je mehr die Minima der Übertragungszeiten in beiden Richtungen übereinstimmen.

Damit kompensiert Gl. 5 zwar nur die konstante Abweichung Δt aus Gl. 3. Daß diese einfache Korrektur dennoch praktisch relevant ist, zeigt folgende Abschätzung: Sei $\alpha_{ij} = \alpha_i - \alpha_j$ die Rate, mit der die Uhren C_i und C_j auseinanderdriften[1]. Sie betrage $\alpha_{ij} = 10$ ppm, was mit knapp 10 s pro Tag realistisch ist für Rechneruhren. Dadurch wachsen die Differenzen, wodurch mit steigender Zeit die Werte von $K_{ij}(e_{kl})$ ebenfalls größer werden. Mit anderen Worten, die freie Fläche zwischen den beiden betrachteten Punktmengen liegt nicht mehr horizontal. Durch diesen Effekt wird die durch Gl. 13 ermittelte Differenz reduziert bis sich beide Intervalle überlappen. Das Minimum der Nachrichtenübertragungsdauer $T_N = \min(t_{Receive} - t_{Send})$ zwischen zwei Benutzerprozessen auf verschiedenen Rechnern betrage 10 ms, ebenfalls ein realistischer Wert. Dann kann eine Messung $T_M = T_N/|\alpha_{ij}| = 10$ $ms/10^{-5} = 1000$ s (etwas mehr als eine Viertelstunde) dauern, bis allein die Drift der Uhren gegeneinander dieser mit wenig Aufwand

---

[1] Die absolute Drift jeder einzelnen Uhr ist irrelevant, da nur Differenzen betrachtet werden.

durchführbaren Abschätzung die Grundlage entzieht. Viele Messungen aber lassen sich in weit kürzerer Zeit durchführen.

Selbst wenn sich die Intervalle aus der Betrachtung der beiderseitigen Kausalbeziehungen überlappen, kann Gl. 14 einen brauchbaren Korrekturwert liefern. Der K_{ij} anhaftende Fehler kann nämlich eingegrenzt werden auf die Summe aus minimalem Abstand kausaler Ereignisse und der Überlappung $\overline{K_{ij}} - K_{ij}$. Erst wenn die Größe dieses Fehlers für die Anaylse nicht mehr akzeptabel ist, bedarf es einer Verfeinerung der Vorgehensweise.

3.3 Linearer Korrekturterm

Die Verfeinerung besteht darin, einen konstanten Wert K_{ij} für die Gesamtdauer der Messung durch einen linearen, zeitabhängigen Term zu ergänzen, der die Drift der Uhren gegeneinander berücksichtigt:

$$G_{ij}(t) = K_{ij} + \beta_{ij}t. \tag{16}$$

Da sich an der grundsätzlichen Problematik nichts ändert, gilt das oben Diskutierte analog, so daß die Bestimmung einer horizontalen Geraden erweitert wird zur Bestimmung einer schrägen Geraden, die im Idealfall genau zwischen den beiden Punktmengen hindurchgeht.

Der einfachste Gedanke, aus den Mengen K_{ij}^{+} und K_{ij}^{-} jeweils die n kleinsten Elemente zu nehmen, und damit eine Regression durchzuführen, muß verworfen werden. Die Steigung der tatsächlichen Geraden liegt zwar nur in der Größenordnung von 10–100 ppm. Dennoch kann dies zur Folge haben, daß sich in beiden Punktmengen die Punkte auf diametral gegenüberliegenden Bereichen häufen.

Abhilfe schafft hier das *Verfahren mit linearem Korrekturterm*; es arbeitet wie folgt:

1. Die Abszisse $C_i(t) = t \in [t_{min}, t_{max}]$ wird in n gleichlange Abschnitte eingeteilt.

2. Das Verfahren mit konstantem Korrekturterm wird auf jedes der n Intervalle separat angewandt[2]. Dabei liefert es Korrekturwerte K_{ij}^{k}, $k \in [0, n - 1]$, die den konstanten Korrekturterm in der Intervallmitte angeben.

3. Eine Regressionsanalyse (Funktion reg) über die Paare $< t_{min} + (t_{max} - t_{min})/n \cdot (k + 1/2)$, $K_{ij}^{k} >$ liefert dann die gesuchten Werte K_{ij} und β_{ij}

$$< K_{ij} , \beta_{ij} > = \text{reg} < t_{min} + (t_{max} - t_{min})/n \cdot (k + 1/2) , K_{ij}^{k} > . \tag{17}$$

Bei diesem Verfahren kann die Varianz der Eingangsdaten benutzt werden, um die Schätzung zu bewerten. Wenn die Übertragungsdauern stark streuen, kann dies auch die Werte K_{ij}^{k} negativ beeinflussen; eine Änderung in der Intervalleinteilung und Wiederholung der Schritte 1–3 führt in der Regel zu anderen Werten mit anderer Varianz. Nachdem der Rechenaufwand — Minimum- und Maximumberechnung ergeben für alle Intervalle zusammen etwa den Gesamtaufwand des einfachen Verfahrens, und für $n < 20$ läßt sich die Regressionsanalyse noch mit dem Taschenrechner durchführen — äußerst gering ist, kann mit der Intervalleinteilung experimentiert werden. Von den verschiedenen sich ergebenden Wertepaaren sollte dann dasjenige mit der geringsten Varianz verwendet werden.

---

[2]Damit das Verfahren mit konstantem Korrekturterm anwendbar ist, muß natürlich jedes Intervall mindestes ein Paar von Werten enthalten. In der Praxis bedeutet dies keine Einschränkung, denn sinnvolle Werte von n ergeben stets viele Wertepaare.

3.4 Bewertung der Verfahren

In Anbetracht der Wichtigkeit quantitativer globaler Aussagen über das Zeitverhalten paralleler und verteilter Systeme und des Fehlens globaler Uhren in solchen Systemen ist es verwunderlich, daß bisher nur die Arbeit von Duda u.a. [DHHB87] sich mit der Abschätzung eines globalen Zeitbezuges aus lokalen Ereignisspuren befaßt. Zugrundegelegt ist dort ein Spezialfall kausaler Abhängigkeit, nämlich Kommunikation über Nachrichten zwischen Stationen mit unabhängigen Uhren C_i und C_j. Korrespondierende Sende- und Empfangsereignisse werden in ein Diagramm mit $C_i(e_k)$ als Abszisse und $C_j(e_l)$ als Ordinate eingetragen, wodurch zwei disjunkte Punktmengen entstehen, nämlich eine für jede Richtung der Kommunikation.

Es werden zwei Verfahren zur Bestimmung von Schätzwerten für die Nullpunktverschiebung und die Steigung einer Geraden angegeben, welche die globale Zeitskala für je zwei Uhren bildet. Bei den Schätzverfahren handelt es sich um die lineare Regressionsanalyse und das auf der geometrischen Anordnung von Punktmengen basierende Schätzen mit konvexen Hüllen.

Für die Regressionsanalyse werden beide Punktmengen einfach zusammengefaßt. Das Verfahren ermittelt diejenige Gerade $a_{ij} + b_{ij}t$, welche die geringste Summe der Abstandsquadrate zu allen Punkten ergibt. Dieses Verfahren weist gegenüber den hier entwickelten Verfahren folgende Nachteile auf:

- Da Punkte mit größerer Entfernung überproportional in die Berechnung mit eingehen und eben diese Punkte aus Übertragungen mit langer Dauer stammen, ergibt die Regressionsanalyse über alle Punkte nur dann befriedigende Ergebnisse, wenn die Übertragungszeit nur wenig streut.

- Es ist zu beachten daß die Anzahl der Punkte in beiden Mengen gleich sein muß, da die Regressionsgerade sich sonst in Richtung der Punktmenge mit der größeren Anzahl bewegt. Dieses Problem tritt genau dann auf, wenn nicht gleich viele Nachrichten in beiden Richtungen verschickt werden

- Das Verfahren selbst bietet keine Möglichkeit, die Güte der Abschätzung zu bewerten.

- Insgesamt kann es bei Anwendung dieses Verfahrens sehr leicht zu Schätzwerten kommen, die die Kausalbeziehungen falsch wiedergeben.

- Der Rechenaufwand ist hoch, da die Regressionsanalyse über alle Punkte durchgeführt wird.

Das zweite Verfahren bedient sich eines geometrischen Algorithmus, welcher für die obere und untere Punktmenge jeweils separat eine konvexe Hülle ermittelt. Eine konvexe Hülle ist ein Polygonzug um eine Punktmenge, deren Ecken alle nach außen zeigen, und die kleinste Anzahl von Eckpunkten aus der Menge der zu umhüllenden Punkte aufweist. Alle Geraden, die zwischen diesen beiden Hüllen hindurchgehen, definieren den Bereich von Schätzwerten $a_{ij} + b_{ij}t$, welche die Kausalbeziehungen korrekt wiedergeben. Als optimalen Schätzwert geben die Verfasser die Winkelhalbierende zwischen denjenigen Geraden an, welche die Grenze dieses Bereiches bilden. Dieses Verfahren vermeidet die meisten Nachteile des vorigen Verfahrens, allerdings um den Preis eines noch höheren Rechenaufwandes.

Obwohl diese Abschätzung garantiert immer die Kausalbeziehungen korrekt wiedergibt, muß man doch einwenden, daß als Grundlage der optimalen Abschätzung die schlechteste aller korrekten Möglichkeiten genommen wurde. Solange das Verfahren mit konstantem Korrekturterm, welches mit sehr geringem Rechenaufwand auskommt — nur Maximum und Minimum von jeweils der Hälfte des Datenmaterials muß gebildet werden — anwendbar ist, bringt das Schätzen mit konvexen Hüllen keinen Vorteil. Ist es nicht mehr anwendbar, läßt das Verfahren mit linearem Korrekturterm dieselbe oder eine höhere Genauigkeit erwarten wie das Schätzen mit konvexen Hüllen, da beim Verfahren mit linearem Korrekturterm die Regressionsanalyse auf den jeweils besten Werten (geringste Nachrichtenlaufzeit) in einem Intervall basiert; dies jedoch mit nur einem geringen Bruchteil des Rechenaufwandes.

4 Anwendungsbeispiel

Mit Hilfe des Monitoring sollte ein File-Transfer über ein ISO-MMS-Protokoll zwischen den beiden Prozeßrechnern L und R untersucht werden. Die Messung wurde mit einem Monitor durchgeführt, der eine gemeinsame globale Ereignisspur für die Vorgänge in L und R erzeugt. Insbesondere weisen alle Zeitstempel dieses Monitors untereinander einen globalen Zeitbezug auf. Aufgrund der Unzugänglichkeit der transportorientierten Protokollschichten, die auf einer separaten Einsteckkarte abgehandelt wurden, konnten nur Ereignisse aus den anwendungsorientierten (oberen) Schichten aufgezeichnet werden [Cra90].

Bei der blockweisen Übertragung von Daten über dieses Protokoll waren die Zeitdauern für Senden und Empfangen im überwiegenden Teil der Zeit gleich. Jedoch gab es auch Fälle mit erheblich größeren Zeitabständen und daraus resultierenden Unsymmetrien; einer davon ist zur Illustration in Abb. 2 in einem Gantt-Diagramm dargestellt. Deutlich erkennt man das

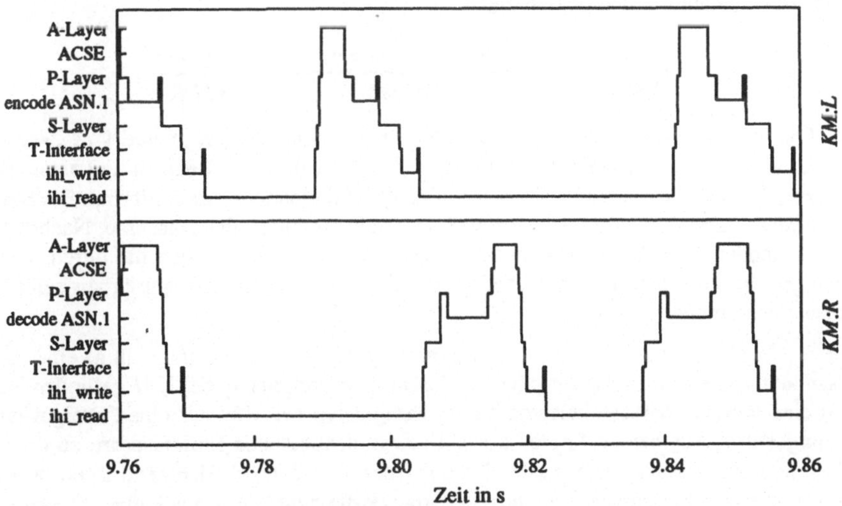

Abbildung 2: Gantt-Diagramm der Ereignisse über zwei Nachrichten

Zusammenspiel zwischen Sender(L) und Empfänger (R) als wechselseitige Folge von Ab- und Aufstiegen in der Protokollhierarchie. Nicht erklärbar ist jedoch die auffällige Unsymmetrie in Sonderfällen wie diesem. Abhilfe schafft hier die zusätzliche Aufzeichnung aller Pakete, die von dieser Applikation ausgetauscht werden, zusammen mit der Anpassung der Zeitskalen beider unabhängig betriebener Monitore.

Gegeben sei hierzu die in Abb. 3 dargestellte Anordnung aus den Prozessoren L und R, dem zu ihrer Beobachtung eingesetzten Knotenmonitor KM und dem Verbindungsmonitor VM

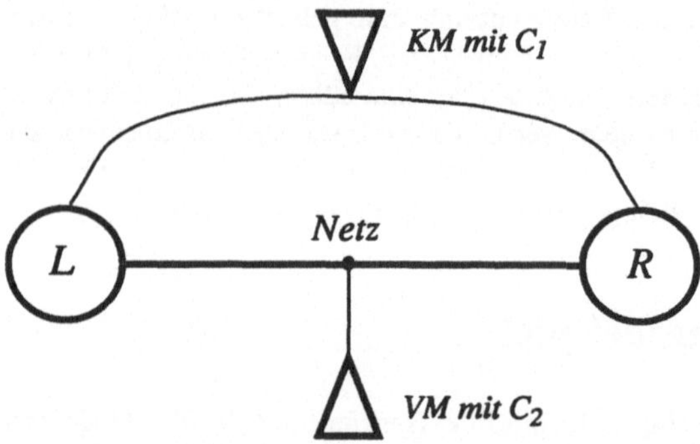

Abbildung 3: Meßanordnung aus zwei unabhängigen Monitorsystemen

zur Beobachtung der Netz-Verbindung zwischen R und L. Beide Monitore verfügen über ihre eigene Uhr, die jeweils unabhängig von der des anderen Monitorsystems die Eigenschaften nach Abschn. 2 haben. Insbesondere gilt $C_1(t) \neq C_2(t)$.

Um die Betrachtungen auf die Herstellung eines globalen Zeitbezuges zu konzentrieren, seien ausschließlich Anfang und Ende von Sende- und Empfangsprozeduren interessant. Besonders wichtig ist das Zusammenspiel der Sende- und Empfangsprozeduren mit den damit assoziierten Vorgängen auf dem Verbindungsmedium zwischen L und R. Dabei treten die Ereignisse *credit*, *data* und *ackdata* auf mit den Beziehungen

$$\underbrace{start\ receive}_{KM:L} \mapsto \underbrace{credit \mapsto data \mapsto ackdata}_{VM:Netz} \mapsto \underbrace{end\ send}_{KM:R}. \tag{18}$$

In der Abb. 4 ist jeweils ein Ausschnitt aus der Aufzeichnung von KM und VM dargestellt. Beide beziehen sich auf denselben Zeitausschnitt in der (globalen) Realzeit und sie enthalten Ereignisse, die über die genannten Kausalbeziehungen miteinander verknüpft sind. Die Einträge in den Zeilen bedeuten von links beginnend: laufende Nummer, Ereignisname, Nachricht mit Nummer, Sender, Empfänger, Zeit in Sekunden. Man erkennt, daß sich die durch die Zeitstempel gegebenen Intervalle nicht überlappen, obwohl beide Ereignisspuren zur selben Zeit aufgezeichnet wurden.

Damit das Verfahren mit dem konstanten Korrekturterm anwendbar ist, muß a) eine kausale Wirksamkeit von einem Ereignistyp bei KM auf einen Ereignistyp bei VM gefunden werden und b) eine kausale Wirksamkeit von einem Ereignistyp bei VM auf einen Ereignistyp bei KM umgekehrt. Aus beiden Spuren korrekt zusammenpassende Ereignispaare zu ermitteln, ist die schwierigste Aufgabe. Sie läßt sich auf jeden Fall dann befriedigend lösen, wenn die zugrundeliegenden Ereignisspuren eine eindeutige Festlegung kausal abhängiger Ereignispaare erlauben. In diesem Beispiel liegt diese Information anhand der aufgezeichneten Nachrichten-Nummer vor, die von beiden Monitoren aufgezeichnet wurde.

Zu a) Da nach Gl. 18 stets KM:*start receive* $\mapsto$ VM:*credit* gilt, sind Ereignispaare dieses Typs bezogen auf jeweils dieselbe Nachricht als Basis für die Richtung KM nach VM geeignet. Damit entstehen die folgenden Ereignispaare

Spur 1: KM	1	5	9	14
Spur 2: VM	1	4	7	10

<table>
<tr><td>

1	*start receive*(N_1, L, R, 8.814)
2	*start send*(N_1, L, R, 8.820)
3	*end send*(N_1, L, R, 8.840)
4	*end receive*(N_1, L, R, 8.845)
5	*start receive*(N_2, L, R, 8.848)
6	*start send*(N_2, L, R, 8.854)
7	*end receive*(N_2, L, R, 8.876)
8	*end send*(N_2, L, R, 8.882)
9	*start receive*(N_3, L, R, 9.768)
10	*start send*(N_3, L, R, 9.770)
11	*end send*(N_3, L, R, 9.788)
12	*start send*(N_4, L, R, 9.802)
13	*end receive*(N_3, L, R, 9.805)
14	*start receive*(N_4, L, R, 9.820)
15	*end receive*(N_4, L, R, 9.837)
16	*end send*(N_4, L, R, 9.842)

Spur 1 aus KM

</td><td>

1	*credit*(N_1, R, L, 13.453)
2	*data*(N_1, L, R, 13.457)
3	*ackdata*(N_1, R, L, 13.466)
4	*credit*(N_2, R, L, 13.486)
5	*data*(N_2, L, R, 13.492)
6	*ackdata*(N_2, R, L, 13.498)
7	*credit*(N_3, R, L, 14.399)
8	*data*(N_3, L, R, 14.407)
9	*ackdata*(N_3, R, L, 14.412)
10	*credit*(N_4, R, L, 14.452)
11	*data*(N_4, L, R, 14.458)
12	*ackdata*(N_4, R, L, 14.465)

Spur 2 aus VM

</td></tr>
</table>

Abbildung 4: Zwei zusammengehörige Ereignisspuren mit unterschiedlichen Zeitreferenzen

Zu b) Dieselbe Überlegung gilt für den Übergang zwischen Netz und Rechner, wobei auch hier die jeweils benachbarten Ereignistypen VM:*ackdata* und KM:*end send* am geeignetsten sind. Hier erhält man die Ereignispaare

Spur 1: KM	3	8	11	16
Spur 2: VM	3	6	9	12

Mit diesen Festlegungen kann Gl. 6 in der folgenden Form angeschrieben werden:

$$K_{12}^+ = \{C_1(\text{start receive}) - C_2(\text{credit})\} ; \tag{19}$$

In derselben Weise gilt für Gl. 10

$$K_{12}^- = \{C_1(\text{end send}) - C_2(\text{ackdata})\} . \tag{20}$$

Daraus ergeben sich für die vier betrachteten Nachrichten $N_1 \ldots N_4$ in diesem Beispiel die in der folgenden Tabelle zusammengefaßten Werte.

Nachricht		N_1	N_2	N_3	N_4
Zeitstempel	KM	8.814	8.848	9.768	9.820
	VM	13.453	13.486	14.399	14.452
K_{12}^+		-4.639	-4.638	**-4.631**	-4.632
Zeitstempel	KM	8.840	8.882	9.788	9.842
	VM	13.466	13.498	14.412	14.465
K_{12}^-		**-4.626**	-4.616	-4.624	-4.623

Bei den in der Tabelle fett gedruckten Feldern handelt es sich um $\overline{K_{12}} = -4.631$ bzw. $\underline{K_{12}} = -4.626$, also die nach Gl. 7 und Gl. 11 sich ergebenden Werte. Aus ihnen kann gemäß Gl. 14

der *konstante Korrekturterm* K_{12} als deren Durchschnitt bestimmt werden zu

$$K_{12} = \frac{-4.631 - 4.626}{2} = -4.6285 \qquad (21)$$

mit der zugrundeliegenden Einheit Sekunden. Dieser Wert ist zu jedem Zeitstempel in der Spur 2 (sie stammt von VM) zu addieren. Dann ergibt die Summe einen Wert, der vom Monitor VM geliefert worden wäre, allerdings mit einer Ungenauigkeit, die sich genau eingrenzen läßt.

Die minimale Zeit zwischen den jeweiligen Partnerereignissen beträgt 2.5 ms, falls sie für beide Richtungen gleich ist, mit einem Maximalwert von 2.5 ms, falls eine von beiden die gesamte Zeit in Anspruch nimmt und die andere keine Zeit benötigt. Die maximal mögliche Ungenauigkeit der korrigierten Zeitstempel beträgt damit 5 ms. Dabei wird durch die Konstruktion des Korrekturwertes garantiert, daß keine Kausalbeziehungen aufgrund der korrigierten Zeitstempel falsch wiedergegeben werden.

Durch die Anpassung der Zeitstempel bei den Ereignissen des Netzmonitors an die Zeitskala des Knotenmonitors können sie über derselben Zeitachse in das Diagramm nach Abb. 2 eingetragen werden. Jetzt erkennt man, daß der Sendevorgang von L nach R zwar vollständig abgewickelt

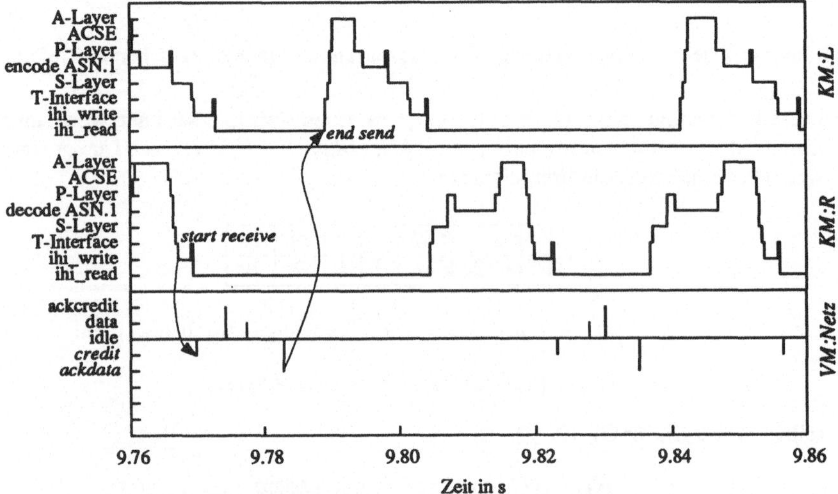

Abbildung 5: Gantt-Diagramm über Knoten- und Netz-Ereignisse

wurde, der Empfänger (R) jedoch in den transportorientierten Schichten auf der Einsteckkarte aufgehalten wurde. Der nachfolgende Sendevorgang in L beginnt natürlich unmittelbar im Anschluß an den vorigen; er muß aber warten, bis in den transportorientierten Schichten von R ein Kreditpaket übermittelt wird, was auf dem Netz das Ereignis *credit* und den Transport der Daten (*data*) sowie dessen Quittierung (*ackdata*) durch den Empfänger auslöst.

5 Zusammenfassung

Kausale Abhängigkeiten über Prozessorgrenzen hinweg können dazu genutzt werden, einen globalen Zeitbezug aus lokalen Ereignisspuren herzuleiten. Hierzu wurde das Ereigniskonzept kurz angerissen, und es wurde gezeigt, daß kausale Abhängigkeiten zwischen Ereignissen deren Reihenfolge bestimmen helfen. Da Ereignispaare, die in einer solchen Kausalbeziehung stehen, stets in derselben Reihenfolge eintreten müssen, ließ sich ein Kriterium ableiten für die Aussage von Zeitstempeln, die solchen Ereignissen aufgeprägt wurden: Der Zeitstempel eines Nachfolgeereignisses steht für einen Zeitpunkt, der nach demjenigen des Vorgängerereignisses kommt. Aus dieser Tatsache wurde zuerst ein einfaches Verfahren konstruiert, welches mithilfe einer additiven Konstante den globalen Bezug zwischen zwei verschiedenen Zeitskalen herstellt. Darauf aufbauend wurde ein Verfahren konstruiert, das zusätzlich zur Korrektur einer konstanten Abweichung die zeitliche Drift der Uhren gegeneinander korrigiert.

Das theoretisch erarbeitete Konzept wurde anhand eines praxisrelevanten Problems, nämlich der Erzeugung einer globalen Zeitskala für die aus zwei unabhängig an derselben Messung arbeitenden Monitoren, erprobt. Dabei ist die als erstes zu lösende Aufgabe die schwierigste, das Finden geeigneter Ereignispaare. Es läßt sich auf jeden Fall dann befriedigend lösen, wenn die zugrundeliegenden Ereignisspuren eine eindeutige Festlegung kausal abhängiger Ereignispaare erlauben. Im vorgestellten Beispiel liegt diese Information anhand der aufgezeichneten Nachrichten-Nummer vor. Basierend auf diesen Informationen konnte dann das Verfahren nach den Vorgaben aus der Theorie einfach durchgerechnet werden.

Literatur

[Cra90]   A. Cramer. Bewertung einer ISO–Protokollimplementierung durch Integration von knoten– und verbindungsorientiertem Monitoring. Diplomarbeit, Universität Erlangen–Nürnberg, IMMD VII, März 1990.

[Cri89]   F. Cristian. Probabilistic clock synchronization. *Distributed Computing*, 3:146–158, 1989.

[DHHB87]   A. Duda, G. Harrus, Y. Haddad, and G. Bernard. Estimating Global Time in Distributed Systems. In *Distributed Systems, Proceedings of 7th Int. Conf.*, Berlin, September 1987.

[ESZ90]   O. Endriss, M. Steinbrunn, and M. Zitterbart. NETMON–II a monitoring tool for distributed and multiprocessor systems. In *Proceedings of the 4th International Conference on Data Communication and their Performance, Barcelona*, June 1990.

[HKLM87]   R. Hofmann, R. Klar, N. Luttenberger und B. Mohr. Zählmonitor 4: Ein Monitorsystem für das Hardware- und Hybridmonitoring von Multiprozessor- und Multicomputer-Systemen. In *Messung, Modellierung und Bewertung von Rechensystemen*, Berlin, Heidelberg, New York, London, Paris, Tokyo, Hong Kong, September/Oktober 1987. 4. GI/ITG-Fachtagung in Erlangen, Springer.

[Hof93]   R. Hofmann. *Gesicherte Zeitbezüge für die Leistungsanalyse in parallelen und verteilten Systemen*, Arbeitsberichte des IMMD (Informatik VII), Universität Erlangen-Nürnberg, 26(3). 1993.

[KQS92]   R. Klar, A. Quick, and F. Sötz. Tools for a Model–driven Instrumentation for Monitoring. In G. Balbo, editor, *Proceedings of the 5th International Conference on Modelling Techniques and Tools for Computer Performance Evaluation*, pages 165–180. Elsevier Science Publisher B.V., 1992.

[Mat89]   F. Mattern. *Verteilte Basisalgorithmen*. Springer Verlag, IFB 226, Berlin, 1989.

[MCNR90]   A. Mink, R. Carpenter, G. Nacht, and J. Roberts. Multiprocessor Performance–Measurement Instrumentation. *Computer*, 23(9):63–75, September 1990.

[Mil90]   D.L. Mills. On the Accuracy and Stability of Clocks Synchronized by the Network Time Protocol in the Internet System. *Computer Communication Review (USA)*, 20(1):65–75, January 1990.

Ein hybrider Computerbus-Monitor

Volkhard Klinger

AB Technische Informatik 2, Technische Universität Hamburg–Harburg
Harburger Schloßstraße 20, D-21071 Hamburg 90
klinger@tu-harburg.dbp.de

Kurzfassung. Es wird ein hybrides Monitorsystem, welches sich sowohl aus Hardware- als auch aus Software-Bestandteilen zusammensetzt, vorgestellt. Die Probleme des Monitoring von Ein-Prozessor/Multi-Tasking- und verteilten Systemen werden aufgezeigt und entsprechende Lösungsansätze vorgestellt. Ferner wird der Prototyp eines hybriden Computerbus-Monitors beschrieben.

1 Einleitung

Die Zustände und Abläufe in einem Ein-Prozessor/Multi-Tasking-System oder in einem verteilten System sind schwierig zu beobachten.

Der Ablauf der verschiedenen Programme bezüglich ihrer Bearbeitungsreihenfolge, ihres Zeitbedarfes und ihres Ressourcenbedarfes bleibt weitgehend unbekannt. Dieses Verbergen von der internen Systemstruktur ist für den Anwender zu begrüßen, bringt jedoch bei der Fehler- oder Performance-Analyse viele Unbekannte mit sich.

Zur Lösung derartiger Probleme lassen sich verschiedene Arten von Monitoren einsetzen. Dabei werden in erster Linie zwei Klassen von Monitoren unterschieden. Die eine Klasse besteht aus den reinen Software-Monitoren. Ein Software-Monitor wird durch ein Programm realisiert, welches sich der Hardware des zu analysierenden Systems selbst bedient, um die Zustände des Systems zu untersuchen. Auf diese Weise können die internen Zustände des Systems erfaßt werden und, im Falle von instrumentierten Anwendungsprogrammen, auch ereignisgesteuerte Analysen durchgeführt werden. Instrumentierung bedeutet dabei, daß der Source-Code eines Anwendungsprogrammes durch Einfügen von Monitorprogrammaufrufen eine spezifische Ereigniserkennung erhält [1]. Die andere Klasse von Monitoren wird von den reinen Hardware-Monitoren gebildet. Ein Hardware-Monitor besteht aus einem physikalisch eigenständigen System, welches die Systemzustände des zu untersuchenden Ziel-Systems mit Hilfe von Meßaufnehmern an verschiedensten Stellen innerhalb dieses Systems aufnimmt [12].
Sowohl die reinen Hardware-Monitore als auch die reinen Software-Monitore besitzen ihre spezifischen Vor- und Nachteile [9].

Im folgenden wird der Prototyp eines intelligenten hybriden Monitor-Systems beschrieben, welcher zur Analyse des Ablaufes von Programmen auf verschiedenen Ziel-Systemen ohne Beeinflussung dieser Systeme konzipiert worden ist. Die Aufgabe liegt in der Erkennung von gültigen Bus-Zuständen des jeweiligen Ziel-Systems, um Speicherzugriffe, Kommunikation und andere auf dem Bus auftretende Ereignisse auch über längere Zeiträume zu protokollieren. Dabei sollen die Ereignisse programmiert werden können, um die Auswahl nicht im voraus einzuschränken und um den Einsatzbereich des Monitors an dieser Stelle nicht zu begrenzen. Ungültige Buszustände, wie zum Beispiel Störungen und Zustandsübergänge werden von dem System nicht registriert. Analysen auf dieser Ebene sollen den Logikanalysatoren und Oszilloskopen vorbehalten bleiben.

Die Realisation des Konzeptes wird durch eine Kombination aus Hardware- und Software-Bestandteilen erreicht. Mit Hilfe dieses hybriden Ansatzes soll vor allem die Rückwirkungsfreiheit der Messung auf das Ziel-System gewährleistet werden. Auf die Verbindung von Software und Hardware zur Realisierung dieses Monitors soll in den nächsten Abschnitten näher eingegangen werden.

Zuerst sollen die Einsatzfelder und die Randbedingungen konkretisiert werden. Anschließend werden das Konzept sowie die Lösungsansätze beschrieben und auftretende Probleme skizziert. In einem weiteren Kapitel soll die daraus resultierende Realisation vorgestellt werden. Zum Schluß folgt eine Zusammenfassung und ein Ausblick auf künftige Vorhaben.

2   Einsatzfelder und Konzepte für einen Bus-Monitor

In erster Linie sollen mit Hilfe dieses Monitors Programmabläufe sowohl von instrumentierter als auch von nicht instrumentierter Software analysiert werden. Multi-Tasking-Software und Programme auf verteilten Systemen bilden die zu untersuchende Zielgruppe. Dabei sollen sowohl summarische Meßwertbehandlungen als auch die detaillierte Beobachtung des Ablaufgeschehens möglich sein.

Die Vielzahl von parallel ablaufenden Programmen erfordert einen komplizierten Steuerungsmechanismus, was wiederum eine optimale Auslastung der Betriebsmittel und der Systemressourcen erfordert. So sollen zusätzlich auch die Belastungsgrenzen eines Systems, die Lokalisierung und Analyse von Systemengpässen, sowie Wartezeiten und Totzeiten ermittelt werden. Dabei sind natürlich auch Zugriffshäufigkeiten auf bestimmte *Devices* von Interesse [2].

Da die fortschreitende Integration in der Halbleiter-Technologie die Möglichkeiten einschränkt auf der Hardware-Ebene allein Informationen über das zu beobachtende System zu erlangen, ist der Hybrid-Monitor das geeignete Instrument eine möglichst tiefe Systemeinsicht mit Rückwirkungsfreiheit zu kombinieren. Um auch zukünftige Generationen von Mikroprozessoren analysieren zu können, dürfte ein on-chip-monitoring notwendig sein [4].

Zur Realisation eines Bus-Monitors muß eine sinnvolle Kombination aus Hardware- und Software-Anteilen gefunden werden. Der Hardware-Aufwand soll dabei so gering wie möglich ausfallen, das System selbst muß jedoch in der Lage sein, Daten zu verwalten und zu speichern, um die Rückwirkungsfreiheit (Interferenzfreiheit) gewährleisten zu können. Zusätzlich muß eine Lösung für die mechanische Kopplung mit dem jeweiligen Bus gefunden werden, die die erforderliche Kompatibilität zu verschiedenen Systemen ermöglicht.

Hier sollen zunächst die wichtigsten Randbedingungen angesprochen und anschließend die daraus folgenden Lösungsansätze gezeigt werden.

2.1   Randbedingungen

Bezüglich des Timings ist sicherzustellen, daß der Monitor beliebige gültige Zustände eines Bus-Systems erkennt und gegebenenfalls aufnehmen kann. Da in jedem Bustakt des Ziel-Systems ein interessierendes Ereignis auftreten kann, muß der Monitor in der Lage sein, in jedem Bustakt des Ziel-Systems ein Ereignis zu erkennen und abzuspeichern. Signale mit beliebiger Phasenlage zum verwendeten Abtasttakt und kurze Steuerimpulse müssen sicher aufgenommen werden. Zusammengehörige Bus-Ereignisse, die zeitlich verschoben auftreten, müssen auch zusammen abgespeichert werden.

Die Kriterien der Beobachtung bestimmen entscheidend das Konzept des Monitor-Systems. Vier verschiedene Arten der Datenaufzeichnung stehen dabei zur Auswahl:

1. zeitgesteuerte Datenaufzeichnung (externer Trigger)

2. kontinuierliche Datenaufzeichnung

3. triggergesteuerte Datenaufzeichnung (einmaliger Trigger)

4. ereignisgesteuerte Datenaufzeichnung (mehrmalige Triggerung)

Bei der zeitgesteuerten Datenaufzeichnung werden die Informationen aus dem Zielsystem in konstanten oder statistisch gewählten Zeitabschnitten ausgelesen. Das bedeutet, Ereignisse werden im Anschluß an den Impuls eines externen Gebers protokolliert. Dadurch läßt sich aber die Anwendung der zeitgesteuerten Datenaufzeichnung auch erweitern. So kann mit Hilfe dieses Triggers jede Überwachung in einem definierten Zeitfenster durchgeführt werden. Auf welche Weise dabei eine Auswahl der Ereignisse stattfindet wird jedoch hinreichend durch die Punkte 2. bis 4. festgelegt, so daß hier keine weitere Differenzierung notwendig ist. Die Möglichkeit eines externen Triggersignals ist jedoch vorzusehen.
Da die kontinuierliche Datenerfassung alle auftretenden Ereignisse aufzeichnet und sich damit bei länger andauernden Messungen eine zu große Datenmenge anhäuft (ganz abzusehen von den benötigten enormen Speicherressourcen), wird nur die triggergesteuerte Datenaufzeichnung der eigentlichen Aufgabe gerecht. Dabei ist jedoch die einmalige Triggerung nicht als brauchbarer Ansatz zu werten, denn bei dieser Art der Datenaufzeichnung findet nach Eintritt des einmaligen Triggerereignisses ebenfalls eine kontinuierliche Datenaufzeichnung statt. Die Reduktion der Datenmenge mit dieser Beobachtungsart ist so nicht sehr groß. Auch die Auswahl der Triggerereignisse ist meist sehr beschränkt, und die Beobachtungsdauer ist aufgrund der anfallenden Datenmenge relativ kurz. Diese Methode wird bei vielen Logikanalysatoren und Speicheroszilloskopen verwendet.
Erst die mehrmalige Triggerung ermöglicht es, verschiedene Ereignisse gezielt zu beobachten und auch ein mehrmaliges Auftreten von Ereignissen über einen längeren Zeitraum zu protokollieren. Hier wird auch die Verwendung eines zeitbezogenen internen oder externen Triggers möglich. Dabei bietet sich eine frühe Reduktion der Datenmenge an, was jedoch zu einer Beschränkung der zur Verfügung stehenden Triggerereignisse führt.
Die Speicherung der 'Vergangenheit' bezüglich eines Ereignisses ist innerhalb des realisierten Prototypen nicht vorgesehen. Dies würde den Speicherbedarf vergrößern, weil eine gewisse Anzahl von Buszuständen ständig in einem Ringspeicher gehalten werden müßten. Die Geschwindigkeitsanforderungen an den Ereignisspeicher würden zusätzlich ansteigen, da bei Auftreten eines Ereignisses auch der Inhalt des Ringspeichers aufgezeichnet werden müßte.

Für verschiedene Aufgaben ist eine Kenntnis der 'Vergangenheit' jedoch sinnvoll, daher wird eine Implementierung dieser Möglichkeit für spätere Realisierungen erwogen.

Eine wichtige Eigenschaft zur Erhöhung der Flexibilität des Monitors muß auf jeden Fall berücksichtigt werden: Die programmierbare Auswahl der Ereignisse auch im laufenden Betrieb des Bus-Monitors ist zu gewährleisten. Dadurch wird der Einsatzbereich weiter vergrößert.

Bei der ereignisgesteuerten Datenerfassung ist eine Zeitetikettierung jedes Ereignisses für die spätere Analyse notwendig. Dabei kann die Zeitmarkierung von einer lokalen Uhr zur Verfügung gestellt werden. Für die Anwendung bei verteilten Systemen müssen Synchronisationsmechanismen für eine globale Zeit realisiert werden (Kapitel 4).

Die zeitliche Auflösung ist mit Bezug auf eine längere Beobachtungsdauer auszuwählen. Eine genaue Dimensionierung des Zeitetiketts und eine Beschreibung der Implementation erfolgt in Kapitel 3.

Für den Datenaustausch des Monitors mit dem Host-System muß eine Kommunikationsschnittstelle zur Verfügung gestellt werden. Die Art der Kommunikationsschnittstelle hängt dabei von verschiedenen Gesichtspunkten ab. Sowohl die Geschwindigkeit als auch der zusätzliche Hardwareaufwand spielen eine große Rolle. Unter anderem wäre es sicherlich sinnvoll, in einem verteilten System die bereits vorhandene Verbindungsstruktur zu nutzen. Bei räumlich nicht getrennten verteilten Systemen oder auch bei der Untersuchung von Einzelsystemen würde hingegen eine Punkt-zu-Punkt Verbindung völlig ausreichen.

Die Abbildung 1 verdeutlicht die verschiedenen Ansätze.

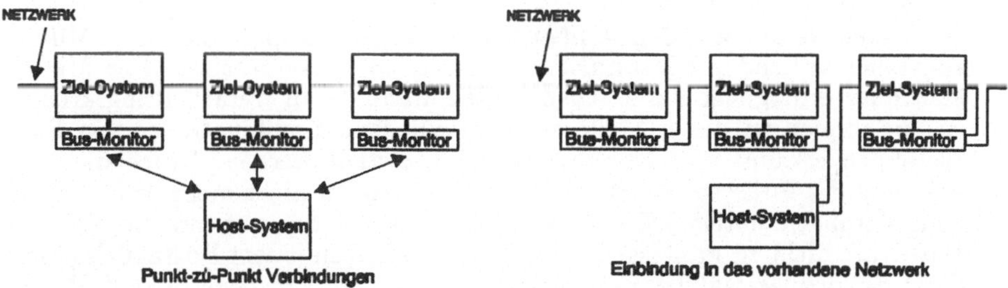

Abbildung 1: Die Verbindung zwischen Host-System und Ziel-Systemen

Auch die mechanischen Randbedingungen müssen zufriedenstellend gelöst werden. Die verschiedenen Ziel-Systeme verfügen über unterschiedliche Anschlußmöglichkeiten an ihren Bus-Systemen. Dieser Tatsache ist, um weiterhin eine möglichst große Anwendungsbreite zu ermöglichen und gleichzeitig den Aufwand zu minimieren, Rechnung zu tragen.

2.2 Lösungsansatz

Ausgehend von den obigen Randbedingungen ist der Bus-Monitor mit einem lokalen Bus realisiert worden, der über einen speziellen Steckadapter mit dem jeweiligen Ziel-System verbunden wird. Auf diese Weise bleibt fast der gesamte Hardware-Anteil des Monitors für eine große Anzahl von Systemen identisch.

Der lokale Bus des Bus-Monitors besitzt dabei getrennte Adreß- und Datenleitungen, um sowohl Systeme mit Multiplexbussen, als auch mit separaten Adreß- und Datenleitungen untersuchen zu können. Zusätzlich werden auf dem lokalen Bus verschiedene Signale bereitgestellt, um Steuersignale des Ziel-Systembusses oder verschiedene spezielle Bus-Zyklen, wie zum Beispiel DMA-Zyklen (Direct Memory Access) oder auch Interrupt-Acknowledge-Zyklen, erkennen zu können.

Um allen Ansprüchen gerecht zu werden, wurde die Datenaufzeichnung und -auswertung in mehrere Abschnitte aufgeteilt. Dadurch konnten die Timing-Anforderungen an einen Teil des Ereignis-Speichers auf dem Monitor-Board vermindert und eine frühzeitige Datenreduktion erzielt werden. Zusätzlich kann dadurch die gewünschte Flexibilität der Systemanalyse erreicht werden.

Insgesamt verläuft die Datenerfassung des realisierten Konzeptes in vier Phasen:

1. Phase

Der Buszustand des Ziel-Systems wird hardwaremäßig nach interessierenden Ereignissen untersucht. Liegt ein programmiertes Ereignis vor, wird dieses mit einem Zeitstempel (lokale Systemzeit) versehen und in einen Pufferspeicher (Ereignisspeicher = Pufferspeicher + Datenspeicher) geschrieben. Dieser Pufferspeicher muß dabei die geforderten Timing-Anforderungen erfüllen und in jedem Bustakt ein Ereignis abspeichern können. (Auf die Art des Pufferspeichers, die Menge an Information, die im Pufferspeicher abgelegt wird, sowie die Größe des Zeitetiketts wird im nächsten Kapitel eingegangen.) Durch die programmierbare Ereignisauswahl werden nur die interessierenden Daten erfaßt, wodurch der Datenstrom bereits in dieser ersten Phase entscheidend vermindert wird.

2. Phase

Die Daten werden aus dem Pufferspeicher ausgelesen und von einem Mikrokontroller anhand programmierbarer Kriterien vorverarbeitet. Der Mikrokontroller ermöglicht dabei einen weiten Rahmen an Verarbeitungskriterien. So können an dieser Stelle auch verschiedene Kombinationen von Buszuständen erkannt und bereits Statistiken erstellt werden. Durch die Verwendung des Pufferspeichers ist der Mikrokontroller nicht mehr den Timing-Anforderungen unterworfen. Dies gilt jedoch nur dann, wenn die mittlere Datenrate nicht zu groß ist. Tritt ununterbrochen in jedem Bustakt des Ziel-Systems ein ausgewähltes Ereignis auf und kann der Prozessor die aufgelaufenen Ereignisse nicht mit dieser Geschwindigkeit abarbeiten, wird der Pufferspeicher sukzessiv gefüllt. Dies kann zu einem Überlaufen des Pufferspeichers führen. Der Zusammenhang zwischen dem Takt des Ziel-Systembusses und dem Takt des Monitors wird im nächsten Kapitel noch kurz angesprochen.

3. Phase

Der Mikrokontroller speichert die bereits vorverarbeiteten gültigen Daten lokal im Datenspeicher des Monitor-Boards ab. Die Timing-Anforderungen an den Datenspeicher sind dabei geringer als an den Pufferspeicher. Sie werden durch das Timing des Mikrokontrollers bestimmt. Das Auslesen des Pufferspeichers, die Vorverarbeitung der Daten und die Abspeicherung der gültigen Daten im lokalen Datenspeicher können vom Mikrokontroller parallel abgearbeitet werden. Auf diese Weise kann der Mikrokontroller in Abhängigkeit der noch verbleibenden Ressourcen des Pufferspeichers auch noch weitergehende Aufgaben übernehmen. So ist es an dieser Stelle möglich, in Abhängigkeit der Ereignisdichte die Daten aus dem Pufferspeicher direkt vom Mikrokontroller bearbeiten zu lassen (on-line-monitoring), um zum Beispiel Zugriffshäufigkeiten direkt nur statistisch zu erfassen, oder auch unbearbeitet in den Datenspeicher zu schreiben (off-line-monitoring).

4. Phase

Der Monitor sendet die Daten aus dem lokalen Speicher an einen Host-Rechner. Der Host-Rechner macht weitergehende Datenanalysen, sammelt die Daten von verschiedenen Monitoren und bereitet diese zum Beispiel für eine grafische Ausgabe auf.

Zum Datenaustausch zwischen den Monitor-Systemen und dem Host-Rechner ist eine Kommunikationsverbindung notwendig. Die Versendung der Daten kann auf zwei unterschiedliche Weisen erfolgen. Die Daten können nach der Beendigung einer Monitoring-Phase komplett als ein Paket versendet oder auch während des Monitorbetriebes in einzelnen Paketen übertragen werden. Die Art der Datenübertragung wird durch die Datenmenge, die Speichergröße des lokalen Datenspeichers sowie durch die Belastung des Mikrokontrollers des jeweiligen Monitor-Systems und der Anzahl der Monitor-Systeme bestimmt (siehe 3. Phase). Werden bereits während des laufenden Monitorbetriebes auf diese Weise Daten übertragen, erhöht sich dadurch natürlich die Anzahl der speicherbaren Ereignisse pro Monitor-System.

Sieht man eine aktive Kommunikation mit dem Ziel-System über den Bus des Ziel-Systems vor, das heißt, kann der Bus-Monitor seinerseits Daten in das Ziel-System übertragen, ergibt sich eine dritte Möglichkeit der Datenübertragung. Nach dem Aufzeichnen der interessierenden Daten wird das Ziel-System zum Host-System. Dies bedeutet, daß das ursprüngliche Ziel-System auf die Daten innerhalb des Datenspeichers des Monitors zugreifen kann. Dadurch können die Daten im Anschluß an eine Messung auf dem Ziel-System auch ausgewertet werden.

Der Host-Rechner übernimmt neben der Datenauswertung auch eine zweite wichtige Aufgabe. Die Programmierung des Monitor-Systems oder der Monitor-Systeme wird vom Host-Rechner aus über die Kommunikationsschnittstelle des Monitors durchgeführt. Im Falle der Auswertung der Daten auf dem Ziel-System wird der Monitor über eine Schnittstelle des Ziel-Systems konfiguriert.

Im folgenden Kapitel soll nun genauer auf die gewählten Lösungen zur Realisation eingegangen werden. Dabei werden auch die verschiedenen Möglichkeiten einer Verbindung der Monitor-Systeme mit einem Host angesprochen und die Probleme beim Betrieb von mehreren Monitoren in einem verteilten System aufgezeigt.

3   Die Realisation eines Prototypen

In diesem Kapitel wird die Realisierung des Bus-Monitors beschrieben. Dazu werden die Konzepte aus dem vorhergehenden Kapitel aufgegriffen und deren Realisierung gezeigt [17].

Es wurden für die Realisierung verschiedene Bus-Systeme zugrunde gelegt, unter anderem der VME-Bus, der ISA-Bus, der NU-Bus und der Multibus II. Dabei wurde dem VME-Bus an dieser Stelle besondere Aufmerksamkeit gewidmet, da er ein genormter 32-Bit Bus ist, der im Gegensatz zu vielen anderen Bus-Systemen (z.B. ISA-Bus) nicht an eine bestimmte Prozessorfamilie bzw. Rechnerarchitektur gebunden, sondern als universeller Backplane-Bus definiert ist. Diese Bus-Systeme wurden auf ihre Beobachtbarkeit hin untersucht, und es wurde daraus das Bus-Modell aus Kapitel 2.2 abgeleitet, das eine möglichst vielseitige Verwendbarkeit des Monitors garantiert.

Zur Erfüllung der Timing-Anforderungen wurde der VME-Bus zugrunde gelegt, der einen Bustakt von 16 MHz aufweist. Dies bedeutet, daß der Bus-Monitor eine Mindestfrequenz von 16 MHz aufweisen muß. Um die Verarbeitungsgeschwindigkeit nicht von der Bus-Frequenz abhängig zu machen, wird der Bus-Monitor mit einer festen Frequenz von 16,777 MHz betrieben. Dies bedeutet, daß der Bus-Monitor eine Auflösung von ungefähr 60 ns besitzt. Sowohl die Ereignisdetektion und -speicherung im Pufferspeicher, als auch die Verarbeitung mit dem Mikrokontroller läuft mit dieser Frequenz. Bei Bus-Systemen höherer Frequenz ist damit eine Auflösung bis auf eine Bustaktperiode nicht mehr gegeben. Die für die Realisierung zur Verfügung stehende Hardware setzte jedoch für den Prototypen an dieser Stelle Grenzen.
Der lokale Monitor-Bus des Prototypen wurde auf 96 Kanäle festgelegt. Dies ermöglicht es, 32 Adreßbits, 28 Steuerleitungen, 16 Datenbits und zusätzliche Leitungen für die Bus-Identifikation oder spätere Erweiterungen zur Verfügung zu stellen. Die Beschränkung auf die unteren 16 Datenbits engt die Analysefähigkeiten nicht wesentlich ein. So werden für die Interruptbehandlung beim VME-Bus nur die unteren 16 Datenbits verwendet. Dies bedeutet, daß der Bus-Monitor sowohl Adreßereignisse, als auch Steuerereignisse und spezielle Bus-Zyklen analysieren kann. Der Datenbus wird nur zur genaueren Beschreibung von Adreß- oder Steuerereignissen verwendet (Interrupts).
In Abbildung 2 wird das vereinfachte Blockschaltbild des Gesamtsystems gezeigt.

Die Verbindung zwischen System-Bus und lokalem Monitor-Bus wird durch das Ziel-System-Interface hergestellt. Der Block *Datenaufnahme*, der die Selektion der Ereignisse vornimmt und diese in den Pufferspeicher schreibt, wird in einem weiteren Blockschaltbild (Abbildung 3) noch näher erläutert. Mit Hilfe der *Zentralen Bus-Steuerung* werden die Buszugriffe aller Busteilnehmer entsprechend der Systemfunktion geregelt. Der *Datenspeicher* (momentan 512KByte) ist der Massenspeicher für die von der CPU bearbeiteten Ereignisse. Die Trace-Tiefe, Gesamtzahl aller speicherbaren Ereignisse, ist von der Weiterverarbeitung der CPU abhängig und beträgt ungefähr 50000 Ereignisse mit vollständiger Zeitmarke. Der *Programmspeicher* (momentan 256 KByte) stellt Speicher für die verschiedenen Anwendungs- und Steuerprogramme der CPU zur Verfügung. Beide Speicherblöcke sind mit statischen RAM-Bausteinen aufgebaut. Die Verbindung *Adressierung für das Ziel-System* (gestrichelt dargestellt) spielt nur im Fall des direkten Zugriffs des Ziel-Systems auf den Datenspeicher eine Rolle (aktive Kommunikation).
Zur Ereigniserkennung (*Datenaufnahme*) werden ebenfalls statische Speicherbausteine eingesetzt, die innerhalb der erforderlichen Zeit einen Ereigniscode liefern, der über eine Speicherung des anliegenden Ereignisses entscheidet. Es existieren RAM-Bausteine, der sogenannte Vordecoder, die die unteren 14 Adreßbits sowie 28 Steuerleitungen überwachen. Die RAM-Bausteine können entsprechend der Vorgabe *während* des Monitor-Betriebes neu programmiert werden. Gleichfalls liefern sie die gewünschte Reduktion der Datenmenge wobei dabei die Einschränkung bezüglich der Menge der zu überwachenden Ereignisse an dieser Stelle durch das Konzept der Programmierbarkeit im laufenden Betrieb und der damit

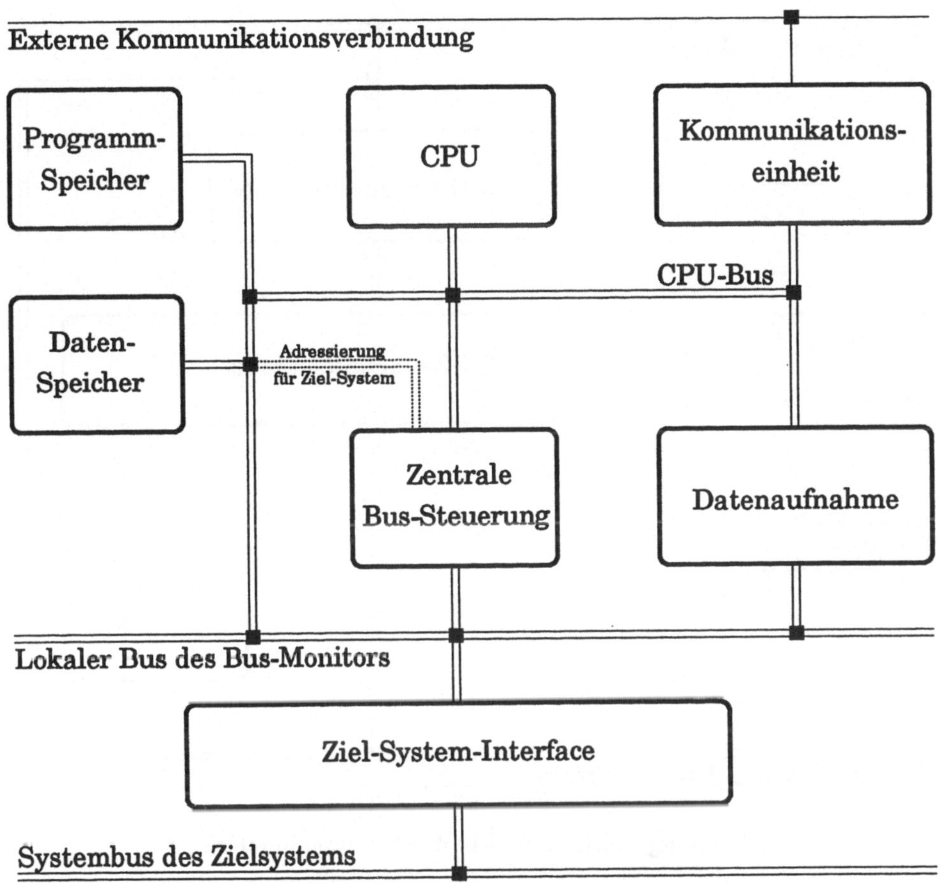

Abbildung 2: Blockschaltbild des Gesamtsystems

verbundenen größeren Flexibilität aufgewogen wird. Insgesamt stehen 45 Ereignisse für Adreß- und Steuerereignisse zur Verfügung. Diese Anzahl dürfte für die meisten Anwendungen voll ausreichen.
Eine Programmierung und Erkennung von Daten-Ereignissen ist innerhalb dieses Prototypen nicht vorgesehen. Dies wird bereits durch die Einschränkung auf dem lokalen Bus auf die 16 unteren Datenbits verhindert. Stattdessen kann bei Adreßereignissen, Steuerereignissen und auch speziellen Buszuständen das untere Datenwort mit dem auslösenden Ereignis gespeichert werden. Dazu ist eine besondere Tabelle implementiert, die sich ebenfalls programmieren läßt. Mit dieser Tabelle kann man für jedes Adreß- oder Steuerereignis festlegen, ob der Datenbus (16 Bit) mit dem Ereignis zusammen abgespeichert werden soll. Gespeichert werden die Daten in einem zweiten Speicherschritt im Anschluß an das auslösende Ereignis. Der Pufferspeicher wird aus drei parallel geschalteten Dual-Port-Memories gebildet. Diese sind als FIFO verschaltet und erlauben den gleichzeitigen Zugriff zum Lesen und Schreiben. So werden die auftretenden Er-

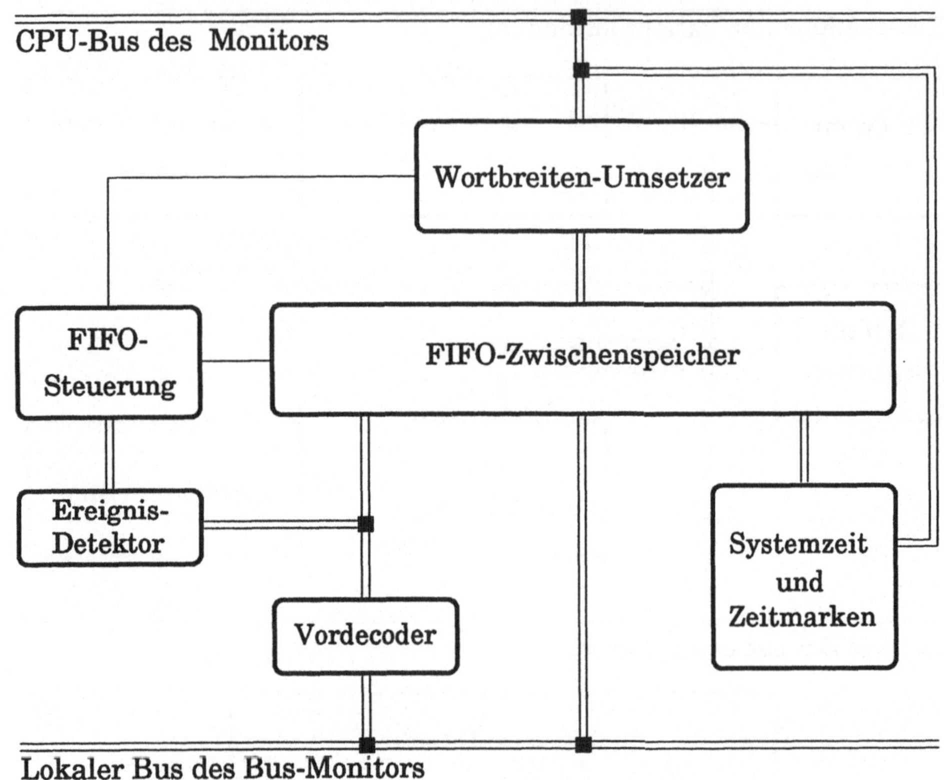

Abbildung 3: Blockschaltbild der Datenaufnahme

eignisse in den Pufferspeicher geschrieben, während sie der Prozessor zur weiteren Verarbeitung wieder ausliest. Der Pufferspeicher ist 2K Worte tief dimensioniert. Diese Dimensionierung der Speichertiefe beruht auf Abschätzungen des tatsächlichen Ereignisaufkommens und wird durch Messungen noch überprüft werden müssen.

Für den Fall eines Pufferspeicher-Überlaufes, das heißt es sind zu viele Ereignisse aufgelaufen und zu wenige vom Prozessor abgearbeitet worden, werden von einer Steuerlogik bestimmte Maßnahmen ergriffen. Diese wirken sich vor allem auf die Zeitmarkierung der Ereignisse aus.
Im folgenden wird der Pufferspeicher nur noch als FIFO bezeichnet.

Das Zeitetikett besteht aus verschiedenen Anteilen. Die Dimensionierung des Zeitetiketts wurde mit Berücksichtigung auf länger andauernde Messungen getroffen. So ist das Zeitetikett insgesamt 44 Bit breit, dies entspricht bei einer Taktfrequenz von 16,777 MHz einer Periodendauer von etwas über 12 Tagen.
Auf dem Monitor-Board wird die lokale Systemzeit verwaltet (Kapitel 4), diese beinhaltet die volle Breite von 44 Bit. Mit jedem Taktimpuls wird die Systemzeit inkrementiert und bildet so für jeden Monitor den lokalen Zeitbezug.
Für die Zeitmarkierung der Ereignisse wäre es theoretisch möglich, die gesamte

Systemzeit (44 Bit) mit dem erkannten Ereignis in die FIFO zu schreiben, jedoch würde daraus ein sehr hoher Speicheraufwand folgen. Um das zu vermeiden, wird nur ein Teil (low-time) der Ereigniszeit in die FIFO geschrieben. Dies erfordert eine Zeitmarke high-time, die den oberen Anteil der Ereigniszeit für die einzelnen Ereignisse beinhaltet. So wird erst beim Auslesen der Daten aus der FIFO die Zeitmarke jedes Ereignisses vervollständigt (Ereigniszeit=high-time+low-time). Dazu ist eine Steuerung realisiert, die garantiert, daß die richtige Ereigniszeit für jedes Ereignis vorliegt.
Zwei wichtige Fälle müssen dabei berücksichtigt werden:

1. Die low-time Zeitmarke in der FIFO ist übergelaufen.
2. Die Kapazität der FIFO ist zu klein und läuft über. Dies macht sich bemerkbar durch Überschreiben von noch nicht ausgelesenen Informationen.

Im Falle des Überlaufes der low-time des Zeitetiketts wird ein sogenanntes Zeitereignis in die FIFO geschrieben. Dieses bewirkt beim Auslesen des entsprechenden Ereignisses aus der FIFO die notwendige Korrektur der oberen Zeitmarke. Durch Hardware wird das Zeitereignis erkannt und entsprechend reagiert. Dadurch muß der Prozessor nicht mit diesen Systemfunktionen belastet werden. Ein normales Ereignis und ein Zeitereignis können völlig unabhängig voneinander in die FIFO geschrieben werden. Das bedeutet, daß die Erfassung von Ereignissen nicht durch den Überlauf der low-time des Zeitetikettes beeinträchtigt wird.
Bei einem Überlauf der FIFO aufgrund eines zu großen Ereignisaufkommens gehen noch nicht bearbeitete Ereignisse verloren. Das im Moment des Überlaufes anliegende Ereignis kann jedoch ganz normal in der FIFO abgespeichert werden. Durch das Überschreiben von Ereignissen können auch Zeitereignisse verloren gehen. In diesem Fall muß die Zeitmarke von einer Logik entsprechend korrigiert werden, um die richtige Ereigniszeit gewährleisten zu können. Generell ist das Auftreten eines derartigen Überlaufes theoretisch auch durch eine beliebig große FIFO nicht auszuschließen.

Ein vereinfachtes Blockschaltbild (Abbildung 3) verdeutlicht die Funktion der *Datenaufnahme*. Der FIFO-Zwischenspeicher ist mit den Ausgängen des Vordecoders, mit dem lokalen Bus des Monitors und mit der Einheit, die die Zeitmarken verwaltet, verbunden. An dieser Stelle wird deutlich, daß die Informationen des Vordecoders, zusätzliche Informationen vom lokalen Bus (zum Beispiel die oberen 18 Adreßbits und Statusbits) und die Zeitmarke (low-time) in die FIFO geschrieben werden.
Die FIFO-Steuerung verwaltet die Schreib- und Leseadressen und berücksichtigt ein angefordertes Speichern der Daten in der FIFO. Ebenso werden das Auslesen der FIFO, die erforderliche Wortbreitenumsetzung und nicht zuletzt die Erkennung und Verwaltung von FIFO-Überläufen, die vor dem Prozessor abgefangen werden, von dieser Logik gesteuert.
Der Block *Systemzeit und Zeitmarken* ist sowohl mit der FIFO als auch mit dem CPU-Bus verbunden. An dieser Stelle wird noch einmal die Verwaltung der Zeitmarken und Systemzeit deutlich.

Die Implementierung der meisten Systemfunktionen, wie zum Beispiel die Realisierung der Systemsteuerung, die Steuerung der FIFO sowie das gesamte Zeitetikett sind bei dem Prototypen mit drei Logic Cell Arrays (LCA) realisiert worden. Diese Logic Cell Arrays der Firma XILINX stellen knapp 8000 Gatteräquivalente in einer Matrixstruktur zur Verfügung. Mit Hilfe von statischen RAM-Zellen

innerhalb dieser Bausteine werden die Ein- und Ausgänge, die einzelnen logischen Zellen sowie die Verbindungsstruktur konfiguriert. Die Konfiguration wird nach jedem Anlegen der Versorgungsspannung oder auch mit Hilfe eines speziellen Konfigurationspins erneut durchgeführt. Die Konfigurationsinformationen werden dabei aus einem EPROM gelesen. Dadurch besteht die Möglichkeit, in Abhängigkeit vom zu überwachenden Bus-System verschiedene Konfigurationen zu laden. Dies kann zum Beispiel durch die Verwendung der am lokalen Bus liegenden Bus-Identifikation geschehen (4-Bit-Kennung).
Durch die Möglichkeit einer einfachen Rekonfiguration dieser Bausteine innerhalb von Millisekunden können verschiedene Konfigurationen für verschiedene Bus-Systeme realisiert werden. Diese unterschiedlichen Konfigurationen werden bei späteren Erweiterungen (Kapitel 5: *Zusammenfassung und Ausblick*) nötig, sie sind für die verschiedenen Bus-Systeme bei der augenblicklichen Version jedoch noch nicht notwendig.

Zur Vorverarbeitung der Daten wurde ein Mikrokontroller eingesetzt, da dieser von seiner Grundkonzeption ideal für den Einsatzzweck auf dem Bus-Monitor geeignet ist. So besitzen Mikrokontroller einen ausreichenden Befehlssatz und die Möglichkeit der Interruptbehandlung. Ferner benötigen diese Bausteine in der Regel sehr wenig externe Hardware für den Betrieb und stellen darüber hinaus verschiedene Signale, wie zum Beispiel Chip-Select Signale zur Verfügung. Dadurch können sie die Vorteile von CISC/RISC-Prozessoren oder Signalprozessoren an dieser Stelle relativieren.
Als Typ wurde der MC68332 von Motorola ausgewählt [14], der durch seine Software-Kompatibilität zum 68010 eine effiziente Programmierung ermöglicht. Zusätzlich besitzt er einen internen Speicher, programmierbare interne Zähler und kann mit verschiedenen Adressierungsarten arbeiten. Insgesamt erfüllt dieser Mikrokontroller die verschiedenen Anforderungen für einen Einsatz auf dem Monitor.

Abschließend sollen das Ziel-System-Interface und das Betriebssystem des Monitors kurz angesprochen werden.
Zu den generellen Aufgaben des Ziel-System-Interfaces gehören die mechanische Anpassung an das Ziel-System, die korrekte Zuordnung der Bussignale auf den lokalen Monitor-Bus und die Erzeugung einer Bus-Identifikation. Außerdem müssen einheitliche Timings von Adreß- und Datenbus gewährleistet sowie fehlende Strobe-Signale erzeugt werden. Darüber hinaus müssen für eine aktive Kommunikation mit dem Ziel-System weitergehende Aufgaben übernommen werden, um den Monitor an das Busprotokoll des Ziel-Systems anzupassen. Die speziellen Aufgaben der verschiedenen Ziel-System-Adapter würden an dieser Stelle zu weit führen.

Für die Funktion des Bus-Monitors ist ein Betriebssystem unerläßlich. Dieses Betriebssystem stellt in seiner Minimalversion verschiedene Error-Behandlungen zur Verfügung und ermöglicht das Laden von Programmen vom Host über die Kommunikationsschnittstelle. Die Erweiterung des Betriebssystems in Verbindung mit einer interaktiven Bedienung, die zusätzlich das Laden von speziellen Programmen erlaubt, ist abgeschlossen.

4 Synchronisation mehrerer Bus-Monitore

Ein grundlegendes Problem beim Analysieren von verteilten Systemen ist die Synchronisation [11]. Das Problem hängt stark von der Verbindungsstruktur zwischen dem Host und den verschiedenen Monitoren ab [8]. Liegt eine Punkt-zu-Punkt Verbindung vor, so kann eine zusätzliche Synchronisationsleitung zu jedem Monitor das Problem lösen. Innerhalb des Monitor-Systems liegt dafür die lokale Systemzeit vor, die für eine Synchronisation herangezogen werden kann. Auf eine Anforderung hin wird diese Systemzeit hardwaremäßig garantiert zu einem definierten Zeitpunkt zwischengespeichert und anschließend je nach Zustand der Monitor-CPU direkt oder im Anschluß an den laufenden Zyklus an das Host-System übertragen. Ist jedoch eine Netzverbindung, zum Beispiel Ethernet, implementiert und soll dieses Netz auch für die Synchronisation genutzt werden, so läßt sich das Problem aufgrund der CSMA/CD Struktur (Carrier Sense Multiple Access/Collision Detection) nur durch häufige Synchronisationen und lokale Vergleiche der Laufzeiten annähernd lösen. Dabei darf die Frequenz der Synchronisationsimpulse nicht zu hoch sein, um die Rückwirkungen auf die System-Kommunikation zu minimieren. Mit Hilfe von Schätzverfahren [3] läßt sich auch nachträglich ein globaler Zeitbezug herstellen, wenn die Kommunikation zwischen den gekoppelten Rechnern aufgrund von Nachrichten erfolgt.
Die Synchronisation ist Gegenstand von Tests und Untersuchungen. Dabei werden auch Ansätze auf der Basis des MAC-Layers (Media Access Control-Layer) zur Verringerung der Kollisionsprobleme untersucht [16].

5 Zusammenfassung und Ausblick

Es ist ein Konzept für einen hybriden Bus-Monitor und eine erste Realisierung des Prototypen beschrieben worden. Die Randbedingungen und die im Prototyp implementierten Lösungen wurden vorgestellt. Der Prototyp wurde, basierend auf ASICs (Logic Cell Arrays), mit einem lokalen Monitorbus und einem Adapter für den ISA-Bus realisiert. Die Zeitmarke ist 44 Bit breit und ermöglicht auch lang andauernde Untersuchungen bei einer maximalen Ereignisrate des Prototypen für den Pufferspeicher von ca. $16{,}7*10^6$ Ereignissen/s. Ebenso wie beim Zählmonitor 4 [7] können mit diesem Monitor lückenlose Meßspuren aufgezeichnet werden, unter der Voraussetzung, daß der Pufferspeicher nicht überläuft (siehe Kapitel 3).
Mit dem Hybrid Monitor werden zur Zeit Computersysteme untersucht. Aktuell werden Messungen an Multitask-Software vorgenommen. Außerdem werden auch Messungen zur Ermittlung der Leistungsfähigkeit des Monitor-Systems vorgenommen. Die Ergebnisse sollen zum Beispiel dazu dienen, die getroffenen Dimensionierungen der Hardware zu bewerten.
Eine zweite Version des Monitors wurde entworfen. Mit dieser Version können auch die Zugriffe auf Speicherblöcke untersucht werden. Dafür sind unterschiedliche Konfigurationen der Logic Cell Arrays nötig, die mit Hilfe der Bus-Identifikation ausgewählt werden.
Als zweites Ziel-System-Interface wurde der S-Bus Adapter entworfen.
Im Anschluß an die verschiedenen Tests sollen Multi-Prozessor-Strukturen untersucht werden. Zu diesem Zweck werden die Monitore über Punkt-zu-Punkt Verbindungen an einen Host-Rechner angeschlossen, der die Monitore steuert

358

und die Datenströme empfängt. Für die Zukunft ist eine Ethernet Verbindung vorgesehen.

Literaturverzeichnis

1. A. Bauch, T. Kosch, E. Maehle, W. Obelöer, *The Software-Monitor DELTA-T and It's Use for Performance Measurements of some Farming Variants on the Multi-Transputer System DAMP*, Parallel Processing CONPAR 90-VAPP IV, Springer Verlag, Berlin, 1992

2. Reinhard Bordewisch, *Messung und Bewertung von Betriebssystem-Komponenten*, In: B. Mertens (Hrsg.): Messung, Modellierung und Bewertung von Rechensystemen, Reihe Informatik Fachberichte, Bd. 41, 14-28, Springer-Verlag, Berlin, Heidelberg, New York 1981

3. A. Duda, G. Harrus, Y. Haddad, G. Bernard, *Estimating Global Time in Distributed Systems*, In: Proceedings of 7th International Conference of Distributed Computing Systems, Sn. 299-306, Berlin, September 1987

4. Wilhelm Föckeler, *Aktuelle Probleme und Lösungen zur Leistungsanalyse von modernen Rechensystemen mit Hardware-Meßwerkzeugen*, In: G. Stiege, J. S. Lie (Hrsg.): Messung, Modellierung und Bewertung von Rechensystemen und Netzen, Reihe Informatik Fachberichte, Bd. 218, 39-50, Springer-Verlag, Berlin, Heidelberg, New York 1989

5. F. Gregoretti, F. Maddaleno, M. Zamboni, *Monitoring Tools for Multiprocessors*, Microprocessing and Microprogramming, 18:409-416, 1986

6. Richard Hofmann, *Gesicherte Zeitbezüge beim Monitoring von Multiprozessorsystemen*, 11. ITG/GI–Fachtagung, München März 1990, VDE–Verlag 1990

7. Richard Hofmann, Rainer Klar, Norbert Luttenberger, Bernd Mohr, *Zählmonitor 4: Ein Monitorsystem für das Hardware- und Hybrid-Monitoring von Multiprozessor- und Multicomputer-Systemen*, In: U. Herzog, M. Paterok (Hrsg.): Messung, Modellierung und Bewertung von Rechensystemen, Reihe Informatik Fachberichte, Bd. 154, 79-99, Springer-Verlag, Berlin, Heidelberg, New York 1987

8. Kang G. Shin, P. Ramanathan, *Clock Synchronization of a large Multiprocessor System in the Presence of Malicious Faults*, IEEE Transactions on Computers, No.1, January 1987

9. Rainer Klar, *Hardware-/Software-Monitoring*, Informatik Spektrum, (8), 37-40, 1985

10. U. Kleinhans, J. Kaiser, K. Czaja, *Sparemints: Hardware Support for Performance Measurements in Distributed Systems*, In: Arbeitspapiere der GMD, No. 717

11. Leslie Lamport, *Time, Clocks, and the Ordering of Events in a Distributd System*, Communications of the ACM, 21(7):558-565,July 1978

12. Daniel Michael Lavery, *The Design of a Hardware Performance Monitor for the CEDAR Supercomputer*, CSRD Report No. 866

13. A. Mink, R. Carpenter, G. Nacht, J. Roberts, *Multiprocessor Performance-Measurement Instrumentation*, IEEE Computer, 9/1990

14. MC68332 SIM, System Integration Module Users's Handbook, CPU32, Central Processor Unit Reference Manual, Motorola Inc. 1989

15. Thomas Raith, *Leistungsuntersuchung von Multi–Bus–Verbindungsnetzwerken in lose gekoppelten Systemen*, 43. Bericht über verkehrstheoretische Arbeiten, Institut für Nachrichtenvermittlung und Datenverarbeitung der Uni Stuttgart, 1987

16. Christophe Vrignaud, *A Communication Concept for a Monitor System on Ethernet*, Diplomarbeit am Institut für Technische Informatik 2, Technische Univerität Hamburg-Harburg 1992

17. Wolfgang Zimmermann, *Konzeption und Aufbau eines universellen Computerbus-Monitors*, Diplomarbeit am Institut für Technische Informatik 2, Technische Universität Hamburg-Harburg 1992

An Analytical Cache–Model for Multiprocessor Systems

Thomas Delica

Siemens Nixdorf Informationssysteme AG
Otto–Hahn–Ring 6, 81739 München

Abstract. A basic cache model for multiprocessor systems is derived and solved in closed form. While details of hardware architecture, cache–coherence protocol, and cache–block replacement strategy are neglected, the results give clear insight in the important dependencies of cache–performance on cache size, number of processors, mixture, and reference characteristics of the tasks contributing to the workload.

1 Introduction

A cache memory main memory hierarchy is a common way to improve the performance of monoprocessor systems by reducing the access times to data referenced by the CPU. Empirical evidence has shown that, due to locality of reference, a high percentage of the CPU's references can be satisfied by accessing only the cache memory which has an access time in general much smaller than those for the main memory. It is obvious that the cache hit ratio, which is the portion of references which can be satisfied by the cache memory, depends directly on the cache size. Therefore, increasing the cache size may be a good idea to improve performance of a monoprocessor system.

The problem becomes more involved in a multiprocessor system, due to the occurrence of cache conflicts. The valid copy of a datum referenced by one of the CPUs may now be located in its own cache, in the main memory, and/or in the cache of another CPU. The latter case, we call a cache–to–cache miss (ctc–miss). A ctc–miss is in general even more costly than an access to the main memory (which is called main–memory miss (mm–miss) throughout this paper), depending on the cache–coherence protocol and the available hardware. Therefore, a large ctc–miss ratio, which is the portion of references that lead to a ctc–miss, will result in a performance degradation of multiprocessor systems and thereby heavily reduce the benefits of increasing cache size.

While important efforts have been made to study the impact of cache features on the performance of a monoprocessor system via analytical models (see, e.g., [1] to [7]), less work has been addressed to multiprocessor systems (see, e.g., [8] to [10] and references therein).

Two reasons may be responsible.

Firstly, the problem of modelling a multiprocessor system is more complex than modelling a monoprocessor system.

Secondly, details of the system which are hardly to be considered in an analytical model often become more important in a multiprocessor system (hardware architecture, cache–coherence protocols etc.).

But also with this problem in mind, it is worthwhile to have a model that gives a first insight in referencing mechanisms of a cached multiprocessor system. Therefore the aim of the present study is the formulation of a primary cache model for multiprocessor systems. It is plain in the sense that we will restrict to features which, in our eyes, are the most important in a rough evaluation of cache performance.

2 Motivation

The smallest units of data which are handled by the memory management system are data blocks of a fixed size. Therefore, the unit of reference will be a block and not a memory word in the remainder of the paper.

Blocks which are referenced by a task in control show up distinct differences. A considerable part of them are from the system–address space (system tables, lock words or other global data structures) and therefore can be referenced by all tasks. They are called *system blocks*. Beyond these, there exists a number of *common blocks*. Common blocks are shared by tasks of a particular *task group* and therefore can be referenced by all tasks of this group. Finally, *private blocks* from the private address space of a given task are referenced by this task exclusively.

In a multiprocessor system, system blocks have the highest conflict probability. Once a task has fetched a block by reference into the cache of its CPU, with high probability this block will be stolen before the next reference by another task running on another CPU. Of course this is not true for blocks containing sharable code, which can run on several processors. We will come back to this problem subsequently, where we will introduce a quantity giving the probability that a reference is a write reference. Nevertheless references of system blocks show a large value of the ctc–miss ratio.

By the same argument, the ctc–miss ratios on common–block references depend on the number of simultaneously running tasks of the same group. This number may increase if the total number of processors increases.

Finally, ctc–misses on private blocks result from starting effects after task migration [10], only.

The main idea of our model is to study the dynamics of the different kinds of data blocks separately and thereby to calculate the mm–miss and the ctc–miss ratio of the system.

3 The Model

3.1 Model Parameters and Basic Notation

Output Parameters. We are mainly interested in the hit ratio as the fraction of references on blocks in the CPU's own cache and the ctc–miss ratio as the fraction of references on blocks in caches of other CPUs.

The related quantity main–memory–miss ratio (as the fraction of references on blocks in the main memory) is obtained by

$$\text{mm\_miss\_ratio} = 1 - \text{hit\_ratio} - \text{ctc\_miss\_ratio} \ . \tag{1}$$

We will also refer to the miss ratio

$$\text{miss\_ratio} = 1 - \text{hit\_ratio} \ , \tag{2}$$

which is the fraction of references on blocks not in the CPU's own cache.

Input Parameters. The multiprocessor system under consideration consists of a total number of M CPUs, each with a private cache of capacity C blocks. We assume that every task addresses exactly one block per instruction. This is not quite correct, since, for example, an analysis of reference traces [12] for the mainframe operating system BS2000$^{\textregistered}$ shows that, in the average, a task references about 1.7 blocks per instruction (64–byte blocks). This however will enter as a simple scaling factor whenever hits, ctc–misses and mm–misses are related to instructions and not to references.

As mentioned above, there are references modifying the addressed block and references for a read access only. In the latter case, several valid copies of the block can exist simultaneously in caches of different CPUs. To take respect of this fact in our model, we denote by p_{write} the probability that a reference is a write reference and therefore intends to modify the block.

Table 1. Definition of the model's input parameters

M	total number of CPUs
C	cache capacity in blocks
G	total number of task groups
g	task–group index, $g = 1, \ldots, G$
N_g	total number of tasks of group g
N	total number of tasks, $N := \sum_{g=1}^{G} N_g$
I_g	average number of references made by a task of group g
w_g^s	average number of different *system* blocks referenced by a task of group g
w_g^c	average number of different *common* blocks referenced by a task of group g
w_g^p	average number of different *private* blocks referenced by a task of group g
w_g	task–group specific working set, $w_g := w_g^s + w_g^c + w_g^p$
$p_{\text{wr},g}$	task–group specific probability that a reference will modify the block

The workload consists of a total number N of tasks. Each of these tasks belongs to exactly one of G task groups. A task group contains all tasks which share a given amount of common memory (see Section 2). The total number of tasks belonging to group g is denoted by N_g, with $\sum_{g=1}^{G} N_g = N$.

$^{\textregistered}$ BS2000 is a registered trademark of Siemens Nixdorf Informationssysteme AG

Let I_g denote the number of references made by a task of group g while it is in control at a CPU. The number of *different* blocks among these I_g blocks is called the group–specific working set w_g. The working set on its part is composed of a certain number of system, common, and private blocks, abbreviated as $w_g^{\mathrm{s}}, w_g^{\mathrm{c}}$ and w_g^{p}, respectively (for the definition of these blocks refer to Section 2). Note that from this the relation $w_g^{\mathrm{s}} + w_g^{\mathrm{c}} + w_g^{\mathrm{p}} = w_g \leq I_g$ follows.

As indicated in the notation, it is assumed that all tasks from a task group show the same reference characteristics, i.e. the same average values for the working set, the number of references while in control, the number of system, common, and private blocks, the write probability etc. This assumption meets well with results from the analysis of CPU–reference strings [12].

The input parameters are summarized in Table 1.

3.2   Formulation of the Model

Let us assume that a task of group g is running at one of the M CPUs, say the CPU 1. To obtain the hit ratio and the ctc–miss ratio, we will determine the dynamics of the following intermediate quantities ($i \in \{1, \ldots, I_g\}$)

- $s_g(i)$: average number of the task's system blocks in the cache after instruction i,
- $c_g(i)$: average number of the task's common blocks in the cache after instruction i,
- $p_g(i)$: average number of the task's private blocks in the cache after instruction i.

In the case of a miss (the addressed block is in the main memory or in the cache of another CPU), the block will be fetched into the cache and the corresponding number will increase by one. Let us denote the probability of this event by

- $\alpha_g^{\mathrm{b}}(i)$ with $\mathrm{b} \in \{\mathrm{s,c,p}\}$: the probability for a miss on a system, common, or private block at instruction i.

The number of system, common, or private blocks will decrease by one if other tasks, running simultaneously on other CPUs, address one of these blocks and intend to modify it:

- $\beta_g^{\mathrm{b}}(i)$ with $\mathrm{b} \in \{\mathrm{s,c,p}\}$: the probability that a system, common, or private block is transferred to another cache at instruction i.

Finally, it may happen that, in the case of a miss, a fetched block replaces a system, common, or private block in the cache. The probability for this event is denoted by

- $\gamma_g^{\mathrm{b}}(i)$ with $\mathrm{b} \in \{\mathrm{s,c,p}\}$: the probability that a system, common, or private block is replaced by a fetched block (in case of a miss) at instruction i.

The dynamics of the above quantities hence are described by the following set of difference equations

$$b_g(i+1) = b_g(i) + \alpha_g^b(i) - \beta_g^b(i) - \gamma_g^b(i) \quad \text{for} \quad b \in \{s,c,p\} , \tag{3}$$

where $i \in \{1,\ldots,I_g\}$. Together with the initial values $s_g(0)$, $c_g(0)$ and $p_g(0)$ these difference equations determine the functions $s_g(i)$, $c_g(i)$, and $p_g(i)$ completely.

Having solved for the Eq. (3), the miss ratio miss_ratio$_g$ for a task of group g can be calculated according to its definition

$$\text{miss\_ratio}_g := \frac{1}{I_g} \sum_{i=1}^{I_g} (\alpha_g^s(i) + \alpha_g^c(i) + \alpha_g^p(i)) \tag{4}$$

from which the overall miss ratio is obtained as the weighted mean

$$\text{miss\_ratio} = \sum_{g=1}^{G} \text{miss\_ratio}_g \frac{N_g}{N} . \tag{5}$$

Furthermore, the quantity

$$\text{ctc\_miss\_ratio}_g := \frac{1}{I_g} \sum_{i=1}^{I_g} (\beta_g^s(i) + \beta_g^c(i) + \beta_g^p(i)) \tag{6}$$

by definition is the ctc–miss ratio of the $M-1$ other CPUs on the cache of CPU 1 where a task of group g is in control. Consequently, the overall ctc–miss ratio is obtained as

$$\text{ctc\_miss\_ratio} = \sum_{g=1}^{G} \text{ctc\_miss\_ratio}_g \frac{N_g}{N} . \tag{7}$$

In Eqs. (5) and (7) we have assumed, that all tasks advance evenly.

3.3 Parameters of the Difference Equations

The difference Eqs. (3) contain parameters which are not known a priori. Thus one is forced to formulate reasonable approximations for the requested functions.

This formulation will be based on two assumptions.

Assumption A1 : The probability that at instruction i a system, common, or private block will be referenced equals the ratio w_g^s/w_g, w_g^c/w_g, and w_g^p/w_g, respectively. Note that this assumption implies independence of i.

Assumption A2 : An important quantity will be the probability $p_{\text{miss}}^{b_g}(b_g(i))$, $b \in \{s,c,p\}$, that a system, common or private block which is referenced at instruction i is not among the $b_g(i)$ blocks that are located in the cache. It is assumed that this probability can be replaced by the linear approach

$$p_{\text{miss}}^{b_g}(b_g(i)) = 1 - \frac{b_g(i)}{w_g^b} . \tag{8}$$

While Assumption A1 seems not to be very unrealistic, Assumption A2 turned out to be quite simple compared to realistic results obtained, for example, from LRU–stack simulations [11]. These results indicate that an exponential decay may be more appropriate for large values of I_g [12].

Nevertheless there are several reasons justifying Assumption A2. Firstly, the setting (8) satisfies the boundary conditions $p_{\text{miss}}^{b_g}(0) = 1$ and $p_{\text{miss}}^{b_g}(w_g^b) = 0$, which is important for the present model and not satisfied for a pure exponential decay. Secondly, Eq. (8) can be regarded as the leading term of a Taylor expansion for any analytical miss probability, thus valid for the dynamics of small values of $s_g(i)$. Thirdly, one will mainly be interested in the integral of $p_{\text{miss}}^{b_g}$, thus details of its explicit form will become less important. Finally, Assumption A2 allows for a complete analytical solution of the model.

Miss Probabilities. By definition, the quantities $\alpha_g^s(i), \alpha_g^c(i), \alpha_g^p(i)$ give the probabilities for a miss on a system, common, or private block at reference i. According to Assumptions A1 and A2, they can be approximated by

$$\alpha_g^b(i) = \frac{w_g^b}{w_g}\left(1 - \frac{b_g(i)}{w_g^b}\right) \quad \text{for} \quad b \in \{\text{s,c,p}\} \tag{9}$$

where stochastical independence of the two events "reference of a given block" and "miss on a given block" is assumed.

Transfer Probabilities. The functions $\beta_g^s(i), \beta_g^c(i), \beta_g^p(i)$ are defined as the probabilities that a system, common or private block in the cache of CPU 1 at instruction i is referenced and modified by a task running at one of the $M-1$ other CPUs.

Again according to Assumption A2, the probability that a task of group g' addresses a system block at instruction i is $w_{g'}^s/w_{g'}$. On the other hand, the probability $a_{g'}$ that a task of group g' is running at a CPU different from CPU 1 is nothing but the portion of the total number of instructions which is consumed by the (remaining) tasks of group g' or

$$a_{g'} := \begin{cases} N_{g'} I_{g'}/\left(\sum_{g=1}^{G} N_g I_g\right) & \text{for } g' \neq g \\ (N_{g'} - 1) I_{g'}/\left(\sum_{g=1}^{G} N_g I_g\right) & \text{for } g' = g \end{cases} \tag{10}$$

Since $M - 1$ other CPUs exist, each of them references a system block with probability $\sum_{g=1}^{G} a_g w_g^s/w_g$, a total number of

$$(M - 1)\sum_{g=1}^{G} a_g \frac{w_g^s}{w_g}$$

system block references on the other CPUs results at instruction i. We now determine, how many of these references address a block located in the cache of CPU 1, modify it and therefore will decrease $s_g(i)$. If one assumes an uniform distribution of these references on the M caches, this entails a factor $1/M$. In addition, the number must be proportional to the number of system blocks located in cache 1. This will be taken into account by the term $s_g(i)/w_g^s$. Finally, even successful references will decrease $s_g(i)$ if and only if they intend to modify the block, which is with probability $p_{\text{wr},g}$. From these arguments

$$\beta_g^s(i) = p_{\text{wr},g}\frac{s_g(i)}{w_g^s}x_{g,M} \tag{11}$$

is obtained, where

$$x_{g,M} := \frac{M-1}{M}\sum_{g=1}^{G}a_g\frac{w_g^s}{w_g} \quad . \tag{12}$$

The function $\beta_g^c(i)$ is defined as the probability that a common block in the cache of CPU 1 at instruction i is referenced and modified by a task *of the same group* running at one of the $M-1$ other CPUs.

According to the argumentation leading to Eq. (11), this probability is given by

$$p_{\text{wr},g}\frac{m-1}{m}\frac{c_g(i)}{w_g^c} \quad ,$$

if $m \in \{1,\ldots,\min(M-1,N_g)\}$ tasks of the same group g are running at the other CPUs. Now, with a_y from Eq. (10), the probability $pg(m)$ that exactly m tasks of the same group are running on the $M-1$ other CPUs simultaneously is

$$pg(m) = \binom{M-1}{m}a_g^{m+1}(1-a_g)^{M-m-1} \quad . \tag{13}$$

So, defining

$$y_{g,M} := \frac{w_g^c}{w_g}\sum_{m=1}^{M-1}pg(m)\frac{m}{m+1} \tag{14}$$

we end with

$$\beta_g^c(i) = p_{\text{wr},g}\frac{c_g(i)}{w_g^c}y_{g,M} \tag{15}$$

for the requested function $\beta_g^c(i)$.

Eventually, since private blocks by definition are blocks that are not used by other tasks

$$\beta_g^p(i) = 0 \tag{16}$$

is valid for all g.

Replacement Probabilities. The quantities $\gamma_g^s(i), \gamma_g^c(i), \gamma_g^p(i)$ are defined as the probabilities that a system, common or private block will be replaced by a block fetched into the cache at instruction i.

Since replacement will take place only if a miss has occurred, the mentioned probabilities are proportional to the total miss probability at instruction i, given by

$$\alpha_g^s(i) + \alpha_g^c(i) + \alpha_g^p(i) \ .$$

Furthermore, if a fully associative cache is assumed, a block will be replaced if and only if $s_g(i) + c_g(i) + p_g(i) \geq C$. Therefore the replacement probability will be proportional to

$$\Theta(s_g(t) + c_g(t) + p_g(t) - C) \ ,$$

where the function $\Theta(x)$ is defined as

$$\Theta(x) := \begin{cases} 1 \text{ for } x \geq 0 \\ 0 \text{ for } x < 0 \end{cases} \ . \tag{17}$$

Finally, the probability that a system, common, or private block is affected by the replacement, is set to $s_g(i)/C, c_g(i)/C$ and $p_g(i)/C$, respectively. This setting corresponds to a random–replacement as well as a LRU–replacement strategy, since both strategies coincide in our model due to Assumption A1.

Collecting the relevant factors one gets

$$\gamma_g^b(i) = \frac{\left(\alpha_g^s(i) + \alpha_g^c(i) + \alpha_g^p(i)\right) b_g(i)}{C} \ \Theta(s_g(i) + c_g(i) + p_g(i) - C) \tag{18}$$

for $b \in \{s,c,p\}$.

3.4 Initial Values

The initial values $s_g(0), c_g(0)$, and $p_g(0)$ are the average number of system, common, and private blocks a task of group g finds in the cache when getting started at the CPU. Obviously these numbers depend on the numbers of blocks which are left in the cache when a task looses control on a CPU. Since in general $I_g \gg w_g$ holds, we will approximate the latter numbers by the stationary values $s_g(\infty), c_g(\infty)$, and $p_g(\infty)$, defined as solutions of the equations

$$\alpha_g^b(\infty) - \beta_g^b(\infty) - \gamma_g^b(\infty) = 0 \ , \tag{19}$$

for $b \in \{s,c,p\}$.

We will assume that only those blocks will contribute to the initial values of a task which are left in the cache by the direct predecessor task on this CPU. It follows that no private blocks are found in the cache. Moreover, with probability $(N_g-1)/N$ the predecessor task is from the same group and leaves $s_g(\infty)$ system blocks and $c_g(\infty)$ common blocks in the cache. With complementary probability however this task was from another group $g' \neq g$. In this case, $s_{g'}(\infty)$ system blocks but no common blocks are left in the cache.

Since the actual working set of the task must be an upper limit for the initial values, we conclude

$$s_g(0) = \min \left\{ \sum_{g=1}^{G} s_g(\infty)(N_g - 1)/N, w_g^{\mathrm{s}} \right\} \quad , \tag{20}$$

$$c_g(0) = \min \left\{ c_g(\infty)(N_g - 1)/N, w_g^{\mathrm{c}} \right\} \quad , \tag{21}$$

$$p_g(0) = 0 \quad . \tag{22}$$

3.5 Solution of the Model

We start the solution of the model by rewriting the difference Eq. (3), now introducing the expressions (9), (11), (15) , (16), and (18). Taking respect of the identity

$$\alpha_g^{\mathrm{s}}(i) + \alpha_g^{\mathrm{c}}(i) + \alpha_g^{\mathrm{p}}(i) = 1 - C/w_g \quad \text{whenever} \quad s_g(i) + c_g(i) + p_g(i) = C \quad ,$$

according to (9), and using the abbreviation

$$\Theta_C(i) := \Theta(s_g(i) + c_g(i) + p_g(i) - C) \quad , \tag{23}$$

the difference equations now read

$$s_g(i+1) = \frac{w_g^{\mathrm{s}}}{w_g} + s_g(i) \left[1 - \frac{1}{w_g} - \frac{p_{\mathrm{wr},g} x_{g,M}}{w_g^{\mathrm{s}}} - \left(\frac{1}{C} - \frac{1}{w_g} \right) \Theta_C(i) \right] \quad , \tag{24}$$

$$c_g(i+1) = \frac{w_g^{\mathrm{c}}}{w_g} + c_g(i) \left[1 - \frac{1}{w_g} - \frac{p_{\mathrm{wr},g} y_{g,M}}{w_g^{\mathrm{c}}} - \left(\frac{1}{C} - \frac{1}{w_g} \right) \Theta_C(i) \right] \quad , \tag{25}$$

$$p_g(i+1) = \frac{w_g^{\mathrm{p}}}{w_g} + p_g(i) \left[1 - \frac{1}{w_g} - \left(\frac{1}{C} - \frac{1}{w_g} \right) \Theta_C(i) \right] \quad . \tag{26}$$

These equations are of the form

$$b(i+1) = \delta + \epsilon b(i) \tag{27}$$

with coefficients δ, ϵ independent of $b(i)$ (in contrast to the coefficients of Eq. (3)). Solving successively for $b(1), b(2), \ldots$ leads to

$$b(i) = \delta + \delta \sum_{j=1}^{i-1} \epsilon^j + \epsilon^i b(0) = \delta \frac{1 - \epsilon^i}{1 - \epsilon} + \epsilon^i b(0) \quad . \tag{28}$$

We need further the arithmetic mean $\overline{b}$ defined and obtained as

$$\overline{b} := \frac{1}{I} \sum_{i=1}^{I} b(i) = \frac{\delta}{1 - \epsilon} - \frac{(1 - \epsilon^I)\delta\epsilon}{(1 - \epsilon)^2 I} + b(0) \frac{(1 - \epsilon^I)\epsilon}{(1 - \epsilon)I} \quad . \tag{29}$$

Due to the occurrence of the Θ-function, two cases have to be separated in the solution of (24) to (26). Either (generally corresponding to $w_g < C$) the cache will not be filled completely at any instruction $i \leq I_g$. Or there exists some critical instruction $i_{g,C}$ where the cache becomes filled, resulting in replacement and a non–zero value of the Θ–function. Let $i_{g,C}$ be the smallest value of i with $s_g(i) + c_g(i) + p_g(i) = C$, that is

$$i_{g,C} := \min \left\{ i \in \{1, \ldots, I_g\} \mid s_g(i) + c_g(i) + p_g(i) \geq C \right\} \quad . \tag{30}$$

For convenience we further introduce the abbreviations

$$\begin{aligned}
\epsilon^{s}_{g,w} &:= 1 - p_{\mathrm{wr},g} x_{g,M} / w^{s}_g - 1/w_g \quad , \\
\epsilon^{c}_{g,w} &:= 1 - p_{\mathrm{wr},g} y_{g,M} / w^{c}_g - 1/w_g \quad , \\
\epsilon^{p}_{g,w} &:= 1 - 1/w_g
\end{aligned} \tag{31}$$

and

$$\begin{aligned}
\epsilon^{s}_{g,C} &:= 1 - p_{\mathrm{wr},g} x_{g,M} / w^{s}_g - 1/C \quad , \\
\epsilon^{c}_{g,C} &:= 1 - p_{\mathrm{wr},g} y_{g,M} / w^{c}_g - 1/C \quad , \\
\epsilon^{p}_{g,C} &:= 1 - 1/C \quad .
\end{aligned} \tag{32}$$

Then from formula (28) for $i \leq i_{g,C}$ the solution of the difference Eqs. (24) to (26) follows as

$$b_g(i) = \frac{w^{b}_g}{w_g} \left[\frac{1 - (\epsilon^{b}_{g,w})^i}{1 - \epsilon^{b}_{g,w}} \right] + (\epsilon^{b}_{g,w})^i b_g(0) \tag{33}$$

for $b \in \{s,c,p\}$. The initial values $s_g(0), c_g(0)$, and $p_g(0)$ are found from Eqs. (20) to (22) and the stationary values

$$s_g(\infty) = \frac{w^{s}_g}{p_{\mathrm{wr},g} x_{g,M} w_g / w^{s}_g + 1} \quad , \tag{34}$$

$$c_g(\infty) = \frac{w^{c}_g}{p_{\mathrm{wr},g} y_{g,M} w_g / w^{c}_g + 1} \quad , \tag{35}$$

$$p_g(\infty) = w^{p}_g \quad . \tag{36}$$

On the other hand, for $i > i_{g,C}$, the solution reads for $b \in \{s,c,p\}$

$$b_g(i) = \frac{w^{b}_g}{w_g} \left[\frac{1 - (\epsilon^{b}_{g,C})^{i - i_{g,C}}}{1 - \epsilon^{b}_{g,C}} \right] + (\epsilon^{b}_{g,C})^{i - i_{g,C}} b_g(i_{g,C}) \tag{37}$$

with stationary solutions

$$s_g(\infty) = \frac{w^{s}_g}{p_{\mathrm{wr},g} x_{g,M} w_g / w^{s}_g + w_g / C} \quad , \tag{38}$$

$$c_g(\infty) = \frac{w^{c}_g}{p_{\mathrm{wr},g} y_{g,M} w_g / w^{c}_g + w_g / C} \quad , \tag{39}$$

$$p_g(\infty) = C \frac{w^{p}_g}{w_g} \quad . \tag{40}$$

Here a remark on the quantity $i_{g,C}$, defined by Eq. (30), is in order. Replacing $s_g(i), c_g(i)$, and $p_g(i)$ by the expressions from Eq. (33), the solution of (30) is simply the problem of finding a root. This can be done easily and effectively on a numerical way. For this reason we here dispense with giving an analytical expression for $i_{g,C}$.

If one now recalls the definitions (4) and (6) of the task group specific miss and ctc–miss ratios, these quantities can be calculated from the arithmetic means $(b \in \{s,c,p\})$

$$\overline{b_g} := \frac{1}{I_g} \sum_{i=1}^{I_g} b_g(i) = \frac{1}{I_g} \sum_{i=1}^{i_{g,C}} b_g(i) + \frac{1}{I_g} \sum_{i=i_{g,C}+1}^{I_g} b_g(i) \ , \tag{41}$$

according to

$$\text{miss\_ratio}_g = 1 - \frac{1}{w_g}[\overline{s_g} + \overline{c_g} + \overline{p_g}] \tag{42}$$

and

$$\text{ctc\_miss\_ratio}_g = p_{\text{wr},g}[x_{g,M}\frac{\overline{s_g}}{w_g^s} + y_{g,M}\frac{\overline{c_g}}{w_g^c}] \ , \tag{43}$$

respectively.

Explicit expressions for the means (41) are found referring to Eq. (29). The initial values $b_g(0)$ are obtained from Eqs. (20) to (22) and (38), the values $b_g(i_{g,C})$ can then be computed from Eq. (33).

4 Particular Results

Due to limited space we will restrict to results that are obtained for the synthetic workloads as given in Table 2. The cache capacity is set to 1500 blocks in both cases.

Table 2. Parameters of the synthetic workloads A and B

Workload A					
g	N_g	I_g	w_g^s	w_g^c	w_g^p	$p_{\text{wr},g}$
1	20	19000	500	800	30	0.15
2	45	12000	700	70	150	0.20
3	30	20000	600	700	100	0.15
4	50	10000	800	500	400	0.25
5	10	5000	300	0	0	0.10

Workload B					
g	N_g	I_g	w_g^s	w_g^c	w_g^p	$p_{\text{wr},g}$
1	40	20000	300	0	1500	0.10
2	30	15000	600	0	700	0.15
3	25	18000	400	100	800	0.20
4	15	10000	200	200	100	0.25
5	10	5000	300	0	0	0.10

While workload A can be seen as the caricature of a conflict–critical load (a database system for example), workload B consists of tasks sharing only a small number of blocks (a batch load for example).

In Figure 1, the mm–miss and ctc–miss ratios are depicted as a function of the total number M of CPUs. The hit ratio can be obtained using Eq. (1).

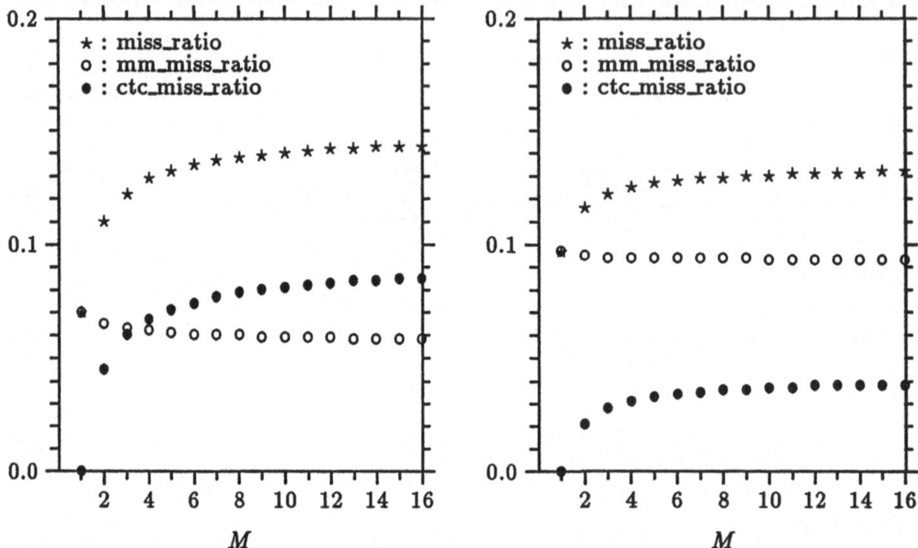

Fig. 1. The miss ratio (⋆) and its composition in the mm–miss ratio (o) and the ctc–miss ratio (•) for workload A (left) and workload B (right) as a function of the total number M of CPUs.

The reader who wants results for workloads of his personal interest might find the relevant parameters $p_{\mathrm{wr},g}, w_g^s, w_g^c, w_g^p$ and I_g from an analysis of CPU–reference strings.

5 Concluding Remarks

The particular merit of the model derived in the present paper is its closed solution and the insight it gives in basic reference mechanisms. Thus it allows for a very quick estimation of the cache performance with arbitrary workloads applied, and, as a first step, may serve as an alternative to more sophisticated but also time–consuming and inflexible methods as trace–driven simulations [13].

Figure 1 shows that the results depend strongly on the workload characteristics. For this reason it is not possible to compare them to data given earlier in the literature, as we do not know the relevant input parameters.

In the future, we will apply our model to workload parameters extracted from reference traces of the operating system BS2000 and compare them to data obtained from trace–driven simulations and measurements. This comparison will serve as a test of our approach and will give useful hints to refine the model as far as necessary.

The most severe restriction in the present model seems to be the linear approach (8) for the cache–miss probability. A more appropriate form [14] could be applied. This however renders a complete analytical treatment impossible and requires a numerical solution of the difference equations. In that case, the numerical solution may be simplified by taking the continuum limit in the difference equations, resulting in a system of coupled differential equations.

References

1. Agarwal, A., Horowitz, M., Hennessy, J.: An Analytical Cache Model. ACM Trans. Comp. Syst. **7** (1989) 184–215
   Agarwal, A.: Performance Tradeoffs in Multithreaded Processors. IEEE Trans. Par. Distr. Syst. **3** (1992) 525–539
2. Aven, O.I., Coffmann, E.G.Jr., Kogan, Y.A.: Stochastic Analysis of Computer Storage. D. Reidel Publishing Company, Dordrecht (1987)
3. Rao, G.S.: Performance Analysis of Cache Memories. J. ACM **25** (1978) 378–395
4. Smith, A.J.: Cache Memories. ACM Computing Surveys **14** (1982) 473–530
   Smith, A.J.: Cache Evaluation and the Impact of Workload Choice. 12th Int. Symp. on Computer Architecture (1985) 64–73
   Smith, A.J.: Second Bibliography on Cache Memories. Comput. Archit. News **19** (1991) 154–182
5. Strecker, W.D.: Transient Behavior of Cache Memories. ACM Trans. Comp. Syst. **1** (1983) 281–293
6. Thiebaut, D., Stone, H.S.: Footprints in the Cache. ACM Trans. Comp. Syst. **5** (1987) 305–329
7. Singh, J.P., Stone, H.S., Thiebaut, D.F.: A Model of Workloads and its Use in Miss–Rate Prediction for Fully Associative Caches. IEEE Trans. Comput. **41** (1992) 811–825
8. Kogan, Ya.A., Boguslavsky, L.B.: Asymptotic Analysis of Memory Interference in Multiprocessors with Private Cache Memories. Performance Evaluation **5** (1985) 97–114
9. Patel, J.H.: Analysis of Multiprocessors with Private Cache Memories. IEEE Trans. Comp. **C–31** (1982) 296–304
10. Squillante, M.S., Lazowska, E.D.: Using Processor–Cache Affinity Information in Shared–Memory Multiprocessor Scheduling. IEEE Trans. Par. Distr. Syst. **4** (1993) 131–143
11. Gecsei, J., Slutz, D.R., Traiger, I.L.: Evaluation Techniques for Storage Hierarchies. IBM Syst. J. **2** (1970) 78–117
12. Bussert, W.: LRU–Stack Analyse von CPU–Referenzstrings. Siemens Nixdorf internal report (1992) in german
13. For example : Kuntz, J.–M., Etiemble, D., Syre, J.–C.: Performance Evaluation of Cache Memories in Tightly Coupled Multiprocessor Systems. Proceedings of PARLE'92, Paris, 15–18 June 1992, Springer, Berlin (1992) 735–750
   Wilson, A.W.Jr.: Multiprocessor Cache Simulation Using Hardware Collected Address Traces. 23th Hawaii Int. Conf. on Syst. Science (1990) 252–260
14. Franklin, M.A., Gupta, R.K.: Computation of Page Fault Probability from Program Transition Diagram. Comm. ACM **17** (1974) 186–196

Übersicht der Kurzberichte [*]

Rechnerarchitektur

Ein Simulator für die Bewertung von parallelen Rechnerarchitekturen
A. Kern, TU Braunschweig

Modelling Memory Access Queues in Multi-Processor Systems
H. Ulrich, IBM Deutschland Entwicklung GmbH

CPU Performance Analysis and Projection
N. Breuer, IBM Deutschland Entwicklung GmbH

Eine generische Lastbeschreibung für frühzeitige Leistungsanalysen beim Prozessor-Entwurf
U. Langer, Universität der Bundeswehr München

Cache-Trefferraten bei LRU-Verdrängung in gemischten Referenz-Strings
L.Frank, Fachhochschule Rosenheim

Zur Leistungsmodellierung von Rechnerinstallationen mit blockierender Ressource
G. Bergholz, Freiberg

Methoden/Modelle

A New Method to Determine the Initial Checkpoint of the Spectral Variance Analysis
Ch. Kelling, Technische Universität Berlin

Analyse stochastischer Petrinetze mit Hilfe der Cox-Verteilung
S. Wild, TU Dresden

Puran2: Ein Zufallszahlengenerator zur Erzeugung von quasi-idealen Zufallszahlen aus elektronischem Rauschen
M. Richter, RWTH Aachen

Konzept für ein regelbasiertes Beratungssystem für das Leistungsmanagement in lokalen Netzen
S. Reul, TU Dresden

Modelling the SDH Management
M. Herpers, S. Tretter, Philips Kommunikations Industrie (PKI), Nürnberg

---

[*] Die Kurzberichte erscheinen getrennt in einem Sammelband der Kurzbeiträge und Werkzeugvorstellungen